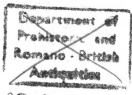

Plate I *Excavations in progress in 1969 on the West Masonry Building, looking south-west.*

THE ROMAN VILLA SITE AT KESTON, KENT.

FIRST REPORT (EXCAVATIONS 1968–1978)

The detailed report on eleven years of rescue-excavations in Lower Warbank Field, in the parish of Keston, now in the London Borough of Bromley, formerly Kent. It covers the prehistoric settlement, including important Iron Age sites, the evolution from a Romano-British farmstead to a substantial Roman Villa, with several major periods and it also covers the minor post-Roman settlement.

By

BRIAN PHILP, KEITH PARFITT, JOHN WILLSON, MIKE DUTTO AND WENDY WILLIAMS

With other main contributions by:

Deborah Cooper,
Peter Couldrey,
Alison Locker,

Richard Reece,
Joanna Bird,
Valerie Rigby.

SIXTH RESEARCH REPORT IN THE KENT MONOGRAPH SERIES
(ISSN 0141 2264)
(ISBN 0 947831 07 X)

Published by: The Kent Archaeological Rescue Unit
C.I.B. Headquarters, Dover Castle, Kent.

1991

Dedicated to

The members of the Bromley and West Kent Archaeological Group, whose tireless and skilled work on excavations at Keston and on another 160 Kent sites for more than 30 years, provides an outstanding contribution to British Archaeology.

ISBN 0 947831 07 X

Produced for the Unit by Alan Sutton Publishing Limited, Stroud, Gloucestershire.
Printed in Great Britain.

The Unit is greatly indebted to the **HISTORIC BUILDINGS AND MONUMENTS COMMISSION (ENGLISH HERITAGE)** for a substantial grant towards the cost of this publication. The Unit also gratefully acknowledges financial contributions from the **COUNCIL FOR KENTISH ARCHAEOLOGY** and the **KENT ARCHAEOLOGICAL TRUST**.

CONTENTS

LIST OF FIGURES

LIST OF PLATES

ABOUT THIS REPORT

This Report is the sixth in the Kent Monograph Series and it largely follows the pattern set by previous volumes. These were:–

Vol. I   Excavations at Faversham 1965 (published by the C.K.A. in 1968).

Vol. II   Excavations in West Kent 1960–70 (published by the Kent Unit in 1973).

Vol. III   The Excavation of the Roman Forts of the Classis Britannica at Dover 1970–77 (published by the Kent Unit in 1981).

Vol. IV   Excavations in the Darent Valley, Kent (published by the Kent Unit in 1984).

Vol. V   The Roman House with the Bacchic Murals at Dover (published by the Kent Unit in 1989).

As with all Reports in this series the entire proceeds from sales go towards covering the printing and publication costs, or into a reserve fund for subsequent volumes. No royalties are paid to any of the authors. Further Reports are already in preparation.

The subject of this Report is an extensive programme of excavation, carried out by the Bromley and West Kent Archaeological Group together with the Kent Archaeological Rescue Unit, on the major Iron Age, Romano-British and Anglo-Saxon site at Warbank, Keston, from 1968–78. A second Report will deal with work on the same site in 1967 and between 1979–1987. Short interim accounts on various aspects of the total work have been published in the *Kent Archaeological Review* and in other journals.

The major structures and features included here are arranged in chronological order by period, whilst the large number of miscellaneous features are listed in tables held in archive. The key dating evidence is presented here and includes reports on all the coins and samian from the site, but selective reports on the coarse pottery, mortaria, small-finds and quernstones. Short reports on the animal bones and some building materials are included, but the small amount of glass recovered has been held over for the second volume on Keston.

As with previous Reports in this series, footnotes have been excluded and the bibliographical references, numbered progressively throughout the text, are listed in that order at the back. These show as numbers placed in round-brackets and prefixed by the letters Ref. (e.g. Ref. 147). Similarly, the illustrated finds are also numbered progressively through the text, this time prefixed by the letters No. or Nos. so as to eliminate recurring finds-numbers and thus hopefully avoiding confusion. Coins (not illustrated) are noted in the text by a unique number (e.g. Coin No. 15) which refers to the number in the table of coins in the appropriate specialist section. References in the text to drawn sections and layers are shown in brackets, prefixed by the letters S. and L., respectively (e.g. S.H, L.18). A key covering all the published sections can be found on Fig. 6. As with other Kent Monographs the main text is set in 11 on 12 point Bembo typeface, at about 800 words to a page. In most cases the excavated features retain their original site feature number. All dimensions have been left in Imperial form, though metric scales are included on most site-plans and sections.

THE AUTHORS: The compilation of this volume required a very substantial input from five people. The basis of much of the descriptive text was a preliminary draft by Keith Parfitt who had not taken part in the excavations covered by this Report. The finished version was then written by Brian Philp who had directed all of the excavations and who also added the discussion. Mike Dutto drew the great majority of the maps, plans and sections whilst Wendy Williams drew almost all the small-finds. John Willson drew the coarse pottery and also added final details to many of the plans and sections.

FOREWORD

It is with considerable pleasure that I write this foreword to the first Keston Report, the sixth volume in the Kent Monograph Series, both as Leader of heritage-conscious Bromley Council and also as a resident of Keston itself over many years.

When I moved to Keston in 1967, the owner of Foxhill Farm took me and my young son one evening to a high point only yards from the Roman villa site. Whilst part of the site was then known, but largely unexplored, my mind soon conjured up three reasons for the location of a Roman villa here. The first related to the impressive ramparts still visible in nearby Holwood Park, of the Iron Age hillfort, clearly a focus of settlement hereabouts for several centuries. The second related to the obvious sight-line from the site to the centre of Roman Londinium, the Roman provincial capital and the third to the close proximity of the Roman arterial road from London to Lewes.

Whether these ideas were simply flights of fancy no-one could then prove me right or wrong, but suffice to say my interest in the programme of excavations on the site has intensified ever since. It is therefore my particular pleasure to write as a way of acknowledging the huge effort on the part of some 500 volunteers who have worked on the site since 1968, led by the indefatigable Brian Philp. Their work confirms the major importance of this site and probably forms the largest area excavation on any archaeological site in South-East London or West Kent. The gradual evaluation of the site's busy domestic occupation, starting with an extensive Iron Age settlement, evolving through a scattered Romano-British farmstead, a proto-villa with an ordered lay-out to a fully fledged Roman villa with masonry buildings, is itself so fascinating. The site incorporated the main house, large barns, paddocks, enclosures, a metalled road, cemeteries and even large mausolea. The estate and its owners must surely have been of some importance, perhaps the principal family across much of the area now known as Bromley. When the Roman Empire in the west collapsed so did the economy of the Keston villa, though there is good evidence for occupation by pagan Saxons about A.D. 500.

It is, therefore, due to the tireless work of so many people that another large facet of Romano-British rural history has been discovered and documented. It is comforting to know that all future generations will now have access to a wealth of detailed information through this written work, which in effect translates the thousands of man-hours given by Brian Philp and his fulltime staff and massed volunteers, thus making a lasting and significant contribution to the totality of the knowledge of our heritage. I shall also look forward to the second Keston Report in the not too distant future.

Councillor E.D. Barkway, O.B.E.,
Leader of the Council,
London Borough of Bromley.   January, 1991.

CHAPTER I.

INTRODUCTION

A. SUMMARY.

A scatter of struck flints suggests limited use of the site in the Late Neolithic or Early Bronze Age (Period I). The first settlement was in the Middle Iron Age, *c.* 600–200 B.C. (Period II), in two discrete areas. Evidence included two shallow storage-pits, a post-hole and quantities of domestic pottery. An unenclosed farmstead is suggested.

The site was resettled in the Late Iron Age, *c.* 50 B.C.–A.D. 50 (Period III a and b), when two ditched enclosures, 13 storage-pits, eleven posted-structures, a possible hut and hearths were constructed. Period IIIa was probably an unenclosed farmstead and the large Period IIIb enclosure resembled an enclosed farmstead of the Farningham Hill type.

A major Romano-British expansion occurred in A.D. 150–160 (Period IV) with chalk quarry-pits (IVa, A.D. 50–100), two rectilinear enclosures, pits, a kiln and a small cemetery (IVb, A.D. 100–160), all associated with pottery. These are the scatterd elements of an extensive farmstead with small-scale industrial activity.

A major reorganisation occurred A.D. 160–200 (Period V) with three large timber-framed buildings (Va) and various lesser features (Vb). The new building layout, framed around a notional courtyard (about 140 x 130 ft.), suggests a 'proto-villa' with the main house at the west end. The buildings, about 60 x 21 ft., 49 x 21 ft. and 37 x 20 ft., consisted of six, five and four bays, respectively. A metalled road to the east was aligned on the east centre of the courtyard and a water storage pond dug north of the road. The flint footings of a structure of uncertain size was built over the in-filled quarry-pits.

At about A.D. 200, until A.D. 300, (Period VI) the 'proto-villa' was superseded by an extensive reorganisation forming the fullest development of the villa complex. The main timber west house, burnt down, was replaced by a larger masonry building; a large new timber barn was built north-east of it; major boundary ditches dug on the north and south sides; fences created across the area; piped water and water storage tanks created and a major cemetery built. Only the timber building (Period V) on the south side survived whilst the new timber barn contained elaborate corn-drying ovens.

The boundary ditches define the main complex whilst the three buildings flank a fan-shaped courtyard at least 150 ft. sq. Fences define a paddock 100 x 45 ft. in the north-west corner of the courtyard. The piped water originated from a spring on the hill and supplied large clay-lined tanks. The cemetery, situated beyond a wide entrance in the ditched enclosure, contained monumental tombs.

At about A.D. 300, through to A.D. 400 (Period VII), the north barn was burnt and not replaced and this suggests a contraction of farming activity. The timber building (Period V) to the south was replaced by a much larger masonry building, domestic in character and perhaps suggesting dual ownership of the estate. The east–west road was re-metalled and may have served the west building. A probable hut, constructed on the ruins of the barn, contained a hearth and traces of iron-working. Two more clay-lined tanks and a small corn-drying oven were built nearby and two short ditches dug to take surface water.

The Roman settlement probably expired at the end of the 4th century. A Saxon grübenhaus was constructed, in A.D. 450–550 (Period VIII) close to the centre of the abandoned Roman site. Apart from robber-pits and shallow field ditches (Period IX) the site appears to have had no settlement on it for the next 1500 years. The settlement focus seems to have moved 500 yds. to the south-east, near to the present Parish church, no later than the 9th century.

B. THE SITE (Figs. 1, 2 and 3).

The Warbank site (N.G.R. TQ 414.632) lies largely in open country at the southern end of the parish of Keston. Until 1965 the parish lay within the historic county of Kent, but in that year it became part of the London Borough of Bromley, the largest of all the Greater London boroughs. The site actually lies about four miles south of the busy town-centre of Bromley and only about one mile from the Surrey border.

The centre of the site lies about 500 yards north-west of the ancient parish church at Keston, the latter being partly of Norman date, but is known to sit over earlier Christian burials. Whilst a late-Saxon settlement at Keston is evidenced by its mention as 'Cheston' in the Domesday Survey (published in 1086), no church was then recorded (Ref. 1). The medieval and later village must have been mainly centred on the church, though the present-day settlement of Keston is largely focused nearly one mile further north. The site seems to have been known locally as Warbank, probably for predictable reasons, for at least 200 years.

In broad geographical terms Keston lies near the southern limit of the Thames Basin only about twelve miles south of the Thames at London Bridge (Fig. 1). It also lies on the dip slope of the North Downs in an area containing many natural springs. The subsoil is mostly Upper

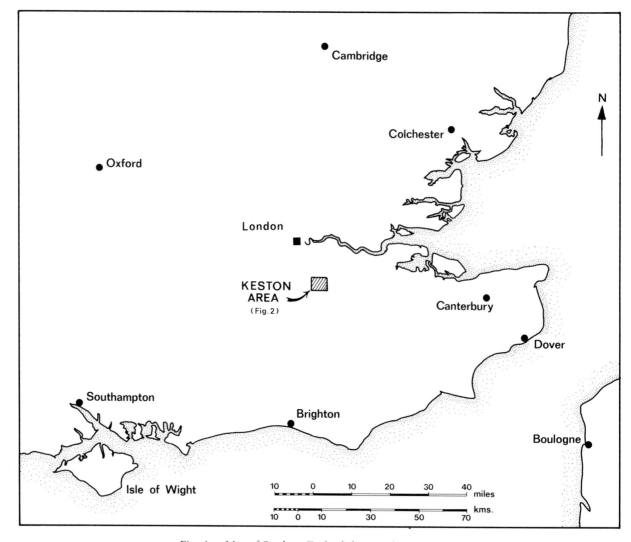

Fig. 1. *Map of Southern England showing the Keston area.*

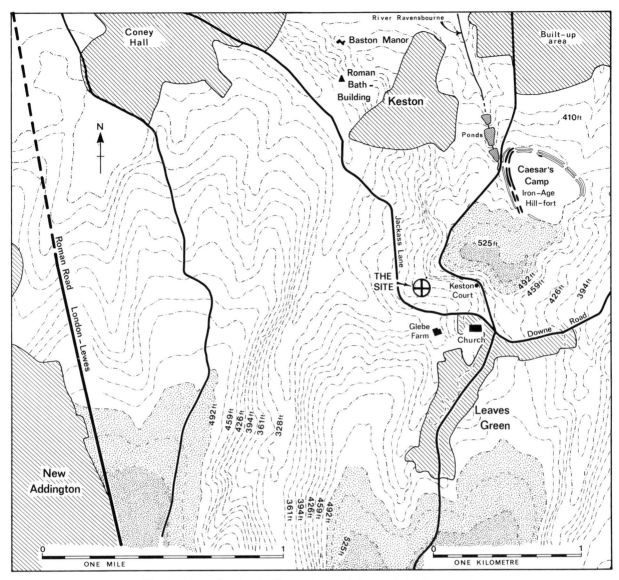

Fig. 2. *Map showing the Keston site in relation to the local topography.*

Chalk, though the upper edge of the site is capped with layers of Woolwich and Blackheath pebble-beds. The site lies between the 395 and 435 foot contours.

The detailed geographical position of the site is of special interest (Fig. 2). It occupies a slight shoulder on the middle slopes of a broad spur which projects from the south-western side of Holwood Hill. This spur has been formed at the junction of a major north-south valley and a very short eastern tributary valley. The main valley must once have contained a stream that eventually joined the River Ravensbourne which, itself, flows from the Downs and ultimately into the Thames. Holwood Hill rises to a maximum height of 541 feet. above Ordnance Datum and its summit is heavily wooded. Immediately to the north-east of the highest part of the hill lies 'Caesar's Camp', a massive Iron Age hillfort originally covering about 42 acres (about 17 hectares). The Warbank site lies some 1000 yards to the south-west of the hillfort's outer defences. The close proximity of these two major sites strongly suggests that they were closely related in some way during at least the later Iron Age.

Several springs rise on the slopes of Holwood Hill and one of these rises directly above the present site. The springs in this region, particularly Caesar's Well, which gives rise to Keston ponds and the River Ravensbourne, have long been known and presumably they also flowed during prehistoric and Roman times. They are, in fact, likely to have been a key factor in establishing both the Caesar's Camp and the Warbank sites.

The precise area of the 1968–78 excavations covered by this Report, lies almost entirely in Lower Warbank Field (Fig. 3; O.S. parcel No. 4518). The area occupied by the Roman mausolea and the related cemetery is at the top of the site, and known locally as Upper Warbank. The western part of the site lies in Eight Acre Field. Neither of the two latter areas is covered by this

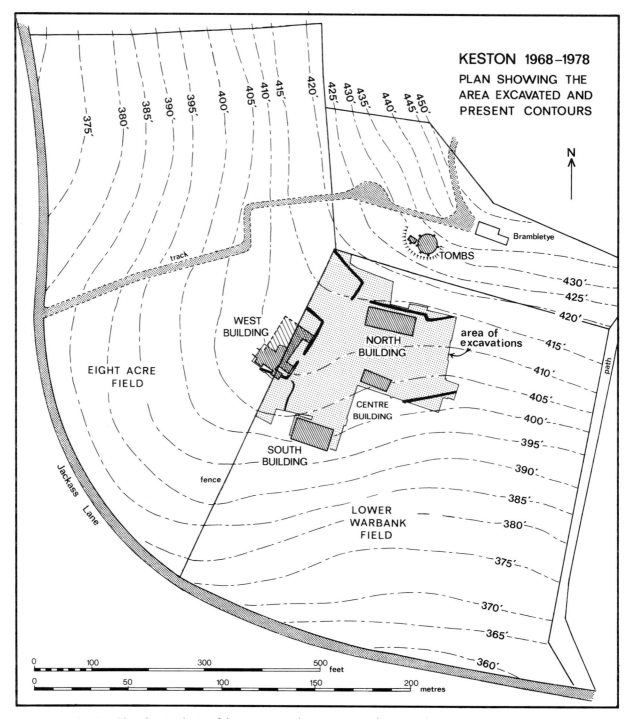

Fig. 3. *Plan showing limits of the excavation, the main Roman features and present-day surface contours.*

Report. The tombs were consolidated by the Bromley and West Kent Group and remain open for public inspection, but all other sites were backfilled on completion and cannot now be seen. The area of the tombs was scheduled sometime between the two World Wars and the whole site in about 1980 (London No. 102).

In archaeological terms the Roman villa at Warbank lay only about twelve miles from *Londinium*, the capital city of Roman Britain. Significantly, it lay about $1\frac{1}{4}$ miles east of the arterial Roman Road (Refs. 2 and 3) which ran from *Londinium* to the proximity of present-day Lewes in Sussex. Presumably, a trackway connected the villa with this road. Several other Romano-British sites have been discovered in the immediate area (Ref. 4), though Keston seems to have been the largest. The only other Roman masonry buildings known nearby are the small bath-house at Baston (Ref. 5), about a mile to the north and the villa at Orpington (Ref. 6), about three miles to the north-east. The villa at Titsey, Surrey (Ref. 7) lies $5\frac{1}{2}$ miles to the south and the Beddington villa, Surrey (Ref. 8) some $7\frac{1}{2}$ miles to the north-west. The line of the presumed prehistoric and later trackway, the North Downs Ridgeway, lies only $4\frac{1}{2}$ miles to the south of Keston.

C. THE HISTORY OF DISCOVERY AND EXCAVATION AT WARBANK.

Prior to the massive 1967–1987 programme of excavation at Keston, the site had witnessed an unusually long and interesting series of discoveries and excavations over some 200 years. Most of the very earliest work took place around the Roman circular mausoleum, then mistakenly called a 'Temple', but even by the mid-19th century the two masonry buildings in Lower Warbank field had been located.

Antiquarian research on the Keston site began with A.J. Kempe and T. Crofton Croker in 1828. Their work here led them to adopt the theories of even earlier antiquaries in identifying the site as being that of the long-lost Roman 'city' of *Noviomagus*. This Roman settlement is mentioned in the Antonine Itinerary as being ten Roman miles from *Londinium* and is today largely thought to have been at Crayford, some nine miles to the north-east of Keston. Kempe, however, was convinced that *Noviomagus* lay at Warbank and he notes (perhaps in his thirst for knowledge) that local tradition said that Warbank was the site of a large town with 16 public houses!

The publication by Kempe in 1829 of a substantial, illustrated paper on his discoveries at Keston, in a national archaeological journal (Ref. 9) was a most useful contribution to Romano-British archaeology at that time. Another important contribution was made by George Corner in 1854, when he produced a second substantial, illustrated report (Plate VII) on his own excavations of the buildings in Lower Warbank Field (Ref. 10). Together, these two 19th century reports, with their carefully engraved drawings and plans, make Keston an important site in the early history of Kentish archaeology and even noteworthy within Romano-British studies, generally.

Keston's early lead in Romano-British studies, however, was not maintained through the following years and it was almost exactly a full century before excavations were resumed at Warbank, this time by a local lady, Mrs. N.P. Fox. The 19th century work on the Keston site had been reviewed in 1932 by Mortimer Wheeler in the Victoria County Histories of Kent (Ref. 11) but significantly, he made no real attempt to interpret the nature of the site. Indeed, steady advances in Romano-British studies during the 20th century made the identification of the site at Keston as that of *Noviomagus* increasingly unlikely. Yet, writing as recently as 1955, Mrs. Fox, who had been involved in local archaeology in the Keston area for about 15 years, considered that her excavations on part of the West Masonry Building had revealed a portion of a 'public building of some kind' (Ref. 12). Elements of the *Noviomagus* identification obviously lingered on in her mind without ever being clearly stated or critically examined.

It was, perhaps, predictable that the 20-year programme of work which started in 1967 would transform knowledge of the site and this has certainly proved to be the case. A settlement sequence of over 1000 years, ranging from the middle Iron Age, through the Roman period and on into pagan Saxon times, has been identified. It is hoped that the publication of this, in two Reports, will itself constitute a notable advance in Romano-British studies, that will prove a fitting sequel to the pioneering work of Kempe and Corner of nearly 150 years ago. The long series of discoveries and excavations at Keston is listed chronologically below:–

1) *c.*1783   Farm workers, digging in a mound of rubble at Warbank, discover a stone coffin. Ditch-digging at the same time is said to have produced coins (including one of Nero), pottery, a dagger, a spur, a key and iron nails, all apparently Roman (Refs. 13 and 14).

2) 1814   A brief illustrated note on the initial discoveries was sent by Mr. A.J. Kempe, F.S.A. to the *Military Register*, a periodical of the time, where it was later published (Ref. 15).

3) 1815   The same information was published again, this time by John Dunkin in his *History and Antiquities of Bromley*, which prompted Thomas Crofton Croker, F.S.A. to consider excavating the site (Ref. 16).

4) 1828   (17th–19th September). Croker carried out a three-day excavation, having invited Kempe to attend. The excavation revealed a circular building, a rectangular tomb (from which the stone coffin had come in *c.* 1783) and a second large stone coffin in a nearby pit (Ref. 17).

5) 1828   (October). Kempe, clearly unhappy with Croker's work, carried out another excavation on the circular building and the adjacent tomb. He then moved into Lower Warbank Field where he briefly examined a series of flint walls, that had been hit during ploughing, at the west side of the field. His detailed and illustrated report was published in *Archaeologia* in 1829 (Ref. 18).

6) 1854   A second excavation was started on the foundations (now identified as the West Masonry Building) at the west side of Lower Warbank Field, this time by Mr. George Corner. He abandoned this in favour of another Roman Building, revealed as a crop-mark, further out in the field. This proved to be substantial and he identified it as part of a 'small Roman villa'; it is now designated as the South Masonry Building. His detailed and illustrated report was published in *Archaeologia* in 1855 (Ref. 19).

7) 1861   An urn containing burnt bones (Ref. 20) was found somewhere at Warbank and must represent a cremation-burial, of Roman date.

8) 1893   Another excavation was carried out on the circular 'Temple' by Mr. G.R. Wright. No excavation report was ever published, but a short note appeared in *The Athenaeum* (Ref. 21). The work was probably of a limited nature.

9) 1936   A third stone coffin was found, well to the west of the other coffins, by workmen digging a post-hole on the Keston Foreign Bird Farm. This was written up by Dr. J.B. Ward Perkins (Ref. 22) and the coffin moved to the old Museum of London, where it was destroyed by wartime bombing.

10) 1951–3   A small-scale excavation was carried out, just beyond Lower Warbank Field's west hedge in what had been Eight Acre Field, by Mrs. Fox. The heavily robbed foundations of a "public building" were then reported (Ref. 23), though these really formed part of the main villa-house (here, the West Masonry Building).

11) 1960–1   Yet another excavation of the Roman 'Temple' was carried out, this time by Mrs. Fox. The excavation was left open for several years and never published.

12) 1962   A Roman 'ritual shaft', west of the 'Temple', was excavated by Mrs. Fox. This was published posthumously in 1967 (Ref. 24).

13) 1967–8   This was the first phase of the major programme of excavations by the West Kent Border Archaeological Group, carried out to save the abandoned site. It involved the complete re-excavation of the circular 'Temple', the tomb and the adjacent area, followed by the consolidation of all the masonry and laying out the site for public inspection. The 'Temple' was soon identified as a major Roman mausoleum, set in a cemetery with other structures and burials (Refs. 25, 26 and 27). This excavation will be published in a second Report dealing with work at Keston.

14) 1968–78   This represents the second and third phases of the major excavation programme, jointly carried out by the West Kent Border Archaeological Group and the Kent Archaeological Rescue Unit. This was largely confined to Lower Warbank Field where the work was done ahead of the proposed Ringway C motorway and because of damage caused by ploughing. These two phases of work form the subject of this Report. They revealed a massive multi-period, multi-phased settlement largely unsuspected by the earlier excavators. Both the previously known masonry buildings were re-excavated and three more timber buildings (including one predecessor of a masonry one) were found and excavated. Over 900 other features of Iron Age, Romano-British and Saxon date were also excavated (Refs. 28, 29, 30, 31 and 32).

15) 1977–8   This was the fourth, smallest phase of the joint West Kent and Kent Unit excavation programme. Circumstances confined this work to the general area of the 1936 burial, then largely abandoned ground (Ref. 33). This revealed a series of minor Roman features that will also be covered in the second Keston Report.

16) 1984–7   This was the fifth phase of the joint Bromley and West Kent Archaeological Group and Kent Unit excavation. This was undertaken in what had formerly been Eight Acre Field, but latterly became part of the Foreign Bird Farm. This site was being developed for a new bungalow and landscaped garden. This revealed the rest of the main villa-house, its large timber predecessor, a second large ritual shaft and many pits, post-holes and ditches (Refs. 34 and 35). These discoveries will also be included in the second Report dealing with the excavations at Keston.

D. THE AIMS AND METHODS OF THE EXCAVATION PROGRAMME.

The first phase and some of the second phase of the programme of excavation at Warbank, Keston, was carried out exclusively by the West Kent Border Archaeological Group under its director, Brian Philp. This work formed part of a broad policy whereby the Group, since its formation in 1960, (Ref. 36) carried out surveys, excavations and prompt publication of sites in the area, mostly ahead of destruction. Most of the work was done at weekends and holidays, but continuous excavation was carried out on some sites as time-scales demanded.

The Group's arrival at Warbank, Keston in 1967 came as a direct result of a joint invitation from the London Borough of Bromley and the (then) Ministry of Public Building and Works. Both these bodies had an official responsibility for the "Temple" area which had been abandoned in 1965 following partial excavation by Mrs. Fox. The Group showed their concern about the deep unfilled trenches across the site and also about the damage to the masonry structures caused by weathering and rapidly growing vegetation. To resolve this situation and to release an official impasse, the Group agreed to re-excavate this part of the site; to consolidate the exposed masonry; then to reinstate the area for public inspection. The site anyway lay on an island of publicly-owned ground, though with only limited access through private property. Limited funds for the work were provided by the Council and the Ministry.

The Group re-excavated the "Temple" using a modified grid system which proved ideal to detect the few remaining unexcavated blocks of soil. The area, confined to the close limits of the flint buildings (soon identified as Roman mausolea), was fully excavated and recorded. The exposed masonry was totally cleaned and all loose flints removed. The upper courses of flint were then consolidated by the Group using specialised mortar-mixes and all the rest firmly pointed. The large circular tomb was then backfilled with soil to match the original form and then turfed.

The ground-level was restored to that of Roman times and this gravelled. The work, which started in May, 1967 was completed in May, 1968. A formal opening ceremony followed and the site opened for a series of public-weekends thereafter, with guided tours given by Group members.

On completion of the Roman cemetery excavation, the Group turned its attention to Lower Warbank Field (second phase of excavation). Here a major motorway, Ringway C, was scheduled to pass east–west through the centre of the field, where it would certainly destroy the Roman buildings found in Victorian times. The field was largely overgrown and only occupied by a horse and two donkeys. This area was therefore given top priority and the Bromley Adult Education archaeology class brought in to assist the work. An initial north–south trial-trench, some 260 feet in length, eventually located the South Masonry Building and suggested that at the upper end of the field little existed or had survived. In fact it was later found that this trench had only missed the unknown North Timber Building by about 10 feet and had actually passed through the wide opening in the outer enclosure ditches! A grid of 10-foot squares suitably lettered and numbered progressively, was laid out across the field and beyond (Plates I and XVIII). This proved ideal for the training excavations and this system remained in use until 1974. Metrification had not then been introduced and the Imperial system of measurement was thus used at the start and continued thereafter.

The re-excavation of the South Masonry Building was largely completed in 1968 and many lesser structures and features recorded. The West Masonry Building was partially examined in 1969 (Plate I) and the Saxon hut in 1970. From 1971–4 the central area of the site was excavated eastwards on the line of the intended motorway and the Centre Timber Building, Iron Age pits and four-post structures and many Roman features found. Again the work was mostly done at weekends throughout the summer and autumn months and the total number of man-days ran into several thousand.

By 1974 the threat from Ringway C had receded, to become the M25 Motorway and no work was carried out in 1975. However, the site soon came back into cultivation and ploughing threatened to destroy the areas not examined. As a result the Department of the Environment agreed to finance a series of area-excavations to substantially complete Lower Warbank Field. This required non-stop excavation for several months each year from 1976–78 and thus the West Kent Group (having dropped the word 'Border') invited the full-time Kent Archaeological Rescue Unit to join in the work. This happy partnership, still directed by Brian Philp, has continued on many sites since that time.

This new (third) phase of work involved open-plan excavation across wide, shallow areas, replacing the grid used by the training-schools. With greater financial resources it was possible to strip off the undergrowth and topsoil so that the maximum effort could be put into the examination of structures and features. The earlier work had anyway shown that little had survived in the topsoil deposits. The Kent Unit's recording system was also adopted at that time.

In 1976 the excavation, in the top north-west corner of the field, revealed the west end of the North Timber Building, some of the villa enclosure ditches, parts of four fence lines and various other minor features.

In 1977 the excavation completed the North Timber Building, a large area at the centre and south-west corner of the site, the latter containing numerous pits and post-holes.

In 1978 excavation took place in the north-east corner of the site where more of the villa enclosure ditch was found, together with a large Roman pond and many minor features. In addition limited work was carried out both east and west of the Roman tombs.

The work for 1976–78 was carried out with the aid of the full-time staff of the Kent Unit, mostly living on site and working every day. These were joined by members of the West Kent Archaeological Group at weekends. Together these teams added several thousand more man-days to the total work on this large site.

By the end of 1978 a major part of the site had been completed as planned. No work was attempted in 1979, but minor supplementary work was carried out in 1980–1. Work had to resume in 1984 and at intervals to the end of 1987, due to new threats from building and landscaping. Only the work from 1968 to 1978 is dealt with in this Report, excluding work in the Roman tombs area.

The archive for the 1968–78 excavations consists of 150 site plans and sections, 550 recorded contexts, 300 photographs, 90 boxes of finds and 10 site-note folders. Of these, 21 plans, 179 sections and 25 photographs of most of the major features are published here. Unpublished sections are either alternative drawings across the main features or relate to minor features which are not considered in any detail here. The large amounts of pottery from the site have been broadly classified by fabric, following the general type-series already established for the area (Ref. 37). The environmental evidence from this dry, chalkland site is largely confined to animal bone and this has been studied and is reported here.

The post-excavation archive contains the analyses and summaries of features, contexts and finds. This archive is stored at the Kent Unit's West Kent office, where it may be consulted upon request. A copy has been placed in the National Monuments Record. Its final destination should (ideally) be in a new Bromley Heritage Centre. In the meantime, however, the ownership of the material remains with the Bromley and West Kent Archaeological Group.

E. ACKNOWLEDGEMENTS.

Thanks are due first and foremost to the part-time members of the Bromley and West Kent Archaeological Group and (latterly) those full-time members from the Kent Archaeological Rescue Unit, who carried out the programme of excavation over all the eleven years. Without their very hard work, enthusiasm and endurance little could have been achieved. More than 300 people were associated with these excavations over the years. The results of their sterling efforts are described in this Report and stand as a tribute to them all. Whilst it is difficult to name each in turn, some deserve a special mention for their particular efforts. Of the site-supervisors Pat Crozier, Edna Mynott (now Mrs. Philp), Jeanne Newbury, Dick Broadfoot, John Willson and Gerald Clewley from the West Kent Group and Derek Garrod, John Doggett and Peter Keller from the Rescue Unit are to be particularly thanked for their excellent work over long periods.

Of the part-time diggers belonging to the West Kent Group, eleven have each earned a very special word of thanks for their work over many weeks. These are: Audrey Button, Thelma Dutton, Pam George, Ann McGary, Roger Cockett, Ronald Fendt, Peter Grant, Maurice Godfrey, Len Johnson, the late D. Jeffries and the late Paul Ryff.

Of the full-time members of K.A.R.U., the extended periods of hard work undertaken by Anthony Emms, Keith Nicol and David Bolton must also be gratefully recorded here.

Special thanks are also due to the late Mr. A.G. Lockley Cook, who readily gave permission each year for the excavations on his land at Keston. The substantial costs of these large-scale excavations were shared and in this respect thanks are due to the Department of the Environment for grants totalling about £10,000 for the work from 1976–78. The balance, probably equivalent to more than £50,000, was generously provided by the Bromley and West Kent Archaeological Group, who supplied the direction, supervision, tools, equipment and volunteers from 1968–75. The equally large task of assessing the results and providing this definitive account for publication cost about £50,000 and this sum was kindly provided, in annual grants, from 1983–88, by the Department of the Environment (now H.B.M.C., English Heritage). The total cost of the 1968–78 excavations and the corresponding post-excavations is thus estimated at about £110,000.

Thanks are also due to the various specialists who have provided reports on a variety of subjects; in particular to Joanna Bird on the samian; Richard Reece on the coins; Valerie Rigby on the Gallo-Belgic pottery and kiln wares; Peter Couldrey on the Iron Age pottery and Alison Locker on the animal bones from the site.

Several members of the Bromley and West Kent Group and the Kent Rescue Unit have also made substantial contributions towards the production of this publication and they must also be thanked here. Wendy Williams has drawn most of the small-finds and decorated samian; Trevor Woodman and Mike Dutto have prepared the site plans and sections from the original field drawings. Deborah Cooper has described the coarse pottery and the catalogue whilst John Willson has drawn most of the illustrated coarse pottery from the site. The text has been typed by Pam Barrett and Alison Borlase carried out all the editorial and many other duties. To everyone concerned the writers extend their sincere thanks.

CHAPTER II.

THE PRE-ROMAN STRUCTURES AND FEATURES (Fig. 4)

This (first) Report deals with the greater part of the excavated area at Keston and the structures and features revealed here are classified into nine main periods (Periods I–IX), some of which contain identifiable phases. The principal elements within each period are generally given a unique identifying name, or number, often in addition to the original site number. The main structures and features located and described include:-

Six major Roman buildings:	The South, North and Centre Timber Buildings. The South and West Masonry Buildings and the Centre Flint Structure.	Periods V–VII
Five ditched enclosures:	West Enclosure	Period IIIb
	South Enclosure	Period IIIb
	East Enclosure	Period IVa
	Centre Enclosure	Period IVb
	Villa Enclosure	Period VI
Six other ditches:	Ditches 2, 3, 4, 5, 14 and 21	Periods VII and IX
Twenty-three pits:	Nos. 1–23	Period II–Period IV
Six clay-lined water storage tanks:	West Tanks (3)	Periods VI–VII
	South Tank	Period VI
	North Tank	Period VII
	North-East Tank	Period VII
Five wooden fences:	South Fence	Period VI
	Centre Fence	Period VI
	North Fence	Period VI
	East Fence	Period VI
	West Fence	Period VI
Ten four-post structures:	Four-Post Structures 1–10	Period III
Two Roman metalled trackways:		Periods V and VII
One Saxon sunken hut:		Period VIII

In view of the fact that work on the site continued after 1978 (to be dealt with as a second Keston Report), the period divisions and date-range offered here should be regarded as provisional. At the moment Periods I and II appear somewhat in isolation, but from the start of Period III (c. 50 B.C.) settlement appears to have been continuous until Period VIII (late-5th to 6th century). Small scale post-Saxon activity constitutes Period IX. Future work on the second Report may refine some of the periods and dates and in particular will include the Roman cemetery, with its walled mausolea, relating to Period VI.

In all over 950 individual features, of very varying sizes, were recorded in Lower Warbank Field. Most of these were either chalk-cut ditches and gullies (Ditches Nos. 1–21), or pits and post-holes. Unfortunately, many of the latter formed no clear patterns or significant alignments and a large number contained either no finds, or just a few nondescript potsherds of doubtful date.

Discrete groups of pits occurred:
1) below the Centre Timber Building
2) below the South Masonry Building
3) in a scatter to the east of the West Masonry Building.

The first two groups lay adjacent to concentrations of post-holes although few coherent structure plans could be reconstructed from these and anyway it seems certain that not all of them are contemporary. A disappointingly small number of the pits, both within these groups and in more isolated positions, produced sufficient pottery to give a very clear indication of their exact date. A total of 23 pits, however, did yield enough material for some idea of their date to be gained. These have been numbered independently and are assigned to the following periods:

Period II, Pits 1–3
Period III, Pits 4–16
Period IV, Pits 17–23.

It seems certain that many of the insecurely dated pits must also be broadly contemporary with these. Others, however, are certainly later. Nevertheless, with many pits and post-holes it is impossible to arrive at any meaningful date. Thus, a good many of these structures have played no further part in the interpretation of the site and they have served merely to emphasise the general level of intensity of ancient occupation across the area examined. Full details of all these miscellaneous minor features are held in archive. The main site plan (Fig. 4) together with the other large-scale plans (Figs. 11, 15, 19, 21, 32, 34, 36 and 37) show the position of every recorded minor archaeological feature with its original site number. It should be noted that missing numbers within a sequence of feature numbers here will reflect those that have been subsequently eliminated as being of natural origin. Generally, each annual excavation season was allocated a specific group of feature numbers. In the following season a new batch of numbers was allocated, regardless of any unused numbers from the previous year's sequence. The feature numbers allocated may be summarised thus:

Year	Feature
1968	= 1–77
1969	= 100–192, 200–263
1970	= 301–381
1971	= 401–511
1972	= 600–693
1973–4	= 700–741
1976	= 800–958
1977	= 1000–1294 (Nos. 1160–9, 1213–49 not used)
1978	= 1501–1562

The stratigraphy of the site in Lower Warbank Field was generally not well preserved and the overall thickness of the archaeological deposits was nowhere very great. In many areas ploughing and burrowing animals had disturbed much, if not all of the stratified levels and over a considerable area on the higher part of the site, a deposit of plough-soil over a thin layer of 'hillwash' were all that sealed the buried, chalk-cut features. Examination of the comparative depths of various linear features indicates that up to 2' of natural chalk may have been eroded by the plough since the Roman period on the higher parts of the site. The worst affected areas largely corresponded with those excavated in 1976 and 1978 and an examination of the overall site-plan (Fig. 4) will quickly reveal a generally lower density of minor features, in the form of pits and post-holes in these areas, when compared with the rest of the site.

Over much of the remainder of the area investigated the plough-soil and 'hillwash' layers rested on a general soil deposit of dark loam. This lay upon the natural chalk and sealed the chalk-cut features. Across most of the site the total thickness of the covering soil above the bedrock was generally 15–18″ and rarely exceeded 2′6″ except where archaeological features occurred. In the lower, south-eastern part of the field, however, a reasonable sequence of deposits up to 4′ thick was located. Excavations in the 19th century, upon the sites of the West and South Masonry Buildings, had removed most of the archaeological deposits which had survived the centuries of ploughing in these areas.

The plough-soil and general soil deposits covering the site must, in fact, largely represent the disturbed remains of the Roman occupational levels. It is not surprising, therefore, that large amounts of the coarse pottery, samian ware, small-finds and coins came from these deposits. Indeed, some 53 coins out of the total of 84 from the whole site came from these deposits. No overall quantitative analysis of the coarse pottery from the unstratified, plough-soil and general soil deposits has been attempted, but some 43 sherds have been illustrated (Nos. 854–896). In addition some 185 samian sherds were also recovered from these deposits and this represents nearly half of the total found. Some 19 illustrated small-finds also came from these layers, together with a flint arrowhead (No. 2).

PERIOD I : THE LATE-NEOLITHIC/BRONZE AGE OCCUPATION.

The earliest evidence of settlement on the Keston site consisted of a scatter of struck flints, found in excavations at both the Tombs and in Lower Warbank Field. None of this material occurred in completely undisturbed contexts and all of it must be regarded as residual. No features relating to the prehistoric occupation implied by this lithic scatter had survived. Only the material from Lower Warbank Field is considered here and eight flints are illustrated (Nos. 1–8).

Some 505 struck flints were recovered from the excavations in Lower Warbank Field and typically 474 of these are either waste flakes or miscellaneous shattered fragments. There are also five cores and three hammer-stones, together with 23 other pieces which show signs of working. The most common tool-type is the scraper and ten of these were recovered (Nos. 3–8). The most interesting pieces are two arrowheads both of rather unusual form (Nos. 1 and 2), one perhaps representing a blank for a barbed-and-tanged arrowhead (No. 1).

The scatter of flints appeared to be slightly more dense in the area of the Tombs and the material there also seemed to be in rather less disturbed contexts, occurring in clay deposits which survived below the Roman levels. Corresponding levels in Lower Warbank Field had not survived the plough. From an analysis of this flint material it seems that the assemblage is of a broad date-range within the late-Neolithic/Bronze Age period (see page 149).

Scatters of similar struck flints are quite common in West Kent and several assemblages have been published (Ref. 38). A late Neolithic settlement-site has been recorded at Baston Manor nearby and two Cornish greenstone axes have been discovered elsewhere in the parish of Keston (Ref. 39). Clearly, more work is required, but it seems certain that this general area was widely inhabited by prehistoric man. It is becoming increasingly clear, however, that on many prehistoric settlement sites in Kent little else other than surface flint scatters are likely to have survived centuries of ploughing. The evidence from Keston, therefore, is probably typical of many other chalkland sites in Kent.

PERIOD II : THE MIDDLE IRON AGE SETTLEMENT, *c.* 600–200B.C. (Figs. 5, 6 and 15).

(i) INTRODUCTION.

Following the activity indicated by the struck flints of late-Neolithic/Bronze Age type (regarded here as Period I), the Lower Warbank site seems to have remained unused for at least the next millenium.

Generally, the earliest features on the site are chalk-cut pits and post-holes and these form part of an overall total of more than 600 such features located during the excavations. From their inter-relationship and their datable contents the majority of these features seem to relate to either the Iron Age (Periods II and III) or to the initial Romano-British farmstead phase (Period IV), although most are not at all closely dateable.

Of special interest are two pits and a post-hole (Pits Nos. 1–3) located in the south-eastern area for their contents seem to show that they are significantly earlier than the majority of the other pits (Figs. 5 and 15). Peter Couldrey has dated the pottery from them to sometime between the 6th and 3rd centuries B.C. and they have been designated here Period II. In addition, several other pits produced only one or a few sherds of the same overall date-range, but generally this was insufficient to show whether or not this pottery was residual (e.g. Pits F.1021 and F.1532).

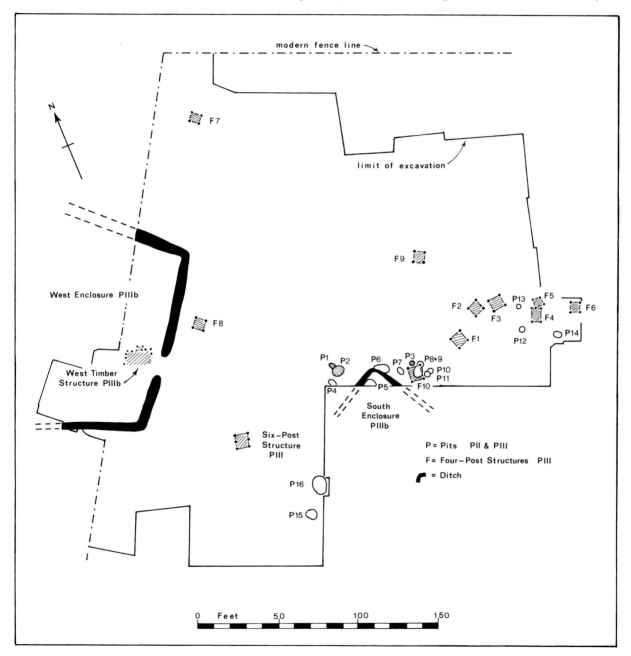

Fig. 5. *Plan of features and structures assigned to Periods II and III.*

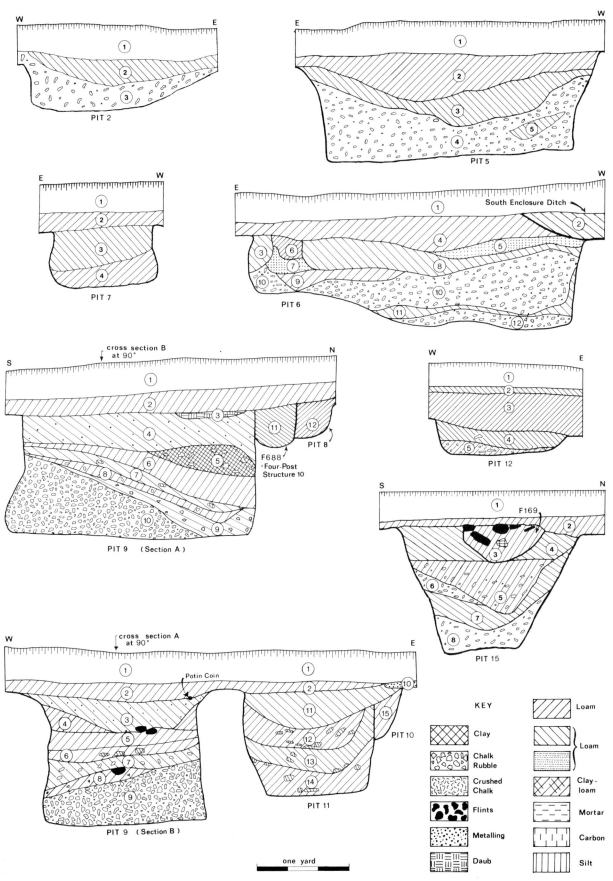

Fig. 6. *Sections across Iron Age pits.*

The full extent of the Period II occupation area is, thus, not entirely clear. The intensive later activity on the site, followed by centuries of ploughing, quite probably has led to the destruction of some minor features associated with this period. It also seems probable that a number of the undated pits and post-holes recorded belong to this period but these cannot be readily identified.

Some indication of the original extent of the Period II occupation area in Lower Warbank Field can be gained from the distribution of the flint-tempered pottery which characterises this period (Fabrics A, B and E in specialist report on the Iron Age pottery). A total of 925 potsherds in these fabrics was recovered, of which 371 came from the three pits assigned here to Period II. The remaining 554 sherds were recovered from miscellaneous and later deposits; 82 of them came from features assigned to Period III. Although it is possible that some flint-tempered wares were being produced in Period III, itself, (e.g. Nos. 241 and 505) the bulk of this material appears, stylistically, to be of the earlier, Period II date. Some 86 flint-tempered sherds have been drawn and although these are somewhat fragmentary they illustrate the range of forms present. Also of a general middle Iron Age date is a complete La Tène I brooch (No. 91), dateable on typological grounds to c. 450–200 B.C., found in a general soil deposit to the north-west of Pit 1. This clearly must have related to the settlement identified as Period II.

Significantly, the bulk of the 554 flint-tempered sherds recovered from post-Period II contexts came from the areas excavated in 1971, 1972 and 1973, on the eastern side of the site and in the general area of the three pits assigned to Period II. The volume of stratified soil deposits on this part of the site was considerable and this will, in part, account for the concentration of material here. Nevertheless, the fact that 85% of all the flint-tempered pottery recovered comes from this part of the site strongly suggests that this area did form a focus of the Period II settlement as known. It is important, also, to note that this area lies close to the southern limit of the excavated area and it seems quite possible that further features of this date remain to be discovered in the unexcavated ground. Whilst it is impossible to estimate the extent of any unlocated features there is some likelihood that the main area of the Period II settlement lay here, with the present discoveries representing just the northern fringes of the main occupation site.

A further 166 potsherds of a similar date were also recovered from the area of the tombs (none illustrated). No contemporary features were located here but the pottery could indicate occupation in this area also. Indeed, it is not impossible that the two areas formed part of one larger complex over 200 feet across.

Clearly some evidence relating to the Period II occupation has been lost to later activity on the site, but the presence of pits and post-holes suggests grain storage and timber structures of uncertain form. There is no indication that this settlement was enclosed, either by a defensive ditch or a palisade, nor were any other related ditches or gullies found. Little more, at present, may be said about this settlement.

(ii) THE PITS ASSIGNED TO PERIOD II.

Pit 1 (F.420).
This shallow pit was situated near the centre of the excavated area (Fig. 15) to the west of the Roman West Fence (Period VI) and below the Centre Timber Building (Period V). The pit was cut by a much larger pit, Pit 2 (F.419) which has also been assigned to Period II (see below). Pit 1 measured a minimum of 4'3" (north-west to south-east) by 3' (north-east to south-west). It was 8" in depth and had steep sides and a flat base. Two deposits of brown loam filled the pit, the upper layer being rather lighter in colour than the lower layer. A total of 73 potsherds (1080 grams) was recovered from the filling of this pit and these represent at least 13 different vessels.

The lower filling of the pit produced a total of 11 potsherds, representing at least six different vessels. All but one of these consist of hand-made domestic wares, clearly of prehistoric date. Two vessels have been illustrated (Nos. 156 and 157). All the vessels are early flint-tempered wares (Fabrics A, B and E, No. 157), except for one grog-tempered sherd (No. 156) which must be a later intrusion (Fabric L).

The upper filling of the pit contained a further 62 potsherds, representing some seven vessels also of flint-tempered fabrics and broadly similar to the material in the lower filling. All of these vessels have been drawn (Nos. 158–164). Much of the pottery from this pit is fragmentary, but a detailed study of the material indicates that it belongs broadly to the middle Iron Age period (see below, page 149). There were no other finds.

Pit 2 (F.419) (Fig. 6).

This substantial pit cut the eastern end of Pit 1 (see above). It was oval in shape, measuring some 7'10" (north-east to south-west) by 6'4" (north-west to south-east) and was 1'6" deep. The sides were vertical and the base flat. The filling consisted of an upper dark brown loam deposit (L.2) over a mixed loam and chalk rubble (L.3). A total of 282 potsherds (2690 grams) representing at least 32 different vessels, was recovered from the filling of the pit.

The lower filling yielded 88 sherds, representing at least 19 different vessels, all of flint-tempered wares and of broadly similar type to the material in the upper filling. A range of domestic hand-made vessels is represented and 13 of these have been drawn (Nos. 165–177).

The upper filling contained a total of 194 potsherds derived from 13 different vessels of flint-tempered wares and nine of these have been drawn (Nos. 178–186). A middle Iron Age date may be broadly assigned here, as for Pit 1. There is also one intrusive shell-tempered sherd of late-Iron Age to early-Roman date (not illustrated).

Amongst the vessels illustrated are a shouldered bowl (No. 179), a vessel with a flaring neck and rounded shoulder (No. 181) and a pedestal base (No.174), together with a number of more fragmentary rims and bases (Nos. 165–173, 175–178, 180 and 182–186).

Several small-finds were also recovered from this pit. The lower filling produced a complete lower stone of a saddle-quern (No. 134). This is made of greensand and rested on the base of the pit. A bone handle (No. 62) was also recovered, together with two flint scrapers which are probably residual (Nos. 3 and 5).

From the size and shape of the pit it seems clear that it represents a storage pit, probably for grain, of a type well-known on many Iron Age sites in southern Britain. The possible ritual significance of quernstones buried in pits has been noted by Merrifield (Ref. 40).

Pit 3 (F.462).

This feature consists of a post-pit, which was located some 47 feet to the east of Pit 2 and lay immediately to the north of Four-Post Structure 10, assigned to Period III. The post-pit was situated on the western side of a cluster of nearly 50 post-holes located in this area. These fairly clearly belong to a variety of different dates: some appear to relate to Period III, whilst others cut features assigned to Periods III and IV, indicating that they are of Roman date. Only the present feature can be reasonably certainly assigned to Period II, although another post-hole (F.673) was demonstrated to be stratigraphically earlier than Pit 10 assigned to Period III. There is no other dating evidence for this feature, however, and it is quite possible that it dates to an earlier phase of the Period III occupation itself. The vast majority of post-holes in this area, however, produced no dateable finds and showed no significant relationships with other features. The dating of Pit 3 to the middle Iron Age (Period II) is based upon the discovery of 16 flint-tempered potsherds within the filling of the post-pit (see below). Just six of the other post-holes produced similar pottery (F.458, 464, 637, 655, 665 and 676) but only F.637 contained more than a single sherd and on other evidence F.464 and 637 must be of post-Period II date.

It may seem reasonable to assume that at least some of the other post-holes in this area relate to Period II, but these cannot now be readily identified. Perhaps significantly, the bulk of the other post-holes do not show a central post-pipe, as does the present feature and only four are of a depth similar to Pit 3. Thus, the characteristics of Pit 3 are not easily matched with any other post-holes in this area and no clear post-hole alignments, which could relate to the present feature, have been recognised. Nevertheless, the existence of just one substantial post-hole in this area during Period II perhaps seems rather unlikely, although it is not impossible.

Pit 3, itself, was circular in shape, with a diameter of 16". It was 17" in depth, with vertical sides and a flat base. Within the pit the outline of a decayed wooden post, about 10″ in diameter was recorded (only two other post-holes in this area, F.457 and 653, showed this). The filling of the post-pit in Pit 3 was a light brown loam with chalk specks. The post-pipe was of a dark brown loam. The 16 flint-tempered potsherds (44 grams) recovered (Fabrics A and E) represent at least three different vessels, of which one decorated sherd has been drawn (No. 187). All of the sherds came from the filling of the post-pit. On stylistic grounds these vessels have been assigned to Period II.

PERIOD III : THE LATE-IRON AGE SETTLEMENT (*c.* 50 B.C.–A.D. 50) (Fig. 5).

(i) INTRODUCTION.

Following the middle Iron Age occupation (Period II) represented by only a few pits, post-holes and associated finds, the Warbank site seems to have been abandoned until the 1st century B.C., a time gap of at least 150 years. The establishment of a new settlement (Period III) on the site around 50 B.C. marked the start of an occupation sequence which continued apparently unbroken for the next half millenium. The full extent of the Period III settlement has not been revealed, but a series of stratigraphically early pits, enclosure ditches and post-hole structures has been assigned to this Period on the pottery dating evidence and on general sequential grounds. It has been possible, to some extent, to subdivide this Period into earlier (Period IIIa) and later (Period IIIb) phases, on the evidence of the site stratigraphy. As with Period II a proportion of the other poorly dated pits and post-holes found are likely to belong with the more certain Period III features.

The majority of the features assigned to Period IIIa were located in the south-eastern part of the excavations, in the area of the Period V, Centre Timber Building (Figs. 15 and 34). Interestingly, this is the same general area as the identifiable Period II features (see above). In this area a series of 13 late-Iron Age pits was located (Pits 4–16) and to the east of these lay a group of seven 'four-post structures' (Nos. 1–6 and 10), fairly certainly of a similar date. Three other examples of four-post structures (Nos. 7–9) and one six-post structure were found, scattered elsewhere on the site and these have also been assigned to Period IIIa. Cutting through the Period IIIa pit-cluster on the south-east side was a ditch, which seemed to form the northern corner of an enclosure lying mainly outside the limits of the excavation (the South Enclosure). A larger, probably contemporary, enclosure lay some 120 feet to the west, below the West Masonry Building and this was more fully examined (the West Enclosure). It contained the probable remains of a small timber hut (the West Timber Structure).

The two ditched enclosures have been assigned to Period IIIb and their construction seems to mark a major change in the organisation of the site. Although at least two phases appear to be represented within the Period III occupation few of the features that were located are closely dateable. Nevertheless, it seems clear enough that the two ditched enclosures post-dated the pits and perhaps also the posted-structures, none of which was enclosed by the ditches. Interestingly, Four-Post Structure 10 cut through one of the pits (Pit 8) hinting at the existence of a third phase within Period III. Perhaps also significant is the fact that there are two instances of Period III pits intercutting. All of this evidence combines to indicate the presence here of a continuously developing settlement. The appearance of ditched enclosures, however, seems to represent the latest phase of the pre-Conquest period (IIIb) and anticipates similar developments after the Roman invasion (Period IV). A total of 13 pits (Nos. 4–16) in Lower Warbank Field have thus been assigned to Period IIIa. These have been numbered following on the sequence begun for the Period II pits. The purpose of these pits, as originally excavated appears, on the evidence of their size, mostly to have been for underground storage, very probably of grain. The bulk of the pits, however, was filled with layers of chalk and loam and it seems clear that once they reached the end of their working life they were backfilled with chalk, soil and domestic rubbish, including over 700 sherds of pottery. On the eastern side of the pit-cluster a scatter of miscellaneous post-holes may include some relating to Period III, although a number are certainly later. Apart from those which constitute Four-Post Structure 10, the purpose of most of these post-holes is not clear.

The ten four-post structures (Nos. 1–10) located on the site have been assigned less certainly to Period IIIa, together with the six-post structure. The ditched enclosures may have served as animal compounds or surrounded domestic structures (or indeed both). One small sub-rectangular hut was located within the West Enclosure (the West Timber Structure) and this has been assumed to be contemporary with the enclosure itself, although it clearly does not represent a major structure.

Five late-Iron Age Potin coins (Coins Nos. 1–5) were recovered from the site and these clearly belong to Period III, even though most came from later contexts. Coins of this type are notoriously difficult to date precisely, but both Class I and Class II types are present and the earliest of these can hardly be later than the mid-1st century B.C.

The pottery associated with the definite Period III features at Keston includes a range of shell-tempered wares (Fabrics C and D of the specialist report on the Iron Age pottery), mostly with simple flat-topped, upright rims, together with footring jars bearing everted rims of burnished sandy wares (Fabric G). Grog-tempered wares (Fabrics J, K and L) occur in rather smaller amounts and it seems clear that 'Belgic' pot forms were first introduced to the site in fairly limited quantities during Period III and become more common in Period IV. Generally, grog-tempered wares are not thought to have been introduced into Iron Age West Kent before the 1st century A.D. Nevertheless, a significant number of the features assigned to Period III produced at least a few sherds of this fabric-type in their filling. Overall, the pottery relating to this Period seems to range between c. 50 B.C. and A.D. 50. Excluding the contexts of the West Enclosure Ditch, a total of 89 vessels from features assigned to Period III have been illustrated. The ditches of the West Enclosure produced considerable amounts of pottery but it is clear that much of this material accumulated in the succeeding Period IV and only some twelve illustrated vessels from here may be regarded as being of truly pre-Conquest forms, although other pieces are likely to span the Conquest period. A further 19 late-Iron Age illustrated sherds come from other features and deposits post-dating Period III.

Of the brooches recovered from the site, only one (No. 94) is more likely to belong to Period III rather than the succeeding Roman periods. Small finds from features filled during Period III, include triangular clay loom-weights found in Pits 5, 7, 9, 11 and 14 (Nos. 9–11), a spindle-whorl (No. 51), two bone toggles (Nos. 58 and 59), an iron spearhead (No. 69) and an iron hammerhead (No. 70) all recovered from Pit 9.

(ii) THE PITS ASSIGNED TO PERIOD IIIa (Figs. 5, 6, 11, 12, 15, 18, 32 and 34; Plates II, III and IV).

Pit 4 (F.485) (Fig. 15).
This was located on the western edge of the group of early pits discovered in the area of the Period V Centre Timber Building. It lay partly outside the line of the excavation and perhaps only half was examined. On the eastern side, the pit merged with Pit F.486. It was not clear, however, which cut which and Pit F.486, itself, produced no dateable finds.

Pit 4 was apparently oval in shape and measured a minimum of 5′ (north-west to south-east) by 3′ (north-east to south-west). It was 22″ in depth with sloping sides and an uneven base. The filling was a dark brown loam with some chalk and it produced a total of just seven potsherds (44 grams), which seem to represent at least five different vessels. Three of the sherds were flint-tempered and may well be residual in this context. There were also four grog-tempered sherds. One grog-tempered wall-sherd has been illustrated (No. 188).

It is hard to date this pit at all closely from the small mixed pottery assemblage it produced. It has been placed in Period III here as it lies adjacent to a number of other pits which have yielded clearer evidence of their pre-Conquest date; the presence of grog-tempered pottery in the assemblage is worthy of note as grog-tempered ware, itself, was a late introduction into Iron Age West Kent and apparently arrived not long before the Roman Conquest.

Pit 5 (F.495) (Fig 6).

This pit was located on the southern side of the group in the area of the Centre Timber Building and also lay partly outside the limits of the excavation. It would seem that about half of the pit was excavated and from this it appears to have had a sub-rectangular shape, overall. The minimum dimensions of the pit were 7'9" (south-east to north-west) by 6'9" (north-east to south-west). It was some 38" in depth with near-vertical sides and a flat base. A total of just 19 potsherds (136 grams) was recovered from the filling of the pit, together with a fragment of a triangular clay loom-weight (not illustrated).

The lower filling of the pit was chalk rubble with a few pockets of dark brown loam (L.4 and 5) and this produced just six potsherds. Four of these are shell-tempered and seem to represent two different vessels. The other two sherds come from a single grog-tempered vessel. All of the sherds are too fragmentary to illustrate. The middle filling of the pit was of brown loam (L.3) and this produced a total of ten potsherds, representing at least seven different vessels. Of these, seven sherds are flint-tempered with single sherds of sandy native ware, shelly ware and grog-tempered ware. The grog-tempered sherd has been illustrated and consists of the rim from a small vessel of uncertain overall form (No. 189). The upper pit filling of brown loam (L.2) produced a further three potsherds, representing as many vessels. These comprise one each of shell, grog and flint-tempered ware, all too small to draw.

Of the 19 potsherds recovered from this pit, a total of eight are flint-tempered and these are very probably residual. The remaining sherds are all of typical late-Iron Age fabrics, although it must again be noted that the presence of grog-tempered wares in the assemblage tends to place the date of the pit filling late in the immediate pre-Conquest period. A triangular clay loom-weight fragment recovered from the middle filling of the pit is also consistent with a pre-Conquest date (not illustrated).

Pit 6 (F.470) (Fig. 6; Plate II).

This large oval pit was situated in the centre of the pit-group located in the area of the Centre Timber Building. It measured some 11' (east to west) by at least 5' (north to south). The south edge remained unexcavated in an east–west baulk. The soil over the upper filling of the pit was cut by the ditch of the South Enclosure (L.2), which has been assigned to Period IIIb (see below). The pit, itself, was some 34" in depth with roughly vertical sides and a sloping base, which dipped down to the west. The filling consisted of a series of chalk and soil deposits (Fig 6). The lower filling was largely chalk rubble with a few pockets of dark brown loam. This material is likely to represent deliberate backfill and produced no pottery finds (L.10, 11 and 12). Above this lower filling were deposits of brown loam with some chalk (L.5, 6, 7, 8 and 9). The most extensive of these deposits (L.5) produced just six sherds of pottery (51 grams), representing at least four different vessels. Four of the sherds are shell-tempered and two are flint-tempered. One flint-tempered sherd (No. 190) has been illustrated, although this is probably residual.

A deposit of brown loam sealing the pit (L.4) produced a total of 19 more potsherds. These represent at least nine different vessels and six of these have been illustrated (Nos. 191–196). There are three shell-tempered sherds, including part of a storage jar (No. 194), eight grog-tempered sherds (Nos. 195 and 196) and six small flint-tempered sherds, including two bases (Nos. 191 and 193), with two more of sandy native ware, one of which is decorated (No. 192). The small amount of dateable material from the pit, itself, is consistent with a broadly pre-Conquest date for its filling. The pottery from the sealing layer is unlikely to be much later. Little more than this can be said.

Pit 7 (F.507) (Fig. 6).

This pit was situated in the middle of the cluster of pits located in the area of the Centre Timber Building. It appeared to be oval in shape but about half was left undug, under baulks. In plan, the pit measured some 5'6" (north-west to south-east) by 3' (north-east to south-west). The sides were undercut slightly and the base was flat, with an overall depth of some 24". The filling consisted of an upper (L.3) and lower (L.4) layer of dark brown loam. The excavated part of the pit filling produced a total of just twelve potsherds (110 grams), representing at least eight vessels (none illustrated). The lower filling produced five sherds; one of sandy native ware, two of flint-tempered ware and two of shelly ware. These are all too fragmentary to draw. The upper filling produced seven sherds and these comprise two each of shelly ware and native sandy ware, two of flint-tempered fabrics and one grog-tempered sherd. In addition, the upper fill also contained a triangular loom-weight of baked clay (No. 11). Together, the fairly limited dating evidence from this pit suggests that it belongs to Period III, along with most of the other pits in this area.

Pit 8 (F.631) (Fig. 6).

This small oval pit was cut on the south-western side by Pit 9 and by a post-hole (F.688) of the Four-Post Structure 10 (S.A, L.11), both of which have also been assigned to Period III. The pit itself, measured a minimum of 4' (north–south) by some 3' (east–west) and was just 8" deep. The sides and base were sloping and flat, respectively. The pit was filled with a black loam (S.A, L.12), which yielded just two sherds (18 grams.) from a single shell-tempered vessel, too fragmentary to illustrate. The position of this pit in relation to Pit 9 and the Four-Post Structure, together with the very limited pottery evidence leaves little doubt that it belongs to an early phase of Period III.

Pit 9 (F.466/509/632) (Fig. 6).

This large pit was located in the area of the Centre Timber Building, under Four-Post Structure 10 and it cut Pit 8 (F.631). The present pit was examined over two seasons. In plan, it was oval and measured some 7'2" (north–south) by 4'2" (east–west). It was some 4'1" deep with slightly undercut sides and a flat base – a profile very characteristic of many pre-Conquest storage pits.

The filling of the pit consisted of a series of chalk and loam deposits. The primary filling, of chalk rubble, consisted apparently of deliberate backfill and seemed to have been thrown in from one side of the feature (see S.A, L.10 and S.B, L.7). Above this, a series of mixed loams, with carbon and some chalk had been deposited (S.A, L.4–9; S.B, L.3–6). A total of 390 potsherds (4646 grams) was recovered; 42 of these have been drawn (Nos. 197–238).

The primary chalk filling produced a total of 58 potsherds, representing at least eight different vessels. Six of these have been illustrated (Nos. 197–202). Some 46 of the sherds are shell-tempered and these represent at least four vessels. All of these have been drawn and comprise three vessels with upright, flat-topped rims (Nos. 197, 199 and 202) and part of a shouldered jar (No. 200). Sandy native wares account for nine sherds from at least two vessels, both apparently footring jars with everted rims (Nos. 198 and 201). Three sherds of flint-tempered ware came from another two vessels, both too fragmentary to illustrate.

The middle, mixed loam fillings of the pit (S.A, L.4–9; S.B, L.3–6) produced a total of 214 potsherds and these represent at least 43 different vessels of which 21 have been drawn (Nos. 203–223). Some 129 sherds representing at least 20 vessels are of shelly wares. Ten of these have been drawn to illustrate the range of types, mostly vessels with simple, upright rims, all typical of the pre-Conquest period (Nos. 205–208, 211, 213, 214, 219, 220 and 223). There are 56 sherds in a sandy native fabric and these represent eleven more vessels. All of these seem to be jars, typically with a footring, everted rim and burnished exterior. Six of these vessels have been drawn (Nos. 204, 209, 212, 215, 218 and 222). There are also 29 small sherds of flint-tempered ware, representing at least twelve more vessels. Five of these are illustrated (Nos. 203, 210, 216, 217 and 221). These comprise three rims (Nos. 210, 216 and 217), a base (No. 203) and a decorated wall sherd (No. 221) from fragmentary vessels of uncertain overall form.

A final deposit of dark brown loam sealed the top of the pit (S.A and B, L.2). This layer produced a total of 118 sherds, representing at least 32 vessels. Fifteen of these have been drawn (Nos. 224–238). Some 34 sherds are of shelly ware and these represent at least ten different vessels. Four typical pre-Conquest rims have been drawn (Nos. 228, 229, 233 and 237). There are in addition 47 sherds in native sandy wares representing at least nine different vessels and seven of these have been drawn. All of them appear to be everted rim jars with footring bases (Nos. 230–232, 234–236 and 238). Thirteen grog-tempered sherds were also recovered and these represent at least seven more vessels of which three have been illustrated. They include a butt beaker (No. 226), an everted rim jar (No. 224) and a large bead rim storage jar (No. 227). There are 22 small flint-tempered sherds and these represent a further six fragmentary vessels. One of these has been illustrated (No. 225). There are also two Roman sherds in this deposit which must be intrusive (not illustrated).

A number of other finds was also recovered from this large pit. In the top of the upper filling (S.B, L.3) a Potin coin of Allen's Type 'L' was discovered; this may be dated to the 1st century B.C. (Coin No. 5). The middle pit filling produced two partially complete skeletons of ovicaprid (S.B, L.5). These have been described in detail by Alison Locker (see below, page 286). Both animals appear to be immature individuals and it is not impossible that they represent some sort of ritual deposit. A considerable quantity of burnt daub was recovered from this pit, together with a number of small-finds.

Level	Flint-tempered Ware	Shell-tempered Ware	Native Sandy Ware	Grog-tempered Ware	Total Vessels
Uppermost Fill	6	10	9	7	32
Middle Fill	12	20	11	0	43
Lower Fill	2	4	2	0	8
Total	20	34	22	7	83

Table 1. Details of vessels recovered from Pit 9.

A fragment of a rotary quern of Greensand was also found (not illustrated). A triangular clay loom-weight (No. 9) came from the middle filling of the pit (S.B, L.6), together with two bone toggles (Nos. 58 and 59) of well-known Iron Age form (S.B, L.5). A pottery spindle-whorl of biconical form (No. 51), an iron hammer-head (No. 70) and a spearhead (No. 69) were recovered from the upper filling (S.A, L.4).

The pottery and other dating evidence from this pit thus combine to make it clear that this substantial feature is of pre-Conquest date. The latest 'Belgic' pottery forms, namely the grog-tempered wares, are confined to the uppermost filling of the pit making it clear that much of the pit had been backfilled by the time these wares arrived in West Kent, presently considered to be sometime just before the Roman conquest. The main pit filling, therefore, may well date to the 1st century B.C. and the Potin coin found above the pit would fit into this period too.

Pit 10 (F.633) (Fig. 6; Plate III).
This pit was located in the area of the Centre Timber Building in 1972. It had been cut by Pit 11 (F.675) and a post-hole (F.655) and itself cut an earlier but otherwise undated post-hole (F.673). Pit 10 was circular in plan with a diameter of some 3'8". (Pit 11, however, had destroyed nearly a half of the feature). Pit 10 had near-vertical sides and a flat base. It was 18" in depth and was filled with black loam (S.B, L.13) which contained very large amounts of burnt daub fragments (not illustrated).

Some 29 potsherds (524 grams) were also recovered from the filling of this pit. These represent at least five different vessels and four of them have been drawn (Nos. 239–242). Twelve sherds, representing three vessels, are of typical pre-Conquest shelly wares (Nos. 239 and 242). A further 16 sherds are from a single everted rim jar of sandy native ware (No. 240). There is also one flint-tempered rim sherd from a small jar (No. 241). No other finds were recovered and from the (limited) pottery dating evidence it seems reasonably certain that this pit belongs to Period III. This dating is largely confirmed by the pit's position relative to Pit 11, also of Period III, and implies that Pit 10 belongs to an early phase of the Period III settlement. The absence of grog-tempered pottery within its filling helps to confirm this.

Pit 11 (F.675) (Fig. 6; Plate III).

This pit cut Pit 10 (F.633) and was oval in shape, measuring some 4′4″ (east–west) by 4′ (north–south). It was some 39″ in depth with slightly undercut sides in places and a flat base. The pit was filled with various deposits of black and brown loam which yielded a total of 102 potsherds (2645 grams) representing at least 20 different vessels. The primary filling of the pit (S.B, L.12) produced ten sherds representing at least six pots. Three of these have been illustrated. Eight of these sherds are of shelly ware and these represent four of the pots (Nos. 243–245), all with simple, upright and undeveloped rims, typical of the pre-Conquest period. In addition there are two sherds from two flint-tempered vessels, too fragmentary to illustrate. The middle filling of the pit (S.B, L.10 and 11) produced a further eight sherds and these represent five more vessels. Sherds from two shelly ware vessels are present, including one slightly out-turned, flat-topped rim (No. 248). There are also four sherds from two vessels of native sandy ware (Nos. 246 and 247) and both consist of fragments from the familiar footring jar with everted rim. In addition, there is one small sherd of flint-tempered ware from the middle filling of the pit (not illustrated).

The bulk of the pottery from this pit, however, came from the upper filling of black loam (S.B, L.9). This deposit produced a total of 84 potsherds and these represent at least 14 vessels, all but one of which have been illustrated (Nos. 249–261). Just over half of the sherds are derived from seven shell-tempered vessels. These include two large storage vessels (Nos. 254 and 256), as well as a number of smaller pots all of typical pre-Conquest forms, with simple, mostly upright rims (Nos. 250, 251, 255, 258 and 260). A further 34 sherds come from at least three different vessels of native sandy ware. Two of these seem to be the bases of footring jars, both with burnished cruciform designs on their underside (Nos. 252 and 253). There is also part of a small jar with an inturned rim (No. 257). Two small flint-tempered sherds from two separate vessels were also recovered. These are, an upright rim (No. 259) and a base (No. 261). In addition, there are three small sherds from a grog-tempered vessel with burnished decoration (No. 249), together with a single sherd of sandy Romanised ware. The Roman sherd is clearly intrusive and the same could be true of the grog-tempered sherds.

Overall, the pottery indicates that this pit is certainly of pre-Conquest date and it may be confidently assigned to Period III. In addition to the pottery, this pit also produced a considerable amount of burnt daub fragments (not illustrated) and the middle filling of the pit produced two small fragments from a triangular clay loom-weight of typical later Iron Age type (S.B, L.10). This unfortunately cannot be usefully illustrated.

Pit 12 (F.733) (Fig. 6).

This Pit lay some 65 feet east of the main pit-group located in the area of the Centre Timber Building. The present pit was circular in shape with a diameter of 4′2″. It had sloping sides and a flat base and was some 12″ in depth. The filling comprised of an upper layer of brown loam (L.4) over a deposit of light brown loam and chalk lumps (L.5). The lower filling of the pit produced a total of 43 potsherds (570 grams) from a single shell-tempered vessel of a typical pre-Conquest type. This has been illustrated (No. 262). There were no finds in the upper filling, but there can be little doubt that this pit is pre-Conquest and it may be quite reasonably assigned to Period III. No other finds were located.

Pit 13 (F.703) (Fig. 34).

This small pit was located in 1973 about halfway between Four-Post Structures 3 and 4. It was circular in plan, with a diameter of 18″ and was just 4″ in depth. The filling was a brown loam and the sides were steep, with a cupped base. The pit-fill yielded some 35 potsherds (280 grams). These are derived from a single large shell-tempered vessel with a flat base but of uncertain overall form (No. 263). No other finds were recovered. This small pit may represent an eroded post-pit. From the slightly limited pottery dating evidence it seems fairly reasonably placed in Period III.

Pit 14 (Pit 'B') (Fig. 18).

This was another easterly outlier to the main pit group. About half of this pit had been cut away by the South-East Villa Enclosure Ditch, assigned to Period VI. Originally, however, the pit was probably circular with a diameter of about 4′6″. The pit had a depth of 28″ with steep/vertical sides and a flat base. It was filled with a series of brown loam (L.15 and 16) and chalk (L.17) largely devoid of finds. The middle filling, however, (L.16) produced seven potsherds (No. 107). These represent at least four different vessels; two shell-tempered, one grog-tempered and one flint-tempered. They are rather fragmentary but include a small base (No. 264), a decorated wall sherd (No. 265) and a slightly recessed rim (No. 266). Part of a triangular clay loom-weight (No. 10) was found with the pottery and together these finds indicate that this pit is broadly of pre-Conquest date.

Pit 15 (F.170) (Figs. 6 and 32).

This pit was situated at the northern end of a cluster of early pits and post-holes located below and to the east of the South Masonry Building in 1968 and 1969. It was the largest pit in this area (Fig. 32) and, from the pottery it contained, also seemed to be one of the earliest. It was cut by two later pits (F.155 and 169).

The present pit was circular in shape, with a diameter of some 7′. It was 4′ in depth with steep/sloping sides and a flat base (Fig. 6). The primary filling was chalk rubble (L.8) and above this was a series of chalk and loam deposits, forming a middle fill (L.5, 6 and 7). The top of the pit was filled with black loam (L.4). A total of 37 potsherds (332 grams) was recovered from this pit and these seem to represent at least 22 different vessels, six of which have been illustrated (Nos. 267–272). The middle filling of the pit also produced the skeleton of a dog and of a human infant.

The lower, primary filling of the pit (L.8) produced just four sherds of shelly ware. These seem to represent at least two different pots and one with an out-turned, flat-topped rim, typical of the pre-Conquest period, has been drawn (No. 267). The upper-middle filling of the pit (L.5) produced some 29 sherds. Thirteen of these are shell-tempered and these represent at least five different vessels. One upright rim, again typical of the pre-Conquest period has been drawn (No. 271), together with a shoulder fragment (No. 272). Another eleven sherds are of sandy native wares and these represent at least three different vessels. One of them has been drawn and this consists of a footring base, presumably derived from one of the familiar everted rim jars (No. 268). There are also three flint-tempered sherds. These represent two different vessels and both are too small for illustration. In addition, there are two Roman sherds. These consist of small pieces of 1st century A.D. Keston Kiln Ware vessels; a butt beaker and a pedestal base. They are clearly intrusive here but have been illustrated for the sake of completeness (Nos. 269 and 270).

The upper filling (L.4) of the pit produced four more potsherds. These represent two sandy native ware vessels and one shell-tempered pot, all too small to illustrate.

Allowing for some intrusive material in this fairly small assemblage of pottery it seems fairly reasonable to assign this pit to the pre-Conquest period.

Pit 16 (Figs. 11 and 12; Plate IV).

This pit was excavated in 1970 and lay some 25 feet north-east of the South Masonry Building (Fig. 11). Its upper levels had been subsequently removed by the early-Roman Quarry Pit Complex of Period IV, which lay in this area. The pottery from the surviving pit fill, however,

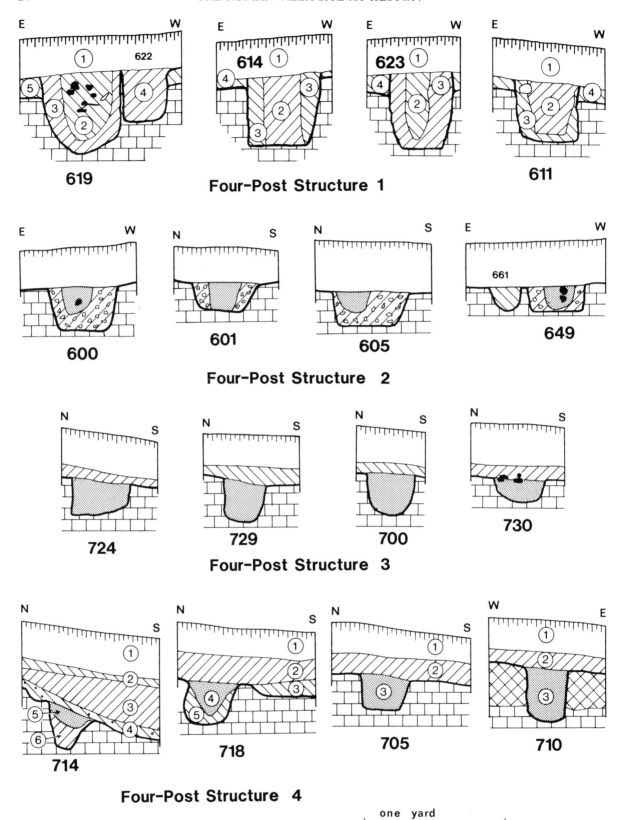

Fig. 7.   *Sections across post-holes of Four-Post Structures 1–4.*

indicated that the present pit was of pre-Conquest date and it has been assigned to Period III. As it survived, the pit was oval in shape and measured a minimum of 11' (north–south) by 6'8" (east–west). Its northern edge was not seen and remained unexcavated in a baulk. The sides of the pit were steeply sloping at about 70° and its original depth overall would have been some 48" into the chalk. The base of the pit was flat and the filling (Fig. 12) consisted of various layers of chalk rubble (S.A, L.11 and 12), with some brown loam (S.A, L.13). Unfortunately, there had been some disturbance of these layers by burrowing animals.

A total of 50 coarse-ware potsherds (485 grams) was recovered from the filling of this pit. These sherds represent at least twelve different vessels and three of them have been illustrated (Nos. 273–275). Some 34 sherds are shell-tempered and these come from at least four vessels, all too fragmentary to draw. A further ten sherds are of sandy native wares; at least three vessels are represented and two of these, both typical everted rim jars, have been drawn (Nos. 273 and 274). In addition, there are three flint-tempered sherds and three small grog-tempered sherds. The flint-tempered sherds come from two fragmentary vessels whilst the grog-tempered pieces represent three different vessels. One rim of a grog-tempered globular jar or bowl has been drawn (No. 275). It is possible, however, that the grog-tempered sherds are intrusive in this pit. The pre-Conquest date of this pit overall seems fairly certain, despite the subsequent disturbance of this area in Period IV. Four late-Iron Age rim sherds from the filling of the Quarry Pit Complex above Pit 16 have also been drawn (Nos. 390–393). These are fairly certainly derived from the filling of the earlier pit and consist of two everted rim jars, one in sandy native ware (No. 393) and the other in a sandy shell-tempered ware (No. 392), together with two other shell-tempered vessels (Nos. 390 and 391).

(iii) FOUR-POST STRUCTURES (Figs. 5, 6, 7, 8, 15, 34 and 36).

Deliberate settings of four post-holes arranged in a regular square or rectangle were recognised in ten instances on the site. These 'four-post structures' range in size from 5' to 9'10" across and fall readily into a class of small timber buildings well known on many Iron Age settlement sites in southern Britain. The ten structures revealed in Lower Warbank Field have been assigned here to the late-Iron Age settlement of Period IIIa, although precise dating evidence is limited. In detail, a group of seven structures was located between 1971 and 1974, set in a broad arc on the south-eastern side of the excavated area (Nos. 1–6 and 10). To the north of this main group a single isolated example was located in 1978 (No. 9) to the south of the North Timber Building. The remaining two structures (Nos. 7 and 8) were widely spaced along the western side of the area excavated. Although the overall dating evidence relating to these four-post structures is limited the general contemporanity of the group on the south-eastern side seems clear enough. The most south-westerly of these structures (No. 10) can be related to one of the early pits located in this area, also assigned to Period IIIa (Pit 8) and demonstrates that the pit predates the posted-structure (see S.A). The relationship of the 'four-poster' to Pit 9, also assigned to Period IIIa and which cuts Pit 8, is less certain, although they clearly cannot have been contemporary. Nor can Four-Post Structures 4 and 5 have stood at the same time, as their sites overlap. These observations help confirm the existence of several phases to the Period III settlement. Indeed, it could be argued, on the strength of Structure 10 cutting Pit 8 (Fig. 6), that all the four-post structures along the south-eastern side of the excavation post-date the pit-cluster. Yet they lie outside the two ditched enclosures of Period IIIb. That the posted structures predate Period IV, however, is indicated by the fact that they cut across the line of the East Enclosure Ditch, assigned to Period IVa.

Other stratigraphical relationships noted are less informative. One post-hole of Structure 4 could be seen to be cut by and therefore, predate the terrace cut for the 4th century Upper East Metalling of Period VII. Two post-holes of Structure 6 had been cut by a later, minor gully (F.738 – Ditch No. 15), which is not securely dated. Structure 9 was cut by a later alignment of post-holes, which again are not securely dated (Fig. 36).

The pottery dating evidence for the four-post structures is considered below and Tables 2 and

Structure No.	Year	Original Feature Nos.	Length (ft.)	Width (ft.)	Main Axis
1	1972	611, 614, 619, 623	7′10″ – 8′0″	7′6″ – 7′8″	NE–SW
2	1972	600, 601, 605, 649	7′6″ – 7′7″	7′0″ – 7′5″	NW–SE
3	1973	700, 724, 729, 730	8′3″ – 8′7″	7′11″	NE–SW
4	1973	705, 710, 714, 718	9′0″ – 9′6″	6′0″ – 6′6″	N–S
5	1973	704, 707, 709, 717	5′0″ – 6′6″	5′3″ – 5′9″	NE–SW
6	1974	734, 735, 737, 740	6′9″	6′0″ – 6′6″	E–W
7	1976	803, 804, 952, 953	6′6″	5′6″	NW–SE
8	1977	1022, 1024, 1026, 1026A	7′3″	7′0″	N–S
9	1978	1522, 1524, 1529, 1533	7′0″ – 7′6″	7′0″	E–W
10	1971/72	465, 662, 677, 688	9′8″ – 9′10″	7′10″ – 8′6″	NW–SE

Table 2. The overall dimensions of Four-Post Structures 1–10.

3, record the basic information on their overall form and details of the individual posts, all of which were oval or circular in shape.

The fillings of the post-holes of the structures produced only meagre dating evidence in the form of an overall total of 35 coarse ware potsherds. All are too fragmentary to draw. No coins (or samian sherds) were recovered. Four-Post Structure 1 produced a total of 16 sherds, representing at least five different vessels. Four of these are shell-tempered, one flint-tempered and the remaining eleven sherds come from a single vessel of native sandy ware. Structure 2 produced five flint-tempered sherds, one shell-tempered piece and two with grog-tempering as well as a flint end-scraper (No. 6). Structure 3 produced only a single shell-tempered sherd. Structure 4 contained a total of five sherds, four flint-tempered and one of sandy native ware. Structure 5 yielded no finds and Structure 6 produced only a single shell-tempered sherd. Four-Post Structure 7 contained two shell-tempered sherds and Structure 8 yielded no finds. Structure 9 yielded only a single Roman sherd which may be intrusive. Structure 10 produced just one grog-tempered sherd. Overall, this pottery merely indicates that the post-holes must be later than Period II.

Structure No.	Feature No.	Shape	Length (ins.)	Width (ins.)	Main Axis	Depth into chalk (ins.)	Sides	Base	Post-Pipe diam. (ins.)
1	611	Oval	21″	16″	E–W	12″	Vert.	Flat	12″
	614	Circ.	19″	19″	–	17″	Vert.	Flat	9″
	619	Circ.	20″	20″	–	15″	Steep	Round	12″
	623	Oval	19″	16″	N–S	16″	Steep	Flat	6″
2	600	Oval	17″	15″	N–S	11″	Steep	Flat	9″
	601	Circ.	17″	17″	–	7″	Steep	Flat	9″
	605	Oval	20″	18″	N–S	9″	Steep	Flat	9″
	649	Oval	18″	16″	E–W	7″	Steep	Flat	12″

Structure No.	Feature No.	Shape	Length (ins.)	Width (ins.)	Main Axis	Depth into chalk (ins.)	Sides	Base	Post-Pipe diam. (ins.)
3	700	Circ.	12″	12″	–	10″	Steep	Cupped	–
	724	Circ.	15″	15″	–	9″	Steep	Cupped	–
	729	Circ.	11″	11″	–	10″	Steep	Cupped	–
	730	Oval	12″	11″	E–W	7″	Steep	Cupped	–
4	705	Circ.	13″	13″	–	8″	Sloping	Flat	–
	710	Circ.	12″	12″	–	15″	Steep	Flat	–
	714	Oval	13″	12″	N–S	12″	Sloping	Flat	5″
	718	Circ.	13″	13″	–	12″	Steep	Flat	9″
5	704	Circ.	18″	18″	–	8″	Sloping	Flat	–
	707	Circ.	16″	16″	–	7″	Steep	Cupped	–
	709	Circ.	12″	12″	–	7″	Steep	Cupped	–
	717	Circ.	17″	17″	–	7″	Sloping	Cupped	–
6	734	Circ.	12″	12″	–	11″	Steep	Flat	–
	735	Oval	21″	20″	E–W	11″	Sloping	Cupped	–
	737	Circ.	12″	12″	–	5″(min)	Steep	Flat	–
	740	?Circ.	10″	?10″	–	6″(min)	Vert.	Flat	–
7	803	Oval	23″	20″	E–W	5″	Vert.	Flat	–
	804	Oval	21″	20″	N–S	3″	Steep	Cupped	–
	952	Oval	20″	!7″	E–W	3″	Steep	Cupped	–
	953	Circ.	21″	21″	–	4″	Steep	Cupped	–
8	1022	Circ.	18″	18″	–	8″	Vert.	Cupped	–
	1024	Circ.	18″	18″	–	13″	Steep	Cupped	–
	1026	Circ.	16″	16″	–	13″	Vert.	Sloping	–
	1026A	Circ.	15″	15″	–	–	–	–	–
9	1522	Circ.	27″	27″	–	10″	Sloping	Cupped	–
	1524	Circ.	24″	24″	–	11″	Steep	Cupped	–
	1529	Circ.	26″	26″	–	5″	Sloping	Cupped	–
	1533	Circ.	22″	22″	–	7″	Sloping	Cupped	–
10	465	Circ.	15″	15″	–	12″	Steep	Flat	–
	662	Oval	15″	12″	N–S	10″	Vert.	Flat	–
	677	Oval	15″	14″	N–S	15″	Vert.	Flat	–
	688	Circ.	15″	15″	–	13″	Steep	Cupped	–

Table 3. Details of the Post-Holes relating to Four-Post Structures 1–10.

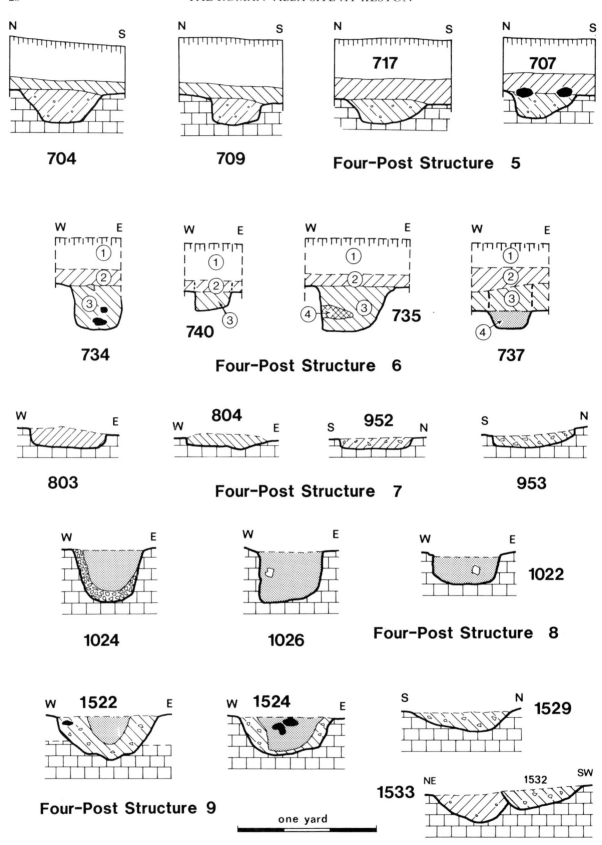

Fig. 8.   *Sections across post-holes of Four-Post Structures 5–9*

In the absence of any clear evidence to the contrary it seems reasonable to place the majority of the four-post structures in Period III, the pre-Conquest, late-Iron Age farmstead. Structure 9, however, produced a Roman sherd and this may have to be assigned to the succeeding Period IV, the post-Conquest farmstead, but this is not certain.

Four-post structures, generally interpreted as raised granaries, are now well known on sites throughout southern Britain. The earliest examples appear to belong to the late-Bronze Age, whilst a number of Roman examples are known. The majority, however, are of Iron Age date. In Kent, until recently, few of these structures had been recorded but they are now known on a number of sites spread throughout the county. At Keston the 'four-posters' seem to relate most probably to the late-Iron Age period.

(iv) SIX-POST STRUCTURE (Figs. 4 and 5).

Only one certain six-post structure was recorded in Lower Warbank Field. This was located in 1969 and lay some 120 feet to the west of Four-Post Structure 10. It comprised six circular post-holes (F.187–192) ranging in diameter from 11″ to 14″. These represent an almost square structure, measuring some 9′6″ to 10′ (north-south) by 9′ to 10′ (east-west).

The dating evidence for the present structure is very limited. The projected line of the East Water Pipe assigned to Period VI runs across the area occupied by the structure and one post-hole is on its exact line, suggesting that the two features could not have been contemporary, but no other sequential evidence is available. The post-holes of the structure, itself, produced no dateable material and thus, the structure cannot be dated on its own merits. The circumstantial evidence, however, strongly suggests that this six-post structure is contemporary with the four-post structures assigned to Period III, both types being well known on Iron Age sites. Interestingly, the present structure could represent a continuation of the arc of seven 'four-posters' found along the south-eastern side of the excavation.

(v) TWO-POST STRUCTURES.

Of the large number of post-holes recorded on the Keston site many could not be linked to form any coherent structure plans. Nevertheless, a number of 'four-post structures', together with one 'six-post structure', both of types well-known on Iron Age sites, have been identified and these have been assigned here to Period III (see above). Also known on other Iron Age sites are 'two-post structures', generally interpreted as drying-racks. One such structure has been identified at nearby Farningham Hill (Ref. 41). At Keston, however, it is more difficult to recognise related pairs of post-holes due to the general scatter of features across much of the site. Two pairs of post-holes set in single oval pits clearly are related but the dating evidence indicates that these are of Roman date and they have been assigned to Period IV (Four-Post Structures A and B). Other possible pairs of post-holes have been dismissed because of differences in individual size and shape.

(vi) THE WEST ENCLOSURE (Figs. 5, 10, 19 and 20).

On the extreme west side of the excavated area and situated on a localised 'shoulder' of high ground, was a substantial ditched enclosure. Excavations over several seasons (1969, 1970 and 1976) revealed the full extent of its silted ditch on the east side, but only short lengths of its north and south sides (Fig. 19). Much later excavations (to be published in a subsequent report) revealed further lengths of the north and south sides, but failed to reach a presumed western ditch. This shows that the excavation in Lower Warbank Field revealed rather less than half the area of the enclosure. However, the east ditch joined the north ditch at an angle of about 95° and joined the south ditch at about 110°. This splayed arrangement precludes a rectangular plan and suggests either a trapezoidal, or pentagonal, arrangement. Coincidentally, or not, the site of the enclosure also formed the site of later, major Roman structures (Period V–VII).

Unfortunately, the Roman activity, extensive later ploughing and antiquarian excavations, have all combined to reduce much of the interior of the enclosure and it is not clear what the ditches enclosed. On the evidence of broadly contemporary enclosures elsewhere, notably at Farningham Hill in West Kent, the enclosure should ideally have contained a substantial round-house and related storage and other features. A 14' wide gap in the east ditch must mark a major entrance, whilst a ditch terminal (discovered in the much later excavations) on the north side seems to mark an uphill entrance of unknown width. In the area under consideration here the ditch enclosed several pits, four gullies (see below) and a number of post-holes, which at one point seemed to define part of a small sub-rectangular structure. The majority of these features, however, failed to yield any significant dateable material and their contemporaneity with the enclosure ditch cannot be certain. Interestingly, the density of such features within the enclosure was in fact no greater than in the adjacent, unenclosed areas and it seems probable that at least some of the features, if not the majority, are of either earlier or later date. Two small pits (F.262 and F.205) produced just sufficient pottery to suggest that they are pre-Conquest (see No. 839) (Period III). Three other pits contained later, Roman cremation burials (Period IV, phase b) and several others seem to be contemporary with the Period VI/VII villa building. One group of post-holes, just within the eastern entrance to the enclosure, formed part of a small sub-rectangular timber structure (West Timber Structure) which could be contemporary with the enclosure ditch, but this is not certain.

Near the south-east corner of the enclosure, three curving, intercutting gullies (Ditches 10, 11, 12) were located. These clearly predated the West Masonry Building but, from their location, did not seem to be contemporary with the West Enclosure. Ditch 11 actually crossed the line of the Enclosure Ditch though whether this was earlier or later than it could not be ascertained. The earliest of these three features was Ditch 12, which was cut by Ditches 10 and 11. The interpretation of these gullies is uncertain; their curved form could suggest that they were drip-gullies around circular huts but this is far from definite. The small number of potsherds from these gullies are all of 1st century A.D. date and include some Romanised fabrics.

Although the full extent of the West Enclosure Ditch was not traced, from the areas examined it could be seen to enclose an area measuring internally 115 feet (north–south) by a minimum of 40 feet (east–west) (work in 1985–87 subsequently located further lengths of the ditch to the west, allowing it to be traced for a total minimum, east-west, distance of about 95 feet).

No trace of any associated bank survived flanking the enclosure ditch, although one quite probably once existed. If so, it was presumably destroyed by the later, Roman building and more recent ploughing. The Enclosure Ditch, itself, cut no earlier features for certain, but several later features cut it, including a post-hole of the Period VI Centre Fence. Most notably a gully, once recut, had been dug along the line of the ditch on the east side after it had completely silted up. This gully (Gully C) seems to form part of a later ditched enclosure lying immediately to the east (the Centre Enclosure of Phase IVb).

The main enclosure ditch, itself, produced pottery in large amounts and this material ranges in date from the late-Iron Age into the early-Roman period (see below). Apart from a few clearly intrusive sherds none of this ceramic material is likely to date much after A.D. 125 and the bulk is no later than *c*. A.D. 85.

a) The Enclosure Ditch, North Arm (Fig. 10).

Work in 1976 revealed that the north ditch of the enclosure joined that on the east at about 95°. The north arm had a minimum length of 38 feet, although it was traced much further to the west in 1985, giving it a total minimum length of over 90 feet. At its western end, in the new area, a terminal was located and this suggests the existence of a second entrance. In Lower Warbank Field, the North Ditch varied in width from 3'9" at the corner to 7' at the western limit of the 1976 excavation. This differential appeared to reflect post-Roman plough erosion rather than any original variation. The ditch had a V-shaped profile with a flat base about 12" across. In depth it ranged between 1'11" and 2'9" as surviving into the chalk. Ploughing had clearly destroyed a considerable amount of its upper part, however, and original dimensions of about 9′ for the width and 4′ for the depth from the original ground surface, seem probable.

The filling of the ditch along the northern side was the only section where the deposits remained largely undisturbed by burrowing animals. The ditch's upper filling (L.2 and 3) and middle filling (L.4 and 5) consisted of layers of brown loam and chalk resting on primary silts of chalky rubble (L.6). This primary silt was clearly mostly natural chalk, weathered from the side of the ditch over a fairly short space of time. This interpretation is generally supported by the few finds from these layers. The upper and middle fills seem to represent secondary chalk and soil silts forming in the ditch naturally, probably with some domestic rubbish dumped here from an adjacent living-area.

The north arm of the enclosure ditch produced a total of 327 coarse-ware potsherds, representing at least 48 different vessels. Twelve of these, all from the upper and middle filling, have been drawn (Nos. 276–287). The lower filling of the ditch produced just six potsherds (too fragmentary for illustration). The middle filling produced 59 sherds and the upper filling 262 sherds. The distribution of this pottery by fabric-type is shown in Table 4.

The upper and middle fillings of the ditch also produced a quantity of animal bone (see below, p. 289) but no small finds were recovered.

b) The Enclosure Ditch, East Arm (Fig. 20).

On the eastern side of the enclosure the ditch was traced in its entirety. It was divided into two unequal parts by a baulk of undug chalk, which formed an entrance causeway some 14′ in width. The lengths of ditch to the north and south of this causeway may be most conveniently described separately.

The ditch length to the north of the entrance was traced for a distance of 70 feet. It varied in width from 3′9″ to 7′, with the narrowest section at the north-east corner adjacent to the narrowest section of the north ditch. It had clearly suffered from the effects of ploughing, like the north arm. The profile of the present length was again V-shaped, with a flat base about 12″ across. The depth ranged from 1′9″ to 2′9″ into solid chalk. The filling at the north end consisted of layers of orange-brown clay and dark brown clay loam with pebbles, which may represent a localised area of deliberate backfilling for it was certainly in contrast to the sequence of deposits found in the rest of this length. The majority of this length of the ditch was filled with brown loam and chalk over a primary chalk silt, again representing largely natural weathering deposits with some domestic rubbish. These ditch deposits, however, had been heavily disturbed by burrowing animals in many places.

The backfill deposits at the north end of this ditch produced a total of 83 coarse-ware potsherds representing at least 19 vessels, of which two have been illustrated (Nos. 289 and 290, from the lower deposit). The remainder of the fill produced a total of 975 potsherds and these represent at least 110 different vessels. Only 26 of these sherds came from the primary filling and just one vessel has been drawn from this small group (No. 288). Some 147 sherds were recovered from the middle filling of this length of the ditch and five of these have been illustrated (Nos. 291–295). The upper filling of the ditch here produced a total of 802 potsherds and 22 have been drawn (Nos. 296–316). The upper filling also produced a bronze brooch (No. 97), a bronze pin (No. 119), a spindle-whorl (No. 48) and a quantity of animal bone. The middle fill produced further animal bone and another bronze brooch (No. 101). Near the north corner, the upper filling of the ditch had been cut by several small pits and post-holes of uncertain significance. An interesting late-Iron Age decorated vessel from one of these has been drawn (No. 838) although it must be residual in its excavated context and is probably derived from the Enclosure Ditch itself. For its whole length the upper filling of this part of the east ditch was also cut by a later Roman gully (Gully C) and its recut (Gully D), running along the western lip. Both these later gullies and the main ditch were cut by another east–west gully of post-Roman date (Ditch 3/4), some 14′ north of the entrance gap.

The length of ditch to the south of the entrance causeway was also fully investigated. It appeared to join the enclosure ditch on the south side at an angle of about 110°. Like its corresponding northern length it was V-shaped in cross-section with a flat base some 9″ to 12″ across. It was traced for its total distance of about 40′ and was some 5′ in width at the top. Where undisturbed, it showed a maximum depth of 2′6″ into the chalk. It had clearly suffered from the effects of subsequent developments in the area and post-Roman ploughing. As originally dug, it may have been twice as deep as the figure given above. Much of the filling of the ditch had been greatly disturbed by burrowing animals and a large medieval pit had almost completely removed the southern corner (Period IX, Pit A/B). The later, Roman gully (Gully C) and its recut (Gully D) continued across the entrance gap and also cut into the upper filling of this present length of the East Ditch. In the few places where the filling of the main ditch was undisturbed the familiar sequence of a primary silt of chalk rubble, overlain by a series of brown loam and chalk silts could be seen. The filling of this length of the East Ditch produced a total of some 158 coarse-ware potsherds, representing at least 51 different vessels. Just ten of these came from primary silts, with 22 from the middle fills and 126 from the upper filling. Four are worthy of illustration (Nos. 317–320). The upper fill of the ditch also produced a Potin coin (Coin No. 1) of Class II.

c) The Enclosure Ditch, South Arm (Fig. 20).

On the south side of the enclosure the ditch was traced for a minimum distance of 43 feet in the present excavation. Its upper levels had been largely destroyed by a terrace cut for the later Roman West Masonry Building, but presumably it was originally of a similar size to the sections recorded elsewhere. Excavations by Mrs. Fox during the 1950s in the area immediately to the west had revealed a further 30′ length of what must have been the same ditch. That was some 2′6″ wide but the published plan (Ref. 42) shows it on a significantly different alignment to the ditch section found in 1969. This seems to be due to a surveyor's error on the earlier plan (subsequently confirmed by re-excavation in 1987). The overall total minimum length for this arm of the ditch, thus, stands at over 70 feet. Only 16 potsherds were recovered from this arm of the ditch in the present excavations and none of these is worthy of illustration. They represent at least nine different vessels.

d) The Dating Evidence from the Enclosure Ditch.

A total of 1,559 sherds was recovered from the filling of the three ditches excavated in Lower Warbank Field and this represents the largest collection of pottery from any feature on the site. The early date of much of the pottery clearly shows that the West Enclosure falls early in the general site-history and the broad similarity of both this pottery and the form of the enclosure, itself, to the nearby Farningham Hill farmstead is at once apparent. Indeed, this initially suggested that the present pottery assemblage could form a correspondingly important group to that recovered from the Farningham enclosure ditch but upon detailed examination such a study has been found not to be worthwhile. The reasons for this are that much of the pottery from the Keston ditch is small and fragmentary; the generally smaller size of the enclosure ditch here has not allowed the development of such well defined levels within the ditch silting and there has been a fairly significant amount of damage by later features and ploughing. Finally, and most importantly, burrowing animals have heavily disturbed and in some places thoroughly mixed the stratigraphy within the ditch. Thus, no especially detailed analysis of the pottery from the ditch has been attempted. Table 4 summarises the distribution of the pottery recovered, in general terms.

A single coin was recovered from the ditch fill. This was a Potin coin of Allen's Type 01 (Coin No. 1). It was found in the upper fill of the east arm (C25–3) and is probably dateable to the first half of the 1st century A.D. or earlier. Another Potin, also of Type 01, was found in ploughsoil nearby (Coin No. 4).

No well stratified samian ware came from the ditch but the mixed upper filling of the ditch and Gullies C and D produced a probable Déch. 72 jar sherd of Central Gaulish ware and of Antonine date. This must be later than the main ditch filling, however. Of the total 1,559 coarse-ware potsherds recovered from contexts within the ditch, at least 184 different vessels could be identified, of which some 45 have been illustrated (Nos. 276–320). Well over three-quarters of this material came from the upper filling of the ditch (Table 4). The bulk of the pottery recovered is of native fabrics and some 820 sherds, representing a minimum of between 60 and 100 different vessels are of shell-tempered fabrics. The bulk of the vessels in these wares are domestic jars and bowls displaying a variety of simple upright and flat-topped rims, typical of the pre-Conquest period (Nos. 283, 302, 303, 305, 306 and 319). Some are decorated with finger-tipping, finger-nail and other impressions (e.g. No. 283). Bead rim jars in shell-tempered wares are more commonly found in early-Roman contexts in West Kent and several of these were also recovered from the filling of the ditch (e.g. Nos. 280, 300, 308 and 318). The majority of these, however, came from the upper filling of the ditch and was associated with some other post-Conquest wares. Less developed bead rim forms, do occur in pre-Conquest assemblages and one (No. 288) from the lower filling of the ditch seems to belong to this earlier type. Sandy non-Roman fabrics are represented by between at least 14 and 30 different vessels (117 sherds). Many of these are fairly small, somewhat abraded, sherds. The recognisable forms however, include shouldered jars (Nos. 276 and 277), one with finger-tip decoration around the shoulder (No. 286) and several everted rim jars with a footring base (No. 278) of typical pre-Conquest type.

	Shell-Tempered Ware		Grog-tempered Ware		Native Sandy Ware		Flint-Tempered Ware		Keston Kiln Ware		Other Roman Ware		Totals	
	Sherds	Vessels (min.)	Sherds	Vessels (min.)	Sherds	Vessels (min.)	Sherds	Vessels (min.)	Sherds	Vessels (min.)	Sherds	Vessels (min.)	Sherds	Vessels (min.)
Upper Fillings	656	60	282	51	76	14	1	1	48	28	195	43	1,258	197
Middle Filling	118	19	63	8	34	9	3	2	6	3	4	3	228	44
Lower Filling	46	22	18	2	7	7	0	0	0	0	2	0	73	31
Total Sherds	820	–	363	–	117	–	4	–	54	–	201	–	1,559	–
Total minimum vessels represented	–	101	–	61	–	30	–	3	–	31	–	46	–	272
Absolute minimum vessels represented	–	80	–	55	–	28	–	2	–	30	–	44	–	239

Table 4. Details of the coarse pottery recovered from the West Enclosure Ditch.

A further 363 grog-tempered potsherds, representing between at least 50 and 60 vessels were also recovered from the filling of the ditch. At pre-Conquest Farningham Hill grog-tempered wares were confined entirely to the upper levels of the ditch filling. At Keston, however, they occurred at all levels in the ditch. The majority from Keston consisted of a range of everted rim jars (e.g. Nos. 282, 290–293 and 301). There is also a large bead rim jar (No. 299), two globular jars with bead rims (Nos. 279 and 285), a probable flagon rim (No. 310) and the base of a pedestal urn (not illustrated). Amongst the sherds of grog-tempered ware are several related to Patch Grove Ware, including a large storage jar rim from the lower filling of the east ditch (north arm – No. 290). Patch Grove Ware, itself, tends to be confined to the post-Conquest period in West Kent. Only four flint-tempered sherds were recovered from the ditch and one finger-tip decorated wall-sherd has been illustrated (No. 294). This small amount of material is all likely to be residual.

Sandy, thoroughly Romanised wares account for 255 of the total potsherds recovered (16%) and these represent between at least 71 and 77 different vessels, of which a minimum of 28 came from the adjacent Keston kiln, presently dated to *c.* A.D. 60–85. These kiln products include a butt beaker (No. 315), a probable pedestal beaker (No. 312), an everted rim bowl (No. 313) and a globular jar (No. 316). Single pieces of mortarium and amphora were recovered (not illustrated). Virtually all of the Roman pottery came from the upper filling of the ditch and at least some must be intrusive (several sherds of late-Roman, Alice Holt Ware were recovered). A large everted rim jar (No. 295) from the middle filling of the ditch has been illustrated, together with a bead rim pie dish (No. 309). The large jar appears to be a typical late-1st to 2nd century type and the bead rim pie dish is of typical 2nd century type.

The precise dating of the ditch filling must be based almost entirely on the coarse pottery but, as has already been noted, much of this material consists of small, abraded sherds not readily assigned to any exact date-range. This problem has been further complicated by the fact that there has been disturbance of the ditch by burrowing animals. The full extent of this disturbance is difficult to gauge but it appears to have been quite extensive along parts of the east ditch. Fairly certainly this animal activity has led to the intrusion of later pottery into the ditch fill and several sherds of late-Roman Alice Holt Ware may be readily excluded from the analysis. More problematical, however, are the earlier Roman wares, mostly found in the upper filling of the ditch, but also in small amounts in the lower and middle fillings. That the West Enclosure Ditch was completely filled by the mid-2nd century A.D. is clear beyond all doubt and the large quantity of late-Iron Age to early-Roman native wares from the filling of the ditch strongly suggest it was substantially filled by the late-1st century A.D. There are also, however, the 255 sherds of sandy Romanised wares to consider, some of which seem to be of 2nd century date. The dating problem, in fact, resolves itself into two alternative questions:

i)   Is the ditch filling dateable essentially to the pre-Conquest period (Period IIIb), with all of the Roman pottery intrusive?

or

ii) Is the ditch filling dateable essentially to the post-Conquest period (Period IV), with most of the 'Iron Age' pottery residual?

The pottery assemblage associated with the other late-Iron Age features of Period III at Keston is dominated by shell-tempered wares (Fabric C of the specialist report on the Iron Age pottery), but significant amounts of sand-tempered wares (Fabric G) also occur, together with some grog-tempered wares and very small quantities of, probably residual, flint-tempered wares. The presence of grog-tempered wares provides the most useful dating evidence, for it is clear that such 'Belgic' fabrics did not reach Iron Age West Kent much before the Roman Conquest. Grog-tempered wares were recovered from throughout the filling of the West Enclosure Ditch, but always in smaller quantities than the shelly wares. Nevertheless, the presence of this fabric type in the ditch tends to preclude a date earlier than the 1st century A.D. for the filling of the ditch. This may be contrasted with the situation at nearby Farningham Hill, where grog-tempered wares were entirely absent from the lower filling of the enclosure ditch, being confined to the upper levels.

Without doubt the ditch at Keston does contain a significant amount of other pre-Conquest pottery fabrics. The shelly ware vessels with flat-topped, upright rims may be easily paralleled by other material from Period III features at Keston, Farningham Hill and other local Iron Age sites, as may be the everted rim, sandy ware jars with footring bases. In later features at Keston, residual Iron Age material has been generally found to be present in the filling and this is also likely to be the case with the West Enclosure Ditch. Some of the pre-Conquest pottery from the ditch is, therefore, most likely to come from any Period IIIa occupation on this part of the site. Indeed, a series of pits excavated in the area in 1985 appear to be of this earlier date. On balance, therefore, it seems clear that much of the filling in the West Enclosure ditches took place in the late-Iron Age, perhaps *c.* A.D. 10–40. The Romanised fabrics appear mostly in the disturbed upper fillings and suggest that the final levelling of the ditch, with soil and domestic rubbish, probably took place mostly between A.D. 50–120 (Period IV).

Four small-finds from the filling of the ditch have been illustrated. These are two brooches (Nos. 97 and 101), a bronze pin (No. 119) and a spindle-whorl (No. 48). Only the two brooches are dateable. No. 101 came from the middle filling of the ditch and consists of a Colchester 'B' type, dated *c.* A.D. 50–75. No. 97 came from the upper filling of the ditch and consists of a small complete 'Dolphin' brooch, dateable to the mid to late-1st century A.D. These two brooches are thus in general agreement with the dating of the coarse pottery.

e) Discussion of the West Enclosure.

Ditched enclosures of this general type are becoming increasingly well-known in Kent. They are generally believed to constitute small farmsteads and the pits and post-holes enclosed at Keston would perhaps agree with this general interpretation, accepting the problems of accurately dating them. In origin, the ditched enclosure tradition is very much pre-Conquest and the example on Farningham Hill (Ref. 43), some 8 miles to the east, has recently been fully excavated. That site, with enclosure ditch, internal storage pits and possible round-house, appears to date from the period 50 B.C. to A.D. 50. Less detailed excavations have also taken place on similar sites in East Kent, at Faversham (Ref. 44) and Dumpton Gap (Ref. 45). The Faversham enclosure appears to be of similar date to Farningham Hill with the ditches being silted up by about *c.* A.D. 50.

Whilst clearly in the same tradition as sites like Farningham Hill, with which the Keston site also shared splayed ditch corners, the latter may be a little later in date. Even so, a pre-Conquest origin seems certain and a construction date at the end of the 1st century B.C. seems the most likely. Quite unlike the Farningham Hill site, which was clearly abandoned at the Roman Conquest in A.D. 43, the Keston site remained in use. Indeed, the West Enclosure may still have continued to be used after the Conquest, but clearly its ditches were already substantially silted by then and were partly used as a dump for domestic rubbish.

At Keston the main West Enclosure appears to have been supplemented by two less substantial ditched enclosures, traces of which were located to the east of the present one (the East Enclosure and the South Enclosure). The East Enclosure seems to be a little later in date and is probably post-Conquest. The South Enclosure may, however, be contemporary with the West Enclosure.

It is worth noting in passing that the main enclosure at Faversham, like Keston, was also superseded by a stone-built villa building, constructed a short distance to the east between A.D. 75 and 100. Thus, a broadly similar sequence to that at Keston seems to have occurred on that site also.

The general sequence of development on this western part of the Keston site is interesting. The West Enclosure, itself, has not yet produced any evidence that it contained a substantial (probably circular) dwelling house of contemporary date; yet this is what may well be expected. Indeed, the presence of two successive Roman houses, one of timber and one of stone could indicate that this was the traditional site of the farmstead's main house. Alternatively, the apparent break in layout (rather than in occupation continuity) between Periods IIIb and V may indicate that the Period V house was erected on a new site, which largely ignored the earlier enclosure. The fact that the Period V house is not centrally placed within the enclosure may support this view. It is not clear, in fact, just how much of the old enclosure still survived at the start of Period V. That the ditch was almost completely silted seems clear enough, but it is likely that some trace of the bank may have remained (though perhaps not on the east side where the digging of Gullies C and D in Period IV had probably removed it). Moreover, if the earthworks of the Period IIIb enclosure had remained substantially complete the Period V house would have been cut off from its ancillary buildings and farmyard area to the east (see below). On balance, therefore, it seems more likely that the Period IIIb earthworks had little direct influence on the positioning of the Period V and VI structures and that the advantages of the topography of this spot were more important factors in influencing the positioning of these later buildings.

(vii) THE WEST TIMBER STRUCTURE (Fig. 19).

A scatter of post-holes was located in 1969 below the foundations of the West Masonry Building, within the West Enclosure. These were largely confined to the area covered by the northern half of the building and they must represent the remains of earlier, largely undefined timber structures. Only one concentration of post-holes was noted. This was located under the east corridor of the Roman building and immediately to its east. The group of post-holes here seemed to form the incomplete remains of a single timber building.

The setting of ten post-holes probably formed the complete north side and parts of the east and west sides of a sub-rectangular structure. A line of six of the post-holes appeared to form the north wall of a building. These were set at intervals at between 2′ and 4′ and ran for a total distance of some 16′. To the north of the middle pair lay two further post-holes (F.228 and 240). This could be the site of the entrance with the two outlying post-holes representing a projecting porch. Four post-holes formed the incomplete west side, about 9′ in length, as surviving. There was just one related post-hole on the east side.

By chance, the line of the north wall of this structure ran exactly across a shallow pit which contained the remains of two complete pots and seemed to be a Roman cremation burial (Burial 1). A second possible Roman burial lay immediately to the north (Burial 2). Although the timber building could not be physically related to the cremation pits, the two sets of features fairly clearly cannot have been contemporary. The main setting of ten post-holes surrounded two, possibly three, slightly smaller post-holes (F. 208, 209 and 235), which may also relate to the structure.

The complete plan of this building is not entirely clear and its date is also somewhat problematical. The hut post-holes, themselves, produced very little dateable material. In fact, only one sherd of pottery was recovered. This comes from Pit F.235 one of the three central post-holes. It is, however, this very same post-hole which is doubtful, bearing more resemblance to an animal burrow rather than a man-made feature. The sherd itself is of a sandy Roman fabric and is likely to be of 2nd century date. In the circumstances, however, little significance can be attached to this. Table 5 below gives details of the individual post-holes.

Feature No.	Shape	Size (ins.)	Depth (ins.)	Sides	Base	Notes
201	Circ.	12″	29″	Vert.	Flat	East side
202	Circ.	10″	21″	Vert.	Flat	North side
208	Circ.	8″	19″	Vert.	Flat	Centre
209	Circ.	6″	14″	Vert.	Flat	Centre
214	Circ.	9″	24″	Vert.	Flat	North Side
215	Circ.	9″	23″	Vert.	Flat	North side
228	Circ.	10″	21″	Vert.	Flat	North side, under wall
229	Circ.	11″	24″	Vert.	Flat	North side, under wall
230	Circ.	11″	24″	Vert.	Flat	North side
231	Circ.	9″	25″	Vert.	Flat	West side
232	Circ.	10″	20″	Vert.	Flat	West side
233	Circ.	9″	20″	Vert.	Flat	West side
234	Circ.	8″	17″	Vert.	Flat	North side
235	Circ.	8″	12″	Steep	Flat	Centre, possibly animal hole
240	Circ.	12″	17″	Steep	Flat	North side

Table 5. Details of the post-holes relating to the West Timber Structure.

On balance, it seems most likely that the present structure stood within the West Enclosure, close to its eastern boundary, although an earlier or later date is not impossible. The late-Iron Age dating of the hut proposed here is somewhat later than has been previously inferred (Ref. 46). Other buildings may also have existed within the West Enclosure, but no definite traces of these have so far been located. It seems unlikely that the present building represents a principal structure of the enclosure.

(viii) THE SOUTH ENCLOSURE (Figs. 5, 6 and 15; Plate II).

Excavations in 1971, close to the south-east limit of the site, revealed two short lengths of ditch that joined each other at about 90°. These appear to form the upper, north corner of an enclosure, most of which seems to lie outside the limits of the excavation (Fig. 15). It is described here as the South Enclosure.

In chronological terms one ditch length cut through the upper filling of Pit 6 which is regarded as being of Period IIIa (see above). In turn, the filling of this same ditch was cut by Post-hole 9 of the Centre Timber Building which belongs to the Period Va farmstead (see below). Hence the enclosure has been assigned here to a late phase of Period III (Period IIIb).

In detail the north-east ditch was traced for a minimum distance of 22′ and it was between 1′ and 2′11″ in width and a minimum of 9″ deep. The north-west ditch was traced for a minimum distance of 14′. It was 2′3″ wide and 4–9″ deep into the natural chalk. Both ditches had sloping sides, cupped bases and were filled with brown loam and chalk specks (Fig. 6).

The filling of the ditches produced only 33 potsherds, representing eight different vessels, of which only one (No. 321) is large enough to be drawn. Seventeen of the sherds are shell-tempered fabrics, two are flint-tempered, 13 are grog-tempered and one is a sandy native ware. This small group of sherds appears to date to about the middle of the 1st century A.D. The absence of later pottery, fairly abundant nearby, suggests that these ditches had completely silted by the middle of the 1st century A.D., but not later.

It is rather unfortunate that more of this enclosure could not be excavated, for without more evidence it is very difficult to determine its size, form or function. The right-angled corner suggests a rectangular, or sub-rectangular form, though whether this was large or small is not clear. The dating evidence suggests that the present enclosure is contemporary with a rather more substantial enclosure located on the western side of the site (the West Enclosure).

CHAPTER III.

THE ROMANO-BRITISH STRUCTURES AND FEATURES

PERIOD IV : THE EARLY-ROMAN FARMSTEAD (A.D. 50–160) (Fig. 9).

It is clear from the evidence of the storage pits, four-post structures, two ditched enclosures and other features, that much of the Lower Warbank site was occupied during the century preceeding the Roman Conquest by an extensive settlement (Period III, see above). It is equally clear, mainly from the associated pottery, that these Period III features were superseded or extended in the century following the Conquest by further major and minor features, here regarded as forming Period IV. The settlement was probably unbroken between Periods III and IV and the Period IIIb West and South Enclosures probably remained in partial or continuous use, into Period IVa. However, the introduction onto the site of distinctive Romano-British pottery fabrics provides clear evidence of new influences and at one stage this included the manufacture of pottery (the Keston kiln) on the site, itself. All the Period III and Period IV features were totally superseded by a major replanning, including large timber-framed buildings, sometime about A.D. 160 (Period V).

   In detail, the Period IV evidence can be subdivided into earlier and later phases (Period IVa and Period IVb). Features were spread widely about the site and certainly appear to have continued at least to the south-east. The north limits were probably found, but subsequent work (to be published later) has shown that the complex extended to the west.

Period IVa
This included an enclosure on the east side (the East Enclosure), a quarry pit complex near the south side with clear evidence of a pottery kiln adjacent to the south-east. The latter was producing distinctive early-Roman coarse and fine-wares, which were found scattered about the site. All these features date from the second half of the 1st century A.D. (see below).

Period IVb
This included an oblong enclosure near the centre of the site (Centre Enclosure) which cut through the largely silted eastern ditch of the Period IIIb West Enclosure. In addition, three cremation burials, forming part of a small cemetery, were found within the disused West Enclosure. Both the Centre Enclosure and the burials probably date from the first half of the 2nd century A.D.

   A group of seven pits (Pits 17–23) also relate to Period IV and the majority probably relates to Period IVa. At least five of these were substantial chalk-cut storage-pits similar to those of Period III, although one (Pit 17) is rather deeper and may have had a special significance (see below) as may the much shallower Pit 23. All but two of these pits produced sherds of Keston Kiln ware and their filling clearly dates from A.D. 60, or later.

PERIOD IVa

(i) THE EAST ENCLOSURE (Figs. 9, 10, 15 and 34).

Excavations at intervals in 1971, 1972 and 1978 revealed sections of two linear ditches which joined to form a neat right-angled corner (Fig. 34). These lay on the east side of the excavated area, south of the North Timber Building. The corner created by these ditches certainly seems to have formed the south-west corner of a substantial enclosure, the rest of which had been ploughed away. In all probability this enclosure was sub-rectangular in plan and it may have had an entrance to the south-east side. It is here described as the East Enclosure. The pottery associated with it suggests that it belongs to Period IV.

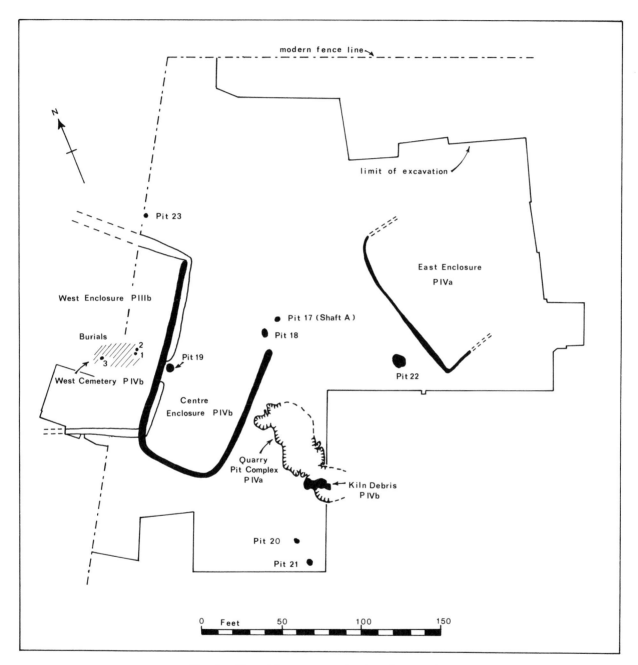

Fig. 9. *Plan of features assigned to Period IV a and b.*

In detail, the western arm of the enclosure was the best preserved. It ran roughly straight, north-west by south-east, but its upper end curved to the east where it seems to have been cut by later Roman terracing. It was actually traced for a distance of about 108 feet and it varied in width between 1′2″ and 3′6″, depending on the differential effect of the ploughing. Similarly, its depth varied from 7″ to 2′ with the largest profiles being at the lower (southern) end. The filling

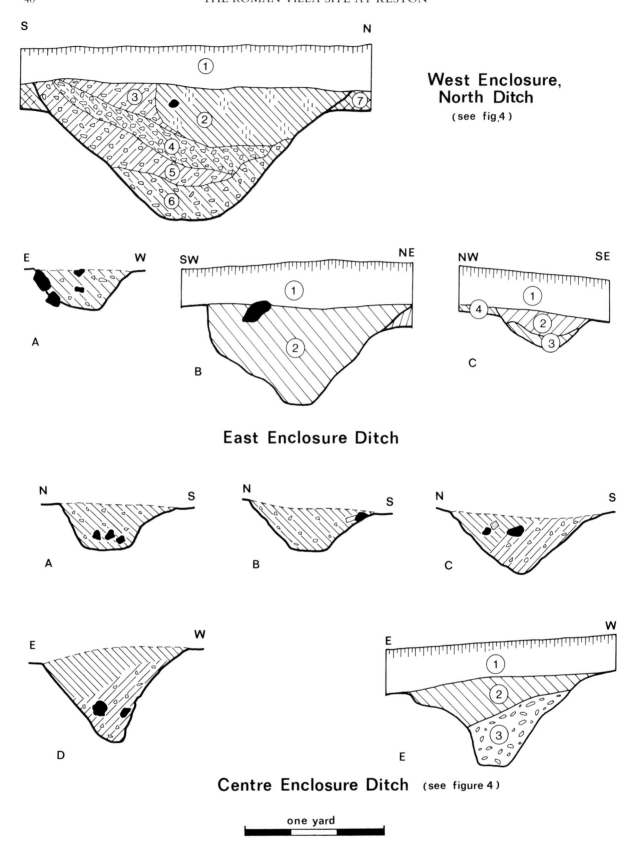

Fig. 10.   *Sections across ditches of West Enclosure, East Enclosure and Centre Enclosure.*

generally consisted of an upper dark brown loam with chalk lumps in places, over a lower fill of light brown loam with chalk rubble (Fig. 10). The finds were largely confined to the upper fill. The ditch had a V-shaped profile, with sloping sides and cupped base.

The south arm of the ditch was traced for a distance of only 17 feet, where it stopped quite suddenly, perhaps marking the position of a causewayed entrance (Fig. 34). It was up to 2′ wide and 10″ in depth and had a similar profile as its joining western arm (Fig. 10). It had later been partly cut by a small, north–south ditch (Ditch 20).

The two enclosure ditches produced a total of 842 coarse-ware potsherds, representing at least 89 different vessels of which 34 have been drawn (Nos. 322–355). Some 564 sherds, representing 62 of the vessels, are of sandy, thoroughly Romanised wares and nearly half of these are attributable to the Keston kiln. The kiln wares include a series of domestic vessels, such as bead rim jars (e.g. Nos. 325, 327, 329, 331 and 333); everted/upright rim jars (Nos. 322, 323, 346, 347 and 350) and lids (Nos. 337 and 341). There were also imitation Gallo-Belgic fine-ware imports including butt beakers (Nos. 348, 349 and 351), platters (No. 342) and globular beakers (Nos. 336 and 344). From the types of vessels being produced the date of the Keston kilns material seems well placed during the period c. A.D. 60–85. Much of the other Romanised sandy ware is fragmentary but includes a familiar range of early-Roman jar and bowl forms (Nos. 339 and 340).

In addition to the Romanised wares a quantity of native pottery was also recovered. There are some 180 sherds representing at least ten vessels of shell-tempered fabrics and these seem to come from bead rim jars of various sizes, all of well-known early-Roman form (Nos. 324, 326, 335 and 338). Forty sherds from at least five vessels in grog-tempered fabrics are also represented and these seem to be large storage jars, some in Patch Grove-type wares (Nos. 328, 330 and 332). There is additionally an upright recessed rim (?) bowl fragment (No. 343). There are four sherds from three vessels of native sandy ware represented. These are all small, abraded fragments and none is illustrated. Finally, some 46 sherds from a minimum of nine vessels of flint-tempered ware are represented. Again most of this material is small and abraded but two pieces have been drawn (Nos. 352 and 355); these are a finger-tip impressed wall sherd (No. 352) and a rim fragment from a vessel with an internally expanded rim (No. 355). All of this flint-tempered ware is probably residual in its present context and is likely to be derived from the occupation of Periods II and III.

Type	Sherds	Min. Vessels	Drawn
Shell-tempered Ware	188	10	4
Grog-tempered Ware	40	5	4
Sandy Native Ware	4	3	0
Flint-tempered Ware	46	9	2
Keston Kiln Ware	245	32	22
Other Sandy Roman Ware	319	30	2
Totals	842	89	34

Table 6. Details of the coarse pottery recovered from the ditches of the East Enclosure.

The presence of the kiln-ware sherds throughout the upper and lower filling the East Enclosure ditch must indicate that it was being filled during and/or after this industrial phase (which is dated c. A.D. 60–85 – see below). The dating of the other pottery is in general agreement and it seems clear that the ditch was completely filled by the end of the 1st century A.D. or c. A.D. 125 at the very latest. No coins or samian ware were recovered to further refine the dating. Two small-finds have been illustrated. These are a spindle-whorl made from a re-used sherd of shell-tempered ware (No. 46) and a bronze brooch of 'Colchester' type (No. 88). The brooch may be dated to *c.* A.D. 20–75 and is, thus, broadly similar to the date of the coarse pottery. The upper filling of the ditch at one point produced part of a human mandible from an individual aged 25–35 years old. A general soil deposit sealing the ditch produced a flint arrowhead (No. 2).

From the limited information on this enclosure it seems that its north–south length was at least 100 feet and its width greater than 25 feet (Fig. 9). Hence its internal area was at least 2,500 sq. ft. and probably twice this size. No related internal structure was found and, if any had existed, then these have since been ploughed away.

The domestic rubbish in the ditches suggests the enclosure probably dates from the middle of the first century A.D. and that the ditches had substantially silted by the end of that century. As an enclosure it seems to have formed part of a discreet group of at least three roughly contemporary enclosures that covered much of the site.

(ii) THE QUARRY PIT COMPLEX (Figs. 9, 11 and 12).

Excavations in 1968 and 1970 towards the centre of the excavated area and north-west of the South Masonry Building, located a major feature dug into the natural chalk. Detailed examination showed this to be an ill-defined area consisting of a mass of shallow, partially superimposed pits and hollows (Fig. 11). This complex lay between the 400 and 405 foot contours and the depth into the chalk varied from between 6″ to 3′ (Fig. 12). The full extent of the complex could not be gauged for it extended beyond the limits of the excavation on its east side. The area excavated measured 75 feet (north-west to south-east) by about 30 feet (north-east to south-west). Most of the sub-divisions within the pit area were filled with mixed layers of light brown loam and chalk rubble. These produced an important collection of domestic rubbish and related objects.

It was largely impossible, due to the frequent superimposition of localised features and the general nature of the fillings, to identify individual pits and hollows. They are thus all treated here as a single composite feature, referred to throughout as the Quarry Pit Complex. Indeed, it seems very likely that these pits and hollows represent a random sequence of quarries, from which the underlying chalk and flints had been extracted. A rough estimation suggests that over 100 cu. yds. of material had been removed from the area within the limits of the archaeological excavation and the total figure may have been as much as 200 cu. yds.

Quite clearly the excavation of this large pit-complex had resulted in the removal of all pre-existing features, though a substantial pre-Conquest pit (Pit 16) had largely survived at the southern end (Fig. 12). The line of a later, curving gully (Ditch 6A) once recut (Ditch 6B) was traced, with difficulty, across the filling of the Quarry Pit Complex. This and the filling of the pits were in turn partly sealed by a general soil deposit which, in its turn, was partly sealed by a Roman metalling of small pebbles (the Centre Metalling, see below). At the southern end of the Quarry Pit Complex its filling was partially sealed by a spread of distinctive burnt clay fragments, apparently representing debris from a nearby pottery kiln (see below).

The filling of the quarry pits and hollows within the complex produced five sherds of samian ware, but no coins. The samian sherds were from Forms 18, 35, 37 and 67 of Flavian date and a Form 29 of pre-Flavian or early-Flavian date. The small-finds included two baked clay objects (Nos. 18 and 20), probably some type of kiln-furniture; five pottery wheels or discs (Nos. 28 and 31), certainly used for decorating some of the Keston Kiln wares found on the site; a pottery counter (No. 40); five fragments of clay crucible (No. 41), perhaps from a small bronze-working area nearby; a spindle-whorl (No. 50); a bronze brooch ('Nauheim derivative', bow type) of 1st century date (No. 87); a small brass bell (No. 114); a bronze link (No. 124) and a flint scraper (No. 8). There were also two pieces of a triangular loom-weight of late-Iron Age or early-Roman date (too fragmentary for illustration), a considerable quantity of iron slag fragments from some nearby blacksmith's forge and 321 fragments of fired clay, probably for a kiln structure (see page 151).

The filling of the quarry pits also produced a total of 1,195 coarse-ware potsherds, representing at least 90 vessels of which 38 are illustrated here (Nos. 356–393). These vessels occur in a range of broad fabrics as shown in Table 7.

Nearly half of the pottery found is in native fabrics. The commonest native fabric is shell-tempered ware and the majority of the vessels in this fabric are bead rim jars and cooking pots of typical early-Roman type (Nos. 378, 379, 381 and 382). An everted rim with sparse shell-tempering also seems to be post-Conquest (No. 387). There are in addition some shelly wares with simple flat-topped, upright rims, which are more typical of the pre-Conquest period (Nos. 390 and 391).

Fabric	Sherds	Vessels rep. (min.)	Drawn
Shell-tempered Ware	418	9	8
Grog-tempered Ware	66	5	0
Sandy Native Ware	21	6	2
Flint-tempered Ware	3	1	1
Gallo-Belgic Imported Ware	24	1	1
Keston Kiln Ware	209	28	26
Other Roman Wares	454	40	0
Totals	1,195	90	38

Table 7. Details of the coarse pottery recovered from the Quarry Pit Complex.

The other native wares occurred in much smaller amounts. Only three small fragments of flint-tempered pre-Conquest ware were recovered (No. 356), although slightly greater quantities of grog-tempered wares and native sandy wares were found. The grog-tempered wares are rather fragmentary with few clearly recognisable forms and none has been illustrated. The native sandy wares include at least two late-Iron Age everted rim jars (Nos. 392 and 393), one decorated with incised grooves (No. 392). There are also a number of sherds from a fine Gallo-Belgic butt beaker import (No. 373), which could just be pre-Conquest in date but is more probably post-Conquest (see page 197).

Just over half of the total pottery recovered, however, is of thoroughly Romanised Sandy Wares. Much of this material consists of undiagnostic wall sherds but within the assemblage there is a group of 209 sherds, representing at least 28 vessels, in a distinctive hard fabric. These seem to be the products of a single kiln site and other good pieces of evidence indicate that this was at Keston itself (see below, p. 199). These kiln wares were discovered throughout the filling of the Quarry Pit Complex and a range of different vessels is present. The most distinctive are imitations of Gallo-Belgic imports, most notably butt beakers (Nos. 357, 358 and 360–364) and platters (one stamped) (Nos. 365–371) but also including a girth beaker (No. 374) and another decorated beaker, probably copying Cam. Form 144 (No. 375), in addition to the upper part of a pedestal beaker (No. 376). Domestic kiln-wares include a series of everted rim bowls and jars (Nos. 384–386 and 388), and a number of bead rim jars and cooking-pots (No. 380). There is also a small cup, possibly a lamp-holder (No. 383), and a probable flagon rim (No. 372). All of the forms of the kiln ware products are typical of the second half of the 1st century A.D., whilst a date range of A.D. 60–85 has been assigned for the production period. The other Roman pottery is of broadly similar date and nothing need be later than A.D. 100. A mortarium sherd (No. 908) from the filling of the quarry pits has also been illustrated.

The soil deposits sealing the quarry pits produced a further large amount of pottery and four coins (Coin Nos. 16, 55, 76 and 77). The coins are: one of Claudius II (A.D. 268–270), one of the House of Constantine (A.D. 335–345) and two illegible Roman coins, one probably late-4th century. A total of 1592 sherds of pottery was recovered and these represent at least 145 different vessels. Some 18 sherds from these deposits have been drawn (Nos. 409–425/902 and 900). Table

8 gives details of the pottery fabrics. Most of this pottery may be dated from the later 1st to the 2nd century A.D., with only a small amount of later material. The bulk of the pottery is clearly derived from the underlying quarry pits filling. Just over 300 sherds, representing at least 30 vessels seem to be in fabrics related to the Keston kilns: ten of these have been illustrated (Nos. 411, 414, 415, 417, 418, 420 and 422–425), including four platters (Nos. 422–425). Two platters are stamped: No. 425 (stamp illustration No. 902) and a vessel not otherwise drawn (stamp illustration No. 900). There was also a butt beaker (No. 414), another possible lamp-holder (No. 418), a decorated flange-rim bowl (No. 417) and a heavily distorted shell-tempered base, quite clearly a kiln-waster (No. 420). Other (non-kiln ware) illustrated vessels of interest are: a grog-tempered bead rim jar with applied bosses on the shoulder (No. 410), a rusticated jar in Romanised sandy ware (No. 412) and a (residual) Iron Age flint-tempered wall sherd decorated with a finger-tip impressed cordon (No. 419).

A quantity of small-finds was also recovered from the soil over the Quarry Pit Complex and twelve of these have been drawn. There are three pieces of probable kiln furniture or fittings (Nos. 15, 17 and 19) and a further 20 fragments of the small pottery wheels or discs used in decorating pottery (Nos. 28 and 30–32). There is also a probable handle fragment from a pottery die (No. 36). Iron objects include an ox-goad (No. 79) and a 1st century A.D. bow-brooch (No. 90). A small annular bead was also recovered (No. 112). There are in addition four unstratified small-finds from the general area of the Quarry Pit Complex; two pottery wheels (Nos. 29 and 33); a bone gaming die (No. 60) and a La Tène III brooch (No. 94), apparently of the rare 'Glastonbury-type'.

Fabric	Sherds	Vessels rep. (min).	Drawn
Shell-tempered Ware	274	23	2
Grog-tempered Ware	244	26	1
Sandy Native Ware	27	5	0
Flint-tempered Ware	2	1	1
Keston Kiln Ware	312	30	11
Other Roman Wares	733	60	3
Totals	1,592	145	18

Table 8. Details of the coarse pottery recovered from the soil over the Quarry Pit Complex.

(iii) THE KILN DEBRIS (Figs. 9, 11 and 12).

Excavations in 1970, to the north-east of the South Masonry Building and within the area of the Quarry Pit Complex, revealed a substantial, dumped deposit of distinctive heavily burnt clay fragments in black ashy loam (Fig. 11). Superficially, this clay material was of similar appearance to the "briquetage" found on coastal salt-working sites; all of the fragments contained voids caused by burnt-out organic material such as straw (see below).

Overall, the deposit was roughly oval in plan and measured 6' (north–south) by a minimum of 14' (east–west), continuing beyond the eastern limit of the excavation. The deposit was between 2″ and 7″ in thickness and lay upon a soil layer which sealed the filled in Quarry Pit Complex (see above, Fig. 12). The dump also sealed a gully (Ditch 6), which cut through the filling of the Quarry Pits. There was no indication that the fired clay material had been burnt in situ and it seems probable that it represents material derived from an adjacent, but otherwise unlocated kiln-site. The dump, itself, was sealed by a thin deposit of dark loam in some places and in others by plough-soil only.

Finds from the layer of burnt clay fragments included many sherds of early-Roman pottery (Nos. 394–408), parts of eight pottery wheels or discs used for decorating pottery (Nos. 23, 24,

29, 31 and 34) and several pieces of probable kiln-furniture (Nos. 16 and 20). A total of 452 coarse-ware potsherds from the deposit represent at least 75 different vessels, of which 15 are illustrated (Table 9). The bulk of this pottery is of sandy Romanised fabrics (360 sherds, representing at least 61 vessels). Some 214 of these sherds are in fabrics that seem to relate to the products of the Keston kilns and they represent at least 41 different vessels. These vessels include a number of the familiar butt beakers and platters (Nos. 398–403). One of the platters has an interesting stamp on its base (drawn stamp No. 901). The kiln-ware fabric also includes two everted rim jars (Nos. 394–408), a bead rim jar (No. 407) and a vessel with a flanged rim (No. 405). The kiln-wares have been dated to *c.* A.D. 60–85.

Fabric Type	Sherds	Vessels rep. (min.)	Drawn
Shell-tempered Ware	83	10	2
Grog-tempered Ware	9	4	1
Sandy Native Ware	0	0	0
Flint-tempered Ware	0	0	0
Keston Kiln Ware	214	41	11
Other Roman Wares	146	20	1
Totals	452	75	15

Table 9. Details of the coarse pottery recovered from the Kiln Debris.

In addition to the Romanised wares, there are also 83 sherds of shell-tempered pottery, representing at least ten vessels. One of particular interest has been illustrated (No. 406). This is a kiln-waster and it provides good evidence that fabrics other than sand-tempered wares were produced at the Keston kiln. The vessel, itself, consists of a small bead rim jar of typical early-Roman type, very familiar on West Kent sites. The pot, however, sagged during the firing process and must have been discarded. Only nine grog-tempered sherds were recovered and these represent four separate vessels; one everted rim jar, typical of the early-Roman period has been illustrated (No. 397).

No coins were recovered from the dump, but the coarse pottery seems to be firmly dateable to the period A.D. 45–85. A single East Gaulish samian sherd of later 2nd to early-3rd century date is clearly intrusive here.

The dark soil which partially sealed the clay dump deposit contained some 93 coarse-ware potsherds, ranging in date from the second half of the 1st century A.D. to the 2nd century A.D. The immediate soil deposit upon which the dump lay produced some 49 potsherds. These also range from the late-1st to early-2nd century in date and it seems likely that some of this material is actually a little later in date than the pottery in the burnt layer above it. This suggests that the burnt clay deposit, itself, was in fact a dump of earlier material brought from nearby.

Some 170 fragments of the burnt clay material were retained for examination. Its superficial resemblance to salt-working briquetage has already been noted but a closer inspection of the material indicates that this similarity is largely coincidental. Its similarity to the St. Albans kiln material is also clear and its identification as part of a pottery kiln superstructure seems fairly certain. Most of the clay fragments are flat or show only a slight curvature. The pieces are generally thin, usually only about 5 mm. in full thickness and none is more than 125 mm. across. The absence of rim and base pieces indicates that the fragments do not form parts of vessels or containers. All of the fragments are fired to a very hard, brittle state and some pieces seem to have been distorted by heat. There are two minor fabric variations, both originally heavily tempered with organic matter now fired out, and one with some sand-tempering also. In colour, the fragments range from yellow, orange and red to black on the surface and dark grey to black at the core.

The precise purpose of this unusual burnt clay material cannot be certain. There is no evidence that it is derived from vessels of any type, nor is there any indication that it had been fixed to a wooden framework in a similar manner to daub. Examination of the finds recovered from other deposits on the site revealed that burnt clay material of this type was not confined solely to the present deposit. A total of 759 fragments of this material was recovered in all including the 170 pieces from the present deposit. Some 321 of the other fragments were scattered throughout the filling of the Quarry Pit Complex and a further 73 fragments were recovered from the soil above the Complex. The remaining fragments came from plough-soil, hillwash, general soil deposits and later features, mostly in the area of the Quarry Pit Complex.

Interestingly, a considerable quantity of similar baked clay fragments, described by the excavator as 'rough clay "plates" and showing impressions of grass and straw' was recovered from Pottery Kiln I at Verulam Hills Field, St. Albans. This material was interpreted as 'part of the temporary dome of the oven built up each time the kiln was fired' (Ref. 47). From the pieces of this material on display in the Verulamium Museum, the St. Albans material appears to be identical to the Keston kiln debris (the writers are grateful to Dr. S. Greep for this reference). The St. Albans kiln is dateable to the 2nd century A.D.

In the absence of any evidence to the contrary, therefore, it may be reasonably suggested that this burnt clay material from Keston is derived from a pottery kiln super-structure. The suggestion that the distinctive burnt clay fragments represent debris from a nearby kiln, is supported by their close association with the Keston kiln products, the pottery wheels and the probable kiln-furniture. No trace of the actual base of a kiln was found anywhere in the extensive area excavated. However, the presence of kiln-debris on the extreme east of the site, suggests that it would have been situated beyond and probably somewhere in the extreme south-east sector.

None of the rather fragmentary pottery from the soil deposits above or below the dump is illustrated, but some unstratified material from this area has been included (Nos. 875–882). This unstratified pottery represents products of the Keston kiln and includes two butt beakers (Nos. 877 and 882); an everted rim jar (No. 875); a flanged rim bowl (No. 878) and a strap handle (No. 880). A stamped platter base (No. 879) is also illustrated (Stamp No. 899).

PERIOD IVb

(i) THE CENTRE ENCLOSURE (Figs. 4, 9, 10, 19 and 20).

Excavations in 1969, 1970 and again in 1977, towards the western side of the investigated area and just to the east of the West Masonry Building, revealed a three-sided ditched enclosure (Fig. 9), astride the 410 foot contour. This is hereafter described for convenience as the Centre Enclosure. This enclosure was roughly rectangular in plan, with parallel east and west ditches, some 60–67 feet apart, forming its width. It had a largely straight south ditch, which joined the long side ditches at about 90°, with rounded corners at the south-west and south-east. The south ditch was cut across by Ditch 1 assigned to Period VII (later villa complex) and the east ditch was cut by two post-Roman ditches (Ditches 3 and 4). There was no fourth (i.e. north) ditch to the enclosure but its total length was between 95 and 125 feet. The enclosure, thus, covered about 800 sq. yds.

The work in 1970 and 1977 located both east and south ditches without difficulty, but the return of the west ditch had been destroyed by a large medieval robber-pit (Pit A). Significantly, however, the 1969 excavation had already located two small, parallel gullies (Gullies C and D) extending north-eastwards from the other side of Pit A (Fig. 19). It is now probable that these represent the west side of the enclosure, with Gully D being a re-cut of Gully C. Both gullies ran partially along the filling of the east ditch of the earlier West Enclosure (Period IIIb) and this presented some difficulty in their recognition during the excavation. In addition, all the ditches of both enclosures here were at least partially disturbed, mainly by burrowing animals that preferred tunnelling through soil rather than through solid chalk.

The eastern ditch of the enclosure was traced for about 95 feet and this was U-shaped in section with sloping sides and a cupped base. It was between 2′6″ and 4′ in width, perhaps reflecting differential later plough-damage, with a slightly broader north-east terminal. It was between 11″ and 22″ in depth and was filled with a dark brown loam containing scattered flints and domestic rubbish (Fig. 10).

The south ditch was 2–3′ wide, but otherwise similar to the east ditch in depth and filling (Fig. 10). The original ditch (Gully C) on the west side (Fig. 19) was traced for a minimum distance of 58 feet, though its northern end had clearly been destroyed by the north-east wing of the West Masonry Building. The ditch was between 1′6″ and 2′ wide, with steeply sloping sides and a rounded base. It was about 1′6″ in depth. Its filling of brown loam was largely mixed, through animal disturbance, with the fill of the West Enclosure Ditch along which it had been dug (Fig. 20). This west ditch had been redug (Gully D) and this re-cut extended further north, having a total minimum length of about 103 feet and ended in a bulbous terminal. It was otherwise similar to Gully C (Fig. 20). It seems probable that this section of the enclosure ditch required re-cutting simply because it was dug along the soft fill of the earlier ditch which would have been weathered quickly. Gullies C and D were cut by three pits to the south-west of Pit 19; two of these contained human infant burials, presumably connected with the later masonry building nearby and one of these produced a sherd of Keston Kiln Ware (No. 837).

No coins were found in any of the ditches relating to this enclosure. Seven samian sherds were, however, found. The north terminal of the east ditch produced a Form 27 of Neronian-Flavian date, a Form 18 of a similar period, a Form 42, 46 or Curle 15 rim fragment of pre- or early-Flavian date and a Form 42 or 46 of Neronian or Flavian date. The south ditch yielded two sherds of Form 18 or 18/31 type (Flavian-Trajanic) and a Walters Form 79 or Lud.Tg of later 2nd century date. In addition, the mixed upper filling of the West Enclosure Ditch and Gullies C and D produced a probable Déch. 72 sherd of Antonine date.

The east and south ditches produced a combined total of 419 coarse-ware potsherds. These represent at least 46 different vessels of which 20 have been drawn (Nos. 426–445). There are some 136 sherds, representing at least eleven vessels, of shell-tempered ware. The majority of these seem to come from bead rim jars of very familiar early-Roman type. Three of them have been illustrated (Nos. 431, 432 and 433). There is also another bead rim jar in a curious 'dual' fabric (No. 428). Superficially this appears to be a typical shell-tempered vessel but closer

Type	Sherds	Min. Vessels	Drawn
Shell-tempered Ware	413	36	9
Grog-tempered Ware	213	19	12
Sandy Native Ware	25	11	0
Flint-tempered Ware	3	2	1
Keston Kiln Ware	31	15	11
Other Roman Sandy Wares	255	16	4
Samian Ware	6	6	0
TOTAL	946	105	35

Table 10. Details of the pottery recovered from the ditches of the Centre Enclosure.

inspection reveals that, to the shell-tempered body of the pot, a bead rim in a sandy ware typical of the Keston Kilns had been added during the manufacturing process. Several such jars were in fact recovered from the excavations and they clearly provide more evidence that shell-tempered wares were being produced on the site (see page 193). In addition to bead rim jars there is also a lid in shelly ware (No. 436) from the east arm of the ditch.

Some 93 sherds, representing at least eight vessels, of grog-tempered ware came from the east and south ditches of the enclosure. These include everted rim jars (No. 430), a Patch Grove storage jar (No. 426), bead rim jars (Nos. 427 and 440) and an upright rim jar (No. 438). All of these vessels are typical of the early-Roman period, although a few, like the Patch Grove jar, could run into the second century. Three flint-tempered Iron Age sherds, from three different vessels, were found. These must be residual, but one small rim has been drawn (No. 444).

Romanised sandy wares account for the remaining 187 sherds (at least 20 vessels) recovered from the east and south arms of the ditch. Within this group there are four amphora sherds (not illustrated) and some 17 sherds of Keston Kiln Ware. Eight kiln-ware sherds have been drawn and these include the bead rim jar noted above (No. 428), two typical platters (Nos. 442 and 443), a lid (No. 435), two bowls (Nos. 434 and 445), a pedestal base (No. 429) and an upright-necked jar, somewhat overfired (No. 441). The products of the Keston kilns have been dated to c. A.D. 60–85.

The remaining Roman wares are rather fragmentary. An everted rim jar (No. 439) and a lid (No. 437) have been drawn. Collectively, the coarse pottery from the ditches mostly falls within the date-range A.D. 50–160, though predictably there are a few earlier Iron Age vessels and these are clearly derived from elsewhere on the site. There is no coarse pottery in the undisturbed deposits from these ditches that need be much later than about A.D. 160, although one samian sherd could be a little later. It is not impossible, however, that this is intrusive and it seems unlikely that the ditch was filled later than c. A.D. 160.

It was not possible in many places to distinguish between the individual fillings of Gullies C and D where they cut into the east ditch of the West Enclosure, due to animal disturbance. The gullies, however, produced a combined total of 521 coarse-ware potsherds. These represent at least 53 different vessels of which 15 have been drawn (Nos. 446–460), together with a further seven pre-Conquest or 1st century A.D. sherds from the mixed upper West Enclosure Ditch and gully fillings (Nos. 461–467). It seems fairly clear that much of the pottery in the two gullies is derived from the filling of the West Enclosure Ditch, through which they are largely cut. Some 277 sherds from the gully fills are of shell-tempered fabrics. These include sherds from a substantially complete storage jar (No. 461) and a number of other, more fragmentary, bead and upright rim jars. One of each of these forms has been drawn (Nos. 451 and 448, respectively). In addition, specifically from Gully C, there is an everted rim jar (No. 453) which is likely to be of pre-Conquest date as is No. 448. The bead rim vessels are typical of the early-Roman period. Some 120 grog-tempered sherds were also recovered. These include typical early-Roman period rolled, bead and everted rim jars (Nos. 446 and 449) and a small beaker (No. 459) as well as several pre-Conquest forms such as the necked jar (No. 452) and a jar/bowl with an upright rim (No. 450). Another 25 sherds are in sandy native wares, all too fragmentary for illustration.

There are, in addition, 99 sherds of Roman fabrics. The bulk of them are of sandy wares and these include a number of sherds of Keston Kiln Ware. Sherds from several butt beakers and platters are present. Two of the platters have been drawn (Nos. 457 and 458), together with a butt beaker (No. 463) and the base of a probable pedestal beaker (No. 462) from the mixed filling of the West Enclosure Ditch and Gullies. Other Roman wares recovered from the gullies include a jar with a rolled rim (No. 455), a bead rim dish (No. 460) a small piece of Nene Valley Ware, not worthy of illustration, and a straight-sided bowl which appears to be of later Roman date and is probably intrusive here (No. 454).

As with the south and east ditches of this enclosure, the bulk of the pottery from this western arm of the ditch appears to date between the mid-1st century A.D. and the mid-2nd century A.D. Several pieces are clearly pre-Conquest and must relate to the earlier settlement in this area.

Several other finds came from the ditch filling of the Centre Enclosure. The fill of the east arm of the ditch produced an iron water-pipe collar fragment in its upper filling (not illustrated). This is presumably derived from the eastern pipe-trench, assumed to have been laid in the succeeding villa period (Period VI) and is, thus, fairly certainly intrusive here. A fragment of red painted Roman wall-plaster also should be intrusive and derived from one of the two masonry buildings. Three small-finds from the enclosure ditch have been illustrated; an iron knife (No. 82) and part of a bronze bracelet (No. 105) from the east ditch and a spindle-whorl from Gully C (No. 44). The bracelet is of late-Roman type and is again probably intrusive, like the water-pipe collar and plaster fragment.

(ii) THE WEST CEMETERY (Figs. 9 and 19).

Excavations in 1969 revealed, at the western edge of the site and within the limits of the West Masonry Building, two probable cremation burials (Fig. 19). Each took the form of a small circular hole dug into the natural chalk. One (Burial 1) contained parts of two pottery vessels. One (No. 481) was a pie-dish, about three-quarters complete, probably dating to the mid-2nd century A.D. The second vessel, a broken globular jar (No. 480), is also probably of 2nd century date.

The second burial (Burial 2), lay about 1′6″ north of the first burial and contained the lower part of a sandy ware jar, broken into many small pieces (not illustrated). This also appears to be of 2nd century date. No trace of cremated bone was found with either burial, but the very damaged state of the vessels suggests that both burials had been severely ploughed down on this very shallow site. None of the super-structure of the superimposed Roman building had survived centuries of ploughing and only those foundations cut into chalk remained.

Excavations in 1970, actually within the central range of the same Roman building, revealed a rather more certain cremation burial (Burial 3), some 23 feet to the west (Fig. 19). This took the form of a rectangular pit with rounded corners which measured 3′3″ (east–west) by 2′3″ (north–south). Its vertical sides cut 11″ into the chalk and it had a flat base. Its filling had been badly disturbed by the roots of large trees, but parts of two pottery vessels were found in it. The first was a substantially complete carinated beaker (No. 482) of late-1st or early-2nd century A.D. date. This lay on its side several inches above the base of the pit and it contained a quantity of calcined human bone. The second vessel was a squat jar, of which only about a quarter survived, of a similar date (not illustrated). Additional fragments of cremated bone were found beneath the carinated beaker.

Excavations in 1987 (to be published later), immediately to the west of Burial 3 revealed an infant inhumation (Burial 4) interred with a complete glass phial. Again this lay in a shallow hollow in the chalk and clearly ground-level here had been substantially reduced by various agencies during the post-Roman centuries.

On the strength of these limited discoveries it is just possible to identify the presence of at least a small Romano-British cemetery on the west side of the site. This certainly contained at least one inhumation and three cremations, but there is every chance that several, or indeed many others, were removed during the later use of the site. The cemetery seems to have had an east–west length of at least 40′ and a narrow width, aligned on the contour of the hill. This part of the site is higher than most of the field to the east, where the contemporary structures (Period IV) have been found and as such it implies a small elevated cemetery marginally overlooking its related settlement.

This cemetery can be seen to fall within the ditches of the West Enclosure, fairly centrally placed within it and not far from its eastern entrance (Fig. 9). The enclosure was probably constructed about A.D. 1 (Period IIIb) and by the late-1st century A.D. its ditches were largely filled with silt and domestic rubbish (see above, p. 29). On this evidence it seems clear that the cemetery was placed within the disused enclosure, probably in the first half of the 2nd century A.D., when the ditches were probably visible only as faint hollows.

It also seems certain that the main West Timber Building and the West Masonry Building (Periods V and VI) were later built over the enclosure and over the burials, thus showing that the cemetery was by then no longer in use. The major cemetery at the north end of the site (to be published later) was anyway already in existence by Period VI and it must certainly have superseded that on the west side. Similarly, the West Timber Building (only discovered in 1987) beneath the West Masonry Building, seems to cut through part of the cemetery and this too implies that the cemetery had been superseded. The West Timber Building (Period Va) appears to have been constructed about the middle of the 2nd century A.D., thus very close in date to the creation of the main cemetery at the north end. The two events probably correspond, but if so then the West Timber Building must have superseded the cemetery on the west side by a comparatively short time. At first glance this could have created a conflict of interests, for traditionally Romano-British structures were seldom consciously built over burial grounds. More likely, however, there were circumstances in time and area, that cannot be revealed by excavation, which account for the occurrence.

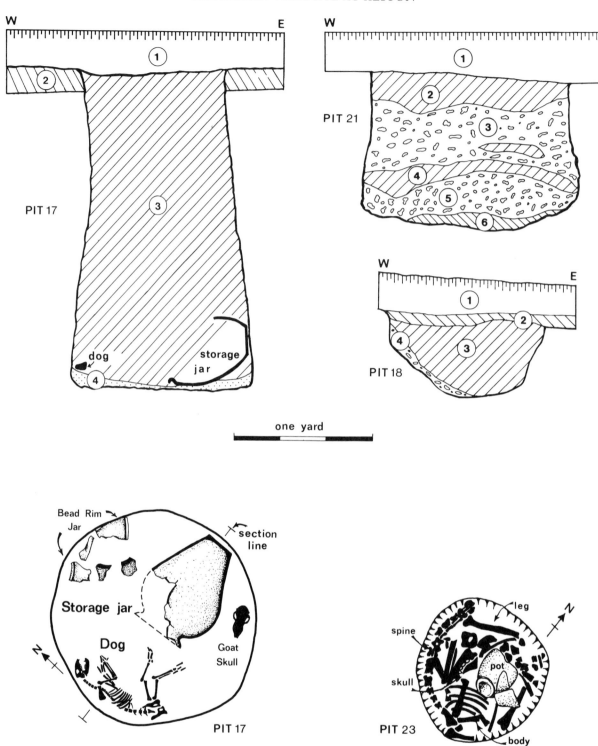

Fig. 13.   *Sections and Plans of Pits 17, 18, 21 and 23.*

(iii) THE EARLY-ROMAN PITS (Figs. 4, 9, 13, 15, 19 and 32; Plates V and VI).

The excavation of pits, either singly or in small groups, appears to have continued from Iron Age times (Periods II and III) into the post-Conquest period (Period IV). At least seven pits (Pits 17–23) belong to this later phase and most were probably dug as storage-pits, though two (Pits 17 and 23) appear to have had a ritual function. Most of these seven pits produced adequate dating evidence and it is this that suggests that they were open and filled mainly during the second half of the first century or early-2nd century A.D. The seven pits are the most significant found, and none was found inside an enclosure. Their numbering follows on from the Iron Age sequence of pits.

Several other pits located on the site may also date from the same general period, but these mostly failed to produce any significant dateable material. More often they yielded a few nondescript sherds only broadly dateable to the first or second centuries A.D. Some other pits contained small amounts of later Roman pottery, which if not intrusive on this shallow site, suggests some minor pit-digging after the first century A.D. Lack of space prevents descriptions of such miscellaneous pits here, but these are listed in the site archive.

Pit 17 (Ritual Shaft 'A') (Figs. 4, 9 and 13; Plate V).

This deep pit, or shaft, was located in 1968 near the centre of the excavated area and just to the south of the (later) South Fence (Fig. 4). It was roughly circular in plan and had been dug through a thin soil layer, into solid chalk to a depth of $6\frac{1}{2}$ ft. The diameter varied from 2'10" at the narrowest and opened out to 3'9" at the base (Fig. 13). Hence the sides were undercut in a manner reminiscent of some Iron Age storage-pits. The bottom of the pit was flat, but there was a small depression in it on the east side. The main filling (L.3) was almost entirely a fine black loam containing domestic rubbish, but the base was covered with a layer of light brown sandy loam (L.4). The lower filling contained the skeleton of a small dog, two goat skulls (see page 287) and three partially complete pots (Nos. 477–479, see Plate V).

The domestic rubbish included well over 300 coarse-ware potsherds, eleven sherds of samian and fragments of fine Roman glass. The main filling (L.3) of the pit produced six of the samian sherds, including three of Form 27 (one with an unidentifiable stamp), two of Form 29 and a rim fragment of Form 42, 46 or Curle 15. All are of either Neronian, pre-Flavian or Flavian date. The lower filling (L.4) yielded the remaining samian sherds including two more of Form 27, a Form 18 and two uncertain sherds from Southern Gaul. These are also of Neronian-Flavian date.

Of some 346 coarse-ware pottery fragments a number were from the three partially complete vessels found at the bottom of the pit (Nos. 477–479). In all, some 36 vessels seem to be represented and of these eleven have been illustrated (Nos. 469–479). Over half of the sherds are of sandy Romanised fabrics, including ten fragments from an amphora. There are also several sherds from the Keston kilns, dated to c. A.D. 60–85, and a platter (No. 473), lid (No. 471), bead rim jar (No. 472) and an everted rim jar (No. 469) in this fabric have been drawn. Of the other non-kiln Roman wares, a vessel with an out-turned bead rim (No. 475), a straight-sided bowl (No. 474) and a beaker (No. 470) have been drawn. The remaining fabrics are of native wares. There are 70 shell-tempered sherds and two large bead rim jars have been illustrated (Nos. 476 and 479). Such bead rim jars are typical of early-Roman sites in West Kent. Some 53 sherds are grog-tempered and a number of these join to produce a substantially complete storage jar of unusually large size, found on the bottom of the pit (No. 478). A smaller jar from the bottom of the pit in a similar grog-tempered fabric has also been drawn (No. 477).

The thin soil layer over the chalk (L.2), through which the pit was cut produced a single shell-tempered rim sherd from a vessel of typical pre-Conquest form. This has been illustrated (No. 468).

The great majority of the coarse pottery seems to date from the second half of the 1st century A.D. and is, thus, in accord with the dating of the samian vessels. The absence of exclusively 2nd century types strongly suggests that the pit was filled with domestic rubbish at the very end of the 1st century A.D. or very early in the 2nd century.

The unusual depth of this pit, taken together with the skeletal evidence and the pots on the bottom, suggests that it had a special function. Larger and deeper shafts, discovered nearby on the site at different times also contained skeletal material. From this it seems likely that a group of pits at Keston had a specialised, perhaps ritual, function and this is discussed below (page 296).

Pit 18 (Figs. 4, 9 and 13).

This shallow pit was excavated in 1970 at a point about 9 ft. south-west of Pit 17 (Fig. 4). It was oval in plan being 5'10" (north-east to south-west) by 3'4" (north-west to south-east) and only 10" deep into the solid chalk. Its south-east side overlapped another, smaller pit with an identical but sterile filling and it was not possible to prove which was the earlier.

Pit 18 had steep sides and a flat base. Its fill consisted mostly of brown loam (L.3) which contained a Potin coin (Coin No. 2), fragments of a triangular clay loom-weight (No. 11), a burnt clay slab (No. 14) and some 277 coarse-ware potsherds. These latter represent at least 34 different vessels of which nine are illustrated (Nos. 483–491).

The coarse pottery provides the main dating evidence with 177 sherds of sandy Romanised wares. Fifty of these fragments, including two strainer bases (No. 486), a flagon rim (No. 489), a platter (No. 487), everted and bead rim jars and bowls (Nos. 483, 484, 488, 490 and 491) are of Keston Kiln Ware, dated to *c.* A.D. 60–85.

The remaning sherds are native fabrics, with 46 shell-tempered sherds, including at least one bead-rim jar (No. 485), 49 grog-tempered sherds, four sandy native ware sherds and one residual flint-tempered sherd (none illustrated). The bulk of this material dates from the second half of the first century A.D. and again suggests that this pit was also filled soon after the end of that century. The Potin coin, although corroded, appears to be a Class I type and is probably of 1st century B.C. date. It is, therefore, likely to be residual in this context.

Whilst Pit 17 seems to have had a ritual function there is no evidence to suggest this for Pit 18. On its merits it was probably dug for storage, but its close association with Pit 17, both in terms of its physical position and its date makes this less certain.

Pit 19 (F.239) (Figs. 4, 9 and 19).

This broad, shallow pit was excavated in 1969 within the Centre Enclosure. It lay close to the Roman West Masonry Building and actually cut into the east entrance causeway of the West Enclosure (Fig. 19). The pit was circular with a diameter of 5'6" and a depth of 20" into solid chalk. It had steep sides and a flat base. Its filling of light brown loam contained 74 potsherds and several small fragments of Roman tile, the latter possibly intrusive.

An examination of the pottery shows that at least 18 vessels are represented, of which five are illustrated (Nos. 492–496). Some 17 of the sherds are in a shell-tempered fabric including two bead rim jars (Nos. 494 and 495) and a flat topped rim of pre-Conquest form (No. 496). Some 19 sherds are in a grog-tempered fabric, twenty are in a native sandy ware and there are only 18 sherds in sandy Romanised fabrics. One lid (No. 492) is a Keston kiln product and another vessel (No. 493) is represented by the rim of an imported Gallo-Belgic butt beaker of Claudio-Neronian date.

Allowing for some residual material the date-range of the pottery seems to be A.D. 50–125. From this it seems likely that this pit was filled by the early-2nd century A.D.

On its merits it was probably dug as a storage-pit, but its position on the site requires some comment. Its early date precludes any association with the adjacent Roman building. Its position across the east causeway of the West Enclosure, however, seems largely accidental for, had the causeway remained in use, then this pit would have substantially blocked it. The badly disturbed nature of the adjacent enclosure ditches makes the precise date of their infilling uncertain. However, it seems likely that these ditches were largely filled by the later first century A.D. The date of the material in the pit filling may suggest that the pit was filled before the Centre Enclosure was dug, probably in the late-1st century or very early-2nd century A.D.

Pit 20 (F.121) (Figs. 4, 9 and 32).
This pit was excavated in 1969 where it was found to be cut and partially sealed by the east wall of the Roman South Masonry Building (Period VII; Fig. 32). It was slightly ovoid in plan, being 3'8" (east–west) by 3' (north–south) and was dug some 19" deep into the underlying chalk. It had vertical sides and a flat base. The filling consisted of brown loam with chalk rubble, which contained a bronze brooch (No. 92), an interesting potter's die (No. 37) and a single potsherd (not illustrated).

The potsherd is of Keston Kiln Ware and consists of an imitation *Terra Nigra* platter fragment. Interestingly, several other platters from Lower Warbank, also from the Keston Kilns and of very similar form to the present sherd, bear a potter's stamp and without doubt a die similar to that recovered from this pit was used. The brooch is an early, 'Thistle'-type and dates from the mid-1st century A.D. The potter's die and potsherd are probably a little later, *c.* A.D. 60–85. From this somewhat limited evidence it seems that this pit, too, was probably filled in the latter part of the 1st century A.D. It seems likely, on its merits, to have been dug originally for storage purposes.

Pit 21 (F.114) (Figs. 4, 9, 13 and 32).
This pit was also excavated in 1969 just to the east of the Roman South Masonry Building (Fig. 32) and only about 12' south-east of Pit 20. It was actually cut by Post-hole 10 of the South Timber Building (Period Va), which was itself beneath the later Masonry Building (of Period VII). The pit was oval in plan, being some 4'2" (north–south) by 3'8" (east–west) and had been dug 2'11" into solid chalk. Its sides were slightly undercut and it had a flat base (Fig. 13). It was filled with alternate layers of chalk rubble (L.3 and 5) and brown loam (L.2, 4 and 6) and together these produced some 179 potsherds. An absolute minimum of 34 vessels is represented, of which eight are illustrated (Nos. 497–504), the latter all from the upper filling of the pit.

The middle and lower fillings (L.3–5) contained 35 potsherds, representing at least 15 vessels, a number of which are also represented in the upper filling. The upper filling (L.2) contained the bulk of the pottery with some 144 sherds being recovered. These represent at least 25 different vessels, some of which are also represented in the lower and middle fillings. At least five of these vessels are in a shell-tempered fabric, including one bead rim jar (No. 497). There are at least nine more vessels in a grog-tempered fabric, including two sherds from a native copy of a Gallo-Belgic platter. These two sherds, too fragmentary for illustration, represent one of the few examples from the site of this vessel-type in a fabric other than Keston Kiln Ware. There is also a grog-tempered jar with an out-turned rim (No. 504). In addition, another seven vessels are in sandy native wares, all too fragmentary to assign to any specific vessel-type. There are another nine vessels in Romanised sandy fabrics and the bulk of these are products of the Keston kiln. They include the three platters illustrated (Nos. 500–502) and two jars (Nos. 498 and 503). These kiln wares have been dated *c.* A.D. 60–85. In addition there is a single flint-tempered rim sherd which is certainly residual. This has, however, been illustrated (No. 499). Allowing for some residual material, most of the pottery seems to date from the latter part of the 1st century or early-2nd century A.D. and it seems clear that this is the period when the pit was filled.

The upper filling of the pit also produced a flint arrowhead (No. 1) relating to the earlier use of the site (Period I). As with most of the other early-Roman pits this present feature could have been dug for storage and indeed, its undercut sides are reminiscent of Iron Age storage pits on this and many other sites.

Pit 22 (F.468) (Figs. 4, 9 and 15).
This broad, shallow pit was excavated in 1971 within the limits of the Roman Centre Timber Building, but otherwise not connected with it. It had a somewhat irregular outline, but was roughly sub-rectangular in plan. It measured 8' (east–west) by 7'4" (north–south) and had been dug some 12" into the underlying chalk. It had sloping sides and a flat base. It was filled with thin layers of black and brown loam which contained 104 potsherds and a fragment of a triangular clay loom-weight (too fragmentary for illustration). The pottery represents at least 25 different vessels and five of these have been illustrated (Nos. 505–509).

In detail, the potsherds included nine, almost certainly residual, pieces of flint-tempered ware, one decorated wall sherd being illustrated (No. 505). There are a further ten sherds of shell-tempered ware and these are from at least four different vessels, all too fragmentary for illustration. A further 30 sherds, representing at least six different vessels, are of grog-tempered wares and another seven sherds are of sandy native ware, representing at least two vessels. None of these sherds is worthy of illustration. In addition, 48 sherds are of sandy Roman fabrics and these come from at least ten different vessels. The Roman wares include an amphora fragment and five sherds of Keston Kiln Ware. Other Roman wares include two bead rim jars (Nos. 507 and 508), an everted rim jar (No. 506) and a flanged-rim bowl (No. 509). The bulk of this pottery again dates to the second half of the first century A.D. Some of the Roman sherds, however, could be of early-2nd century A.D. date and there is little material in the group that is exclusively post-A.D. 100 (e.g. No. 506). It is, thus, likely that this feature was filled during the mid or later 2nd century A.D. The function of this somewhat irregular pit is not clear, but storage is a possibility.

Pit 23 (F.946, Sheep/goat burial) (Figs. 4, 9 and 13; Plate VI).

This small and very interesting pit was excavated in 1976 at the extreme west edge of Lower Warbank Field, some 14′ north of the north ditch of the West Enclosure. The pit was circular in plan with a diameter of only 1′5″ and it had been cut some 6″ into the natural chalk. Its filling of brown loam contained the contracted skeleton of a sheep/goat and six joining sherds of the lower half of a pottery vessel (not illustrated).

There can be little doubt that this pit was dug specifically to contain the body of the animal which substantially filled it (Fig. 13). The spine of the animal curved along the west side of the pit and was tightly against it. The left leg was on the north side, the rib-cage correspondingly on the south side, but the head had been tucked back into the centre where only the jaw survived intact. The body had clearly been placed with some care, for, as the body length was longer than the pit, the dead animal was effectively tucked in to create a ball-like arrangement. Of special interest was the pot, for it had occupied the only available space left, namely on the east side between the legs and the upper body. The pot was found crushed on its side and it is likely that more of it was removed by ploughing in the post-Roman period. Indeed it is likely that it may have been complete and stood upright when originally deposited.

The pot is in a sandy Roman fabric and may broadly be of second century A.D. date. Without the rim and more of it little else can be said and it is not now worthy of illustration. However, it seems certain that the skeleton and the pot were deliberately placed in the pit at the same time. On this evidence a ritual deposit seems to be indicated, and with the close proximity of the various shafts with their skeletal deposits this now seems highly likely. The ritual implications of the site are discussed below (page 296).

Analysis of the bones from this pit has shown that the complete animal skeleton had not survived. When living, however, the creature probably stood to a height of about 21″. No butchery was apparent except for a number of knife-cuts (see page 288).

PERIOD V : THE 'PROTO-VILLA' COMPLEX (A.D. 160–200; Figs. 4 and 14).

It seems clear that the Romano-British farmstead (described above as Period IV), with its enclosures, pits, burials and kiln, evolved through two main phases between about A.D. 140–160. It is equally clear that many of these features were superseded by at least three major timber buildings that appear to belong to a single overall scheme. This much more ordered arrangement must represent a major reorganisation of the whole site and this is designated as Period V. This reorganisation, from the relative evidence of earlier and later structures, seems to have taken place between about A.D. 160 and 200.

It included:–

(A) The construction of a large West Timber Building in a dominant position on the west side of the site, partly over the small cremation cemetery (Period IVb).
(B) The construction of the Centre Timber Building, partly across the South Enclosure (Period IIIb).
(C) The construction of the South Timber Building over at least two pits (Period IV), at the southern edge of the site.
(D) The construction (here regarded as Period Va) of the Centre Flint Structure over the infilled Quarry Pit Complex.
(E) The formation of the Lower East Metalling, a road or trackway running east–west.
(F) A patch of isolated metalling to the north (F.873).
(G) A Water Storage Pond in the north-east corner of the site.
(H) A pair of Two Post Structures in the general area of the new buildings.

Of the three major buildings designated Period Va, only the South and Centre Timber Buildings are discussed in detail here. The third, the West Timber Building, was not fully excavated until 1987 and will be dealt with in the second Keston report, but a brief outline is included here.

(i) THE SOUTH TIMBER BUILDING (Figs. 14, 32 and 33).

This building was located during the 1968 excavations at the south edge of the site and largely beneath the later Roman South Masonry Building (Period VII, see below). The eastern half of this area contained a large number of features (Fig. 32), mostly pits and post-holes of late-Iron Age and Roman date cut into the underlying chalk. These continued east of the building in the small area excavated in 1969 and probably beyond. No overall sequence could be established for these numerous features, largely because the area had been heavily ploughed and previously cleared during the 1854 excavation, but also due to the presence of the overlying Roman Masonry Building.

It is, however, possible to identify a regular group of ten substantial post-pits, filled with brown loam (Table 11) as forming the outline of a single large timber building (South Timber Building). This is itself very similar in form and scale to the two other large timber buildings found higher up on the site (West Timber Building and Centre Timber Building). The post-pits described an oblong structure consisting of two parallel rows of five posts each, creating a building of four bays (Fig. 32). Measuring from the centre-points of the post-pits the building was 36′6″ in east–west length and 19′9″ in north–south width, thus having an area of about 720 sq. ft. It lies across the slope of the hill on about the 400 foot contour. Two of the post-pits (Nos. 4 and 10) cut earlier pits (Pits 19 and F.132) and the structure itself lay at about 9–10° off the main axis of the later masonry building constructed over it.

In detail the post-pits varied in shape, but the majority were oval or sub-rectangular and ranged from 2′1″–3′9″ by 2′5″–3′11″ in size. There were no obvious traces of vertical post-pipes, as survived in post-pits elsewhere on the Lower Warbank site, but it seems highly probable that these had once existed; presumably, either one or other of the later disturbances to which the area has been subjected led to their destruction here, or the posts had been deliberately pulled out in the Roman period. The depth of the post-pits varied. As surviving, those along the north wall were between 18″ and 30″ deep into the chalk (Fig. 33, S.P, L.22), whilst those along the south wall were between 9″ and 28″. This variation appears to be caused by later erosion of the original chalk surface in this area. Plough damage is likely to account for the shallower depth of Post-pits 5 and 10, which lay beyond the confines of the later masonry structure. In the absence of the

No.	Shape of Pit	Size of Pit (ins.)	Depth (ins.)	Original Feature No.
1	L-Shaped	33 × 41	25	9
2	Sub-rectangular	29 × 31	26	19
3	L-Shaped	45 × 48	30	25
4	Rectangular	26 × 37	21	131
5	Oval	33 × 38	18	127
6	Oval	39 × 47	28	45
7	Circular	37 × 37	15 (min.)	31
8	Oval	29 × 30 (min.)	12	29
9	Oval	32 × 35	14	111
10	Sub-rectangular	25 × 41	9	113

Table 11. Details of the post-pits relating to the South Timber Building.

actual post-pipes the precise dimensions of the building cannot be certain. Nevertheless, the spacings of the post-pits, from centre to centre, are fairly evenly arranged, varying from 8′4″ to 9′7″, which seems entirely acceptable as a margin of error. The average spacing of the post-pits is 9′1″ and it may be more than just coincidence that 10 Roman feet equate with about 9′8″. (For a discussion of the probable use of the Roman foot in this structure and the Centre Timber Building, see below, page 298). Details of the post-pits and of the inter-post spacings for the South Timber Building are given in Tables 11 and 12.

No floor-levels or demolition deposits associated with the South Timber Building had survived and these may have been removed during the construction of the later masonry structure (Fig. 33). A small spread of burnt daub, however, located between Post-pits 3 and 4 could represent part of the collapsed north wall of the structure and this deposit contained 17 sherds of pottery (No. 510). Four of the post-pits also contained some small fragments of burnt daub. There seems insufficient evidence, however, to suggest that this building was destroyed by fire as happened at the West Timber Building (see below, page 61).

North Wall	South Wall
Bay 1 (Pits 1–2) = 9′5″ Bay 2 (Pits 2–3) = 9′5″ Bay 3 (Pits 3–4) = 8′4″ Bay 4 (Pits 4–5) = 9′7″	Bay 1 (Pits 6–7) = 8′10″ Bay 2 (Pits 7–8) = 9′6″ Bay 3 (Pits 8–9) = 8′8″ Bay 4 (Pits 9–10) = 9′2″
Total Length = 36′9″	Total Length = 36′2″

Table 12. The bay sizes of the South Timber Building as calculated from the post-pit centres.

Collectively, the post-pits were found to contain 42 sherds of pottery and one coin. Little can be said as to the likely superstructure, but substantial circular upright posts forming the main frame, with 20' tie-beams and large horizontal wall-plates, seem likely. The infilling between the main wall frame-work was probably wattle and daub. The roof was probably timber-framed and thatched, as no trace of roof-tile was found in association. (For a further discussion of this and other timber structures at Keston see page 296).

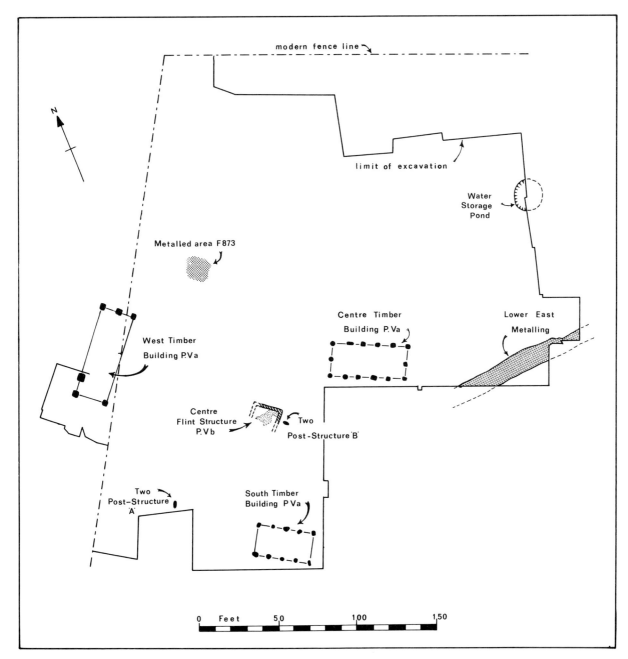

Fig. 14.   *Plan of features and structures assigned to Period V a and b.*

As regards dating evidence, the structure cut two earlier pits (Pits 21 and F.132) which contained later 1st to early-2nd century A.D. pottery, including Keston Kiln Ware and clearly it cannot have been constructed before the end of the first century A.D. In addition, the post-pits contained a coin (Coin No. 6) of Claudius I (A.D. 43–54) from Post-pit 5, a mortarium (No. 909) from Post-pit 5, a sherd of Neronian samian ware (from Post-pit 3) and 40 other coarse-ware sherds. The latter represent 17 vessels, of which four have been illustrated (Nos. 511–514). The majority appears to date from the second half of the 1st century A.D. and consists of native shell and grog-tempered wares. Two rims of Patch Grove Ware jars have been illustrated (Nos. 511 and 513). Some Romanised wares were also recovered and these include a few Kiln Ware sherds. Two Roman sherds have been drawn, a small bead rim jar in Keston Kiln Ware (No. 512) and a jar in fine sandy ware (No. 514). Although most of these sherds are likely to be of 1st century A.D. date some, notably the Patch Grove Wares, could well belong to the 2nd century. No. 514 is dateable to the first half of the 2nd century A.D.

The sherds from the daub layer are also of late-1st to early-2nd century date; one Patch Grove storage jar is illustrated (No. 510). In view of this evidence and the general absence of associated late-second century pottery, a construction date in the mid-2nd century seems the most likely. The bulk of the associated pottery would, therefore, have been derived from slightly earlier deposits on, or adjacent to, the site chosen for the building. The single coin recovered (Coin No. 6) came from the upper filling of Post-pit 5 and is likely to be of similar origin. It is just possible that six smaller post-holes (F.32, 128, 17, 21, 140 and 141) could represent additional related post-holes, as they fall on the main lines of the structure. However, it is equally possible that they form part of the large group of unassociated pits and post-holes and that their apparent coincidence with the main timber building is fortuitous. The large group of miscellaneous features probably contains post-holes and pits that are both earlier and later than the timber-building, but the general absence of finds makes this difficult to ascertain. Either way, they suggest the presence of several other structures, of unknown size and form, in this immediate area.

A large rectangular clay-lined water-storage tank was also located at the west end of the structure (South Tank). This lies hard against the presumed line of the building's west wall and is likely to be of a later date. The general site evidence indicates that this tank is unlikely to have been constructed before the late-2nd century A.D. and it has been assigned here to Period VI. The date at which the South Timber Building itself was demolished is not certain. It was clearly gone by the time the South Masonry Building was erected in Period VII. The fact that these two structures are on slightly different axes and that their positions do not exactly correspond, may suggest that the timber structure was not directly replaced by the masonry building (as happened with the West Timber Building); this in turn would imply that the timber building disappeared sometime before the masonry building's construction. The absence of any major building here in Period VI, however, could indicate that the South Timber Building, survived into the early villa period.

The function of the South Timber Building cannot be certain. There was no evidence, in the form of painted wall-plaster, window glass or roof-tile, to suggest that it was a dwelling (as seems fairly clearly to have been the case with the West Timber Building). An agricultural function of some kind may, thus, perhaps be more likely for the present structure. If the Period VI water tank, built immediately to the west of the South Timber Building, was constructed whilst the building was still in use it may well indicate that a considerable quantity of water was needed for some reason within the building (for animals perhaps). The inference that the Period VI water tank is a later addition could suggest that the building had another purpose in Period V when water was not required there in any great amount.

(ii) THE CENTRE TIMBER BUILDING (Figs. 14, 15 and 16).

This building was located and excavated in 1971, close to the centre of the area so far investigated and only some 8' east of the Anglo-Saxon hut, itself found in 1970 (Fig. 15, see below). The building was defined by a regular series of large post-holes, totalling 14 in all, and took the form of an oblong structure. The East Fence and the West Fence, associated with the main Roman villa complex (Period VI) crossed the west end of the building, actually cutting Post-hole 2. This shows that the building had by then been removed, in part or whole. In addition Post-hole 9 of this building cut an earlier ditch (the South Enclosure Ditch) which is assigned by reasonable dating evidence, to Period IIIb. Post-hole 8 cut an earlier Post-hole, F.503. For these reasons the Centre Timber Building is regarded as being of Period V and indeed it largely matches the form and construction of the South Timber Building, also classified as Period V (see Fig. 14).

In detail, the shape of the Centre Timber Building is described by a regular setting of 14 substantial post-pits forming a building 5 bays long. All but two of the pits contained a central post-pipe. Measuring from the centre of these post-pipes, the building is some 49 feet in east–west length and 21'3" in north–south width, thus having an area of about 1041 sq. ft. It lies across the slope of the hill on the 405 foot contour. In overall layout there are six pairs of post-holes along the north and south walls of the building with single post-holes in the middle of

Post-Hole No.	Original Feature No.	Pit Shape	Pit Size (ins.)	Pit Depth (ins.)	Pit Sides	Pit Base	Pipe Shape	Pipe Size (ins.)
1	425	Circ.	34 × 34	20	Vert.	Flat	Circ.	16 × 16
2	–	Oval	31 × 54	27	Steep	Flat	–	–
3	446	Sub-Rect.	37 × 40	25	Vert.	Flat	Circ.	15 × 15
4	452	Sub-Square	37 × 37	20	Steep	Flat	Circ.	14 × 14
5	454	Sub-Rect.	39 × 43	22	Vert.	Flat	Circ.	18 × 18
6	455	Sub-Rect.	34 × 40	13	Steep	Flat	Oval	15 × 17
7	–	Sub-Rect.	35 × 36	12	Steep	Flat	–	–
8	502	Sub-Rect.	36 × 42	10	Vert.	Flat	Oval	17 × 18
9	501	Sub-Rect.	34 × 36	14	Vert.	Flat	Circ.	14 × 14
10	496	Sub-Rect.	42 × 49	16	Vert.	Flat	Circ.	17 × 17
11	492	Sub-Rect.	36 × 39	19	Vert.	Flat	Oval	14 × 16
12	488	Sub-Rect.	43 × 47	16	Vert.	Flat	Circ.	13 × 13
13	484	Circ.	37 × 37	29	Vert.	Flat	Circ.	19 × 19
14	424	Oval	31 × 36	21	Steep	Flat	Circ.	12 × 12

Table 13. Details of the post-holes relating to the Centre Timber Building.

the east and west sides. The post-pits, themselves, were generally sub-rectangular in plan and were between 2'7" and 4'1" across. At the west end four of the post-pits (Nos. 1, 12, 13 and 14) were oval or circular. These had a similar size-range to the other post-pits and apparently represented nothing more than a minor constructional variation. The pits ranged in depth from 13" to 27" along the north wall and from 10" to 29" along the south wall. The single pits in the east and west walls were 12" and 21" deep, respectively. Plough erosion of the original chalk surface is likely to account for these variations in depth to a large extent. The post-pits were filled with chalk rubble mixed with a little brown loam. Some also contained a few flint lumps packed around the post-pipes. The post-pipes were all oval or circular in shape and varied in diameter between 12" and 19". They were filled with dark brown loam and were the same depth as their respective post-pits (Fig. 16).

The presence of the actual post-pipes in the Centre Building allows the true size of the structure to be fairly accurately calculated. The posts were spaced, centre to centre, between 9′6″ and 10′6″ along the north wall and between 8′9″ and 10′1″ along the south wall. In the west wall the posts were set 10′7″ apart, whilst the exact spacing in the east wall is not certain since the pipe of the central post-pit (No. 7) had not survived. The average spacing of the posts is thus about 9′9″. As with the South Timber Building, the spacing of the posts of the present building suggest that it was constructed using a standard measurement of 10 Roman feet (9′8″) (see discussion, page 298). Details of the post-pits and post-pipes and the inter-post spacings are given in Tables 13 and 14.

North Wall	South Wall
Bay 1 (P.H. 1–2) = ?⎫ 19′9″ Bay 2 (P.H. 2–3) = ?⎭ Bay 3 (P.H. 3–4) = 9′6″ Bay 4 (P.H. 4–5) = 10′0″ Bay 5 (P.H. 5–6) = 10′6″	Bay 1 (P.H. 12–13) = 10′1″ Bay 2 (P.H. 11–12) = 8′9″ Bay 3 (P.H. 10–11) = 10′0″ Bay 4 (P.H. 9–10) = 9′7″ Bay 5 (P.H. 8–9) = 10′1″
Total Length 49′9″	Total Length 48′6″
West Wall	East Wall
(P.H. 1–14) = 10′7″ (P.H. 13–14) = 10′7″	(P.H. 6–7) = ? (P.H. 7–8) = ?
Total Length 21′2″	Total Length 21′3″

Table 14. The bay sizes of the Centre Timber Building as calculated from the post-hole centres.

No floor levels or demolition deposits associated with the building had survived the centuries of ploughing in this area. Enclosed within the walls of the building were five pits (Nos. 1, 2, 6, 7 and 22). On the pottery dating evidence, however, these seem to be earlier, belonging to Periods II, III and IV. There are also several smaller post-holes, mostly of uncertain date, but none is obviously related to the main building. Also seemingly unrelated is a series of six parallel slots which run across the building (see below, page 101).

The dating of the Centre Timber Building is based upon the horizontal stratigraphy outlined above, the finds from the post-holes and general considerations. The ditch of the South Enclosure cut by Post-hole 9 of the Centre Timber Building produced pottery dateable to the middle years of the 1st century A.D. (Period IVa) and clearly the building must post-date this. No coins or samian ware were found in the post-holes of the building but 151 coarse-ware potsherds were recovered. Some 65 of these came from the filling of post-pits and 86 from the post-pipes. The sherds from the packing deposits in the post-pits represent at least 24 different vessels. Just over half of these are of late-Iron Age/early-Roman native shell, flint and grog-tempered fabrics, whilst the remainder are of sandy Romanised wares, of later 1st to 2nd century A.D. date. One residual flint-tempered rim sherd (No. 519) together with an everted rim jar in Roman sandy ware (No. 517) have been drawn. The filling of the post-pipes produced sherds representing at least 29 vessels and three of these have been drawn (Nos. 515, 516 and 518). Again, just over half of them are of late-Iron Age/early-Roman native fabrics, with the rest in sandy Romanised wares. Two bead rim jars have been drawn, one shell-tempered (No. 516) and one sand-tempered (No. 515) together with a Patch Grove rim sherd (No. 518). As with the material from the post-pits, all these sherds may be dated to the later 1st to 2nd centuries A.D. A single prehistoric flint scraper (No. 4) was recovered from the filling of Post-hole 13. The bulk of the pottery associated with the post-holes is likely to be derived from slightly earlier deposits in the same general area.

Since the packing deposits in the building's post-pits produced sherds broadly dateable to the later 1st to 2nd centuries A.D. it seems clear that the structure cannot have been erected before A.D. 100 at the earliest. On general grounds a construction date in the mid-2nd century seems most likely.

The date at which the Centre Timber Building went out of use is not certain. The presence of the undisturbed post-pipes indicates that at least the bases of the building's main uprights rotted *in situ* and the structure was certainly never superceded by a stone building on the same site, as happened on the sites of the West and South Timber Buildings. It has been suggested above that the South Timber Building continued in used into the main villa period (Period VI, see page 66). Whether this happened with the Centre Building is not clear. What is known is that the East and West Fences of Period VI crossed the site of Centre Building apparently destroying one of its post-holes (Post-hole 2). Thus, the building must have been abandoned and at least partially demolished by then. It is not certain, however, whether the fence-lines relate to the earliest part of the Period VI or whether they are subsequent additions. Either way, it would seem that, if the Centre Building did last into Period VI, it was not for long.

The function of the Centre Timber Building is not known. As with the South Timber Building there was no evidence that it was a dwelling and an agricultural use is perhaps most likely. It seems highly probable, in fact, that the massive North Timber Building of Period VI represents the subsequent replacement for this structure, built on an entirely new site. In Period VI, this new building clearly assumed the role of one of the principal agricultural structures on the site and it must be significant that the total floor area of the North Building is considerably greater than the combined area of the two earlier (presumed agricultural) timber structures of Period V.

(iii) THE WEST TIMBER BUILDING (an interim note) (Figs. 14 and 19).

This structure was located on the western edge of the site, beneath the West Masonry Building (Period VI). At least two of its post-pits were encountered during the 1951–3 excavation, but were identified as 'soakaways' and another was partially excavated in 1969. It was not, however, until 1987 that the whole area became available and a large-scale excavation was undertaken. This revealed almost the complete structure largely masked by the later masonry. As this excavation falls outside the scope of this volume only an outline description is provided here (full details will be published in the second report on the site).

The West Timber Building (Fig. 14) was rectangular in plan, with a major north–south axis, measuring overall some 59′8″ by 21′4″. Its wooden frame consisted of seven massive posts, each set in much larger pits, running down each side of the building and creating six bays. A single post was found in the centre of the north side, but no trace was found of a corresponding south post. The side posts were spaced, on average, at 10′2″ centre to centre and the whole structure covered an area of about 1270 sq. ft.

There was clear evidence that this building had been burnt down and the fire debris included a mass of daub, much of it coated with painted plaster. From this it seems likely that the building had a domestic function and its large size shows that it was, when built, the paramount structure on the site. Its basic structural similarity to the Centre Timber Building and the South Timber Building, together with the organised layout of the three buildings, strongly suggests that they were all erected at the same time and perhaps even by the same workforce.

(iv) THE CENTRE FLINT STRUCTURE (Figs. 4, 11 and 14).

This structure was located in 1968 near the centre of the excavated area (Fig. 11). It lay just above the 405 foot contour very roughly midway between the three major timber buildings of Period Va. Only an L-shaped section of unmortared flint foundation survived of a presumed timber-framed building of unknown overall size.

The structure overlay the filled in Quarry Pit Complex (Period IVa) and it had been cut through by a post-medieval ditch (Period IX, Ditch 4). The late-Roman metalling (Period VII) extended to the north-east corner of the foundations and appeared to spill over it. One part of the foundation was also cut by the shallow trench of the east water-pipe (Period VI). On this evidence the structure seems to belong to Period V and its position relative to the large timber buildings tends to support this.

The remaining flint foundations were poorly preserved and indeed only survived through having settled into the filling of the underlying quarry pits. The rest of the structure seems to have been robbed or ploughed away. As surviving, the L-shaped foundations appear to represent the north-east corner of a rectangular building. Its north wall was traced for 14'6". It was 1'6" wide and composed of numerous flint nodules set neatly in a shallow foundation-trench two courses deep. The east wall joined the north wall at marginally less than 90°, but only survived for a length of about 4'. It was similarly constructed, but later disturbance had caused it to spread to a width of 2'6". No related floor, occupation or destruction levels were found.

Of special interest, however, was an irregular spread of flints, largely enclosed within the walls of the structure, that measured about 14' (north-east to south-west) by about 7' (north-west to south-east). This seems to have been laid down to consolidate the upper filling of the quarry-pits and it contained 180 fragments of pottery. On its surface was a circular hearth of burnt clay, some 2' in diameter (F.71), that may have served the building itself.

As regards dating evidence no objects were found in the actual flint foundations. The main filling of the underlying quarry pits dates from the latter part of the 1st century A.D. (see page 42 above). In addition, a thin layer of soil beneath the flint rubble spread contained 51 potsherds, representing at least 19 vessels. These include two pieces of a Keston Kiln Ware butt beaker, an everted rim jar also in Kiln Ware, part of a pedestal-urn base in grog-tempered ware and fragments from two mortaria. All but the everted rim jar (No. 522) is too fragmentary for illustration, but most appears to date from the late-1st to 2nd century A.D. Clearly, the flint foundations were laid after this. Of even more relevance is the pottery in the flint spread associated with the structure. This large group contained fragments of at least 22 coarse-ware vessels, two mortaria (No. 910) and a single sherd of samian ware (a Walters 79R/Lud. TgR). Ten of the coarse-ware vessels (Nos. 520–529) and one of the mortaria (No. 910) have been illustrated. The samian sherd is of mid to late-Antonine date.

The coarse pottery includes a significant number of late-Iron Age/early-Roman native ware vessels and two shell-tempered bead rim jars have been drawn (Nos. 526 and 529), together with part of a grog-tempered jar, possibly a pedestal-urn (No. 520). Just over half of the vessels are of Romanised wares, however, and these include two amphora sherds (not illustrated), sherds from two rusticated beakers (No. 523), two bowls with outcurved rims (Nos. 527 and 528), a cup (No. 524), an everted rim jar (No. 521) and a few sherds of Keston Kiln Ware (No. 525). Most of this pottery seems to date from the period *c*. A.D. 50–150 and was probably derived from adjacent areas when the surface of the quarry pits was consolidated. However, the samian sherd suggests that this was not done before about A.D. 150–180 and this, together with the total absence of later pottery, suggests that this structure was probably built sometime in the second half of the 2nd century A.D. A hone (No. 131) was also recovered from the flint layer.

The 'hillwash' deposit over the flint rubble layer produced a total of 74 coarse-ware potsherds and these represent a minimum of 18 vessels. The bulk of this material appears to be of early-Roman date and includes significant amounts of shell-tempered and grog-tempered wares and Keston Kiln products. Three late-Roman flanged rim bowls also occur, however.

The precise nature and function of the structure represented by these damaged foundations is difficult to gauge. No overall size can be ascertained, but presumably the unmortared foundations supported a stout timber frame. The method of construction does set the building apart from the three major timber buildings, whose main frames were earth-fast. In this respect it could be regarded as an intermediate stage between these buildings (Period Va) and the mortared buildings of Periods VI and VII. Indeed the dating evidence, placing its construction in the second half of the 2nd century, suggests that it formed a second phase, hence Period Vb. Its position within the notional yard of Period Va is also of interest. Not only does it lie in a roughly central position between the three timber buildings, but its east wall seems to line up with the west wall of the South Timber Building. In addition its north wall seems to line up with the centre of the West Timber Building. This seems to suggest that the notional yard was further sub-divided (see Fig. 14). At the very least the construction of the Centre Flint Structure in Period Vb, shows that the original layout was substantially changed. More than this cannot be said.

(v) THE LOWER EAST METALLING (Figs. 14, 18, 34 and 35).

Excavations in 1973 and 1974, on the eastern side of the site, immediately to the south of the group of seven Four-Post Structures (1–6 and 10), revealed two levels of Roman metalling (Fig. 34). The lower one of these, from its position in the site sequence, is likely to be contemporary with the buildings which formed the Period V farmstead (see above). The Lower Metalling consisted of a layer of small flint pebbles set in brown loam and clearly represented a road or trackway leading onto the site. This trackway was aligned north-east by south-west and ran along the side of the hill, just above the 400 foot contour. It was traced for a minimum distance of 73 feet in the main excavation. It continued beyond the area investigated in both directions but did not re-emerge within the 1970 excavated area, further to the south-west. Two trial-trenches dug to the east of the main excavation limit produced further traces of this metalling, giving it a total minimum length of about 125 feet.

The roadway had subsequently been cut through by a large ditch, running on a similar axis (Figs. 18 and 35). This ditch is likely to form part of the later (Period VI) villa enclosure, (South-East Ditch of the Villa Enclosure). Both the ditch and the Lower Metalling were later sealed by dumps of orange clay, chalk and loam, which supported the late-Roman, Upper East Metalling (Period VII), also on the same alignment (Figs 18, L.6; Fig. 35, L.6, 7, 9 and 10).

The Lower Metalling was best preserved on the south-eastern side of the ditch. Here, it was up to 10′ in width. Traces of pebbling on the opposite side of the ditch, however, indicated that it was originally much wider, perhaps some 15–20′. A probable wheel rut 4″ to 6″ wide and about 2″ deep was located on the surface of the metalling, towards its south-eastern edge (Fig. 34).

Upon excavation the metalling was found to be about 2½″ thick and to rest upon 1–3″ of brown loam, plough soil, over the natural chalk (Fig. 18, L.14; Fig. 35, L.18). It also partially sealed an east–west gully cutting through this brown loam. The excavation of the Lower Metalling produced a total of 88 coarse-ware potsherds. These represent at least 34 different vessels, of which five are illustrated (Nos. 532–536). Some 61 of the sherds are of late-Iron Age/early-Roman native grog and shell-tempered wares. The grog-tempered wares include a number of jars (Nos. 532–535). There are a further 25 sherds of coarse, sandy, fully Romanised fabrics. These include Keston Kiln Ware fragments (No. 536). The date-range of this material, thus, seems to be from the second half of the 1st century A.D. into the 2nd century A.D. The rather fragmentary nature of the sherds makes more precise dating difficult.

The shallow soil layer beneath the Lower Metalling produced a Flavian samian ware sherd (Form 18) and 83 coarse-ware potsherds, representing at least 30 vessels, of which two are illustrated (Nos. 530 and 531). Most of these sherds are late-Iron Age/early-Roman native wares and a shelly ware bead rim jar (No. 530), together with a Patch Grove storage vessel (No. 531) are drawn. Again there are also a few sherds of sandy Romanised fabrics. These include an amphora fragment and four sherds of a decorated Keston Kiln Ware vessel (not illustrated). The fragmentary nature of the pottery makes precise dating difficult, but it seems clear that this layer could not have been sealed by the metalling much before about A.D. 100, and indeed this is likely to have occurred later, in the second century A.D.

From this combined evidence, both direct and circumstantial, it seems likely that the Lower Metalling was laid down sometime during the middle of the 2nd century A.D. The soil over the metalling, which contained an iron stylus (No. 72), samian ware (Nos. 138–141) and coarse pottery of later date, also supports this dating and as such the metalling fits neatly into Period V. Clearly this metalled trackway went out of use as soon as the enclosure ditch was dug (Period VI). The general absence of soil deposits above the metalling when the ditch was dug suggests that the former was replaced immediately by the latter, probably towards the end of the 2nd century A.D.

The alignment of the Lower Metalling and the later Villa Enclosure Ditch are of interest, especially when compared with the overlying late-Roman Upper Metalling, for all three of these features, to within a degree or two, are on precisely the same axis along the side of the hill (Fig. 34). This must surely be more than coincidence. The implication seems to be that some sort of boundary line influenced the positioning of these features. In the earliest phase, perhaps, the Lower Metalling was following the line of a pre-existing fence, hedge or some less visible boundary. The excavation of the ditch seems to have maintained and formalised this boundary line but ultimately, after the ditch had been filled in and the area levelled, the metalled roadway was relaid at a higher level. Thus, this (presumed boundary) line was maintained for some two centuries, throughout Periods V, VI and VII.

(vi) THE ROMAN WATER STORAGE POND (Figs. 4, 14 and 16).

The excavations at the top north-east corner of the site in 1978 revealed a very large, but shallow hollow cut into the natural chalk, some 65 feet east of the main North Timber Building (Fig. 4). Part of this feature actually lay outside the limits of the excavation and it seems that only about half of it was examined. It had been cut partly horizontally into the chalk, but had a dished base. At its north end it was about $2\frac{1}{2}'$ deep, but its south end coincided with the natural slope of the chalk (Fig. 16). Its maximum north–south measurement was thus about 25 feet and its east–west width only 11 feet as excavated, but if circular this would increase to about 25 feet. It is here regarded as part of the Period V layout (see below).

The base of this large hollow was found to have been lined on its north and west sides with a thick, sticky layer of orange-yellow clay (L.9). This was covered by extensive layers of black and brown loam (L.5–8), some 15″ deep and containing domestic rubbish. These layers were in turn sealed by a consolidating deposit of chalk rubble (L.4), probably thrown down to level off what would have become a wet soil-filled hollow. Even this left a marked hollow below the adjacent Roman ground-level and this became filled with dark loam (L.3) some 4″ to 10″ in depth, containing quantities of domestic rubbish and four coins.

In terms of dating evidence, the clay lining was found to contain a single pot base and a bronze 'Dolphin' brooch (No. 96) of 1st century A.D. date. The primary filling contained a single sherd of samian ware of Hadrianic-Antonine date and some 96 coarse-ware sherds, representing at least 17 vessels, of which five have been drawn (Nos. 538–542). All of this pottery dates from the late-1st to the late-2nd centuries A.D. and includes a sherd of probable Nene Valley Ware (No. 541), several jars (Nos. 538, 539 and 542) and a bead rim pie dish (No. 540). It seems from this that the pond was probably constructed in the mid-2nd century A.D. and that it was filled in no later than the end of the 2nd century A.D. (hence Period V). The chalk layer produced no finds, but the final soils over the largely filled pond produced four coins and 392 potsherds. These represent at least 60 different vessels of which six are illustrated (Nos. 543–548). A considerable number of these vessels are of late-3rd or 4th century date (Nos. 546, 547 and 548), whilst the remainder are of forms and fabrics which suggest that they are residual. The latter includes a samian Form 33 of late-2nd or 3rd century date. The four coins (Coin Nos. 18, 47, 56 and 67) are one each of Postumus (A.D. 260–268), Helena (A.D. 337–341), House of Constantine (A.D. 335–345) and of Valens (A.D. 364–378). From this evidence it seems clear that the final hollow was being used as a domestic rubbish dump during most of the late-3rd and 4th centuries, probably from a fairly nearby source.

It seems clear from the size of the excavation in the chalk and the very substantial clay lining, that this feature was deliberately constructed as a water-storage tank, or pond. It seems to have become filled by the end of the 2nd century A.D. when it could have been superseded by the series of rectangular clay tanks across the area. These, too, had thick clay linings and were apparently fed by piped water. The tanks are shown, on independent evidence, to relate to Periods VI and VII and the dating of this Pond as Period V, thus, agrees with this. The domestic rubbish found over the pond would then come from Period VI or Period VII.

(vii) TWO-POST STRUCTURES (Figs. 4, 11, 14, 16 and 37).

Large numbers of post-holes were located over much of the Lower Warbank site. Many of these cannot be interpreted with any confidence, although it has been possible to recognise one six-post structure, ten 'four-posters' and several larger structures.

Two-post structures, generally interpreted as drying racks or similar structures, have also been recorded on many native farmstead sites. With so many scattered post-holes at Keston it is very difficult to be certain if any two post-holes can be related to form such a 'two-poster'. In most instances it has been considered best not to attempt this, but in at least two cases, it has been possible to recognise related pairs of post-holes by the fact that they were both set in a common construction pit. Details of these 'two-post structures' are given below.

Two-Post Structure 'A' (F.1131) (Figs. 16 and 37).

This was located in 1977, just to the north-west of the South Masonry Building (Fig. 37). Two circular posts were set in a sub-rectangular pit with its main axis aligned north-east by south-west. The pit measured 5′1″ by 2′ and had steep sides and a base sloping to the south. It was about 12″ to 14″ in depth and was filled with a light brown loam and chalk lumps, which showed the outline of two post-pipes, filled with dark brown loam (Fig. 16). These post-pipes were the same depth as the pit with steep or vertical sides and flat bases. The southern post was 11″ in diameter, whilst the northern was 12″. The two posts were 3′5″ apart (centre to centre) and clearly formed a pair of contemporary wooden uprights. The fill of the south post-pipe produced two potsherds, one shell-tempered fragment and a sandy grog-tempered ware rim sherd of late-1st to 2nd century A.D. date, which is illustrated (No. 537).

Two-Post Structure 'B' (Fig. 11).

A similar structure was found in 1968 over the filled in Quarry Pit Complex, which contained late-1st century material (Fig. 11). Structure 'B' was somewhat smaller than 'A' with the posts being 10″ in diameter and only 2′ apart (centre to centre). It was aligned north-west by south-east with the most westerly post being 20″ in depth and the other 27″ in depth. They were set in a single pit some 3′10″ by 1′2″.

No finds were recovered from it, but as the Quarry Pit Complex relates to Period IV this structure must be later. However, the 4th century Roman metalling in this area, assigned to Period VII, appeared to seal the south-eastern end of the construction pit indicating that Structure 'B' is earlier. It is here regarded as belonging to Period V, though it could equally well relate to Period VI.

(viii) METALLED AREA (F.873) (Figs. 4, 14, and 29).

An isolated sub-rectangular area of pebble metalling was located just within the western limits of the Centre Enclosure, some 15′ to the north-east of the north-east corner of the West Masonry Building, in 1976. It measured 15′ (north-east by south-west) by 13′ (north-west by south-east) and consisted of flint pebbles, chalk and flint lumps set in a brown loam. This metalling, which was generally 2″–6″ thick, had been partially disturbed by later ploughing. It is clear, however, that it originaly sealed part of the filled in West Enclosure Ditch (Period IIIb) and was itself cut by the western water-pipe trench (Period VI, see Fig. 29). It has, thus, been placed here as part of the

Period V layout/scheme. A group of post-holes along the western side of the metalling may have related to it, but this could not be proved. Indeed, the exact purpose of this metalling is not clear. It could represent an external hard-standing or just possibly the floor of a small timber hut. The post-holes recorded are, however, not really sufficient to postulate a structure. The proximity of the metalled area to metalling laid along the northern side of the West Masonry Building may alternatively suggest that the two areas were originally connected, but that they were subsequently separated by plough-damage. The pebbling along the edge of the building however, seems likely to be later, probably belonging to Period VII, as it seals the Period V Centre Enclosure Ditch and two post-holes of the Period VI Centre Fence.

It has been assumed that the western water-pipe is contemporary with the Period VI West Building and the clay-lined West Tank 1. Clearly if the two areas of metalling were contemporary, then the pipe-line must be later (possibly a subsequent replacement feeding West Tanks 2 or 3 dug on the same spot as Tank 1). On balance, therefore, it seems most likely that the two areas of metalling are not related and are of different dates.

There was little dating evidence found in association with this metalling. Of seven sherds, none is sufficient for illustration, one was a samian fragment of early to mid-2nd century A.D. date. The other six represent a minimum of four coarse-ware vessels, of which two are grog-tempered native wares and a third an imitation Gallo-Belgic platter of Keston Kiln Ware. The other three sherds are sandy Romanised fabrics and the whole group (none illustrated) is unlikely to date any later than the mid-2nd century. From this, the metalling cannot have been laid down much before about A.D. 150 and this agrees well with its identification as Period V.

PERIOD VI : THE MAIN VILLA COMPLEX (A.D. 200–300 – Fig. 17).

It is clear from the evidence on the site that the 'proto-villa' layout (described above as Period V), with its three large timber buildings, was substantially superseded by an even larger reorganisation at about A.D. 200. This new era (Period VI) is dated on stratigraphic, artefactual and circumstantial evidence, broadly to A.D. 200–300. It represents the Roman villa site at its most extensive and opulent, with perhaps an increased status, or even new owners. It included:

(A)   The excavation of large enclosing ditches on the north and south sides.
(B)   The construction of the West Masonry Building to replace the West Timber Building on the same site.
(C)   The construction of a massive North Timber Building replacing the Centre Timber Building, but on a new site about 100 km. further north.
(D)   The construction of substantial fences to create compounds and enclosures, probably to restrict cattle or horses.
(E)   The construction of water storage-tanks and pipe-lines.
(F)   The construction of masonry tombs in a new cemetery at the north end of the site.

These are described in detail below, though the North Cemetery has been held over for publication in the second Report on the site.

(i) THE VILLA ENCLOSURE DITCH (Fig. 17).

The three substantial ditch lengths apparently enclosing the villa complex are individually described below.

a) The North-West Ditch (F.800 and 801) (Figs. 4, 17 and 18; Plate XV).
Excavations in 1976 revealed a substantial length of a long ditch, L-shaped in plan, to the north of the West Masonry Building and close to the northern limit of the excavations (Fig. 4). The ditch

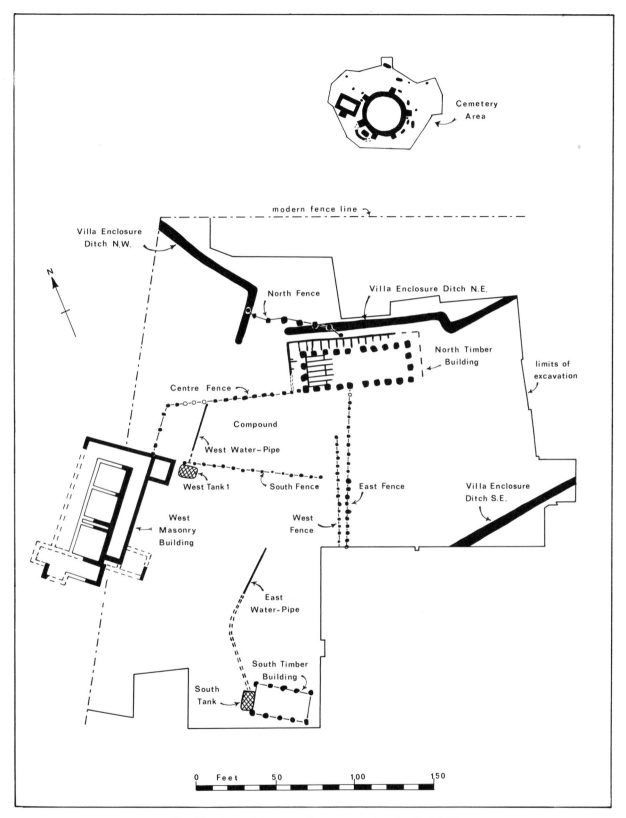

Fig. 17. *Plan of features and structures assigned to Period VI.*

seems to have formed part of the main villa enclosure and was first located during trenching in 1968. The two arms of the ditch joined at an angle of about 107°. No trace of any accompanying bank was located and whether one ever existed is not clear. The north arm of the ditch ran along the side of the hill between the 415 foot and 420 foot contours and was traced for a minimum distance of 76 feet in the recent excavations. Subsequent work in 1984 and 1986 revealed a further significant length in an adjacent area to the west. As excavated in 1976, the north arm of the ditch was between 5'3" and 7' wide at the top (due to plough erosion) and 9" to 1'6" across the base, with a V-shaped profile overall. This arm was between 2'4" and 3'2" deep. At the north-west end it cut an earlier gully (F.943), which produced no dateable pottery. The lower and middle fillings of the main ditch were mostly layers of light brown loam with chalk lumps (Fig. 18, S.A, L.4–7; S.B, L.2) overlain by an upper deposit of brown loam with chalk specks all apparently representing largely natural silts with some dumped domestic rubbish. There were suggestions of a later, shallow recut in the top of one ditch but this was not clearly defined (S.A, L.3; S.C, L.1).

The east arm was traced for its full distance of 39'8". It was about 4'9" wide across the top and between 10" and 12" across the bottom, again with a V-shaped profile. The lower fill was a brown loam with chalk rubble (Fig. 18, S.C, L.2) with deposits of brown loam and chalk specks above (S.C, L.1). It was between 2'1" and 2'5" deep. There was no sign of a recut. This east arm of the ditch was cut by a pair of shallow U-shaped gullies or ruts. Where parallel these were between 59" and 60" apart. They diverged at the west. The ruts were between 6" and 10" wide and 3" to 6" in depth. They have been interpreted as wheel-ruts but there is no dating evidence for them. They are in fact probably quite recent and are not shown on Fig. 4.

More certainly of Roman date is a large post-hole, which cut the eastern arm of the ditch. This appears to be the first in a slightly sinuous line of post-holes, running up to the North Timber Building of Period VI and are termed here the 'North Fence'.

The Dating Evidence for the North-West Ditch.

No coins were recovered from the filling of the North-West Ditch of the Villa Enclosure, but five samian sherds were found. Trenching in 1968 along the north arm produced a Central Gaulish dish-base (Form 36 etc.), probably of Antonine date and two other burnt Central Gaulish sherds. Work in 1976 yielded two sherds of a decorated Form 37, dateable to c. A.D. 175–210. These sherds (No. 137) came from the upper filling of the east arm of the ditch and apparently came from the same vessel as a sherd found in the corn drying ovens in the North Timber Building.

Five mortaria came from the north arm (Nos. 911–913). Large amounts of coarse pottery were also recovered from the ditch. The east arm produced a total of 204 sherds. These represent at least 29 different vessels and 12 have been drawn (Nos. 549–560). Although over half of these sherds are of thoroughly Romanised fabrics there is also a significant proportion of earlier, native wares, which are clearly residual. There are 40 sherds of early shell-tempered ware (none illustrated), 27 sherds of early grog-tempered ware (including an upright rim jar, No. 551) and three sherds in a sandy pre-Roman fabric (none illustrated).

The bulk of the Roman wares were from coarse sandy domestic vessels and included straight-sided bowls and dishes (Nos. 549 and 557), bead rim dishes (Nos. 552 and 560), out-turned and everted rim jars (Nos. 550, 553, 555 and 558), a lid (No. 556) and two flagons (Nos. 554 and 559). Several sherds of late-Roman Alice Holt Ware are present within this material (none illustrated). Finer Roman wares are represented by two colour-coated vessels, including a sherd of Nene Valley Ware from the primary filling of the ditch (not illustrated). The bulk of the pottery from this arm of the ditch ranges in date from the mid-1st to late-2nd centuries A.D. with some later material. The early pottery must be residual, however. The smaller amount of later material present indicates that the ditch cannot have been filled before the end of the 3rd century A.D., but the general absence of 4th century material suggests that it was not long after A.D. 300.

Much larger amounts of coarse pottery were recovered from the north arm of the ditch. Some

893 sherds, representing at least 119 different vessels have been recorded and 47 of these have been illustrated (Nos. 561–607). Well over three-quarters of this material came from the upper filling of the ditch, which seems to represent a late recut. Although some early Roman residual material is again present within the assemblage, the bulk of the pottery (664 sherds) is of later Roman wares and these include: 28 sherds of Alice Holt domestic grey ware (Nos. 563, 567, 569, 572, 574, 575, 584, 587, 589, 590, 592 and 594; 14 probable Oxfordshire Ware sherds (Nos. 595, 598, 603 and 607); 14 other colour-coated sherds (Nos. 593, 599 and 604) and four of Nene Valley type (not illustrated). A few sherds of New Forest ware were also noted, including a bowl which is illustrated (No. 591). There are 85 sherds of late-Roman grog-tempered ware (Nos. 566, 573, 576 and 578).

Of the earlier, residual material, some 59 fragments are shell-tempered, including a decorated rim of pre-Conquest date (No. 600). There are some 85 early-Roman grog-tempered sherds (none illustrated) and five fragments of sandy native ware (none illustrated). Of particular interest is a fragment from a *Terra Nigra* platter, dated to *c.* A.D. 50–75 (No. 606).

The bulk of the pottery recovered from this arm of the ditch is of late-3rd to 4th century date and includes a whole range of typically late-Roman vessel-types, such as straight-sided bowls, flanged bowls and colour-coated fine-wares, like Oxfordshire Ware. The majority of this pottery was obtained from the upper (recut?) filling of the ditch. The lower and middle fillings also produced some late-Roman material, but only small amounts of pottery overall.

A number of small-finds came from the north arm of the ditch (F.800). Nine have been illustrated. These are: two bronze brooches, one of 1st century A.D. date (No. 93) and one possibly of 3rd century A.D. date (No. 95); a pair of bronze tweezers (No. 123); two jet bracelet fragments of later Roman type (Nos. 109 and 110); a shale bracelet (No. 104); a bronze bracelet (No. 106) and an antler fragment (No. 53). The east arm (F.801) of the ditch yielded an iron pruning-hook (No. 68).

From the date of the coarse pottery and other finds it seems clear that the North-West Ditch of the Villa Enclosure was filled during the late-Roman period. The east arm of the ditch seems to have been completely filled soon after the end of the 3rd century A.D. and definite 4th century material is largely absent from it. The north arm of the ditch produced a considerable amount of material which is dateable to the 4th century. It seems possible, however, that this arm of the ditch was recut at a later date, unlike the east arm. The most likely sequence is, therefore, that both arms of the ditch were excavated at the same time, probably at the start of the 3rd century A.D. By the end of that century both ditches must have become largely silted. The east arm seems to have remained in this state and the North Fence was constructed partially across it. The north arm of the ditch, however, seems to have been recut and continued in use well into the 4th century (Period VII). By the end of that century this recut ditch also seems to have been filled with accumulations of domestic rubbish and natural silt.

It seems clear that the North-West and North-East Ditches represent the northern boundary of the Roman Villa complex (Fig. 17). The gap between the two ditches was some 28 feet across and this must have facilitated a trackway leading to the cemetery and land to the north of the villa site. Subsequently this track was either wholly or partially blocked by the North Fence (which may or may not have had a gate through it). This fence-line, itself, cut the silted east arm of the North-West Ditch and also the North-East Ditch. Although this fence seems to have terminated at the North-West Ditch, a linear boundary appears to have continued along the north arm of the ditch, where the possible recut remained open well into the 4th century A.D. It is quite likely that the spoil thrown up when the ditches were excavated was formed into an internal bank. If so, this would have extended the overall height of the ditch and helped create a formidable barrier. This would have served a dual role in that it would have helped retain the animals and help prevent others getting into the main area of the villa.

b) The North-East Ditch (F.832) (Figs. 4, 17, 18 and 21).

Near the upper limit of the excavations, immediately to the north and north-east of the North Timber Building, work between 1976 and 1978 revealed another substantial ditch, running east–west, just below the 415 foot contour (Fig. 4). This ditch was traced for a distance of 176 feet and at the east end it continued beyond the excavated area. About one third of the way along its length from the east end it dog-legged northwards for a short distance before resuming its general east–west alignment. This kink in the ditch line occurs close to the north-east corner of the North Timber Building and indicates that the ditch had to be diverted to avoid this existing structure. There was no evidence to suggest that the ditch alignments were not contemporary. That this ditch and the building are roughly contemporary is suggested by the fact that the north wall of the building and the ditch run almost parallel. In addition the west end of the ditch finished in a neatly rounded terminal exactly in line with the west end of the building.

In detail, the ditch had a V-shaped profile and was between 4′6″ and 7′ in width and 2′3″ to 2′6″ in depth (Fig. 18). Its main filling consisted of a series of brown loam and clay deposits containing small chalk lumps (S.A, L.1 and 2; S.B, L.3 and 4; S.C, L.2–9; S.D, L.3–8 and S.E, L.1–5); occasional zones of pure weathered chalk also occurred (S.E, L.2 and 4). These various deposits clearly represent largely natural silts, containing some domestic rubbish. When the ditch was fully silted it was cut by three post-pits of the North Fence (S.B, L.1 and 2) and by a second ditch (S.C, L.1 and S.D, L. 1 and 2) which cut through the 'dog-leg'. This later ditch (Ditch 13) was traced for a minimum distance of 40 feet and was between 1′2″ and 3′4″ in width. It had sloping sides and a cupped base and was filled with dark brown loam containing small chalk lumps and pebbles. It does not appear to have been related in function to the earlier ditch. Its filling produced a small amount of coarse-ware pottery dateable to the 2nd to 4th centuries A.D.

It seems fairly clear that the North-East Ditch of the Villa Enclosure was dug just after the North Timber Building was erected, or at least its intended position had been marked-out. It also seems clear that the ditch represents part of the enclosure ditch along the northern side of the villa site (Fig. 17).

The Dating Evidence for the North-East Ditch.

No coins were recovered from the filling of the ditch and only four sherds of samian ware were found. These were: a Central Gaulish sherd of uncertain form but probably a Form 18/31 or 31; a Central Gaulish Form 31; a later 2nd century A.D. mortarium sherd and an uncommon Central Gaulish piece, probably a flagon. Most of these sherds are of Antonine date, but the mortarium can only be broadly dated to the later 2nd century A.D.

A total of 338 coarse-ware potsherds was also recovered from the ditch. These represent at least 36 different vessels of which 18 have been drawn (Nos. 608–625). Some 233 sherds are of thoroughly Romanised fabrics, whilst 105 are of earlier native wares. These native wares are fairly certainly residual in their present context; over half are from grog-tempered vessels (none illustrated). One flint-tempered base is illustrated (No. 624).

The Roman wares make up the bulk of the pottery recovered but there is also a significant proportion of residual pieces. One rouletted beaker of 1st century A.D. Keston Kiln Ware is present (not illustrated). Part of a Hunt Cup of Nene Valley Ware and dateable to the later 2nd century to early-3rd century is drawn (No. 615), together with the base of a colour-coated beaker (No. 610). Much of the other pottery recovered appears to be broadly dateable to the 2nd to mid-3rd centuries A.D. (e.g. Nos. 611, 620, 622 and 625). Later material, however, is also present. There are two Alice Holt Ware sherds from the upper filling of the ditch (not illustrated), together with a rim of 4th century cream sandy ware (No. 623). Other illustrated vessels of interest are: the neck of a flask (No. 609) with a white slip coating from the lower filling of the ditch and the complete profile of a small everted rim jar (No. 613). A single small-find from the North-East Ditch is illustrated and this is a large glass bead (No. 111).

The small ditch (Ditch 13), cutting the North-East Ditch, produced some 25 sherds of coarse pottery. These represent at least nine different vessels, all too small to illustrate. They include one sherd of Alice Holt Ware and one Oxfordshire Ware fragment. The material seems to broadly

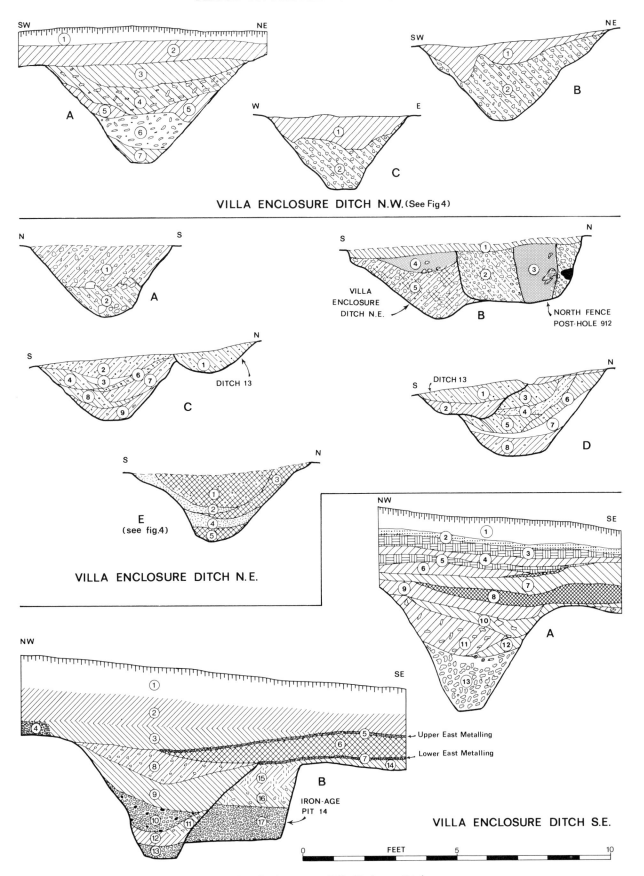

Fig. 18. *Sections across Villa Enclosure Ditches.*

range in date from the 2nd century to the 4th century A.D. and most probably is derived from the earlier ditch.

The coarse pottery from the filling of the North-East Ditch, itself, ranges in date from the later 1st to the 4th centuries A.D. and much of it appears to belong to the 2nd and 3rd centuries. The amount of late-Roman material present is fairly small and only a little of this material need be of definite 4th century rather than later 3rd century date. The Cream Sandy Ware sherd (No. 623) appears to be of definite 4th century date. On balance, it seems probable that the North-East Ditch was completely silted by the mid-4th century A.D. and there is no evidence that it was ever recut. Thus, it seems probable that this ditch was filled about the same time as the east arm of the North-West Ditch or only a short time after. Certainly both ditch fills were cut across by the line of the North Fence.

The construction date of the North-East Ditch of the Villa Enclosure seems likely to have been broadly contemporary with that of the North-West Ditch and the present ditch was also fairly certainly contemporary with the erection of the North Timber Building. On other evidence this event has been dated to the early-3rd century A.D. The North-East Ditch, therefore, is unlikely to have been dug before the start of the 3rd century but probably not much later. It seems likely that much of the 3rd century pottery in the ditch is derived from the North Timber Building. From the evidence of the North Fence, which seems to respect the north wall of the North Timber Building, it seems that the ditch was filled in before the building was destroyed by fire. The absence of burnt material within the ditch tends to confirm this.

c) The South-East Ditch (Figs. 17, 18, 34 and 35).

This substantial ditch was first located in 1972 in the south-eastern part of the excavation and further lengths were traced in 1973 and 1974 (Fig. 34). It ran roughly north-east by south-west, following the contour of the hillside, on about the 402 foot level. A total length of some 80 feet was located on the main site. The ditch continued beyond the limits of the main excavation in both directions and two outlying trial-trenches to the north-east located it again allowing it to be traced for a total distance of about 130 feet. On the main site the stratigraphy was fairly well-preserved in the area of the ditch and this allowed the feature to be tied closely to a local sequence of deposits (Figs. 18 and 35). On this evidence it could be seen that the ditch was cut through a layer of earlier, Roman metalling (the Lower East Metalling assigned to Period V; Fig. 18, S.B, L.7), a gully (F.716) and a pre-Conquest pit (Pit 14; S.B, L.15–17). The ditch had eventually silted and was buried by a series of dumped soil, clay and chalk deposits (Fig. 18, S.A, L.2–8; S.B, L.6; Fig. 35, L.10), upon which a later Roman metalled trackway had been laid in Period VII (the Upper East Metalling; Fig. 18, S.B, L.5; Fig. 35, L.5).

In width, the ditch varied from 4' to 7' across the top. It had sloping sides, set at an angle of between 50° and 70° and these joined a flat base between 11" and 18" across, giving a broad V-shaped profile overall. The ditch was between 3' and 3'9" in depth and was generally filled with a primary silt of chalk rubble (Fig. 18, S.A, L.13; S.B, L.13) or occasionally clay (Fig. 35, L.16), overlain by further chalk rubble silt deposits (Fig. 18, S.B, L.10; Fig. 35, L.15) and layers of soil containing small chalk lumps (Fig. 18, S.B, L.8, 9, 11 and 12; S.A, L.10–12; Fig. 35, L.11–14). These deposits seem to represent a largely natural series of silt layers but were found to contain domestic rubbish in the form of pottery and animal bone. A complete dog skeleton was recovered from the top of the primary chalk filling at one point (see animal bone report, page 289).

Dating Evidence for the South-East Ditch.

No coin was recovered from the filling of the ditch, but one of the soil dumps above it produced a coin, somewhat corroded, of late-1st to early-2nd century date (Coin No. 10).

The upper filling of the ditch produced three samian sherds from two separate Form 37 bowls of Hadrianic-Antonine date and the middle fill of the ditch produced a samian Form 33 cup of similar date. A number of other samian sherds was recovered from the soil deposits above the ditch and most of these are of 1st century date, with nothing later than the Antonine period.

The ditch produced no mortarium sherds, but two pieces were recovered from soil layers above the ditch (Nos. 917 and 918). One of these is stamped (No. 917) and is dated to the period A.D. 65–100 (see page 281).

An overall total of 280 coarse-ware potsherds was also recovered from the ditch. These represent at least 45 different vessels and 13 of them are illustrated (Nos. 626–638). Much of the material is small and abraded. Over half of the sherds came from the upper filling of the ditch (133 sherds). Of these, 57 are of Roman sandy fabrics, which include three amphora sherds too fragmentary for illustration; several everted rim jars (Nos. 634, 636 and 638) and bead rim jars (No. 637). There is also one early-Roman fine-ware in the form of a 'rough cast' beaker sherd (not illustrated). Some 39 sherds from the upper filling were of native grog-tempered wares, all too fragmentary to draw and 27 further sherds were shell-tempered. These shelly wares include several bead rim jars of typical early-Roman form (No. 635). In addition there are seven sherds of sandy native ware and three flint-tempered sherds, all too small to draw. All of the coarse pottery in the upper filling of the ditch seems to range in date from the mid-1st to the mid-2nd centuries A.D.

The middle filling of the ditch produced just 34 sherds. Twelve of these are of sandy Roman fabrics, including a bead rim jar of Keston Kiln Ware (No. 632). The remaining sherds are of early native wares, but only one is illustrated, an everted, bead rim jar of shelly ware (No. 633). This complete group may be dated to the second half of the 1st century A.D.

The lower filling of the ditch yielded 81 potsherds. Some 23 of these are of sandy Roman wares including a small bead rim bowl (No. 631); much of this material is fragmentary, but a single amphora sherd and a fine-ware beaker sherd should be noted (not illustrated). The remaining pieces are of early native wares. These include shelly ware jars with bead rims (Nos. 626 and 628) and upright rims (Nos. 629 and 630). Of particular interest is a large grog-tempered vessel with corrugated walls (No. 627). This is a classic 'Belgic' form seldom found in West Kent. All of this material from the lower ditch filling is of 1st to early-2nd century date and includes several pieces of essentially pre-Roman forms (e.g. Nos. 627 and 629).

There were two small-finds: one came from the primary filling of the ditch and this was a bronze necklace (No. 103) whilst the middle filling produced a spindle-whorl (No. 49).

None of the pottery recovered from the ditch seems to be later than mid-2nd century in date. The position of the ditch in the site sequence, however, indicates that it cannot have been dug before the second half of the 2nd century A.D., for it cuts through the Lower East Metalling assigned to Period V and this appears to have been laid sometime around the middle of the 2nd century. It would thus appear that all of the pottery contained within the ditch is residual and that it weathered in from adjacent areas. The generally small and abraded nature of much of the pottery tends to confirm this as does the fairly large number of vessels that the sherds represent. On balance, a date for the excavation of the ditch sometime very late in the 2nd century seems most likely and this may have been a little before the northern enclosure ditches (North-West and North-East Ditches).

The deposits above the South-East Ditch produced a single coin (Coin No. 10), 11 samian sherds, two mortaria (Nos. 917 and 918) and 669 sherds of coarse-ware pottery, representing at least 109 vessels. All of this material dates from the 1st and 2nd centuries A.D., with some pre-Conquest material. This is clearly all residual. The eight illustrated coarse-wares include: two bead rim jars of shelly ware (Nos. 721 and 724); four flint-tempered vessels of pre-Conquest date (Nos. 722, 723, 725 and 728) and two sandy Roman vessels, one an everted rim jar (No. 727) and the other a small bead rim vessel (No. 726).

Discussion of the South-East Enclosure Ditch.

Although the precise purpose of this ditch is not certain it seems highly likely from its position, both stratigraphically and spacially, that it formed part of the southern boundary of the Period VI villa (see Fig. 17). It may be more than coincidence, therefore, that its alignment is parallel to the eastern end of the North-East Ditch. No trace of the South-East Ditch was located in the 1968 or 1970 areas dug to the west and it seems clear that the ditch must have either ended or turned to the south (see Fig. 4). The fact that the ditch cut the Period V East Metalling certainly places it within the main villa period on the site (Period VI). It seems likely that this ditch was completely filled by the end of the 3rd century A.D. Indeed, the general absence of later Roman material in the filling of this ditch suggests that it could have been some time earlier.

(ii) THE WEST MASONRY BUILDING (Figs. 4, 17, 19 and 20; Plates VII–X).

1) Introduction.

This major Roman masonry building lay along the extreme western edge of the excavated area and continued under the hedge on that side of Lower Warbank Field (Fig. 19). It was largely set on a localised level area just above the 410 foot contour (see Fig. 3). The building had been previously examined by Mr. G.R. Corner in 1854 (Ref. 52), although Mr. A.J. Kempe had first located its walls in 1828 (Ref. 53). Corner's work recovered only a partial plan of the building and as published this cannot easily be reconciled with the present plan. Further small-scale work on the building in 1951–53 was undertaken by Mrs. N.P. Fox (Ref. 54). The eastern side of the building was, however, fully explored during the recent programme of excavation in 1969 and 1970. A substantial part of the western side of the structure nevertheless remained unexcavated until access was possible in 1986–87. Resumption of this later work must be held over and reported in a second Report on the Keston site.

The excavations by Mrs. Fox, and also those of 1969–70, showed that by the middle years of this century the structure was very poorly preserved, having suffered from Victorian excavation, medieval and post-medieval stone-robbing and centuries of ploughing. Very little Roman masonry or stratigraphy had survived much above foundation-level and virtually no floors remained *in situ*. Fortunately, the larger scale of the most recent work has allowed the general form of the overall structure to be seen and understood for the first time. The small-scale earlier work by Mrs. Fox had led to a confusing and unclear site report and conclusions.

The building as revealed (Fig. 19) in 1969–70 appeared to consist of the front portion of a 'winged-corridor' villa of well-known Romano-Britsh type, with an (added) bath-suite at one end and this was largely confirmed by the subsequent work here. The main axis of the building was roughly north-east by south-west and from the position of the frontal wing-rooms it seems clear that it faced in the prefered south-easterly direction. The building had an overall length of some 102′6″ and overlay an earlier timber house (see Period Va), as well as overlying pits, post-holes and gullies, some of which must relate to the substantial ditched enclosure (the West Enclosure) belonging to the immediately pre-Conquest period (Period IIIb). The discovery of three early-Roman cremation burials and one inhumation burial below the villa building, indicates that it was also constructed upon the site of a, presumably forgotten, cemetery (Period IVb). The villa building, itself, originally seems to have been positioned on the western side of an open courtyard which was first established in Period Va and around which at least four other large Roman buildings stood at different times (Figs. 14 and 17).

The poor preservation of the West Masonry Building was in part due to stone-robbing after the abandonment of the site. Three large pits (Pits A, B and D) produced sherds of medieval pottery and seems fairly certainly to have related to this process. Writing in 1854, Corner records that "about two years since, Mr. Smith, the farmer, grubbed-up a narrow shaw which extended along the hedge and took the opportunity of removing the foundations which were met with, out of the ground" (Ref. 55). In addition, a probable field boundary-ditch (once recut) had been dug across the building at some time in the post-medieval period (Ditches 3 and 4, Period IX). Later ploughing had steadily eroded much of what survived these events.

2) The Structural Evidence (Fig. 19).

(For convenience here it will be assumed that this building was aligned north–south, rather than the actual north–east by south–west). In detail, the structural evidence found in 1969–70 consisted of a central range, comprising originally three rooms (Rooms A, B and C), with a flanking gallery or corridor on the north and east sides. A contemporary rectangular wing-room (North-East Room) projected eastwards at the north end of the eastern corridor and possible traces of a second occurred at the south end of the corridor (South-East Room). Another, added, room (South Wing Room) was located at the south end of the building. This addition appeared to form part of the later bath-suite, which occupied the southern end of the structure. This bath was partially excavated by Mrs. Fox and some further work was undertaken here in 1970. It was not, however, until 1987 that the entire bath-suite and central range were fully excavated. The walls located during the excavation of the West Masonry Building appear to belong to three or four different phases of construction (Phases 1–4). These are described below.

Phase 1 – The Central Range.

The main central range appears to be the earliest part of the building and as originally constructed seems to have had an overall length of 64'6" by 18'3" (internal). It has been assigned here to Period VIa. The layout of this central range closely followed that of an earlier timber building which had previously occupied this site in Period Va and which had been destroyed by fire. Ploughing had destroyed most of the walling of the central range and generally only the foundations survived, though no floors remained (Fig. 20). Cross-walls divided this central range into three main rooms (Rooms A, B and C). Work prior to 1986 revealed about half of Room C, but only small parts of Rooms A and B. Full descriptions of these rooms must, therefore, form part of the second Report concerned with the 1981–87 work.

The east wall of the central range survived only at the north-east and south-east corners. It was 2'4" to 2'6" wide here and stood to a height of about 6" above foundation-level. The foundation of the east wall, where the superstructure was missing, was found to be of a similar width and up to some 20" deep. In construction, the foundation consisted of flint nodules set in a light grey loam with some chalk lumps. The wall was composed of flint nodules set in a coarse cream mortar with many small blue and black pebbles.

Only a short length of the north wall of the central range was located in 1969 and this appeared to be of a similar type and construction to the east wall. The south wall of the range had been completely replaced by the north wall of the Phase 2 bath-suite, which itself had been built at a lower level, on a terrace cut into the chalk hillside.

The cross-walls dividing the central range were of seemingly similar construction and of one build with the outer walls. The original room sizes may be summarised as follows:-

	(east–west)		(north–south)
Room A	18'3"	×	16'6"
Room B	18'3"	×	17'6"
Room C	18'3"	×	24'1" (Later reduced to 20'3")

(Information partly based on 1987 excavations).

Phase 2 – Room 'D' and the Southern Bath-Suite (Fig. 20; Plate IX).

A bath-suite was subsequently added to the southern end of the central range (presumably in Period VIb). This was set on a chalk-cut terrace at a slightly lower level than the main range, although to some extent this reflected the natural slope of the ground (Fig. 20, S.F). Part of this bath-suite was excavated by Mrs. Fox in the 1950s. Another portion was excavated in 1970 during the present programme of work and in 1987 rescue-work led to the complete excavation of the entire suite.

The bath-suite, itself, had suffered extensive robbing and plough damage, to the point where even the base of the wall-footings had been destroyed in many places. The hypocausted room (Room D) dug in 1970 was, however, rather better preserved, being protected under the headland along the eastern boundary of what was formerly 'Eight Acre Field', which adjoined Lower Warbank Field on the west side (Plate IX). From what little survived generally it would seem that the bath-suite consisted of the familiar, axially arranged set of rooms, with the furnace at the west end (located in 1987). This report is only concerned with that part of the bath-suite excavated in 1970, namely Room D, located under the hedge, and predictably the best preserved part of the baths.

Originally, Room D was set at the eastern end of the bath block and probably measured about 10'6" square internally. The east, north and south walls of the room were comparatively well preserved. They consisted of flint nodules set in hard, sandy cream-yellow mortar with many small blue and black pebbles. The west wall had, however, been almost totally destroyed. The north wall of Room D survived to a height of some 21" (5 courses) and was some 2'6" in width. It rested on a foundation of flint nodules set in rammed chalk and grey clay loam with some chalk lumps. This foundation was 3–6" deep and 3' in width. The south wall was 2'4"–2'7" wide and survived to a height of 15". It stood on a foundation which consisted of mortared flint nodules some 5" deep. Here, there was no clear division between the wall and the foundation and they were of the same width. The east wall of the room was narrower, just some 11" in width and merely formed a retaining wall for the hypocaust cut-out. It was only about 8" high as surviving and had suffered some damage. Only very slight traces of the west wall survived.

In its earliest phase Room D was hypocausted. Its floor (now missing) had been supported by a series of large stone-built piers. There were probably 16 of these piers originally (arranged 4 by 4). Only six, on the northern side of the room, had survived. The piers were built of mortared flint and squared greensand blocks and had been built on the natural chalk of the terrace. A thin layer of orange clay was generally used to fix the pier bases to the chalk. The piers were separated by hypocaust channels between 11" and 15" wide. In two of the piers against the north wall, angled slots in the top of the supports seemed to mark the bases of vertical heating ducts. The piers survived to a height of up to 20", but no trace of the suspended floor above the piers was found.

Although Room D was clearly heated originally, there was no evidence of a furnace arch leading through any of the three surviving walls. Since each of these walls was reasonably well preserved, some trace of such an arch should have survived. It, thus, seems most likely that the missing arch was in the effectively destroyed west wall, the direction in which the furnace was later found.

The hypocaust piers in the southern half of Room D had subsequently been removed to make way for a small sunken plunge-bath. Internally this measured some 5'10" (north–south) by 7'9" (east–west), although its west edge had been almost completely destroyed. As surviving this bath was up to 15" in depth and was lined with *opus signinum* on the floor and walls, with traces of a quarter-round moulding at their junction. In the north-east corner of this bath there was the base of a rectangular stone-built seat or step. This measured some 14" (north–south) by 37½" (east–west), but survived only an inch or two above floor-level. The quarter-round moulding ran around the front of this step. In the south-east corner traces of a drain-hole with an impression of a missing lead pipe were noted in the *opus signinum*. The base of the drain-hole was some 3" below the level of the floor and a curved drainage gully led away downhill to the south on the outside. This gully had been filled and built over, when the South Wing Room was later constructed.

An earlier *opus signinum* floor with traces of its own quarter-round moulding was located below the upper floor of the bath. There were also two separate skins of *opus signinum* on the walls and it seems clear that the entire bath was completely re-lined on at least one occasion.

With the construction of the sunken bath, the earlier hypocaust seems to have gone out of use and its surviving channels on the north were partially blocked with rough masonry.

It would appear that when Room D of the hypocausted bath-suite was first built, a second hypocaust was inserted in the adjoining Room C of the central range. All that survived of this was a broad chalk-cut pit, occupying the southern two-thirds of the room. A new wall seems to have been built at the same time across the width of this room, along the northern edge of the hypocaust pit, effectively reducing the length of the room from 24'1" to 20'3". This hypocaust may have been abandoned when that in Room D went out of use.

Phase 3 – The Corridors and Wing Room (Plate VIII).

Work in 1969 revealed that the central range of the West Building was flanked by broad corridors on the north and east sides. Beyond this corridor at the north-east corner lay a wing room (Plate VIII) and possible traces of a corresponding wing were located near the south-east corner. Work in 1977 subsequently suggested that the corridor also continued along the western side of the building.

It seems probable that the corridor and wing rooms were all added to the central range at a later date and as the east corridor appeared to stop short of the bath-suite this could be after Phase 2. Vital wall junctions, however, had been largely destroyed and the phasing of the building sequence cannot now be certain. In favour of the suggestion that the corridors were later than the main central range is the point that the corridor walls were a little narrower and the mortar a slightly different colour. More significantly, the corridor along the north side was not quite parallel to the main range. None of these points, however, can be taken as conclusive proof. The corridor and wing room walls were all of a similar construction and of one build, consisting of flint nodules set in a hard cream-white gritty mortar containing many small blue pebbles.

The broad corridors or galleries which apparently enclosed two, if not three, sides of the central range of the West Masonry Building seem to show influence from North Gaul, where structures with similar features are fairly well-known (Ref. 56). This point is further discussed below, but clearly it forms a significant feature of the building. In detail, the broad corridor running along the eastern side of the central range was 9'6" wide (internally) and at the northern end joined a similar corridor running along the north end of the range. At the southern end most of the east corridor wall and its foundation had been destroyed by ploughing and robbing, but from the surviving sections it seems probable that the corridor ended, in line with the south end of the central range, leaving the bath-suite as a projecting range to the south. There does not appear to have been any access into the bath-suite from the corridor. The corridor had a total length of 77 feet. The external wall was some 2' wide and stood to a maximum height of just 6". It rested on a foundation generally some 12" deep. At one point, however, the wall foundation was cut through an area of disturbed sandy soil filling an apparently natural hollow in the chalk (Pit C, S.B, L.6 and 7). The foundation here had a depth of some 36" and clearly had been built deeper to compensate for this soft ground. The soil filling the disturbance produced three 2nd century samian sherds and some 280 sherds of coarse pottery, representing at least 77 different vessels. Some three coarse-ware sherds from this feature have been illustrated (Nos. 834–836). There is a little pre-Conquest material (Nos. 835 and 836), but most of the pottery ranges in date from the 1st to 2nd centuries A.D. There are some 50 sherds of sandy Roman wares (No. 834) including an amphora fragment, together with a substantial amount of pottery in early-Roman shell and grog-tempered native fabrics (not illustrated). It is not clear to what extent this feature represents a disturbed pre-villa pit. Some later disturbance seems quite likely and it does not seem safe to date the building's construction as being after the date of the pit's contents.

No floor-levels had survived in the east corridor except for a small area of mortar at the north-east end (see below). The amount of loose tesserae discovered in the corridor area, however, strongly suggests that it once had a red tesellated floor.

Towards the northern end of the east corridor, largely in line with the north wall of the central range, was a substantial rectangular pit occupying the full width of the corridor (Fig. 20; S.A and G). This has been interpreted as a contemporary cellar and it measured 11'6" (north–south) by 10' (east–west). It was some 4' in depth, with steeply sloping sides and a slightly cupped base. The fill consisted of a series of brown loam, chalk and mortar rubble deposits (S.A, L.9 and 10; S.G, L.15–20). No trace of a lining or floor was noted. The cellar cut the north-east corner post-pit of the earlier West Timber Building of Period Va. The filling of the cellar yielded some 131 pieces of tesserae and 59 potsherds, representing at least 23 different vessels. One mortarium sherd has been illustrated (No. 914), together with a flanged rim dish of typical later Roman form (No. 643) and a jar with a squared rim (No. 642). All of these sherds may be dated from the late-2nd to the late-3rd centuries A.D.

Immediately to the north of the cellar a shallow slot some 2" in depth, with a rectangular cross-section, was located (S.G) cut into the natural chalk. This ran the full width of the corridor and two short arms projected southwards from it. The western arm joined the north-east corner of the central range. A small area of mortared floor survived within its north-east angle. The exact interpretation of this feature is not clear, but it seems possible that it represents a beam-slot for some sort of wooden structure, perhaps a partition, associated with the cellar entrance. The loam filling of the slot yielded six potsherds representing at least four different vessels. None of these is worthy of illustration, but all appear to be broadly of later 2nd to early-3rd century A.D. date. A rectangular rubble base of uncertain purpose had subsequently been built over the filled in slot on the north side. This was about 2' square and was constructed of flint, tile and chalk.

The North Corridor (Fig. 20; Section G).
Of the north corridor little was seen in 1969. It was between 9' and 10' in width. The outer wall was not quite parallel to the main range and the corridor narrowed towards the west. The outer wall was some 2' wide and stood to a height of 9". The floor did not survive, but an elongated pit (F.225) cut into the chalk, measuring 5' by 1'6", appeared to represent an oven or hearth-pit. It was 16" deep and was filled with ash and carbon, which produced some 17 sherds of coarse pottery. These sherds represent at least eight vessels and these are of 4th century A.D. date. This feature thus seems to be late in the villa's occupation sequence. Three sherds from this feature have been drawn (Nos. 639–641) and these are all typical late-Roman forms.

The North-East Room (Fig. 20, Section A; Plate VIII).
A rectangular wing room projected from the north-east corner of the east corridor. This was not quite a true rectangle and internally measured 12'3" to 13' (north–south) by 10'11" to 11'5" (east–west). Its walls were about 3"–6" high, 2' wide and, on the east side, their foundations were cut into the filled in Gullies C and D of Period IVb. Again no trace of any floor remained.

The Possible South-East Room (Fig. 20; Section E).
A short length of wall foundation located well to the east of the east corridor, towards the southern end of the West Masonry Building, seems likely to be related to it. The foundation ran north–south and was traced for a minimum distance of 9'4". It was cut into the fill of the West Enclosure Ditch and had been cut by a later medieval robber-pit (Pit B). It seems likely that it was only preserved here because the builders had cut deeper into this soft ground than for the rest of its walls. It consisted of a loosely mortared foundation, built of roughly-coursed flints, chalk and tile some 2' wide. The function of this foundation is not entirely clear but it is likely to be significant that it is almost in line with the eastern wall of the North-East Room and its southern end corresponds with the projected eastern line of the south end of the east corridor wall. These points suggest that this wall fragment had formed part of a second wing room, corresponding with the North-East Room, with later disturbances and ploughing having removed all other traces of it. If this reconstruction is correct, it is possible that this wing room was actually destroyed in later Roman times when the Phase 4 South Wing Room was added to the bath-suite.

Phase 4 – The South Wing of the Bath-Suite (Section C; Plate X).
A wing room was subsequently added to the south-east corner of the bath-suite. This was built over the drain from the plunge-bath in Room D and clearly represents a later addition. The wing room only partially survived, but it measured internally between 12'6" and 13'6" (east–west) by some 8'10" (north–south). The walls were up to three courses high (14") and were constructed of flint nodules set in a yellow-cream mortar with occasional chalk grits and many small blue-grey pebbles. The north-east and south-east internal corners were turned in rectangular greensand blocks. The walls were of different widths. The complete east wall was 2'6"–2'9" wide, whilst the (largely destroyed) north wall was 2'4" and the west wall, 3'3" wide. The south wall was almost totally destroyed but at the south-east corner it was about 2'8" wide. The east and west walls of the room were cut through the filling of the West Enclosure Ditch. The mortared flint foundations of the room had been dug deeper here with extra layers of flints and mortar to

compensate for the soft ditch fill. The interior of the room had been completely robbed. It seems likely, however, that it was originally hypocausted and that it formed an extension to the bath-suite, just possibly being a *laconicum*.

In the east corridor a new cross-wall was inserted about 4' inside the south end wall. This new wall had been partially destroyed by ploughing, but a length survived to a height of 15" on the west side. It was between 2' and 2'2" wide and consisted of flint nodules with some chalk, tile and *opus signinum* lumps set in cream mortar. The overall internal length of the corridor would, thus, have been shortened by about 6'. The reason for this modification is not clear; it could have created a narrow passageway between the South-East Room and Room C, perhaps relating in some way to the alterations in the immediately adjacent bath-suite.

Metalling along the North Wall (Fig. 20; Section G, L.21).
Along the outside wall of the north corridor of the West Masonry Building a spread of pebbles seemed to represent a metalled pathway. This was not an original feature since it overlay two post-holes of the wooden Centre Fence, which itself once ran up to the north wall of the building. The pebble layer was mostly about 6'6" in width but its north-east end had been removed so that its width was reduced to about 2'. It was only an inch or two thick and it produced eleven potsherds ranging in date from the 2nd to 3rd centuries (none illustrated).

The Dating Evidence for the West Masonry Building.
Virtually no undisturbed stratified deposits survived within the building and the extensive damage which has occurred to this structure makes its precise date of construction and occupation difficult to ascertain. Two coins were recovered from the immediate area of the building during the latest excavations. An unstratified barbarous radiate dated to A.D. 270–290 (Coin No. 32) came from the 1970 excavations in the central range and a coin of Constantius II, A.D. 345–348 (Coin No. 52), was recovered from a post-Roman robber pit, also in the 1970 area. Excavations by Mrs. Fox on an adjacent part of the building had produced two coins of Constantine I (A.D. 306–337) and another of Constantius II (A.D. 337–361). Another barbarous radiate (Coin No. 28) was found in 1969 in the topsoil a little to the east of the building. A total of five coins, all of late-3rd or 4th century date are, thus, now recorded from the area of the West Masonry Building.

No samian ware was recovered from any stratified Roman deposit within the building, but eight sherds came from various post-Roman robber-trenches and pits located in 1969. These were: a Déch. Form 72 of Antonine date; two form 31 sherds, both of probable Antonine date; a decorated sherd of a Form 37 bowl (No. 142), dated *c.* A.D. 140–160; a Form 37 or 30 rim sherd of Antonine date; a Form 43/Lud. RSMd of late-2nd to early-3rd century date; a mortarium or Curle Form 21 sherd of the late-2nd century and an uncertain sherd of Hadrianic-Antonine date. In addition, a disturbed area (Pit C) produced a Form 18/31 or 31 sherd and another uncertain fragment both of Central Gaulish manufacture and of probable Hadrianic-Antonine date. A rubble layer over the southern end of the building yielded an East Gaulish sherd of late-2nd to mid-3rd century date.

The hillwash deposits over the West Masonry Building produced another five samian sherds. These are: a Form 33 of Antonine date; a Form 18 of Neronian-Flavian date; a Form 31R of Antonine date; a mortarium base of the late-2nd to mid-3rd century and an uncertain East Gaulish sherd. Five more samian sherds, all of Hadrianic-Antonine or Antonine date except one later 1st century sherd, were recovered from the plough-soil above the building. A (non-samian) mortarium sherd was recovered from a robber-trench and this has been drawn (No. 915).

The hillwash deposits over the West Masonry Building also produced some 277 coarse-ware potsherds. These represent at least 61 different vessels of which nine have been drawn (Nos. 644–652). The assemblage is rather mixed. The bulk of this pottery ranges from the 1st to 4th centuries A.D., but also includes some pre-Roman sherds and some medieval material. Of the pre-Roman material one flint-tempered rim is illustrated (No. 651). The early-Roman sherds include a typical range of shell and grog-tempered wares. These are all too fragmentary for illustration. Several wall sherds from an imported Gallo-Belgic butt beaker were also recovered. These are not worthy of illustration, but may be from the same vessel as the rim illustrated from Pit 19 nearby (No. 493). Later Roman sherds include both Alice Holt Wares (Nos. 648 and 652) and Oxfordshire Wares (none illustrated). Familiar late-Roman flanged rim bowls (Nos. 644 and 648) and straight-sided dishes (Nos. 646 and 650) are amongst this material. Three other vessels of typical Roman sandy fabrics have also been drawn (Nos. 645, 647 and 649). An iron key (No. 76) came from the hillwash layer a little to the east of the building.

A further 248 coarse-ware potsherds were recovered from the plough-soil over the building (Fig. 20, L.1). The material represents a thoroughly mixed group of Roman and medieval sherds. Many are small and abraded and only one is worthy of illustration, a mortarium sherd (No. 916). A Roman tile with a graffito (No. 40) came from the topsoil over the West Masonry Building in the 1970 area. The post-Roman robber-pits (Pits A, B and D) cutting the West Masonry Building also produced sherds of Roman and medieval pottery (see page 136, Period IX).

The construction date of the West Masonry Building cannot be precisely determined. The sequence of earlier structures and features in this area, however, can give some guidance. It is clear that the West Masonry Building replaced the earlier West Timber Building of Period Va (dated c. A.D. 160–200). Since the line of the walls of the timber building were closely followed by the masonry building, after the former had been destroyed by fire, it is beyond all reasonable doubt that the West Masonry Building was constructed shortly after the fire. There is, unfortunately, no direct dating evidence for the West Timber Building itself, but it is clear that it was built over an earlier cemetery site, apparently still in use during the first half of the 2nd century A.D. (the West Cemetery, Period IVb. See page 49).

Allowing for the subsequent construction of the West Timber Building over the cemetery, its occupation, followed by its destruction by fire, it seems clear that the West Masonry Building could not have been built much before A.D. 200.

The West Masonry Building, itself, seems to have developed through four phases of expansion and additions, which clearly imply a fairly lengthy span of occupation. The presence of a hearth-pit (F.225) in the north corridor, containing 4th century pottery, indicates the building was occupied at least until that time. The five coins from the area of the West Masonry Building, all of late-3rd and 4th century date, tend to confirm this. The latest coins are two of Constantius II, of mid-4th century date (Coin No. 52 and one earlier discovery).

The fairly small and somewhat mixed coarse pottery assemblage from the area of the building is of little value in determining the date of its occupation. The samian, however, is more useful. The general absence of Flavian samian is immediately apparent, whilst virtually all of the material is of Hadrianic-Antonine or later date. It seems likely, therefore, that the bulk of this material relates to the occupation of the Period Va West Timber Building and the earliest phases of the succeeding masonry building of Period VI. In the absence of more critical dating evidence, due largely to the very extensive robbing and plough damage, the overall date-range of the West Masonry Building is between A.D. 200–400/450.

(iii) THE NORTH TIMBER BUILDING (Figs. 17, 21, 22, 23, 24 and 31; Plates XI–XIV).

1) Introduction.

This large rectangular timber building was located at the northern end of the excavated area, set on a slight terrace cut into the hillside between the 410 and 415 foot contours (Fig. 21). Its main axis was largely east–west and it was bounded on the northern side by a substantial ditch (North-East Ditch of the Villa Enclosure). The building was excavated over two seasons, in 1976 and 1977. Unlike the South and West Masonry Buildings, the present structure had never been previously recorded and its discovery formed a significantly new addition to the Roman villa's layout.

The building originally consisted of two main structural elements, namely a massive central framework of upright timbers, flanked on at least two sides by a wide corridor, also timber-framed. At the west end of the main structure were three large corn-drying ovens. There was clear evidence that this timber building had eventually been destroyed by fire and that subsequently two clay-lined water storage tanks and a small wooden hut had been constructed (Period VII) on its site. Later still, a large ditch (Ditch 21) was cut through some of these structures. This had been recut once and seems to have formed part of the villa's later enclosure earthworks (Period VII). No earlier features were found below the North Timber Building apart from the undated pit (F.1211) and it may be that the building was constructed on a previously unused part of the site, although insubstantial features could have been terraced away during the building work. The evidence suggests that the North Timber Building was purely agricultural in function and that it was contemporary with the West Masonry Building.

2) The Main Structure (Figs. 23 and 24).

The main framework of the North Timber Building consisted of 24 massive circular posts set in a clear rectangular pattern following the contour of the hill. Each post was set in an upright position in an individual post-pit (Post-holes 1–24). The rectangular framework was 72 feet in overall east–west length and consisted of two lines of ten posts (Post-holes 1–10 and Post-holes 13–22). Its overall north–south width was 25 feet and consisted of four posts at each end (Post-holes 1 and 22–24 and Post-holes 10–13). The framework covered a total area of some 1,800 square feet.

Post-pipes survived in all the pits (Figs. 23 and 24) and these pipes were generally filled with brown loam and burnt debris. They were all circular in plan suggesting that the posts were uncut tree trunks and varied in diameter between 1'8" and 2'9". The posts were spaced at intervals of between 6' and 8'11" (centre to centre) – see Table 15, except in the middle of each long side where the gap between the fifth and sixth posts was 9'9" in the north wall and 11'3" in the south wall. These wider spacings suggest the position of centrally placed entrances. The post diameters on either side of these entrance gaps were within the general range of those found in the rest of the structure and do not suggest the presence of larger posts here. There was no trace of any infilling between the main posts and indeed it seems most likely that there were open bays between the posts allowing access into the flanking corridor, at least on the north and west sides.

The pits which held the substantial upright posts were very large and were generally sub-rectangular in plan. They were generally about 4' square, but ranged in size from 3'7" to 5'2" and were between 2'3" and 5'6" in depth (see Figs. 22–24). Each was filled with chalk rubble with some brown loam, indicating that they had been backfilled immediately after the posts had been set in position. Table 16 summarises the details of the post-pits and post-pipes. Two successive post-holes (F.1182 and 1183) later dug on the uphill side of the main north wall (by Post-hole 4) may represent later attempts to support post No. 4. These two holes contained posts only slightly smaller than the originals. No trace of any flooring survived within the main building. At some time after the erection of the structure, a complex of three large corn-drying ovens was constructed in the west end of the main building. The oven walls partially sealed several of the main post-pits.

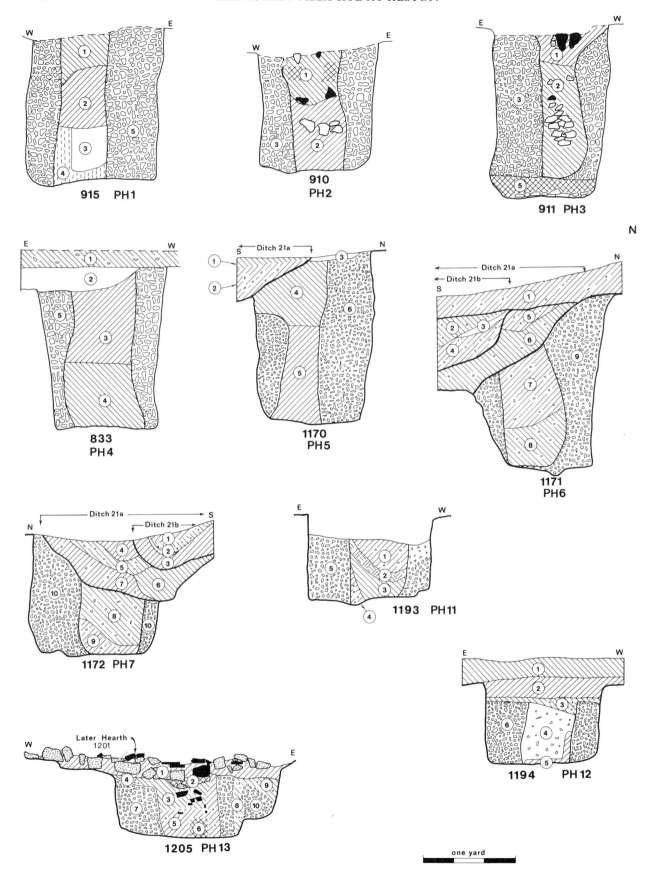

Fig. 23.   *Sections across main post-holes of North Timber Building.*

Post-hole No.	Centre to Centre	Bay Width	Notes
1– 2	7′ 0″	5′ 2″	North Wall
2– 3	7′ 6″	5′ 7″	
3– 4	7′ 9″	5′ 5″	
4– 5	7′ 6″	5′ 3″	
5– 6	9′ 9″	8′ 1″	(entrance)
6– 7	8′ 0″	6′ 3″	
7– 8	7′ 0″	5′ 1″	
8– 9	7′ 6″	5′ 6″	
9–10	8′ 1″	5′10″	
Average	7′ 9″	5′ 9″	
Total	70′ 1″	–	
10–11	7′10″	6′ 0″	East Wall
11–12	7′ 0″	4′11″	
12–13	8′ 1″	6′ 1″	
Average	7′ 7″	5′ 7″	
Total	22′11″	–	
13–14	6′10″	4′11″	South Wall
14–15	8′ 3″	7′ 0″	
15–16	7′ 2″	5′ 2″	
16–17	6′ 0″	4′ 6″	
17–18	11′ 3″	9′ 7″	(entrance)
18–19	7′ 9″	4′ 2″	
19–20	8′ 3″	6′ 3″	
20–21	6′ 9″	4′ 7″	
21–22	7′ 8″	5′ 7″	
Average	7′ 9″	5′ 9″	
Total	69′11″	–	
22–23	8′11″	6′ 1″	West Wall
23–24	7′ 9″	5′ 5″	
24– 1	7′ 8″	5′ 4″	
Average	8′ 0″	5′ 7″	
Total	24′ 4″	–	

Table 15. The spacing of the main posts of the North Timber Building.

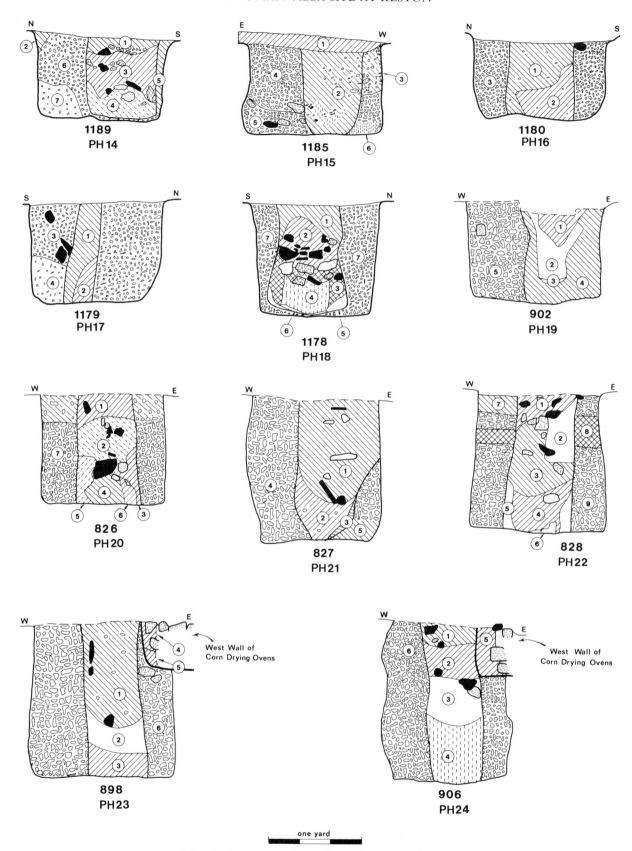

Fig. 24.   *Sections across main post-holes of North Timber Building.*

Post Hole No.	Size E–W	N–S	Depth	Sides	Base	Deposit No.	Feature No.	Post-pipe size	Post-pipe depth	Deposit No.
				POST-PIT				**POST-PIPE**		
1	4′3″	4′3″	4′7″	Vert.	Flat	76–202	915	2′ ×1′10″	4′7″	76–166
2	3′11″	3′11″	3′9″	Steep	Flat	–	910	2′	3′9″	76–162, 172
3	3′9″	3′9″	5′3″	Vert.	Flat	–	911	2′2″	5′1″	76–163, 171
4	4′3″	4′3″	4′4″	Steep	Flat	–	833	2′2″×2′	4′4″	76–79, 168
5	4′5″	4′	5′4″	Vert.	Flat	–	1170	1′10″	5′4″	–
6	4′	3′9″	5′4″	Vert.	Flat	–	1171	1′8″	5′4″	76–236
7	4′2″	3′7″	4′8″	Vert.	Flat	–	1172	1′11″	4′8″	–
8	4′6″	3′10″	5′6″	Vert.	Flat	77–209	1173	2′9″	5′5″	77–208
9	4′8″	4′2″	4′2″	Vert.	Flat	77–267	1190	–	–	–
10	5′2″	4′4″	4′4″	Vert.	Flat	–	1191	1′9″×6″	4′3½″	–
11	4′	3′10″	2′11″	Vert.	Flat	–	1193	1′10″	2′11″	77–252
12	4′5″	3′9″	2′11″	Vert.	Flat	–	1194	1′6″	2′4″	77–257, 258
13	4′	3′11″	2′3″	Vert.	Flat	–	1205	2′	2′4″	77–271
14	4′7″	4′7″	2′9″	Vert.	Flat	–	1189	2′3″	2′8″	77–248
15	4′6″	4′3″	3′	Vert.	Flat	–	1185	2′2″	3′	77–233
16	4′5″	4′	2′5″	Vert.	Flat	–	1180	2′	2′5″	–
17	4′4″	3′11″	3′3″	Vert.	Flat	77–235	1179	1′11″	3′3″	77–234
18	4′2″	3′11″	3′5″	Vert.	Flat	–	1178	2′×1′9″	3′4″	77–230
19	4′3″	4′3″	3′1″	Steep	Cupped	–	902	2′4″	2′10″	76–169
20	4′	4′	3′8″	Vert.	Flat	76–205	826	2′	3′8″	76–29, 147
21	4′	4′	4′5″	Steep	Flat	–	827	2′3″×1′10″	4′5″	76–30
22	4′	4′	4′4″	Vert.	Flat	–	828	1′10″	4′4″	76–31, 170
23	4′7″	4′7″	4′11″	Vert.	Flat	–	898	2′	4′11″	76–148
24	4′	4′	4′10″	Uneven	Flat	76–201	906	1′10″	4′10″	76–158

Table 16. Details of the post-pits and post-pipes of the main frame of the North Timber Building.

3) The Corridors (Fig. 22; Plate XI).

There was evidence that the main wooden framework of the North Timber Building had been enclosed by a corridor, some 7′ wide. This corridor was traced on the north and west side only and was bounded externally by a shallow slot for a beam set in a broader construction-trench. On the north side, the cut for the beam was traced for its full distance of some 91 feet. On the west side, the corridor beam-slot joined the north beam-slot at 90°. Only about two-thirds of its length, however, had survived ploughing. The southern end of the west corridor wall was accordingly missing and there was no evidence of any southern corridor, though this may have been ploughed away. The line of the west corridor was cut across by the Centre Fence, which ran up to the south-west corner post (P.H. 22) of the main central structure. One post-hole of the fence-line (F.830) lies exactly upon the projected line of the west corridor wall and this suggests that it may have held a post that served as both a fence support and the end-post of the corridor wall. Two further post-holes (F.829 and F.835), of the fence-line occur across the width of the west corridor. The fact that the north arm of the Centre Fence runs up to the south-west corner of the North Timber Building and that it is exactly upon the same alignment as the southern row of timbers of the building, indicates that the two structures are complementary. The arrangement, however, is unusual and the evidence is not sufficient for the precise relationship to be understood. Several possibilities suggest themselves. These are that: (a) the fence-line is slightly earlier than the building, with the timbers of the North Building subsequently destroying further traces of the fence-posts eastwards, whilst following their precise alignment; (b) the west corridor never continued beyond the line of the Centre Fence, leaving the south side of the west corridor open and (c) the fence line is later and cuts across the west corridor, the latter being partly demolished. Of these three possibilities the most likely is that the fence and building are contemporary and that there was no corridor along the south side of the North Timber Building.

Along the north side of the North Timber Building the trench for the beam was between 2' and 4' wide and up to 7" deep. It was largely filled with brown loam and chalk (Fig. 22). Running along the southern edge of this trench were the outlines of the beam-slot itself. This could not be traced at the eastern end of the cut where it had been removed by the later North-East Tank and was recorded for a minimum distance of about 70 feet. It was 1'5" to 1'9" wide and was of a similar depth to the construction-trench. It was filled with brown loam and much burnt daub and was sealed by an extensive spread of daub. In profile, this beam-slot had sloping or vertical sides and a flat base. It produced a small amount of 2nd to 4th century A.D. pottery. A Hunt Cup of Nene Valley Ware has been illustrated (No. 654), together with a 4th century grog-tempered ware dish (No. 653).

On the west side, the construction-trench for the beam was traced for 24'6", the south end having been destroyed by ploughing. It was 3'3" to 3'6" wide and up to 10" deep. It was again filled with brown loam and chalk (Fig. 22). Running along the centre of this cut was the shallower beam-slot, filled with brown-black loam and burnt daub fragments. No finds were recovered from either the construction-trench or the beam-slot. The beam-slot had also been destroyed at the south end, but the surviving part was about 1'5" wide and some 4" deep, with sloping sides and a cupped base. Sealing the construction-trench along the outside of the west beam-slot was a line of burnt daub.

Joining the two main beam-slots at right-angles was a series of smaller slots cut into the chalk. There were 13 of these meeting the main north slot and they were spaced (centre to centre) at intervals of between 3'10" and 5'11" (Slots 1–13). The average spacing was just under 5'. They were between 5" and 10" in width and were generally no more than 2" deep. The fill of these slots varied from brown loam with chalk to black loam and carbon with daub lumps (Fig. 22). No dateable material was recovered from them. The surviving lengths of the slots varied, but there seems little doubt that they all originally ran across the full width of the north corridor, probably holding horizontal wooden joists to support a raised planked floor, perhaps for storing grain as at Gadebridge Park (Ref. 57).

In the western half of the north corridor another shallow slot (F.948) ran along its south side, touching the north edge of the main posts of the building and cutting their post-pits (Fig. 22). This probably held a beam which supported the southern ends of the joists. This slot, as excavated, was just over 32' long and was 1'6"–2'2" wide. It was about 7" deep and ended at the east just short of the central entrance gap (by Post-hole 5). At the west end this slot terminated at joist-slot 1, in line with the start of the west corridor. It was filled with dark brown loam and chalk and daub lumps, which produced 17 potsherds of late-1st to 2nd century date. These are all too fragmentary to draw. No trace of a similar beam-slot had survived in the eastern half of the corridor, probably having been destroyed by later features.

Traces of just three cross-joist slots (Slots 14–16) were located in the west corridor. Of these the two at the north were only 1'6" apart, but there seems no doubt that they served a similar purpose to those in the north corridor. There was no sign of a supporting joist along the east side of the corridor here. Table 17 contains details of the various joist-slot spacings.

	Joist-Slots	Spacing (centre to centre)
North Corridor	1– 2	5′
	2– 3	3′10″
	3– 4	5′11″
	4– 5	5′
	5– 6	4′11″
	6– 7	4′ 9″
	7– 8	5′
	8– 9	5′
	9–10	4′10″
	10–11	4′10″
	11–12	5′ 1″
	12–13	5′
West Corridor	14–15	1′ 6″
	15–16	4′11″

Table 17. The spacing of joist-slots in the north and west corridors of the North Timber Building.

4) The Corn Drying Ovens (Figs. 21 and 22, Plates XI–XIV).

At the west end of the main barn structure was a block of three elaborate and integral corn-drying ovens (Fig. 21). These had been built in a slight cutting into the natural chalk and partially sealed the filling of the post-pits holding the building's main timber framework (Figs. 22 and 24). The main ovens (the North Oven and South Oven) consisted of two long, parallel structures each fed from a stoke-hole on the east side (Plate XII). The stoke-hole area, itself, had been partially destroyed by later features, although a small part at the northern end remained. It is not certain, however, whether the ovens were served by separate stoke-pits, or whether there was a single large pit, since removed. The latter arrangement would seem to be most convenient. Between the two main ovens a rather unusual third oven had been fitted (the Centre Oven), although all three appeared to be contemporary in date. It, too, must have had a stoke-hole on the east side.

The two main ovens were similar, each consisting of a set of three parallel-sided channels; the central channel, which was longer than the other two, received the direct heat from the stoke-pit end. In the north oven the two side chambers measured 1′10″ in width, and were 10′ (north) and 10′5″ (south) in length, respectively. The central chamber was 2′ wide and 17′3″ long and led back into the stoke-pit area. The South Oven had side chambers measuring 2′ by 10′ (south) and 1′8″ by 10′ (north) (see Plate XIII). The central chamber was 2′ wide and had a minimum length of 15′3″ to where it had been subsequently cut away by the North Tank.

The heated air passed from the firing point in the main channels into the side channels by means of lateral vents, spaced along the dividing walls. These dividing walls were 1′2″ to 1′3″ in width. The vents were between 8″ and 12″ wide and were arranged, at least in the complete South Oven, with three apertures in the south wall and five in the north (Plate XIV). The arrangement in the North Oven had been partially obscured by a large modern robber-trench, but the four surviving vents mirrored the arrangements in the South Oven. The heating vents in the partition walls were of two forms and again the arrangements within the two ovens seem to have been identical. Between the central flue and the outer side chamber the three vents had ridged bases. The five vents into the inner side chambers had alternating ridged and flat bases.

The arrangements of the third Centre Oven had been partially destroyed by the modern robber-trench and also the south-west terminal of the late-Roman Ditch 21a, which cut through the building. This oven as surviving, however, consisted of a single rectangular chamber, measuring 5'9" wide by at least 6' long. No vents pierced the walls of this chamber and it seems clear that all the heat was received direct from the stoke-pit.

The whole elaborate oven structure was built of chalk, flints and tile fragments set in clay. The floors of the oven chambers were of unburnt yellow clay. The inner faces of the main flue walls had been rendered with clay that had baked by the heat. The walls survived to an average height of about 12". The main outer walls of the structure were between 1'2" and 1'8" thick. The superstructure of the ovens had not survived, but originally would probably have consisted of an extensive floor of stone, or wood, supported probably some 2–3' above the base of the heating channels. Upon this flooring, farm produce could have been spread out and dried by the hot air circulating in the channels below.

The soil filling of the corn-drying ovens (L.5–30) produced a total of 168 small coarse-ware potsherds, representing at least 35 vessels (none illustrated). These are of 2nd to 4th century A.D. date. Three samian sherds were also recovered (see below).

The corn-drying ovens located in the North Timber Building at Keston represent a fairly elaborate version of a type of structure known on many Roman rural sites. These have been studied in some detail by Morris (Ref. 58) who concludes that they were used mainly for drying grain, although other produce could also have been processed in them. Such ovens are often found within aisled buildings and most excavated examples are of 3rd or 4th century A.D. date. In Kent, a broadly comparable structure to Keston has been recorded in the mid-3rd century masonry aisled building at Darenth (Ref. 59).

It seems clear that the Keston ovens were capable of processing fairly large quantities of produce as the surface area of the drying platform above the ovens would have been at least 185 sq. ft. It may be significant that in Period VII, after the destruction of the North Building and its large ovens, a new, much smaller and simpler corn-drying oven was constructed a short distance to the south (Fig. 36). This oven seems to have been open to the air, or at least was only protected by a lean-to structure which had left no trace (Plate XXV). It seems clear that this oven could never have coped with the quantities of material that would have been possible with the earlier driers. This could reflect changes in either the amount of grain produced in the later period, or in the methods used to process it.

5) The Fire.

Burnt material filled a number of the main post-pipes of the building and the surrounding joist-slots were frequently filled with and buried under spreads of orange-red burnt daub (Fig. 21). This provides very clear evidence to show that a large part of the North Timber Building had burnt down, never to be rebuilt. This fire preserved details of the construction of the building, particularly in the corridors on the west and north sides. The extensive spreads of burnt daub following the line of the outer corridor joist-slots suggest that, originally, horizontal timber ground-beams, set in the slots, held a wooden frame which supported wall panels of wattle and daub. Large numbers of iron nails were found in the daub spreads in the joist-slot of the north corridor wall. These presumably once secured some part of the superstructure of the building. A quantity of nails was also discovered in the joist-slots crossing the corridor and these could have been used to fix the floor boards to the joists.

The cause of the fire in the building is not certain, but, if it was indeed accidental, the corn drying ovens at the west of the structure are very probably the cause. It is just possible, however, that the building was deliberately burnt down once it had reached the end of its useful life. Subsequently, it seems to have been replaced by the South Masonry Building, built some 200 feet to the south in Period VII. The destruction of the building by fire appears to have occurred around the start of the 4th century A.D.

The Dating Evidence for the North Timber Building.

Five 4th century coins were found in soil deposits over the North Timber Building. The soil over Post-hole 15 (F.1185) produced a coin (Coin No. 36) of Constantine I (dated A.D. 313–317) (see Fig. 24, L.1); a coin (Coin No. 71) of the House of Valentinian (A.D. 364–378) came from the plough soil above the building; a general soil layer sealing the structure on the west side produced a coin (Coin No. 53) of the House of Constantine (A.D. 330–345) and the brown loam filling the terrace-cut of the later hut built over the remains of the main building produced a coin (Coin No. 50) of Constans (A.D. 345–348) (Fig. 22; S.C, L.19). There is also an unstratified Constantinopolis coin (Coin No. 46, dated A.D. 330–345).

A number of samian sherds was also recovered. The filling of the corn-driers produced single sherds of Form 31, Form 33 and Form 37. The Form 31 and 33 fragments are of Antonine date, whilst the Form 37 is dated c. A.D. 175–212 (another sherd from this same vessel, No. 142, came from the upper filling of the North-West Villa Enclosure Ditch). The soil in the top of the post-pipe of Post-hole 12 (F.1194) produced a burnt Antonine sherd (Fig. 23; L.3) whilst the lower filling of the post-pipe in Post-hole 2 (F.910) produced a Form 33 of mid to late-Antonine date (Fig. 23; L.2).

The general soil deposits over the building (Fig. 22; S.A, L.3 and S.B, L.2) produced a total of eleven more samian sherds. These consist of a Form 37 of Hadrianic to early Antonine date; two Form 38 sherds, one Form 33, one Form 31 and a Form 31 or Form 31R, all of Antonine date; together with less certain fragments from vessels of South, Central and East Gaulish manufacture. The three East Gaulish sherds may be dated to the late-2nd to mid-3rd centuries A.D. and include a mortarium sherd and a probable Form 37 fragment. Two more East Gaulish sherds of a similar date came from the hillwash deposit sealing the building (Fig. 22; S.C, L.1).

Coarse pottery was more abundant. The backfilling of the main post-pits of the North Timber Building however, produced little dateable material. Only Post-holes 1, 8, 17 and 20 contained any pottery within the filling of the pit. In each case this was just one or two sherds and there are only six sherds in all, most of which are probably residual. Two sherds have been drawn: a large everted rim storage jar from Post-hole 17 of later 1st or early-2nd century A.D. date (No. 655) and a small jar of 2nd century A.D. date (No. 656) from Post-hole 20. The remaining four sherds are also of 1st or 2nd century date.

The post-pipes produced a total of 174 coarse-ware potsherds. These represent at least 50 different vessels and six have been drawn (Nos. 657–662). Most of this material ranges from the 2nd to 4th century A.D. in date and is of sandy, Romanised fabrics. Noteworthy pieces recovered include: single sherds from Nene Valley colour-coated vessels in Post-holes 19 and 23 (not illustrated); an Alice Holt sherd from Post-hole 8 (not illustrated); an early-3rd century bead rim dish from Post-hole 19 (No. 658); a straight-sided dish of New Forest Ware (No. 659); a flanged rim bowl of 4th century date (No. 660) and two jars with out-turned rims, all from Post-hole 12 (Nos. 657 and 661). Also recovered was a small everted rim jar from Post-hole 18 (No. 662). Since all this pottery came from the pipes formerly occupied by the wooden upright posts of the building, it need not reflect the actual date of construction. It could be either residual material derived from the general area, or pottery relating to the period after the destruction of the building.

The burnt filling of the outer beam-slot on the north side of the building produced 23 coarse-ware potsherds. These represent at least twelve different vessels and two have been drawn (Nos. 653 and 654). The latest of these is a grog-tempered dish of 4th century A.D. date (No. 653). Again these need not reflect the date of the building but could be either residual or later.

The filling of the corn-drying ovens produced a further 168 coarse-ware potsherds. These represent at least 35 different vessels, but none is worthy of illustration. The bulk of the material is of sandy Roman fabrics (136 sherds) with some residual grog and shell-tempered pieces. The Roman material again ranged in date from the 2nd to 4th centuries A.D. and clearly included a large residual element. Later Roman wares identified are: four sherds of Alice Holt Ware; an Oxfordshire Ware fragment; a single piece of Nene Valley Ware and two sherds of New Forest Ware (none illustrated).

The general soil deposits over the North Building (Fig. 22; S.A, L.3 and S.B, L.2) produced a total of 719 sherds, representing at least 75 different vessels. Four have been drawn (Nos. 663–666). Well over three-quarters of the coarse pottery is of thoroughly Romanised fabrics, with the remainder consisting of residual native wares. The overall date-range of the Roman wares is 2nd to 4th century A.D., although the earlier material in this range tends to predominate (Nos. 664 and 665). The later Roman wares include 64 sherds of Alice Holt Ware, ten pieces of New Forest Ware, along with eleven fragments of Oxfordshire Ware (none illustrated). A flanged rim dish of typical later 3rd to 4th century A.D. date has been drawn (No. 666), together with a straight-sided dish of similar date (No. 663). One sherd of Rhenish Ware may also be noted (not illustrated). In addition, there are also eight mortarium sherds (none illustrated).

Several small-finds were recovered from the area of the North Timber Building. The soil over the building produced a finger-ring (No. 119) and a spatula (No. 122). The filling of the post-pipe from Post-hole 18 produced four fragments of a large millstone (not illustrated) and a quernstone fragment (No. 135) came from the filling of the central channel of the North Oven. The post-pipe of Post-hole 3 produced an iron key (No. 77) and the outer joist-slot on the north side yielded part of a shale palette (No. 130). The post-Roman robber-trench cutting the corn-drying oven produced part of a chalk basin (No. 129). A chalk spindle-whorl or weight (No. 43) was recovered from a general soil layer just to the south of the building in 1978 and a bronze stud (No. 117) from a similar layer to the west of the building in 1968. The plough-soil in the same general area yielded a bronze buckle (No. 116).

The absence of any dateable earlier features below the North Timber Building and of any useful contemporary deposits within the structure makes the date of its construction difficult to ascertain. There seems little doubt that it belongs to the general Period VI villa complex and the fact that it is connected with the West Masonry Building by a substantial timber fence (the Centre Fence) makes it clear that these two buildings were contemporary. The West Masonry Building appears to have been constructed about A.D. 200 and it must be assumed that the present building was also erected around this time, though not necessarily exactly at the same time as the West Masonry Building. There is little independent evidence from the North Timber Building, itself, to confirm this. The few 2nd century A.D. sherds from the filling of the post-pits (Nos. 655 and 656), indicate that the building was not constructed earlier than the middle of that century and the relatively small amounts of 1st century A.D. pottery in this area tend to confirm this. On balance, therefore, it does seem likely that the North Timber Building was constructed at the end of the 2nd century A.D. or early in the 3rd century A.D. The destruction of the building by fire seems to have taken place sometime around the start of the 4th century A.D. and it was clearly before a series of later features (Period VII) were cut through its site.

(iv) THE FENCE-LINES (Fig. 17).

Excavations in the areas between the Roman buildings of Period VI revealed a large number of smaller features and structures. These included the lines of four substantial timber fences (the Centre, South, East and West Fences) which were marked by alignments of post-pits and post-holes. It is not entirely certain if all these fence-lines were of exactly the same date but this seems the most likely arrangement. The East and West Fences, however, probably represent successive replacements of a single fence-line. From their general arrangement and positioning it seems clear that all of these fence-lines were broadly related to Period VI and they apparently served to delimit and sub-divide the central yard area, around which the main villa buildings were set. A probable stock compound seems to have been thus created in the north-west corner of the yard, between the West and North Buildings.

A fifth fence-line (the North Fence), of apparently slightly later date, was erected over the silted North-East Ditch of the Villa Enclosure, along the north side of the North Building. This fence-line also cut the east arm of the North-West Ditch of the Villa Enclosure and it seems clear that it was primarily intended to close the gap between these two earlier ditches, which must have restricted access to the tombs and cemetery area, north of the main villa complex.

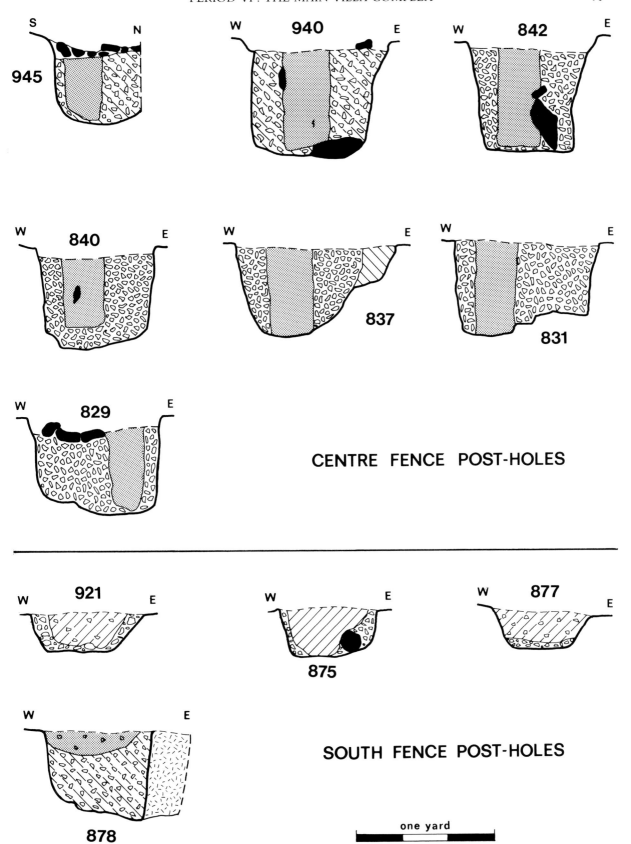

CENTRE FENCE POST-HOLES

SOUTH FENCE POST-HOLES

one yard

Fig. 25.   *Sections across post-holes of Centre and South Fences.*

a) The Centre Fence (Figs. 4, 17, 19, 21 and 25; Plate XVI).

An L-shaped alignment of substantial post-pits ran westwards from the south-west corner of the North Timber Building, turned south and then continued up to the north wall of the main West Masonry Building (Figs. 4 and 17). These pits seem to mark the line of a stout timber fence and the bulk was excavated in 1976, with a few in the area of the West Building having been previously located in 1969. The two arms of the fence-line joined at about 110° and were of unequal lengths. The north arm was 90 feet long and contained at least twelve post-pits (probably originally 15 – the sites of perhaps two or three were obscured by a modern shed). All of the excavated post-pits of the north arm were sub-rectangular in shape and still preserved the shape of the circular wooden post they had once held (Fig. 25; Plate XVI). An extra post-hole (F.835) between post-pits F.829 and F.830 at the east end is also likely to belong to this same fence-line, perhaps a late addition (see Fig. 21).

The west arm was only 35 feet long. It contained four or five post-pits (it is not entirely clear if Pit F.257 belongs here or not: on balance, this seems unlikely, however). The pits were again sub-rectangular in shape, but only one contained a post outline within its filling (F.945). Pit F.945 also cut through the filled in north ditch of the West Enclosure. The two pits nearest the West Masonry Building (Pits F.255 and 256) had later been covered by a spread of pebbles laid along the north wall of the building (Fig. 19). The last pit of the alignment (F.255) had slightly undercut the north wall of the building. Details of the post-holes are given in Table 18. The spacings of the post-holes are given in Table 19.

The spacing of post-pipes (centre to centre) along the north arm varied between 4'2" and 6'8". The average was about 5'11" (Table 19 below gives the precise details). Along the west arm the pit spacings were between 6' and 10'6".

From the general layout of this fence-line it seems clear that it need be only slightly later than the construction of the two buildings which it connected. It is of interest to note two points of detail in the layout. Firstly, the north arm of the fence continues the exact line of the posts of the south wall of the North Timber Building (see above) and secondly, the west arm continues the line of the east corridor wall of the West Masonry Building (Fig. 17). These points clearly indicate the two buildings and this fence-line formed parts of a common plan. In fact, this fence-line would have created the same effect as the stone boundary walls, revealed on a number of villa sites, linking separate structures.

The precise arrangement at the junction of the fence-line and the North Timber Building is not clear. Since the fence ran across the line of the building's outer west corridor in order to join up with the internal south aisle timbers it must be inferred that the corridor wall never came any further south and it may thus be implied that the North Timber Building was open on its southern side, rather like a modern Dutch barn. If this is correct, Post-hole F.830 of the fence-line may also have acted as the end-post of the villa's west corridor.

The contemporanity of the Centre Fence with the Period VI North and West Buildings seems certain enough, but there is little material from the post-holes of the fence-line to provide more precise dating. No dateable material came from the packing of the post-pits. The filling of the post-pipes, however, produced 26 fragmentary coarse-ware potsherds between them (Fig. 25). These represent at least twenty vessels and two have been illustrated (Nos. 667 and 668). Five of the sherds are shell-tempered and a further five are grog-tempered (No. 667); there is one flint-tempered sherd. The remaining 15 sherds are of sandy wares, apparently including both pre-Roman, native sandy wares and Romanised fabrics. Amongst the Roman wares there is a single amphora sherd (not illustrated) and a bead rim dish of 2nd century A.D. date (No. 668). It seems clear that the bulk of this pottery is residual in its present context and the majority seems to be of 1st or 2nd century A.D. date.

The discovery of timber fence-lines at Keston, can be paralleled at several recently excavated villa sites, e.g. Gorhambury (Ref. 60), Frocester Court (Ref. 61), Upmarden (Ref. 62), Chilgrove 1 (Ref. 63) and more recently at Orpington (Ref. 64). The erection of the Centre Fence at the present site would have effectively blocked access to the northern part of the site and it thus seems likely that there was a gate somewhere along its length, of which no certain trace remained.

Post Pit Feature No.	Shape	Length (ins.)	Width (ins.)	Main Axis	Depth into chalk (ins.)	Sides	Base	Post-pipe diameter (ins.)
829	Sub-Rect.	35″	29″	N–S	24″	Steep	Flat	9″ × 10″
835	Oval	20″	16″	N–S	18″	Steep	Flat	–
830	Sub-Rect.	29″	23″	N–S	14″	Vert./ Sloping	Flat	9″
831	Sub-Rect.	36″	31″	E–W	24″	Steep/ Sloping	Stepped	11″
846	Sub-Rect.	36″	25″	NW–SE	14″	Steep	Cupped	12″ × 18″
836	Sub-Rect.	35″	24″	E–W	22″	Steep	Flat	16″
837	Sub-Rect.	36″	24″	E–W	24″	Steep	Cupped	12″ × 16″
839	Sub-Rect.	43″	30″	E–W	24″	Steep	Rounded	13″ × 15″
840	Sub-Rect.	30″	28″	N–S	24″	Steep/ Sloping	Flat	14″
841	Sub-Rect.	37″	30″	E–W	24″	Sloping	Pointed	19″ × 25″
842	Sub-Rect.	31″	26″	E–W	28″	Steep	Flat	14″
944	Sub-Rect.	25″	24″	N–S	24″	Vert.	Flat	12″
940	Sub-Rect.	30″	23″	E–W	27″	Vert.	Irreg.	12″
945	Sub-Rect.	26″	24″	E–W	20″	Vert.	Cupped	10″ × 12″
260	Sub-Rect.	28″	21″	E–W	26″	Vert.	Flat	–
256	Sub-Rect.	37″	30″	N–S	28″	Vert.	Flat	–
255	Sub-Rect.	32″	29″	E–W	27″	Steep	Flat	–

Table 18. Details of the post-pits relating to the Centre Fence.

North Arm, Feature No.	Spacing (centre to centre)
F.940–944	6′0″
(positions of 3 post-holes not seen)	–
842–841	6′8″
841–840	6′2″
840–839	6′8″
839–837	6′2″
837–836	6′8″
836–846	6′0″
846–831	6′6″
831–830	5′4″
830–829	5′3″
829–PH 22, North Timber Building	4′2″
Average	5′11″

West Arm, Feature No.	Spacing (centre to centre)
F.940–945	6'9"
945–260	10'3"
260–256	10'6"
256–255	6'0"
Average	8'4"

Table 19. The spacing of post-holes of the Centre Fence.

b) The South Fence (Figs. 4, 15, 17 and 25).

This fence was again represented by a line of substantial post-holes, running eastwards from the north-east corner of the Roman West Masonry Building and roughly continuing the line of its north corridor wall. It met the West Fence some 61 feet south of the North Timber Building (Fig. 4). The post-hole alignment was excavated during 1970 and again in the 1976 season. It consisted of 15 circular or oval post-pits, varying in diameter from 12" to 45". There were no obvious post-pipes surviving (Fig. 25). The total length of the fence-line was some 92 feet and the spacing of the post-pit centres was between 5'11" and 7'5". The most westerly post-pit (F.921) was 6'6" east of the corner of the West Villa Building, whilst the last post-pit at the east end (F.306) was some 12' from the West Fence (Fig. 15). The projected line of the South Fence strikes the West Fence at pit F. 406. The greater than average spacing between these two posts may indicate the presence of a gate here. Full details of the post-holes and their spacings are given in Tables 13 and 14.

It is not clear that this fence-line is exactly contemporary with the Centre and West Fences. The probability that they are, however, seems high and, if this is correct, these fences would have formed a trapezoidal enclosure, set between the West and North Buildings of Period VI (Fig. 17). This enclosure would have measured between 35 feet and 61 feet (north–south) by some 115 feet (east–west) and perhaps with an entrance gap at the north-east corner. Such fenced enclosures are becoming increasingly common in villa excavations and presumably they represent animal compounds of some sort.

Whilst clearly broadly contemporary with the North and West Roman Buildings of Period VI precise dating evidence for this fence-line is again very limited. The fillings of the various post-holes produced a total of 36 coarse-ware potsherds, representing at least 21 different vessels (one drawn). No coins or samian ware were recovered and most of the coarse pottery appears to be residual. There are eight shell-tempered ware sherds, six are grog-tempered and one is flint-tempered. A further 21 sherds, generally rather small and abraded, include both pre-Conquest native sandy wares and thoroughly Romanised fabrics. A beaker in a Roman fabric has been drawn (No. 669). All of the pottery recovered seems to be of 1st or 2nd century A.D. date and is likely to pre-date the construction of the fence-line itself.

c) The East and West Fences (Figs. 15 and 17).

Two not quite parallel north–south fence-lines were located to the south of the North Timber Building. These were represented by individual lines of circular post-pits, most of which contained a central post-pipe. The two fence-lines were about 8' apart at the north end, tapering to about 5' at the south. They cut across the Centre Timber Building of Period Va and continued on, beyond the southern limit of the excavation. The West fence-line also cut through two of a series of parallel slots in the area of the Centre Building (see below). The relative date of the two fence-lines to each other is not clear from the site evidence (see discussion below).

Post Pit Feature No.	Shape	Length (ins.)	Width (ins.)	Main Axis	Depth into chalk (ins.)	Sides	Base
921	Oval	30″	28″	N–S	9″	Sloping	Flat
916	Oval	29″	22″	N–S	13″	Sloping	Cupped
875	Circ.	25″	25″	–	16″	Sloping	Cupped
876	Circ.	27″	27″	–	20″	Steep	Flat
877	Circ.	26″	26″	–	10″	Sloping	Flat
878	Oval	45″	30″	N–S	22″	Sloping	Flat
879	Circ.	30″	30″	–	14″	Sloping	Cupped
880	Oval	28″	25″	N–S	9″	Sloping	Cupped
311	Circ.	25″	25″	–	10″	Steep	Flat
313	Circ.	13″	13″	–	8″	Steep	Flat
310	Circ.	12″	12″	–	9″	Steep	Flat
309	Circ.	30″	30″	–	11″	Steep	Flat
308	Circ.	28″	28″	–	10″	Steep	Flat
307	Circ.	25″	25″	–	8″	Steep	Flat
306	Circ.	30″	30″	–	6″	Steep	Flat

Table 20. Details of the post-pits relating to the South Fence.

Feature No.	Spacing (centre to centre)
West Masonry Building –921	6′9″
921–916	6′3″
916–875	6′7″
875–876	6′5″
876–877	5′11″
877–878	7′5″
878–879	6′2″
879–880	6′5″
880–311	6′2″
311–313	6′9″
313–310	7′5″
310–309	5′0″
309–308	6′6″
308–307	6′9″
307–306	6′0″
306–406	12′0″
(F.406 = West Fence)	
Average	6′5″

Table 21. The spacing of the post-holes of the South Fence.

The West Fence (Figs. 15, 17 and 27; Plate XVII).

This was excavated during 1971 and 1976 and consisted of a row of 14 substantial post-pits, generally circular or oval in plan. The fence-line was traced for some 80 feet and appeared to continue into the unexcavated area at the south end (Fig. 15). Most of the pits contained post-pipes (Fig. 27). The post-pipes themselves were generally spaced at about 5' intervals (centre to centre). Where surviving, the post-pipes indicated the post diameters as being generally between 7" and 9", rather smaller than the posts of the East Fence. Full details of the post-pits and post-pipes are contained in Table 22 and their spacings are noted in Table 23.

The packing of the post-pits yielded just six potsherds, of which one is grog-tempered and three are sandy native wares. Only two, somewhat indeterminate, Roman sherds were recovered (not illustrated). None need be later than the 2nd century A.D. in date. The filling of the various post-pipes produced a further 62 coarse-ware potsherds, representing at least 25 different vessels. No coins or samian ware were recovered. The coarse-wares included five shell-tempered sherds, eleven grog-tempered sherds, twelve of sandy native ware (none illustrated) and 21 flint-tempered sherds (Nos. 683–685). None of this material need be later than the early-2nd century A.D. and much is certainly pre-Conquest. The remaining 13 sherds are of sandy Roman fabrics and these include the jar and straight-sided dish illustrated (Nos. 681 and 682).

Post Pit Feature No.	Shape	Length (ins.)	Width (ins.)	Main Axis	Depth into Chalk (ins.)	Sides	Base	Post-Pipe Diameter (ins.)
489	Circ.	20″	20″	–	17″	Steep	Flat	18″
426	Oval	22″	19″	N–S	15″	Sloping	Cupped	7″
428	Oval	26″	22″	NE–SW	16″	Steep	Flat	8″
430	Circ.	20″	20″	–	14″	Steep	Flat	8″
433	Circ.	21″	21″	–	16″	Vert.	Flat	7″
435	Circ.	20″	20″	–	15″	Vert.	Cupped	9″
437	Oval	21″	19″	E–W	14″	Vert.	Flat	6″
406	Oval	28″	20″	E–W	9″	Steep	Flat	7″
405	Oval	29″	22″	E–W	10″	Sloping	Cupped	7″
404	Oval	26″	20″	E–W	9″	Sloping	Flat	7″
407	Oval?	30″	11″ (min.)	E–W	12″	Sloping	Cupped	13″
864	Oval	22″	21″	N–S	6″	Sloping	Uneven	–
863	Oval	19″	17″	E–W	7″	Steep	Cupped	–
862	Oval	21″	17″	E–W	4″	Steep	Cupped	–

Table 22. Details of the post-pits relating to the West Fence.

More significant for dating purposes is a Form 18/31 samian sherd of Hadrianic-Antonine date found in an earlier slot (F.427, Slot No. 4 – see below), which was cut by F.426 of the present fence-line. From this it seems clear that the West Fence cannot have been erected before the late-2nd century A.D. at the earliest.

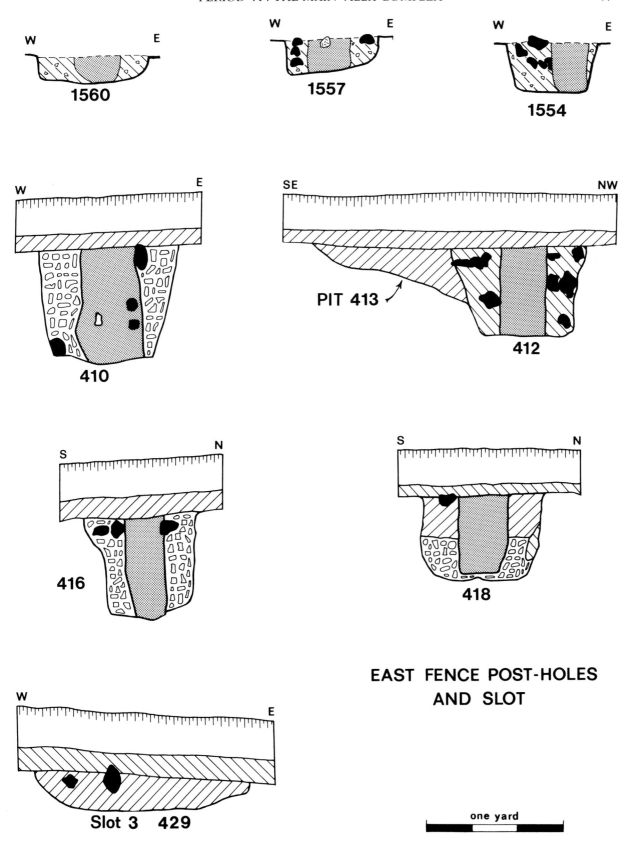

Fig. 26. *Sections across post-holes of East Fence and Slot 3.*

Feature No.	Spacing (centre to centre)
489–426	9'8" (one post missing)
426–428	4'8"
428–430	5'3"
430–433	5'1"
433–435	4'6"
435–437	4'10"
437–406	5'3"
406–405	4'6"
405–404	4'8"
404–407	5'3"
407–864	4'8"
864–863	4'11"
863–862	4'8"
Average	4'10"

Table 23. The spacing of the post-holes of the West Fence.

The East Fence (Figs. 15, 17 and 26; Plate XVII).
This fence-line was revealed during the 1971 and 1978 seasons. It consisted of a row of 19 post-pits, generally oval or circular in plan (Fig. 15). The line was traced for a distance of 103 feet and again seemed to continue into the unexcavated area at the south. It appears that originally the north end of the alignment joined the south wall of the North Timber Building on the west side of the central doorway, at an approximate right-angle (Fig. 17). An unexcavated baulk of soil between the 1978 and 1977 areas, however, seems to have covered the northernmost post-hole. All but two of the post-pits contained post-pipes (Fig. 26); from these it would seem that the posts were originally spaced between 4' and 6' apart. The posts had diameters of 9" to 16", somewhat larger than the West Fence posts. Full details of the post-pits and post-pipes are contained in Table 24. Their spacings are noted in Table 25. One significant relationship occurs; post-hole F.414 cuts Post-hole 2 of the Period Va Centre Timber Building, clearly indicating that the fence-line post-dates Period V (see Fig. 15).

The packing of the various post-pits produced a total of 92 coarse-ware potsherds, together with a single samian ware sherd of Flavian-Trajanic date, found in the post-pit of F.414. Of the coarse pottery, five sherds were shell-tempered (No. 670), 36 were grog-tempered (Nos. 671, 674 and 676), nine were of sandy native fabrics and seven sherds were flint-tempered (none illustrated). These pieces are clearly residual and none need be later than the early-2nd century A.D. The remaining 35 sherds were of Roman fabrics and include a bead-rim dish of later 2nd century date (No. 672), part of a carinated bowl (No. 673), a poppy-head beaker (No. 677) of 2nd century date and a jar of late-Roman Alice Holt Ware (No. 675). Several fragments of an indented beaker were also recovered, together with a single sherd from a mortarium (not illustrated). The bulk of the sherds is of the 2nd century A.D. but the presence of an Alice Holt Ware jar indicates that the fence-line cannot have been erected before c. A.D. 250 at the earliest.

The filling of the post-pipes produced a total of 69 potsherds, representing at least 28 different vessels. No coins or samian were recovered. Of the coarse pottery some ten sherds were shell-tempered, 31 were grog-tempered (No. 679), ten were of sandy native wares and a further six were flint-tempered (Nos. 678 and 680).

Post–pit Feature No.	Shape	Length (ins.)	Width (ins.)	Main Axis	Depth into chalk (ins.)	Sides	Base	Post-pipe diameter (ins.)
508	Circ.?	28″	9″(min.)	–	Not exc.	Not exc.	Not exc.	–
491	Circ.	28″	28″	–	23″	Vert.	Flat	11″
418	Circ.	31″	31″	–	23″	Vert.	Flat	13″
417	Oval	30″	28″	N–S	30″	Vert.	Flat	12″
416	Oval	32″	29″	E–W	27″	Vert.	Flat	10″
415	Oval	47″	34″	E–W	27″	Sloping	Cupped	14″
414	Circ.	32″	32″	–	27″	Vert.	Flat	14″
412	Oval	38″	36″	N–S	24″	Vert.	Flat	16″
411	Oval	35″	31″	E–W	26″	Vert.	Flat	10″
410	Oval	41″	36″	N–S	29″	Vert.	Flat	15″
409	Circ.	27″	27″	–	7″	Vert.	Flat	9″
408	Circ.	25″	25″	–	15″	Vert.	Flat	10″
1554	Oval	26″	24″	NW–SE	13″	Sloping	Flat	10″
1555	Oval	26″	25″	E–W	14″	Steep/ Sloping	Flat	10″
1556	Circ.	27″	27″	–	10″	Sloping	Flat	10″
1557	Circ.	24″	24″	–	10″	Vert.	Sloping	11″
1558	Circ.	20″	20″	–	7″	Vert.	Flat	–
1559	Circ.	24″	24″	–	6″	Vert.	Flat	–
1560	Oval	29″	26″	E–W	6″	Vert.	Flat	12″

Table 24. Details of the post-pits relating to the East Fence.

All of these pieces are of 1st or early-2nd century A.D. date, if not earlier, and must be residual in their present contexts. A further twelve fragmentary sherds of sandy Roman fabrics were recovered. These are all too fragmentary to be illustrated but they include a single sherd of late-3rd or 4th century Oxfordshire Ware from F.417.

Also of significance for dating purposes is the fact that post-hole F.412 cut an earlier pit (F.413) which contained two sherds of a grey ware bowl or lid, probably Keston Kiln Ware, dated c. A.D. 60–85 (No. 850). A late-3rd century date is thus indicated for the erection of the East Fence.

Discussion of the East and West Fences.

There seems no doubt that these two features are broadly similar, both in terms of date and function, to at least two other such linear features located on the site. It is possible that the present two lines are precisely contemporary, representing a (rather narrow) fenced track or droveway running north–south across the site and leading into the compound formed by the Centre and South Fences (Fig. 17). Several points argue against this, however: (a) The East and West Fences are not quite parallel and if they continued southwards on the same alignments they would ultimately meet; (b) Towards the northern end, the post-pits of the two lines do not form regular pairs; (c) The West Fence seems rather shorter than the East Fence and (d) The East Fence post-pits and pipes are larger. All of these points suggest that the two fence-lines are of slightly different dates and that one was replaced by the other. From the limited evidence available it is not certain which of the two fence-lines is the earlier but there are some minor details which indicate that the East Fence was the original structure. It seems significant that the East Fence is aligned exactly upon the western entrance post in the south wall of the North Timber Building. The shorter West Fence line, if projected, strikes the south wall of the building less precisely between Post-holes 19 (F.902) and 20 (F.826). The post-holes of the fence-line, however, ended some 33 feet south of the building, others perhaps being destroyed by ploughing, as may be indicated by the comparatively shallow depth of the most northerly post-hole surviving (F.862). The rather more precise alignment of the East Fence may, thus, reflect the neat, original design, with the West Fence representing a later replacement. It is not clear, however, just why this fence-line should have been replaced and moved only a few feet westwards. The larger size of the East Fence posts could also indicate that these are the earliest.

In absolute dating terms, the samian sherd from the fill of the earlier slot (F.427) cut by a post-hole (F.426) of the West Fence indicates that F.426 can have been dug no earlier than about A.D. 150. Virtually all of the pottery from within the post-pits and post-pipes of both fence-lines, however, appears to be residual and only the Alice Holt sherd from the packing of F.414 and the Oxfordshire Ware sherd from the post-pipe of F.417, both in the East Fence seem to be later than the 2nd century. Circumstantially, the fence-lines must belong to the later 3rd century and must be contemporary with the North Timber Building.

Feature No.	Spacing (centre to centre)
508–491	4'6"
491–418	5'0"
418–417	4'6"
417–416	4'9"
416–415	4'8"
415–414	5'3"
414–412	4'5"
412–411	4'6"
411–410	4'6"
410–409	6'10"
409–408	5'5"
408–1554	6'3"
1554–1555	6'3"
1555–1556	5'11"
1556–1557	5'10"
1557–1558	6'5"
1558–1559	6'1"
1559–1560	3'8"
1560–1178 (North Timber Building)	11'6" (one between missing)
Average	5'3"

Table 25. The spacing of the post-holes of the East Fence.

d) The Parallel Slots in the Area of the Centre Timber Building (Figs. 15, 26 and 27; Plate XVII).

A series of at least six parallel slots (Nos. 1–6) cut into the chalk in the area of the Centre Timber Building (Fig. 15 and Plate XVII) appear to have held pairs of wooden posts originally. This group of rather problematical features may be conveniently described here, under Period VI, although their date is not entirely clear. The slots are parallel-sided, with rounded terminals. One (No. 5) contained a definite post-hole at one end and two others (Nos. 1 and 2) have swollen terminals, suggesting that these too once contained posts. The slots lie immediately to the west of the East Fence of Period VI and two (Nos. 4 and 6) are cut by the post-holes of the West Fence, which probably represents a subsequent replacement of the East Fence (see above). Four of the slots (Nos. 2–5) lie within the confines of the Centre Timber Building; Slots 1 and 6 lay immediately outside the building. It is possible that further slots remain to be discovered beyond Slot 6 in the unexcavated area.

The individual slots were all roughly parallel and were between 4'11" and 6' apart (centre to centre) – see Table 27. Their main axis was east–west and they ranged in length from 4'2" to 4'8" and in width from 1'2" to 1'10". In depth, they varied from 6" to 11"; most having flat or cupped bases with steep or sloping sides. The features were all filled with brown loam containing chalk specks (Figs. 26 and 27; for details of the individual slots, see Table 26). Slot 5 (F.490) contained a post-pipe at its eastern end. This was some 10" in diameter and was filled with brown loam (Fig. 27).

The filling of the slots produced a combined total of just nine coarse-ware potsherds, representing at least eight different vessels. None of these is worthy of illustration. In addition, Slot 4 (F.427) also produced a samian sherd of Hadrianic-Antonine date. The coarse pottery may all be broadly dated to the late-1st to 2nd centuries A.D. and includes three grog-tempered sherds and seven fragmentary sherds in sandy Roman fabrics, not closely dateable.

The exact purpose of these unusual slots is not at all clear. That they originally held pairs of upright posts seems reasonably certain but what purpose these served is unknown. Even the Period to which the features belong is not clear. The options are: (a) the slots predate the Centre Timber Building and the fence-lines; (b) the slots in some way relate to the structure of the Centre Timber Building or (c) the slots post-date the building (whilst clearly predating at least the West Fence). In view of the general axis of the slots it is perhaps unlikely that they predate all the other timber structures in this area and it is difficult to see exactly what function they could have served if they formed part of the Centre Timber Building. Perhaps a more reasonable idea is that these slots represent a line of two-post drying racks, constructed adjacent to the East Fence. With the removal of the East Fence and its replacement by the West Fence these 'two-posters' must also have been removed. The location of further slots in the unexcavated area to the south may well provide further evidence as to their date and interpretation but at present these structures remain enigmatic.

Slot No.	Feature No.	Length (East–West)	Width (North–South)	Depth	Sides	Base
1	434	4'5"	1'10"	6"	Steep	Flat
2	431	4'8"	1'7"	6"	Sloping	Cupped
3	429	4'7"	1'10"	10"	Sloping	Cupped
4	427	4'2"	1'8"	10"	Steep	Flat
5	487	2'8"(min.)	1'6"	8"	Steep	Flat
6	490	3'1"(min.)	1'2"	11"	Steep	Uneven

Table 26. Details of parallel slot Nos. 1–6 in the area of the Centre Timber Building.

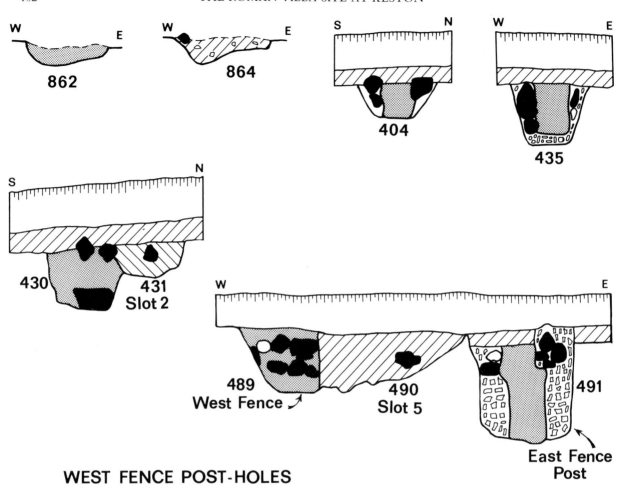

WEST FENCE POST-HOLES

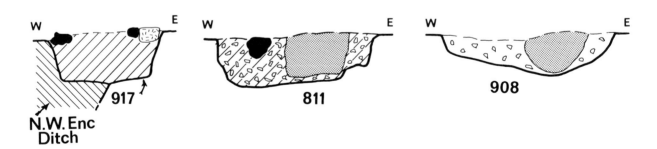

NORTH FENCE POST-HOLES

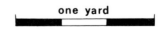

one yard

Fig. 27. *Sections across post-holes of West and North Fences.*

Slot No.	Spacing (centre to centre)
1–2 2–3 3–4 4–5 5–6	5'6" 4'11" 6'0" 5'0" 5'7"
Average	5'5"

Table 27. The spacing of parallel slot Nos. 1–6 in the area of the Centre Timber Building.

e) The North Fence (Figs. 17, 21 and 27; Plate XV).

A slightly sinuous line of eight substantial post-pits was located at the northern end of the site during the work of 1976 and 1977 (Fig. 17). These pits were aligned north-west by south-east and three were cut through the fill of the North-East Villa Enclosure Ditch, whilst the most westerly cut the silted up eastern arm of the North-West Villa Enclosure Ditch (Plate XV). The post-pits presumably represent another line of timber posts forming a fence, which extended for a distance of some 65 feet across the long established access point between the two old enclosure ditches (now apparently largely silted up).

The spacing of the post-pits was between 4'7" and 10'6" but was generally around 10'. The pits were all fairly large and were mostly rectangular or sub-rectangular in plan. They were filled largely with chalk rubble and some flint packing stones and all but one contained the outline of its original timber post (Fig. 27). These posts were all circular in plan and all were over 12" in diameter. The most easterly of the post-pits was positioned close to the north wall of the North Building and it seems clear that the fence originally ran up to this wall. The tables below give details of the post-holes and pits and their spacings (Tables 28 and 29).

The packing of post-pits yielded just four sherds, of which one is shell-tempered and three are of sandy Roman wares, all too fragmentary to draw. It seems clear that the majority of the sherds is residual and of later 1st to 2nd century A.D. date. The filling of the post-pipes produced a further nine coarse-ware sherds, representing as many different vessels. No coins or sherds of samian ware were recovered. Two of the potsherds are shell-tempered and two are grog-tempered, whilst the other five are of Roman fabrics, including a decorated sherd from a colour-coated beaker (No. 686) of late-2nd or 3rd century A.D. date. Nevertheless, it is clear from the dating evidence from the villa enclosure ditches through which the post-holes were cut, that this fence-line cannot have been constructed much before the early-4th century A.D.

Although the pottery dating evidence is of limited value, the horizontal stratigraphy places this fence-line fairly late in Period VI. Both the North-East Ditch of the Villa Enclosure and the north arm of the North-West Ditch of the Villa Enclosure had almost completely silted up before this fence was constructed. From its position, however, it seems clear that the main function of this fence was to close the entrance gap existing between the northern enclosure earthworks, implying that the entrance was still reasonably well defined. Since the eastern end of the fence ran up to the north wall of the North Timber Building this structure was still clearly standing and no doubt served to continue the boundary line eastwards. How the western end of the fence-line terminated is not so clear. It seems possible, however, that the north arm of the North-West Enclosure Ditch, with its supposed accompanying bank was still sufficiently clear to act as a barrier; if not, some sort of hedge may have existed. The North Fence would, thus, effectively have blocked the entrance gap. There could, however, have been a gateway in this fence (perhaps between post-pits F.811 and F.907 in view of the wider gap here). Since the North Timber

Building was still standing when the North Fence was erected it would seem that the present fence-line belongs to a late phase within Period VI, sometime prior to the burning down of the North Building, an event which effectively marks the end of Period VI and the beginning of Period VII.

Post Pit Feature No.	Shape	Length (ins.)	Width (ins.)	Main Axis	Depth into chalk (ins.)	Sides	Base	Post-Pipe diameter (ins.)
917	Oval	33″	32″	NW–SE	14″	Steep/Sloping	Cupped	–
810	Sub-Rect.	33″	29″	N–S	7″	Steep	Cupped	13″
809/907	Rect.	40″	30″	N–S	8″	Sloping	Flat	15″
811	Sub-Rect.	50″	42″	N–S	13″	Steep	Flat	19″
908	Sub-Rect.	47″	42″	N–S	9″	Sloping	Cupped	15″ × 19″
912	Sub-Rect.	52″	36″	N–S	22″	Steep/Sloping	Cupped	18″
914	Sub-Rect.	36″	30″	N–S	18″	Sloping	Cupped	12″
913	Sub-Rect.	58″	42″	E–W	28″	Steep	Flat	15″

Table 28. Details of the post-pits relating to the North Fence.

Feature No.	Spacing (centre to centre)
917–810	4′7″
810–809/907	9′7″
809/907–811	10′6″
811–908	10′2″
908–912	9′6″
912–914	10′3″
914–913	7′3″
913–North Wall, North Building	3′6″
Average	8′10″

Table 29. The spacing of the post-holes of the North Fence.

(v) THE WATER SUPPLY

a) The West Water Pipe-Line (Figs. 4, 17 and 29).

This was located in the 1976 excavation just to the north-east of the Roman West Masonry Building (Fig. 4). It consisted of a shallow gully, running north-north-east by south-south-west. This was U-shaped in cross-section, being some 10″ wide and 4–6″ deep (Fig. 29). The gully was traced for a minimum distance of 31 feet and was destroyed by ploughing beyond this, in either direction. The gully was filled with a brown loam and contained a number of iron water-pipe collars (Fig. 92).

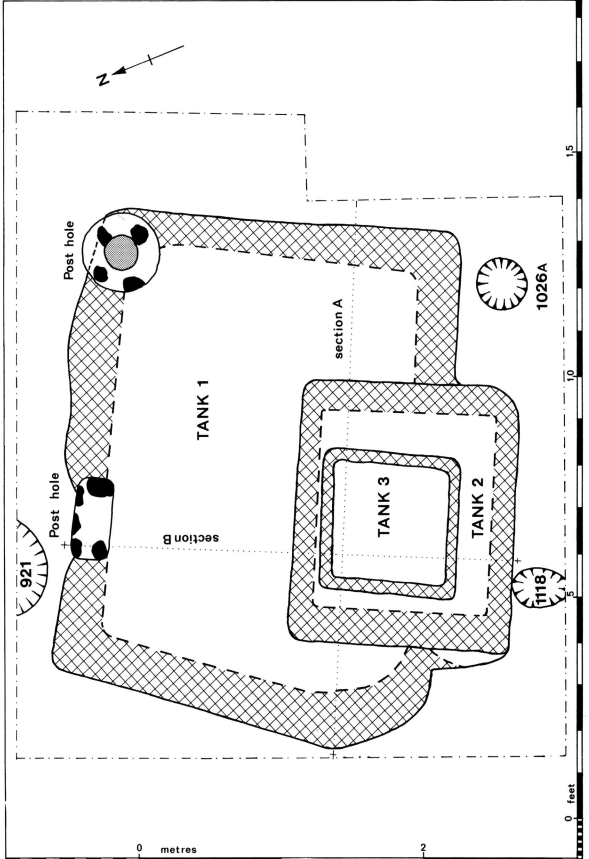

Fig. 28. *Plan of West Tanks adjacent to West Masonry Building.*

Traces of six iron collars, each about 3″ (75mm.) in diameter internally, were noted (No. 938) together with two fragments of lead sheeting pierced by iron nails (No. 937). These sheets probably represent late repairs to (by then) rotting wooden pipes, which the iron collars would have joined. A fairly long period of use for the pipe-line is, thus, implied. The spacing of the iron collars varied between 5′ and 5′8″ and this must reflect a fairly standard pipe length. The two lead fragments were discovered at points between the iron collars and must have been used to cover splits in the wooden pipe-work between the joints.

For about half of the total length traced, the pipe-gully was cut through an earlier sub-rectangular area of pebble metalling (Period V). A total of eleven coarse-ware potsherds was recovered from the gully filling and these seem to represent at least five different vessels, all dateable to the late-1st to 2nd centuries A.D. (none is worthy of illustration). The earlier metalling produced just six sherds of the later 1st century A.D. It has, however, been assigned to Period V.

The function of this water pipe-line seems fairly certain. The flow was clearly from north to south, following the slope of the hill and it must be significant that the line of the pipe, if projected just 10′ southwards from its last surviving point, strikes the group of three successive clay-lined tanks excavated in 1970 and 1977 (Fig. 28). These are immediately adjacent to the north-east corner of the West Masonry Building and it seems reasonable to suppose that fresh water was brought in from springs higher up the hillside (where springs, significantly, still exist today) via the pipe-line, to these tanks. A good supply here could have provided all the water needed for domestic purposes in the main villa building and may also have catered for animals held in the Period VI fenced compound immediately to the north.

Although the three water tanks at the southern end of the present pipe trench were successive, there is only evidence for this one line of pipes feeding them. It thus seems likely that the same pipe-line supplied each of the tanks in turn and it must, therefore, have been of some considerable age when it was finally abandoned. The lead sheeting repairs found in the pipe-trench reinforce this view.

Several villa sites have produced evidence for a piped water supply, including Chilgrove 1 (Ref. 65), Bignor (Ref. 66), Eccles (Ref. 67) and Cobham (Ref. 68). At these sites the water brought in seems to have been primarily for use in the bath-suites and it is of interest to note that this was not apparently the case at Lower Warbank.

b) The West Tanks (Nos. 1, 2 and 3) (Figs. 17, 19, 28 and 29).

Three superimposed pits or tanks lined with clay were located in 1970, just east of the north-east corner of the West Masonry Building. The largest and earliest of these was Tank No. 1 and this had been cut by the smaller Tanks 2 and 3 and also by two minor, apparently unrelated, post-holes.

Tank 1 (F.348).

This was a large, sub-rectangular pit, measuring between 11′6″ and 12′ (east–west) by 9′ to 9′9″ (north–south). It had been dug to a depth of some 2′8″ into the natural chalk and was then lined with a thick deposit of clay 10–15″ thick, leaving a tank with an internal capacity of at least 120 cu. ft. (min.). This tank was apparently intended to hold water and could have held about 720 gallons. Later it had been deliberately filled in with black loam, mortar lumps (of a similar type to that used in the West Masonry Building), building rubble and pebbles. It had been subsequently replaced by a smaller clay-lined tank (Tank 2) cut through the south side of the original structure. Two post-holes had also cut through the edge of the tank on the north side, although these could not be related to any definite structure. It seems likely that the original Tank 1 was supplied with fresh water by the western water pipe-line, which heads in this direction and would have discharged into it on the north side (see above).

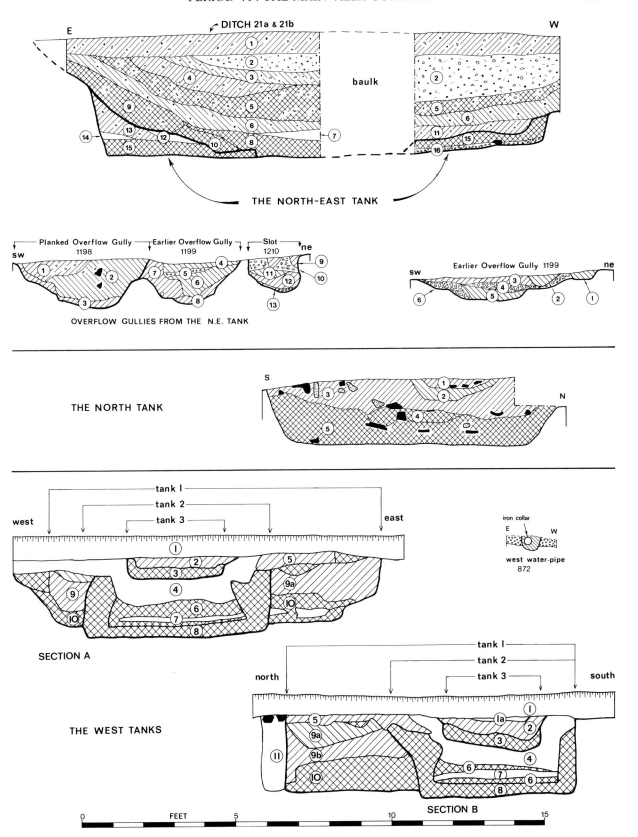

Fig. 29. *Sections across Tanks, Overflow Gullies and West Water Pipe-line.*

Stratigraphically, it was clear that Tank 1 was the earliest of the group (Fig. 29). Its fill produced three samian sherds (a Form 31 of late-2nd to mid-3rd century date, a Flavian Form 33 and an East Gaulish fragment, possibly from a Form 36). No coins were recovered. A total of 50 coarse-ware potsherds was also discovered in the fill and representing at least twelve diferent vessels. Six sherds have been drawn (Nos. 701–706). The bulk of the coarse pottery is of sandy Roman fabric and includes two amphora sherds (not illustrated). Some clearly residual material, in native shell and grog-tempered wares, also occurs (none illustrated). All of the drawn material is of sandy Roman fabric and includes a bead rim pie dish of 2nd century A.D. date (No. 703), a flanged rim dish of later 3rd to 4th century A.D. date (No. 706), a straight-sided bowl (No. 704) and three jars with everted rims (Nos. 701, 702 and 705). The date of all the pottery material ranges from the late-1st to the late-3rd/4th centuries A.D. The latest pieces (No. 706, and the Form 31 samian sherd) indicate that the tank could have been filled in before about A.D. 260. It is not, however, likely to have been filled much after this. The date of the tank's construction may be assumed to be broadly contemporary with the construction of the West Masonry Building probably in the early-3rd century A.D.

It may also be noted here that one of the minor post-holes cutting the north side of the tank produced a Form 36 samian sherd of Antonine date.

Tank 2 (F.349).

This was almost square in plan and was considerably smaller than Tank 1. The pit, as originally excavated, measured 6′ (east–west) by 5′2″ (north–south) and had been partly dug through Tank 1 to a depth of some 3′2″, before being lined with a similar clay layer to that in Tank 1. The capacity of this tank was only about 27 cu. ft. (min.) (c. 160 gallons), but it seems very probable that it continued to be supplied with water by the west pipe-line. Tank 2, like Tank 1, had been eventually backfilled and replaced by a third smaller tank (Tank 3). The fill of Tank 2 consisted of soil with tiles, flint and general rubble and produced five samian sherds, all somewhat fragmentary (a Form 31R of late-2nd to early-3rd century A.D. date, a Curle Form 15 dated to the late-2nd to early-3rd century A.D., a Form 31R of the mid to late-Antonine period, a mortarium base of the late-2nd to mid-3rd century A.D. and a Central Gaulish sherd). Only seven coarse-ware potsherds were recovered, representing five vessels. Three sherds have been drawn (Nos. 707–709). The sherds include three fragments of late-Roman grog-tempered ware (not illustrated), one Rhenish sherd, a straight-sided dish of 3rd to 4th century date (No. 707) and a rolled rim storage jar in a sandy ware (No. 708), together with an early, Belgic grog-tempered sherd (No. 709). From the latest of this material and the tank's relationship to Tank 1 it seems clear that this tank could not have been filled in before the end of the 3rd century A.D. This tank also produced a 'lamp chimney' fragment in its primary filling (No. 133).

Tank 3 (F.350).

This had been cut into the top of the filled in Tank 2 and measured only 3′2″ square. It was up to 12″ deep and was lined with about 3–4″ of clay, which gave an internal capacity of only some 6 cu. ft. (min.) (c. 36 gallons). This tank appears to have silted up naturally and was presumably still supplied by the western water pipe-line, until it went out of use – perhaps at the same time as the final abandonment of the West Masonry Building at the end of Period VII.

The fill of Tank 3 produced a single sherd of samian ware, a Form 45 of late-2nd to early-3rd century A.D. date. Some ten coarse-ware potsherds were also recovered, representing at least seven different vessels. Three of these have been drawn (Nos. 710–712). There are also two mortarium fragments (Nos. 925 and 926). All the pottery is of sandy Roman fabric and most seems dateable to the later 2nd to mid-3rd century A.D. There are a few later vessels however; a flanged bowl (No. 711) of late-3rd to 4th century date is illustrated. The dateable material from the earlier tanks indicates that the present Tank 3 is unlikely to have been dug before the early-4th century A.D.

Assuming that these three clay-lined tanks represent successive replacements of a single structure and that this structure did hold water, it seems clear that the amounts capable of being stored have decreased with the passage of time. It must be remembered, however, that erosion of the upper parts of the tanks has occurred so their precise size cannot be certain. The figures here are all minimum amounts. It seems most likely that these tanks held water for use in the main West Masonry Building but the lack of an overflow system in any phase may suggest that the water entering the tanks was not a continuous flow and it was presumably turned off somehow once the tank was full. It may also be significant that the tanks are adjacent to the fenced compound formed by the Centre and South Fences. It is possible that water stored in the tanks was also used for animals kept within this compound. The Centre Fence, and by implication the complete compound, seems to have been dismantled at the end of Period VII, well before the general abandonment of the villa site and it, therefore, seems likely that just Tank 1 had this dual purpose. It is certainly much larger than the two later tanks and could hold more than twice the amount of Tank 2.

c) The East Water Pipe-Line (Figs. 4, 11 and 17).

Traces of another water-pipe trench were located some 75 feet to the south-east of the west pipe trench in the 1968 and 1969 seasons, near the early-Roman Quarry Pit Complex (Period IV). This pipe-line again consisted of a shallow U-shaped gully, some 12″ wide and up to 5″ deep. The gully was filled with brown loam and a number of iron pipe collars were located along its length (Fig. 92). The pipe gully, where surviving, was aligned north-east by south-west but ploughing had again destroyed much of its course. The actual gully survived for a minimum distance of about 40 feet, although a single isolated iron pipe collar was located in disturbed soil some 35 feet to the north-east of its north end, exactly on the projected line. This presumably represents a continuation of the pipe-line and gives a total minimum length of about 75 feet.

Parts of five iron pipe collars were located *in situ* and four of these have been illustrated (Nos. 933–936). They were set at intervals of between 7′3″ and 11′5″, indicating longer but less standard pipe lengths than those used in the west pipe-line. The internal diameters of the collars were between 2½″ and 3″ (66–77 mm.) and are thus broadly similar to the other pipe-line.

The east pipe-line was cut through by two post-Roman ditches (Ditches 3 and 4). Its relationship with the early-Roman Centre Flint Structure of Period Vb, however, was not certain. It seems most likely, that the pipe-line formed part of the later villa complex (Period VI or VII) and it, therefore, would have cut through this earlier structure, but this was not completely clear on the ground.

The origin of the pipe-line is unclear but again it is likely to have been at a spring higher up the hill (perhaps the same one as supplied the western pipe-line). If the alignment of the present pipe is projected south-westwards it strikes the Roman South Masonry Building of Period VII, near its north-west corner, perhaps hinting that it might have provided water for that building. It is, however, implicit that some sort of collecting tank would exist at the end of a water pipe-line and no such structure was recorded in this area. However, an earlier clay-lined tank, the South Tank, very suitable for holding water, was located under the middle of the South Masonry Building. The presence of this tank, very similar to Tank 1, strongly suggests that the eastern pipe-line is contemporary with it and that it, in fact, originally fed the tank. If this is correct it must be inferred that, at some point now destroyed, the pipe-line changed direction to a more southerly course in order to reach the tank (Fig. 17). It seems likely that the east pipe-line was, in fact, laid more or less at the same time as the west pipe-line, sometime during Period VI. There is no useful independently dateable material to confirm this, however. The fill of the east pipe-line produced just three rather indeterminate potsherds of general Roman date (not illustrated).

d) The South Tank (Figs. 17, 32 and 33; Plate XX).

This was located under the central part of the Period VII South Masonry Building, in 1968, sealed by three of its walls (Fig. 32). It lay immediately to the west of the earlier South Timber Building of Period Va. The pit was roughly rectangular in shape and measured 12'6" (north–south) by 8'8" (east–west). It was lined with a grey clay, mostly 6–12" thick. Excluding the lining, the Tank was about 2' deep (Fig. 33). A series of 19 stake-holes, generally rectangular in cross-section, were discovered within the clay and these probably originally helped to keep the lining in position. The bulk of the stakes were 3" to 4" in width (Table 30). The pit had been filled in with loam and rubbish deposits and then flint rubble had been packed into the top.

The purpose of this pit would seem to have been as a water-storage tank, in view of the thick, waterproof clay lining and it may, therefore, be regarded as being of a similar type to the pits found by the Roman West Masonry Building. Certainly it is very similar in size to West Tank 1. There is, however, no definite evidence of a water-pipe discharging into the present pit. It does seem likely, though, that the east water pipe-line changed its alignment to a more southerly course (Fig. 17) and did, in fact, once bring water to this tank (see above). Leading from the south side of the present tank was a gully, some 12–14" wide and 2–6" deep, with almost vertical sides. It was filled with brown loam and carbon and was traced for some 11' to the southern limit of the excavation. This gully almost certainly represents an overflow from the tank and clearly suggests a fairly continuous in-flow of water. From the surviving remains it would seem that, as a collecting tank, the pit could have held at least 800 gallons of water at any one time.

Stratigraphically, this clay-lined tank clearly predates the construction of the South Masonry Building in Period VII. In position, it lay at the west end of a large timber building assigned to Period Va (the South Timber Building) which occupied the same site before the masonry building. It seems likely that these two earlier structures were in use together for some time during Period VI (see above, page 58). This view is reinforced by the fact that the long axis of the tank is the same as the short axis of the timber building, implying that the tank was aligned on an existing wall line.

Stake-hole No.	Shape	Size (ins.)	Depth (ins.)	Sides	Base
1	Rectangular	4" × 3"	10"	Steep	Pointed
2	Rectangular	4" × 3"	12"	Steep	Pointed
3	Square	3" × 3"	8"	Steep	Pointed
4	Square	2" × 2"	6"	Steep	Pointed
5	Square	3" × 3"	8"	Steep	Pointed
6	Rectangular	4" × 3"	10"	Steep	Pointed
7	Rectangular	4" × 3"	9"	Steep	Pointed
8	Rectangular	4" × 3"	9"	Steep	Pointed
9	Rectangular	3" × 3"	7"	Steep	Pointed
10	Rectangular	3" × 2"	7"	Steep	Pointed
11	Square	3" × 3"	11"	Steep	Pointed
12	Square	3" × 3"	6"	Steep	Pointed
13	Square	3" × 3"	9"	Steep	Pointed
14	Rectangular	4" × 3"	10"	Steep	Pointed
15	Square	3" × 3"	8"	Steep	Pointed
16	Square	4" × 4"	11"	Steep	Pointed
17	Rectangular	4" × 3"	10"	Steep	Pointed
18	Rectangular	4" × 3"	9"	Steep	Pointed
19	Square	$2\frac{1}{2}$" × $2\frac{1}{2}$"	7"	Steep	Pointed

Table 30. Details of the stake-holes relating to the South Tank.

No coins were recovered from the filling of the tank and there were only three samian sherds. These were: a Form 37, dated A.D. 75–95 (No. 143); a Form 27 of Flavian date and an uncertain South Gaulish sherd of later 1st century A.D. date. A total of 93 coarse-ware potsherds was also recovered. These represent at least 27 different vessels and 14 of these have been drawn (Nos. 687–700). Over two-thirds of this material is of sandy Roman fabrics. These include seven amphora sherds (not illustrated); there are two sherds of Keston Kiln Ware (Nos. 688 and 699), dateable to c. A.D. 60–85. Several jars with everted rims are present (Nos. 693, 696 and 697) and there are also two sherds from a rusticated beaker, too fragmentary to illustrate. Two ring-necked flagons are present (Nos. 690 and 691), both of earlier 2nd century A.D. date. One large vessel of 4th century A.D. Cream Sandy Ware is clearly intrusive and must relate to the Period VII occupation of the area (No. 698). Fine-wares are represented by a wall sherd from a roulette-decorated beaker (No. 689). Other illustrated Roman wares include a bowl with a flanged rim (No. 694), the rim of a flagon or flask (No. 692) and a dish with a curving wall and upright rim (No. 695). Some grog-tempered wares of earlier Roman date are also present and these include two vessels of Patch Grove Ware (Nos. 687 and 700), dateable to the later 1st to 2nd century A.D. Apart from one clearly intrusive sherd it seems clear that all of the pottery from the filling of the South Tank dates to the later 1st century or 2nd century A.D. and most must be residual. The general site evidence indicates that the tank is unlikely to have been constructed much before the end of the 2nd century A.D. at the earliest and it was probably not filled in until at least A.D. 250.

Two small-finds came from the filling of the Tank. These were a baked clay container (No. 21) and a bronze bracelet (No. 102). The bracelet is of a typical later Roman type and the form is common from the late-3rd century onwards, but some 2nd century examples are known.

The overflow gully leading from the tank produced a total of just 18 potsherds representing at least three vessels. All of these sherds are too small for illustration and 15 of them come from an amphora. The other three sherds are likely to be of later 1st or 2nd century A.D. date and must all be residual in their present context.

PERIOD VII : THE LATER ROMAN VILLA COMPLEX (A.D. 300–450) (Fig. 30).

It seems clear that the major Period VI structure and features represent the fullest development of the Roman Villa complex, dated about A.D. 200–300. The next major sequence of structural events appears to start with the destruction of the North Timber Building by fire at about A.D. 300, here regarded as Period VII.

The West Masonry Building seems to have continued in use as the main house, with only minor alterations at its south end. The North Timber Building was not replaced, though its precise site was used, but a corresponding building (the South Masonry Building) was constructed to replace the South Timber Building. Various other structures and features, mostly dated by pottery and circumstantial evidence, were introduced in the fourth century and can be divided into two broad phases within Period VII, as follows:

Phase A   Ditches 1 & 7
          Probable late hut on site of North Timber Building
          North-East and North Tanks
          South Masonry Building (Phases 1 and 2)
          Upper East Metalling and Centre Metalling
          External Corn-drying Oven

Phase B   Ditch 21 (a and b recut)
          South-West Timber Structure
          Late Chalk Structure.

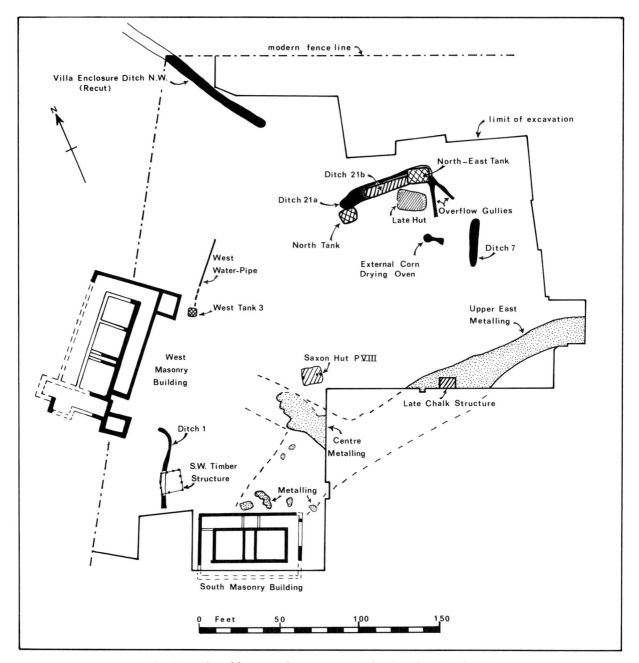

Fig. 30.   *Plan of features and structures assigned to Periods VII and VIII.*

(i) THE LATER ROMAN VILLA BOUNDARY DITCHES (Fig. 30).

Apart from the villa's main boundary ditches (Period VI), several other lengths of ditch produced quantities of late-Roman pottery and these features must have been filled late in the history of the Roman site. This implies that these ditches were open and in use during the 4th century A.D. (Period VII). Only one recut ditch, however, is demonstrably later that Period VI on the evidence of the site stratigraphy (Ditch 21 a and b). Four ditches have been grouped together here in Period VII, and these are described below. These are: Ditches 1, 7, 21 (a and b) and a partial recutting of the North-West Ditch of the main Villa Enclosure. Two of these ditches are very short and it is difficult to see exactly how they fitted into the overall scheme (Ditch 7 and Ditch 21). It seems reasonably clear, however, that the Period VI North-East Ditch of the Villa

Enclosure and the east arm of the North-West Enclosure had largely silted up by the beginning of Period VII.

The north arm of the North-West Ditch of the Villa Enclosure, in contrast, seems to have remained open (or was more probably recut) and it apparently continued to mark the northern boundary of the villa complex throughout much of Period VII. To the east of this ditch lay Ditches 7 and 21. These may have been dug at different dates and cannot alone have formed any continuous boundary to replace the North-East Enclosure Ditch of Period VI, although they could have been supplemented by hedges or fences that have left no trace. The purpose of Ditch 1, well to the south, is unclear. It is less substantial than the other ditches and it does not seem to mark any major boundary.

Ditch 1 (Figs. 19, 30, 37 and 38).

This small ditch was located between the West Masonry Building and the South Masonry Building in 1977 (Fig. 30). Its main axis was roughly north–south, with the northern end curving round to the north-west and ending just short of the West Masonry Building in such a way as to suggest that the two were complimentary. The ditch's northern terminal had been previously located and excavated in 1969 (Fig. 19). On the south side the ditch continued beyond the excavation limits. In all, the ditch was traced for a total length of 56 feet. It varied in width from between 1'6" and 3'4", being wider at the southern (downhill) end and it seems likely that plough damage has caused these variations. In depth, the ditch was between 6" and 13" and the sides were vertical in places and steep, or sloping, in others. The base was flat and this measured between 15" and 18" across. The filling of the ditch consisted of dark brown loam with chalk (Fig. 38) and this produced a quantity of Roman pottery, but no other finds.

The ditch, itself, cut through the Centre Enclosure Ditch assigned to Period IVb, but was cut through by five post-holes of the South-West Timber Structure, which has been assigned to Period VIIb (Fig. 37). The ditch was also cut by a substantial post-pit (F.1133) of uncertain function. This pit produced an Antonine samian sherd (Form 30) and 13 early-Roman coarse pottery sherds, all clearly residual.

The filling of the ditch produced no coins, but two samian sherds were recovered; one a Form 27 of Flavian date and one Form 18, or 18/31, of Flavian-Trajanic date. These, however, must be residual in the light of the coarse pottery dating. A total of 146 coarse-ware potsherds was recovered from the ditch and these represent at least 35 vessels, the majority of which seem to be residual, early-Roman types and include a few pieces of Keston Kiln Ware. Three sherds have been drawn (Nos. 777–779). They comprise: a single sherd from a crudely made bowl of 4th century grog-tempered ware (No. 777); a globular jar of kiln ware (No. 778) and an unusual grog-tempered vessel with a simple upright flat-topped rim (No. 779). More relevant dating evidence is provided by 13 sherds of grey, sandy Alice Holt Ware. This material may be broadly dated to the late-3rd to 4th centuries A.D., but all of the sherds are unfortunately too fragmentary to illustrate.

From its relationship to the Centre Enclosure Ditch it seems clear that Ditch 1 cannot have been dug any earlier than the mid-2nd century A.D. and it was very probably at least a century and a half later. It seems clear, however, that the ditch was filled before the end of the Roman period, when the South-West Timber Structure was erected partially over it. The purpose of this ditch is not clear but, from its fairly insubstantial nature, it seems likely that it formed part of some local boundary, or drainage, ditch within the later villa complex of Period VII.

Ditch 7 (Figs. 4, 30, and 38; Plate XXIV).

Excavations in 1978 to the south-east of the North Timber Building revealed a length of ditch running north–south across the site (Fig. 4). This was just 32 feet long and both terminals were located. The north terminal was squared off, whilst that at the south tapered to a rounded point. Ploughing had clearly reduced this feature, particularly towards the southern end. As surviving, the ditch was between 4' (south) and 5'2" (north) wide and ranged in depth between 2" (south) and 23" (north). It had sloping sides and a cupped base and was filled with deposits of brown loam and chalk (Fig. 38) which produced a coin, samian and coarse pottery.

The filling of the ditch yielded a single coin and two (residual) samian sherds (of Form 37 and 18/31R). The East Gaulish Form 37 samian sherd is dated to the later 2nd to the first half of the 3rd century A.D. while the other is of 2nd century A.D. date. The coin (Coin No. 61) is of the House of Constantine (c. A.D. 350–360). A mortarium sherd was recovered and this has been illustrated (No. 920). A total of 165 coarse-ware potsherds, representing at least 47 different vessels was also recovered and six of these have been drawn (Nos. 771–776). Virtually all of this material is of late-Roman forms and fabrics and includes several pieces of 4th century A.D. grog-tempered ware (Nos. 771 and 773). The bulk of the sherds, however, are of sandy fabrics (No. 774) and these include a few pieces of Alice Holt Ware (Nos. 772 and 775). Overall, most of the pottery seems to date from the late-3rd to the 4th centuries A.D. with a little earlier, residual material. The residual material includes two sherds from platters of 1st century A.D. Keston Kiln Ware (not illustrated) and an Iron Age rim of flint-tempered ware (No. 776).

It seems likely that this ditch formed part of the later boundary earthworks delimiting the eastern side of the Period VII villa complex (Fig. 30). From the pottery dating evidence, it would seem that the North-East Ditch of the Villa Enclosure of Period VI had completely silted up before this present ditch was dug. They cannot, therefore, have belonged to the same system. More closely related in date to the present ditch is Ditch 21, cutting through the North Timber Building. This too is of a fairly short length and it is not clear how the two would have functioned together as any useful boundary. One slight piece of evidence could, moreover, suggest that the two ditches, though both late, are not in fact precisely contemporary, at least in construction date. It seems possible that an overflow gully leading from the North-East Water Tank originally discharged into the northern end of Ditch 7, which would have acted as a sump. Unfortunately, ploughing has destroyed part of the gully so this point cannot be certain. If this is what did happen though, it would make the North-East Tank and Ditch 7 contemporary. Since the North-East Tank was cut away by Ditch 21, it must follow that this was the later ditch to be dug. This is not to say, however, that Ditch 7 did not remain open once Ditch 21 was completed. The coin and pottery dating evidence indicates that Ditch 7 was not filled until the second half of the 4th century A.D. Ditch 21 may have been dug about this time and it is not entirely impossible that one ditch replaced the other, for reasons which are not obvious.

(ii) PROBABLE LATE HUT OVER THE NORTH TIMBER BUILDING (Figs. 21, 22, 23 and 30).

A slight terrace, between 9″ and 12″ in depth, had been cut into the chalk across the south-east corner of the demolished North Timber Building (Fig. 21). This feature clearly post-dated the building, for it actually cut through one of its post-pits (Post-hole 11, F.1193). The terrace predated the substantial Ditch 21a which likewise cut through the remains of the burnt down building and had also destroyed the north-west corner of the terrace.

The surviving terrace-cut measured some 28′ (east–west) by 10′ (north–south), though ploughing may have reduced the southern edge. A cluster of over 60 stake-holes (see Table 31), two post-holes (F.1187 and F.1206) and a small pit (F.1200) had been cut into the surface of the terrace (Fig. 22), although these formed no obvious pattern. To the south of these features a roughly sub-rectangular hearth (F.1201) had been laid over one of the earlier North Timber Building post-holes (Post-hole 13, F.1205; see Fig. 23). It seems highly likely that this hearth was related to a building which may also be reasonably inferred from the stake-holes and terracing. This building presumably took the form of a fairly insubstantial wooden hut which, if it enclosed the hearth, would have roughly measured some 25′ (east–west) by about 20′ (north–south).

The hearth, itself, had been cut by a later pit (F.1209) but measured some 9′2″ (east–west) by 6′1″ (north–south). It was constructed of chalk lumps and Roman tiles and bricks set in a brown (burnt) loam (Fig. 23). The underlying natural chalk had been burnt in places due to the intense heat and from the large size of the structure an industrial, rather than domestic function, is implied. Perhaps significantly, 19 substantial pieces of iron smithing hearth-bottom slag were recovered from the soil filling the terrace-cut as compared with just one piece from the rest of the area of the North Timber Building. This could suggest that the conjectured hut enclosed an iron working forge, but this cannot be certain.

The terrace-cut was flanked on the north and west sides by a shallow ditch (Ditch 14). This cut through two of the post-pits of the main building (Post-holes 11 and 16, F.1180 and F.1193) and it had, itself, been destroyed at the corner by the later ditch (Ditch 21b). Originally, the two arms of the ditch would have met at about 95°.

Stake Hole No.	Shape	Size (ins.)	Main Axis	Depth (ins.)	Sides	Base
11	Oval	$3'' \times 3\frac{1}{4}''$	E–W	$2\frac{1}{2}''$	Steep	Flat
12	Circ.	$3'' \times 3''$	–	$2''$	Steep	Flat
13	Oval	$4'' \times 5''$	E–W	$4\frac{1}{4}''$	Steep	Flat
14	Irreg.	$5'' \times 6''$	E–W	$3''$	Steep	Flat
15	Oval	$4\frac{1}{4}'' \times 4\frac{1}{2}''$	N–S	$4\frac{1}{2}''$	Steep	Round
16	Oval	$2\frac{1}{2}'' \times 3''$	E–W	$3''$	Steep	Round
17	Oval	$3'' \times 3\frac{1}{2}''$	E–W	$2''$	Steep	Round
18	Circ.	$3'' \times 3''$	–	$4\frac{1}{2}''$	Steep	Cupped
19	Oval	$2\frac{1}{2}'' \times 3''$	N–S	$2''$	Vert.	Flat
20	Circ.	$3\frac{1}{2}'' \times 3\frac{1}{2}''$	–	$2''$	Steep	Flat
21	Circ.	$4'' \times 4''$	–	$7''$	Vert.	Round
22	Oval	$2'' \times 3''$	E–W	$4''$	Vert.	Round
23	Oval	$2'' \times 2\frac{1}{2}''$	E–W	$3\frac{1}{2}''$	Vert.	Round
24	Oval	$2'' \times 3\frac{1}{2}''$	E–W	$3''$	Steep	Cupped
25	Oval	$2'' \times 3''$	E–W	$4''$	Vert.	Round
26	Sub-Rect.	$5\frac{1}{2}'' \times 6''$	E–W	$4''$	Steep	Round
27	Oval	$4'' \times 5''$	N–S	$5''$	Steep	Round
28	Sub-Triangular	$5'' \times 5''$	–	$6''$	Steep	Pointed
29	Circ.	$5'' \times 5''$	–	$4''$	Steep	Round
30	Oval	$4'' \times 4\frac{1}{2}''$	E–W	$5''$	Vert.	Round
31	Oval	$6\frac{1}{2}'' \times 8''$	N–S	$6''$	Steep	Round
32	Oval	$4\frac{1}{2}'' \times 5''$	N–S	$4''$	Vert.	Round
33	Oval	$3'' \times 3\frac{1}{2}''$	N–S	$5\frac{1}{2}''$	Steep	Round
34	Sub-Triangular	$3'' \times 3''$	–	$2''$	Steep	Round
35	Sub-Triangular	$4'' \times 5''$	E–W	$5\frac{1}{2}''$	Steep	Round
36	Oval	$3'' \times 4''$	N–S	$2\frac{1}{2}''$	Steep	Cupped
37	Oval	$3\frac{1}{2}'' \times 4''$	N–S	$4''$	Steep	Cupped
38	Oval	$3'' \times 4''$	N–S	$3''$	Steep	Round
39	Circ.	$5\frac{1}{2}'' \times 5\frac{1}{2}''$	–	$9''$	Steep	Round
40	Circ.	$3\frac{1}{2}'' \times 3\frac{1}{2}''$	–	$3\frac{1}{2}''$	Steep	Cupped
41	Oval	$4'' \times 4\frac{1}{2}''$	E–W	$3''$	Steep	Round
42	Circ.	$3'' \times 3''$	–	$2''$	Steep	Flat
43	Oval	$4\frac{1}{2}'' \times 5''$	E–W	$3\frac{1}{2}''$	Steep	Cupped
44	Circ.	$4\frac{1}{2}'' \times 4\frac{1}{2}''$	–	$5''$	Steep	Round
45	Oval	$4\frac{1}{2}'' \times 5''$	E–W	$4\frac{1}{2}''$	Steep	Round
46	Oval	$3'' \times 3\frac{1}{2}''$	E–W	$4\frac{1}{2}''$	Vert.	Round
47	Oval	$2\frac{1}{2}'' \times 3''$	N–S	$1\frac{1}{2}''$	Steep	Round

Stake Hole No.	Shape	Size (ins.)	Main Axis	Depth (ins.)	Sides	Base
48	Oval	3″ × 3½″	E–W	4″	Steep	Round
49	Oval	3″ × 3½″	N–S	2″	Steep	Round
50	Circ.	3″ × 3″	–	3½″	Steep	Cupped
51	Oval	2″ × 3″	N–S	2½″	Steep	Cupped
52	Circ.	3″ × 3″	–	5″	Steep	Cupped
53	Circ.	2½″ × 2½″	–	6″	Steep	Cupped
54	Oval	4″ × 4½″	E–W	3½″	Steep	Cupped
55	Oval	4″ × 5½″	N–S	4½″	Steep	Cupped
56	Circ.	2½″ × 2½″	–	4″	Steep	Cupped
57	Circ.	2½″ × 2½″	–	4½″	Steep	Cupped
58	Circ.	4″ × 4″	–	8″	Steep	Cupped
59	Circ.	2″ × 2″	–	5½″	Steep	Cupped
60	Circ.	3″ × 3″	–	4″	Steep	Cupped
61	Oval	3½″ × 4½″	E–W	4″	Steep	Cupped
62	Circ.	3″ × 3″	–	3½″	Steep	Cupped
63	Circ.	2½″ × 2½″	–	2″	Steep	Cupped
64	Circ.	3″ × 3″	–	2½″	Steep	Cupped
65	Circ.	2½″ × 2½″	–	3½″	Steep	Cupped
66	Circ.	3″ × 3″	–	5″	Steep	Cupped
67	Circ.	2″ × 2″	–	5″	Steep	Cupped
68	Sub-Square	2½″ × 2½″	–	5″	Steep	Cupped
69	Circ.	4″ × 4″	–	5″	Steep	Cupped
70	Circ.	3″ × 3″	–	4″	Steep	Cupped
71	Circ.	5″ × 5″	–	6″	Steep	Cupped
72	Oval	3″ × 3½″	E–W	6″	Steep	Cupped
73	Circ.	2½″ × 2½″	–	5″	Steep	Flat

Table 31. Details of stake-holes on late hut terrace over North Timber Building.

Considering the evidence of the horizontal stratigraphy, together with its general position, it seems fairly certain that this ditch (F.1197/1175) was of the same date as the hut-terrace.

On the north side, the ditch (F.1197) was traced for a minimum distance of 15′. It was some 1′4″ wide and just 7″ deep. It had sloping sides and a flat base and was filled with a light brown loam, devoid of finds. There was a neatly rounded terminal at the east end, corresponding roughly with the north-east corner of the terrace-cut.

It seems likely, in fact, that both this ditch and the hut-terrace respect the north–south overflow channel leading from the north-east water tank nearby. This overflow channel would, thus, have effectively provided a corresponding gully on the east side of the hut. Water for use in the supposed iron forge could also have been brought from the water-tank, via this channel and the juxtaposition of these two structures may thus be more than coincidence.

The west arm of the ditch (F.1175) was also traced for a minimum distance of 15′. It had a U-shaped profile with sloping sides and a cupped base. It was 1′3″ to 1′5″ wide and just 5″ deep. Its fill was a dark brown loam with Roman tile fragments and it produced a total of 19 coarse-ware potsherds, representing 13 different vessels. One of these, a straight-sided dish, has been illustrated (No. 832). Nearly all of these sherds are of sandy Roman fabrics, but many are fragmentary and of somewhat indeterminate date. Some are quite likely to be residual and three early-Roman grog-tempered sherds are certainly residual. The latest sherds seem to be broadly of late-3rd to 4th centuries A.D. date.

The Dating Evidence for the Probable Late Hut.

The position of this supposed hut structure within the overall site sequence has been described above. It is clearly a late feature and this is confirmed by the finds within it.

The dark brown loam forming the general filling of the terrace-cut produced no coins or samian ware, but three mortaria have been illustrated (Nos. 922–924). This soil filling also produced a total of 692 coarse-ware potsherds and these represent at least 67 different vessels. Five of these have been drawn (Nos. 827–831). The bulk of this ceramic material is of late-3rd to 4th century A.D. date and includes 48 sherds of grey Alice Holt Ware (No. 828), some 30 small sherds of Oxfordshire Ware (not illustrated) and three small sherds of New Forest Parchment Ware (not illustrated), as well as 27 late-Roman grog-tempered ware sherds of 4th century A.D. date (Nos. 827 and 831), a probable Cream Sandy Ware sherd (No. 330) also of 4th century A.D. date and a range of other less distinctive Roman sandy wares (No. 829). A bone counter also came from this layer (No. 61).

The hearth (F.1201) produced 19 coarse-ware sherds representing at least ten different vessels. Included within this material were three sherds of late-Roman grog-tempered ware and a burnt Oxfordshire Ware sherd. All are too small to illustrate but the group may be broadly dated to between A.D. 250 and A.D. 400. The pit (F.1200) produced just three sherds, all of probable 3rd century A.D. date including a fragment of colour-coated ware (not illustrated). A localised soil deposit sealing the top of this pit yielded a further 65 potsherds and these represent another 13 vessels. A flanged dish has been drawn (No. 845). Significantly, this layer (S.C, L.19) also produced a 4th century A.D. coin (Coin No. 50) of Constans (dated A.D. 345–348), along with an iron knife blade (No. 73). All of the pottery from this may be dated broadly to the late-3rd to 4th centuries A.D.

It seems clear from the pottery and coin dating evidence that the terracing from this structure was filled with domestic rubbish by the mid to late-4th century A.D. and it must be that any hut had been abandoned by then. From the small amount of pottery recovered from the make-up of the hearth (F.1201) it seems that this structure cannot have been laid before about A.D. 250 and on general grounds a date of A.D. 300 seems likely for the construction of the hut.

(iii) THE NORTH-EAST AND NORTH TANKS (Figs. 21, 22, 29, 30 and 31).

Two clay-lined pits, or tanks, had been cut through the abandoned site of the North Timber Building (Fig. 21). Whether these two features were of precisely the same date is not certain, but both were clearly later than the destroyed building. It is possible that one tank represents a replacement of the other. The clay linings within these tanks suggest that they were for water storage and may, thus, be compared with the earlier South and West Tanks.

The North-East Tank (Figs. 21, 29 and 31).

This was rectangular in plan and measured about 14′6″ (east–west) by 10′ (north–south) in overall size. It had, however, been largely removed by the north-eastern terminal of the late-Roman Ditch 21a (F.1174). As originally dug for the tank the pit was some 3′3″ deep with vertical sides and a flat base (see sections on Fig. 31). The sides and base of the pit had been lined with a layer of puddled clay some 5–6″ thick. This clay was mustard-brown in colour and probably represented a water-proof lining, as seen in several other rectangular pits on the site. The lined tank thus created had a capacity of over 330 cu. ft. (*c.* 2000 gallons). It had eventually been abandoned and became filled with grey and brown loam with chalk, carbon and daub specks before being largely dug away by Ditch 21a. The lower filling of the tank, where it survived, produced two coarse-ware potsherds from a grog-tempered vessel of otherwise indeterminate date (not illustrated).

At the south-eastern corner of the tank a gully (F.1198) led downhill to the south. This appears to represent some sort of overflow arrangement and at the north end it cut through an earlier gully (F.1199) running south-east to north-west, which seems to have had a similar purpose (Fig. 29). The gully running southwards was traced for a minimum distance of about 25 feet before it had been destroyed by ploughing. It was 22–35″ wide with sloping sides and a flat base. The base of the gully entered the tank at a level 10″ higher than the top of the lining of the tank's base and was itself some 14″ deep. Four pairs of square stake-holes, just over 12″ apart, set at intervals of about 5′ were cut into the base of the gully and these suggest that this overflow channel originally had planked sides; the planks being held in place by vertical wooden stakes.

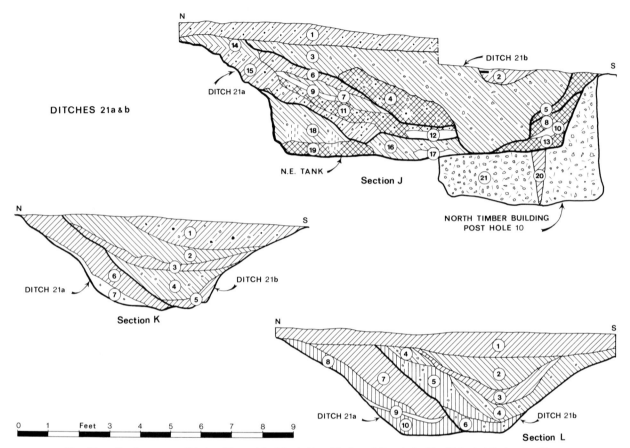

Fig. 31.   *Sections across Ditches 21a and b, North-East Tank and Post-hole 10 of North Timber Building.*

It is interesting to note that this gully occupies almost the exact line of a beam-slot which, it is supposed, once formed the outer wall of an east corridor of the North Timber Building. Whether this positioning is deliberate is not clear, but if old, rotten wooden ground-beams had been dug out and removed, the resulting trench would only require a little recutting and lining to form a very serviceable drainage gully. No other traces of the beam-slot were noted.

The earlier overflow gully running to the south-east was traced for a minimum distance of 20′ and it was between 12″ and 27″ wide and some 5″ deep. Ploughing had destroyed the south-eastern (downhill) end of the gully, but it may be significant that its projected line strikes the north end of Ditch 7, suggesting that this ditch acted as a drainage sump. There was no trace of a planked lining in this gully. The two overflow channels produced no coins, but two samian sherds came from Gully F.1198. These were a Form 33 of Hadrianic-Antonine date and a Form 31R/Lud. Sb of the later 2nd century to the first half of the 3rd century A.D. A combined total of just 42 coarse-ware potsherds, representing at least 17 vessels, was also recovered from these channels. Three mortaria sherds were also found. One mortarium sherd has been drawn (No. 927) along with one coarse-ware sherd. The coarse-ware pottery is mostly of sandy Roman fabrics of broadly 2nd to 3rd century A.D. date. There are also eight 4th century A.D. grog-tempered sherds of which one is drawn (No. 720).

The provision of overflow channels for this tank implies that it was intended to take a continuous inflow of water. If this is correct, a wooden water pipe-line bringing in fresh water from higher up the slope would have existed, as in the case of the South and West Tanks but no trace of such a pipe leading to this tank was found. From the pottery in the overflow gullies it seems that the tank went out of use sometime in the 4th century A.D.

Stake Hole No.	Shape	Size (ins.)	Main Axis	Depth (ins.)
1	Oval	$2\frac{1}{2}'' \times 3\frac{1}{2}''$	E–W	$6\frac{1}{2}''$
2	Sub-Rect.	$2'' \times 2\frac{3}{4}''$	E–W	$5''$
3	Sub-Rect.	$2\frac{1}{4}'' \times 2\frac{3}{4}''$	E–W	$5''$
4	Sub-Rect.	$2\frac{3}{4}'' \times 3''$	N–S	$5''$
5	Rect.	$2'' \times 2\frac{1}{4}''$	N–S	$5\frac{1}{2}''$
6	Rect.	$2'' \times 6\frac{1}{2}''$	E–W	$6\frac{1}{2}''$
7	Oval	$1\frac{1}{2}'' \times 3\frac{1}{4}''$	E–W	$7''$
8	D-shaped	$2\frac{1}{2}'' \times 3\frac{1}{2}''$	E–W	$8\frac{1}{2}''$
9	Oval	$3\frac{1}{2}'' \times 4\frac{1}{4}''$	E–W	$8\frac{1}{2}''$
10	Oval	$3'' \times 4''$	N–S	$8\frac{1}{2}''$

Table 32. Details of stake-holes relating to the North-East Tank overflow gully F.1198.

The North Tank (Figs. 22 and 29).

A second tank, some 40 feet to the west of the North-East Tank, was located cutting through the east of the corn-drying ovens. This tank was roughly rectangular in shape and measured 10'6" (east–west) by between 8' and 9'6" (north–south). It was just 24" deep with sloping sides and a flat base. A lining of yellow clay with some tile fragments, between 9" and 16" thick, had been placed upon the sides and base of the pit, again suggesting that the structure was intended to hold water (Figs. 22 and 29). The volume of the lined tank was about 60 cu. ft. (about 340 gallons), substantially less than the North-East Tank. This partly reflects the differential preservation of the two structures. On the northern side of this tank a short length of a possible water inlet channel was located but no overflow channels were found.

The soil filling of the tank consisted of brown loam and chalk. No coins were recovered from this filling, but a single samian sherd was discovered. This was a Dr.31/Lud. Sa. of late-2nd to mid-3rd century date. Some 71 coarse-ware potsherds were also recovered. These represent at least 20 vessels and seven of them have been drawn (Nos. 713–719). The bulk of these vessels is of sandy Roman fabrics and includes the rim of an amphora (No. 714) and a range of other fully Romanised types. Most of this material seems to be broadly dateable to the 2nd to 3rd centuries A.D. No. 716 could be of 4th century date, however. In addition, there are a few residual pieces of early, grog-tempered ware. A post-hole cutting the fill of the tank produced two later 2nd century A.D. samian sherds, two coarse-ware flanged bowls of 3rd century type (Nos. 841 and 842) and three sherds of Rhenish Ware (not illustrated).

From the pottery dating and the fact that the North Tank was cut through the remains of the burned down North Timber Building it seems clear that this tank was not filled in before the earlier 4th century A.D. It is not possible to precisely relate this tank to Ditch 21 or to the North-East Tank. Both could be either contemporary or represent successive replacements of a single structure. The pottery dating suggests that they had both gone out of use by the mid to late-4th century A.D.

(iv) THE SOUTH MASONRY BUILDING (Figs. 30, 32 and 33; Plates VII and XVIII–XXIII).

This major Roman building was situated at the extreme southern end of the excavated area, set up on a slight terrace cut into the hillside on the 400 foot contour (Fig. 32). It lay some 70 feet south-east of the West Masonry Building and was largely excavated in 1968, with the east end being completed in 1969. The supposed southern wall of the building lay beyond the limits of the excavation and this has not been investigated. The structure had previously been located in 1854 by Mr. G.A. Corner and a small-scale plan and short report on this work was published in *Archaeologia* the following year (Ref. 69). It would appear that the building was rather better preserved then, although it is likely that some stone-robbing had already taken place (Plate VII). Subsequent ploughing had caused considerably more damage to the structure since this first excavation and much of the building did not survive above foundation-level in 1968. Very little Roman stratigraphy had survived the heavy ploughing and earlier excavation (Plate XIX).

As revealed in 1968–69, the structure consisted of a large, rectangular masonry building with overall dimensions of 691 feet by an estimated 43 feet (Fig. 32). It partially overlay an earlier timber building of Period Va (the South Timber Building). The axis of the masonry structure was east–west across the slope of the hill. In plan, it consisted of a central range, surrounded by a wide corridor on at least three sides. There are some difficulties in reconciling the present site-plan with that of 1854 and it is clear that much was missed in the 19th century excavations, but it is just possible that the earlier plan records some walls totally destroyed by 1968–69.

The Victorian plan also shows a rectangular central range surrounded by a wide corridor on only the north and west sides. The main range is shown sub-divided by four cross-walls and a single cross-wall centrally divides the north corridor. In size and shape, the main range of the Victorian plan closely matches the central range of the structure as drawn on the present plan. The overall dimensions of the Victorian plan, however, show the building as being rather shorter in both length and width than revealed by the recent excavations.

The best way to reconcile the two plans is to assume that the true outer walls of the building on the east and south sides were not actually located in the 1854 excavations. The south and east walls shown on the 19th century plan, in fact, seem to be those of the central range rather than the outer corridor. If this is correct then the walls shown on the 19th century plan linking the north corridor wall with the main east wall of the main range, and linking the west corridor wall with the south wall of the main range would probably represent dividing walls within the outer corridor. No trace of either of these walls survived in 1968. Assuming that they did originally exist (and, given the standard of Victorian excavation and recording, this need not be the case) it seems possible that they are late additions, similar to the three cross-walls located in the recent excavations (two of which were missed by the Victorians).

Two walls, forming a passage across the central range, were recorded in 1968 and these can be recognised on the earlier plan, together with two others. These two other walls, of which only the slightest traces survived in 1968, appear to be later additions, probably contemporary with those dividing the corridor.

In conclusion then, it seems clear that the Victorian excavators failed to recognise robbed or heavily plough-damaged walls and they assumed they had reached the limits of the building when the obvious masonry came to an end. This produced an incomplete plan, which was in any case published at too small a scale to be very clear. The present excavations have thus added greatly to our knowledge of this heavily damaged structure.

1) The Structure (Figs. 32 and 33).

The building had been constructed on a slight terrace cut to a depth of up to 1'6" into the sloping chalk hillside. This terracing had led to the reasonable survival of the walls on the northern, uphill side, whilst on the downhill side ploughing had progressively destroyed virtually everything except very faint traces of foundations (Fig. 33).

At least two phases of construction (Phases 1 and 2) were recognised in the 1968–69 excavations. In Phase 2, cross-walls had been added to the central range and the outer corridor surrounding it had been divided by at least three short cross-walls on the north and west sides. The Victorian plan suggests that there could originally have been more of these, of which no trace now survives.

a) The Outer Corridor Wall (Phase 1).

The central range was surrounded on the north, east and west sides by a wide corridor or gallery, between 7'1" and 7'11" in width (internally). Its outer walls were best preserved on the north side and here consisted of a mortared flint wall of two distinct widths (Plates XXI–XXIII). The lower part of the wall was 2' wide and about 1' high. This was surmounted by a second stage, only 1'6" wide, which survived to a height of between 6" and 1'9". This was offset on the lower wall by some 3" on either side. In the central sector, this upper wall appeared to have been subsequently removed for a distance of some 14'; either to enlarge or create an entrance into a new passage which had been formed by two walls inserted across the corridor at this point in Phase 2 (see below, Plate XX).

The west wall of the outer corridor was less well-preserved, but appeared to be of a similar construction to the north wall. Only a short length of the upper level survived near the north-west corner, but at the south end all trace of the wall had been destroyed by ploughing. The east wall of the corridor had been almost completely robbed, but was presumably of similar character. The presence of this broad corridor is similar to the West Masonry Building and may again show some Gallic influence. It may be reasonably assumed that the corridor continued along the southern side of the building, but this was not excavated.

b) Later Additions to the Corridor (Phase 2).

The excavations in 1968 revealed three walls running across the width of the outer corridor. Two of these occurred in the centre of the north side and the other ran between the north-west corner of the central range and the west wall of the corridor. All of them appeared to be later additions.

The Entrance and the two Cross-Walls in the North Corridor.

These were situated close to the centre of the north corridor and were just 9'9" apart. Each was 1'5" in width, the west one surviving to a height of 12" and the east to about 9". They were constructed of flints set in white mortar and were clearly later additions, running over the lower wall of the corridor on the north side and apparently butting up to the outside wall of the central range on the south (although this has been largely robbed here).

It seems fairly clear that these two walls represent a cross-passage built through the corridor at a late date. At the same time, the upper (external) wall of the corridor on the north side appears to have been removed in order to form a doorway into the passage, which itself seems to have led to a middle room now created in the central range. Outside the north corridor wall, a spread of flint rubble probably represented a metalled area outside the new entrance and this contained two indeterminate Roman potsherds. Two thin layers of rammed chalk over a mixed layer of chalk, mortar and flints between the two passage walls probably represent successive floor levels to the passage (Fig. 33; S.P, L.16). A thin soil layer between these produced 14 Roman potsherds, including a sherd of 4th century A.D. New Forest Parchment Ware (not illustrated).

The Cross-wall at the North-West Corner of the Main Range.

This cross-wall was also a later addition and extended the line of the north wall of the central range across the west corridor (Plate XXI). It was 1'6" in width and survived to a height of just 7", again being constructed of mortared flints. The construction of this wall created a long, narrow room (the North-West Room) in the north-west angle of the building, which measured 27'9" (east–west) by 7'1" (north–south), being bounded on the east side by the northern cross-passage.

Other Cross-walls.

Study of the 19th century plan and engraving of the building suggests that two other cross-walls may have once existed in the outer corridor. One of these ran from the south-west corner of the central range across the west corridor in a similar fashion to the wall of the north-west corner. The other ran from the north-east corner of the central range across the north corridor. No trace of either of these walls was noted in 1968, unless the small projection on the south-west corner of the central range represents the last remains of a cross-wall there. The purpose of these added walls seems to have been to create one, if not a series, of narrow rooms within the corridor. It is likely that these were store rooms.

c) The Corridor Floors.

No trace of a solid floor was noted in any part of the corridor, although a limited series of brown loam and carbon deposits did seem to represent occupational layers (Fig. 33; S.N, L.6) over the natural chalk. These produced a total of just three potsherds, all probably of later-3rd or 4th century A.D. date and including one Alice Holt fragment. These were all too fragmentary for illustration.

The Shallow Slots (North-West Room).

A series of six parallel gullies or slots cut into the underlying chalk and running north–south were located in the north corridor (Fig. 33; S.P, L.8–10). They were confined to the North-West Room created by the added cross-walls. These gullies were all filled with a brown loam and varied in width from between 1'3" and 2'. Each had sloping sides and a rounded base, but none was more than 6" deep. The gullies were evenly spaced between 4' and 5' apart (centre to centre) and it seems likely that they originally held wooden cross-beams supporting a raised timber floor. A similar supported floor arrangement was found in the Period VI North Timber Building at Keston and also at Gadebridge Park villa, Hertfordshire (Ref. 70). Three shallow gullies in the west corridor of the South Masonry Building, running east–west, could represent similar floor supports. A total of twelve potsherds was recovered from the filling of the slots. All of these seem to be of late-3rd to 4th century A.D. date and include two Alice Holt sherds (none illustrated).

d) The Central Range (Phases 1 and 2).

The corridor enclosed a central range measuring some 45' (east–west) by 19' (north–south) internally. The walls were constructed of flint nodules set in white mortar with a single tile bonding course surviving in places. In general, the walls were poorly preserved and only the foundation course survived in many areas. Where surviving, the outside walls were 1'11" to 2' in width and were up to 12" high. The Central Range, in Phase 1, was subdivided by a pair of contemporary cross-walls which created an East Room and a West Room of broadly similar size, separated by a narrow passage.

The West Room was 19' square and traces of a rammed chalk floor survived in places on the northern side (Fig. 33; S.O, L.12). This floor produced a total of ten potsherds, all probably of late-3rd to fourth century A.D. date and including two sherds from an Alice Holt vessel (none illustrated). A thin carbon occupation layer over this floor produced two more potsherds (not illustrated), one being of Alice Holt Ware. Below the chalk floor a layer of flint pebbles and yellow mortar (S.O, L.13) seems to represent an earlier floor or construction level. This mortar layer produced four potsherds, three of Alice Holt Ware and one Oxfordshire Ware sherd, all probably of early-4th century A.D. date (none illustrated). It sealed a thin layer of brown loam (S.O, L.14) which produced five potsherds, all late-Roman, and including two colour-coated fragments, perhaps New Forest Ware, also too small to draw.

A later (Phase 2) north–south wall line was traced on the eastern side of the West Room. This was badly damaged, but its width seems to have been 1′4″ to 1′6″. The base of this added wall stood at a higher level than the other walls. It was set in a yellow mortar and butted up to the outer north wall of the range (S.O, L.16). The construction of this wall would have reduced the width of the room to about 14′.

The East Room measured 18′ (east–west) by 19′ (north–south). No trace of a floor survived, although a thin layer of brown loam adjacent to the west wall probably represents an occupation deposit (Fig. 33; S.O, L.31). This produced two Alice Holt sherds (too small for illustration). There were slight traces of a shallow, linear, north–south depression at one point along the north wall, which seems to suggest the line of a later (Phase 2) cross-wall, corresponding to that in the West Room. If this is correct, the East Room seems to have been reduced in width to some 11′ (the plan of 1854 does show a wall here).

The central passage between the two rooms was originally (in Phase 1) 5′ wide and was defined by two walls, between 1′11″ and 2′ in width and surviving to a height of only 2–3″. Traces of a rammed chalk floor survived between these. The two probable later walls, built on either side of the passage, seem to represent a widening of that passage in order to form a new central room, some 16′9″ across, in Phase 2. Access to this central room appears to have been from a new passage across the north corridor.

Under the central range a large clay-lined tank (the South Tank) was located (S.O, L.23–29). This clearly pre-dated the structure and contained pottery of late-1st to early-2nd century A.D. date. A series of pits and post-holes was also located beneath the building. At least some of these seem to relate to a substantial, early-Roman timber building (the South Timber Building), probably of early-2nd century A.D. date (S.P, L.22). The rest of the post-holes are also probably of earlier Roman date, although most did not produce any dateable material.

2) The Dating Evidence.

Stratigraphy in and around the South Masonry Building had been largely destroyed and the dating for the structure is, thus, somewhat imprecise. The site evidence, however, showed that the South Masonry Building post-dated the earlier Timber framed Structure of Period Va and also a clay-lined pit or tank assigned to Period VI. The post-holes of the timber building produced finds of the second half of the 1st century A.D., including a coin of Claudius I (Coin No. 6). This dating material, however, appears to be residual and the building has been assigned to Period V (c. A.D. 160–200). The clay-lined tank seems to be a little later and has been assigned to Period VI (the main villa complex, c. A.D. 200–300). It thus seems fairly clear that the present structure was not erected earlier than the late-3rd century A.D. The few stratified deposits which survived within the South Masonry Building, in the form of floors and occupational layers produced small amounts of broadly late-3rd to 4th century A.D. pottery, including Alice Holt, Oxfordshire and New Forest wares (all too fragmentary for illustration).

Six coins were found, all in the soil over the South Masonry Building during the present excavations. Four late-Roman coins came from the plough soil above the building (Coin Nos. 14, 17, 37 and 57), with a barbarous radiate (Coin No. 29) coming from the hillwash on the north side of the building and an illegible late-Roman coin (Coin No. 73) from a deposit over the cross-passage in the central range (S.O, L.30). The earlier excavation of the building in the last century produced a coin of Valens. Previously found coins of Victorinus, Claudius-Gothicus, Carausius, Allectus, Clodius Albinus (one each) and two of Constantine I had been found on the surface here (Ref. 71).

The demolition deposits over the South Masonry Building also produced 22 samian sherds. These were: a mortarium fragment of late-2nd century A.D. date; six Form 31 sherds of Antonine date; two of Form 37 of c. A.D. 75–95 (No. 145) and c. A.D. 100–125 (No. 146); a

Form 45 of late-2nd to mid-3rd century A.D. date; a Form 18/31 or 31 of Antonine date; a Walters 79R or Lud. TgR sherd of later 2nd century A.D. date; a Form 31R/Lud. Sb sherd and a sherd of Form 31/Lud. Sa, both of the late-2nd to mid-3rd century A.D.; two sherds of Form 36, one Hadrianic-Antonine, the other Flavian; three sherds of Form 33 of Antonine date; two of Curle 21 (Antonine) and two uncertain fragments, one South Gaulish and one Central Gaulish. The fill of the terrace-cut for the building produced a further two samian sherds; a Form 36 (etc.) fragment of probable Antonine date and a Form 31 sherd of the Antonine period. Two more sherds came from the plough soil. Several coarse-ware mortarium sherds were also recovered. One (unstratified) example has been illustrated (No. 921).

A total of 1619 sherds of coarse-ware pottery was recovered from the various soil deposits over the South Masonry Building. These represent at least 166 different vessels and some 31 of these have been illustrated here (Nos. 780–808). Residual, early-Roman material is quite extensively represented within the assemblage, no doubt being derived from the earlier structures located below the main building and adjacent areas. A quantity of sherds from the Keston kilns, including Gallo-Belgic platters and butt-beakers occur within this early material. One lid of kiln ware is illustrated (No. 808). An early-Roman bead rim bowl has also been drawn (No. 805). Over half of the pottery recovered, however, is of late-Roman fabrics. These are mainly sandy wares with 182 Alice Holt grey-ware sherds (Nos. 803 and 806); six sherds of 'cream sandy ware' of 4th century A.D. date (No. 786); seven Oxfordshire Ware sherds (Nos. 798 and 801); eight sherds of New Forest Ware (No. 804); three sherds of Much Hadham Ware (not illustrated) and one piece of Argonne Ware (not illustrated). Considerable amounts of late-Roman grog-tempered ware, dateable to the 4th century A.D., were also present (Nos. 780, 781, 794, 795 and 799). Of special interest amongst this material is a large hand-made storage jar (No. 780).

Apart from the obviously earlier material it would seem that the pottery from the soil over the South Masonry Building may be dated to the late-3rd to 4th centuries A.D., a whole range of typical late-Roman forms and fabric types being present.

Eight small-finds from the deposits over the South Masonry Building have also been illustrated. These are: a late-3rd to 4th century A.D. cross-bow brooch (No. 100); a sheet bronze fragment (No. 128); a buckle (No. 115); a penannular brooch (No. 99); a bead fragment (No. 113); an antler pick (No. 54); a stylus (No. 74) and a pottery wheel (No. 34). There is also an unstratified bronze chain segment (No. 126) and the general soil layer immediately to the north of the building produced a bronze fitting (No. 124) and an iron spike (No. 83). The plough soil immediately to the north of the building produced a spindle-whorl (No. 47).

There seems little doubt from the coin and pottery dating that the South Masonry Building was occupied until the end of the Roman period. Overall, it seems clear that the South Masonry Building was intensively occupied throughout the 4th century A.D. Exactly when the structure was first built however, is less certain. It clearly post-dated the clay-lined tank apparently relating to Period VI. More significantly, a floor or construction level in the West Room of the central range sealed a thin deposit of brown loam which must represent either a pre-building soil deposit or an occupation layer associated with an early phase of the building's use. This soil layer produced five pottery sherds (none illustrated), including two fragments from a colour-coated vessel, perhaps New Forest Ware, probably of late-3rd to 4th century A.D. date. From this it would seem likely that the South Masonry Building was constructed no earlier than c. A.D. 275 and perhaps some significant time after this. The floor layers directly above this soil deposit produced further fragments of late-3rd to 4th century A.D. coarse pottery which tends to confirm this view.

From the general layout of the South Masonry Building, it seems fairly clear that it represents a domestic, rather than agricultural structure. There was no evidence of any hypocausted rooms here, however, nor of any bath-suite and it is probable that the West Masonry Building baths continued to be used throughout the period of the South Masonry Building's occupation. The demolition deposits over the South Masonry Building produced a number of fragments of painted wall-plaster, underlining the domestic nature of the building. The apparent absence of hypocausted rooms and any evidence for tessellated floors, however, suggests that the structure was soundly constructed but not pretentious. In general plan, the Keston building, covering an estimated 2967 sq. ft., may be compared with the Block 'A' of the Roman villa complex at South Darenth (some ten miles to the north-east). There, a slightly larger structure with a similar layout has been interpreted as a 'guest-house' (Ref. 72).

In view of the previous site layout (Fig. 17) and of the present building's apparently late date, it seems possible that in some way, the South Masonry Building at Keston represents a later replacement of the destroyed North Timber Building, for there is no evidence to assume that the West Masonry Building was abandoned at this time. The North Timber Building, however, appears to have had a purely agricultural function and was rather larger than the South Masonry Building. This point, together with the fact that the South Masonry Building seems to have been primarily a dwelling without any obvious agricultural functions, suggests that the South Masonry Building was not a direct rebuild in stone of the earlier timber structure on a new site. Yet there are some interesting similarities in the ground plans (see above). Both structures consist of a central area, surrounded by an outer corridor. The corridors and central range are, interestingly, both of similar widths. The South Masonry Building is, however, fairly exactly three-quarters the length of the North Timber Building. Also significant, perhaps, is the fact that on a number of other villa sites, excavation has shown that an original aisled barn of purely agricultural function developed over the centuries into a stone-built domestic dwelling. The same sequence may occur at Keston, but with a marked change in the siting of the successive structures.

BABY BURIALS ADJACENT TO THE SOUTH MASONRY BUILDING (Fig. 32).

A group of four very shallow pits containing baby burials (Burials A–D) was located in 1969, to the east of the South Masonry Building. Burials B and C were set close to (though not under) the line of the east wall of the building, with the other two being further to the east and well apart.

These burials are assumed to be contemporary with the occupation of the South Masonry Building. Table 33 below summarises the details. It seems probable that the burials were made by the occupants of the South Masonry Building. None of the grave-pits produced any pottery and cannot, therefore, be securely dated. No detailed examination of the human remains has yet been undertaken, but it may be possible to incorporate such a study in the next volume.

Burial	Grave Shape	Size (ins.)	Main Axis	Depth below Ground Level (ins.)	Notes
A	Circ.	7″ × 7″	–	12″	Body Disturbed
B	Oval	5″ × 13″	NE–SW	12″	Head at N.E.
C	Oval	7″ × 9″	NE–SW	16″	Head at N.E.
D	Oval	7″ × 10″	SE–NW	23″	Head at S.E.

Table 33. Details of baby burials outside the east wall of the South Masonry Building.

(v) THE UPPER EAST METALLING AND THE CENTRE METALLING (Figs. 4, 11, 12, 18, 30, 34 and 35).

These two areas of late-Roman metalling both relate to the upper level of metalling found in 1973–4, on the eastern side of the site (p. 63, Fig. 30). The most extensive (the Upper East Metalling) clearly overlay the corresponding Lower East Metalling (Figs. 18 and 35) and also extended roughly north-east by south-west. This, too, seems to represent a laid road, or track, leading from the villa site. It had a maximum width of 21 feet, was traced for a minimum distance of 104 feet and clearly continued beyond the limit of excavation in both directions (Fig. 34). A slight terrace, (cut-out A and B) some 4″ to 8″ deep, on the north-west side had been cut into the hillside just above the 400 foot contour to allow the construction of this trackway (Fig. 35).

The metalling consisted of large to medium sized flint pebbles with tile, bone and some flint nodules and was 1″ to 3″ thick. This road was partially laid on a dump of clay, soil and chalk, which sealed the South-East Ditch of the Villa Enclosure and an earlier road both, interestingly, on the same alignment (Figs. 18 and 35). The later metalling had subsided into the fill of the ditch and towards the western end of the exposed length a spread of flint nodules, roughly 12 feet in diameter, appeared to represent a partial repair of this hollow.

A probable continuation of this metalling had been previously noted some 80 feet further to the south-west (the Centre Metalling). Work in 1968 and 1970 towards the southern side of the excavated area had revealed a heavily damaged, irregular spread of metalling (Figs. 11 and 12), partly sealing the filled in first century Quarry Pit Complex. This metalled area measured some 20 feet (north-east to south-west) by 50 feet (north-west to south-east) and it seems likely that it had only been preserved here because it had subsided into the earlier features. The metalling consisted of flint pebbles, flint nodules, tiles and chalk fragments and was 1″ to 3″ thick. Part of this metalling had been cut away by a later ditch (Ditch 5) of post-Roman date.

To the south and south-west of this main Centre Metalling several small isolated patches of pebbling occurred. Together, all these areas probably represent a continuation of the road or track and suggest that ploughing and burrowing animals have destroyed most of its south-west extension. From the surviving fragments, however, it seems likely that this trackway originally led to the north side of the South Masonry Building. An entrance to the building existed here, at least in its Phase 2 arrangement. Towards the eastern end a chalk-block structure (Fig. 34) had been cut into the surface of this trackway after it had gone out of use.

The Dating Evidence for the Upper East Metalling and the Centre Metalling.

There is clear evidence to show that this trackway was of late-Roman date. Above the South-East Ditch of the Villa Enclosure at the east end, a coin (Coin No. 58) of the House of Constantine (A.D. 350–360) was found lying on the surface of the road. Above the Quarry Pits the two isolated patches of metalling contained a coin (Coin No. 12) of Gallienus (A.D. 260–268) and an issue (Coin No. 42) of Urbs Roma (A.D. 330–345) within their make-up.

The soil over the metalling also produced several coins. At the east end a (residual) coin (Coin No. 8) of Trajan (A.D. 98–117) was found. In the Quarry Pits area the soils directly over the roadway produced: a coin (Coin No. 7) of Claudius I (A.D. 43–54); one (Coin No. 15) of Claudius II (A.D. 270); two (Coin Nos. 20 and 21) of Tetricus I (A.D. 270–273); two (Coin Nos. 26 and 33) Barbarous Radiates (A.D. 270–290); one (Coin No. 35) of Constantine I (A.D. 318–320) and another (Coin No. 39) of the same emperor (A.D. 337–340); one coin (Coin No. 41) of Constantine II (A.D. 335–337) and another (Coin No. 60) of the House of Constantine (A.D. 350–360). The hillwash deposit sealing this layer here produced two more coins, another Barbarous Radiate (A.D. 270–290; Coin No. 27) and an issue of Gratian (Coin No. 68; A.D. 367–378). This coin is one of the latest coins from the site. The hillwash above the road metalling at the east end produced a coin (Coin No. 65) of Valentinian I (A.D. 365–375).

Several samian sherds were recovered from the make-up of the roadway (Nos. 147 and 149) and the soil directly above it (No. 148). The latest of this material is of later 2nd to mid-3rd century A.D. date, but in view of the coin evidence it seems clear that all this samian is residual.

On the eastern side, the trackway produced some 315 sherds of coarse pottery and these represent at least 52 different vessels. The great majority of this material appears to be residual and ranges in date from the 1st to the 2nd century A.D. A few sherds of Keston Kiln Ware are included in this material (not illustrated). Some later material is, however, also present and this includes typical late-Roman sandy wares (Nos. 809 and 812) and grog-tempered vessels (No. 810), together with a single sherd of Oxfordshire Ware (not illustrated). A residual sherd from a flint-tempered vessel (No. 811) is also drawn.

A further 208 coarse-ware sherds were recovered from the metalling in the Quarry Pits area. These represent at least 46 different vessels and again most of these seem to be residual and are dateable to the 1st and 2nd centuries A.D. Much of the material is small and abraded. None may be usefully illustrated.

The brown and black loam deposits sealing the trackway at the eastern end produced over 800 sherds of coarse pottery (Fig. 18, L.2 and 3; Fig. 35, L.3 and 4). These represent at least 74 different vessels and nine of these have been drawn (Nos. 813–821). This material ranges in date from the late-1st to the 4th centuries A.D., but a very large residual element is present, as with the actual make-up of the road. Two Iron Age flint-tempered sherds have been drawn (Nos. 819 and 821) together with an everted rim jar (No. 813) of typical pre-Conquest form. Later wares present in the assemblage are all somewhat fragmentary but include a small number of sherds of Oxfordshire Ware (none illustrated), Alice Holt Ware (none illustrated) and 4th century A.D. Cream Sandy Ware (No. 814) as well as a few sherds of Nene Valley Ware, too small to draw. A number of 4th century A.D. grog-tempered sherds are present and one vessel has been illustrated (No. 818). One earlier grog-tempered vessel has also been included (No. 817). The majority of the sherds, however, is of several Romanised wares and include everted rim jars (No. 816), flanged dishes (No. 815) and a jar with a rolled rim (No. 820).

The soil sealing the metalling in the area of the Quarry Pit Complex produced a total of 377 potsherds (Fig. 12; S.B, L.4). These represent at least 40 vessels (none illustrated). Once again a very high proportion of the material represents earlier residual pieces. There are some late wares present, however, and these include 14 sherds of Alice Holt Ware, three Oxfordshire Ware sherds and eight pieces of late-Roman grog-tempered ware.

The soil under the metalling on the eastern side (Figs. 18 and 35) produced a total of 828 coarse ware potsherds. These represent at least 64 different vessels of which just eight have been drawn (Nos. 721–728). The bulk of this material is dateable from the pre-Conquest period to the late-1st to 2nd century A.D. and is clearly residual. A small amount of later material is, however, also present and this includes a single Oxfordshire Ware sherd (not illustrated). Of the illustrated material there are: four flint-tempered sherds all clearly from vessels of pre-Roman date (No. 722, 723, 725 and 728); two shell-tempered bead rim jars (No. 726) and a sandy everted rim jar (No. 727).

The soil directly under the metalling in the central part of the site yielded only a few early-Roman potsherds (Fig. 12). More importantly it also contained a coin (Coin No. 13) of Gallienus, dated A.D. 260–268.

Several small-finds have also been illustrated. From the actual make-up of the trackway came a small baked clay container (No. 42) and an iron ferrule (No. 71), both from the Centre Metalling. The East Metalling produced an antler rake-head (No. 56). The soil over the East Metalling produced two iron implements (Nos. 66 and 67); a bronze bow-brooch of 1st century A.D. date (No. 86) and a bronze bracelet (No. 107). The soil below the East Metalling yielded: a flint scraper (No. 7); a Hod Hill-type brooch (No. 85) of 1st century A.D. date and a bronze stud (No. 127). The soil below the Centre Metalling contained an iron fitting (No. 84) and a bronze bracelet (No. 108). In addition, two more 1st century A.D. brooches (Nos. 89 and 98) came from the overlying general soil deposits south of the East Metalling.

Despite the considerable amounts of residual material recovered, the date of this trackway seems fairly clear. Unusually, the coins provide the most useful evidence. Of the two coins discovered within the metalling, one is of mid-4th century A.D. date (Coin No. 42) and the other is of the mid-3rd century A.D. (Coin No. 12). Another 4th century coin was actually found lying on the surface of the road (Coin No. 58) and a late-3rd century A.D. coin was found in the soil under the Centre Metalling (Coin No. 13). From these coins it seems clear that the trackway could not have been laid before the period A.D. 330–345 (the date of Coin No. 42) and would have been in use at least during the period A.D. 350–360 (when Coin 58 was dropped on its surface). A number of other coins was found in the soil over the metalling. Two of these are of 1st century A.D. date and are certainly early survivals (Coin Nos. 7 and 8). There are also five late-3rd century A.D. coins (Coin Nos. 15, 20, 21, 26 and 33) which must also be residual. The other four coins are of 4th century date, all of the House of Constantine (Coin Nos. 35, 39, 41 and 60). Allowing for large residual elements in the coarse pottery assemblage associated with the metalling, the dating of the ceramic material is generally in agreement with the coin evidence.

(vi) THE EXTERNAL CORN-DRYING OVEN (Figs. 30, 36 and 38; Plate XXV).

Excavations in 1978, just outside and to the south of the North Timber Building, revealed another corn-drying oven (Fig. 36). It consisted of two large pits joined by a narrow channel, all dug into solid chalk. The main axis of the structure was east–west. The west pit (F.10) was circular in plan with a diameter of 4'6". It had partly vertical sides and a roughly flat base. Its depth was 25". Slight traces of an unburnt clay lining were noted on the sides of the pit, which was filled with a black loam. The east pit (F.8) was D-shaped in plan and measured 3'2" by 3'2". It again had vertical sides and a roughly flat base. It was 20" deep and traces of an unburnt clay lining were again observed. It was also filled with black loam.

A rectangular channel connected these two pits. It was 4'6" in length (east–west) by 1'4" in width (north–south). It was 20" deep and had a yellow clay lining, some 7" thick, which had been burnt red by fierce heat. Two groups of tiles were found in the channel and these seemed to represent some collapsed part of the superstructure of the oven, which did not otherwise survive.

The precise arrangements of this structure above ground cannot now be certain, but it seems likely that the west pit represents a stoke-pit with the central channel as the actual furnace and the east pit as the heating chamber of the oven. This arrangement would then closely compare with a bowl furnace, well-known on a number of Roman sites (Ref. 73). No trace of any cover-building over the structure was found.

The filling of this corn-drying oven (Fig. 38) produced a total of 217 coarse-ware potsherds and these represent at least 45 different vessels. Five of these have been drawn (Nos. 822–826). All of this material is of late-3rd to late-4th century A.D. date and includes: some 45 sherds of 4th century A.D. grog-tempered ware (Nos. 823 and 824); three Oxfordshire Ware fragments (No. 822); 62 pieces of Alice Holt Ware (No. 825) together with three New Forest Ware sherds (not illustrated). There is also a mortarium fragment which has been drawn (No. 928). It seems most likely that this oven was abandoned and filled with domestic rubbish and some residual material sometime in the mid to late-4th century A.D. An antler fragment from the heating chamber has been drawn (No. 57), together with a bone pin (No. 63) and a quernstone fragment (No. 135) from the stoke-pit.

It is of interest to note that the later of two overflow channels leading from the North-East Tank (Period VII) heads straight towards this oven (Fig. 30). It seems highly unlikely that waste water would have been allowed to discharge in the area of the corn-drying oven when in use and from this it follows that these two features were not contemporary. The earlier overflow channel heading to the south-east could, however, have been in use when the oven was functioning.

This corn-drying oven clearly represents a much smaller, less elaborate, structure than those ovens built within the North Timber Building during Period VI (Fig. 21). Whether it also represents a direct replacement of the earlier structures is not clear. What is clear is that the later corn-drying oven was only able to deal with much smaller quantities of material than those of the earlier period. This could imply that some major changes had taken place in grain production, or its processing, during Period VII.

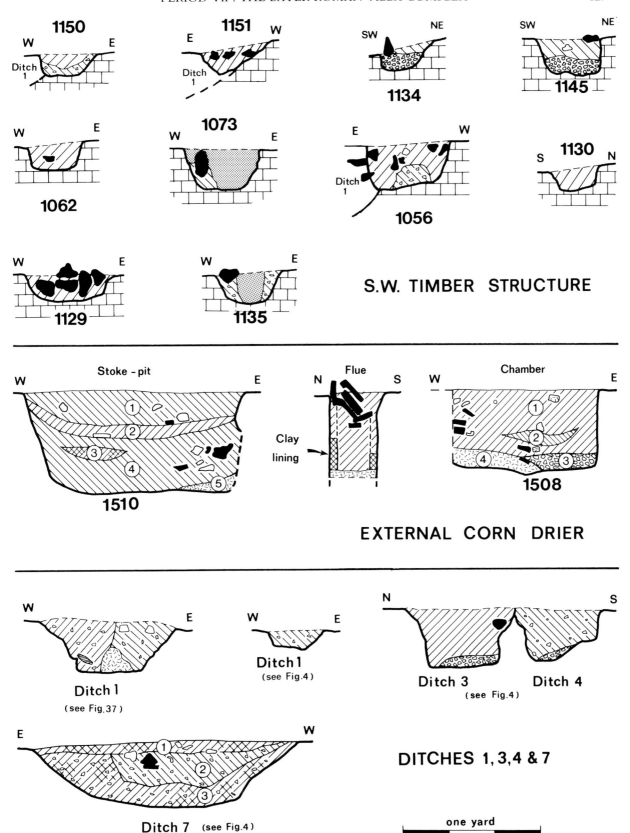

Fig. 38. *Sections across post-holes of South-West Timber Structure, External Corn Drying Oven and Ditches 1, 3, 4 and 7.*

(vii) THE LATE DITCHES CUTTING THROUGH THE NORTH TIMBER BUILDING – DITCHES 21a and 21b (F. 1174 and F.1177) (Figs. 21, 22, 30 and 31).

Excavations in 1976–77 on the site of the North Timber Building revealed the full length of a substantial ditch cutting through the remains of both the main (Period VI) structure, the North-East Tank and the late hut terrace, which themselves post-dated the North Timber Building (Ditch 21a, F.1174; Fig. 21). The ditch was some 65 feet in length and ran almost east–west, cutting through six of the post-holes forming the north side of the central range of the North Timber Building (Nos. 6–10). It removed most of the upper part of the later North-East Tank (Fig. 22) and also destroying the north-west corner of a late-Roman hut terrace and its associated gully (Ditch 14). In width, the ditch varied from 8′ to 11′ and it was between 2′7″ and 3′3″ deep. It had sloping sides and a cupped base and was filled, for the mostpart, with layers of brown and grey loam with chalk lumps (Figs. 22 and 31).

On its southern side, a second ditch (Ditch 21b, F.1177), on the same axis, had been cut through the fill of this first ditch (Figs. 22 and 31). It was not as long, being only some 41′ in length. The western terminal of the second ditch was some 18′ east of that of the earlier ditch, whilst its eastern terminal was 5′ to the west of the original east end. There seems little doubt that this second ditch represents a re-cutting of the earlier one. In width, the later ditch was between 6′ and 7′6″ and was some 2′3″ to 3′1″ in depth. The sides were sloping and the base was cupped. The filling of the later ditch was mostly of brown loam and chalk.

Some indication of the construction date of Ditch 21 is given by a coin (Coin No. 50) of Constans (A.D. 345–348) which was recovered from the filling of the hut terrace that was cut by the ditch. From this, it would seem that Ditch 21a was dug no earlier than c. A.D. 350.

The Dating Evidence from the Ditches.

No coin was recovered from the filling of the main ditch (21a), or its recut (21b). On the evidence of the coin (Coin No. 50) from the filling of the hut terrace cut by the ditches, however, Ditch 21a cannot be earlier than about A.D. 350).

A number of samian sherds was discovered in the filling of Ditch 21a. Its lower filling produced a small sherd of Central Gaulish samian of uncertain form and a later 2nd century A.D. mortarium base. The upper filling contained a Form 31 (Antonine), a Form 31R (mid to late-Antonine), an East Gaulish sherd of later-2nd to mid-3rd century A.D. date, a Form 37 (No. 144, of later 2nd to early-3rd century A.D.), a Form 38 of similar date and a Form 31R/Lud. Sb of later 2nd to mid-3rd century A.D. date. All of this samian, however, must be residual in the light of the coarse pottery and coin evidence.

The fill of Ditch 21a produced a total of 539 coarse-ware pottery sherds. These represent at least 54 vessels and 22 of these have been drawn (Nos. 729–749). The bulk of this ceramic material (479 sherds) came from the upper fill of the ditch, with a further 54 sherds from the middle fill and just six fragments from the lower fill.

A total of 105 sherds is of early-Roman native wares, predominantly grog-tempered (none illustrated). These are clearly residual in the present context. Virtually all of the rest of the pottery recovered (426 sherds) is of coarse, sandy Roman wares, mainly everted rim jars (Nos. 732, 737, 738, 742, 745 and 746), flanged rim bowls (Nos. 733, 736, 739, 744 and 749) or straight-sided dishes (Nos. 731 and 748). There are seven sherds of grey Alice Holt Ware (Nos. 729, 741 and 743). In addition, there are three sherds of late-Roman grog-tempered ware, all too small to illustrate. Roman fine-wares are represented by five colour-coated sherds comprising three of Nene Valley Ware (Nos. 730 and 734), one of New Forest type and one of Rhenish type (not illustrated).

This pottery ranges in date from the late-1st/2nd to the 4th centuries A.D. The sherds in the lower fill are somewhat indeterminate, but seem to be of late-1st to 2nd century date and must be residual. The pottery from the middle fill is mostly of 2nd to 3rd century date, though one Alice Holt Ware sherd (No. 729) could date to the 4th century. The material in the upper filling includes a significant amount of 1st to 2nd century A.D. material as well as 3rd and 4th century pottery. Overall, it seems likely that the ditch was completely silted up by the late-4th century

A.D. Some of the earlier pottery contained within its filling is likely to be derived from the North Timber Building of Period VI.

No coins or samian ware were recovered from the filling of the recut Ditch 21b. A total of 4 mortarium sherds was recovered, however, and one of these has been drawn (No. 919). A total of 490 coarse-ware potsherds was also recovered. These represent at least 48 vessels, of which six certainly occur also in the filling of Ditch 21a. Some 21 sherds have been illustrated (Nos. 750–770).

Early-Roman native wares account for some 72 sherds and these again must be residual. One platter base of Keston Kiln Ware has been illustrated (No. 762). There are some 385 sherds of sandy Roman wares. These include flanged bowls (Nos. 755, 758, 761, 764 and 767), bead rim dishes (Nos. 750, 765 and 770), straight-sided dishes (No. 769) and vessels with everted rims (No. 768). There are at least 39 sherds of Alice Holt grey wares (No. 764). In addition, there are 20 sherds of 4th century grog-tempered ware. Some 20 sherds of Oxfordshire Ware were also recovered. These include a dish or bowl with a small bead rim (No. 756). There are a number of other colour-coated pieces, mostly from beakers (Nos. 752, 760, 763 and 766) but also including Nene Valley Wares (Nos. 751 and 757). A piece of green-glazed medieval pottery from the uppermost fill of the ditch must be intrusive.

The upper filling of Ditch 21b produced the bulk of the pottery, as with Ditch 21a. Some 373 potsherds were recovered from the upper levels, with some 85 fragments coming from the middle fill and only 32 sherds from the lower filling. The date-range of the pottery is again largely from the late-1st/2nd to the 4th centuries A.D. All of the pottery in the lower ditch fill appears to be of 2nd to 3rd century A.D. date, whilst most of the middle fill pottery dated to the 2nd century A.D., with a little later material (No. 753). The upper ditch fill contained some earlier, late-1st to 2nd century A.D. material together with a considerable amount of later material. It seems clear from the contents of the filling of Ditch 21a, however, that it cannot have been recut much before the end of the 4th century A.D. Most of the debris in the recut ditch, therefore, must have collected here during the earlier 5th century A.D. The absence of any obviously post-Roman pottery within the ditch filling must be significant in the light of the Period VIII Anglo-Saxon occupation (see below, page 133).

Ditch 21 produced two small-finds. The original ditch produced a bone pin from its middle filling (No. 65), whilst the upper filling of the recut ditch yielded another (No. 64). No. 65 is of Crummy's Type 1 dated to c. A.D. 70–250 and must be residual. No. 64 is of Type 3 and this form has been dated to the 3rd and 4th centuries A.D. The upper filling of Ditch 21b produced some carbonised plant remains (see page 292).

The precise purpose of this late ditch and its recut is not immediately clear. It seems most likely, however, that they formed some part of the northern boundary earthworks of the villa enclosure sometime late in Period VII (Fig. 30). The very fact that the ditch was recut indicates that it served some useful and specific purpose which continued beyond the life of the original ditch.

(viii) THE SOUTH-WEST TIMBER STRUCTURE (Figs. 30, 37 and 38).

This was located in 1977 between the South and West Masonry Buildings and consisted of a simple rectangular outline formed by eleven substantial post-holes (Fig. 37). It measured 13′8″ to 15′6″ (east–west) by 14′3″ to 15′ (north–south). The post-holes were either circular or oval in plan and some still retained flint packing stones in their tops (Fig. 38). The spacings of the posts varied between 3′8″ and 5′6″ (on the south side one post-hole was missing). A series of other post-holes occurred in this area, but it is not clear whether any of them relate to the present structure. No trace of a floor survived to indicate whether this present structure was a true building; it could represent a small animal pen or compound.

The north and west walls of this structure cut through Ditch 1, which produced Alice Holt Ware of late-3rd to 4th century A.D. date (Period VIIa). The post-holes, themselves, produced just 16 potsherds, representing as many vessels. These were all of late-1st to early-2nd century A.D. date and, thus, must be residual in this context. None is, therefore, illustrated.

Table 34 below summarises the details of the post-holes. In view of the apparently late date of this structure it is just possible that it is Saxon rather than Roman, but there is no other evidence to support this idea.

Post-pit F. No.	Shape	Length (ins.)	Width (ins.)	Main Axis	Depth into chalk (ins.)	Sides	Base
1151	Circ.	13	13	–	8	Sloping	Cupped
1150	Circ.	14	14	–	6	Steep	Flat
1062	Circ.	13	13	–	7	Vert.	Flat
1073	Circ.	16	16	–	11	Steep	Flat
1129	Oval	23	20	N–S	9	Sloping	Flat
1145	Oval	18	16	N–S	8	Steep	Flat
1134	Oval	16	12	N–S	12	Steep	Flat
1135	Circ.	14	14	–	7	Sloping	Cupped
1157	Circ.	9	9	–	8	Vert.	Flat
1130	Oval	19	14	E–W	6	Steep	Flat
1056	Oval	18	16	E–W	10	Steep	Uneven

Table 34. Details of the post-pits relating to the South-West Timber Structure.

(ix) THE LATE CHALK STRUCTURE (Figs. 30 and 34).

In 1972 work on the south-eastern side of the site revealed a short length of chalk-block wall set at an angle to and cut into the top of the Upper East Metalling (Fig. 34). The wall was aligned north–south and was traced for a minimum distance of 4'9". At the north end it had been destroyed by ploughing, but it continued beyond the limit of the excavation on the south side. It was sealed by a layer of dark occupational soil, which also sealed the Upper Metalling.

The wall was constructed of chalk lumps set in soil. It was about 11½" in width and survived to a height of only a few inches. A roughly rectangular spread of chalk rubble, measuring about 6'9" (east–west) by 5' (minimum, north–south) was located some 2'6" to the west. This may be a foundation raft related to the wall. The western edge of this rubble spread was straight and it could have incorporated the base of another wall, corresponding to that on the east. The two elements can, in fact, be joined to form the reasonably regular outline of a rectangular structure, measuring some 11' (east–west) by at least 5' (north–south). Some 5' to the north-east of the east wall another spread of rubble, roughly sub-rectangular in shape and measuring about 9'6" (north–south) by 6' (east–west) was located. This could be the base of a second structure, but too little survived to be clear on this point. The first structure, however, is more certainly identifiable as the remains of a small building.

On the coin evidence, the Upper East Metalling was in use in the mid to late-4th century A.D. This must imply that the chalk building was constructed no earlier than A.D. 360 and very probably much later in the 4th century A.D., or even in the 5th century A.D. It should, thus, belong to the very end of the Roman occupation on the site, but only a little more can be said at present. It is unfortunate that the full size and shape of the structure could not be revealed during the excavations. The general absence of building debris around the structure and the narrow wall width tends to imply that its upper parts were of timber and a construction broadly similar to that employed for the much earlier Period Vb Centre Flint Structure may be envisaged, with timber uprights fixed in a horizontal wall-plate, set upon a sleeper wall of chalk blocks. Despite its late date, this method of construction seems typically Roman and tends to preclude a Saxon date. From the part of the structure which was examined, it seems likely that the remains are those of only a small building.

CHAPTER IV

THE POST-ROMAN STRUCTURES AND FEATURES

PERIOD VIII : THE ANGLO-SAXON OCCUPATION (A.D. 450–550) (Fig. 30).

1) Introduction.

The extensive excavations on the Lower Warbank site have revealed only one certain Anglo-Saxon structure. This was a sunken hut located in 1970. It was first published in 1973 (Ref. 74), but is re-published here for the sake of completeness. The pottery dating suggests that the disused hut pit was filled with domestic rubbish in the period A.D. 450–550. It thus seems likely that a phase of early-Saxon occupation followed fairly directly on from the late villa period (Period VII), albeit seemingly upon a much reduced scale when compared with the previous occupation.

The hut was situated just about in the middle of the former villa's courtyard (Fig. 30) and it may be significant that it lay just to the north of a 4th century metalled area which may still have been serviceable in part. There was no trace of any other definite Saxon structures and examination of the 25,000 plus sherds of pottery from the site has revealed only a few more possible examples of Saxon ceramic material (No. 895). Unless the main area of Saxon occupation lay beyond the limits of the present extensive excavations, it would seem that there was, in fact, only limited early-Saxon activity on the villa site. The villa site, thus, may well have been abandoned as an occupation area by the middle of the 6th century A.D. There was certainly no trace of a Mucking (Ref. 75) or Chalton (Ref. 76) type of early-Saxon village here.

The actual place-name of Keston, written Chestan in the Domesday Book, is likely to be of 5th century A.D. origin and probably derives from 'Cyssi's stone' or, perhaps more likely, 'Cyssi's stone-building'. This may well suggest that the actual Roman villa ruins stood on land belonging to one Cyssi, although this name is not otherwise documented (Ref. 77) and the problem of relating early place-names to the known archaeology of an area is notoriously difficult.

2) The Anglo-Saxon Hut (Figs. 15, 30 and 39).

The hut was first detected as a large rectangular pit cut into the underlying chalk near the centre of the site in 1970 (Fig. 15). In detail, it measured 13'3" (east–west) and 11'8" (north–south) with its longer axis following the contour of the slope. The sides had been cut almost vertical and the corners at about 90°. The base had been cut horizontally so that on the uphill (north) side it lay 1'4" beneath the surface of the solid chalk, whilst on the downhill side it was only about 8" (Fig. 39). It seems that originally it had been dug to a depth of about $1\frac{1}{2}$–2'.

Within the hut were three large post-holes and a series of 29 small stake-holes, all cut into the hard chalk floor. Externally, on the east side, was a rough arc of smaller holes which must have held small posts, but not necessarily connected with the hut. The large post-holes on the east and west sides (A and B) were each 1'8" in diameter, 1'8" in depth and had steep or vertical sides. Both were filled with compact chalk rubble which had been packed around a large upright post. No trace of the actual posts survived, but circular columns of black-brown loam, 9" in diameter, clearly indicated the positions of the wooden uprights. Post-hole C was broadly similar, but was only 1'5" in diameter and 1'6" deep. It too had contained a wooden post, $9\frac{1}{2}$" in diameter, packed around with chalk, but here the post appeared to lean slightly to the east.

An arc of four stake-holes, more or less evenly spaced, was found between Posts A and C. These appear to divide the hut into two unequal parts and it seems probable that they represent the line of a thin barrier or partition. The area to the south of this arc contained a further series of stake-holes cut into the chalk floor. These were mostly circular, about 1–3" in diameter and 2–9" deep and may have been drilled with a metal tool. Four were rectangular in shape, about 2" by 2", and probably held posts driven into the floor. No comprehensive pattern emerges, but there are several possible alignments across the hut, though these may be fortuitous. It seems possible that these stake-holes could relate to a series of looms constructed within the hut at different times (they have been considered in more detail previously: Ref. 74). No stake-holes were recorded to the north of the partition.

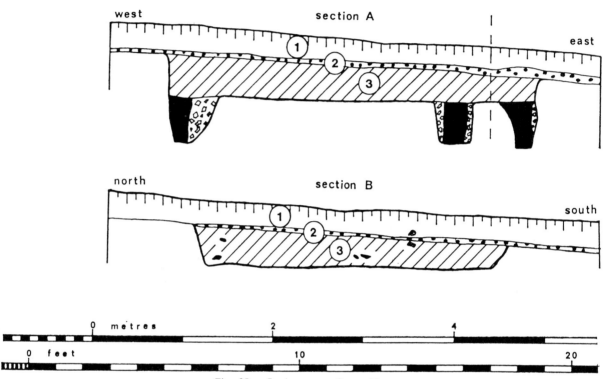

Fig. 39. *Sections across Saxon Hut.*

The filling of the hut consisted of an even black-brown loam, partially disturbed by burrowing animals (Fig. 39). There was no trace of any prepared floors, or of debris from collapsed walls or roof, or of a hearth. A total of about 360 potsherds was recovered from the filling of which about 230 were Saxon, about 125 Roman and at least four were Iron Age. There were 90 pieces of Roman tile and about 380 bones. Of the Saxon pottery, at least twelve vessels can be identified, of which only three were decorated (West Kent Nos. 467, 471 and 472: Ref 74) and all found within 6″ of the hut floor. The fragmentary nature of these vessels suggests they were deposited as domestic rubbish.

The primary layer also produced a number of other interesting objects. These include two bone pins, weaving needles of antler and bone, a bone comb, a pair of bronze tweezers and a probable lead loom-weight. Several of these items relate to a weaving process, probably carried out in the immediate vicinity or, more probably, in the hut itself. A Roman coin of Tetricus I (c. A.D. 270) was found 10″ above the hut floor and this may have been washed into the hut sometime after it was abandoned.

Three small-finds from the filling of the Saxon hut have been illustrated for this report. These are; two antler tines (Nos. 55 and 57) and a bronze toilet spoon (No. 117). None of these objects may necessarily be Saxon, however. Eight small-finds from the hut were previously published (Ref. 74, Nos. 473–480). These objects include a characteristic Saxon bone comb, but are not re-published here.

The Dating Evidence for the Anglo-Saxon Hut.

It is at once clear that this hut belongs to the Anglo-Saxon *grubenhaus* class as noted at a number of British sites, mostly of the 5th to 7th centuries A.D. (Ref. 78), having originated in northern Europe. Its size, shape and depth are typical of the *grubenhäuser* elsewhere, the major parallels being at Mucking, Essex (Ref. 79), Sutton Courtenay, Berkshire (Ref. 80) and West Stow, Suffolk (Ref. 81). The posts set partly into the sides on the long axis are characteristic features of many of these huts and must have supported a ridged roof. The middle post is not a constant feature in these huts, but it certainly occurs in huts at Sutton Courtenay, though at Keston it may have been inserted at a later date, at an angle to help support the roof or the east post.

This hut was one of the very first of its type to be found in rural Kent though Saxon huts found at Canterbury seem to have had sunken floors (Ref. 82). It seems likely that the hut was used for weaving. The bone pins, weaving needles, lead weight and bone comb all provide some evidence for this and, indeed, many of the sunken huts at Mucking and West Stow have been identified as weaving huts. The various groups of stake-holes in the Keston hut suggest light wooden structures of vertical form which may have been looms. In particular, two groups appear to relate to a single structure with a length of about 4'6". This corresponds very well with a Saxon loom identified at Sutton Courtenay (Ref. 83) which had a length of 4'6". Another similar cluster of four stake-holes found in a Saxon sunken hut at Bishopstone, Sussex (Ref. 84) in 1968 could also represent the frame of a loom. Much of the domestic rubbish in the hut appears to have been dumped into it probably after the hut had gone out of use. The large proportion of Roman material, nearly 50% of the dateable objects, must represent residual debris from the nearby Roman buildings. The animal bones include those of pigs, cattle, sheep, red and roe deer, with a considerable preference for the former, though here again a large element of Roman residual material may be present. If the bones do fairly reflect the Saxon occupation of the site then the pastoral form of farming may be indicated with sheep providing both meat for eating and wool for weaving.

The provision of a precise date for this hut, based upon the material in it, is at this early stage, somewhat difficult and a complete discussion will be published at a later date. Some of the more significant pieces of pottery have, however, been examined by Dr. J.N.L. Myers who has suggested that these may date from the 6th century A.D. Dr. Myers has also remarked that the stamped pieces look like 6th century A.D. Saxon pottery, rather than anything specifically Kentish, resembling material from Saxon sites along the Thames estuary.

Several of the other vessels seem to parallel pots recovered from 5th century A.D. huts at Mucking. The bone comb is noted on other early Saxon sites, including a 5th century A.D. hut at West Stow.

As regards the lead ring, probably a loom-weight, somewhat similar ones have been found in Saxon huts of the 5th–7th centuries A.D. at Mucking (Ref. 85). Some had already been found in the adjacent Linford Quarry excavation by Mr. K.J. Barton in 1955. Mrs. M.U. Jones has kindly supplied drawings of some of those found at Mucking and remarked that they were found with 5th century A.D. pottery and melted lead in one hut. Mrs. Jones has also noted that lead rings have been found at Hanwell, Middlesex (Ref. 86) and at Ezinge terp, Holland (Groningen Museum).

It seems from the available evidence that the material found in the hut at Keston is both 5th and 6th century A.D. in date and this may well represent rubbish, as the fragmentary nature suggests, discarded over a period of time. In view of the comparatively small number of finds, it is perhaps wiser at this stage to offer a tentative date of *c.* A.D. 450–550 for the Saxon hut at Keston.

PERIOD IX : THE MEDIEVAL AND POST-MEDIEVAL FEATURES (Fig. 40).

With the abandonment of the early-Saxon hut, occupation in Lower Warbank Field seems to have come to an end. Some post-Saxon activity, however, has been revealed. Three large pits (Pits A, B and D), one producing medieval pottery, were located cutting into the ruins of the Roman West Masonry Building. These are likely to be the work of stone-robbers and it is no doubt significant that about a dozen pieces of Roman tile are presently visible, built into the fabric of Keston's medieval parish church, only a short distance to the south-east. Three ditches (Ditches 3, 4 and 5) also appear to be of post-Roman date and it seems likely that these represent field boundaries belonging to medieval or post-medieval times. The small amounts of dateable material recovered from their filling, however, makes it difficult to say much more.

A scatter of medieval and post-medieval pottery found throughout the plough-soil and hillwash deposits across the site, suggest that, after the settlement was abandoned, the area ultimately became plough land (as it remains today), periodically spread with manure and domestic rubbish derived from nearby dwellings. In post-medieval times Lower Warbank Field has always formed part of Keston Court Farm. Keston Court Farm is situated immediately to the east of Lower Warbank Field, close to the parish church which seems to have acted as the focus of medieval settlement in this area.

1) ROBBER-PITS CUT THROUGH THE WEST MASONRY BUILDING (Figs. 19 and 20).

At least three pits cutting through the remains of the West Masonry Building were located. These are described below.

Pits A and B.

These two conjoining pits covered an area roughly L-shaped in plan and measured overall some 24' (north–south) by 17'6" (east–west). They cut through the West and Centre Enclosure Ditches and also through the south-east corner of the West Masonry Building's inferred South-East Room. The pits were dug some 2'2" into the chalk and their filling indicated that they had both been filled in at the same time (Fig. 20; S.E, L.2 and 3; S.G, L.2–6). The upper fill of the pits consisted of dark brown loam with tile and flint lumps and this overlay a deposit of heavy flint rubble with mortar, tile and some brown loam. The lower courses of the South-East Room's east wall survived in the base of Pit A (S.E). A quantity of Roman pottery, including samian ware (none illustrated), ranging in date from the 2nd to the 4th centuries A.D., was recovered from the pits, together with several tesserae and a number of painted wall-plaster fragments. These two pits clearly post-date the Roman period and are perhaps robber-pits, dug to obtain stone from the remains of the villa building. A date sometime in the medieval period seems an appropriate time for their digging, although there is no direct pottery dating evidence for this.

Pit D.

This pit was located cutting into the natural chalk of the east corridor of the West Masonry Building (Fig. 20; S.B, L.2–5). It was sub-square in plan and measured some 8' across. It had steep sides and a sloping base and was 1'2" in depth. The lower filling of the pit (S.B, L.5) consisted of light brown loam and orange sand and produced some 80 pieces of tessera. The upper filling of the pit (S.B, L.3 and 4) consisted of brown loam, mortar and flint rubble. Some 28 sherds of pottery were recovered from this pit. Most is of Roman date, including an Antonine samian sherd, but there are also several sherds of Iron Age date (No. 833) and a few medieval pieces, includng a probable Cheam Ware jug of about 14th century date (No. 840). A hone was also recovered (No. 132).

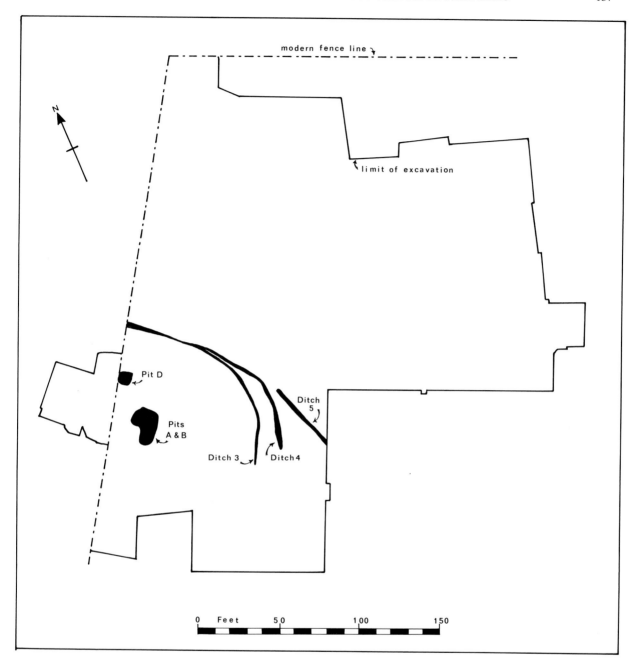

Fig. 40.   *Plan of features assigned to Period IX.*

In addition to these pits, another large, ill-defined pit had been cut through the south wing added to the bath suite (Fig. 20; S.C, L.2 and 3) and this produced 40 sherds of pottery, including part of a medieval vessel together with a piece of medieval peg-tile (none illustrated). This feature presumably represents another robber-pit.

2) DITCHES 3 AND 4 (Figs. 4, 11, 19, 30 and 38).

A pair of curving ditches (Ditches 3 and 4) was discovered which merged and cut through the remains of the West Masonry Building (Fig. 19). They ran across the western half of the site and were excavated over several seasons (1968, 1969, 1970 and 1977). Both ditches initially ran roughly north–south and then curved westwards (Fig. 4). They merged at a point about two-thirds of the way along their length and continued as a single ditch, traceable as far as the western limit of Lower Warbank Field. It seems very likely that they in fact represent successive recuts of the same feature. Which ditch is the earlier, however, is not clear (Fig. 38).

Ditch 4.

The most easterly ditch was Ditch 4 and this was traced for a total distance of about 106 feet from its junction with Ditch 3. It was between 1'8" and 3'2" wide across the top with a V-shaped profile. The base was flat and about 9" across. The ditch was up to 1'3" in depth and was filled with dark brown loam and chalk rubble. It cut through the Centre Flint Structure, the Centre Enclosure Ditch and the Roman East Water Pipe-line and is, thus, clearly late in the site sequence. The southern terminal of this ditch was not located precisely but it seems to have been within the area of the early-Roman Quarry Pit Complex of Period IV.

The ditch produced a total of 152 sherds of coarse-ware pottery, representing at least 43 different vessels. Three samian sherds were also recovered. These were: a Form 18 and a Form 27 of 1st century A.D. date and a Curle 21 or Form 43 of later 2nd to mid-3rd century A.D. date. The coarse pottery ranges in date from the 1st to the 4th centuries A.D. and all must be residual. Some of the latest Roman material is represented by sherds of Alice Holt Ware. A single mortarium sherd has been illustrated (No. 929). One small-find has also been drawn; an iron key (No. 75).

Ditch 3.

This ditch lay to the west of Ditch 4 and ran almost parallel to it. It was traced for a total distance of about 108 feet from the point where it merged with Ditch 4. In detail it was between 1' and 2' in width, with near-vertical sides and a flat base between 6" and 13" across. The ditch measured between 10" and 1'3" in depth and was filled with dark brown loam, chalk and flint. The southern terminal of this ditch has been destroyed by a rectangular pit, which contained a single (apparently residual) Roman potsherd. Stratigraphically, a late date is indicated for this ditch by the fact that it cut through the Centre Enclosure Ditch (Period IV), the East Water Pipe-line (Period VI) and a pit (F.1110) which contained three early-Roman coarse-ware potsherds and a samian sherd dateable to the later 2nd to the first half of the 3rd century A.D.

Ditch 3 produced a total of just 47 coarse-ware potsherds representing at least 15 different vessels (none illustrated). This material ranges in date from the 2nd to the 4th centuries A.D. and includes a single sherd of Alice Holt Ware. More significantly for dating, a fragment of post-medieval tile came from well down in the fill of this ditch and strongly suggests that it is of post-Roman date.

Some distance along their length Ditches 3 and 4 merged, to form a single U-shaped ditch with steeply sloping sides. It seems likely, in fact, that this length of ditch represents both the line of an original ditch and a later recutting of it (assuming that Ditches 3 and 4 are in fact successive rather than truly contemporary). This length of ditch cut through the West Enclosure Ditch and the West Masonry Building. It was between 1' and 4' wide and 6" to 2' deep. The filling was a fairly uniform brown loam with chalk specks (Fig. 38). The ditch was traced from the point where it split in two for a minimum distance of 45' and it continued beyond the western limit of the excavations.

This section of the ditch produced a total of 44 coarse-ware potsherds, representing at least 17 different vessels. None is worthy of illustration but all are of Roman date and are most probably residual.

The discovery of a post-medieval tile fragment in Ditch 3, together with the horizontal site stratigraphy, leaves little doubt that Ditches 3 and 4 are of post-Roman date and that they are completely unrelated to the main villa site. It seems most likely that they in fact represent successive lines of some minor field boundary ditch. Ditch 5, apparently less extensive, could also be broadly contemporary (see below).

3) DITCH 5 (Figs. 11, 12 and 40).

This straight ditch was located just to the north of the early-Roman Quarry Pit Complex (Period IV) and it continued beyond the eastern limit of the excavation (Fig. 11). It was dug over two seasons, in 1968 and 1970. The ditch ran north-west by south-east and was traced for a minimum distance of 55 feet, its northern terminal being discovered in 1968. It was between 2'3" and 4' wide and was about 9" deep. The sides were sloping and the base was cupped. It was filled with a light brown loam, with chalk and pebbles (Fig. 12; S.B, L.2). The ditch cut through a late-Roman metalled surface, located on this part of the site (Centre Metalling) and also the layer of dark soil sealing it. It also cut the Roman East Water Pipe-line (Period VI) and clearly comes late in the site sequence.

The ditch produced a total of 72 coarse-ware potsherds representing a minimum of 20 vessels (none illustrated). The bulk of these are of 1st or 2nd century A.D. date but a single sherd of white ware with a dark green glaze seems to be of medieval or Tudor date. This, together with the site stratigraphy, indicates that the ditch is a post-Roman feature, unrelated to the main villa complex. No coins or samian ware were recovered but one small-find has been drawn, an iron T-clamp (No. 81). It seems likely that Ditch 5 forms part of a post-Roman field boundary and, as such, may be related in some way to Ditches 3 and 4 which seem to have had a similar function.

CHAPTER V

THE EXCAVATED OBJECTS

The excavations in Lower Warbank Field, Keston have produced a considerable amount of (mostly) Roman objects and each main class of find is described in the following pages. The objects which provide the key dating evidence are reported in full. The coins from the site have been listed chronologically in two tables (Tables 35 and 36). The samian ware and coarse pottery have been described quantitively by feature and deposit. The small-finds are catalogued by material and/or function. Details of the fairly small quantities of Roman glass and mortaria recovered from the site must be held over until the second Report. The excavated finds are all noted in the main site text, allowing easy cross-referencing with the relevant section of the finds report.

The finds from the Warbank site could form a good basis for a new Bromley Museum or Heritage Centre. Until all work on the site is completed, however, the material will remain in store at the Kent Unit's West Kent Office. It may be consulted there upon written request.

A) THE COINS.

The excavations at Keston between 1967 and 1978 produced a total of 85 coins. This number includes nine coins from the Roman tombs area (Coin Nos. 9, 25, 30, 34, 45, 48, 49, 62 and 81) and one of Tetricus I already published from the Anglo-Saxon hut (Ref. 87), together with four coins (Coin Nos. 44, 64, 66 and 69) from surface deposits in the adjacent areas. The 84 previously unpublished coins from the present excavations are listed below (Table 35). Five of these (Coin Nos. 1–5) are Iron Age coins of the Potin type, 72 are Roman (Coin Nos. 6–77) and another seven (Coin Nos. 78–84) are medieval or later. Each of these three groups is considered below. Dr. Richard Reece has identified the Roman coins and kindly provided some general comments on their significance.

In addition to the 85 coins recovered from the current excavations, another 20 are recorded from earlier work on the same site. All 105 coins now recorded are shown below in a consolidated list (Table 36).

Most of the Roman coins from the earlier work at Warbank are not provenanced exactly and sadly, many of the coins from the present excavations are not well stratified. Fifteen of the Roman coins from the present excavations came from the plough-soil and unstratified deposits; a further nine came from the hillwash deposit under the plough-soil and another 23 came from the general layers of dark soil over the site, which probably represent plough-disturbed Roman occupational levels. Thus, well over 75% of the Roman coins from Lower Warbank Field came from these essentially non-stratified contexts. Only six coins came from features (Coin Nos. 6, 22, 38, 52 and 61, and the third century coin from the Anglo-Saxon sunken hut). A further eight coins came from reasonably well-stratified deposits (Coin Nos. 10, 12, 13, 36, 42, 50, 58 and 76). All of the coins are of bronze, except one (Coin No. 66) which is silver.

(i) The Iron Age Coins (Coin Nos. 1–5).
Five late-Iron Age Potin coins were recovered from the Lower Warbank site. Of these, one came from the upper filling of the Period IIIb West Enclosure Ditch (Coin No. 1) and another came from an unstratified context above it (Coin No. 4). Pit 18, assigned to Period IV, produced a single coin (Coin No. 2) and a general soil deposit immediately to the north of the South Masonry Building yielded another (Coin No. 3). Coin No. 5 came from a soil layer over late-Iron Age Pit 9 (F.632) which has been assigned to Period IIIa. Only three of the Potins can be identified with accuracy. Coin Nos. 1 and 4 belong to Class II, whilst Coin No. 5 is of Class I.

Coin Nos. 2 and 3 are too corroded to allow them to be classified. All of the coins appear to be residual in their excavated contexts though from their general date-range it seems clear that they were all derived from the pre-Roman settlement (Period III) at Keston.

The Potin coin from the West Enclosure Ditch (Coin No. 1) was first published in 1970 (Ref. 88), with a note by the late D.F. Allen. The coin is of his type 01 (Class II), which he dated to somewhere in the first half of the first century A.D. Indeed, this very coin was re-published by Allen in 1971 as the type-specimen in his classification of British Potins (Ref. 89). The unstratified coin from nearby is also of this type (Coin No. 4). There is at least one earlier Potin, of Type L (Class 1), in the collection (Coin No. 5) and this probably dates to the mid-first century B.C. Allen considered that the latest British Potins (i.e. Types O and P of the Class II series) continued to be made until the eve of the Roman Conquest. Haselgrove, however, has more recently doubted this late dating and considers them to have ceased production well before the invasion (Ref. 90).

Potin coins are anyway a well-known Kent type, with discoveries from over 25 locations in the county. They are, however, not closely dateable because they lack a legend and have no well-defined sequence of development. Such coins are found on native farmstead sites like Keston, but never in large numbers. Excavations at the Faversham farmstead produced just one example (Ref. 91), whilst the total excavation of the settlement on Farningham Hill produced only two (Ref. 92). Work at the Greenhithe farmstead revealed three examples (Ref. 93). Two Potins were recovered from the Lullingstone Roman Villa site (Ref. 94) and both of these are a late type (Type O) broadly comparable to Keston Coin Nos. 1 and 4. These unusual coins were probably of little monetary value and are generally regarded as representing the 'small change', used in trading by a society which had just begun to develop some kind of rudimentary money-economy (see Ref. 95). The small numbers of these coins found on farmstead sites is probably due to their general lack of use in such rural contexts, which must have lain well away from the main market centres.

(ii) The Roman Coins (Coin Nos. 6–77)
by Richard Reece.

With the comparatively small numbers of Roman coins involved there is no point in taking comments to any numerical extreme; instead a few more general points may be made. The most obvious feature of the list is its gentle continuity. The five Potin coins together with the two Claudian copies make it quite clear that there is occupation by the middle of the first century A.D. at the latest and that that occupation was in at least economic contact with the early Roman presence in Kent. The three worn coins of the second century could have been lost at any time up to the middle of the third century so that if the archaeology of the site suggests a break in occupation during the second century these coins by themselves would not contradict this. However, there is archaeological continuity and it is no surprise at all that there are no freshly minted and lost coins to support it, for sites with small numbers of coin losses rarely show much coin activity during the second century. The total absence of coins of the early-third century is absolutely normal, their presence would in fact be highly remarkable, so that the coin list rarely has any comment to make on this period.

After the debasement of the silver coinage in the middle of the third century all sites in Britain show an increase in coin loss so that the sudden rise in coin loss in this list is not in any way an index of renewed activity on the site. Gallienus is the first Emperor who would be expected and the issues carry on through the latest radiates of Carausius to the early and middle issues of Constantine I, so that there is no break in the sequence here. Coins of 330 to 348 are not particularly numerous but they are there in moderate numbers. If they are compared with the 5 coins of Constantine struck between 317 and 330 then they are slightly low in numbers, so that the modest list of 330 to 348 might suggest that no great changes or expansions were happening on this site, in contrast to many other sites which appear, from their coins, to blossom at just this time. The modest level of coin loss is continued through the 360s and 370s with a surprise in the silver coin of Valens. It is not really possible to quantify this surprise for silver coins of this period do occur as site finds at the very rough rate of one per thousand finds, but the incidence of such finds does not seem to have any spatial or social pattern. There are no coins identified for the House of Theodosius, struck after 388, and this might mean an end to the occupation of the site somewhere soon after 375 or 380, but not all sites which continue to the end of the fourth century use the latest coins so that occupation post-dating the Valentinianic coins could not be particularly surprising.

In sum this is the list of coins lost at a modest Roman site which seems to have fairly continuous occupation and which kept directly in touch with economic exchange of the surrounding area through the use of coins until at least the last quarter of the fourth century.

The Roman coins are listed in chronological order according to the usual works of reference:

R.I.C. = Edd. Mattingly, Sydenham and others, *Roman Imperial Coinage*, 1923 ff.
HK = Carson, Hill and Kent, *Late Roman Bronze Coinage*, 1960, part I.
CK = The same, part II.

When the coin cannot be completely identified it is given a reference which is the nearest in the list to what can actually be seen and described, for example, in the terms 'HK as 52'. Those coins that are not issues of the regular mints are described as copies either 'of' a particular reference when all details are clear, or 'as' a particular reference, when there is some doubt.

(iii) The Post-Roman Coins (Coin Nos. 78–84).

A total of six post-Roman coins was discovered during excavations at Warbank (Coin Nos. 78–84). These include a farthing of James I (Coin No. 79); two halfpennies of George II (Coin Nos. 80 and 81) and a French jetton, probably of fourteenth century date (Coin No. 78). The remaining coins (Coin Nos. 82 to 84) are of nineteenth and twentieth century date.

No.	Obverse	Date (A.D.)	Notes (R.I.C. No. etc.)	Context	Deposit No.	K.F. No.
1	Potin	First half of 1st cent. A.D.	Allen Type 01 (Mack 24)	1969: W. Enc., Upp. Fill E. Ditch	LWB–C25–3	69–8
2	Potin	Late-Iron Age	Corroded	1970: Fill of Pit 18 (F.18)	LWB–J21–3	70–17
3	Potin	Late-Iron Age	Corroded	1970: General soil N. of S. Masonry Build.	LWB–M32–3	70– 25
4	Potin	First half of 1st cent. A.D.	Allen Type 01 (Mack 24)	1969: Unstrat., W. Enc.	LWB–C24–1	–
5	Potin	Mid 1st cent. B.C.	Allen Type L (Mack 17a)	1972: Soil over Pit 9 (F.632)	LWB–U24–4	72–2
6	Claudius I	43–54	Copy R.I.C. as 67	1969: S. Tim. Build. – Fill of Post-pits (F.127)	LWB–N34– 5	69–6
7	Claudius I	43–54	Copy R.I.C. as 66 or 68	1970: Soil over Centre Metall.	LWB–M28–3	70–28
8	Trajan	98–117	Sestertius, Reverse Illegible	1973: Soil over Upp. E. Metall.	LWB–CC21–4	73–1
9	Hadrian	117–138	Sestertius, Reverse Illegible	1968: Late-Roman Dump, Tombs area	WB–79	68–10

No.	Obverse	Date (A.D.)	Notes (R.I.C. No. etc.)	Context	Deposit No.	K.F. No.
10	?	Late-1st to early 2nd cent.	As, worn and illegible	1972: Soil over S.E. Villa Enc. Ditch	LWB–X24–6	72–1
11	Gallienus	260–268	R.I.C. 166	1970: Disturbed soil N.E. of Anglo-Saxon hut	LWB–N23–2	70–6
12	Gallienus	260–268	R.I.C. 179	1970: Centre Metalling	LWB–L30–5	70–14
13	Gallienus	260–268	R.I.C. 230	1970: Soil under Centre Metall.	LWB–L31–4	70–20
14	Gallienus	260–268	R.I.C. 166/245	1969: Unstrat. S. Masonry Building	LWB–F35–1	69–1
15	Claudius II	270	R.I.C. 266	1968: Soil over Centre Metall.	LWB–L27–3	68–17
16	Claudius II	268–270	Reverse Illegible	1970: Soil over Quarry Pit Comp.	LWB–L28–3	70–8
17	Claudius II	268–270	Reverse Illegible	1968: Unstrat. S. Masonry Build.	LWB–L36–1	–
18	Postumus	260–268	R.I.C. 59	1978: Soil over pond, E. of N. Tim. Build.	LWB–78–47	78–8
19	Tetricus I	270–273	R.I.C. as 88	1970: Hillwash N. of S. Masonry Build.	LWB–131–2	70–2
20	Tetricus I	270–273	R.I.C. 90	1968: Soil over Centre Metall.	LWB–M27–3	68–13
21	Tetricus I	270–273	R.I.C. as 100	1970: Soil over Centre Metall.	LWB–N27–3	70–31
22	Tetricus I	270–273	R.I.C. as 100	1977: Fill of Post-hole (F.1089)	LWB–77–102	77–1
23	Probus	276–282	R.I.C. 29	1970: Gen. soil, S. of Anglo-Saxon hut	LWB–N26–3	70–32
24	Carausius	289–293	R.I.C. as 878	1970: Plough soil, N. of S. Masonry Build.	LWB–L31–2	70–13
25	Carausius/ Maximian I	290–293	R.I.C. 44	1968: Late-Roman Dump, Tombs Area	WB–79	68–12
26	Barbarous Radiate	270–290	–	1968: Soil over Centre Metall.	LWB–L27–3	68–12
27	Barbarous Radiate	270–290	–	1968: Hillwash over Centre Metall.	LWB–L27–2	68–11
28	Barbarous Radiate	270–290	–	1969: Unstrat. W Masonry Build. area	LWB–C25–1	69–2

No.	Obverse	Date (A.D.)	Notes (R.I.C. No. etc.)	Context	Deposit No.	K.F. No.
29	Barbarous Radiate	270–290	–	1968: Hillwash above S. Masonry Build.	LWB–K33–2	68–3
30	Barbarous Radiate	270–290	–	1978: Late-Roman Dump, Tombs Area	LWB–78–405	78–22
31	Barbarous Radiate	270–290	–	1970: Disturb. Soil N. of Saxon hut	LWB–L21–2	70–12
32	Barbarous Radiate	270–290	–	1970: Unstrat. W. Masonry Build.	LWB–Z–1	70–9
33	Barbarous Radiate	270–290	–	1970: Soil over Centre Metall.	LWB–N27–3	70–23
34	Constantine I	313–317	R.I.C. 7, London as 69	1978: Tombs Area	LWB–78–501	78–23
35	Constantine I	318–320	R.I.C. 7, London as 156	1968: Soil over Centre Metall.	LWB–L27–3	68–17
36	Constantine I	313–317	R.I.C. 7, Trier as 39	1977: Soil over Post-hole 15 (F.1185) N. Tim. Build.	LWB–77–232	77–6
37	Constantine I	320–323	R.I.C. 7, Trier 306	1968: Unstrat., S. Masonry Build.	LWB–134–1	68–10
38	Constantine I	324–330	R.I.C. 7, Arles Copy of 286.	1977: Pit fill (F.1096)	LWB–77–104	77–2
39	Constantine I	337–340	HK 114	1970: Gen. soil layer, cut by Ditch 5, over Centre Metall.	LWB–N28–3	70–26
40	Constantine II	335–337	HK 88	1976: Unstrat.	LWB–76–1	76–7
41	Constantine II	335–337	HK 93	1970: Soil over Centre Metall.	LWB–N27–3	70–21
42	Urbs Roma	330–345	HK copy of 184	1970: (disturb.) Centre Metall., over Quarry Pits	LWB–L29–3	70–22
43	Constantinopolis	330–345	HK copy as 52	1977: Unstrat., Area 'A'	LWB–77–1	77–4
44	Constantinopolis	330–345	HK copy as 52	1969: Field survey, W. of Lower Warbank Field	RF–K203	–
45	Constantinopolis	330–335	HK 66	1978: Late Roman Dump, Tombs Area	LWB–78–405	78–21
46	Constantinopolis	330–345	HK copy of 191	1977: Unstrat. N. Tim. Build.	LWB–77–1	77–5

No.	Obverse	Date (A.D.)	Notes (R.I.C. No. etc.)	Context	Deposit No.	K.F. No.
47	Helena	337–341	HK as 112	1978: Soil over Pond, E. of N. Tim. Build.	LWB–78–47	78–6
48	Constans	337–341	HK 131	1967: Late Roman Dump, Tombs Area	WB–79	67–11
49	Constans	345–348	HK 150	1968: Late Roman Dump, Tombs Area	WB–79	68–15
50	Constans	345–348	HK 160	1977: Fill of late hut terr., N. Tim. Build. (Over Pit F.1200)	LWB–77–256	77–11
51	Constantius II	337–341	HK 126	1968: Hillwash N. of S. Masonry Build.	LWB–K32–2	68–6
52	Constantius II	345–348	HK 152	1970: Robber-pit, W. Masonry Build.	LWB–Z9	70–11
53	House of Constantine	330–345	HK copy as 48	1976: Soil over N. Tim. Build.	LWB–76–40	76–2
54	House of Constantine	330–348	HK copy as 48	1978: Unstrat. S. of N. Tim. Build.	LWB–78–1	78–3
55	House of Constantine	335–345	HK copy as 48	1971: Soil over Quarry Pit Complex	LWB–M30–4	71–41
56	House of Constantine	335–345	HK as 87	1978: Soil over Pond, E. of N. Tim. Build.	LWB–78–47	78–2
57	House of Constantine	345–355	HK copy as 137	1968: Unstrat., S. Masonry Build.	LWB–G34–1	68–11
58	House of Constantine	350–360	CK copy as 25	1973: On surface of Upper E. Metall.	LWB–Z24–7	73–5
59	House of Constantine	350–360	CK copy as 25	1969: Hillwash N. of S. Masonry Build.	LWB–I31–2	69–4
60	House of Constantine	350–360	CK as 256	1970: Soil over Centre Metall.	LWB–M28–3	70–38
61	House of Constantine	350–360	CK copy as 256	1978: Fill of Ditch 7	LWB–78–39	78–7
62	Magnentius	350–353	CK as 8	1968: Late Roman Dump, Tombs Area	WB–79	68–14

No.	Obverse	Date (A.D.)	Notes (R.I.C. No. etc.)	Context	Deposit No.	K.F. No.
63	Magnentius	350–353	CK 238	1968: Hillwash N. of S. Masonry Build.	LWB–K32–2	68–5
64	Valentinian I	364–375	CK as 501	1969: Unstrat. from hillside immediately above the tombs	–	69–9
65	Valentinian I	364–375	CK as 1014	1973: Hillwash over Upper E. Metall.	LWB–Y23–2	73–2
66	Valens	364–378	Silver, R.I.C. 9, Lyon 6f.	1967: Found in garden abou 200 ft. N.E. of tombs	–	67–9
67	Valens	364–378	CK as 97	1978: Soil over Pond, E. of N. Tim. Build.	LWB–78–47	78–4
68	Gratian	367–378	CK as 318	1968: Hillwash over Centre Metall.	LWB–L27–2	68–18
69	House of Valentinian	364–378	CK as 96	1969: Field survey, Eight Acre Field	K202	–
70	House of Valentinian	364–378	CK as 96	1978: Unstrat., S. of N. Tim. Build.	LWB–78–1	78–1
71	House of Valentinian	364–378	CK as 96	1977: Unstrat. N. Tim. Build.	LWB–77–1	77–10
72	–	3rd–4th cent.	Illegible	1969: Gen. soil, N. of S. Masonry Build.	LWB–I32–3	69–5
73	–	3rd–4th cent.	Illegible	1968: Soil over S. Masonry Build.	LWB–J35–3	68–22
74	–	3rd–4th cent.	Illegible	1973: Soil over Post-hole (F.712)	LWB–Z20–4	73–3
75	–	3rd–4th cent.	Illegible	1970: Hillwash, N. of S. Masonry Build.	LWB–I30–2	70–1
76	–	1st–4th cent.	Illegible	1970: Soil over Quarry Pit Complex	LWB–N31–7	70–29
77	–	Late 4th cent.?	Illegible	1970: Gen. soil above Quarry Pit Complex	LWB–N29–3	70–30
78	French counter (jetton)	14th cent.?	–	1978: Unstrat., S. of N. Tim. Build.	LWB–78–1	78–9

No.	Obverse	Date (A.D.)	Notes (R.I.C. No. etc.)	Context	Deposit No.	K.F. No.
79	James I	1603–1625	Farthing	1970: Hillwash, N. of Anglo-Saxon hut	LWB–M21–2	70–15
80	George II	1752	Halfpenny	1969: Unstrat., over W. Enc. Ditch	LWB–D23–1	69–7
81	George II	1727–1760	Halfpenny	1968: Unstrat.	WB–2	68–13
82	Victoria	1877	Halfpenny	1976: Unstrat.	LWB–76–1	76–3
83	George V	1911	Penny	1976: Disturbed upper fill of Post-hole	LWB–76–2	76–1
84	George V	1917	Halfpenny	1970: Unstrat., over Quarry Pit Complex	LWB–L29–1	70–4

Table 35. Catalogue of coins from Warbank, Keston (1967–78).

Emperor/Type	Date	Discoveries Pre-1967	1967–78 Excavations	Totals
Potin Coins	Pre-Conquest	–	5	5
Claudius I ⎫	A.D. 41–57 (?)	1	–	1 ⎫
Claudius I ⎭	43–54	–	2	2 ⎭ 3
Nero	54–68	1	–	1
Trajan	98–117	–	1	1
Hadrian	117–138	2	1	3
Faustina II	161–180	1	–	1
Albinus	193–194	1	–	1
Unident. Late-1st to early-2nd cent.	c. 70–140	–	1	1
Gallienus	260–268	–	4	4
Victorinus	265–267	1	–	1
Claudius II	268–270	2	3	5
Postumus	260–268	–	1	1
Tetricus I	270–273	–	5	5
Probus	276–282	–	1	1
Carausius	287–293	2	1	3
Carausius/Maximian I	290–293	–	1	1
Allectus	293–296	1	–	1
Barb. Radiate	270–290	–	8	8
Constantine I	306–340	6	6	12
Constantine II	335–337	–	2	2
Constantius II	337–361	1	2	3
Helena	337–341	–	1	1
Constans	337–341	–	3	3
Urbs Roma	330–345	–	1	1
Constantinopolis	330–345	–	4	4
House of Constantine	330–360	–	9	9
Magnentius	350–353	–	2	2
Valentinian I	364–375	–	2	2
Valens	364–378	1	2	3
Gratian	367–378	–	1	1
House of Valentinian	364–378	–	3	3
Illegible	3rd to 4th cent.	–	5	5
Illegible	Roman	–	1	1
Med. and Post-Med. coins	14th to 20th cent.	–	7	7
TOTALS	–	20	85	105

Table 36. Table of coins from Warbank, Keston.

B) THE PREHISTORIC FLINT WORK (Fig. 41, Nos. 1–8).

A collection of over 500 prehistoric struck flints was recovered during excavations in Lower Warbank Field between 1968 and 1978. Just eight worked examples of these have been illustrated (Nos. 1–8). Out of the total assemblage of 505 pieces, 474 are either waste flakes (458) or shatter-fragments (16). In addition, there are five cores or fragments of cores. Three hammer-stones can be identified and a further 23 pieces show some signs of secondary working. Of these worked pieces, ten are scrapers (Nos. 3–8) and there are two arrowheads, both of rather unusual form (Nos. 1 and 2). All the remaining worked pieces show areas of miscellaneous retouching, but cannot be classified as any recognisable tool-type.

This flint material was recovered from various features and soil deposits across the field and all of it apeared to be in residual contexts. Indeed, it seems possible that a certain amount of the flint-work actually derived from higher up the hill, perhaps from the area of the Roman tombs, where a further quantity of lithic material was recovered (to be reported in the second Report). In view of this it seems clear that the material from Lower Warbank Field cannot be regarded as anything more than a mixed assemblage, quite possibly containing material of more than one period. Of the tools present, the two most diagnostic pieces are the arrowheads (Nos. 1 and 2), both of which appear to be of late-Neolithic/Bronze Age date. All the remaining flint material would fit reasonably well into this same general date-range, but little more may be said.

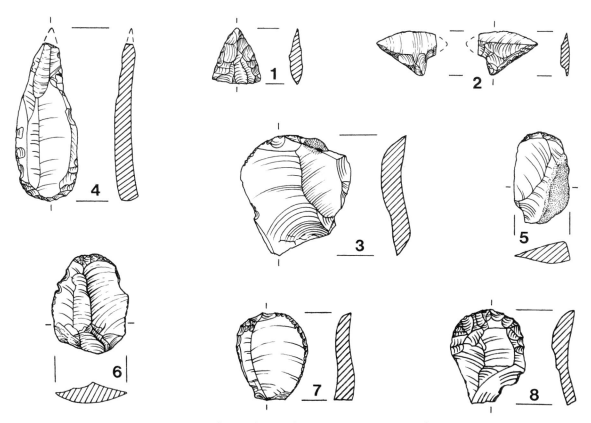

Fig. 41. *Flint implements from Lower Warbank Field* ($\frac{1}{2}$).

No. 1   Unusual triangular arrowhead worked over both faces and coated with a grey-white patina. Three similar triangular forms are illustrated by Evans (Ref. 96) and another comes from Winterton, Lincs., (Ref. 97). Green (Ref. 98) has suggested that these triangular forms are often blanks for barbed-and-tanged arrowheads, typical of the Bronze Age. From fill of early-Roman Pit 19. (LWB–M36–3).

No. 2   Chisel-ended arrowhead, with one corner broken. The cutting edge is unworked, whilst the other two have been retouched on both faces. Mottled white and dark grey flint. Green's recent work on flint arrowheads suggests that chisel-ended forms were in use from the earlier part of the third millenium b.c. and they seem to have disappeared by *c.* 1500 b.c. at the latest (Ref. 99). From general soil deposit over the East Enclosure Ditch. (LWB–U22–7).

No. 3   Scraper made on a broad flake. The convex edge, opposite the platform, shows signs of steep retouch. Blue-white patina with one small area of cortex surviving. From fill of Pit 2 (F.419), dateable to the middle-Iron Age. (LWB–023–6).

No. 4   End-scraper made on a blade, with a white patina. The working end has been steeply retouched to an angle of about 90°. From Post-hole 13 (F. 484) of the Centre Timber Building. (LWB–024–6).

No. 5   End-scraper made on a short blade. An area of original cortex survives on one side and there is an area of steep retouching at the working end. It has a light blue patina. From fill of Pit 2 (F.419), dateable to the middle-Iron Age. (LWB–023–6).

No. 6   End-scraper made on a broad flake. There is a small area of steep retouch opposite the platform. Mottled blue patina. From Post-hole (F.649) of Four-Post Structure 2, probably of late-Iron Age date. (LWB–Y19–3).

No. 7   Scraper made on a thin flake. The end has been steeply retouched (about 70°) and the working extends along both sides of the flake. Mottled dark and light blue patina with a light green staining. From soil beneath the fourth century A.D. Upper East Metaling. (LWB–X24–6).

No. 8   End-scraper made on a thin flake. The working on the end is at an angle of about 45°. White patina with light green staining. From filling of first century A.D. Quarry Pit Complex. (LWB–L29–5).

C) THE SMALL-FINDS (Figs. 42–55, Nos. 9–133).

The excavations in Lower Warbank Field produced a total of just over 180 objects which are generally regarded as small-finds and 125 of these are illustrated here (Nos. 9–133). These consist mostly of the better preserved and more significant pieces from the excavations and together they form a largely representative selection of the finds recovered. The objects are grouped according to their material or composition (e.g. baked clay, bone, antler, iron, bronze and stone) and specific object-types within these general groupings are illustrated together. In a few cases, objects with a similar function, such as spindle-whorls, brooches and bracelets, have been grouped together regardless of the material used in their production. All of the illustrated objects are described individually and short general notes are included on most of the more significant groups and single objects. All copper-alloy pieces have been described as being of 'bronze', unless analysis during conservation work has specifically indicated that they are of brass. The description of an object is followed by a note of its context, the general date of that context and the individual site code (in brackets). Many finds appear to be residual and a significant number, unfortunately, do not come from well dated deposits. Nevertheless, together they form an important collection of material from a major Romano-British settlement in rural West Kent. Eight small-finds from the Saxon 'grübenhaus' first published in 1973 (Ref. 100) have not been republished here. All measurements are in millimetres and weights are in grams.

Clay Loom-weights (Fig. 42).

The Lower Warbank site produced a total of 28 baked clay loom-weight fragments, representing at least 20 separate weights. No complete example was recovered. Five of the fragments are illustrated here (Nos. 9–13). Eighteen of the pieces came from ten pits and post-holes and were generally associated with pottery of either immediately pre-Conquest, or immediately post-Conquest date. Of the ten features, Pits 5, 7, 9, 11, 14 and 15 are dated to the pre-Conquest period and Pits 18 and 22 to the post-Conquest period. Features 253 and 658 are not securely dated. The post-Conquest East Enclosure Ditch, produced a single loom-weight fragment (not illustrated) and the filling of the Quarry Pit Complex, also of early-Roman date, produced two fragments (not illustrated). A further seven pieces, all too fragmentary for illustration, came from various general soil deposits across the site and were probably residual in these contexts.

Many of the pieces are small, but it seems clear that they are all of the triangular type, well-known on sites of the Iron Age in southern Britain. It seems that most were between 190 mm. and 210 mm. across, originally. This form of loom-weight belongs essentially to the later part of the Iron Age, replacing an earlier pyramidal form (Ref. 101) not represented at Keston. There is some evidence that the triangular type goes on into the early-Roman period and the evidence from Keston may partially confirm this view. Excavations at Newhaven, in Sussex, produced a triangular loom-weight in an early-Roman context, on a site that yielded no evidence of pre-Conquest occupation (Ref. 102). Work at the Roman settlement at Flaggrass, in the Fens, also produced a loom-weight of triangular form (Ref. 103). Kent sites producing triangular loom-weights include: Crayford (pre-Conquest, unpublished); Farningham Hill (pre-Conquest, Ref. 104); North Pole Lane at West Wickham (pre-Conquest, Ref. 105) and a site on the Isle of Grain (pre-Conquest, unpublished).

Kiln Furniture (Fig. 43).

A group of seven deliberately shaped baked clay objects (Nos. 14–20), recovered from the excavations in Lower Warbank Field, appear to have no obvious domestic function and it seems probable that they represent material used as pottery kiln-furniture. Other evidence for pottery manufacture on the site, in the early-Roman period (Period IV), is convincing and it seems reasonable to suppose that the present objects are also derived from this industry. All but one of the pieces came from either the Quarry Pit Complex or the 'Kiln Debris' and soil deposits over it. These are precisely the areas where much of the (presumed) kiln ware pottery was also recovered. The other piece (No. 14) came from the filling of the first century A.D. Pit 16 which also produced a significant amount of the kiln-ware pottery.

The fragments recovered comprise a variety of types, each clearly with a different purpose. They include slabs (Nos. 14 and 15), small wedges (Nos. 16, 17 and 19) and possible spacers (Nos. 18 and 20).

One essential characteristic of kiln-furniture of the early-Roman period is its portability (Ref. 106) and it seems likely that the slab fragments (Nos. 14 and 15) represent parts of pedestals used to support kiln floors. Such slabs are fairly well known on kiln sites in the North Kent marshes (Ref. 107). Swan (Ref. 108) accepts that at least some of the Belgic 'bricks' from Wheeler's excavations at Prae Wood, Herts., also had a similar function (Ref. 109). The small wedge-shaped pieces from Keston (Nos. 16, 17 and 19) have a rather less clear function, but perhaps represent some sort of floor support. The roughly shaped ring (No. 20) appears to be a stacking-spacer, used when loading the kiln. The rod (No. 18) may also have acted as some sort of small spacer.

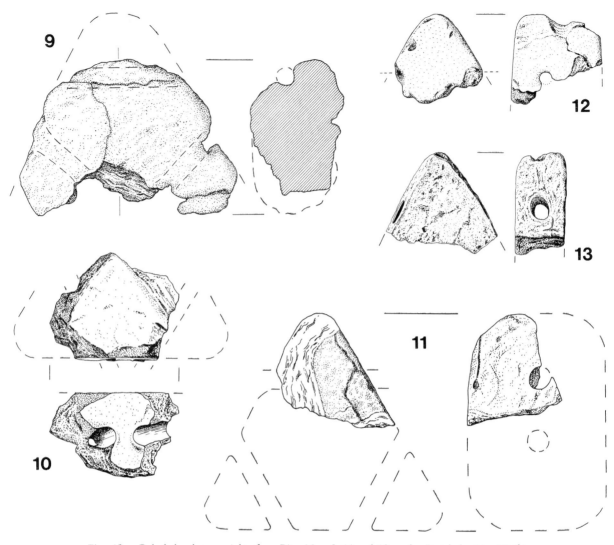

Fig. 42.   *Baked clay loom-weights from Pits, Nos. 9–11 and 13, and a Post-hole, No. 12 ($\frac{1}{3}$).*

No. 9   Substantial part of a triangular baked clay loom-weight. This is of the well-known later Iron Age type and two of the three perforations across the corners, through which the warp threads were passed, survive. From filling of Pit 9 (F.632/509/466) in the area of the Centre Timber Building and dated to the late-Iron Age. (LWB–U24–8).

No. 10   Part of a triangular clay loom-weight. Traces of two of the original corner perforations survive and these are between 14 mm. and 16 mm. in diameter. The loom-weight is made from a fairly hard, slightly sandy buff-brown fabric. From filling of Pit 14 cut by the South-East Villa Enclosure Ditch and dated to the late-Iron Age. (LWB–DD21–7).

No. 11   Fragment of a triangular clay loom-weight of hard, slightly sandy orange-buff fabric, with very occasional small flint pebble inclusions. Traces of one corner perforation survive. From filling of Pit 7 (F.507), dated to the late-Iron Age. (LWB–S24–9).

No. 12   Corner fragment of a triangular clay loom-weight. Traces of one corner perforation survive and there is a rubbed groove on the outside corner (see also No. 13). The fabric is a fairly soft, slightly sandy clay of buff-brown colour. Voids left by the burning out of organic matter occur within the body of the weight. From filling of a Post-hole (F.658), cutting the East Enclosure Ditch. (LWB–V22–12).

No. 13   Corner fragment of a triangular clay loom-weight, in a soft, orange-red slightly sandy fabric, with orange-brown surfaces. A single corner perforation survives and this is about 15 mm. in diameter. There is a slight rubbed hollow on the outside corner. From filling of Pit 18 (F.318), dated to the late-first century A.D. (LWB–J21–4).

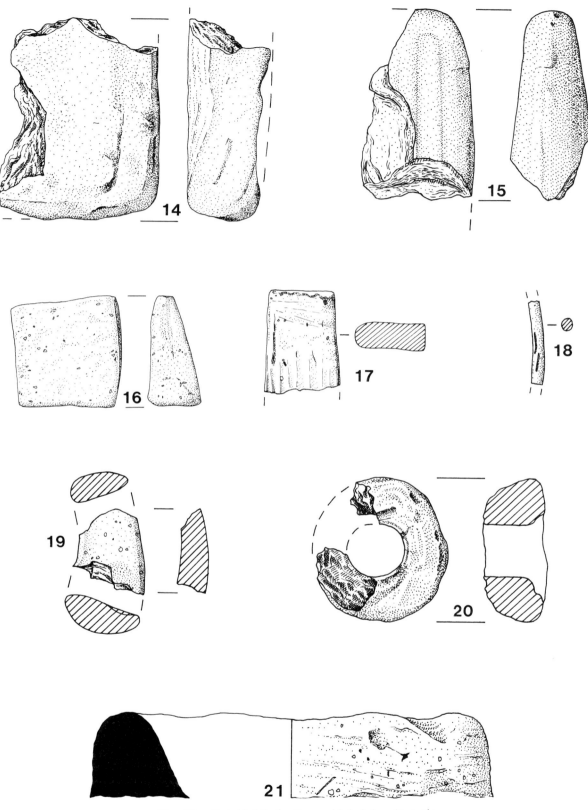

Fig. 43.   *Probable kiln furniture and baked clay objects ($\frac{1}{2}$).*

No. 14   Corner fragment of a large rectangular slab of baked clay. Soft, dark grey-brown, grog-tempered fabric with orange-buff surfaces. The piece has a thickness of 45 mm. It seems fairly certain that this object was a piece of kiln-furniture. Similar fragments, described as 'bricks', were discovered in Belgic contexts at Prae Wood, St. Albans (Ref. 110). From filling of Pit 18 (F.18), dated to the late-first century A.D. (LWB–J21–4).

No. 15   Corner fragment of a large sub-rectangular slab of baked clay. Hard orange-pink, slightly sandy fabric with light grey surfaces. The piece has a thickness of 42 mm. and seems to be of a similar type to No. 14. From soil over the first century A.D. Quarry Pit Complex. (LWB–L29–4).

No. 16   Small, rectangular 'wedge' of orange-brown shell-tempered baked clay. The piece is complete and has a maximum thickness of 29 mm. The exact purpose of this object is not clear but it is probably a piece of kiln-furniture of some sort. From first century A.D. Kiln Debris over the Quarry Pit Complex. (LWB–N31–8).

No. 17   Part of a thin baked clay wedge with a sub-rectangular cross-section and a maximum thickness of 14 mm. The fabric is a dark grey-brown shell-tempered ware. Again, the purpose of this piece is not clear but it may have been similar to No. 16. From soil over the first century A.D. Quarry Pit Complex. (LWB–L29–4).

No. 18   Part of a small rod of baked clay, broken at both ends. The object has a circular cross-section and varies in diameter from 5 to 6 mm. It is of a pink-buff, slightly sandy fabric and does not appear to have been made with great care. The precise purpose of this object is not clear, but it may have been a piece of kiln-furniture, presumably some kind of small spacer. From filling of first century A.D. Quarry Pit Complex. (LWB–N29–5).

No. 19   Fragment of a probable curved wedge, of a hard, dark grey shell-tempered fabric with orange-grey surfaces. It has a maximum thickness of 17 mm. and may be broadly comparable with Nos. 16 and 17. From soil over the Quarry Pit Complex. (LWB–N31–3).

No. 20   About three-quarters of a ring of heavily burnt clay. There is a central hole some 30 mm. in diameter. The object has been crudely shaped and it seems probable that it represents a stacking spacer-ring used for loading pottery kilns. The piece has been broken, with some fragments coming from the filling of the first century A.D. Quarry Pit Complex and some from the Kiln Debris above. (LWB–N31–10 and N31–19).

A Clay Container (Fig. 43).

No. 21   Part of a crude container, or tray, of baked clay. The fabric is fairly soft with chalk and flint inclusions (some large). The core is black and the outer surface buff-brown, whilst the inner surface is orange-red. The piece has clearly been fired but its purpose is not clear. A broadly similar tray fragment was discovered at the Romano-British farmstead at Brockworth in Gloucestershire (Ref. 111). From filling of the South Tank under the South Masonry Building, dated to the late-second to early-third century A.D. (LWB–I36–4).

Pottery Wheels (Fig. 44).

Excavations on the central part of the site, during 1968 and 1970, in the area of the early-Roman Quarry Pit Complex, produced a total of 51 fragments from small pottery discs or wheels. These fragments seem to represent over 40 different wheels and thirteen of them have been illustrated here (Nos. 22–34). The general filling of the Quarry Pits produced five of the wheel fragments and eight more were found in the 'Kiln Debris' over the Quarry Pits. The dark soils above the Quarry Pit Complex produced 24 more fragments and the general soils above these produced a further six fragments. The unstratified and plough-soil deposits in the Quarry Pits area produced another three pieces. A further four pieces were recovered from general soil deposits beyond the limits of the Quarry Pit Complex and one other fragment had been incorporated into an area of late-Roman metalling to the north of the South Masonry Building. Few complete wheels have been reconstructed from the fragments.

The wheels themselves, are made of fired clay and their fabrics closely resemble those of the imitation Gallo-Belgic butt-beakers and platters which were found on the site in some quantity. The wheels, in profile, are all thickest near their centre and both faces taper evenly towards the edge. They have shallow cuts around their circumference consisting of angled lines, incised generally in one direction but sometimes in two, producing either a narrow 'cord' or 'fern-leaf' pattern. They range in diameter from 32 mm. to 100 mm. Only two (see No. 22) have traces of a small central perforation, although many are dished at the centre, usually on one side only.

These somewhat unusual objects have been studied in some detail both by the present writers and Dr. Valerie Rigby. Their function now seems clear. Examination of the vertical roulette decoration on many of the butt beakers from the site suggested that the wheels were, in fact, used to produce this effect and experiments in plasticine confirmed this by producing designs identical to those visible on the butt beakers sherds. The individual zones of decoration on the beakers rarely exceed 70 mm. and it was established in the experiments that generally a half, or less, of one revolution of a wheel would produce the appropriate length of design. Thus, the wheels could be easily used between the thumb and forefinger without any need for mounting on a central spindle with a handle device; hence the general absence of central holes in the wheels. Various features relating to the bad spacing of the impressed lines were exactly reproduced by the experimental work. The final proof that the pottery wheels were used for decorating these early fine-wares is that they are of essentially the same fabric as the butt beakers themselves. A band of rouletting noted on the base of a copy of a Gallo-Belgic platter (No. 879) also seems to have been produced with such a wheel, clearly indicating platter manufacture, here too, (see p. 201) and a small beaker with similar decoration has also been noted (No. 873).

Thus, there can be no doubt that these pottery wheels were used in the on-site production of fine-wares in the later first century A.D. (Period IV). This is further reinforced by the discovery of two pottery dies (Nos. 35 and 36) with similar stamps to those found on some of the platter bases. It is of great interest to note that another Kentish rural site has produced some very similar evidence. Work at Eccles, near Rochester, has revealed a dump of pottery waste material and it seems clear that imitations of Gallo-Belgic platters and butt-beakers were also being produced there in the later first century A.D., together with a variety of other vessels, including flagons and mortaria (Ref. 112). Even more significantly, amongst the debris from that site, part of a potter's rouletting wheel was recovered (Ref. 113). This was identified as having been used to decorate the butt beakers that were made on the site. It is rather smaller than the Keston examples and has a central perforation for a handle device. It clearly represents a slightly different method of producing roulette decoration.

No. 22   About half of a small pottery wheel with a diameter of 32 mm. Hard orange-buff, slightly sandy, fabric with orange-buff surfaces. Deeply incised almost horizontal lines, have been cut around the circumference of the disc. Unusually, a central perforation, some 3 mm. in diameter, occurs in this example. From filling of the Quarry Pit Complex, dateable to the late-first century A.D. (LWB–N30–8).

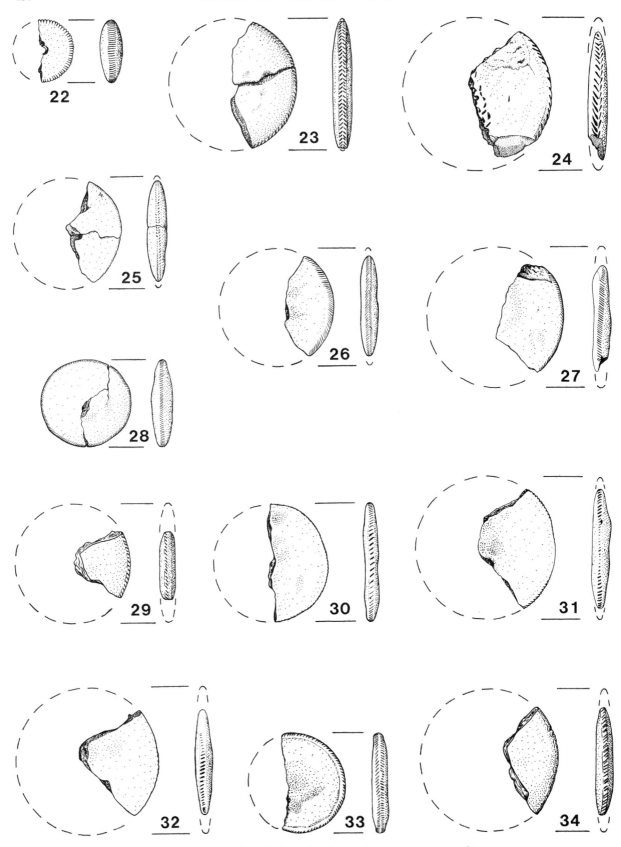

Fig. 44.   *Baked clay wheels used to decorate Keston Kiln Pottery* ($\frac{1}{2}$).

No. 23   Two joining fragments of a pottery wheel with a diameter of about 70 mm. Hard, slightly sandy fabric with grey core and orange-pink surfaces. A 'fern-leaf' design has been cut around the circumference of the disc. From Kiln Debris, dateable to the late-first century A.D. and plough soil above. (LWB–N31–18 and N31–2).

No. 24   Fragment of a pottery wheel with an estimated original diameter of about 88 mm. Hard, slightly sandy fabric with mottled orange-grey core and surfaces. A bold 'fern-leaf' pattern has been cut around the circumference of the disc. From Kiln Debris dateable to the late-first century A.D. over the Quarry Pit Complex. (LWB–N31–2).

No. 25   Fragment of a pottery wheel with an estimated original diameter of about 65 mm. Hard, dark grey-black, slightly sandy, fabric with dark grey-black surfaces. A fine 'fern-leaf' pattern has been cut around the circumference of the disc. From Kiln Debris, dateable to the late-first century A.D., over the Quarry Pit Complex. (LWB–N31–18).

No. 26   Fragment of a pottery wheel with an estimated original diameter of about 64 mm. Hard, light grey sandy fabric with orange-grey surfaces. A fine 'fern-leaf' pattern had been cut around the circumference of the disc. From Kiln Debris, dateable to the late-first century A.D., over the Quarry Pit Complex. (LWB–N31–18).

No. 27   Fragment of a pottery wheel with an estimated original diameter of about 80 mm. Hard grey, slightly sandy fabric, with patchy orange-buff surfaces. Closely spaced angled lines have been quite boldly cut around the circumference of the disc. From Kiln Debris, dateable to the late-first century A.D., over the Quarry Pit Complex. (LWB–M31–2).

No. 28   Complete pottery wheel (now broken in two) with a slightly oval shape, 45–48 mm. in diameter. Hard, grey-brown, slightly sandy fabric with grey-brown surfaces. Closely spaced, shallow angled lines have been cut around the circumference of the disc. Unstratified, Quarry Pit Complex. (LWB–N29).

No. 29   Fragment of a pottery wheel with an estimated original diameter of about 60 mm. Hard, light grey-brown, slightly sandy fabric with light grey-brown surfaces. Angled lines have been cut around the circumference of the disc. Unstratified, Quarry Pit Complex. (LWB–M27–7).

No. 30   About half of a pottery wheel with a diameter of about 63 mm. Hard, orange-buff, slightly sandy fabric with orange-buff surfaces. Angled lines have been cut around the circumference of the disc. From soil over the late-first century Quarry Pit Complex. (LWB–L30–3).

No. 31   Fragment of a pottery wheel with an estimated original diameter of about 76 mm. Hard, light grey, slightly sandy fabric with dull buff surfaces. Bold angled lines have been cut around the circumference of the disc. From soil over the late-first century Quarry Pit Complex. (LWB–L30–3).

No. 32   Fragment of a pottery wheel with an estimated original diameter of about 80 mm. Hard, light grey, slightly sandy fabric with dull buff surfaces. Faint angled lines have been cut around the circumference of the disc. From soil over the late-first century Quarry Pit Complex. (LWB–L30–3).

No. 33   Just over half of a pottery wheel with a diameter of 53 mm. Hard, light grey, slightly sandy fabric with buff-grey surfaces. A well formed 'fern-leaf' pattern has been cut around the circumference of the disc. From disturbed soil in the area of late-first century Quarry Pit Complex. (LWB–L32–5).

No. 34   Fragment of a pottery wheel with an estimated original diameter of about 80 mm. Hard, slightly sandy, orange-grey fabric with orange-grey surfaces. Bold angled lines have been cut around the circumference of the disc. From a demolition deposit over the South Masonry Building. (LWB–M33–2).

Potter's Dies (Fig. 45).

Two inscribed potter's dies of fired clay were recovered from the site (Nos. 37 and 38), together with probable handle fragments from two others (Nos. 35 and 36). As with the pottery wheels, their fabric is very similar to that used in vessels assigned to the Keston Kilns and these dies provide further clear evidence for pottery manufacture at Keston. Dr. Valerie Rigby has kindly provided notes on the two inscribed dies.

No. 35   Probable handle of a potter's die, in a light grey, slightly sandy fired clay, with orange surfaces. The lower, presumably inscribed, end of the die has broken away. (See Nos. 37 and 38). Unstratified. (LWB–1).

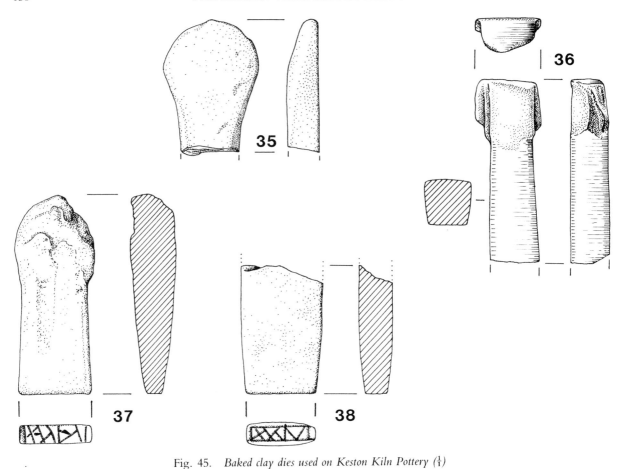

Fig. 45.   *Baked clay dies used on Keston Kiln Pottery* (⅟₁)

No. 36   Probable handle of a potter's die, in a grey, slightly sandy fired clay. The lower, presumably inscribed,
           end of the die has broken away. From soil over the Quarry Pit Complex. (LWB–N29–9).

No. 37   Complete die in fired clay; originally oxidised, with traces of burning. Overall length 52 mm; die-face 22
           mm. × 5 mm.
           The unbordered inscription was executed in cursive letters making it difficult to read and to decide
           whether it is simply a Mark, i.e. a selection of meaningless motifs, or a Name Copy, i.e. an attempt by an
           illiterate or unskilled die-maker to produce the potter's name. It can be read both ways, and in both
           directions, normally left to right, or retrograde, right to left; occasionally even reversing individual letters!
           The possibilities are innumerable; however for the purpose of listing and future researchers, two
           alternatives have been chosen:
           a) IANNEFI ?reading IANNE F(EC)I(T) retrograde
           b) VENANI
           The die was not used for any of the six stamped platters found amongst the settlement material. In Britain
           generally, Name Copies on locally made cups, platters and bowls in quartz-tempered coarse-wares are
           comparatively rare, it was apparently more normal for Marks to be used. The date range for Name Copies
           extends throughout the Roman period, on coarse-wares from the mid-first to early-third centuries and
           from third to fourth centuries on metallic colour-coated and red-slipped products. From filling of Pit 20
           (F.121) under the South Masonry Building, dated to the late-first century A.D. (LWB–M34–30).

No. 38   Broken but still functional fired clay die. Overall surviving length 31 mm.; die face 20 mm. × 5 mm.
           A bordered Mark, with two repeats each of two simple motifs – X and V. The die is not represented on
           platters in the settlement material. Although a simple arrangement, there are no recorded close parallels.
           From filling of a small, undated pit, F.163, South Masonry Building area. (LWB–N33–9).

Clay Crucibles and Metal-Working Residues (Fig. 46).

Some 264 fragments of (mostly iron) slag were recovered from the excavations in Lower Warbank Field. Much of this material was fairly evenly spread throughout the many deposits on the site. The two largest groups of iron slag came from the soil deposits over the South Masonry Building, which produced 79 fragments and the filling of the first century A.D. Quarry Pit Complex, which produced 34 fragments. Only two fragments came from the area of the West Masonry Building. Six pieces came from the filling of the North-East Ditch of the Villa Enclosure but only one from within the adjacent North Timber Building, although 19 fragments came from the fill of the late hut terrace cut into its ruins. No slag was recovered from sealed pre-Conquest deposits.

All of the iron slag appears to be from blacksmithing hearths, where iron was forged into its final shape. Smithies with such hearths must have been very common on farmsteads and villa estates. Here nails, fittings and tools such as those illustrated (Fig. 46) could be manufactured and old implements repaired; yet smithing hearths are rarely found in excavations (probably due to the fact that they were built above ground-level and, thus, they generally do not survive). McDonnell (Ref. 114) has recently described a typical smithing-hearth bottom-slag. These are generally plano-convex in form, often with a slight depression in the upper, flat surface caused by the blast from the bellows. There are a number of complete examples from Lower Warbank of this typical 'bun' form. Most are not very large (generally 50 to 100 mm. across).

In addition to the iron slag, a few pieces of probable copper-alloy slag were also recorded at Keston. Other evidence for brass/bronze-working on the site comes from seven small clay crucible fragments, one of which contained traces of a copper-alloy residue. Six of the crucible fragments were derived from the filling of the Quarry Pit Complex dated to the later first century A.D. (Period IV). All of these fragments are heavily burnt, with the vitrified surfaces often having a red colour due to the inclusion of copper. There is one pinched pouring spout fragment. The filling of the ditch of the West Enclosure (dated to the mid to late-first century A.D.) produced a single small rim fragment. One crucible fragment from the filling of the Quarry Pit Complex, has been drawn (No. 39). It, thus, seems fairly clear that a small-scale bronze or brass working industry was established on the Keston site in the later first century A.D. (Period IV). What was being produced, however, is not entirely clear; brooches, toilet instruments and small fittings are all possibilities.

Small-scale iron and bronze working such as that evidenced at Keston are likely to have been among the common, day-to-day activities carried out on many rural sites during the Roman period.

No. 39   Part of a small, fired clay crucible, probably originally oval in shape. It has a simple upright rim and the exterior has been vitrified by intense heating. The core and interior of the vessel are dark grey-black and the exterior is light grey. There are traces of a copper-alloy residue on the inside of the vessel, indicating that it was used for melting bronze or brass. From the filling of the Quarry Pit Complex, dated to the late-first century A.D. (LWB–N31–4).

Miscellaneous Baked Clay Objects (Fig. 46).

No. 40   Fragment of a Roman (?)box-flue tile bearing a grafitto, scored into the surface of the wet clay before firing. It consists of two angled downward strokes forming a probable letter 'A'. To the left is another angled line, originally perhaps belonging to a repeat of this letter, but it is now partially broken away. Unstratified, West Masonry Building. (LWB–Z–1).

No. 41   Small, undecorated pottery counter made from a potsherd of light grey-brown sandy ware. Diameter 21 mm. From filling of the Quarry Pit Complex, dated to the late-first century A.D. (LWB–N29–8).

No. 42   Small, crudely-made pottery vessel or container, of an orange-red sandy fabric. The function of this vessel is not clear but it does not appear to belong to the normal range of domestic pottery used on the site. It shows no sign of intensive heating as might be expected with a crucible for melting metal. From the Centre Metalling, over the Quarry Pit Complex, dated to the fourth century A.D. (LWB–N29–11).

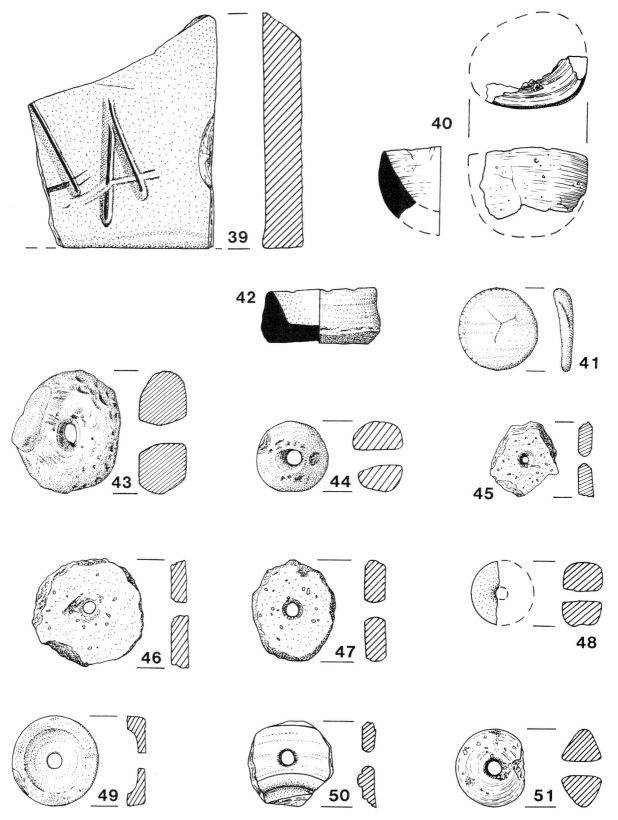

Fig. 46. *Miscellaneous, objects of baked clay, Nos. 39–40 and 42 ($\frac{1}{2}$); pottery counter, No. 41 ($\frac{1}{4}$) and spindle whorls, Nos. 43–51 ($\frac{1}{2}$).*

Spindle-whorls (Fig. 46).

A small collection of spindle-whorls came from the excavations in Lower Warbank Field. Such objects are commonly found on Iron Age and Roman sites and are clearly connected with textile production. A representative selection of nine probable spindle-whorls is illustrated (Nos. 43–51), although No. 43 may be considered too large and heavy to be included here as a true spindle-whorl. The majority of the spindle-whorls from the site are of baked clay, quite frequently being made from a re-used potsherd (e.g. Nos. 46, 47 and 49). There are also a few examples in chalk (e.g. Nos. 43 and 44). Only one spindle-whorl from a certain pre-Roman context was recovered (No. 51) and this is of a well-known Iron Age type.

No. 43 Crudely-shaped chalk disc with a diameter of 60–65 mm. and a roughly central perforation. The perforation is oval in shape and measures 6–10 mm. across. The object may be too large and heavy to be considered as a true spindle-whorl and it is possibly a weight of some other kind. From a general soil deposit south of the North Timber Building. (LWB–78–47).

No. 44 Plain chalk spindle-whorl, with a diameter of 36 mm. It is ovoid in cross-section with a slightly off-centre perforation, 8 mm. in diameter. From the filling of Gully C of the Centre Enclosure, dateable to the early-second century A.D. (LWB–C25–5).

No. 45 Very crude pottery spindle-whorl, with a diameter of 36–40 mm., made from a re-used sherd of grey-brown shell-tempered ware. The central perforation is 4 mm. in diameter. From filling of a post-hole (F.378) cutting the fourth century A.D. metalling over the Quarry Pit Complex. (LWB–M29–9).

No. 46 Crude pottery spindle-whorl, with a diameter of 55–60 mm., made from a re-used black shell-tempered ware pot base. The central perforation is 6 mm. in diameter. From filling of the East Enclosure Ditch, dateable to the late-first century A.D. (LWB–X22–3).

No. 47 Pottery spindle-whorl, slightly oval in shape, with a diameter of 45–54 mm. The object is made from a re-used sherd of black shell-tempered ware. The central perforation is 9 mm. in diameter. From plough-soil north of the South Masonry Building. (LWB–J31–1).

No. 48 About half of a cylindrical pottery spindle-whorl with an estimated original diameter of 34 mm. The object is made of a hard, sandy clay, fired orange-brown. The central perforation is partially broken away but it probably had an original diameter of about 6 mm. From upper filling of the West Enclosure Ditch, dateable to the mid to late-first century A.D. (LWB–E18–2).

No. 49 Pottery spindle-whorl, with a diameter of 48 mm., made from a re-used pot base of smooth grey-black ware with orange surfaces. The central perforation is neatly drilled and has a diameter of 8 mm. From middle filling of the South-East Ditch of the Villa Enclosure, probably dateable to the later second to earlier third century A.D. (LWB–BB22–7).

No. 50 Roughly made pottery spindle-whorl, with a diameter of about 45 mm., made from a re-used basal sherd of an orange-buff Keston Kiln Ware platter. The central perforation is 6–7 mm. in diameter. From the filling of the Quarry Pit Complex, dateable to the late-first century A.D. (LWB–N30–8).

No. 51 Pottery spindle-whorl of biconical cross-section and diameter of 41 mm. The object is made of clay, tempered with flint and shell and fired dark brown. The central perforation is 7 mm. across. Spindle-whorls of this general form are well-known in Iron Age contexts. From the upper filling of Pit 9, dateable to the late-Iron Age. (LWB–T24–9).

Objects of Antler (Fig. 47).

A total of six pieces of Red Deer antler have been illustrated in this report (Nos. 52–57). Of these, two are definite tools; a pick (No. 54) and a rake-head (No. 56), whilst the remainder (Nos. 52, 53, 55 and 57) probably represent off-cuts and waste products. The presence of these probable waste pieces seems to indicate that small-scale antler-working actually took place on the site. Presumably, implements like the pick and rake-head illustrated were produced. Two of the illustrated waste tines (Nos. 52 and 55) came from the filling of the Anglo-Saxon sunken hut and another tine from here has been published previously (Ref. 115, No. 475). It is not clear, however, if these are residual Roman pieces or whether they represent antler-working in the Saxon period. The other antler pieces (Nos. 53 and 57) and the two implements (Nos. 54 and 56) came from late-Roman contexts.

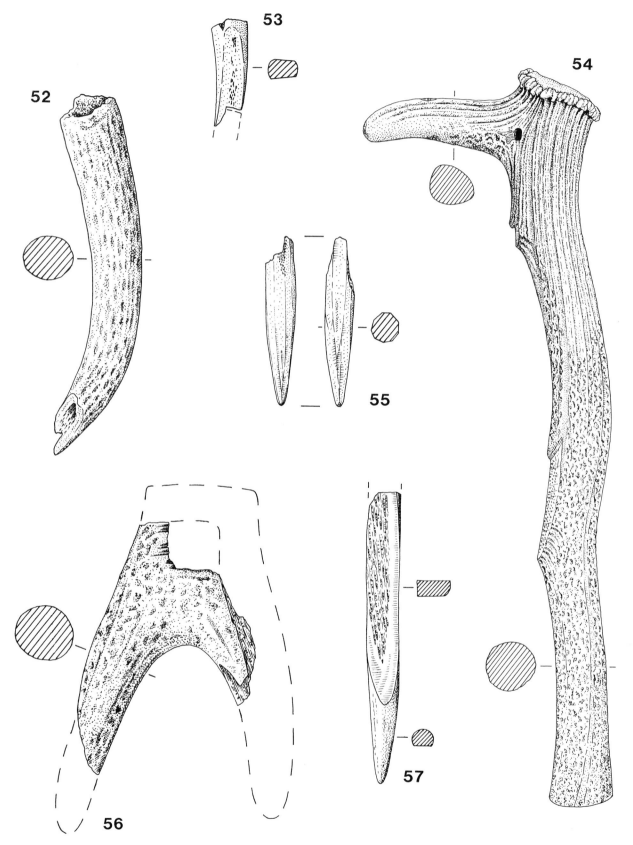

Fig. 47.   *Antler tools and waste products ($\frac{1}{2}$), No. 54 (about $\frac{1}{3}$).*

No. 52   Largely complete antler tine. The piece has been broken away from the main shaft and the tip is also broken off. There is no indication of any human working, but it is perhaps most likely that it represents waste from antler working. From upper filling of the Anglo-Saxon sunken hut. (LWB–M24–3).

No. 53   Small piece of an antler tine. A thick strip has been cut away on two opposite sides of the piece and the ends have been partially sawn through, then broken away. This piece has clearly been worked and seems to indicate that small-scale working of antler took place on the Keston site in the Roman period. From upper filling of the North-West Ditch of the Villa Enclosure, dated to the late-third to fourth century A.D. (F.800; LWB–76–3).

No. 54   Pick made from a shed Red Deer antler. The short brow-tine was left at the base to form the working end. Scars of where the two other main tines have been removed remain higher up on the beam but the crown has been cut away completely. The length of the beam as surviving is 522 mm. This implement is of a crude but apparently effective type and the form is well-known from as early as the Neolithic period. Similar tools are also well-known in Roman contexts, however, and examples come from Corbridge and Wroxeter (Ref. 116), Maiden Castle (Ref. 117) and Dover (unpublished). From a demolition deposit over the South Masonry Building. (LWB–F34–4).

No. 55   Broken tip of an antler tine, with a surviving length of 90 mm. The piece has been roughly sharpened at one end by the removal of long slivers from the outer surface, using a knife. From lower filling of the Anglo-Saxon sunken hut. (LWB–M24–4).

No. 56   Part of a rake or hoe made from two tines of a Red Deer antler. Only one tine survives substantially complete but its tip is broken off. Three slivers of bone had been cut lengthwise from its end, suggesting that the tip had originally been sharpened into a point. Only the base of the other tine remains. Above the projecting tines are traces of a square hole, cut through the thickness of the beam. This would have originally held the wooden handle of the implement. Rakes of this general type are known from a number of Roman sites, including the nearby villa at South Darenth, where three very similar examples have been published (Refs. 118 and 119). From the Upper East Metaling dated to the fourth century A.D. (LWB–Z23– 4).

No. 57   Antler tine with a broad strip cut away from two opposite sides. Perhaps used as a peg but more probably this is a piece of waste. From filling of the heating chamber (F.8) of the External Corn Drying Oven, dateable to the fourth century A.D. (LWB–78–9).

Iron Age Bone Toggles (Fig. 48).

Two small bone objects (Nos. 58 and 59) identifiable as 'toggles' were recovered from the filling of Pit 9 (F.632), dated to the late-Iron Age. These objects can be paralleled by finds from several other Iron Age sites in Britain, most notably Danebury hillfort in Hampshire (Ref. 120). Here, some 28 very similar bone and antler examples have been recorded and these constitute the largest collection so far found. They include both plain pieces and others decorated with ring-and-dot motifs. Many are burnt to some degree and Lyn Sellwood in her detailed study of these objects has suggested that this burning was deliberate and done in order to produce a more desirable colour. Interestingly, this idea seems to be borne-out by the two Keston examples, both of which show signs of burning. At Danebury, the bulk of the toggles came from later Iron Age contexts, dating between the fourth and first centuries B.C. The function of these toggles is not entirely clear but it seems most likely that they represent some kind of dress fastening.

No. 58   About one third of a cylindrical toggle of burnt bone, with a length of 33 mm. The outer surface has partially flaked off but, where surviving, it is polished and decorated with three rows of a double ring-and-dot motif. There is a lateral groove around either end externally. From middle filling of late-Iron Age Pit 9. (F.632; LWB–U24–6).

No. 59   Substantially complete cylindrical toggle of burnt bone, with a length of 30 mm. The exterior is plain but well polished, with an oval, counter-sunk hole bored through the centre of one side. A shallow longitudinal groove occurs on either side of this hole externally. From middle filling of late-Iron Age Pit 9. (F.632; LWB–U24–6).

Other Objects of Bone (Fig. 48).

No. 60   Small bone gaming die, measuring 8 mm. × 9mm. × 10 mm. The numerals are marked by double ring-and-dot motifs. The numbers shown on opposite sides, if added, total seven, which is the norm. Unstratified, Quarry Pit Complex. (LWB–L26–6).

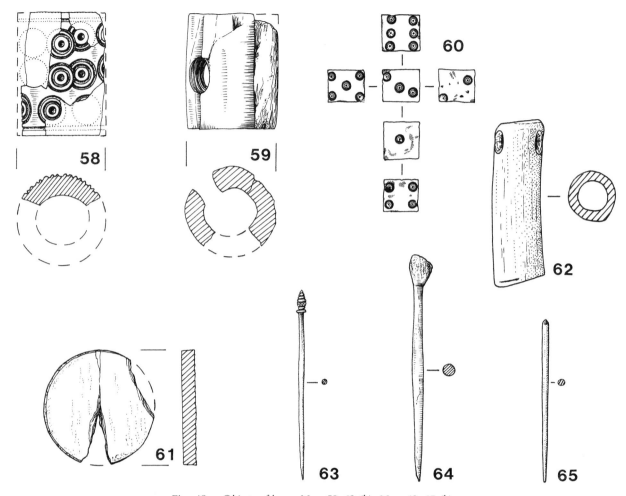

Fig. 48.   *Objects of bone, Nos. 58–62 ($\frac{1}{1}$); Nos. 63–65 ($\frac{1}{2}$).*

No. 61   Plain, crudely fashioned bone counter with a diameter of 30 mm. and a rectangular cross-section. The piece has been broken in two but may never have been finished. From filling of the late-Roman hut-terrace cutting through the North Timber Building. (LWB–77–246).

No. 62   Small bone object with an overall length of 44 mm. and a circular cross-section. A hole has been bored lengthwise down the centre of the piece and there is a smaller horizontal counter-sunk perforation through one end. The outer surface has been well polished. Probably a handle of some kind. From lower filling of Pit 2 (F.419), dated to the middle Iron Age. (LWB–024–4).

No. 63   Complete bone pin. The ovoid head is decorated with horizontal grooves and lattice-work and there is a single reel below this. The shaft tapers slightly towards both ends and has a length of 101 mm., with a circular cross-section. From filling of the stoke-pit (F.10) of the External Corn Drying Oven, dated to the fourth century A.D. (LWB–78–11).

No. 64   Complete bone pin, with a very roughly shaped spherical head formed from the original knuckle-end of the bone. The shaft tapers towards both ends and has a length of 120 mm., with a circular cross-section. It is well polished. The form of this pin places it within Nina Crummy's Type 3, which is dated *c*. A.D. 200–400 (Ref. 121). From upper filling of Ditch 21b, dated to the fourth to earlier-fifth century A.D. (F.1177; LWB–77–205).

No. 65   Complete bone pin with a crudely formed conical head. The shaft tapers towards the point and has a length of 86 mm. It is well polished. The form of this pin places it within Nina Crummy's Type 1, which is dated *c*. A.D. 70–200/250 (Ref. 122). From middle filling of Ditch 21a, dated to the fourth century A.D. (F.1174; LWB–77–225).

   Surprisingly, few bone pins were recovered from the excavations in Lower Warbank Field, although the reason for this is not clear.

Objects of Iron (Figs 49 and 50).

A total of 26 iron objects from the excavations in Lower Warbank Field have been illustrated (Nos. 66–84, 89, 90, 934–938). For the most-part these are typical of what would be expected from an Iron Age/Romano-British rural settlement site. There are two iron brooches of first century A.D. date (Nos. 89 and 90), a small collection of keys (Nos. 75–78) and a number of other typical household objects, such as styli (Nos. 72 and probably 74) and kitchen knives (Nos. 73 and 82). Specifically agricultural implements, such as would be in everyday use on a working farm, include a bill-hook (No. 66), two small pruning-hooks (Nos. 67 and 68), and an ox-goad (No. 79). Of more particular interest is the spearhead (No. 69) and the small hammer-head (No. 70) recovered from Pit 9 (F.632), which has been dated to the late-Iron Age. Five iron water-pipe collars (Nos. 934–938), associated with two separate Roman pipe-lines are illustrated in the section on building materials (page 284).

A quantity of iron slag recovered from the site indicates that black-smithing took place at Warbank and it seems highly probable that equipment, like that illustrated, was actually made on the site (see page 295).

No. 66	Iron bill-hook with an open socket for a wooden handle. The blade is axe-shaped, although the cutting edge has broken away. This form is one of the less common types found on Romano-British sites. Similar, but larger, examples come from Dicket Mead, Herts (Ref. 123), Cirencester (Ref. 124) and London (Ref. 125). From soil over the fourth century A.D. Upper East Metalling. (LWB–BB21–3).
No. 67	Small iron pruning-hook with a curved blade and an open socket for a wooden handle (see also No. 68). From soil over the fourth century A.D. Upper East Metalling. (LWB–CC20–3).
No. 68	Small iron pruning-hook with a curved blade. Traces of a socket for a wooden handle survive. This implement is broadly similar to No. 67 but it is slightly smaller and must have been used for fairly delicate work. From upper filling of the North-West Ditch of the Villa Enclosure, dated to the late-third to early-fourth century A.D. (F.801; LWB–76–4).

Similar sized hooks to those described above come from Barnsley Park (Ref. 126), Bignor (Ref. 127), Chilgrove 2 (Ref. 128) and Shakenoak (Ref. 129). At Barnsley Park the implement was suggested as a grape-hook. |
No. 69	Iron spearhead with a narrow, leaf-shaped blade and a closed, circular socket. The object is now somewhat corroded but it seems clear that it originally had a blade some 143 mm. in length, with a central mid-rib. The context of the piece indicates that it is of pre-Conquest date. Several broadly similar examples come from Hod Hill (Ref. 130) and these are dated to the late-Iron Age to early-Roman period. From upper filling of Pit 9 (F.632), dated to the late-Iron Age. (LWB–U23–13).
No. 70	Small, rectangular sectioned, iron hammer-head with a central, sub-rectangular hole for a wooden handle. It has a flat striking face at the end of one arm, whilst the other arm has a chamfered upper surface, with a flat or slightly domed striking face. The object has an overall weight of just 67 grams and its small size indicates that it was something of a specialist tool, intended for fairly delicate work. Its precise purpose, however, remains unknown. From upper filling of Pit 9 (F.632), dated to the late-Iron Age. (LWB–U23–13).
No. 71	Long iron ferrule with a split socket, pierced by a square-sectioned iron nail or rivet. The object has a length of 186 mm. and would be suitable for the end of a spear or staff of some kind. From the Centre Metalling over the Quarry Pit Complex, dated to the fourth century A.D. (LWB–N28–5).
No. 72	Plain iron writing stylus with a length of 120 mm. It has a shaft with a circular cross-section and a flattened, rectangular head. The form of this implement places it in Manning's Group II or III (Ref. 131). There is, however, no cronological significance to this classification and these objects cannot be accurately dated stylistically. From soil above the Lower East Metalling, dated to the second to third century A.D. (LWB–CC23–3).
No. 73	Part of a small iron knife with a surviving length of 79 mm. The tang remains largely intact and this has a rectangular cross-section. Conservation work revealed traces of an organic handle around the tang but this was too fragmentary to identify. Only the upper part of the blade has survived and this is slightly bent. It seems fairly clear that this was a small domestic implement with many uses in the Roman home. From filling of the late-Roman hut-terrace cutting through the North Timber Building. (LWB–77–256).
No. 74	Possible iron writing stylus. The shaft is broken and has a surviving length of 50 mm., with a square cross-section. The head has been flattened out to form a straight-edged blade. The identification of this broken object is not certain. If it was a stylus it seems to have been of a rather more crude type than No. 72. From a demolition layer over the South Masonry Building. (LWB–F34–2).

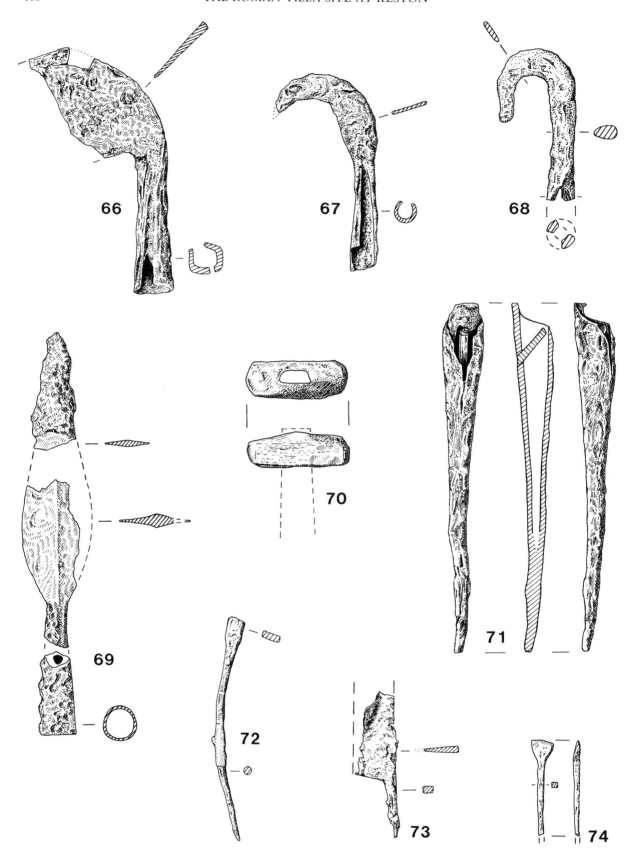

Fig. 49.   *Objects of iron, including tools and spearhead* ($\frac{1}{2}$).

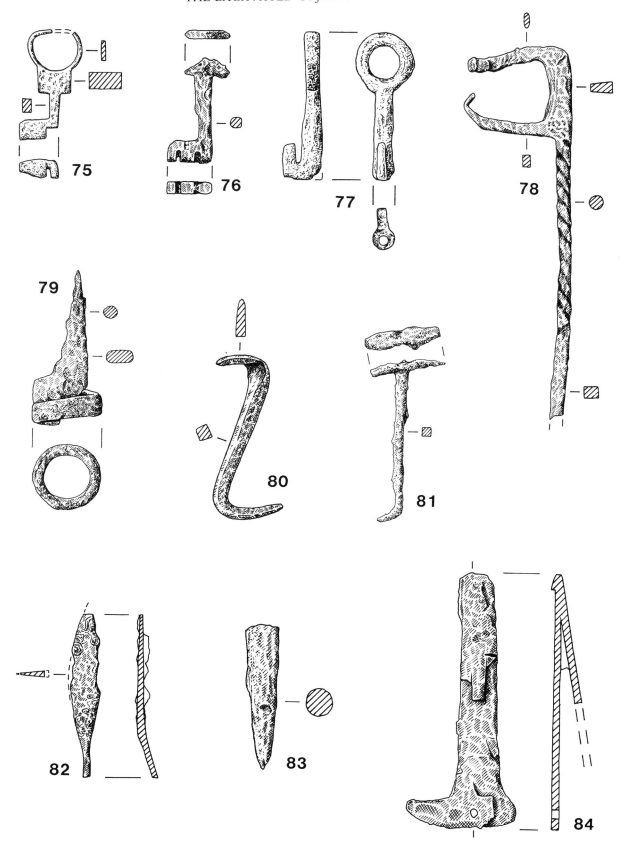

Fig. 50. *Objects of iron* ($\frac{1}{2}$), *No. 79* ($\frac{1}{1}$).

No. 75   Iron key with a large, round loop partially broken away. The bit is heavily corroded and the precise arrangement of the teeth is not clear. The key, itself, appears to be for use with a tumbler lock and many similar examples are known from Roman sites. The context of the present example, however, could indicate that it is of post-Roman date. From filling of Ditch 4, dated to the medieval or post-medieval period. (LWB–K25–11).

No. 76   Small iron slide key, now rather corroded. The handle loop has broken away. The shaft has a sub-square cross-section and the rectangular bit shows traces of cut grooves which engaged the lock mechanism. From hillwash deposit east of the West Masonry Building. (LWB–77–8).

No. 77   Heavy iron key for a rotary lock. There is a round loop for suspension at the end and the shaft is circular in cross-section. The simple L-shaped bit is complete and there is a central longitudinal hole bored in this end of the shaft. An x-ray examination indicated that this key was made from a single piece of metal. From lower filling of post-pipe, Post Hole 3 of the North Timber Building. (LWB–76–171).

No. 78   Large iron lift-key with two long teeth set at right angles to the shaft. The handle is broken away. The shaft has been spirally twisted for a distance of some 90 mm. below the lower tooth. This is a well-known type of simple Roman key. From filling of miscellaneous Pit F.1096, dated to the fourth century A.D. (LWB–77–104).

No. 79   Iron ox-goad consisting of a spiralled loop in two turns, continuing on into a sharp, projecting spike. The loop would have been fitted onto the end of a wooden pole or stick. A bone example of an ox-goad comes from Lydney Park (Ref. 132) and other iron examples are known from Woodcutts (Ref. 133), Verulamium (Refs. 134 and 135) and Maiden Castle (Ref. 136). From general soil above the late-first century Quarry Pit Complex. (LWB–M28–3).

No. 80   Iron S-shaped wall hook, with a tapering rectangular shaft and a flattened head. From filling of miscellaneous post-hole, F.1004, of uncertain date. (LWB–77–8).

No. 81   Small, iron T-clamp or staple, with a shaft of square cross-section. Such clamps had a number of uses, including holding hypocaust box-flue tiles in place (Ref. 137). From filling of Ditch 5, dated to the post-Roman period. (LWB–N28–4).

No. 82   Small iron knife with tip missing. The tang is rectangular in cross-section and the overall length surviving is 86 mm. From filling of the Centre Enclosure Ditch, dated to the second century A.D. (LWB–J23–6).

No. 83   Tip of a solid iron spike, with circular cross-section and surviving length of 77 mm. Since the object is solid it seems improbable that it is part of a ferrule like No. 71. From general soil deposit north of the South Masonry Building. (LWB–J32–2).

No. 84   Iron fitting, or bracket, now partially broken and corroded. Originally the object appears to have consisted of two T-shaped strips, joined at the base. Only one of these now survives largely complete. Both strips seem to have had a rectangular cross-section and there is a small rivet-hole in the centre of the cross-piece on the complete example. The precise function of this fitting is not clear. From soil under the fourth century Centre Metalling, above the Quarry Pit Complex. (LWB–L27–5).

Brooches (Figs. 51 and 52).

A collection of just less than 20 brooches was recovered from the Keston excavations and nearly all of these are illustrated here (Nos. 85–101). The majority of the brooches are of early-Roman date and they are generally of bronze, with just two iron examples (Nos. 89 and 90). There is one late-Roman crossbow brooch (No. 100). Of special interest is the La Tène I Iron Age brooch (No. 91) and a probable La Tène III 'Glastonbury' type brooch (No. 94).

No. 85   Bent and damaged bronze strip-brooch of the Hod Hill type. The bow tapers towards a narrow, knobbed foot, with a solid catch-plate above. The upper part of the bow is decorated with longitudinal grooves and at the top it is rolled under to house the pin, which is now missing. The lower part of the bow is plain. The type is well-known on early-Roman sites and is largely confined to the Claudian-Neronian period in date (Ref. 138). From soil below the Upper East Metalling, dated to the third century A.D. (LWB–Z24–6).

No. 86   Bronze bow-brooch of the 'Nauheim derivative' type. The bow is flattened and bears decoration in the form of a punched longitudinal cable motif. The edge of the solid catch-plate is broken away and only the beginning of the spring remains at the top. This is a very well-known type of brooch, dateable to the first century A.D. (Ref. 139). From soil over the fourth century A.D. Upper East Metalling. (LWB–AA24–12).

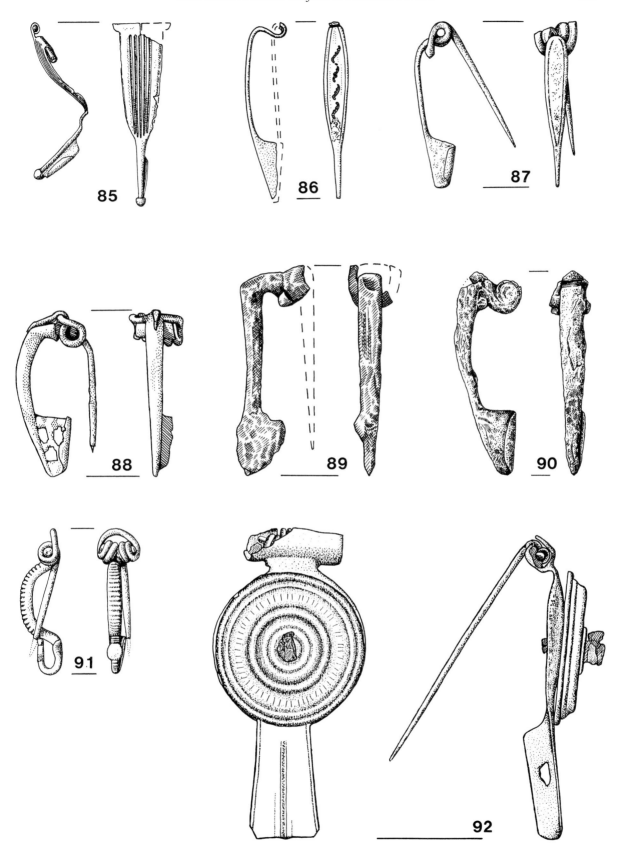

Fig. 51.   *Iron Age and early-Roman brooches* (¼).

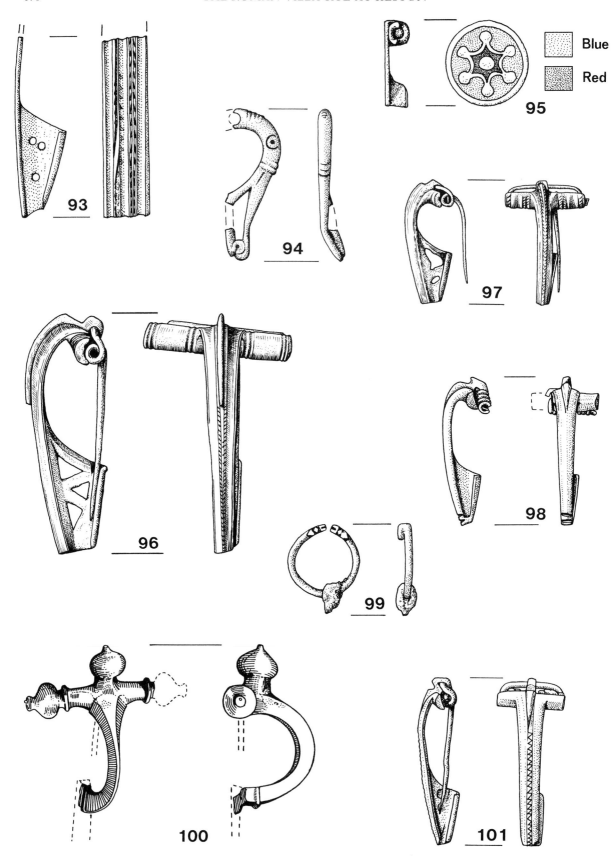

Fig. 52.   *Iron Age and Roman brooches* (⅟₁)

No. 87   Complete but slightly corroded bronze bow-brooch of the well-known 'Nauheim derivative' type, similar to No. 86. The bow is flattened and undecorated and the catch-plate is solid. The pin is broken in two. Dateable to the first century A.D. From filling of the Quarry Pit Complex, dated to the late-first century A.D. (LWB–N28–12).

No. 88   Complete bronze bow-brooch of the 'Colchester' type (Camulodunum Type III, Ref. 140). The bow is plain and has an oval cross-section, whilst the catch-plate is perforated by three irregular holes. The type of brooch was very common in the first century A.D., production lasting from *c*. A.D. 20 to 75 (Ref. 141). From filling of the East Enclosure Ditch, dated to the late-first century A.D. (LWB–T21–4).

No. 89   Corroded iron bow-brooch of the 'Nauheim derivative' type. The bow is straight and has a sub-rectangular cross-section. The catch-plate is solid and the pin is missing. This type of brooch is more frequently made of bronze (e.g. Nos. 86 and 87) and is dateable to the first century A.D. (see Ref. 142). From general soil over the fourth century A.D. Upper East Metalling. (LWB–CC24–3).

No. 90   Corroded iron bow-brooch, with a solid catch-plate and only part of the spring surviving. This is a form typical of the first century A.D., although bronze is more commonly used for the manufacture of such pieces. From soil over the late-first century A.D. Quarry Pit Complex. (LWB–L28–4).

No. 91   Complete La Tène I fibula of bronze, with an iron hinge-pin through the spring. The bow is arched and is decorated with closely spaced lateral grooves. The foot is turned back on itself and is parallel to the catch-plate. Near the end it is expanded into a small, plain circular disc. The spring is in four turns.

    This type of brooch is fairly rare and most of the examples from Britain come from the southern half of the country. The general form is of continental origin or at least inspiration (Ref. 143) although the hinged pin, as on the present example, is an insular British feature. Within the British material are three main sub-types. The most common of these is the 'Wessex' form and it is to this group that the Keston example belongs (Ref. 144). The precise date of these brooches has yet to be decided but they seem to be broadly dateable to the period *c*. 450–200 B.C. The present brooch, thus, seems to be of a similar date to the earliest pottery from the site, which is associated with a small group of pits and post-holes (Period II, see page 12). From a general soil layer, north-west of the Anglo-Saxon sunken hut. (LWB–L23–2).

No. 92   Complete bronze brooch of 'thistle' type (Camulodunum Type XI, Collingwood Group W, Refs. 145 and 146). The applied, upper plate of the central rosette survives and is decorated with a series of concentric circular mouldings. The broadest of these bears an incised pattern of short cross-lines. The rosette-plate is held in place by a large central rivet. The spring and pin of the brooch also survive, although the spring casing is damaged on one side. The catch-plate is solid, except for one sub-triangular perforation.

    This type of brooch is descended from Gallic and German types and some examples may have been imported into Britain during the pre-Conquest era. More generally, they occur on early-Roman sites but seem to have gone out of use by the end of the Claudian period. From filling of Pit 20 (F.121), under the South Masonry Building, dated to the late-first century A.D. (LWB–M34–30).

No. 93   Part of a bronze brooch of 'Langton Down' type (Camulodunum Type XII, Ref. 147). The head is missing and only the lower part of the bow and catch-plate survive. The bow is longitudinally ribbed and the catch-plate is solid, except for three small, round perforations. This type of brooch was imported into Britain on a small scale before the Roman Conquest, but became more common with the Claudian invasion, dying out by the Flavian period (Ref. 148). From upper filling of the North-West Ditch of the Villa Enclosure (F.800), dated to the fourth century A.D. (LWB–G6–2).

No. 94   Damaged La Tène III bronze brooch, apparently belonging to Hull's uncommon 'Glastonbury' type (Type 6 – see Ref 149). The foot has been cast as one with the bow leaving an opening above the pin-catch. This forms an open catch-plate now partially broken away. At the foot of the catch-plate, on one side only, there is a single, punched ring-and-dot motif. This motif occurs again on both sides of the bow, just above a pair of moulded cross-ridges, which imitate the foot attachment-collar of earlier La Tène forms. The top of the bow is broken away, across a small perforation which once would have housed an axial rod, holding the pin-spring in place. This brooch-type is likely to be of immediately pre-Conquest date. Unstratified, Quarry Pit Complex. (LWB–L26–6).

No. 95   Small, flat, enamelled bronze plate-brooch, with missing pin. A central flat disc of metal is surrounded by a shape of five concave sides, filled with red enamel. This is enclosed within a raised area of bronze, consisting of a six-pointed star with a lobe at each point, projecting into an outer field of turquoise enamel. A similar brooch came form Lullingstone, where it was dated to the third century A.D. (Ref. 150) and another very similar example (unprovenanced) is illustrated by Hattatt (Ref. 151). From upper filling of the North-West Ditch of the Villa Enclosure (F.800), dated to the fourth century A.D. (LWB–76–178).

No. 96   Complete bronze broch of the 'Dolphin' type, with a catch-plate pierced by three triangular perforations. The bow has a central mid-rib, the lower part of which is decorated with incised angled lines. The horizontal spring-case bears four pairs of lateral grooves and the spring and pin remain largely intact. This

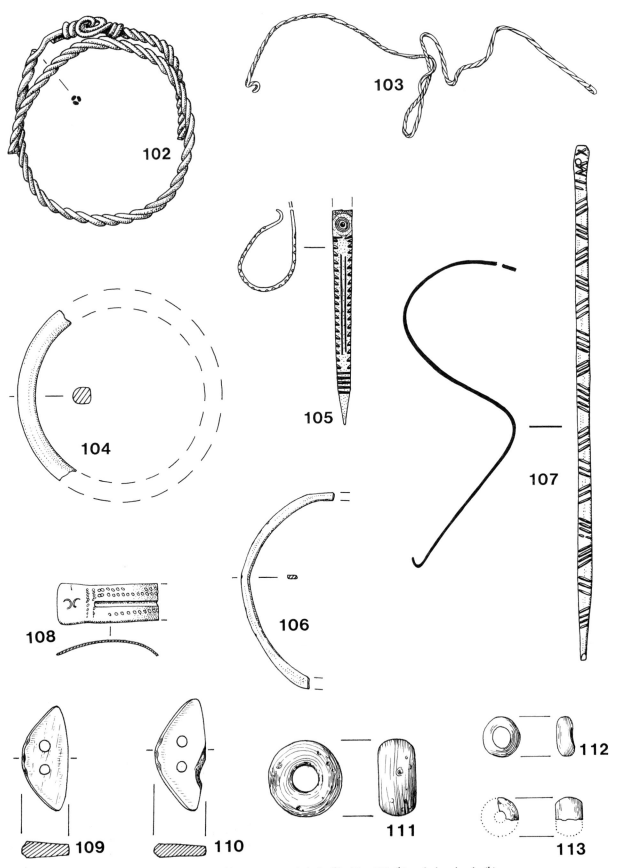

Fig. 53. *Bracelets of bronze, jet and shale (⅟₁), No. 103 (½) and glass beads (⅟₁).*

type of brooch is well-known on sites of the Roman period and is dateable to the mid to late-first century A.D. (Ref. 152). From the lining of the Water Storage Pond, probably constructed in the second century A.D. (LWB–78–57).

No. 97   Small, but complete bronze brooch of the 'Dolphin' type, with a perforated catch-plate. The bow has a central mid-rib decorated with incised angled lines. The horizontal spring-case arms have vertical ridges which also show incised decoration. Dateable to the mid to late-first century A.D. (Ref. 153). From upper filling of the West Enclosure Ditch, dated to the mid to late-first century A.D. (LWB–77–101).

No. 98   Small bronze brooch of Colchester 'BB' type, with a solid catch-plate. Only one of the short horizontal arms protecting the spring survives. Most of the spring itself, together with a very short section of the pin, remains. The bow is undecorated, except for two lateral grooves at the foot. This type of brooch is dateable to the mid to late-first century A.D. (Ref. 154). From general soil, south of the fourth century A.D. Upper East Metalling. (LWB–BB24–5).

No. 99   Small, penannular brooch of brass, with a sub-square cross-section. The terminals have been turned back and decorated, perhaps to represent animal heads. A deposit of iron corrosion opposite the terminals probably represents the last remains of a central iron pin. Brooches of this type are generally not closely dateable (Ref. 155). From a demolition deposit over the South Masonry Building. (LWB–H33–4).

No. 100   Upper part of a bronze brooch of 'cross-bow' type, with well developed, disc-necked, globular terminals on the arms (only one of which survives complete). There is another globular terminal on the head without a neck-disc. The lower part of the brooch has broken away and the remaining bow has been bent to one side. No trace of the pin survives. This type of brooch was very popular in later Roman Britain and the present example is likely to be of late-third or fourth century A.D. date. From soil over the South Masonry Building. (LWB–I34–6).

No. 101   Small, complete bronze brooch of Colchester 'B' type (Camulodunum Type IV, Ref. 156), with a solid catch-plate. The bow has been slightly bent, distorting the profile. There is a longitudinal mid-rib on the bow, decorated with an incised zig-zag pattern. This type of brooch may be dated to c. A.D. 50–75 (Ref. 157). From middle filling of the West Enclosure Ditch, dated to the mid to late-first century A.D. (LWB–E19–3).

Bracelets and Necklaces (Fig. 53).

No. 102   Bronze bracelet made of three strands of twisted wire. The piece originally had at least two hoops, of which only one now remains complete. One original fastening survives, with the individual wire strands here being coiled to form an elaborate 'knot'. Bracelets of this general type belong mostly to the late-Roman period but some second century examples are known, as at Lullingstone (Ref. 158). From filling of the South Tank under the South Masonry Building, dated to the late-second to early-third century A.D. (LWB–J35–4).

No. 103   Bronze necklace of square-sectioned, twisted wire. The piece is heavily distorted and is now broken in two. The necklace was originally closed by means of two simple, hooked terminals, each bearing two incised horizontal grooves. From primary filling of the South-East Ditch of the Villa Enclosure, dated to the late-second to early-third century A.D. (LWB–BB22–8).

No. 104   About one quarter of a small shale bracelet, with sub-rectangular cross-section. The original internal diameter may be estimated as about 47 mm. From upper filling of the North-West Ditch of the Villa Enclosure (F.800), dated to the fourth century A.D. (LWB–76–3).

No. 105   Part of a decorated bronze bracelet with simple, hooked terminal. The terminal is plain, but above this there are five horizontal grooves. Following these there is a 32 mm. long zone decorated by two central, longitudinal grooves with angled notches cut along both edges. Beyond this, a single ring-and-dot motif is probably all that remains of the main decoration of the band. This type of bracelet is dateable to the later Roman period and is probably intrusive in its present context. From filling of the Centre Enclosure Ditch, dated to the second century A.D. (LWB–I27–2).

No. 106   Nearly half of a plain bronze bracelet made from a flat strip of metal, with rectangular cross-section. The original diameter may be estimated as being about 55 mm. From upper filling of the North-West Ditch of the Villa Enclosure (F.800), dated to the fourth century A.D. (LWB–76–3).

No. 107   Complete bronze bracelet made from a thin strip of metal, with a rectangular cross-section. The outer surface is decorated with groups of angled, punched lines running across the width of the band. One end of the band has been hammered out and a small hole drilled through, allowing the insertion of the opposite end, which tapers to a hooked terminal. The original bracelet would have had a diameter of just 40–50 mm., suggesting that it was for a child. The style indicates that it is probably late-Roman in date. From soil over the fourth century A.D. Upper East Metalling. (LWB–Z23–3).

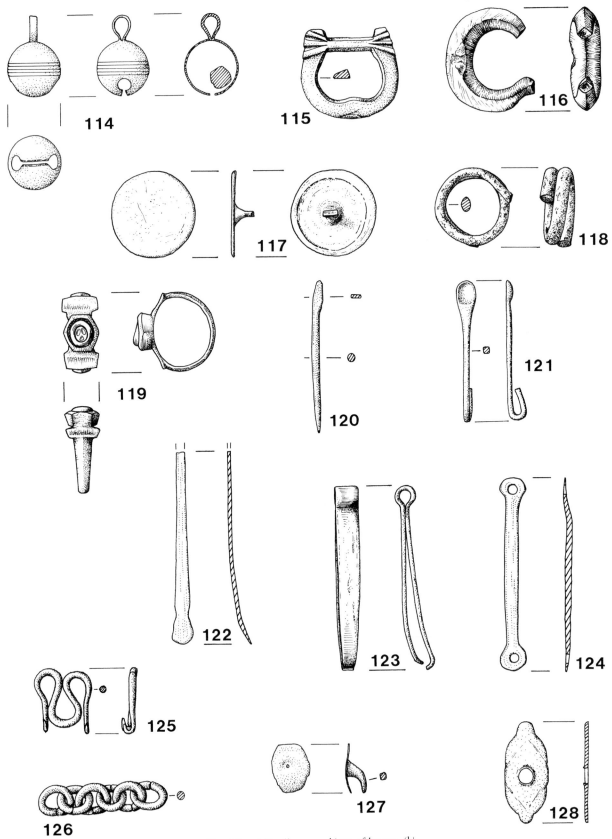

Fig. 54.   *Miscellaneous objects of bronze* ($\frac{1}{1}$).

No. 108 Terminal fragment of a bracelet, made from a thin strip of bronze. The strip widens towards the terminal and the outer surface is decorated with a centrally placed longitudinal groove and rows of punched dots and circles. Part of a similar bracelet came from Baldock (Ref. 159). From soil under the fourth century A.D. Centre Metalling, over the Quarry Pit Complex. (LWB–L27–5).

Nos. 109 and 110 Two sub-triangular segments from an articulated jet bracelet. Each segment is perforated by two centrally placed holes for attachment and the curved outer edges on both are decorated with three pairs of opposed, V-shaped, cut notches. Each segment has a wedge-shaped cross-section, which reflects the curve of the bracelet. Crummy (Ref. 160) considers the type to be of late third to fourth century A.D. date. In Kent, similar pieces have come from Ospringe (Ref. 161) and Springhead (Ref. 162). From upper filling of the North-West Ditch of the Villa Enclosure Ditch (F.800), dated to the fourth century A.D. (LWB–76–3).

Beads (Fig. 53).

No. 111 Large, plain annular bead with a diameter of 20 mm. Pale blue-green translucent glass. The central perforation has a diameter of 7 mm. From upper filling of the North-East Ditch of the Villa Enclosure, dated to the later third to early-fourth century A.D. (LWB–76–63).

No. 112 Small, plain annular bead with a diameter of 10 mm. Pale blue translucent glass. The central perforation has a diameter of 5 mm. From soil over the late-first century A.D. Quarry Pit Complex. (LWB–L28–4).

No. 113 About a quarter of a small bead with an estimated original diameter of about 10 mm. Royal blue glass, with heavily abraded surfaces. The central perforation had a diameter of about 5 mm. From a demolition deposit over the South Masonry Building. (LWB–N33–2).

Miscellaneous Objects of Bronze and Brass (Fig. 54).

No. 114 Complete small bell of brass with a suspension loop on the top. Inside is a small iron ball which served to make the bell sound. The outer sphere of the bell was made from two separate halves, which analysis during conservation has shown to be soldered together with a white tin-solder. The loop is also soldered in position.

    The precise purpose of small bells such as this is not clear but it seems likely that many were attached to the halters or collars of pets or possibly farm animals, whilst others could have been personal ornaments (Ref. 163). From filling of the Quarry Pit Complex, dated to the late-first century A.D. (LWB–N31–17).

No. 115 D-shaped buckle of brass, with traces of surface tinning. On the upper surface, the base of the loop at its junction with the cross-bar is decorated with punched, angled lines. At the head there is a widening of the loop and traces of iron corrosion at this point could indicate the position of the lost central pin. The back of the buckle is plain. From a demolition deposit over the South Masonry Building. (LWB–M36–2).

No. 116 Loop of a stout buckle of bronze. The piece is undecorated and has a diamond-shaped cross-section. A slot cut into the top of the loop probably once housed the point of the central pin, now lost. From plough-soil, west of the North Timber Building. (LWB–76–1).

No. 117 Stud of bronze with a plain, flat circular head, 23 mm. in diameter. The shaft is broken and has a rectangular cross-section. From general soil west of the North Timber Building. (LWB–K12–3).

No. 118 Coil of bronze, made from a length of metal with an oval cross-section. The coil is in two turns, with an internal diameter of about 15 mm. It is possible that the object is a finger-ring. From filling of the Quarry Pit Complex, dated to the late-first century A.D. (LWB–L29–5).

No. 119 Finger-ring of bronze with an hexagonal bezel. On either side of the bezel is a sub-rectangular plate. The bezel, itself, contains a blob of royal blue glass, bearing an uncertain impression. This is presumably imitating an engraved gemstone. A similar ring came from the Lullingstone Villa site (Ref. 164). From soil over the North Timber Building. (LWB–76–46).

No. 120 Small pin of bronze, with a circular cross-section. The shaft is straight and the head has been formed at one end by hammering the metal flat. From upper filling of the West Enclosure Ditch, dated to the mid to late-first century A.D. (LWB–77–101).

No. 121 Small toilet spoon of bronze, with a length of 38 mm. The handle has a square cross-section and one end has been bent around to form a suspension loop. At the opposite end is a small bowl. From lower filling of the Anglo-Saxon hut. (LWB–M24–4).

No. 122 Small spatula of bronze, with a surviving length of 51 mm. The object has been made from a strip of sheet-metal and has a rectangular cross-section. One end is broken, whilst the other has been hammered out, to form a flat, circular disc, set at a slight angle to the main shaft. From soil over the North Timber Building. (LWB–76–46).

No. 123 Pair of bronze tweezers with a length of 49 mm. The undecorated blades are tapered and curve inwards.

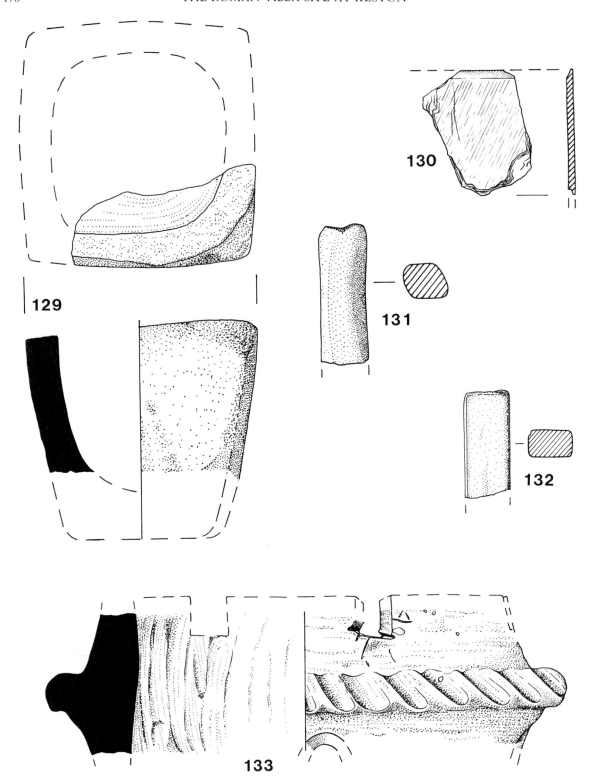

Fig. 55. *Objects of stone, Nos. 129–132, and a clay 'lamp chimney', No. 133 ($\frac{1}{2}$).*

There has been some distortion of the object, however. From upper filling of the North-West Ditch of the Villa Enclosure (F.800), dated to the fourth century A.D. (LWB–76–178).

No. 124   Fitting of bronze, consisting of a flat strip of metal, with a rectangular cross-section and an overall length of 51 mm. The two ends have been hammered out and a small circular hole, some 2 mm. in diameter, has been drilled through each. A similar piece, suggested as a handle of some kind, came from Colchester (No. 2122, Ref. 165). From general soil north of the South Masonry Building. (LWB–M32–3).

No. 125   Elaborately shaped link or fastening made from a bronze rod of circular cross-section, which tapers towards both ends. The two ends of the object have been turned back to form hooks. A similar link came from a Neronian context at Baldock (Ref. 166), where it was suggested as a dress-fastener. From upper filling of the Quarry Pit Complex, dated to the late-first century A.D. (LWB–N30–3).

No. 126   Six links of a small bronze chain. The oval links are made from short lengths of rod with a circular cross-section. Each link varies between 3 and 6 mm. in diameter and has a join in one of the longer sides. No attempt seems to have been made to solder these closed. Unstratified, South Masonry Building. (LWB–M34–13).

No. 127   Small stud of bronze, with an almost flat head and a bent shaft. The shaft has a square cross-section and tapers to a point. There has been some corrosion of the head but it seems probable that it was originally circular in shape. From soil below the Upper East Metalling, dated to the third century A.D. (LWB–CC22–5).

No. 128   Decorated fitting of sheet-bronze, with a central perforation presumably for attachment. Surrounding the hole is a slightly raised lozenge-shaped area. The precise purpose of this object is not clear. From a demolition deposit over the South Masonry Building. (LWB– J34–7).

Objects of Stone (Fig. 55).

In addition to building stone, prehistoric flints and querns, the excavations in Lower Warbank Field produced several other miscellaneous stone artefacts. Four of them have been illustrated. These are, a chalk basin (No. 129), a shale palette (No. 130) and two hones (Nos. 131 and 132).

No. 129   Part of a chalk container or basin. This appears to have been of sub-rectangular shape when complete and was at least 80 mm. deep. There is no trace of the contents of this vessel, nor evidence of its function. From filling of the deep, post-Roman robber-trench cutting the North Timber Building. (LWB–76–200).

No. 130   Fragment of a rectangular shale object. The shale is a dark brown colour and has the laminated structure typical of this rock-type. It seems probable that the piece has, in fact, split laterally and that its full thickness is not represented here, with only one original surface remaining. There is a short length of one straight edge surviving and this has a bevelled upper surface. It is likely that this fragment formed part of a small palette of a type well-known on Roman sites, used for mixing ointments or pigments. Such palettes often have bevelled edges to allow them to be slotted into grooved containers of metal (Ref. 167). From filling of the outer beam slot, North Timber Building, dated to the third to early-fourth century A.D. (LWB–77–204).

No. 131   Rectangular hone, with one end broken away. It has a sub-rectangular/oval cross-section and consists of a fine, hard light grey sandstone. All of the sides and the unbroken end are well worn through use. From spread of flint rubble associated with the Centre Flint Structure, dated to the second century A.D. (LWB–J27–5).

No. 132   Rectangular hone, with one end broken away. It has a rectangular cross-section and consists of a fine, light grey-brown sandstone. All of the sides and the unbroken end are well worn through use. From filling of Pit 'D', cutting the West Masonry Building and dated to the medieval period. (LWB–A24–7).

A Fired Clay 'Lamp Chimney' (Fig. 55).

No. 133   Fragment of a so-called 'lamp chimney', of a smooth orange-buff fired clay, with occasional red grog inclusions. A raised horizontal cordon, decorated with deeply incised angled lines, is present and in the wall of the object above this, part of an original rectangular knife-cut aperture remains. There are traces of a second, round-headed opening below the cordon. Another unstratified chimney fragment from the site (not illustrated), has a similar horizontal cordon and is likely to be from the same specimen.

The precise purpose of these objects is not at all clear: they are sometimes alternatively described as 'roof-ventilators'. A similar example to the present one came from the nearby villa site at New Ash Green, Kent (Ref. 168). From primary filling of West Tank 2, adjacent to the West Masonry Building, dated to the late-third century A.D. (LWB–F19–9).

D) THE QUERNSTONES AND MILLSTONES

(i) Quernstones (Figs. 56 and 57, Nos. 134–136).

A considerable number of fragments of stone, foreign to the immediate area, were recovered from the Warbank excavations. Out of these pieces, many of which are small, shapeless lumps, only some 57 can be positively identified as forming parts of quernstones, but it is very likely that many of the other pieces are also of this origin. Several of the miscellaneous small fragments, not recongiseably parts of querns, bear worn areas indicating their casual, or secondary use as whetstones and rubbers. Most of the 57 certain quernstone fragments are not very large and most appear to be from rotary querns. A complete saddle quern (No. 134) came from the fill of middle Iron Age Pit 2 (F.419) and a fragment from another came from the hillwash deposit on the east side of the site (not illustrated).

Due to their rather fragmentary nature no detailed examination of the quernstones from the site has been undertaken. Tentative identifications of the rock types have, however, been

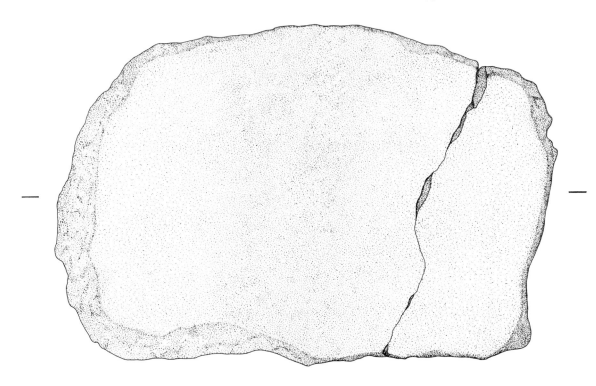

134

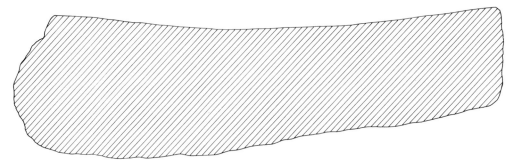

Fig. 56.   *Middle-Iron Age saddle-quern from Pit 2 (⅓)*

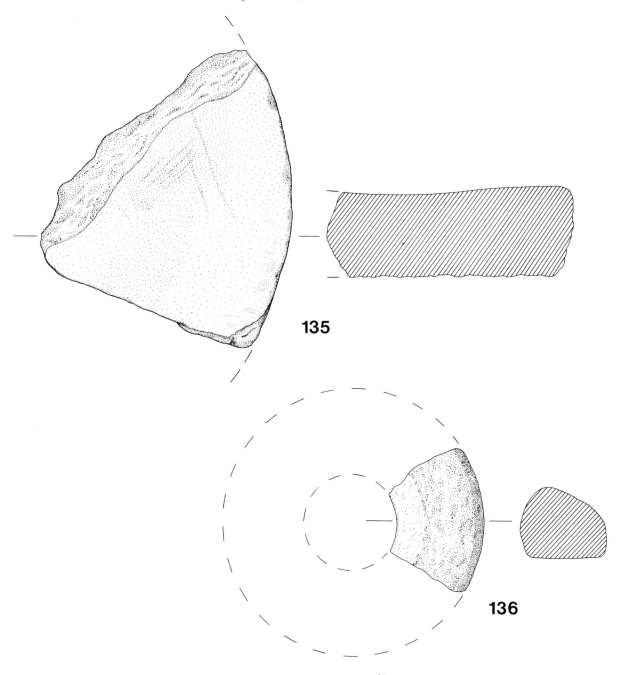

Fig. 57. *Rotary quernstones* ($\frac{1}{3}$).

attempted. From this it seems clear that nearly half of the quernstone fragments (22) are of sandstones derived from the Lower Greensand Beds of the nearby Wealden District (Nos. 134, 135 and 136). A further 19 fragments are of hard brown quartz sandstone, probably belonging to the Millstone Grit series of the Pennines (none illustrated). Continental imports are represented by 13 small pieces of grey lava-stone from the Mayen district of Germany (none illustrated). There are in addition two large pieces of dark red Puddingstone, from north of the Thames (not illustrated) and one other uncertain fragment. Querns of German lava-stone, Puddingstone, Greensand and Millstone Grit have all been noted on a number of other Iron Age/Roman sites in the West Kent area (Ref. 82) and E.W. Black has recently recorded their distribution more generally in the south-east (Ref. 169).

In site distribution, the quernstone fragments were fairly evenly spread across the Lower Warbank excavations, being found in ditch silts, re-used as packing stones in post-holes, discarded in rubbish pits and in the general soil and demolition deposits. One or two more quernstone fragments came from the Tombs area (not included here). Apart from the typologically earlier saddle querns, the stones themselves cannot generally be closely dated, but there seems little doubt that they relate to periods covering the entire time that the site was occupied.

No. 134   Complete lower stone of a saddle-quern, broken in two. This is a good example of a type well-known on pre-Roman sites in Britain. It is made of Greensand, obtainable from within a few miles of the Keston site, and has the characteristic dished upper surface, slightly smoothed through use. It has a length of 405 mm. and a thickness of 110 mm. A fragment from a similar example came from the pre-Conquest farmstead on Farningham Hill, a short distance to the east (Ref. 172), although the present stone seems to be of rather earlier date. From middle Iron Age Pit 2 (F.419); found lying on its base. (LWB–O24–4).

No. 135   Part of a rotary quern of Greensand, with an estimated original diameter of about 500 mm. The stone has a rectangular cross-section and the edge and one side of the fragment show rough, unworn tooling. The other side bears an undulating surface worn smooth through use. It seems unlikely, however, that such an uneven surface could have been produced by a normal rotary action and it appears that this side of the stone was re-used as some kind of grinding surface after it was broken. From filling of the stoke-pit (F.10) of the External Corn Drying Oven, dated to the fourth century A.D. (LWB–78–27).

No. 136   Fragment of a small rotary quern of a dark grey-green sandstone, probably a type of Greensand. The original diameter of the stone may be estimated as being at least 215 mm. and there seems to have been a large central spindle hole/hopper. Unstratified. (LWB–1).

(ii) Millstones (not illustrated).

It seems likely that the bulk of the quernstones noted above served the domestic needs of the settlement at Keston but there are in addition several fragments which seem to be from bigger millstones and these suggest that milling on a larger, perhaps commercial scale took place at some time on the site. Four fragments are of particular interest. These form about one third of a massive stone, of Millstone Grit, originally some 950 mm. in diameter and 110–120 mm. in thickness, with a large central spindle hole. They came from the filling of the post-pipe of Post-hole 18, North Timber Building. (LWB–77–230).

Millstones of a similar size have been recorded from the nearby Roman villa site at South Darenth (Ref. 170). The close proximity of that site to the River Darent suggested that these may be from a water mill, located somewhere in the immediate area (Ref. 171). Clearly this cannot be the case at Keston, situated high on the side of a chalkland spur. It seems more likely that animal power was used on this site for turning such large stones.

E) THE SAMIAN WARE (Figs. 58 and 59, Nos. 137–155)

by Joanna Bird, B.A., F.S.A., with notes on the stamps by B. Dickenson, B.R. Hartley and G.D. Marsh.

Just under 400 sherds of samian ware were recovered from Lower Warbank Field and the majority of this is plain. The material ranges in date from the mid-first century to at least the early third. Although there is not enough stamped and decorated ware to permit a detailed and statistical analysis by date, it is clear that the bulk of the samian falls into two groups, of early to mid-Flavian date and of Antonine date, following the normal pattern for British sites (Ref. 173).

The first century samian all comes from South Gaul and includes three identifiable stamps, all on plain forms: Crestus (*c.* A.D. 65–90) (No. 155), Passienus (*c.* A.D. 50–65) and Pontheius (*c.* 70–85) (No. 156). Apart from two examples of form Dr. 29 of pre- or very early Flavian date, the decorated pottery is Flavian: seven bowls of Dr. 29 dated *c.* A.D. 70–85, including one having some stylistic links with stamped bowls of Felix; seven Dr. 37 bowls, including one in the style of the M Crestio group and one having stylistic links with the 'Large Rosette' potter; and a single decorated fragment of a Déch 67 beaker. The majority of the plain vessels are of Flavian date; definately pre-Flavian forms are represented by single sherds of Ritt 12 and of Dr. 24/25 or Ritt 9 and four of Ritt 8. This date is also indicated by the apparent absence of Dr. 15/17, a common form on sites with pre-Flavian occupation.

Trajanic samian from Les Martres-de-Veyre consists of only two decorated bowls, attributed to Drusus I and Donnaucus, and a single example of Dr. 18/31. The rest of the Central Gaulish ware comes from Lezoux, and dates after A.D. 125. The decorated pottery includes a stamped Dr. 37 by Cinnamus, at least two other bowls attributed to him, one each by Mercator II and Censorinus, at least one by Advocisus and perhaps one by Sacer; there is also a bowl with an ovolo shared by Cinnamus, but no stamps survive; late forms such as Dr. 45 and Walters 79 or Ludowici Tg are well represented.

There is a relatively high proportion – approximately 13% – of East Gaulish ware, taking the samian dating into the third century. The decorated ware consists of a bowl by Ianu or Ciriuna, of Heiligenberg, dated c. A.D. 140–160, a stamped bowl of Comitialis VI of Rheinzabern, dated c. A.D. 175–210 (not illustrated), a bowl of Reginus I of Rheinzabern, a sherd from La Madeleine of Hadrianic to early-Antonine date, and two further fragments from Rheinzabern which are not closely dateable. No stamps survive on the plain ware, which consists largely of Dr. 31 and 31 R (Ludowici Sa and Sb) and mortaria forms; other late forms such as Dr. 32 are rare.

Fill of Quarry Pit Complex (LWB–K27–5, M29–7, N29–5 and N31–9).

Dr. 29, South Gaul, pre-or early Flavian.
Déch 67, South Gaul, basal band or panel of two rows of trilobed leaves, Flavian.
Dr. 18, South Gaul, Flavian.
Dr. 35, South Gaul, Flavian.
Dr. 37, South Gaul, Chevron wreath at base, Flavian.
Dr. 31, East Gaul, later C2–early C3.

Fill of Centre Enclosure Ditch (LWB–K22–3, 77–10, 77–11 and C24–2).

Dr. 18, South Gaul, Neronian-Flavian.
Dr. 27, South Gaul, Neronian-Flavian.
Dr. 42 or 46, South Gaul, Neronian-Flavian.
Rim fragment, Dr. 42, 46 or Curle 15, South Gaul, pre- or early Flavian.
2 × Dr. 18 or 18/31, South Gaul, Flavian-Trajanic.
Walters 79 or Lud Tg, Central Gaul, later C2.
Jar sherd (Déch 72 etc), Central Gaul, Antonine.

Fill of Pit 17 (LWB–K20–3 and K20–4).

Dr. 29. Same as vessel No. 139 (p.183).
Dr. 29, South Gaul, pre-Flavian.
Rim fragment, Dr. 42, 46 or Curle 15, South Gaul, pre-or early Flavian.
4 × Dr. 27, South Gaul, Neronian–early Flavian.
Dr. 18, South Gaul, Neronian-Flavian.
South Gaulish footring, probably Dr. 15/17 or 18.
South Gaulish sherd.
Dr. 27 probably, stamped IO[. Unidentifiable. Not illustrated.

Soil Under Lower East Metalling (LWB–AA24–15).

Dr. 18, South Gaul, Flavian; burnt.

Fill of Post-pit 3, South Timber Building (LWB–L34–3).

Ritt 12, South Gaul, Neronian.

Deposits in Area of Centre Flint Structure (LWB–K26–7 and J27–5).

Walters 79R or Lud TgR probably, Central Gaul, mid-later Antonine (flint spread).
Dr. 33, East Gaul, later C2–mid C3 (soil north of foundation).

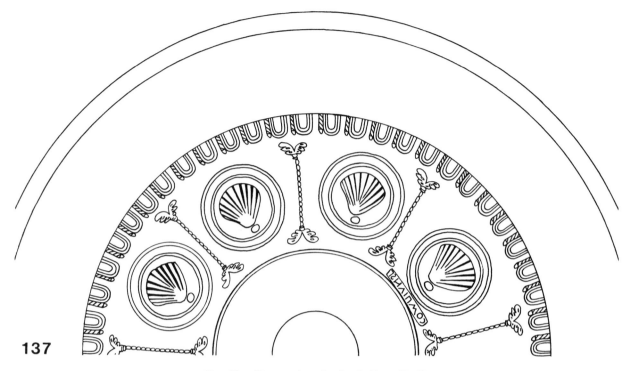

137

Fig. 58.   *Decorated samian bowl, Form 37 (½).*

Fill of Roman Water Storage Pond (LWB–78–56).

Central Gaulish sherd, Hadrianic-Antonine.

Soil over Roman Water Storage Pond (LWB–78–47).

Dr. 33, East Gaul probably, later C2–first half C3; burnt.

Fill of North-West Ditch of the Villa Enclosure (LWB–76–4, E4–3 and E4–5).

No. 137   Dr. 37 in the style of Comitialis VI of Rheinzabern, with his mould-stamp COMITIALISF retrograde
Rheinzabern (this die has been found at the kiln site). Decorated bowls with this stamp occur at
Niederbieber and the Brougham cemetery, where the samian is mainly late-Antonine. The shell
(LRF.020) in the medallion (K20a), the ovolo (E25) and vertical beads (O263) with acanthus terminals
(P145) are on Ludowici and Ricken 1948, taf. 106, nos. 9, 14, 20, but not in this exact arrangement. *c.*
A.D. 175–210.

Dr. 37, Rheinzabern: an additional sherd of the stamped Comitialis bowl from 76–4 and 76–78 above.

Dish base (Dr. 36 etc.), Central Gaul, probably Antonine.

Dish sherd, probably Central Gaul, burnt.

Burnt Central Gaulish sherd.

Fill of North-East Ditch of the Villa Enclosure (LWB–76–61, 76–66, 78–37 and 78–53).

Dr. 31, Central Gaul, Antonine.

Central Gaulish sherd, probably Dr. 31 or 18/31; Antonine.

Mortarium sherd, Central Gaul, later C2.

Small flagon, probably (cf. Oswald and Pryce 1920, pl. 83, no. 2) (Ref. 174); Central Gaul, Antonine.

Fill of South-East Ditch of the Villa Enclosure Ditch (LWB–X24–10, BB22–6, AA23–13).

Dr. 33, Central Gaul, Hadrianic-Antonine.

Dr. 37, Central Gaul, with part of an animal (probably a bear); Hadrianic-Antonine.

Two sherds of Dr. 37, La Madeleine. The ovolo is shown on Ricken 1934, taf. 7, B; the boar and beads on
taf. 7, no. 115 (Ref. 175). Hadrianic-early Antonine.

Soil above South-East Ditch of the Villa Enclosure/Lower East Metalling (LWB–X24–6, CC22–6, AA24–5, AA24–6, AA24–9, AA24–12, BB22–5, Z24–6, BB23–14, BB23–11, BB23–16, BB24–3, BB24–5, CC22–5, CC23–3, CC24–3, DD21–4).

No. 138   Dr. 37, South Gaul. The narrow friezes are characteristic of much of the Pompeii Hoard material (Atkinson 1914, Ref. 176); the chevrons and short gadroons are on pl. 7, no. 40, the s-gadroons on no. 39, both by the 'Large Rosette' potter. The ovolo is double-bordered with a small rosette tongue, c. A.D. 70–85.

Dr. 27 probably, South Gaul, second half C1.

South Gaulish sherd, second half C1.

3 × Ritt 8, South Gaul, pre-Flavian.

Dr. 18, South Gaul, pre- or early Flavian.

5 South Gaulish platter sherds, probably all from the Dr. 18.

South Gaulish sherd, probably a second Dr. 18.

11 × Dr. 18, South Gaul, Flavian.

Dr. 18, South Gaul, Neronian-Flavian.

Dr. 18, South Gaul, second half C1.

Dr. 18(R), South Gaul, Flavian.

Dr. 27, South Gaul, Flavian.

Dr. 27, South Gaul, second half C1.

Dr. 18/31, Central Gaul, first half C2.

Central Gaulish sherd, Hadrianic-Antonine.

No. 139   Dr. 29, South Gaul. Scroll in upper frieze, with rosette terminals and small circles in the field, c. A.D. 50–75.

No. 140   Dr. 29, South Gaul. Panels of narrow arrowheads and (fragmentary) running animals in upper frieze, c. A.D. 70–85.

No. 141   Two sherds of Dr. 29, South Gaul. Narrow arrowheads in upper frieze, wreath of (probable) chevrons round the base, c. A.D. 70–85. The motif beneath the boar resembles a signature in the mould, but it has no parallel and may be simply a fragment of stylised vegetation. The chevron wreath is common to forms 29 and 37 at Pompeii (Ref. 177). The boar (F. Hermet, 1934, pl. 27, 40, Ref. 178), and the alternating panels of animals and of leaf tips with diagonal wavy lines are normal Flavian motifs (cf. for example, R. Knorr, 1912, taf. ix, 11, Ref. 179), c. A.D. 70–85.

Dr. 36, South Gaul, Flavian.

South Gaulish platter foot, probably Flavian.

South Gaulish platter sherd.

2 × South Gaulish sherd.

Dr. 31, Central Gaul, Antonine.

Fill of post-Roman pits, West Masonry Building (LWB–A24–6, A27–2, A28–4, B24–3, B28–2, B28–3 and C27–2).

Mortarium or Curle 21 sherd, Central Gaul, late C2; slightly burnt (Pit A).

Central Gaulish sherd, Hadrianic-Antonine (Pit A).

Dr. 43/Lud RSMd, with barbotine decoration; East Gaul (probably Trier), late C2–first half C3; slightly burnt (Pit A).

Dr. 18/31 or 31, Central Gaul, Hadrianic-Antonine (Pit C).

Central Gaulish sherd (Pit C).

Dr. 31, Central Gaul, Antonine (Pit C).

Déch 72 probably, with trace of barbotine decoration; Central Gaul, Antonine (Pit D).

Dr. 31, Central Gaul, Antonine (Robber-pit, south wing of bath-suite).

Dr. 31 sherd, perhaps the same vessel; Central Gaul (Robber-pit, south wing of bath-suite).

Dr. 37 or 30 rim, Central Gaul, Antonine (Robber-pit, south wing of bath-suite).

Dr. 31, Central Gaul, Antonine (Robber-pit, south wing of bath-suite).

Dr. 31 sherd, perhaps the same vessel; Central Gaul (Robber-pit, south wing of bath-suite).

Dr. 37 or 30 rim, Central Gaul, Antonine (Robber-pit, south wing of bath-suite).

Fill of Robber-Trench, West Masonry Building (LWB–Z31).

No. 142   Dr. 37 in a style used by Ianu at Heiligenberg. The wreath and bifid leaf are on Forrer 1911, taf. 29, no. 8, the star-shaped leaf on taf. 28, no. 17 (Ref. 180). The motif to the left is probably the cup on taf. 29, no. 7. The dog is not recorded for Ianu but was used by Ciriuna (taf. 20, no. 3), c. A.D. 140–160. Identified by Brenda Dickenson.

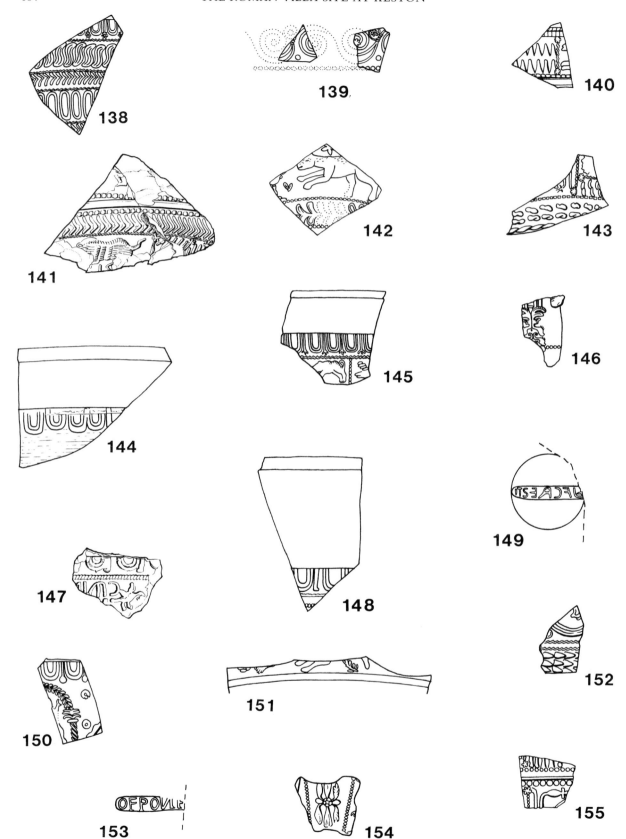

Fig. 59.   *Decorated samian ware* ($\frac{1}{2}$) *and stamps* ($\frac{1}{1}$).

Soil over West Masonry Building (LWB–B27–2).

Dr. 32, East Gaul, late C2–mid C3.

Fill of Corn Drying Ovens, North Timber Building (LWB–76–58 and 76–78).

Dr. 31, Central Gaul, Antonine.
Dr. 33, Central Gaul, Antonine; burnt.
Dr. 37. Same vessel as No. 137 (p. 182).

Fill of Main Post-pipes, North Timber Building (LWB–76–172 and 77–258).

Dr. 33, Central Gaul, mid-late Antonine (Post-hole 2).
Bowl foot, Central Gaul, Antonine; burnt (Post-hole 12).

Fill of West Tanks (LWB–F19–3, F19–4 and F19–9).

Dr. 33, South Gaul, Flavian (Tank 1).
Dr. 31(R), Central Gaul, mid–late Antonine (Tank 2).

Fill of South Tank (LWB–J35–4).

No. 143   Dr. 37, South Gaul. Panels, including shallow one with double row of narrow arrowheads below one
with an animal; basal wreath of trifid leaves, *c.* A.D. 75–95; burnt.
Dr. 27, South Gaul, Flavian.
Dish with offset on interior; South Gaul, second half C1.

Fill of North Tank (LWB–76–136).

Dr. 31/Lud Sa, East Gaul, later C2–mid C3.

Fill of Ditch 1 (LWB–77–9).

Dr. 27, South Gaul, Flavian.
Dr. 18 or 18/31, South Gaul, Flavian-Hadrianic.

Fill of Ditch 7 (LWB–78–24 and 78–25).

Dr. 18/31R, Central Gaul, Hadrianic-Antonine.
Dr. 27, East Gaul (Rheinzabern), later C2–first half C3.

Fill of Ditch 21a (LWB–76–46, 76–182, 77–207, 77–218 and 77– 220).

Central Gaulish sherd, Hadrianic-Antonine.
Dr. 31, Central Gaul, Antonine.
Dr. 31(R), Central Gaul, mid-late Antonine.
Mortarium base, Central Gaul, late C2; heavily worn inside.
East Gaulish dish sherd, later C2–mid C3.
Dr. 31R/Lud Sb, East Gaul, later C2–mid C3.
No. 144   Dr. 37, Rheinzabern. The ovolo is too smudged to identify, but it seems to be tongueless. Later C2–early
C3, on rim form.
Dr. 38, probably, East Gaul, later C2–mid C3.

Demolition Soil Over South Masonry Building (LWB–F34–6, G33–3, G34–4, H33–6, H34–6, I33–4, I34–6, J35–2, L33–2, M33–3, M33–4, M34–3, N33–2, N33–4, K33–2, L35–3, H33–12, F33–4 and I36–7).

Dr. 36, South Gaul, Flavian.
South Gaulish sherd, later C1.
No. 145   Dr. 37, South Gaul. The ovolo was used by M Crestio. There is no exact parallel for the boar, but cf.
Dannell 1971, fig. 129, no. 32 (Ref. 181); the next panel probably contains a saltire with foliage motif, *c.*
A.D. 75–95.
Dr. 36, Central Gaul, Hadrianic-Antonine.
Central Gaulish sherd, probably Dr. 31 or 18/31, Hadrianic-Antonine.
Mortarium sherd, Central Gaul, late C2; worn inside.

Curle 21, Central Gaul, mid–later Antonine; burnt.

Dr. 31, Central Gaul, Antonine.

3 × Dr. 33, Central Gaul, Antonine.

Dr. 18/31 or 31 base, Central Gaul, Antonine.

3 × Dr. 31, Central Gaul, Antonine.

Dr. 31 foot, Central Gaul, Antonine.

Dr. 31 foot, Central Gaul, later C2–mid C3.

Walters 79R or Lud TgR, Central Gaul, later C2.

Dish base (Dr. 36 etc.), Central Gaul, probably Antonine.

Curle 21 or similar, later form such as Chenet form 324h.

No. 146   Dr. 37 in the style of Drusus I of Les Martres-de-Veyre. The arcade supported on an acanthus on a series of paired dolphins is shown on Stansfield and Simpson, 1958, pl. 12, no. 146 (Ref. 182), c. A.D. 100–125.

Dr. 31/Lud Sa, East Gaul, later C2–mid C3.

Dr. 31R/Lud Sb, East Gaul, later C2–mid C3.

Dr. 45, East Gaul, later C2–mid C3.

Upper East Metalling (LWB–Y23–5 and BB21–4).

Dr. 18, South Gaul, Flavian-Trajanic.

Dr. 37, South Gaul, Flavian-Trajanic.

No. 147   Dr. 37, stamped (IMAИИIƆ in the mould. Die 5b of Cinnamus ii; the die has been found at Lezoux. The ovolo and bird are shown on Stansfield and Simpson, 1958, pl. 160, 35, Ref. 182), c. A.D. 150–180.

Soil Over Upper East Metalling (LWB–CC21–3 and CC21–4).

Dr. 35/36, South Gaul, Flavian.

2 South Gaulish sherds, 1 possibly from Dr. 29; second half C1.

No. 148   Dr. 37, Central Gaul. The ovolo was used by Cinnamus, Carantinus and Illixo (Rogers, 1974, type E145, Ref. 183), Antonine.

Mortarium sherd, East Gaul, late C2–mid C3.

Centre Metalling Over Quarry Pit Complex (LWB–L27–4, L29–3, N28–5, N33–14 and N29–11).

Dr. 27 probably, South Gaul, later C1.

Dr. 27, South Gaul, Neronian-early Flavian; slightly burnt.

Dr. 29 or 37, South Gaul; Small double festoons with trifid pendants between. Early–mid Flavian.

No. 149   Crestus 33a OFCRESTI retrograde La Graufesenque (kiln-site presumed from the fabric or distribution etc.). Most of this potter's output is later than that of the better-known Crestio. The stamp is noted, once, on form 24 and there are many examples from Flavian contexts, including the Saalburg and Period IIA at Verulamium (after A.D. 75). It appears occasionally on Flavian Dr. 29s, c. A.D. 65–90.

Dr. 33, Central Gaul, Hadrianic-Antonine; burnt.

Dr. 33, Central Gaul, Antonine; slightly burnt.

Dr. 37, East Gaul, later C2–mid C3.

East Gaulish sherd, probably from Dr 31/Lud Sa; later C2–mid C3.

Metalling north-east of West Masonry Building (F.873) (LWB–76–119).

Dr. 18/31, Central Gaul, early–mid C2.

Fill of Saxon Hut (LWB–N23–3).

Dr. 33, Central Gaul, Antonine.

Fill of Miscellaneous Pits and Post-Holes (LWB–K23–2, K24–2, M33–19, L23–8, F19–10, L31–3, P23–5, W24–14, 76–176, 77–102, 77–113, 77–142, 77–81, 77–116 and 77–305).

Dr. 37, South Gaul, Flavian-Trajanic, (F.414, East Fence).

Dr. 18, South Gaul, Flavian-Trajanic, (Pit F.1080).

South Gaulish sherd, second half C1, (Post-Pit, F.1259).

2 × Dr. 18/31, Central Gaul, Hadrianic-Antonine. (Post-Hole, F.1089 and Slot No. 4, F.427).

Central Gaulish cup sherd, Hadrianic-Antonine, (Pit, F.664).

Dr. 31(R), Central Gaul, mid-late Antonine, (Hollow, K24–2).

Dr. 18/31 or 31, Central Gaul, Antonine, (Hollow, L31–3).

No. 150   Dr. 37, Central Gaul. The ovolo (Rogers 1974, type B85, Ref. 183) was used by Secundus V at Toulon-sur-Allier and probably also at Lezoux. It also occurs on bowls with stylistic connections with Cinnamus ii, but was almost certainly used by other lesser-known potters, one of whom is likely to have made this bowl. The column is Rogers P76, but he has no exact parallels for the arcade and rosettes, *c.* A.D. 140–170. (Identified by Brenda Dickenson), (Hollow, K23–2).

No. 151   Dr. 30, Central Gaul. The design apparently includes running animals and leaf motifs, Antonine, (Post-Hole, F.1133).

Dr. 33, Central Gaul, Antonine, (Pit, F.154).

Dr. 36 probably, Central Gaul, Antonine, (Post-Hole, F.355).

Lud Tg, Central Gaul, later C2, (Post-Hole, F.955).

Central Gaulish mortarium sherd, late C2; very little wear inside, (Post-Hole, F.955).

Dr. 44, East Gaul, later C2–mid C3; rivetted, (Post-Hole, F.1089).

Dr. 31R/Lud Sb, East Gaul, later C2–mid C3, (Post-Hole, F.1089).

East Gaulish sherd, probably Walters 79; later C2–first half C3, (Post-Hole, F.1110).

Fill of Miscellaneous Ditches and Gullies (LWB–K26–3, 77–244 and 77–260).

Dr. 18, South Gaul, Flavian, (Ditch 4).

Dr. 27 probably, South Gaul, later C1. (Ditch 4).

Dr. 33, Central Gaul, Hadrianic-Antonine. (Overflow Gully, North-East Tank, F.1198).

Dr. 33, Central Gaul, Antonine. (Overflow Gully, North-East Tank, F.1198).

Curle 21 or Dr. 43, East Gaul, later C2–mid C3. (Ditch 4).

Dr. 31R/Lud Sb, East Gaul, later C2–first half C3. (Overflow Gully, North-East Tank, F.1198).

General Soil Deposits
i) Centre Flint Structure/Quarry Pit Area (LWB–L28–3, L28–4, L29–4, L30–3, L32–3, M23–25, M28–3, M28–4, M29–5, M29–4, M30–4, M31–5, M32–3, N29–3, N29–4, N30–2, N28–3, N32–3 and L26–3).

No. 152   Dr. 29, South Gaul. Lower frieze panels with small triple medallions and small circle motifs, and massed arrowheads, *c.* A.D. 70–85.

4 base sherds, Dr. 15/17 or 18, South Gaul, pre- or early Flavian (probably 2 vessels).

Dr. 15/17 or 18, South Gaul, pre- or early Flavian.

No. 153   Dr. 15/17 or 18, South Gaulish sherd, probably a platter form, stamped OFPOИTHE[I] La Graufesenque (this die has been found at the kiln site). Pontheius used this die, and a broken version of it, in the Flavian period. A stamp from the complete die (Ia) occurs in the Inchtuthil Gutter and, almost certainly, on Dr. 29 from Hofheim, which it will have reached before *c.* A.D. 75. Stamps from the broken die are known from Binchester and the main site at Corbridge. Ia will have been in use *c.* A.D. 70–85, therefore.

At least 3 × Dr. 18, South Gaul, early-mid Flavian.

Dr. 27, South Gaul, Flavian.

South Gaulish sherd with part of beadrow; second half C1.

Dr. 18 probably, South Gaul, Flavian.

3 × Dr. 29, South Gaul, pre- or early Flavian.

Dr. 18, South Gaul, early-mid Flavian.

4 × Dr. 18, South Gaul, Flavian.

Dr. 18 probably, South Gaul, second half C1.

Dr. 27, South Gaul, second half C1.

2 × Dr. 27, South Gaul, Flavian.

Déch 67, South Gaul, Flavian.

2 × Dr. 27, South Gaul, pre- or early Flavian.

2 × Dr. 27, South Gaul, second half C1.

Dr. 29, South Gaul. Pendant scrolls in upper frieze, *c.* A.D. 70–85.

Dr. 33, South Gaul, Flavian.

Dr. 36, South Gaul, Flavian.

South Gaulish sherd, cup form.

South Gaulish sherd, probably a platter form.

South Gaulish platter foot sherd.

3 × South Gaulish sherd.

Footring, small bowl or dish, Central Gaul, Antonine.

Dr. 33 (large example), Central Gaul, Hadrianic-early Antonine.

Dr. 37, Central Gaul. The broken ovolo is certainly not identifiable. Hadrianic-early Antonine.

Bead rim fragment, Central Gaul, Hadrianic-Antonine.

Central Gaulish sherd, Hadrianic-Antonine.

3 sherds and one foot fragment, Dr. 31, Central Gaul, Antonine; possibly all one vessel.

Dr. 33, Central Gaul, Antonine.

Mortarium sherd, Central Gaul, late C2; unworn inside.

Central Gaulish sherd, dish form, Antonine probably.

Central Gaulish sherd.

Dr. 37. Same as vessel from plough soil in Quarry Pit Area (p. 189).

Dr. 45 probably, East Gaul, late C2–mid C3.

Dr. 30 or 37, East Gaul (Rheinzabern), later C2–first half C3.

Dr. 31/Lud Sa, East Gaul (Rheinzabern), later C2–first half C3.

Dr. 31/Lud Sa, East Gaul, later C2–mid C3.

Dr. 33, East Gaul (Argonne), later C2–mid C3.

East Gaulish sherd, later C2–mid C3.

ii) Area North of South Masonry Building (LWB–I32–2, J32–2 and J32–5).

Dr. 30, Central Gaul. The satyr (0.606) ovoid beads and circles were used by Censorinus (Stansfield and Simpson 1958, pl. 101, nos. 1, 10, Ref. 182). Mid-later Antonine.

Central Gaulish sherd.

2 × Dr. 31/Lud Sa, East Gaul, later C2–mid C3.

Dr. 38, East Gaul (Trier probably), later C2–first half C3.

East Gaulish sherd, later C2–mid C3.

iii) 1971–1974 Areas (LWB–S23–3, S23–5, Y22–3, AA22–3, BB21–3, BB24–5, CC23–3, DD20–3, EE21–3, EE20–3).

2 South Gaulish cup sherds, pre- or early Flavian.

Déch 67, South Gaul, Flavian-Trajanic.

South Gaulish platter base, probably Dr. 18 and Flavian-Trajanic.

South Gaulish sherd.

Dr. 37, Central Gaul; the large vine leaf may be one used by Sacer (Stansfield and Simpson 1958, pl. 83, no. 11, Ref. 182). Hadrianic-early Antonine.

Dr. 37, Central Gaul, Hadrianic-early Antonine.

Dr. 37 or 30, Central Gaul, Hadrianic-Antonine.

Central Gaulish sherd, Hadrianic-Antonine.

Dr. 37, Central Gaul. The broken ovolo may be one used, with similar terminals, by Advocisus (Stansfield and Simpson 1958, pl. 114, no. 29, Ref. 182). Antonine.

Déch 72 with incised floral motif; Central Gaul, Antonine.

Dr. 37, Central Gaul, with an ovolo used by Advocisus (Stansfield and Simpson 1958, pl. 114, no. 29, Ref. 182); the beads beneath are rather squarer than his usual ones. Antonine; burnt.

2 × Walters 79 or Lud Tg, Central Gaul, later C2.

3 × Central Gaulish sherd.

Curle 23, East Gaul, later C2–mid C3.

2 East Gaulish mortaria sherds, late C2–mid C3; very worn inside.

Dr. 37R, East Gaul, Hadrianic-Antonine; rivetted.

iv) Area of North Timber Building (LWB–76–37, 76–53, 76–71, 76–75, 76–77, 77–210 and 77–211).

South Gaulish sherd, second half C1.

Dr. 37, Central Gaul, Hadrianic-early Antonine.

Central Gaulish sherd, Hadrianic-Antonine.

Dr. 31 or 31R, Central Gaul, mid-later Antonine; burnt.

Dr. 31, Central Gaul, Antonine.

Dr. 33, Central Gaul, Antonine.

2 × Dr. 38, Central Gaul, Antonine.

East Gaulish sherd, later C2–mid C3.

Mortarium sherd, East Gaul, late C2–mid C3; very worn inside.

East Gaulish sherd, probably Dr. 37; later C2–first half C3.

Hillwash Deposits
i) Centre Flint Structure/Quarry Pit Area (LWB–G33–2, I30–2, I31–3, M30–2, N24–2, L26–2, K32–2, J27–2, J29–2, K26–2, K31–2 and L32–2).

Dr. 18, South Gaul, Flavian.

Base, Dr. 27 or 35, unstamped; South Gaul, Flavian.

Dr. 18 or 18/31, South Gaul, Flavian-Trajanic.

Footring fragment, probably Dr. 27, South Gaul, second half C1.

Dr. 18/31 probably, South Gaul, Flavian-Trajanic.

South Gaulish cup sherd, second half C1.

South Gaulish sherd.

2 × Dr. 31, Central Gaul, Antonine.

Dr. 33, Central Gaul, Hadrianic-Antonine; burnt.

Mortarium sherd, Central Gaul, late C2.

2 × Central Gaulish sherds.

Dr. 31/Lud Sa, East Gaul, later C2–mid C3.

Dr. 38 probably, East Gaul, later C2–first half C3.

Mortarium foot, East Gaul, later C2–mid C3; worn inside.

ii) 1971–1974 Areas (LWB–O22–2, O24–2, Q24–2, T24–2, V24–6 and EE21–2).

Dr. 37 in the style of Mercator II of Lezoux. The lion and tiny figure are on Stansfield and Simpson 1958, pl. 146, no. 10, and the other motif may be the cornucopia also shown there; the corded borders are on Stansfield and Simpson 1958, pl. 146, no. 12 (Ref. 182), c. A.D. 160–190.

Dr. 18, South Gaul, probably pre-Flavian.

Dr. 27, South Gaul, second half C1.

Dr. 18(R), South Gaul, Flavian.

Worn South Gaulish sherd.

Dr. 31, Central Gaul, Antonine.

Dr. 33, Central Gaul, Antonine.

Dr. 33, Central Gaul, Hadrianic-early Antonine.

iii) Area of West Masonry Building (LWB–A25–2, A26–2, F19–2 and Z2).

Dr. 18, South Gaul, Neronian-Flavian.

Dr. 31R, Central Gaul, mid-late Antonine.

Dr. 33, Central Gaul, mid-late Antonine.

Mortarium base, East Gaul, late C2–mid C3.

East Gaulish dish or bowl sherd.

iv) Area of North Timber Building (LWB–77–203 and 77–217).

Dr. 33, East Gaul, later C2–first half C3.

Mortarium, East Gaul probably, late C2–mid C3; slightly burnt.

v) 1977 Area (LWB–77–301).

Dr. 31, Central Gaul, mid-late Antonine.

Plough soil
i) Centre Flint Structure/Quarry Pit Area (LWB–L29–2, L30–2, K25–4, N31–2, J27–1, M29–2, M30–1 and M32–2).

Two sherds of Dr. 37 in the style of 'Donnaucus' of Les Martres-de-Veyre. The saltire of fine beads, vertical ovoid beads, chevron, acanthus and tendrils are on Stansfield and Simpson, 1958, pl. 46, no. 533 (Ref. 182), the beaded medallion and rosette are no. 538 and the wavy line no. 547. The figure is not identifiable, *c.* A.D. 100–125. A third sherd of this vessel comes from the general soil deposit over the Quarry Pit Area (LWB–N32–3).

Cup sherd, South Gaul, second half C1.

South Gaulish platter sherd, second half C1.

Dr. 31R, Central Gaul, mid-later Antonine.

2 × Dr. 31, Central Gaul, Antonine.

Foot, probably Dr. 31, Central Gaul, Antonine.

(Probably all one vessel) Large Dr. 33, Central Gaul, Hadrianic-early Antonine.

Dr. 33 foot, Central Gaul, Hadrianic-Antonine.

Central Gaulish cup or dish sherd, Hadrianic-Antonine.

Dr. 33, East Gaul, later C2–mid C3.

ii) Area of West Masonry Building (LWB–B17–1, B17–2, E4–1 and C24–1).

Cup sherd, South Gaul, later C1.

Dr. 31R, Central Gaul, mid-late Antonine.

Dr. 33, Central Gaul, Antonine.

Dr. 33 probably, Central Gaul, Hadrianic-Antonine.

Central Gaulish sherd, Hadrianic-Antonine.

iii) Area of South Masonry Building (LWB–I34–1 and M33–1).

South Gaulish platter sherd, second half C1.

Dr. 31R, Central Gaul, mid-late Antonine.

iv) Other Areas (LWB–J20–1, O24–1 and X34–9).

Dr. 18(R), South Gaul, Flavian.

Dr. 27, South Gaul, Flavian.

Burnt sherd, probably a South Gaulish platter.

Bowl sherd, East Gaul, later C2–mid C3.

East Gaulish sherd, later C2–mid C3.

General Unstratified Material
i) 1968 (LWB–M27–5, M27–7 and L26–6).

Dr. 27, South Gaul, Neronian-early Flavian.

South Gaulish cup sherd, second half C1.

Central Gaulish platter sherd.

2 × Dr. 31/Lud Sa, East Gaul, later C2–mid C3.

ii)1969 (LWB–J32–3, M33–7, M33–21 and M33–2).

Dr. 18R or 15/17R, South Gaul, second half C1.

Dr. 36, Central Gaul, Antonine.

Dr. 31R, Central Gaul, mid-late Antonine.

Dr. 31R/Lud Sb, East Gaul, later C2–mid C3.

iii) 1970 (LWB–Z1, N24–3, N24–4, L32–4, N32–3 and 70–1).

Dr. 18, South Gaul, Flavian.

Dr. 27, South Gaul, Flavian.

Dr. 33, Central Gaul, Antonine.

Central Gaulish sherd, Hadrianic-Antonine.

Dr. 18/31, Central Gaul (Les Martres), early C2.

Dr. 33, East Gaul, later C2–first half C3.

Foot, Dr. 31, East Gaul, later C2–mid C3.

iv) 1971 (LWB–1).

Dr. 18, South Gaul, later C1; burnt.

Dr. 31, East Gaul, later C2—early C3.

v) 1976 (LWB–76–1).

Dr. 31, Central Gaul, Antonine.

Dr. 33, Central Gaul, Antonine.

Dr. 31 or 18/31 rim, Central Gaul, Hadrianic-Antonine.

Central Gaulish sherd, early C2.

2 Central Gaulish sherds

Dr. 37 foot, East Gaul, second quarter C3 probably.

Dr. 33, East Gaul, late C2–mid C3; very worn inside.

vi) 1977 (LWB–77–1).

No. 154   Dr. 37, Central Gaul. Trophy used by Cinnamus (Stansfield and Simpson 1958, pl. 160, nos. 41, 45, Ref. 182) with ovoid beads (pl. 159, no. 34), *c.* A.D. 145–175.

Dr. 37, Central Gaul, Antonine.

vii) (LWB–1).

3 × Dr. 18, South Gaul, Flavian.

Foot, Dr. 27, South Gaul, Flavian.

No. 155   Dr. 29, South Gaul. Narrow arrowheads in upper frieze panel, medallion in lower with poppyhead tendril. *c.* A.D. 70–85.

2 × Dr. 36 – 1 South Gaulish and Flavian, the other burnt.

One South Gaulish, one Central Gaulish sherd.

Walters 79 probably, Central Gaul, later C2.

Dr. 37, Central Gaul, Antonine.

Curle 15, Central Gaul, Antonine probably.

Footring fragment, Central Gaul, Antonine probably.

Dr. 45, Central Gaul, late C2.

Mortarium, East Gaul, late C2–mid C3; heavily worn inside.

F) THE COARSE POTTERY (Figs. 60–89, Nos. 155–907)

by Deborah Cooper and Keith Parfitt

Introduction.

The stratified deposits in Lower Warbank Field produced a total of 25,991 coarse ware potsherds of all periods. To these must be added an estimated 6,000 additional sherds from the general high-level, soil deposits, hillwash and plough-soil which were effectively unstratified. Thus, about 32,000 sherds were recovered in total and the great majority is either Iron Age or Romano-British in date, with only some 261 sherds being of Saxon or medieval date. Exact numbers of vessels represented by this major collection are difficult to calculate, but perhaps 3,000–3,500 seems likely. Of these some 740 vessels (Nos. 156–896) are illustrated here, mainly to provide the basic dating evidence, but these also seem to be a fairly representative selection.

In view of the large volume of material involved only the stratified pottery (anyway about 81% of the total) has been analysed quantatively. This has been done under eight broad fabric-types, four (Fabrics 1–4) being essentially Iron Age and four more (Fabrics 5–8) being Romano-British. Several of the fabric-types have been further subdivided. In addition, the contents of 16 pre-Roman pits (Pits 1–16) and all the flint-tempered wares (Fabric 4, some 925 sherds), have been studied by Mr. Peter Couldrey in detail and his report appears below (page 206). About 10% of the Keston Kiln Ware (Fabric 5, ii) has been examined by Dr. Valerie Rigby, together with all the corresponding Gallo-Belgic imports of this type (only 29 sherds) and her report is also included (page 200).

Of the stratified material considered here large assemblages, consisting of over one thousand sherds, came from seven separate contexts, of which four were chalk-cut features (the West Enclosure Ditch, the Quarry Pit Complex, the North-West Ditch of the Villa Enclosure and the late-Roman Ditches 21A and 21B); the other three assemblages were from horizontal soil deposits (the soils over the Quarry Pit Complex, the soils over the South Masonry Building and the soils over the Upper Metalling).

Together these seven pottery groups account for over one third of the total pottery recovered from the stratified levels of the excavation. The table below gives the precise numbers of these seven groups, together with three other smaller but significant assemblages.

Contexts	Sherds	Minimum Vessels	Drawn
Soils over South Masonry Building	1,619	166	29
Soils over Quarry Pit Complex	1,592	145	17
Filling West Enclosure Ditch	1,559	184	45
Filling Quarry Pit Complex	1,195	90	38
Soils over Upper Metalling (East and Centre)	1,177	114	9
Filling N.W. Villa Enclosure Ditch	1,097	148	59
Filling Ditches 21A and 21B	1,029	102	42
Filling East Enclosure Ditch	842	89	34
Soils over North Timber Building	719	75	4
Kiln Debris	452	75	15
Totals	11,281	1,188	292

Table 37: Details of major stratified pottery assemblages from Lower Warbank Field.

The classification and dating of the Lower Warbank Romano-British pottery, which constituted by far the largest volume of material, is largely based upon the local typology developed in the West Kent report of 1973 (Ref. 184). Details of the earlier, native wares have been amplified by the work of Mr. Peter Couldrey on the material from Farningham Hill, some 8 miles to the east of Keston (Ref. 185) and in his special study here of the Keston material. No attempt at an in-depth study of all the Roman coarse-wares has been made at this stage, although Pollard has recently produced such a study for the pottery from the Lullingstone Roman Villa site (Ref. 186). The major type-series of wares and forms for this nearby Roman site, presented by Pollard, clearly represents a significant contribution to pottery studies in West Kent and it seems fairly likely that many of the general observations and comments made about the material from Lullingstone, located only 7½ miles to the south-west of Keston, will eventually also be found to apply to the pottery from the Keston site. The material from the implied Keston kiln will provide another area for detailed work at a later date.

Brief notes about the main fabric types from Keston are given below and Peter Couldrey's work on the Iron Age material provides further details on the pre-Conquest wares. Pollard's most recent study (Ref. 187) of the Roman pottery of Kent will greatly assist in the general understanding of Romano-British wares and the present notes should be taken in conjunction with the information in this new volume. The full implications of this new study, however, have not been considered here as the volume appeared too late during the preparation of the present report.

The Late-Iron Age Local Native Pottery (Fabrics Types 1–4).
This class, which is associated with the pre-villa farmsteads of Periods II, III, IV and V comprises fabric groups 1, 2, 3 and 4 (see separate notes below) and constitutes some 49% of the total stratified assemblage. The pottery fabrics and types within this class essentially belong to those traditions which were indigenous to the region prior to the Conquest, although most types continued to be made into the early-Roman period. Mr. Peter Couldrey has undertaken a more

detailed study of the pre-Conquest material associated with Periods II and IIIa and this includes a more detailed fabric analysis.

Fabric Type 1: Shell-Tempered Wares.

This fabric type consists of wares in which varying amounts of crushed shell have been included in the clay as a temper before firing. Sherds in such shell-tempered fabrics occasionally occur with additional grog, sand, vegetable matter or flint inclusions but the predominant tempering agent is always shell. Peter Couldrey in his more detailed study of the Iron Age pottery from the site has defined a flint and shell-tempered fabric (his Fabric B), but in these wares the flint tends to predominate and this material is grouped here with the Type 4 fabrics (see below).

The Type 1 shell-tempered wares are very common in West Kent, appearing in the 1st century B.C. and continuing throughout the 1st century A.D. and probably into the early-2nd century A.D. They occur in definite late-Iron Age contexts at nearby Farningham Hill (there, Fabrics H, L and M) and on the present site (Period III), mostly as plain, simple, upright rimmed vessels in a range of sizes (e.g. Nos. 197, 199, 202, 205, 208 and 211), although there is one decorated jar (No. 838). Bead rimmed vessels, which occur at nearby Fox Hill and Baston Manor in association with later 1st and early-2nd century A.D. pottery, generally seem to be a post-Conquest development and such forms are very well represented at Keston (e.g. Nos. 288, 296, 300, 324, 326, 379, 413, 416, 431–433 and 451).

In the present excavations shell-tempered wares constituted nearly one quarter of the total stratified pottery recovered. This is some 5450 sherds, representing an absolute minimum of 200 vessels of which 109 have been drawn. In post-Conquest contexts bead rim jars of various sizes are the predominant form and these clearly represent a range of kitchen vessels used for cooking and storage purposes. Most post-Conquest vessels are undecorated and most sherds retain their shell-tempering, the 'corky' wares caused by the firing-out of the shell particles are rare here.

Three sherds in this fabric are of especial interest as they are sufficiently mis-shapen to suggest that they represent wasters from pottery production. One is a rim-sherd (No. 406) from a typical post-Conquest bead rim vessel, which has sagged during the firing process. The other two sherds form a base which had totally collapsed in the kiln (No. 420).

Significantly, all three sherds come from the area of the early-Roman Quarry Pits of Period IV, which also produced other evidence for a kiln site nearby (see discussion, page 294) including probable kiln-furniture fragments (Nos. 14–20) and a deposit of burnt clay debris. This burnt clay layer (Kiln Debris) produced the waster rim fragment.

Thus, these waster fragments, together with other evidence, strongly suggest that somewhere immediately to the east of the excavated area was an early-Roman pottery kiln, producing some, at least, of the shell-tempered vessels which are so well represented on the site. It is also clear that Gallo-Belgic imitations were also manufactured here (see below), together with a range of sandy domestic wares. In a few cases, a sandy fabric rim seems to have been added to an otherwise shell-tempered vessel, e.g. Nos. 311 and 428 (see below).

Generally, it seems fairly clear that early-Roman shelly wares were not the product of one kiln site, but were made by many local potters throughout West Kent. Indeed, very similar wares were also being produced in southern Essex (see Ref. 188). From the evidence recently recovered from Keston there can be no doubt that this settlement was one of these local production sites, although it probably did not produce pottery for very long.

Fabric Type 2: Patch Grove and Other Early Grog-Tempered Wares.

This fabric type consists of wares containing small particles of crushed pottery or 'grog', which was added to the clay before firing to render the fabric more elastic and thus suitable for the production of more elaborate forms. A typically 'Belgic' trait, beginning in the West Kent area very late in the Iron Age, the bulk of this fabric group occurs at Keston in immediately post-Conquest contexts, as well as residually in later deposits. Only a fairly small amount comes from the pre-Conquest pits of Period III (Fabrics J, K and L in specialist report here). A total of some 4,220 sherds was recovered, representing an absolute minimum of 150 vessels and 75 have been illustrated here. In general, the fabrics are relatively soft, are often 'soapy' to the touch and are usually grey or grey-brown in colour, with surfaces varying from orange-buff to brown or grey-black. A proportion of these grog-tempered wares contain other tempering agents, including occasionally shell, flint, chalk and other burnt-out organic material but most frequently sand. The other tempers, however, always occur less frequently than the grog.

Grog-tempered ware is generally taken as being of 'Belgic' origin and the Keston site lies well to the west of the general distribution of such wares (Ref. 189). Indeed, it is clear in West Kent, generally, that grog-tempered wares were a late introduction into the region, arriving only a little before the Roman Conquest and supplementing the long established, shell-tempered wares, widely used in the area. At the Farningham Hill farmstead grog-tempered wares (there, Fabrics F and N) were exclusively confined to late contexts on the site, indicating their use probably no earlier than the start of the 1st century A.D. (Ref. 190).

Vessels in this fabric type include large numbers of plain, everted rim jars and bowls (e.g. Nos. 282, 284, 291, 293, 301 and 307), bead rim jars and other vessels (e.g. Nos. 227, 285, 334, 410, 494 and 679) and a platter, together with some more elaborate cordoned vessels (e.g. Nos. 627 and 671). No. 627 is of Thompson's Type D3–5 (Ref. 191) and is generally dateable to the 1st century B.C. This type of vessel seems to be confined to Kent in its distribution and is usually found in rich burial contexts. Its occurence at Keston is, therefore, somewhat unexpected. It was unfortunately recovered from a later, Roman context. The base of a typical 'Belgic' pedestal urn was recovered from the filling of the West Enclosure Ditch (not illustrated) and the upper part of another vessel probably of this type has been illustrated (No. 520).

Large storage jars of so-called Patch Grove Ware, frequently with stabbed or finger nail impressed decoration around the shoulder, form a significant sub-group among the grog-tempered wares. Vessels in this particular fabric-type seem to appear immediately after the Roman Conquest and continue the grog-tempered tradition to the end of the 2nd century A.D. Some ten sherds of Patch Grove Ware have been drawn (Nos. 426, 510, 511, 513, 518, 531, 534, 687, 700 and 709). Grog-tempering reappears in West Kent in the 4th century A.D. (see below) but there appears to be no direct link with the earlier wares in this fabric.

Fabric Type 3: Native Sandy Wares.

This fabric type comprises a very generalised group of wares not always easily distinguishable from the truly Romanised sandy wares, especially when abraded. Over 1,000 sherds have been assigned to this fabric type and these must represent an absolute minimum of 55 vessels of which 34 have been illustrated. They are generally of hard, grey, brown or black fabrics, noticeably sandy to the touch and can often be seen to contain fine grey or white calcite grits.

From their general associations, it seems clear that the fabrics essentially belong with the native wares and seem to span the period from the 1st century B.C. to the later 1st century A.D. (effectively, site Periods III and IV). The forms represented include both those influenced by the 'Belgic' potting tradition, as well as earlier forms.

The present general group may be aligned with Peter Couldrey's fabrics A to E in the Farningham Hill Report and include his fabrics F, G and H in his present report on the Iron Age material from Keston.

Within this category, the most characteristic class of material is a collection of everted rim bowls and jars, mainly from the pre-Conquest pits (e.g. Nos. 230, 231, 235, 238, 240 and 247). These have been discovered at Farningham Hill in primary contexts, and several other West Kent sites including the Iron Age hillfort in Holwood Park, just above the Lower Warbank site (Ref. 192). These jars are characterised by footring bases (e.g. Nos. 232, 234, 236, 246, 252 and 253), everted rims and a smooth S-shaped profile. Their outer surfaces are quite often burnished (see below) and one vessel of this general form is decorated (No. 392). There are also three decorated wall sherds from vessels of uncertain form (Nos. 192, 222 and 868). A vessel with a plain inturned rim has also been illustrated (No. 257). It would appear that this fabric type includes the 'native burnished wares' discovered at nearby North Pole Lane (Ref. 193). The vessels there included small beakers, everted rim jars and bowls.

Fabric Type 4: Flint-Tempered Wares.

The Lower Warbank excavations produced a total of 925, often fragmentary, potsherds whose main tempering was calcined flint. Some 86 of these have been illustrated. Flint-tempering is essentially a characteristic of prehistoric pottery in West Kent. Much of the present material, however, was scattered in small amounts throughout the Roman and general soil deposits across the site. The only significant stratified groups came from the two inter-cutting pits (Nos. 1 and 2) in the area of the Centre Timber Building (354 sherds). A considerable number of other features produced small amounts of flint-tempered pottery but most of this is likely to be residual.

Of the residual and unstratified flint-tempered pottery, proportionally the largest collection came from the excavations of 1970–1974. These excavated areas correspond with the area occupied by the two pits which produced the main stratified groups. From this it seems likely that the distribution of the residual material reflects fairly well the position of an original prehistoric settlement focus.

The flint-tempered wares from the site have been subjected to a more detailed study by Mr. Peter Couldrey. From this it seems that these wares, which he subdivides into three groups (Fabrics A, B and E), are essentially related to a middle Iron Age occupation on the site, dated to somewhere between the 6th and 3rd centuries B.C. (Period II). Some flint-tempered wares, however, seem to have also been produced in the late-Iron Age (Fabrics J and L at Farningham Hill), but the problems of defining residual material make it difficult to estimate the actual proportions involved at Keston. The bulk of the flint-tempered pottery from the site consists of small, somewhat abraded, sherds and this has not allowed the precise identification of many of the fragments. A more detailed discussion of this material will be found on page 208.

The Roman Coarse Pottery (Fabric Types 5–8).

This class encompasses the whole range of basic post-Conquest, thoroughly Romanised wares found on the site and constitutes almost 51% of the total stratified ceramic assemblage. The class comprises Fabric types 5–8, although Fabric type 5 (sandy wares), itself, accounts for the bulk of the sherds. The date range of the material covers the full length of the Roman period, essentially site Periods IV to VII.

Fabric Type 5: Coarse, Sandy Romanised Wares.

This large composite group of sandy fabric types includes all of the hard, thoroughly Romanised wares where sand has been used as a tempring agent. The products of a number of different kiln sites (mostly unidentified) are clearly represented within this group and one fairly distinctive fabric sub-group, used for imitations of Gallo-Belgic imports seems actually to have been produced at Keston. A total of more than 11,000 sherds are of Fabric type 5 and these sherds represent nearly half of the total pottery analysed. A number of distinctive vessel forms/fabrics occur within the group, of which the following significant types may be noted.

i) Rusticated Ware: Some 20 sherds of this type, representing at least two different vessels were recovered. In form, these consist of sandy grey ware pots on which a thick slip has been worked up into rough knobs and ridges. Vessels of this type were generally produced between A.D. 50 and 120. Both vessels from Keston have been illustrated (Nos. 412 and 523).

ii) Keston Kiln Ware: A distinctive group of sandy wares appears to have been produced at Keston itself during the period c. A.D. 60–85. Both Gallo-Belgic imitations and a range of domestic wares were made and these are considered in more detail below (see page 199). Over 2,100 sherds in kiln ware fabrics have been recorded from the site so far and 127 vessels have been drawn (Nos. 270, 311–316, 322, 323, 325, 327, 329, 331, 333, 336, 337, 341, 342, 344–351, 353, 354, 357–372, 374–377, 380, 383–386, 388, 394, 398–403, 405, 407, 408, 411, 414, 415, 417, 418, 422–425, 428, 429, 434, 435, 441–443, 445, 457, 458, 462, 463, 469–473, 483, 484, 486–492, 498, 500–503, 512, 522, 525, 536, 577, 604, 632, 688, 699, 762, 778, 808 and 872–882). Together, these drawn pieces illustrate the bulk of the forms presently recognised as coming from the Keston kilns.

iii) Alice Holt/Farnham Grey Wares: The products of the Alice Holt kilns, which lay some 38 miles to the south-west of the Keston site, were widely spread across south-east England in the late-3rd and 4th centuries A.D. A range of grey, sandy kitchen wares was produced, sometimes decorated and quite often with a black or white burnished slip. The products of the Alice Holt industry have been extensively studied by Lyne and Jeffries (Ref. 194). At Keston some 641 sherds of this type have been identified and the ware occurs consistantly in all later contexts on the site. Some 19 vessels have been illustrated (Nos. 563, 567, 569, 572, 574, 584, 589, 590, 592, 594, 648, 652, 675, 729, 743, 775, 806, 825 and 828) including jars with everted and squared rims, straight-sided dishes and flanged bowls. The majority of these vessels are of 3rd or 4th century date but a few could be late-2nd century (e.g. No. 563).

iv) Cream Sandy Wares: During the early-4th century A.D. a number of production centres south of the Thames began making vessels in hard, sandy cream-buff or yellow fabrics. The most common products were horizontally rilled jars. A considerable quantity of this ware was produced at the Alice Holt site (Ref. 195) but there were also kilns in south-east Hampshire, supplying the Saxon Shore Fort at Portchester, and apparently somewhere in mid Surrey, producing 'Surrey Buff Ware'. At Portchester this fabric type (Fabric 'D') does not appear before *c.* A.D. 325. At Alice Holt the earliest vessels in this fabric date to about A.D. 330. Some 30 sherds of this general type have been identified at Keston and 13 of these have been illustrated (Nos. 548, 623, 698, 784, 786, 814, 830, 886–890 and 894). In view of the small quantities involved, no attempt has been made to distinguish between the products of the Alice Holt and (supposed) mid Surrey kilns. Production of these Cream Sandy Wares appears to have continued well into the 5th century A.D.

v) Amphorae: Some 147 sherds of amphora were recovered from the site including a single stamped handle (No. 903). The sherds seem to represent at least three different vessels, although the bulk is made up of small fragments. All are apparently derived from the common Dressel 20 globular South Spanish amphora (or its variant). Such vessels are well-known on sites in southern Britain in contexts ranging from the pre-Conquest period to the 3rd century A.D. In addition to the illustrated stamped handle, a rim has been drawn (No. 714).

Fabric Type 5A: Smooth Grey Ware, probably from the North Kent Marshes.

Although common in much of Kent, this fabric type was rare at Keston. Four sherds have been illustrated (Nos. 482, 612, 677 and 884). No. 482 consists of a complete carinated vessel from Burial 3 of the West Cemetery (Period IV). No. 612 is an upright necked jar or beaker. A poppy-head beaker seems to be represented by No. 677, whilst No. 884 is from a vessel with compass-scribed decoration in the style of the so-called 'London Ware'. All of these sherds are probably of later 1st or 2nd century A.D. date.

Fabric Type 6: Late-Roman Grog-Tempered Ware.

A total of 385 sherds, representing a minimum of 40 different vessels belong to this fabric type. Some 31 of these vessels have been drawn (Nos. 546, 565, 566, 568, 571, 573, 576, 578, 579, 580, 581, 639, 640, 653, 657, 660, 720, 771, 773, 777, 780, 781, 794, 810, 818, 823, 824, 827, 831, 845 and 856). The fabric type itself is generally hard, granular and tempered with grog and sometimes a little coarse sand or flint. It is usually grey or black in colour with brown and black grog inclusions. The surfaces range from grey-black to grey-brown in colour and they are often burnished. The relatively poor construction of some of the vessels reflects their essentially hand-made nature. The vessel types identified are limited, being confined to everted rim jars and cooking pots (e.g. Nos. 640, 781, 794 and 818), straight and convex-sided dishes (e.g. Nos. 653 and 810) and flanged rim bowls (e.g. Nos. 546, 660, 771 and 824) together with two large storage vessels (Nos. 780 and 856).

Late-Roman grog-tempered wares are being increasingly recognised on sites in the south-east. In West Kent the fabric type is paralleled at nearby West Wickham (Ref. 196), Lullingstone (Ref.

197) and Darenth (Ref. 198). It seems clear that these wares are the products of several different kiln sites, at least one of which ought to be in Kent. Another kiln site must have been in south-east Hampshire, near Portchester. Fabric 'A', identified there at the late-Roman fort site appears to be broadly comparable with the Keston material (Ref. 199).

As regards dating, the earliest vessels seem to belong to the later 3rd century A.D. in eastern Kent, but in the West Kent area it was not until the 4th century A.D. that these wares became at all widespread. It seems clear that they continued on for some time into the 5th century A.D. The genral 4th century A.D. dating, however, is in agreement with the otherwise rather imprecise evidence from the Keston site itself.

Roman Fine-Wares (Fabric Types 7 and 8).

In addition to the extensive range of sandy Roman coarse-wares (Fabric Type 5), small quantities of a number of Roman fine-wares were also recovered from the site. The majority of these is of the later Roman period (Fabric Type 8) but some earlier wares are also present (Fabric Type 7). The main types are briefly noted below (the fine-ware products of the inferred Keston kiln are not included here as these are discussed elsewhere, see page 199).

Fabric Type 7: earlier Roman Fine-Wares.

Three early fine-ware types are worthy of note:

i) Gallo-Belgic Imported Wares.

True Gallo-Belgic imports are rare on the Keston site and only some 29, representing at least three different vessels have been identified (Nos. 373, 493 and 606). These were submitted to Dr. Valerie Rigby who has kindly provided the report below.

a) Terra Nigra

1. (No. 606) Rim Sherd from a platter of Cam. form 14. Fine white matrix; worn grey surfaces, little finish survives. Source – import, workshop unknown. One of the most common and widely found platter-types, with a distribution extending from Norfolk into Wales and at least as far north as North Farriby, North Humberside. The date-range appears to be entirely post-Conquest, c. A.D. 50–70. This form can perhaps be considered as one of the prototypes for the range of foot-ring platter made at Keston (see page 201). Fill of North-West Villa Enclosure Ditch (F.800). (LWB–76–3).

b) White Ware Butt Beakers

1. (No. 493) Rim sherd from a butt beaker, Cam. form 113, in typical white ware. The rim has an internal cornice, but no cordon outside, therefore not an early variant; Claudio-Neronian. Fill of Pit 19 (LWB–D23–2).
2. (No. 373) 23 sherds from a butt beaker, Cam. form 113, in typical softer, pink ware, with soapy burnished finish on the rim and neck. The rim has an internal cornice and an external cordon; the rouletted zones are defined by a cordon at the neck base and a burnished and grooved band at the maximum girth. Although the rim is typologically early, overall it is a comparatively tall and slim variant which it unlikely to date to the period before A.D. 40, and so could just about be a pre-Conquest import. Fill of Quarry Pit Complex (LWB–N29–5 and N29–8).
3. Body sherd from a butt beaker (not illustrated), probably from the same source as No. 2. Fill of Quarry Pit Complex (LWB–M30–8).
4. Body sherds from a butt beaker (not illustrated), possibly from the same vessel as No. 1 above. Soil over the West Masonry Building (LWB–C23–2).

Previously considered as products of workshops at Camulodunum, recent evidence suggests that it is more likely that pre-Conquest versions, at least, were made in Gallia Belgica (Ref. 200).

Keston can now be added to the list of sites where definite Gallo-Belgic imports have been identified, although, with only a maximum of one platter and four butt beakers, it is not possible to judge their significance when estimating the size, scope and date of trade in Gaulish pottery. The forms are predictable since the platter is one of the most common post-Conquest types, while butt beakers, Cam. form 113, are the most common and widely found thin-walled, closed vessel-type.

Gallo-Belgic imports have been identified on ten sites in Kent, most of which lie on or near the coast. With the exception of Canterbury, Eccles and perhaps also Richborough, no more than a sprinkling of sherds, or even a single sherd, have occurred on each. Moreover, except for Canterbury, Deal and Springhead, the vessels were all manufactured and imported in the post-Conquest period, so that until recently, Kent did not figure in any distribution map of early imports. Excavations at Canterbury have produced a sizeable group of early-Gaulish pottery, although it has proved disappointing because it occurred residually in later contexts. There is hope for more early material at Springhead and Deal where late Augustan T.R. has been found. Deal is also significant because a cremation burial found at Mill Hill (Ref. 201) provided the sole example of the earliest variant of the white ware butt beaker, Cam form. 113, to be identified south of the Thames until the recent excavations in Canterbury.

ii) Rough Cast Ware: Four sherds of this early-Roman fine-ware were identified and these came from at least two different vessels, both too fragmentary to illustrate. The fine fabric is buff in colour with an orange-brown colour-coat. The Keston sherds are likely to come from the most common vessel-type, which is the cornice rim beaker, with surfaces sprinkled with small particles of dried clay. This ware may be dated to the 1st to 2nd centuries A.D.

Fabric Type 8: Later Roman Fine-Wares.
Five later Roman fabric types have been identified:

i) Rhenish Ware: Only six certain sherds of this imported fine-ware were recorded and all are too fragmentary to illustrate. A single sherd was recovered from the filling of West Tank 2, whilst the remainder came from various deposits in the western half of the North Timber Building. This ware may be dated to the later 2nd to 3rd centuries A.D.

ii) Nene Valley Ware: This occurred on a number of the later contexts on the site, but only some 39 sherds were recovered in all. Just nine of them have been illustrated (Nos. 615, 654, 730, 734, 751, 757, 790, 891 and 892). At least three of these (Nos. 751, 891 and 892) certainly came from 'Hunt Cups', typical of the industry. The products found at Keston may all be dated to the later 2nd to 4th centuries A.D. and all are from fine-ware cups and beakers.

iii) Oxfordshire Ware (Ref. 202):
a) Late imitation samian. About 100 sherds of this type were recovered and nine of these have been illustrated (Nos. 595, 598, 603, 607, 749, 756, 798, 801 and 822). The wares generally consist of an orange-pink micaceous fabric with a dark red or brown-red slip and sometimes with impressed rosette, slipped or horizontal rouletted decoration. The date-range for this type of ware is late-3rd to 4th centuries A.D.
b) Parchment Ware. A few sherds of this characteristic fine, white, powdery fabric with red or brown painted decoration were recovered, although all are too fragmentary for illustration.

iv) New Forest Ware (Ref. 203):
a) Late imitation samian. This ware is not as common in Kent as the Oxfordshire imitations and only two sherds have been identified from Keston. These are from a cream-buff fabric with a brownish-orange slip. Both pieces are too fragmentary for illustration.
b) Parchment Ware. Four sherds of this ware have been identified. The fabric consists of a sandy, off-white ware, rough to the touch and with painted orange or red decoration. All the pieces are too fragmentary for illustration.
c) Fine colour-coated wares. Some 38 sherds were recovered from the Keston site. Their fabrics

vary in colour from buff to grey and the colour-coats vary from matt-red to metallic purple (depending on the firing temperature). The forms occurring at Keston include shallow bowls, dishes and beakers. Three pieces have been illustrated (Nos. 591, 659 and 734).

v) Much Hadham Ware (Ref. 204): This very distinctive late-Roman ware was manufactured in the area of Much Hadham, Hertfordshire in the later 4th century A.D. The ware is easily recognisable with a dense blue-black fabric and well burnished, red-orange surfaces. A total of six small sherds was recovered from the site at Keston from five different vessels (none illustrated). The bulk of the material produced was traded into East Anglia, Essex and the East Midlands: from the published sources, it appears that Much Hadham Ware is comparatively rare in Kent. Recent work, however, on the Roman settlement at Springhead has shown the type to occur in considerable quantities here, whilst a single sherd has been recorded at Orpington (Ref. 205); a complete Much Hadham Ware flagon was recovered from St. Richard's Road, Deal (Ref. 206) and it seems possible that the 'streak-burnished' ware identified in Canterbury (Ref. 207) may also have derived from the Much Hadham kilns.

Thus, it may be suggested that the distribution of the ware throughout Kent is more extensive than has hitherto been supposed. It is obvious, nonetheless, that more work on the distribution in the area is needed.

KESTON KILN WARES.

During the analysis of the ceramic material from Lower Warbank Field it became clear that an unusually large number of imitation Gallo-Belgic vessels in the form of platters and butt beakers was represented, particularly in the earlier Roman features and especially those of Period IV. Six of the platters bore apparently illiterate stamps on their bases (Nos. 897–902) and the presence of two pottery dies, or poinçons, with broadly similar stamps (Nos. 37 and 38) immediately suggested that these vessels were actually made at Keston. The fabrics of the platters were essentially the same as those of the butt beakers and the discovery that a group of small pottery 'wheels' or discs found on the site (Nos. 22–34) had actually been used to decorate the butt beakers (see below) reinforced the evidence for on-site production. The identification of several fired clay objects, fairly certainly derived from a kiln (Nos. 14–20), along with several probable waster fragments (Nos. 406 and 420) seems to clinch the argument and this has led to a more detailed (though not total) study of the relevant material in order to more closely define the products of the (presumed) Keston kiln(s).

A further examination of the site notes relating to the excavated features showed that there was nothing that might be reinterpreted as the remains of an early kiln. The distribution of the 'kiln' products, in fact, suggested that any kiln lay beyond the south-eastern limits of the present excavations. The kiln apparently operated during site Period IV.

The following preliminary observations have been made at this stage but further study of the material is being undertaken. The present notes must, therefore, be regarded as provisional only.

i) The Fabrics.

In the absence of any still-loaded kiln or large quantities of definite wasters, the full range of Keston kiln products and fabrics has been difficult to determine. The work so far, however, has defined three different fabric sub-types, all fairly certainly from the kilns. The most common fabric type consists essentially of a hard sandy ware. A similar, though less common fabric, appears to be of the same clay matrix but without added sand tempering. Small (often red or black) grog particles occur in both these fabrics in fairly small amounts along with some glauconitic grit and there is, in fact, no clear-cut division between these two fabric types: one tends to merge gradually into the other depending entirely on the amount of sand tempering added to the matrix. The majority of the butt beakers and platters are in the sandy fabric. A range of domestic wares also seems to have been produced and these include vessels in both these fabric types. The sandy wares, however, were still the most common.

The third fabric type is completely different and consists of the well-known local, native, shell-tempered ware. Apart from a few waster fragments (Nos. 406 and 420) and some unusual 'dual fabric' sherds (Nos. 311 and 428) it has not been possible to determine which of the shelly wares were produced at Keston. It seems unlikely that all of the large number of vessels in this fabric which are represented on the site were produced here and it seems clear that shelly wares were in use on the site well before the kilns were established. Nevertheless, at least some bead rim jars seem to have been produced (e.g. No. 406).

Well over 2100 sherds in the non shell-tempered fabrics have been identified but the generally fragmented nature of the material, together with the similarity of the fabrics and forms make the precise number of vessels represented difficult to ascertain. From the large number of sherds, however, it seems unlikely that less than 200 individual pots are present and 134 separate vessels have been illustrated. Kiln ware fabrics were discovered within many features and deposits on the site. Large stratified groups came from: the East Enclosure Ditch (245 sherds); the Quarry Pit Complex (209 sherds) and the Kiln Debris (214 sherds). The soil over the Quarry Pits produced a further 312 sherds and the hillwash and general soil deposits across the central part of the site contained several hundred more sherds.

ii) The Date of the Keston Kiln Wares.

The range of products assigned to the Keston kilns may be readily dated to the 1st century A.D. Indeed, some of the most characteristic vessel types of this period, including platters, butt beakers and bead rim jars are present. A pre-Conquest beginning to the kilns, nevertheless, appears unlikely and overall, Dr. Rigby considers that a production period sometime between c. A.D. 60 and 85 is most probable. This would place such an industrial phase within Period IV on the site. It seems unlikely that this industrial phase was long-lived, since the range of pot types produced appears to cover a limited time-span. It is interesting to note that only a short time before this, pottery of similar forms was being made at the Eccles villa site just outside Rochester. Pottery making there is dated to the period c. A.D. 45–65 (Ref. 208). Dr. Rigby notes "the platters and butt beakers being produced at Keston are not close copies of the commoner Gallo-Belgic imports; rather they are hybrid/derived forms" and probably do not belong to the earliest years of the Roman occupation (see below).

iii) General Comments on the Keston Kiln Products, by Valerie Rigby.

The discovery of pottery marking and decorating equipment at Keston is extremely important. Poinçons or dies in fired clay for marking a potter's products have been found on the site of the great samian manufactures in Gaul, but this is the first time that they have definitely been found in Britain. Although simple tools, they make crisp impressions. Potters working at West Stow, Suffolk, are known to have made stamped cups, bowls and platters, but no dies were found during the excavations; nor have they been identified in or around the many workshops making stamped mortaria in Britain in the late-1st and 2nd centuries A.D. The dies from Keston are, therefore, unique.

The discs from Keston have provided the first evidence of how long lengths of simple cord impressed and fern-leaf motifs were executed. A 'molette' was found in Gaul, but this is a more complex tool comprising a pierced cylinder of fired clay, with the decorative pattern on the circumference, mounted on a wooden handle, like the modern pastry cutter. This particular example was used for producing the large and more complex patterns typical of the Argonne samian potteries. A fragment from a similar tool was found at Eccles, Kent, on the site of an early-Roman pottery workshop (Ref. 209).

Although no actual kiln structures have been found at Keston, pottery must have been produced in the vicinity. The range of forms appears to have included a number of fairly close copies of Gallo-Belgic imports: footring platters, Cam. forms 8 and 14 (six stamped centrally with a maker's mark); close copies of girth, butt and globular beakers, Cam forms 84, 112 and 91 and pedestalled cups, Cam. form 74/79 and barbotine beakers of Cam. form 114. The detailed formation of the rim and base shapes is less precise than those of the imports, and the incised decoration tends to be simpler and coarser in texture, but there is no doubt that potters working locally had handled the prototypes and they were not trying to produce vessels from mere verbal descriptions. The results are perhaps not yet sufficiently exact in form, fabric techniques and die associations to support the idea of a potter migrating directly from continental production centres to the exclusion of all other hypotheses.

Seven different dies are represented, two by dies and five by platters, and they are all unique to Keston: hopefully, in time, examples will be found at other settlements. Each exhibits a rather different range of motifs, although four are simple and common arrangements which can be paralleled. The range of motifs is also well within the range of those commonly used by Gallo-Belgic potters but it is difficult to estimate the connection. Did some migrant potters arrive with their original dies, or did local potters take impressions from imported vessels? Did die-makers try to copy specific Names, Marks or Name Copies, or just follow the general idea of the impression a die should produce? Even when there is evidence that a particular die was used to stamp both genuine T.R. and coarse-ware platters, it is still open to different interpretations: to date, only two different dies have been identified, while there is evidence that a wide variety of coarse-ware vessels were imported, as well as fine table wares, throughout the Roman occupation (see for example Ref. 210).

The range of forms produced at Keston overlaps to varying degrees with those of early-Roman production centres, both locally and some distance away. Similar footring platters with Marks and butt beakers were made at Eccles about 24 miles distant. However, there are some notable geographical and chronological differences in the choice of other prototypes. At Keston, the potters relied on traditional Gallo-Belgic prototypes, which had originally been imported in the pre-Conquest period, while those at Eccles chose to copy more up-to-date, post-Conquest fine-wares which originated in Central and South Gaul. It is possible that the differences reflect different markets, with Eccles aiming at the more Romanised, even military market, and Keston, the native population.

There may be chronological factors involved, with Keston just possibly being somewhat earlier or short-lived. Archaeological factors cannot be ignored though the samples recovered so far may not be sufficiently comprehensive. The early-Roman workshops at Chichester produced a wide range of traditional Gallo-Belgic copies as well as Central and South Gaulish types 1–12 (Ref. 211), while at Rushden, Northants, unusual forms, possibly of Mediterranean origin, were copied and added to the traditional Gallo-Belgic range (Ref. 212).

It is of course always difficult to estimate output and distribution, but since seven different dies are represented at Keston, one interpretation could be that seven different potters and/or workshops were involved over a fairly short period of time, in which case output would have been considerable and the need for other markets essential. Examples of roulette-disc decorated beakers at Crayford, Kent (unpublished excavation by K.A.R.U.), demonstrate at least a limited local trade in Keston products of perhaps the proverbial single-day's cart journey. It is tempting to see London as a likely market since the distance is not much greater. The Keston potters may have aimed to fill the gap in the market caused by the drastic reduction in the supply of Gallo-Belgic products *c*. A.D. 60, so that they were satisfying a demand created by imported pottery which was, therefore, native, traditional and was being superceded by new trends.

iv) The Forms.
The material attributed to the Keston kilns has been divided into seven basic forms (Forms 'a–g'):

Form 'a' – Imitation Gallo-Belgic Platters (Cam. forms 8 and 14).
Together with the butt beakers, these are the most recognisable products of the inferred kiln, although no obvious platter waster-fragments have been found to date. Some 208 platter sherds have been recorded and these seem to represent at least 70 different vessels. Some 31 of these have been drawn (Nos. 342, 365–371, 398–403, 422–425, 442, 443, 457, 458, 473, 487, 500–502, 536, 762, 879 and 881). Six of these vessels were marked with a single stamp (Nos. 897–902), although only three of these stamps survive essentially complete.

The fabrics of all these vessels are broadly similar, they are hard, well-fired and are generally tempered with fine to very fine quartz sand, together with occasional larger inclusions of grog and glauconitic grit (up to 0.5 mm. in diameter). The grits are usually black or dark red but are occasionally dark grey. The grog tends to be orange or red in colour. The surface colour of the platter sherds varies but they may be divided into two broad groups: i) those with dark grey, black or dark brown surfaces and; ii) those with orange-brown, buff or red surfaces. The core of the vessels is generally dark grey, frequently with an outer zone of orange-brown, which on the lighter coloured sherds continues through to the surface while on the dark coloured pieces it gives way to the outer black/brown/grey surfaces. Occasionally, pieces have been fired either black or orange-brown throughout. Some sherds have the appearance of being over-fired.

A number of decorative techniques have been applied to these platters. Those with dark coloured surfaces (group i) are often burnished, especially on the exterior. Pieces with light coloured surfaces (group ii) are often coated with a dark red (or very occasionally orange-brown) slip. This slip is generally applied to the whole of the vessel and is sometimes burnished to produce a most attractive surface finish. Internally, on the base, a few vessels have a concentric band of rouletting. Three examples of this have been noted. One (No. 762) consists of eight concentric rings of small punched dots producing a zone about 15 mm. wide. This band is enclosed on either side by a single incised groove. The other two bases are more significant, for their rouletting has been produced using impressed lines which have been applied by means of one of the small pottery wheels also used to decorate the butt beakers (see below). This observation thus provides an important link between the two types. One of the bases so decorated has a centrally placed, illiterate stamp enclosed by the rouletted band (No. 879/stamp No. 899).

These illiterate marks or stamps may be divided into two general types: 1) fern-leaf and 2) an apparently meaningless series of mock 'I's, 'V's and 'X's. Two potter's dies for making these marks were also recovered from the excavations (Nos. 37 and 38). These fall into the type 2 group, although they are different from each other and neither can be exactly matched with any of the stamped bases. Nor can any of the stamped bases be positively matched with each other. The fern-leaf, type 1, marks do not seem to have been made with a pottery wheel, despite their similar appearance.

The platters exhibit an infinite variety of details in rim profiles, although an internal quarter-round moulding/offset is the norm. These vessels are clearly copying a well-known late-Iron Age/early-Roman import. The Gallo-Belgic orignals are of two main types; those of the red *Terra Rubra* and those of the dark grey *Terra Nigra*. The colour variations noted in the Keston versions clearly reflect this. Application of the dark red slip was probably an attempt to copy the finish on the *Terra Rubra*, although the slip is very similar in colour to 'Pompeian Red Ware' and the burnishing on the dark coloured vessels gives them some resemblance to *Terra Nigra*. From the material recovered it would seem that the two versions were produced in roughly equal amounts. Only one sherd of a genuine *Terra Nigra* vessel was recovered from the site (No. 606) and nothing of *Terra Rubra*. Two sherds of an imitation Gallo-Belgic platter in a grog-tempered ware were also recovered (not illustrated). There is no reason to think that this vessel was made at Keston, however.

Form 'b' – Butt Beakers (Cam. form 112).
These were the other readily distinguishable products of the Keston kilns. Over 200 sherds from butt beakers have been identified and these represent at least 40 different vessels of which 19 have been drawn (Nos. 269, 315, 348, 349, 351, 357–364, 373, 414, 463, 874, 877 and 882). In general terms the fabric of these butt beakers may be readily compared with that used for the platters. The wares are generally thinner, however. The surface colour of the beakers is varied and ranges from cream to light grey, dirty buff, orange-buff and pale orange-red. No dark wares are present. The core may range from light to dark grey or it may be the same colour as the surface of the vessel.

The surface decoration of these butt beakers is interesting. Several vessels seem to have been coated in a dark red slip, like a number of the platters (No. 364), and several other vessels were coated with a light grey slip. One vessel was decorated with deeply cut, angled slashes on the neck (No. 882). This appears rather crude when compared with the other butt beakers, although the fabric is similar. As with Gallo-Belgic imports, the majority of the Keston butt beakers were decorated on the body of the vessel with horizontal bands of vertical 'rouletting'. The 'rouletted' decoration was of two main types: Type a) fine, plain vertical combing divided by impressed horizontal lines. This was the simplest method of decoration and, although having the superficial appearance of 'rouletting', was seemingly produced with a comb rather than a wheel. It occurred fairly frequently on the Keston butt beakers and several examples are illustrated (Nos. 269, 874 and 877). Type b) vertical rouletting applied with small pottery wheels. This was a more advanced method of decoration and is particularly significant because the actual rouletting wheels used to produce the decoration were also recovered from the site in some numbers (see above, page 155).

Several different forms of butt beaker seem to have been produced at Keston, although the fragmentary nature of the surviving sherds makes these difficult to define in great detail. They are clearly intended as copies of Gallo-Belgic imports of which just three or four genuine examples were recovered from the excavations. No detailed study of the distribution of Keston kiln products in West Kent has yet been attempted but, already, two butt beakers from excavations at Perry Street, Crayford have been located which have the fabric and characteristic pottery wheel rouletting of the Keston products. This suggests that the kiln at Keston provided wares for local market centres and perhaps for London itself. Clearly more work is required, however, before the details can be worked out.

Form 'c' – Girth Beakers (Cam. forms 84 and 85).
Another fine-ware form apparently produced at Keston was the 'girth beaker'. As yet only one certain example has been identified but virtually a complete profile of this is available (No. 374). It has burnished dark red surfaces with a brown core and is in the now familiar hard sandy fabric. Red and black grits, however, are a little more common within the fabric of this vessel than in most other pieces examined. There were no obvious traces of a slip on the vessel. The body of the vessel is decorated with four rows of impressed, elongated triangles. A number of wall sherds with similar type of decoration may be from other vessels of this form but this cannot be certain. In general terms, the form of the substantially complete vessel may be compared with Cam. forms 84 and 85.

Form 'd' – Reeded Rim Bowls.
At least six examples of reeded rim bowls in the standard sandy 'kiln-ware' fabric have been noted so far. These are mostly rather fragmentary, however (see Nos. 405, 417 and 878). The surface colour of the sherds falls into two main groups: a) those of dark grey-black colour (two sherds) and b) those of buff-brown colour (four sherds). The core colour ranges from dark to light grey. The top of the rim is the only area selected for any decorative treatment. On the two dark sherds a pair of incised concentric grooves delimit a zone of decoration consisting of either a continuous wavy line, rather irregularly incised, or a close-set incised lattice pattern, also poorly executed. Of the lighter sherds two are plain (No. 405) except for the two concentric grooves, whilst the other two also have the incised wavy line motif and an additional dark red slip applied to the rim (No. 417).

From the fragments examined so far it seems probable that all of these sherds come from vessels of just one standard form. This seems to have been mildly carinated and was broadly similar to Cam. form 246A etc.

Form 'e' – Pedestal beakers (Cam. form 74/79).
Only two certain examples of this vessel type have been found in the Keston kiln fabric (Nos. 312 and 376) but a complete profile for neither is available. Fragments of a possible third example have also been noted. The surface colour of the sherds ranges from buff to orange and red. The cores are either grey or orange-red. All of the sherds are coated with a dark red slip and one vessel has been burnished. From the colouring of the Keston examples they seem to be copying *Terra Rubra*.

Form 'f' – Other Fine-Ware Vessels.

From the large number of 'kiln-ware' sherds it has been possible to reconstruct several other fine-ware vessel-types. Generally, only single examples of each have been located so far and it seems likely that they were not produced in such large numbers as the platters and butt beakers.

A small, high-shouldered beaker has been reconstructed from fragments (No. 873). This is of particular interest because it is decorated with the vertical rouletting produced by the pottery wheels also used on the butt beakers. From this it now seems clear that many small, indeterminate wall sherds decorated in this manner could come from either type of vessel, rather than just butt beakers as was originally thought. The single vessel so far reconstructed has orange-red surfaces and a light grey core. The interior surface is coated with a red-brown slip. This may once have also coated the outside of the vessel but it is now somewhat weathered. This seems to be a local copy of a Gallo-Belgic globular beaker (Cam. form 91) but this is not certain.

Part of a hemispherical bowl has been illustrated (No. 434). This is in the typical sandy kiln ware and has an orange-brown core and surfaces. The exterior is decorated with horizontal grooves and coated in the by now familiar dark red slip. The type is perhaps copying a girth-grooved, pedestalled beaker.

Another small jar (No. 375) may also be noted here. This is of a cream-buff colour with a grey-buff core. On the exterior, two rows of deeply incised angled lines occur below the shoulder. On the rim and neck, an orange-brown slip has been applied and then burnished. It seems likely that this vessel type is imitating Gallo-Belgic imported material represented by Cam. form 114.

A considerable amount of small fragments in kiln-ware fabrics remain to be studied. It seems likely that a number of other forms are represented by this material but the fragmentary nature of the sherds makes these difficult to isolate. A variety of other beaker types may be included, however, and at least some of these seem to have been decorated. There are two rim fragments apparently from flagons of Cam. form 140 etc. These are in orange-brown and buff coloured wares which seem to be of Keston kiln fabric (Nos. 372 and 489). There are also at least three handles (No. 880) which may be related.

Form 'g' – Domestic Wares.

A series of plain vessel fragments, representing a variety of normal domestic types also occurs in sandy fabrics similar to those used for the platters, butt beakers and other fine-ware forms. These domestic forms do not seem to occur in great quantities and many of the vessels are represented by only a few somewhat fragmentary sherds. The general form and fabric of these sherds strongly suggest, however, that they were also produced on the Keston site (although perhaps not in so great a quantity as the platters and butt beakers etc.). The following provisional observations have been made and apparent vessels defined.

The main vessel types appear to be:

i) A series of small bead rim jars (e.g. Nos. 316, 329, 344, 472, 484, 488, 512 and 525).

ii) A series of larger bead rim jars and cooking pots (e.g. Nos. 325, 327, 380, 407 and 428).

At least six vessels with bead rims (e.g. Nos. 311 and 428) have a curious dual fabric construction on their rim and neck. The actual beading of the rim and the outer part of the neck below are typical sandy kiln ware. The inner wall, however, is made of a familiar shell-tempered fabric. It would, thus, appear that for some reason a number of essentially shell-tempered pots had a bead rim applied to them in a sandy ware (perhaps the sandy ware was easier to shape than the shell-tempered fabric). The shell-tempering itself ranges from sparse to moderate; the individual inclusion being 1–3 mm. across.

iii) Carinated jars and bowls with everted rims and often incised decoration on the body (e.g. Nos. 313, 384, 778 and 837).

iv) A variety of everted rim bowls/jars, often of uncertain form (e.g. Nos. 323, 347, 350, 385, 386, 388, 394, 396, 408, 415, 490, 491 and 875 etc.). Some of these seem to have been quite large (e.g. No. 388).

v) Several lids have been identified (e.g. Nos. 337, 341, 435, 471 and 808).

vi) Other vessels represented include bead rim bowls (No. 445), globular jars (No. 411), a pedestal base (No. 429) and at least two collander bases (No. 486).

The vessels in the form 'g' series range in colour from black to dark grey, brown and orange-buff. The red colours seen in other kiln ware groups are mostly absent here. Decoration is largely confined to a little light burnishing and incised linear decoration, including broad lattice designs (e.g. No. 313 etc.). Vessels are also occasionally decorated with a red slip.

vii) Two small cups (possibly lamp holders) have been illustrated (Nos. 383 and 418). These are not well made but are of typical kiln ware sandy fabric.

It thus seems fairly clear that a range of domestic wares was being produced at Keston to supplement the more specialised fine-wares being produced here. There is evidence, in the form of waster sherds, that some of the shell-tempered wares recovered from the Keston site were also made here. An interesting link with the present range of material seems to be provided by the half-dozen bead rim vessels noted above, with both shelly and sandy fabrics used in their manufacture. The waster rim in shelly ware (No. 406) and base (No. 420) are clearly significant discoveries.

h) Conclusion on Pottery Manufacture at Keston.

Although no definite *in situ* kiln structure was identified at Lower Warbank, there seems very good circumstantial evidence for pottery manufacture on the site in the early-Roman period. It appears that the kiln(s) here were producing both shell-tempered kitchen wares and a range of finer sandy wares, including Gallo-Belgic imitations. The Quarry Pits and East Enclosure Ditch located on the site seem to have provided a convenient dump for some waste material from the kiln site, which may well have been located immediately to the south-east of the excavated area.

The situation of the Lower Warbank site must have been suitable for the operation of a kiln. Indeed, the three basic raw materials required: clay, water and wood for firing the kiln all seem to have been readily available close to the site. The higher chalkland above Lower Warbank Field is capped with a thick deposit of Eocene rocks in the form of Thanet Sands, Woolwich Beds and Blackheath Pebble Beds. These beds include deposits of clay which would probably have been suitable for potting. It is of interest to note that analysis of three samples of shell-tempered pottery from the Iron Age farmstead at Farningham Hill, a few miles to the east of Lower Warbank, showed that the source of the clay there was the so-called Black Shelly Clays of the Woolwich Beds. Today, the higher ground above Warbank is heavily wooded and study of fossil soil preserved under the rampart of the Iron Age Hillfort situated here showed that, prior to its construction, the area was occupied by long-established oak woodland. It, therefore, seems likely that this hilltop remained wooded throughout the Roman period. Thus, both firewood and potting clay were probably available on this hilltop and could have been easily brought from here to the kiln site. Water for the preparation of the clay could have been obtained from the springs which rise just above the site.

Coincidentally, another early kiln seems to have existed at the 1st century A.D. villa site at Eccles, near Rochester. Interestingly, this kiln also seems to have been producing a range of early-Roman fine-wares (Ref. 213).

Chaff-Tempered Ware (Nos. 906 and 907).

The site in Lower Warbank Field produced a total of 19 small fragments of chaff-tempered ceramic material, of the same general type as that recently defined by Nigel Macpherson Grant whilst working on early-Roman material from Canterbury (Ref. 214). This material is always associated with Belgic/early-Roman pottery and has now been recognised on at least five Kentish sites (Ref. 215). The few fragments from Keston add little new information about the overall shape of the crude vessels which this material seems to represent and there is still some doubt about the precise forms, due to the consistently small size of the fragments which survive. It has been possible to draw two rim profiles from the Lower Warbank material (Nos. 906 and 907) and both of these appear to belong to Macpherson Grant's open form (Type 2). Seven other small rim fragments were also recovered.

This material is the first to be published from West Kent and most of it was again associated with pottery of early-Roman date. Six fragments were recovered from the fill of the Quarry Pit Complex (Period IV), which contained large amounts of pottery dateable to the second half of the 1st century A.D. One small fragment came from the soil over the Quarry Pit Complex. The filling of Pit 17 (Period IV) produced a single fragment and this was again associated with pottery of later 1st century A.D. date. Another small sherd came from Pit 18 (Period IV) and was associated with similar early pottery. The filling of the West Enclosure Ditch of later 1st century A.D. date produced a further five fragments. The remaining five fragments occurred in residual material in later features and deposits, together with residual 1st century A.D. pottery.

The precise function of these small baked clay containers is still being discussed but it currently seems most likely that they represent containers used to package salt. Salt production is well attested on the North Kent and Essex coasts and it seems that such production centres may have been exporting their wares in these small vessels. Without doubt, more sites in West Kent will produce this material in the next few years and further light may be shed on its purpose.

G) THE IRON AGE POTTERY (associated with Periods II and III)

by Peter Couldrey, B.Sc.

The pre-Conquest pottery from the excavations in Lower Warbank Field has been studied in greater detail than has been attempted for the much larger amounts of later Romano-British wares recovered. A total of 1328 sherds (18.0 kg.) of Iron Age pottery was submitted to the present writer for analysis and this comprises all of the flint-tempered wares and the more diagnostic pieces in other fabrics found residually in Roman contexts, but principally the entire contents of a series of stratigraphically early pits (Pit Nos. 1–16) assigned to site Periods II and III.

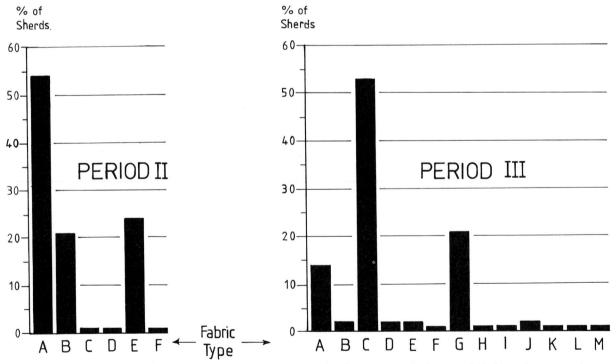

Table 38. Graph showing percentage distribution of Fabrics in Periods II and III based on number of pottery sherds.

For the purposes of the overall site pottery-study the early native wares were sub-divided into four broad fabric types (Fabric Types 1–4). In the detailed study here they have been re-grouped into twelve more specific fabric types (Fabrics A–L). The shell-tempered wares of Fabric type 1 have been sub-divided into two (Fabrics C and D). The grog-tempered wares of Fabric type 2 have been sub-divided into 3 (Fabrics J, K and L) as has Fabric type 3, the native sandy wares (Fabrics F, G and H). The flint-tempered wares of Fabric type 4 have also been sub-divided into three (Fabrics A, B and E). Intrusive Roman material is represented here by Fabrics I and M.

During the study of the Iron Age pottery each sherd was examined. Within each deposit, those sherds which appeared to be derived from the same vessel were grouped together and regarded as a single pot. For each of these pots were recorded: the weight, wall thickness, number of non-fitting sherds, surface treatment, colour and fabric. These details are held with the site archive. This report describes the main fabrics, forms, styles of decoration, discusses the chronology and ends with a brief general discussion. Vessels have been selected for illustration to show the main groups on which the discussion is based and to demonstrate the range of forms and decoration present.

The Iron Age pottery examined appears to represent two distinct periods of occupation on the site. The first (site Period II) probably dates to somewhere between the 6th and 3rd centuries B.C., whilst the second (site Period III) probably belongs to the 1st century B.C. or a little later.

The Fabrics

The fabric of each sherd was examined macroscopically. The main inclusions were recorded together with their size and frequency. These detailed descriptions of fabrics are held with the site archive. For the purposes of this report each fabric has been assigned to one of eleven groups which are described here. The distribution of these fabric groups is shown in Table 39. Two final Groups (I and M) have been created for all Romano-British fabrics, which are here presumably intrusive.

Pit No.	A	B	C	D	E	F	G	H	I	J	K	L	M	Total
1	598	12	–	–	450	–	–	–	–	–	–	20	–	1080
2	1581	61	–	7	1041	–	–	–	–	–	–	–	–	2690
3	38	–	–	–	6	–	–	–	–	–	–	–	–	44
4	27	–	–	–	–	–	–	–	–	17	–	–	–	44
5	50	–	41	–	18	–	6	–	–	21	–	–	–	136
6	–	–	35	–	16	–	–	–	–	–	–	–	–	51
7	27	4	54	11	–	11	–	–	–	3	–	–	–	110
8	–	–	18	–	–	–	–	–	–	–	–	–	–	18
9	484	36	2801	54	9	20	1064	35	–	95	24	–	24	4646
10	3	–	289	–	–	–	232	–	–	–	–	–	–	524
11	64	–	1983	28	–	–	423	69	–	73	–	–	5	2645
12	–	–	570	–	–	–	–	–	–	–	–	–	–	570
13	–	–	280	–	–	–	–	–	–	–	–	–	–	280
14	–	–	88	–	11	–	–	–	–	–	–	8	–	107
15	19	3	105	15	35	–	146	–	1	–	–	–	8	332
16	6	49	273	32	–	–	80	–	–	13	16	16	–	485
Total	2897	165	6537	147	1586	31	1951	104	1	222	40	44	37	13762

Table 39. Pottery from the Iron Age pits showing distribution by fabric and weight in grams.

Fabric A – Flint

This group includes fragments of calcined flint as the main inclusion. The accompanying matrix may also contain, in various quantities: iron oxide, small fragments of shell, very sparse chalk and organic-tempering. The size of the flint inclusions is generally less than 3 mm., though moderate occurrences up to 5 mm. and rarely up to 7 mm. are found.

Fabric B – Flint in sandy matrix

As in Group A, the main inclusion is calcined flint, and accompanying inclusions may be iron oxide and organic tempering. In this instance, however, the flint, although the main tempering material, is generally sparse and moderate and the sandy texture of the fabric is particularly noticeable. The clay matrix may contain grains of either quartz or glauconite.

Fabric C – Shell

This group is characterised by abundant inclusions of fossiliferous shell. It also contains iron oxides, quartz grains, grog and organic inclusions, in varying quantities.

Fabric D – Shell in sandy matrix

This group includes fabrics with sparse to moderate amount of fossiliferous shell in a sandy matrix. Occasional grains of iron oxides are also found.

Fabric E – Shell and Flint

This group contains common to abundant inclusions of shell, as in group C, but with additional inclusions of calcined flint, generally up to 3 mm. in size.

Fabric F – Sandy and Organic tempered

This group is characterised by a sandy matrix containing moderate to common voids, up to 3 mm. in size, representing the former presence of organic tempering.

Fabric G – Glauconitic sandy

This sandy fabric is characterised by the presence of abundant grains of glauconite, up to 1 mm. in size, with just four sherds with grains up to 2 mm. in size.

Fabric H – Quartz sandy

This sandy fabric is characterised by the presence of abundant grains of quartz, generally up to 0.1 mm. in size, though occasionally up to 0.3 mm.

Fabric I – Fine grained sandy

This fabric was used for one vessel only, a butt beaker (No. 269) with walls just 3 mm. thick from Pit 15. This is an intrusive sherd of Keston Kiln Ware, dated *c.* A.D. 60–85.

Fabric J – Grog

This group is characterised by abundant inclusions of grog. Additional inclusions of shell, iron oxides, flint or organic tempering occasionally appear.

Fabric K – Grog and Shell

This group is similar to Fabric J except that the shell fragments are more prominent, being common up to 2 mm. in size.

Fabric L – Grog in sandy matrix

This group contains common inclusions of grog and sparse to moderate inclusions of shell up to 1 mm. in size in a noticeable sandy matrix.

Fabric M – Romano-British fabrics

This code is used to refer to any Romano-British fabric other than Keston Kiln Ware, appearing in the contexts being described.

The Forms

The Iron Age pottery from the site was very fragmentary. Only two complete profiles could be reconstructed (Nos. 240 and 838) and most of the recognisable forms consisted of rims and bases. These form the basis of this typology. Distinctions drawn using just rim profiles offer only a very broad guide to the type represented. Nevertheless, they do provide some indication of vessel form and it will be shown below that they also provide a general indication of chronology. The following types are distinguished by shape, angle and wall thickness:

Inturned rims – convex neck

Form 1 – Plain sharply inturned, with wall thickness of 5–7 mm:
    a. Dia. *c.* 20 cm: (No. 216)
    b. Dia. unknown: (Nos. 257, 275 and 444)

Form 2 – Jar with inturned flat top with slight external expansion, and wall thickness of 4–5 mm:
    Dia. 9.5 cm: (No. 226).

Form 3 – Plain slightly inturned, almost open form, with wall thickness of 7 mm:
    Dia. *c.* 11 cm: (No. 819)

Form 4 – Slightly inturned, flat top with external expansion and wall thickness of 8–15 mm:
    a. Dia. 16 cm: (No. 251)
    b. Dia. *c.* 30 cm: (No. 229)
    c. Dia. 44 cm: (No. 254)
    d. Dia. unknown: (No. 205)

Form 5 – Inturned lightly recessed rim with slight internal and external expansion, and wall thickness of 8–9 mm:
    a. Dia. 36 cm: (No. 208)
    b. Dia. unknown: (No. 266)

Form 6 – Inturned internally bevelled rim with external expansion and wall thickness of 11–14 mm:
    a. Dia. 23 cm: (No. 262)
    b. Dia. 30 cm: (No. 255)

Form 7 – Inturned rim with thick internal rounding and external projection, and wall thickness of 5–7 mm:
    a. Dia. 13–14 cm: (No. 189)
    b. Dia. 18 cm: (Nos. 195 and 196)

Inturned rims – straight neck

Form 8 – Inturned, lightly recessed, rim with slight external projection, and wall thickness of 9–10 mm:
    Dia. 14 cm: (No. 223)

Form 9 – Slightly inturned, almost bead, rim with external projection and wall thickness of 4 mm:
    Dia. *c.* 22 cm: (No. 186)

Form 10 – Slightly inturned rim with external flange, and wall thickness of 5 mm:
    Dia. 30 cm: (No. 860)

Inturned Rims – concave neck

Form 11 – Plain inturned rim with wall thickness of 5–6 mm:
    a. Dia. 18 cm: (No. 861)
    b. Dia. unknown: (Nos. 158 and 863)

Form 12 – Inturned rim with flat top with external expansion and a wall thickness of 5–7 mm:
    a. Dia. *c.* 20 cm: (Nos. 228 and 684)
    b. Dia. 24–26 cm: (No. 219)

Form 13 – Inturned recessed rim with external expansion and internal bevel, and wall thickness of 4 mm:
    Dia. 11 cm: (No. 241)

Form 14   – Inturned rim with internal bevel and external expansion, and wall thickness of 6 mm:
           Dia. unknown (No. 245)
Form 15   – Slightly inturned rim with a plain or flat top, and wall thickness of 5–7 mm:
           a. Dia. 10.5 cm. (not illustrated)
           b. Dia. unknown (Nos. 161, 169 and 499)
Form 16   – Slightly inturned rim with a flat top, similar to form 15, but with wall thickness of 11–18 mm:
           Dia. unknown: (No. 859)
Form 17   – A shouldered vessel with an inturned rim with flat top and slight internal projection, with wall thickness of 7–8 mm:
           Dia. 13 cm: (No. 200)
Form 18   – Inturned rim with a flat top and internal and external projections, and wall thickness of 10–13 mm:
           Dia. 32 cm: (No. 862)
Form 19   – Slightly inturned rim with flat top and external expansion, and wall thickness of 8–11 mm:
           a. Dia. 16 cm: (No. 237)
           b. Dia. 20 cm: (No. 233)
           c. Dia. unknown: (No. 214)
Form 20   – Inturned rim with flat top and external expansion, and wall thickness of 12 mm:
           Dia. *c.* 50 cm: (No. 256)
Form 21   – Inturned thick bead rim of a storage jar, with wall thickness of 11 mm:
           Dia. 37–40 cm: (Nos. 194 and 227)

Upright Rims
Form 22   – Plain rim with slightly concave neck and wall thickness of 6–7 mm:
           Dia. 12 cm: (No. 243)
Form 23   – Upright externally thickened rim with plain or flat top, and wall thickness of 6–9 mm:
           a. Dia. 12 cm: (No. 244)
           b. Dia. unknown: (No. 220)

Out-turned Rims
Form 24   – Slightly out-turned with plain or flat-topped rim, and wall thickness of 5–6 mm:
           a. Dia. *c.* 14 cm: (No. 185)
           b. Dia. unknown: (Nos. 217, 225 and 250)
Form 25   – Out-turned with expanded flat-topped rim, and wall thickness of 5–8 mm:
           a. Dia. *c.* 12 cm: (No. 260)
           b. Dia. 16–18 cm: (Nos. 170 and 211)
           c. Dia. 28–30 cm: (Nos. 178 and 267)
           d. Dia. 40 cm: (No. 180)
           e. Dia. unknown: (Nos. 159, 181, 258 and 858)
Form 26   – Straight flaring rim with wall thickness of 7–9 mm:
           a. Dia. 15 cm: (No. 651)
           b. Dia. 34 cm: (No. 833)
           c. Dia. unknown: (No. 355)
Form 27   – Slightly everted rim with plain top, and wall thickness of 4–6 mm:
           a. Dia. *c.* 12 cm: (No. 844)
           b. Dia. 20–22 cm: (No. 198)
           c. Dia. 26–30 cm: (No. 811)
           d. Dia. unknown: (Nos. 164, 173 and 725)
Form 28   – Slightly everted rim with plain top, and wall thickness of 13 mm:
           a. Dia. *c.* 26 cm: (No. 213)
           b. Dia. unknown: (No. 272)

Form 29 – Slightly everted rim with flat top, and wall thickness of 4–6 mm:
      a. Dia. 11–12 cm: (Nos. 356 and 871)
      b. Dia. 22 cm: (not illustrated)
      c. Dia. 30 cm: (No. 865)
      d. Dia. unknown: (Nos. 157, 162, 166, 182, 183 and 853)
Form 30 – Slight eversion with expanded flat-topped rim, and wall thickness of 4–7 mm:
      a. Dia. 17 cm: (No. 190)
      b. Dia. 20–22 cm: (Nos. 163, 248 and 678)
Form 31 – Everted rim with finger-tip impressions, and wall thickness of 4–6 mm:
      a. Dia. 20 cm: (No. 849)
      b. Dia. unknown: (No. 776)
Form 32 – Everted rim with plain rounded top, and wall thickness of 5–9 mm:
      a. Dia. 13 cm: (not illustrated)
      b. Dia. 16–17 cm: (Nos. 215, 273 and 393)
      c. Dia. 18–22 cm: (Nos. 212, 218, 230, 235, 238, 240, 274, 453 and 813)
      d. Dia. 23–25 cm: (Nos. 224 and 839)
      e. Dia. uncertain: (Nos. 232 and 247)
Form 33 – Short everted rim with rounded top, and wall thickness of 7–10 mm:
      a. Dia. 16 cm: (Nos. 209 and 392)
      b. Dia. unknown: (not illustrated)
Form 34 – Bowl with slightly everted plain rim, with wall thickness of 4 mm:
      Dia. 18 cm: (Nos. 179 and 231)
Form 35 – Jar with slightly everted plain rim, and wall thickness of 4–6 mm:
      Dia. 15–16 cm: (No. 838)
Form 36 – Jar with everted rim, a slightly inturned, straight neck, and wall thickness of 6–7 mm:
      Dia. 11 cm: (No. 452)

Plain Open Bowls

Form 37 – An open bowl with a plain rim with flat top, with wall thickness of 9–11 mm:
      a. Dia. 22–25 cm: (Nos. 197, 202 and 239)
      b. Dia. 30 cm: (No. 199)
      c. Dia. unknown: (No. 259)
Form 38 – Plain rim of an open bowl, with wall thickness of 7 mm:
      Dia. 16–18 cm: (Nos. 271 and 519)

Miscellaneous Forms

Form 39 – Open bowl or lid with short out-turned rim, and wall thickness of 6–7 mm:
      Dia. *c.* 16 cm: (No. 821)
Form 40 – Shallow dish:
      Dia. uncertain: (No. 171)
Form 41 – Handle
      (No. 683)

Bases

B1 – Tall pedestal:
      a. Dia. 8 cm: (No. 270)
      b. Dia. 10 cm: (not illustrated)
B2 – Low Pedestal:
      Dia. 11 cm: (No. 278)
B3 – Footring:
      a. Dia. 7–8 cm: (Nos. 201, 204, 234, 236, 246, 268 and 324)
      b. Dia. 9.5 cm: (No. 253)
      c. Dia. unknown: (No. 252)

Decoration
Some 44 sherds were decorated (of which 38 have been illustrated) and the styles of decoration are described here, grouped according to the position in which they occur on the vessel.

Rim decoration
a. Finger-tip impressions on the outside of the rim: (Nos. 158, 161, 168, 849 and 870).
b. Finger-tip impressions along the top of the rim: (Nos. 271, 600 and 776).
c. Light groove along the top of the rim: (No. 195).
d. Two horizontal grooves around the outside of the rim: (No. 275).

Neck decoration
e. Two light horizontal burnished grooves: (No. 189).
f. Lightly burnished vertical grooves: (No. 452).

Shoulder decoration
g. Finger-tip impressions: (Nos. 294, 352, 833 and 862).
h. Stamped and grooved interlocking arcs: (No. 838).
i. Light horizontal grooves and cordon: (No. 226).
j. Linear grooved motif, comprising a horizontal line and diagonal grooves: (No. 392).

Wall decoration
In addition to genuine wall decoration, this category also includes decoration on sherds which are not certainly from the shoulder or neck of a vessel.
k. Finger-tip impressions: (No. 683).
l. Finger-tip impressions on cordon: (No. 419).
m. Stamped and grooved design: (Nos. 222 and 868).
n. Groups of short diagonal grooves forming part of an uncertain design: (No. 187).
o. Light horizontal groove: (No. 272).
p. Pair of light horizontal grooves: (No. 869).
q. Horizontal groove with diagonal burnished lines: (No. 249).
r. Two light curvilinear grooves: (No. 265).
s. Two adjacent horizontal grooves with residual cordon: (not illustrated).
t. Light broad grooves: (Nos. 156 and 188).
u. Fine 'combed' designs: (No. 505).
v. Light broad 'combing': (not illustrated).

Internal surface
w. Burnished lines from an uncertain design: (No. 177).

Beneath Base
x. Linear cruciform design: (No. 253).
    Straight line probably from part of a cruciform design: (Nos. 204, 246, 252 and 268).

Chronology
In considering the chronology of this pottery it is recognised that the sample is small and that the typology defined above is built on fragmentary rims and bases. Nevertheless, these forms, together with the fabrics and styles of decoration, provide the main dating evidence for the Iron Age occupation. An analysis of the material suggests that the pottery falls into two groups, corresponding with site Periods II and III. Only four of the early pits (Pit Nos. 1, 2, 9 and 11) contained more than four recognisable forms and in several cases the relative chronological sequence of a deposit is based on the presence of one vessel. Much of the Iron Age pottery was found in residual contexts. Some was recovered from Roman features, and some Period II vessels

appeared in Period III deposits. Those features which contained only a few Iron Age sherds may be later than indicated by the pottery and many cannot be securely dated.

Table 39 shows the distribution of fabrics in pits assigned to Periods II and III. During Period II the fabrics employed were predominately flint-tempered: fabrics A and B account for 48% by sherd count, and 75% by weight. When shelly clay was used, flint fragments were added to it – fabric E accounts for 51% by sherd count and 24% by weight. The only sherd of sandy grog-tempered fabric (fabric L) is regarded as being intrusive from Period III or later.

In Period III a wider range of fabrics is employed. Shell-tempered fabric (fabric C) is commonly used for cooking and storage vessels, accounting for 55% by sherd count and 62% by weight. Sandy fabrics are used for finer vessels, with glauconitic sandy fabric (fabric G) accounting for 21% by sherd count and 20% by weight. Flint continues to be used, but it is evident that some of this is residual from Period II.

In the following discussion, the date of each period is established using forms and identifying typological parallels with pottery from recently published material. The range is then extended to include fabrics and decoration to identify other vessels which may belong to the period.

Fabric Decoration	A	B	C	D	E	F	G	I	J	K	L
a	5										
b	1				2						
c										1	
d									1		
e									1		
f										1	
g	1	1	2								
h				1							
i									1		
j				1							
k	2										
l	1										
m							2				
n	1										
o	1		1	1		1					
p	1										
q									2		
r					1						
s									1		
t									1		1
u	1										
v									1		
w	1										
x							5				

Table 40. The association of decoration and Iron Age fabrics. (No sherds found in fabric H were decorated)

Fabric	A	B	C	D	E	F	G	H	I	J	K
Form											
1	1	1						1		1	
2										1	
3	1										
4			3	1							
5			2								
6			2								
7										1	2
8			1								
9	1										
10	1										
11	2				1						
12	1		2								
13	1										
14				1							
15	4	1									
16	1		1								
17			1								
18			1								
19			3								
20			1								
21			1								1
22			1								
23			3								
24	3		1		1						
25	3		4		3						
26	1	1	1								
27	5	1						1			
28			1	1							
29	10	1									
30	1	1	1		1						
31	2										
32			1				15			1	
33				1			2				
34	1						1				
35				1							
36											1
37	1		5								
38	1				1						
39	1										
40	1										
41	1										
B1							1				
B2								1			
B3		1					9				

Table 41. The association of Iron Age Forms and Fabrics.

The Dating of the Period II Pottery.

In spite of the small sample size and the fragmentary nature of the evidence from the Period II pit deposits, a sufficient number of recognisable forms exists to enable a general chronology of the period to be proposed.

The shouldered bowl from Pit 2 (No. 179; form 34) is broadly similar to vessels from Orsett, Essex (Ref. 216) and St. Catherine's Hill, Surrey (Ref. 217). The latter falls within Cunliffe's Park Brow-Caesar's Camp (Wimbledon) group, dated from the 5th to 3rd centuries B.C.; and the Orsett bowl has been placed between the 6th and 4th centuries B.C. (Ref. 218).

Vessels resembling No. 181 (form 25), with a flaring neck and rounded shoulder, are found in the Upper Thames region – e.g. from Old Marston and Mount Farm, Oxfordshire and Blewburton Hill, Berkshire (Ref. 219). Cunliffe places these forms within his Long Wittenham-Allens Pit and Chinnor-Wandlebury groups (Ref. 220) in the 5th to the 3rd centuries B.C. Harding, however (Ref. 221), has argued for an earlier date in the 6th century B.C., seeing the origins of these 'round-bodied' bowls in continental late-Hallstatt assemblages, such as Saint Vincent, Belgium, where broadly similar forms appear from the HaC1 to La Tène 1 periods (Ref. 222).

Bead or 'developed' rims, such as No. 186 (form 9), from Pit 2 are found on biconical bowls in Late Bronze Age contexts at Runnymede Bridge (Ref. 223), but become more common in the 7th and 6th centuries B.C., for example at Petter's Sports Field, Egham where they are found stratified above a Ewart Park hoard (Ref. 224). They are also associated with the 6th to 4th century B.C. assemblage at Orsett (Ref. 225).

Pedestal bases of form B1 are found from the same period – e.g. at Orsett (Ref. 226) and Chinnor, in Cunliffe's Long Wittenham-Allens Pit group (Ref. 227). They are also found in later Iron Age contexts.

The remaining forms from this period are either too small or too simple to receive special comment and, with one exception, all are likely to date between the 6th and 3rd centuries B.C. The exception is the fragment of a shoulder decorated with two broad horizontal grooves: No. 156 from the lower fill of Pit 1. It is in sandy grog-tempered fabric (Fabric L). Both the fabric and the style of decoration are typical of 'Belgic' pottery and this sherd is quite evidently intrusive from the Period III or later occupation.

Styles of decoration occuring in fabrics A–E are shown in Table 40. Those in use during this period include finger-tip impressions on the rim (a and b), shoulder (g) and wall (k). These are commonly found on pottery from the late-Bronze Age and gradually fall out of use in the early-Iron Age, becoming rare by about the 3rd century B.C. Sherds with this style of decoration are attributed to Period II. These include No. 221, which is residual in Pit 9.

Applied cordons with finger-tip impressions (style l) are found in the necks of storage jars – e.g. at South Rings, Mucking (Ref. 228) – and, less frequently, on smaller vessels. Its appearance here seems to represent a late use of this style. The form of the vessel on which it appears here, No. 419 is uncertain.

Intersecting groups of grooves, as on No. 187, are not common in Britain, though they occur in late-Hallstatt and early-La Tène contexts on the continent – e.g. at Lede, Belgium (Ref. 229). Similarly, open bowls with internal decoration (style w), such as No. 177, are known from a few unpublished assemblages of the 5th to 3rd centuries B.C. in East Kent.

The excavation recovered flat bases with flint fragments protruding from underneath. Such bases are known from late-Bronze Age assemblages – e.g at Farnham Green, Surrey, between the 11th and 9th centuries B.C. (Ref. 230) and at South Rings, Mucking, Essex (Ref.231) – and are believed to be the result of resting the base of the pot on a bed of calcined flint grits during manufacture. At Warbank, examples have been found in pit F.205 and Pits 1 and 2, and they appear as a residual element in Period III deposits (e.g. Pits 9 and 11 etc.) and later. Of the 21 examples from the site, two are in sandy flint-tempered fabric (fabric B); two are in shell and flint-tempered fabric (fabric E) and the remaining 17 are in flint-tempered fabric (fabric A). Their occurrence in these fabrics supports their attribution to Period II and suggests that this technique continued in use at least until the 6th century B.C.

The Dating of the Period III Pottery.

A larger sample is available from the Period III pit deposits (Pits 4–16). The forms most commonly represented are footring bases (form B3) and everted rims (form 32). These occur together on bowls and jars, as illustrated here by No. 240, and confirmed at other sites. But on occasions, similar bases have been employed with different forms – e.g. No. 257, from the upper fill of Pit 11. In this instance, the inturned rim (form 1) and footring base (form B3) have been associated because they are both in a distinctive fabric consisting of sparse flint-tempering in a quartz sandy matrix; though it is of course possible that they belong to different vessels.

Everted rim footring vessels are characteristic of middle Iron Age pottery in Essex, Kent and Sussex, and form an important element of Cunliffe's Mucking-Crayford style (Ref. 232). While we await large samples from closely dated deposits, a chronology based on detailed differences of these vessels is premature. Nevertheless, it is perhaps significant that half of the footring bases from Period III features are decorated with linear burnished designs underneath (style x). Such decoration appears to be associated with vessels during the later Iron Age, perhaps from the 1st century B.C. onwards, since they are known from assemblages which immediately precede or overlap with 'Belgic' forms (e.g. Farningham Hill, decoration style b; Ref. 233).

In Pit 11 these vessels are associated with cooking and storage jars in shell-tempered fabrics, such as Nos. 254–256. The use of shell-tempered fabrics, while present in Period II becomes more popular for larger vessels in the middle and late-Iron Age in West Kent. The use of inturned, flat-topped expanded rims, as seen here, is known from Farningham Hill (e.g. Nos. 138 and 142, Ref. 234).

Pit 10 (which is cut by Pit 11) shares forms with Pit 11, but also includes a thin-walled jar with an inturned, recessed rim, No. 241 (form 13), in flint-tempered fabric. The development of recessed rims is generally a feature of late-Iron Age pottery and is more commonly found on shell-tempered jars, as in Pit 9 etc. (forms 5 and 8, see below). At Farningham Hill they appear in Phase 2 (Ref. 235).

In addition to an everted rim No. 274, Pit 16 contained a related vessel with a short everted rim (form 33, not drawn) and a jar with a plain, inturned rim, No. 275 (form 1). The latter is distinguished from the others of the same type by having two horizontal grooves (decoration style d) around the outside of the rim and by being in grog-tempered fabric (Fabric J). Both this style of decoration and fabric enable it to be classified as 'Belgic'. While decoration with two horizontal grooves around the rim is not common, it is broadly similar to bead rim jars of Thompson's type B5–1, 3 and 5 (Ref. 236).

From the evidence presented here it is clear that the pottery from Period III embraces middle to late-Iron Age forms. Applying close dates, however, is problematical. Very little 'Belgic' pottery was contained within the 13 pit groups examined. Grog-tempered fabrics J, K and L were represented by just 35 sherds (5%) weighing 357 gm. (4%), and only a short time-span would be required to account for its deposition in the late-Iron Age features. Such pottery is generally scarce in this part of West Kent, and the identification of early and late types within the general repertoire of 'Belgic' forms remains uncertain and subject to local variation. It is possible that the use of everted rim footring vessels, characteristic of the middle-Iron Age, continued in use in this area up until shortly before the arrival of Roman pottery. The whole of Period III could then be accommodated within the first half of the 1st century A.D. It is probably more likely, however, that the Period III occupation came to an end shortly after the arrival of 'Belgic' forms, during the 1st century B.C. The quantity of 'Belgic' pottery is small, and the sherds mostly appear in the upper fills of the pits. It is even possible that many are intrusive and belong to the early-Roman occupation of Period IV and later. Certainly a significant amount of grog-tempered ware was recovered from the early-Roman features on the site.

Other forms which may belong to Period III, or which may be just post-Conquest, include the low pedestal base (form B2), No. 278 which has fine horizontal striations and has evidently been wheel-turned; and the necked jar, No. 452 (form 36), in grog-tempered fabric. The latter is decorated with at least one group of vertical burnished grooves around the neck, a trait shared by vessels in post-Conquest deposits from North Kent, at Springhead and Stone (Ref. 237).

Vessel No. 838 in sandy shell-tempered fabric, decorated with an elaborate grooved and dotted design, was found in a post-hole cut into the West Enclosure Ditch of the Conquest period (Period IIIb). This style of decoration (h) is normally found in late-Iron Age contexts, as at Farningham Hill (Ref. 238). This and sherd Nos. 222 and 868 all fall within Elsdon's group from the Thames Estuary and Lower Thames Region (Ref. 239) and probably belong to the Period III occupation. No. 838 is most probably derived from the filling of the Enclosure Ditch itself which has produced other late-Iron Age material.

Form 7, the internally thickened rims with external expansion, from Pit 5, and the soil over Pit 6 is clearly related to thickened bead rims – Thompson's type C1–4 (Ref. 240). It is a well-known form from the late-Iron Age and post-Conquest periods, as at Elm Farm and North Pole Lane, West Wickham (Ref. 241).

Pit 9 contained a new range of vessels in its upper filling. Jars with recessed rims in shell-tempered fabric (forms 5 and 8), Nos. 208 and 223 are joined by Belgic forms: No. 226 (form 2) and the thickened bead rim of a storage jar, No. 227 (form 21). The former is of grog-tempered fabric (fabric J) and is similar to Thompson's barrel jar forms (type B5–3 and B5–5, Ref. 242), which are common in Kent from pre-Conquest assemblages. The latter is of grog and shell-tempered fabric (fabric J), paralleled at Farningham Hill in phase 2 (type 12, Ref. 243) and is of Thompson's type C6–1 (Ref. 244).

In addition to the styles of decoration already mentioned, the use of pairs of adjacent horizontal grooves, with a residual cordon (style s) is commonly found on 'Belgic' pottery, as are 'combed' surfaces (styles u and v). Both these are found at Farningham Hill. It is possible the No. 505 which is in flint-tempered fabric (fabric A), belongs to Period II – a few examples are known from this early period (e.g. at Wilmington Gravel Pit, report in preparation). But combed decoration was found on flint-tempered vessels at Farningham Hill and it is likely that this example belongs to Period III.

CATALOGUE OF THE ILLUSTRATED COARSE POTTERY (Figs. 60–89, Nos. 156–907).

Middle Iron Age Pit 1, Lower filling (LWB–023–5).

No. 156   A shoulder of sandy grog-tempered fabric. It is decorated with two broad shallow grooves. The internal surface is dark grey (N3) and smooth. The external surface and core are light brown (7.5YR7/6) and there is an orange-brown (2.5YR6/8) internal margin. (Fabric L). This sherd appears to be intrusive.

No. 157   An everted rim in flint-tempered fabric. The sherd is worn and the diameter uncertain. It has been fired dark grey (N3) throughout. Both surfaces have been wiped with flint fragments protruding. (Form 29, fabric A).

Middle Iron Age Pit 1, Upper filling (LWB–023–3).

No. 158   An inturned rim of flint-tempered fabric. It is decorated with light finger-tip impressions around the outer edge. Both surfaces are wiped, with flints visible and protruding. The internal surface is dark grey to brown (N3–5YR6/4). The external surface and core are dark grey (N3). (Form 11, fabric A).

No. 159   A rim with internally projecting flat top, of flint-tempered fabric. The sherds are black (N2) throughout and the surfaces have been wiped with flints protruding. (Form 25, fabric A).

No. 160   A small, everted rim with flat top and a slight external projection, in sandy flint-tempered fabric. The diameter is uncertain. The internal surface is red-brown (2.5YR6/6) and although worn, appears to have been burnished with few flints visible. The external surface has been wiped with flints protruding. Both it and the core are black (N2). (Fabric B).

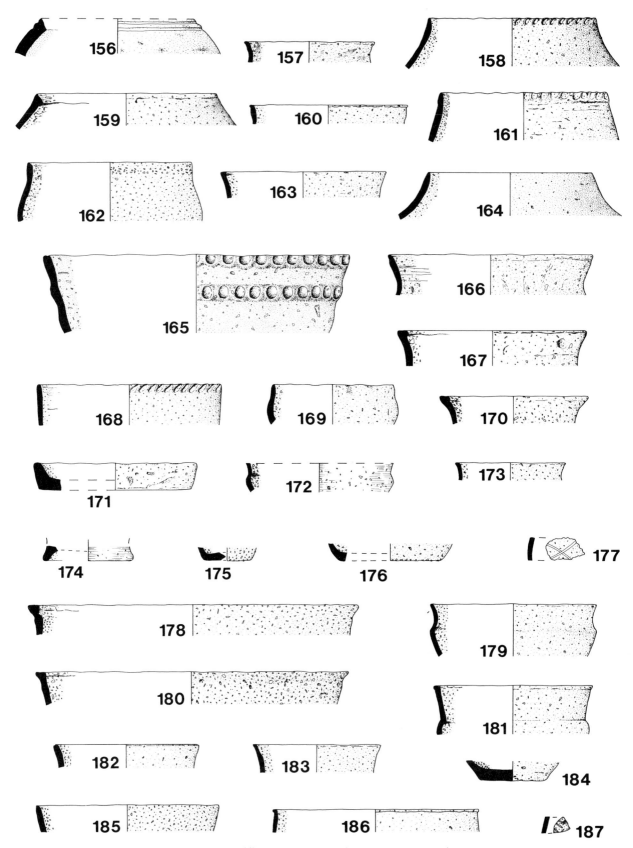

Fig. 60.   *Middle-Iron Age pottery from Pits 1, 2 and 3* ($\frac{1}{4}$).

No. 161 An inturned rim of flint-tempered fabric. It is decorated with light finger-tip impressions along the outer edge; and this sherd may belong to the same vessel as No. 158. Both surfaces are worn with flint grits protruding. The internal surface is brown to light orange (5YR5/3–2.5YR6/8). The external surface and core are dark grey to grey (N3–N5). (Form 15, fabric A).

No. 162 A slack shouldered vessel with a slightly out-turned rim in flint-termpered fabric. The rim is small and the diameter uncertain. The sherd is worn and though it was evidently wiped smooth, flint inclusions protrude. It appears to have had brown (5YR5/3) surfaces and a grey (N4) core; though it has been refired and now has orange (2YR6/8) patches. (Form 29, fabric A).

No. 163 An out-turned rim with flat top and internal projection in sandy flint-tempered fabric. The rim is small and the diameter uncertain. Both surfaces have been wiped with flints protruding. The internal surface and core are black (N2). The external surface appears to have been brown (5YR7/4), but most of it is worn with the black core showing through. (Form 30, fabric B).

No. 164 A rim of flint-tempered fabric. The sherd is small and the angle and diameter uncertain. Both surfaces are worn with flints visible. The internal surface is light grey (N6). The external surface is light to dark grey (N6–N3), and the core is dark grey to brown (5YR4/2). (Form 27, fabric A).

Middle Iron Age Pit 2, Lower filling (LWB–024–4 and 023–7).

No. 165 Large jar with upright, slightly flared rim in a hard, flint-tempered fabric. Black core, dark brown internal surface and medium brown exterior surface. There is a faint, thumb-pressed horizontal cordon below the rim. The rim itself, also bears faint thumb-pressed decoration on the outer surface. (Fabric A).

No. 166 A gently everted rim in flint-tempered fabric. The sherds have been fired dark grey (N3–N2) throughout. The internal surface is wiped smooth with flints visible and protruding. The external surface has been wiped and is rough with flints protruding. (Form 29, fabric A).

No. 167 An out-turned rim with internally projecting flat top in flint and shell-tempered fabric. The sherd is dark grey to black (N3–N2) throughout. Both surfaces have been wiped with flints and shell protruding. (Fabric E).

No. 168 Two sherds, possibly from the same vessel as No. 158, with an upright or slightly inturned rim of flint-tempered fabric. Finger-tip impressions decorate the outer edge of the rim. The surfaces have been wiped smooth with few flints visible or protruding. The sherds are light brown (5YR7/6) and dark grey (N3) throughout and have evidently been refired. (Fabric A).

No. 169 An open bowl with rounded shoulder in flint-tempered fabric. The sherd is small and the diameter uncertain. It has been fired grey-brown (7.5YR5/3–6/2) throughout. Both surfaces are worn and flints protrude. (Form 15, fabric A).

No. 170 An everted rim with flat top and slight internal expansion in flint and shell-tempered fabric. The internal surface is black (N2) and worn with flint and shell inclusions protruding. The external surface is dark grey to dark brown (N3–7.5YR5/4) and smooth with fragments of shell and flint visible. The core is black (N2). (Form 25, fabric E).

No. 171 A shallow dish of flint-tempered fabric. The internal surface is dark grey to brown (N3–5YR6/3) and smooth with flints visible. The external surface is brown (5YR6/6) with grey (N4) patches. The core is dark grey to black (N3–N2). (Form 40, fabric A).

No. 172 The shoulder of a small cup or bowl in flint and shell-tempered fabric. The surfaces are smooth with flint and shell fragments visible. The internal surface and core are dark grey (N3) and the external surface is grey (N4). (Fabric E).

No. 173 An out-turned rim in flint-tempered fabric. The sherd is small and the angle and diameter uncertain. The surfaces are orange (2.5YR6/8) and worn with flints protruding. The core is dark grey (N3). (Form 27, fabric A).

No. 174 A fragment of a pedestal base of flint-tempered fabric. The sherd is small and the diameter uncertain. The surfaces are dark grey (N3) and smooth, almost burnished, with flints visible. The core is dark grey (N3) and there is a brown (2.5YR6/6) internal margin. (Fabric A).

No. 175 A flat base in flint-tempered fabric. The internal surface is worn away. The external surface is grey (N4) and wiped with flint visible and protruding. The core is light grey (N6). (Fabric A).

No. 176 A flat base in flint-tempered fabric. The internal surface is black (N2) and wiped with flint grits visible and protruding. The external surface is dark grey (N3) and smooth with flint visible. Beneath the base the surface is brown (5YR6/4) and worn with flint inclusions protruding. (Fabric A).

No. 177 A wall sherd, possibly from an open bowl or dish, in flint-tempered fabric. The internal surface is dark red-brown (2.5YR4/3) and smooth. It has a burnished cross, possibly added as deliberate decoration. The external surface is dark grey (N3) and smooth with few flints visible. The core is dark grey to black (N3–N2). (Fabric A).

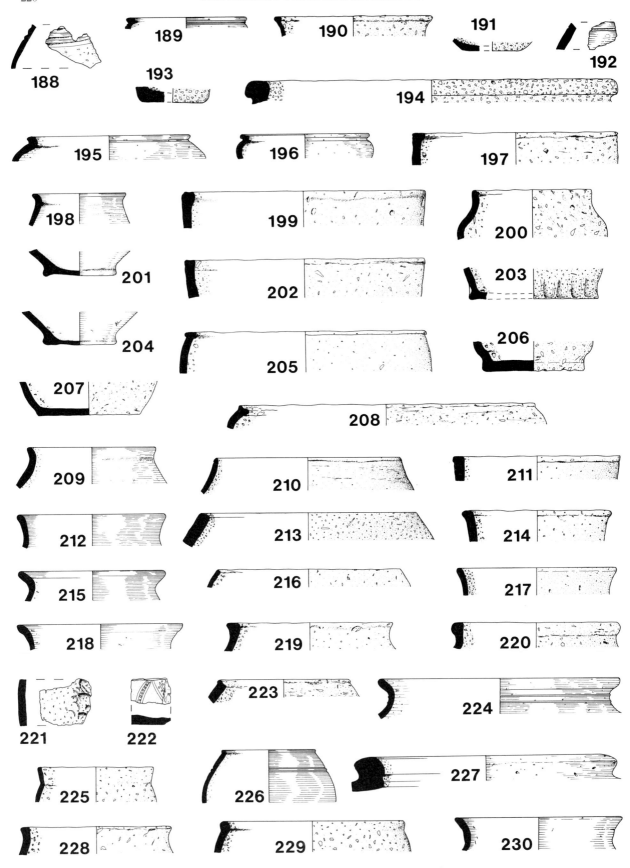

Fig. 61.   *Iron Age pottery from Pits 4, 5, 6 and 9 ($\frac{1}{4}$).*

Middle Iron Age Pit 2, Upper filling (LWB–023–6).

No. 178   An out-turned rim with flat top and internal projection in shell and flint-tempered fabric. The sherd is small; the rim irregular and the diameter uncertain. It is black (N2) throughout and the surfaces have been wiped with flint grits protruding. (Form 25, fabric E).

No. 179   A bowl with a carinated shoulder in flint-tempered fabric. The sherds have been fired dark grey to black (N3–N2) throughout. Both surfaces are now worn with flint inclusions visible and protruding. However, the external surface appears to have been smooth and partially burnished with few flints visible. (Form 34, fabric A).

No. 180   An out-turned rim with flat top and external expansion, in flint and shell-tempered fabric. The rim is irregular and the diameter uncertain. The sherd is dark grey to black (N3–N2) throughout, the surfaces have been wiped with flint and shell fragments visible and protruding. (Form 25, fabric E).

No. 181   A flaring rim with a flat top on a rounded shoulder in flint-tempered fabric. The surviving rim is small and the angle and diameter uncertain. The sherd is black (N2) througout and both surfaces have been wiped with flints protruding. (Form 25, fabric A).

No. 182   A gently everted rim in flint-tempered fabric. The sherds are small and the diameter uncertain. The surfaces are dark grey to brown (N3–2.5YR4/2) and wiped with flints visible or protruding. The core is dark grey to black (N3–N2). (Form 29, fabric A).

No. 183   A gently everted rim in flint-tempered fabric. The sherd is small and the diameter unknown. The surfaces are black (N2) and smooth with flint visible. The core is light grey (N6). (Form 29, fabric A).

No. 184   A flat base in flint-tempered fabric. The surfaces are red-brown (2.5YR5/6) and wiped with flint grits protruding. The core is black (N2). (Fabric A).

No. 185   A plain out-turned rim in flint-tempered fabric. The surfaces are worn and flint temper protrudes. The internal surface is dark grey (N3); the core is black (N2) and the external surface dark brown (5YR5/3). (Form 24, fabric A).

No. 186   An upright rim with a flat top and external projection in flint-tempered fabric. The surfaces are brown (5YR5/3) and smooth with flints visible. The core is black (N2). (Form 9, fabric A).

Middle Iron Age Pit 3 (LWB–T23–14).

No. 187   A small wall sherd in flint-tempered fabric with incised and grooved decoration. Three deep parallel cuts are set obliquely to two light grooves. The sherd has been fired light grey (N6) throughout. (Fabric A).

Late-Iron Age Pit 4(LWB–024–7).

No. 188   Sherd from neck of a vessel in grog-tempered fabric. The internal surface is worn away. The external surface is black (N2) and smooth and decorated with horizontal burnished grooves and cordons. The core is dark grey (N3) (Fabric J).

Late-Iron Age Pit 5 (LWB–R24–9).

No. 189   An inturned, externally projecting rim with flat top in grog and organic-tempered fabric. The surfaces are dark grey (N4) and smooth. The core is light grey (N6). Beneath the rim the external surface is decorated with two light grooves. (Form 7, fabric J).

Late-Iron Age Pit 6, Upper filling (LWB–R23–4).

No. 190   An everted rim in flint and shell-tempered fabric. The sherd is small and the diameter uncertain. It has been fired light brown (7.5YR6/4) throughout. The surfaces have been wiped smooth and the flint temper is visible. (Form 30, fabric E).

Soil over Late-Iron Age Pit 6 (LWB–R23–3).

No. 191   A shallow flat base in flint-tempered fabric. The surfaces are dark grey (N3) and smooth with flints visible. The core is grey (N4). (Fabric A).

No. 192   A wall sherd in sandy fabric. It is dark grey (N3) throughout. The internal surface is worn and the external surface is decorated with a light horizontal groove, 2.5 mm. wide. (Fabric F).

No. 193   A flat base in shell and flint-tempered fabric. All the surfaces are smooth with shell fragments visible. The internal surface is orange (10R6/6). The external surface and that beneath the base are dark grey (N3) and the core is grey (N4). (Fabric E).

No. 194   The flat top of a thick rim from a storage jar in shell-tempered fabric. The sherd is small and the diameter uncertain. The surfaces are brown (2.5YR6/6) and wiped with shell fragments visible. The core is dark grey (N3). (Form 21, fabric C).

No. 195   An inturned, externally projecting rim in grog and sparse shell-tempered fabric. The surfaces are light brown (7.5YR7/6) and smooth with few shell fragments visible. The core is light grey (N5) and the margins are black (N2). (Form 7, fabric K).

No. 196   A vessel with a high shoulder and an inturned, externally projecting rim in grog and sparse shell-tempered fabric. The surfaces are black (N2) and smooth with few shell fragments visible. The core is grey-brown (5YR4/2). (Form 7, fabric K).

Late-Iron Age Pit 9, Lower filling (LWB–U24–9).

No. 197   An upright, internally thickened, rim with flat top in shell-tempered fabric. Both surfaces are wiped with shell fragments visible and protruding. The internal surface is grey (N4), the external surface and rim brown (5YR5/3) and the core dark grey (N3). There is an orange-brown (2.5YR6/6) external margin. (Form 37, fabric C).

No. 198   A small fragment of an everted rim in quartz sandy fabric. The sherd has been fired dark grey to black (N3–N2) throughout. Both surfaces are highly burnished. (Form 27, fabric H).

No. 199   A rim with flat top and internal expansion in shell-tempered fabric. The sherd is small and the diameter uncertain. Both surfaces have been wiped with few shell fragments visible. The sherd has been fired dark grey (N3) throughout. (Form 37, fabric C).

No. 200   An inturned rim of a shouldered jar with concave neck in shell-tempered fabric. The sherd is small and the diameter uncertain. Both surfaces have been wiped with shell fragments visible. The internal surface is light grey (N5–5YR7/4), the external surface brown (5YR6/6) and the core grey (N4). (Form 17, fabric C).

No. 201   A footring base in sandy glauconitic fabric. The internal surface is grey (N4) and smooth. The external surface is grey-brown (N4–7.5YR5/2) and burnished. Beneath the base the surface is grey (N3–N4) and partially burnished. The core is grey (N4). (Form B3, fabric G).

No. 202   An upright rim with flat top in shell-tempered fabric. The rim is irregular and the diameter uncertain. Both the surfaces have been wiped smooth and few shell fragments are visible. The sherd is grey (N4–N5) throughout. (Form 37, fabric C).

Late-Iron Age Pit 9, Middle filling (LWB–U23–17, U24–6, U24–8 and U24–16).

No. 203   A flat base in flint-tempered fabric. The sherd is small and the diameter uncertain. Both surfaces are wiped with flints visible and protruding. The internal surface is light grey (N6–N5) and the external surface and core are dark grey (N3). Beneath the base numerous flint fragments, up to 1 mm. in size, protrude. The external surface has clear finger or thumb impressions where the wall has been joined to the base. (Fabric A.)

No. 204   A worn footring base in fine glauconitic sandy fabric. The internal surface is dark grey to black (N4–N2) and smooth, with horizontal wipe marks visible. The external surface is brown (7.5YR5/4) and burnished. Beneath the base the surface is black (N2) and is decorated with a burnished groove. The colour of the core varies from grey to brown (N4–7.5YR5/4). (Form B3, fabric G.)

No. 205   An inturned rim with flat top, internal expansion and external projection in sandy shell-tempered fabric. The rim is irregular and the diameter uncertain. The internal surface is light brown (7.5YR7/4) and wiped smooth with voids representing dissolved shell fragments. The external surface is dark grey (N3) and wiped with few shell fragments visible. The core is grey (N4–N3). (Form 4, fabric D.)

No. 206   A flat base in shell-tempered fabric. Both surfaces have been wiped. The internal surface is light brown (7.5YR7/4) and there are voids where the shell has been dissolved away. The external surface is grey (7.5YR5/2) and the shell is visible. The core is dark grey (N3). (Fabric C.)

No. 207   A fragment of a flat base in shell-tempered fabric. The internal surface is dark grey (N4) and smooth with a few shell fragments visible. The external surface is dark grey to brown (N4–7.5YR5/4) and has been wiped smooth with shell fragments visible. The core is dark grey (N3). (Fabric C.)

No. 208   An irregular fragment of an inturned rim with flat top and an internal bevel in shell-tempered fabric. The internal surface is red-brown (2.5YR5/4) and has been wiped with a slurry leaving few shell fragments visible. The external surface is dark grey (N4) and wiped smooth with shell fragments visible. The core is dark grey to black (N3–N2). (Form 5, fabric C.)

No. 209   An everted rim in sandy fabric containing quartz and glauconite. The sherd has been fired dark grey (N3) throughout. The internal surface is smooth and the external surface is burnished. (Form 33, fabric G.)

No. 210   A fragment of plain rim in flint-tempered fabric. The sherd is small, the rim irregular and the angle uncertain: it could be everted or inturned. The internal surface is dark grey-brown to grey (7.5YR4/2–N4) and wiped with flints protruding. The external surface is dark grey (N3) and wiped with a slurry leaving few flints visible. The core is dark grey-brown (7.5YR4/2) and there is a brown (2.5YR5/4) internal margin. (Fabric A.)

No. 211 A slightly out-turned rim with flat top and external projection, in shell-tempered fabric. The surface has been wiped smooth with a few shell fragments visible, the internal surface is dark grey (N3) to grey-brown (10YR6/2) and the external surface and core are dark grey (N3). (Form 25, fabric C.)

No. 212 An everted rim in fine glauconitic sandy fabric. Both surfaces are light brown (7.5YR7/4) and burnished and the core is dark grey (N3). (Form 32, fabric G.)

No. 213 A rim in fine shell-tempered fabric. The angle and diameter are uncertain. The surfaces are orange-brown (5YR5/3–2.5YR6/6) and wiped smooth with shell visible. The core is dark grey (N3). (Form 28, fabric C.)

No. 214 A slightly out-turned rim with external expansion in shell-tempered fabric. The surfaces are grey-brown (7.5YR5/2) and have been wiped smooth. Voids are now visible where shell has been dissolved. The core is dark grey (N3). (Form 19, fabric C.)

No. 215 An everted rim in fine glauconitic sandy fabric. The internal surface is brown (5YR6/6) and burnished around the rim, and dark grey (N3) and smooth from the neck down. The external surface is brown (5YR6/6) and burnished. The core is dark grey (N3). (Form 32, fabric G.)

No. 216 A small fragment of an irregular, plain rim with flat top in flint-tempered fabric. The surfaces have been wiped smooth with few flints visible or protruding. The internal surface is light grey-brown (2.5YR6/2– 7/4) and the external surface is light grey (N6) with a patch of brown (7.5YR7/4). The core is grey (N4). (Form 1, fabric A.)

No. 217 An everted rim in flint-tempered fabric. The sherd is small and the diameter uncertain. Both surfaces are wiped with flints protruding. The internal surface is dark brown (2.5YR4/2), the external surface dark grey (N3) and the core grey (N4). There are brown (5YR6/6) margins. (Form 24, fabric A.)

No. 218 An everted rim in fine glauconitic sandy fabric. Both surfaces are worn, but appear to have been burnished. The internal surface and top of the rim are light brown (5YR7/6), the external surface is grey (N5–N6) and the colour of the core varies from grey to brown (N5–5YR7/6). (Form 32, fabric G.)

No. 219 A rim with flat top and external expansion in shell-tempered fabric. The rim is irregular and the diameter uncertain. Both surfaces are wiped smooth with shell fragments visible. The internal surface and the top of the rim are orange (10R6/8), the external surface is dark grey-brown (2.5YR4/2) and the core is dark grey (N3). (Form 12, fabric C.)

No. 220 A fragment of an externally thickened everted rim in shell-tempered fabric. The sherd is small and the angle uncertain. The internal surface is brown (7.5YR4/2–5/2) and smooth with few shell fragments visible. The external surface is dark red-brown to grey (10R5/6– N4) and wiped with few shell fragments visible and protruding. The core is black (N2). (Form 23, fabric C.)

No. 221 A flint-tempered sherd, apparently from the wall of a vessel, with finger-tip and finger-nail impressions forming part of an unknown design. Both surfaces are wiped with flint fragments protruding. The internal surface is dark grey (N3), the external surface dark brown (7.5YR4/2) to light grey (N5) and the core is light grey (N5). (Fabric A.)

No. 222 A wall sherd in fine glauconitic sandy fabric. The internal surface is dark grey (N3) and smooth. The core is grey (N4). The external surface is dark grey and appears to have been smooth, though it is now worn. It is decorated with two pairs of light parallel grooves on either side of curves of circular stamped decoration. The stamps do not follow the curve of the grooves exactly and have evidently been applied after the grooves. There is no repeated pattern of spacing between the stamps visible on this sherd, and it is possible that they were made individually. (Fabric G.)

No. 223 An inturned rim with flat top in shell-tempered fabric. The sherd is fired dark grey (N4) throughout. The internal surface has been wiped with shell fragments visible and the external surface is smooth with few shell fragments visible. (Form 8, fabric C.)

Late-Iron Age Pit 9, Upper filling (LWB–T23–8, U23–13 and U24–5).

No. 224 An everted rim in grog-tempered fabric. The surfaces are brown (5YR4/2–5/3) and burnished, and the core is light grey-brown (7.5YR6/2). There are two light horizontal grooves around the neck. (Form 32, fabric J.)

No. 225 A slightly everted rim in flint-tempered fabric. The sherd is small and diameter uncertain. Both the surfaces are wiped smooth with large flint fragments visible and protruding. The internal surface is light brown (7.5YR7/4–7/6), the external surface is light brown (7.5YR7/4–7/6) around the rim and dark grey (N3) on the shoulder. The core is light grey (N6). (Form 24, fabric A.)

No. 226 A butt beaker in grog-tempered fabric. The internal surface is grey (N5) and has been wiped smooth. The external surface is orange-brown (2.5YR6/8) and lightly burnished. It is decorated with a light horizontal cordon between two light grooves. The core is grey (N5). (Form 2, fabric J.)

No. 227 A thickened bead rim of a storage jar in grog-tempered fabric, with sparse inclusions of shell up to 1 mm.

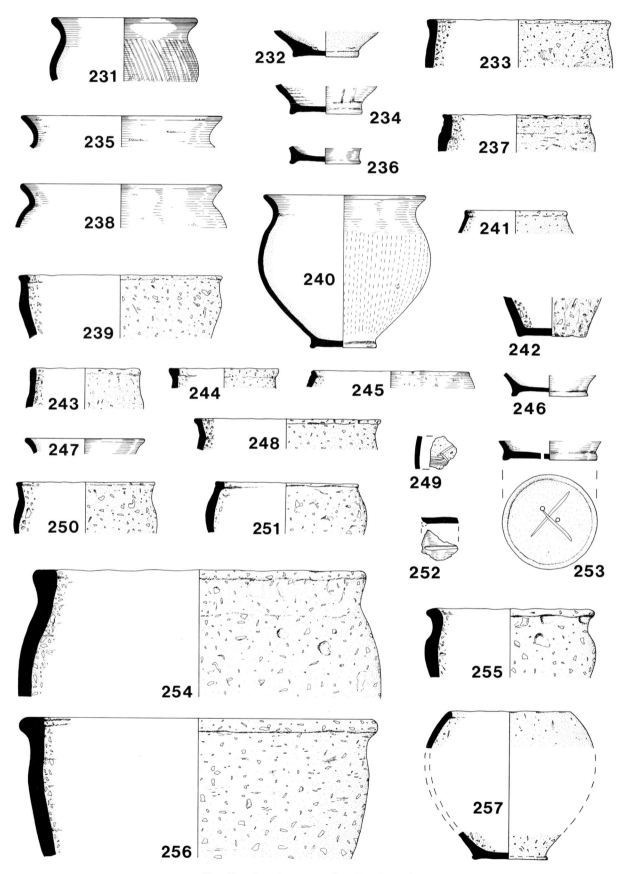

Fig. 62. *Iron Age pottery from Pits 9–11* ($\frac{1}{4}$).

in size. The surfaces are worn but appear to have been black (N1) and burnished. The core is dark grey (N3) with an orange (2.5YR6/6) external margin. (Form 21, fabric J.)

No. 228   An upright rim with flat top and with external projection in shell-tempered fabric. The colour of the surfaces and core varies from light brown (7.5YR6/4) to dark grey (N3), probably as a result of refiring. The internal surface is smooth with voids where the shell has dissolved away. The external surface is wiped with few shell fragments visible. (Form 12, fabric C.)

No. 229   An inturned, externally expanded, rim in shell-tempered fabric. The sherd is small and the diameter uncertain. The sherd has been fired light brown (5YR7/6) throughout. Both surfaces have been wiped smooth with shell fragments visible. (Form 4, fabric C.)

No. 230   An everted rim in fine glauconitic sandy fabric. Both surfaces are burnished. The internal surface is dark grey (N3) with a brown-grey (10YR5/2) patch. The external surface and core are dark grey (N3) and there is a brown (7.5YR5/4) external margin. (Form 32, fabric G.)

No. 231   An everted rim in fine glauconitic sandy fabric. The rim is warped and the diameter uncertain. The internal surface is grey (N4) and burnished. The external surface is dark grey (N2) and clear diagonal burnish marks, applied after horizontal burnishing, are visible beneath the neck. The core is light grey (N6) and there are partial brown (5YR5/4) margins. (Form 34, fabric G.)

No. 232   A footring base in fine glauconitic sandy fabric. Both surfaces are worn and light orange-brown (5YR6/6) in colour. Traces of the original surface show that the exterior was smooth or burnished. The core is dark grey (N3). (Form 32, fabric G.)

No. 233   An upright rim with flat top and external expansion in shell-tempered fabric. The sherd is small and the diameter uncertain. Both surfaces have voids where shell fragments have dissolved. It has been fired dark grey (N3) throughout. The internal surface is smooth and the external surface has been wiped. (Form 19, fabric C.)

No. 234   A footring base in fine glauconitic sandy fabric. All the surfaces are burnished. The internal surface is black (N2) and the external surface is dark grey (N3). The core is grey (N4) and there is an orange-brown (5YR6/6) external margin. Beneath the base the surface is grey (N6–N3). (Form B3, fabric G.)

No. 235   An everted rim in fine glauconitic sandy fabric. The sherd is dark grey (N3) throughout and both surfaces are burnished. There is a light groove running along the top of the rim. (Form 32, fabric G.)

No. 236   A footring base in fine glauconitic sandy fabric. All the surfaces have been burnished. The internal surface is black (N2). The external surface and core are dark grey (N4) and beneath the base the surface is grey (7.5YR6/2–5/2). (Form B3, fabric G.)

No. 237   A slightly inturned rim with flat top and small external projection in shell-tempered fabric. The sherd is dark grey (N3) throughout. Both surfaces have been wiped with few shell fragments visible or protruding. (Form 19, fabric C.)

No. 238   An everted rim in fine glauconitic sandy fabric. Both surfaces are burnished. The internal surface is light grey-brown (10YR5/2) and the external surface and core are dark grey (N3). There is a brown (7.5YR6/4) external margin. (Form 32, fabric G.)

Late-Iron Age Pit 10 (LWB–U23–9).

No. 239   The rim of an open bowl in shell-tempered fabric. The sherd has been fired dark grey to grey-brown (N4–5YR5/2) throughout. Both surfaces have been wiped smooth with the shell tempering visible (Form 37, fabric C.)

No. 240   A jar with everted rim and footring base in a fine glauconitic sandy fabric. The surfaces are burnished. The colour of the sherds varies from dark grey (N3) to brown (5YR6/6) throughout, as a result of having been refired. (Form 32, fabric G.)

No. 241   An inturned recessed rim from a small jar in flint-tempered fabric. Both the surfaces are smooth, even polished, with very few flints visible. The internal surface and core are dark grey (N4) and the external surface black (N2). The rim, however, is light brown (7.5YR6/4) inside and out, apparently as a result of refiring. (Form 13, fabric A.)

No. 242   A flat base in shell-tempered fabric. The surfaces are brown (5YR6/6–7/6) and have been wiped with shell visible and protruding. The core is dark grey (N3) to brown (5YR6/6–7/6). (Fabric C.)

Late-Iron Age Pit 11, Lower filling (LWB–U24–15).

No. 243   A plain slightly inturned rim with concave neck in shell-tempered fabric. The sherd is black (N2) throughout and the surfaces have been wiped with few shell fragments visible. (Form 22, fabric C.)

No. 244   An internally thickened, everted rim in shell-tempered fabric. The rim is irregular and the angle and diameter uncertain. The surfaces have been wiped smooth, with shell fragments visible. The internal surface is grey-brown (N4–5YR6/4) and the external surface and core are dark grey (N3). (Form 23, fabric C.)

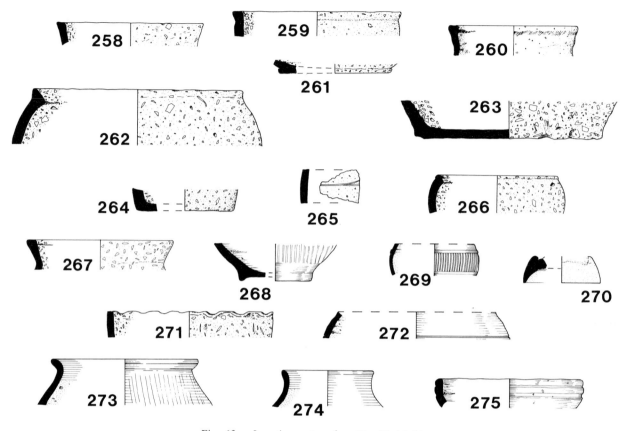

Fig. 63.   *Iron Age pottery from Pits 11–16 ($\frac{1}{4}$).*

No. 245   An inturned rim of sandy shell-tempered fabric. The sherd is small and the angle and diameter are uncertain. The surfaces are brown (5YR7/4) and smooth with very few shell fragments visible. The core is black (N2). (Form 14, fabric D.)

Late-Iron Age Pit 11, Middle filling (LWB–U24–14).

No. 246   A footring base in fine glauconitic sandy fabric. The external surface is burnished, and both it and the core are dark grey (N3). The internal surface and that beneath the base are light grey (N5) and smooth with fine striations suggesting that the vessel was finished or even wholly manufactured on the wheel. (Form B3, fabric G.)

No. 247   An everted rim in fine glauconitic sandy fabric. Both the surfaces are dark grey (N3) and slightly worn; though it is clear that the external surface was originally burnished. The core is grey (N4). (Form 32, fabric G.)

No. 248   An out-turned rim with an externaly projecting flat top in shell-tempered fabric. The surfaces are dark grey-brown (5YR4/1) and have been wiped smooth with few shell fragments visible. The core is dark grey (N3). (Form 30, fabric C.)

Late-Iron Age Pit 11, Upper filling (LWB–U24–10).

No. 249   A wall sherd in grog and sparse flint-tempered fabric. Both the surfaces are smooth. The external surface is decorated with a linear burnished design. The internal surface and core are grey (N5) and the external surface is dark grey to black (N3–N2). (Fabric J).

No. 250   A plain, slightly out-turned rim with a flat top from a jar of shell-tempered fabric. The sherd is small and the diameter uncertain. The internal surface has been wiped smooth and few shell fragments are visible. It and the core are dark grey (N3). The external surface is dark grey-brown (2.5YR5/2) and wiped with shell fragments visible. (Form 24, fabric C).

No. 251   A vessel with a high shoulder, inturned neck and expanded flat-topped rim in shell-tempered fabric. The surfaces are dark grey-brown (2.5YR4/2–5YR4/2) and the core is dark grey (N3). The internal surface is smooth with few shell fragments visible. The external surface has been wiped with more shell visible. (Form 4, fabric C).

No. 252   A fragment of a base, which evidently had a footring, in fine glauconitic sandy fabric. Beneath the base the surface is grey-brown (N4–5YR6/4), burnished and appears to be decorated with a faintly burnished line radiating from the centre. The internal surface is either worn away, or untreated. It and the core are grey (N5–N4) to grey-brown (5YR5/4). (Form B3, fabric G).

No. 253   A worn footring base in fine glauconitic sandy fabric. The sherd has been fired dark grey (N3) throughout. The internal surface is worn away. The external surface appears to have been burnished. Beneath the base the surface is smooth and has been decorated with two burnished lines forming a cruciform design. The surviving sherds show that at least two holes, 5 mm. in diameter have been drilled through the base. (Form B3, fabric G).

No. 254   An inturned rim with expanded flat top in shell-tempered fabric. Both surfaces are worn and the shell inclusions are visible and protrude. The sherds are grey to orange-brown (N5–2.5YR6/6) throughout. (Form 4, fabric C).

No. 255   An extremely worn rim and shoulder from a storage jar in shell-tempered fabric. The sherd has been fired dark grey to grey (N3–N5) throughout. (Form 6, fabric C).

No. 256   A rim with flat top and external expansion belonging to a storage jar or cauldron in shell-tempered fabric. Both the surfaces are brown (7.5YR6/4) and wiped with shell fragments visible and protruding. The core is dark grey (N3). (Form 20, fabric C).

No. 257   A plain inturned rim in quartz sandy fabric, with sparse flint-tempering. The sherd is small and the angle and diameter are uncertain. The surfaces have been wiped smooth. The internal surface is grey-brown (7.5YR6/3). The external surface is dark grey (N4–N3) with patches of brown (7.5YR5/4). The core is black (N2). The base shown here is of the same fabric and colour and is assumed to belong to the same vessel as the rim. (Form 1, fabric H).

No. 258   A fragment of an out-turned rim with externally expanded flat top in shell-tempered fabric. The sherd is small and the diameter uncertain. Both surfaces are wiped with shell fragments visible. It has been fired dark grey (N3), with a patch of dark brown (5YR5/3) on the rim and a dark brown (5YR5/3) internal margin. (Form 25, fabric C).

No. 259   An upright rim with flat top in flint-tempered fabric. The sherd is worn and the angle and diameter are uncertain. The internal surface has been worn away. The external surface is grey-brown (5YR5/2) and wiped with few flints visible or protruding. The core is light orange (5YR7/6). (Form 37, fabric A).

No. 260   An out-turned rim with flat top in shell-tempered fabric. The sherd is small and the diameter uncertain. The surfaces have been wiped smooth and are dark grey-brown (7.5YR5/2) to dark grey (N3). The core is black (N2). (Form 25, fabric C).

No. 261   A flat base in flint-tempered fabric. The sherd is small and the diameter uncertain. The internal surface is dark red-brown (10R5/3) and wiped with flints visible. The external surface and core are dark grey (N4). Beneath the surface is light grey (N6) and abundant flint grits protrude. (Fabric A).

Late-Iron Age Pit 12, Lower filling (LWB–BB21–7).

No. 262   A jar with an internally thickened inturned rim of shell-tempered fabric. The internal surface is grey-brown (N4–5YR6/4) and worn with shell inclusions visible. The external surface is orange-brown (10R6/6) to grey (N4) and wiped with shell visible and protruding. The core is dark grey (N3). (Form 6, fabric C).

Late-Iron Age Pit 13 (LWB–AA19–3).

No. 263   A flat base in shell-tempered fabric. Both the surfaces are wiped with shell fragments visible and protruding. The external surface is dark grey to dark red-brown (N4–2.5YR5/4). The internal surface and core are dark grey to black (N4–N2). (Fabric C).

Late-Iron Age Pit 14, Middle filling (LWB–DD21–7).

No. 264   A flat base in shell-tempered fabric. The internal surface is brown (7.5YR6/4), the external surface dark grey (N3) to dark brown (7.5YR5/4) and the core black (N2). Both surfaces have been wiped smooth with shell fragments visible (Fabric C).

No. 265   A wall sherd in shell and flint-tempered fabric. The internal surface is dark grey (N3) and smooth with few flint or shell fragments visible. The external surface is dark grey (N3) to light brown (7.5YR6/6). It has been burnished and decorated with two light grooves forming part of a curvilinear design. The core is grey (N4). (Fabric E).

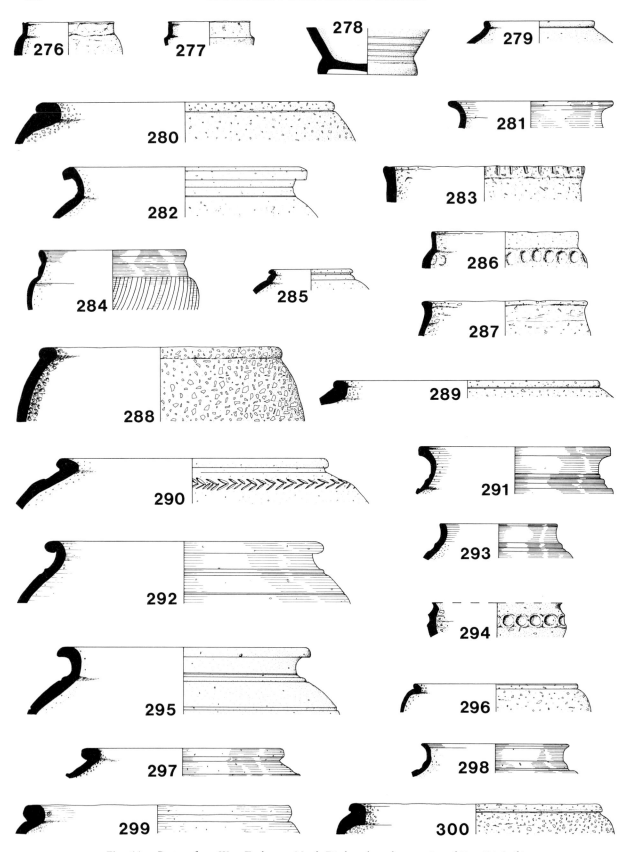

Fig. 64.   *Pottery from West Enclosure, North Ditch and northern section of East Ditch ($\frac{1}{4}$).*

No. 266 An inturned, slightly recessed rim in shell-tempered fabric. The sherd is small and the angle and diameter are uncertain. The surfaces are light orange-brown (5YR6/6) and smooth with shell fragments visible. The core is black (N2). (Form 5, fabric C).

Late-Iron Age Pit 15, Lower filling (LWB–M33–27).

No. 267 An out-turned rim with flat top in shell-tempered fabric. The sherd is small and the diameter uncertain. The surfaces have been wiped smooth with shell fragments visible. The internal surface and top of the rim are light brown (7.5YR6/4–7/6). The external surface is red-brown (2.5YR5/4–5/6) and the core is dark grey (N3). (Form 25, fabric C).

Late-Iron Age Pit 15, Upper filling (LWB–M33–10).

No. 268 A footring base in fine glauconitic sandy fabric. All surfaces are dark grey to black (N3–N2) and have been burnished. Beneath the base, after the surface was burnished, an additional burnished groove was added, radiating from the centre, possibly as part of a cruciform design. The core is grey (N4) and there are brown (7.5YR6/4) margins. (Form B3, fabric G).

No. 269 A wall sherd from a butt beaker in fine sandy fabric. The core and internal surface are orange (5YR6/6–7/6). Fine striations on the internal surface suggest that the vessel was wheel turned. The external surface is coated with a grey-brown slip (2.5YR5/2) and is decorated with a band of almost vertical fine combed grooves. These are bounded above by a broad horizontal groove, and below, by a light horizontal cordon. This is a piece of Keston Kiln Ware dated A.D. 60–85. (Fabric I).

No. 270 A pedestal base in fine sandy fabric. The surfaces are brown (7.5YR6/4) and smooth and the core is light grey (N5). Both surfaces have light horizontal striations. This is a piece of intrusive Keston Kiln Ware dated A.D. 60–85, as No. 269. (Form B1, fabric G).

No. 271 An upright rim in shell and flint-tempered fabric. The sherd is small and the angle and diameter uncertain. The top of the rim has a finger-tip impression which may represent deliberate decoration. The internal surface is brown (5YR6/4) and wiped smooth with few shell or flint fragments visible. The external surface is red-brown (10R5/6) and wiped with shell and flint inclusions visible and protruding. The core is dark grey (N3). (Form 38, fabric E).

No. 272 A shoulder of a sandy shell-tempered fabric. The sparse shell fragments, up to 1 mm. in size, have dissolved away and are now represented by voids. The sherd has been fired dark red (10R5/6) throughout. The internal surface is smooth with fine horizontal striations, suggesting that the vessel was wheel made. The external surface is polished and is decorated with a light horizontal groove. (Form 28, fabric D).

Late-Iron Age Pit 16 (LWB–N31–11, N31–13 and N31–14).

No. 273 An everted rim with fine glauconitic sandy fabric. The internal surface is grey to dark grey (N4–N3) and burnished around the rim to a depth of about 2.5 cm. Below this, the surface is smooth. The external surface is dark grey (N3) and highly burnished. The core is dark grey (N3) and there is a narrow brown (5YR6/4) external margin. (Form 32, fabric G).

No. 274 An everted rim in fine glauconitic sandy fabric. The sherd is small and the diameter uncertain. The internal surface is dark grey (N3) and appears to have been burnished. The external surface is grey (10YR4/1) and highly burnished. The core is light grey (N6) and there is a brown (5YR6/6) margin. (Form 32, fabric G).

No. 275 An upright or inturned rim of a globular jar in grog-tempered fabric. Both surfaces are light brown (5YR7/6) and the core is light grey (N6). The internal surface is smooth and the external surface is burnished, with two horizontal grooves and a cordon around the outside of the rim. (Form 1, fabric J).

West Enclosure, North Ditch, Middle filling (LWB–76–195 and 76–196).

No. 276 Small, hand-made bowl or jar with upright rim and rounded shoulder of gritty ware. Brown-black core and surfaces. Pre-Conquest.

No. 277 Small, hand-made jar or bowl with upright rim and angled shoulder. Hard, gritty ware with grey-black core and brown-black surfaces. Pre-Conquest.

No. 278 A low pedestal base in a fine quartz sandy fabric. The internal surface is smooth and dark grey to black (N3–N2) with a rusty brown (2.5YR6/6) patch. Horizontal striations on the wall and circular striations around the internal surface of the base suggest that it has been wheel-turned. The external surface is brown (5YR6/6–7/6) with a dark grey (N3) patch. It is decorated with three light horizontal grooves, 2 mm. wide and about 5 mm. apart. Beneath the base the surface is dark grey to black (N3–N2) and smooth or even polished. Traces of light circular striations beneath the base suggest that the underside of the base was smoothed on a wheel. Fracture marks indicate that the foot of the pedestal was added as a coil to a flat base. The core is dark grey (N4). (Form B2, fabric H). Pre-Conquest.

West Enclosure, North Ditch, Upper filling (LWB–76–180 and 76–184).

No. 279   Globular jar with bead rim of slightly sandy, grog-tempered ware. Light grey and orange-buff surfaces. Dateable to the first century A.D.

No. 280   Large storage jar with flat-topped bead rim of shell-tempered ware. Grey-brown core and surfaces. The form is typical of the later first to early-second centuries A.D.

No. 281   Jar with everted rim of sandy ware. Grey core and abraded orange-brown surfaces showing traces of burnishing. Similar to No. 273. Probably from a pre-Conquest vessel.

No. 282   Large jar with under-cut, everted rim of hard, grog-tempered ware. Blue-grey core and orange-buff surfaces. Later first to second century A.D.

No. 283   Upright, externally thickened rim of shell-tempered ware. Grey-brown core and orange-buff surfaces with slashed decoration around rim. Pre-Conquest.

No. 284   Jar with everted rim of grog-tempered ware. Grey-brown core and grey-brown, burnished surfaces with shoulder cordon. First century A.D.

No. 285   Globular jar with bead rim of slightly sandy, grog-tempered ware. Dark grey-black core and pink-brown surfaces. Later first century A.D.

No. 286   Hand-made jar with upright rim and rounded shoulder of gritty ware. Grey-buff core and yellow-buff surfaces with finger-impressed decoration on the shoulder. Pre-Conquest.

No. 287   Externally expanded, upright rim of shell-tempered ware, grey-brown core and brown-black surfaces. Probably hand-made. Pre-Conquest.

West Enclosure, Northern Section of East Ditch, Lower filling (LWB–E19–4 and 76–143).

No. 288   Large jar with bead rim of shell-tempered ware. Grey-brown core and orange-brown surfaces. Later first to early-second century A.D.

Storage vessels, jars and bowls with bead rims are amongst the commonest forms of shell-tempered wares represented in early-Roman deposits at Keston and a considerable number have been illustrated. Both the fabric and the form are well-known in West Kent and East Surrey, generally. Although the shelly wares go back well into the pre-Roman period, vessels with well-developed bead rims do not appear much before the Conquest and they are not common at the Farningham Hill Iron Age settlement site. Their production seems to have ceased entirely by the mid-second century A.D. and they are essentially a product of the second half of the first and early-second centuries A.D. There is evidence that some of the vessels were being made at Keston during the first century A.D.

No. 289   Large jar with flat-topped, bead rim of shell-tempered ware. Brown-black core and surfaces. Later-first to early-second century A.D.

No. 290   Storage jar with bead rim of grog-tempered ware. Grey-buff core and buff-brown surfaces with incised chevrons around the neck and black 'pitch' beneath the rim.

Storage jars of very similar form have been identified in late pre-Conquest levels at Farningham Hill (Form 12, Nos. 81, 82, 83 and 88). The form continued into the post-Conquest period, although the beaded rim was frequently replaced by one of the everted type (Ref. 245).

West Enclosure, Northern Section of East Ditch, Middle filling (LWB–E18–3 and E19–3).

No. 291   Jar with squared, everted rim of grog-tempered ware. Brown core and grey-brown burnished surfaces. Slight cordon between shallow grooves on neck. Traces of a more pronounced cordon on shoulder. First century A.D.

No. 292   Large jar with rolled rim of hard, grog-tempered fabric. Blue-black core and buff-brown surfaces. Slight cordon on neck between broad horizontal grooves. Later first to early-second century A.D.

No. 293   Jar or bowl with slightly everted rim of grog-tempered ware. Brown-black core and burnished surfaces. Horizontal cordon on neck. First century A.D.

No. 294   A sherd from the neck of a vessel in sandy flint-tempered fabric. It has a raised cordon decorated with finger-tip impressions. It is dark grey to black (N3–N2) throughout and both surfaces have been wiped smooth with few flints visible. (Fabric B). Pre-Conquest.

No. 295   Large storage jar with out-turned rim of sandy ware. Buff-brown core and buff surfaces. Faint cordon on upper shoulder. Late-first to second century A.D.

West Enclosure, Northern Section of East Ditch, Upper filling (LWB–E18–2, E19–2, 76–39, 77–88 and 77–101).

No. 296   Jar with bead rim of shell-tempered ware with some grog inclusions. Grey-brown core and brown-black surfaces. Later first to early-second century A.D.

No. 297 Jar with internally thickened, flat-topped bead rim of fine shell fabric with grog inclusions. Grey-brown and red-brown surfaces with black 'pitch' underneath the rim. Slight traces of incised decoration upon a raised cordon on the shoulder. Later first to early-second century A.D.

No. 298 Jar with everted rim of sandy ware. Brown core and grey-brown surfaces with a cordon above the shoulder. Keston Kiln Ware, dateable to c. A.D. 60–85.

No. 299 Large jar with internally thickened, flat-topped bead rim of grog-tempered ware. Grey-brown core and brown-black surfaces with 'pitch' painted underneath the rim. First century A.D.

No. 300 Large jar with bead rim of shell-tempered ware. Orange-buff core and surfaces.

No. 301 Large storage jar with everted rim of grog-tempered ware. Grey-brown core and heavily weathered, reddish-brown surfaces. Two shallow cordons on neck. Later first to early-second century A.D.

No. 302 Open bowl with slightly thickened, flat-topped rim of coarse, shell-tempered ware. Grey-brown core and red-brown surfaces. Probably pre-Conquest.

No. 303 Open bowl with slightly thickened, bevel-topped rim of coarse, shell-tempered ware. Light brown core and orange-brown surfaces. Similar to No. 302. Probably pre-Conquest.

No. 304 Storage jar with squared bead rim of coarse, shell-tempered ware. Orange-brown core and orange surfaces. Later first to early-second century A.D.

No. 305 Plain, straight-sided vessel with simple, upright rim of hard, coarse shell-tempered ware with occasional flint inclusions. Dark grey-black core and mottled, light orange-brown surfaces, frequently pitted where shell-inclusions have fired out. Pre-Conquest.

No. 306 Flat-topped, upright rim of shell-tempered ware. Brown-black core and surfaces. Pre-Conquest.

No. 307 Jar with squared, everted rim of sandy, grog-tempered ware. Grey-brown core and brown-black surfaces and a shoulder cordon. First century A.D.

No. 308 Small jar with bead rim and high, rounded shoulder of shell-tempered ware. Grey-brown core with brown-black surfaces and a hole in the wall just beneath the rim. Later first to early-second century A.D.

No. 309 Dish with bead rim of sandy ware. Light grey core and patchy grey surfaces.
        Vessels of this general type are mainly dateable to the second century A.D. and are largely absent from later first century A.D. contexts in this part of West Kent. The present example may, therefore, be intrusive.

No. 310 Probable flagon with undercut, squared, everted rim of sandy, grog-tempered ware. Grey-brown core and brown-black surfaces. Later first to early-second century A.D.

No. 311 Small jar with bead rim. The body of the pot is of a dark grey shell-tempered fabric. The rim, however, is of a grey, slightly sandy ware and this has clearly been added to an otherwise finished vessel. This feature has been noted on several other sherds from the site (No. 428) and appears to be a feature of the Keston Kiln products, dated c. A.D. 60–85. The surfaces of the vessel are dark grey-black with traces of burnishing on the exterior.

No. 312 Pedestal beaker with out-turned rim of sandy ware. Grey-brown core and orange-red surfaces, in imitation of *Terra Rubra*. The form can be broadly paralleled at Colchester (Camulodunum Form 74/79), dated there to c. A.D. 10–65 (Ref. 246). Keston Kiln Ware, dateable to c. A.D. 60–85.

No. 313 Small, carinated bowl with everted rim of sandy ware. Sandwiched grey and brown core and dark grey surfaces. Exterior burnished with a zone of irregular lattice decoration on the lower part of the body. Cordon on neck. The fabric is typical of the products of the Keston Kiln which have been dated to c. A.D. 60–85.

No. 314 Slightly everted rim of sandy ware. Brown-black core and surfaces with cordon on neck. Keston Kiln Ware, dateable to c. A.D. 60–85.

No. 315 Butt beaker of sandy ware. Grey-black core and pink-buff surfaces decorated with wheel rouletting. Keston Kiln Ware, dateable to c. A.D. 60–85.

No. 316 Globular jar with small bead rim of fine, sand-tempered ware. Brown-black core and surfaces. Tooled horizontal grooves around shoulder. Keston Kiln Ware, dateable to c. A.D. 60–85.

West Enclosure, Southern Section of East Ditch, Lower filling (LWB–C25–8).

No. 317 Hand-made vessel with straight, out-turned rim, rolled over internally. Hard, shell-tempered ware with light brown exterior. An essentially pre-Conquest form.

West Enclosure, Southern Section of East Ditch, Upper filling (LWB–C25–7 and C26–9).

No. 318 Hand-made jar with thickened, externally projecting rim of shell-tempered ware. Dark grey core with orange-brown interior surface and dark grey-brown burnished exterior. First century A.D.

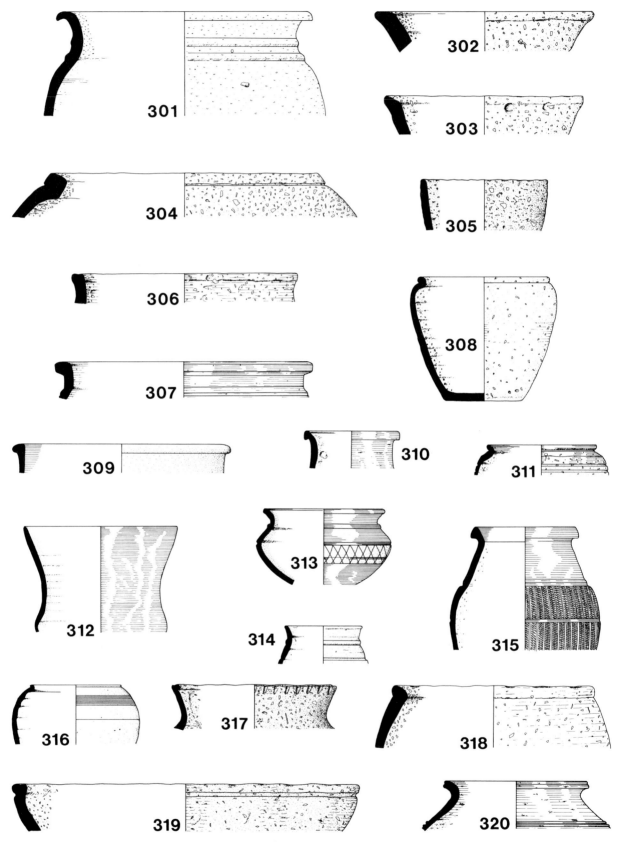

Fig. 65.   *Pottery from West Enclosure, East Ditch* (¼).

No. 319   Large bowl with upright, slightly thickened, flat-topped rim of hard, shell-tempered ware. A broad shallow groove on the exterior gives the rim the appearance of being slightly beaded. Light grey-brown core with orange-brown interior surface and dark brown exterior. The fairly irregular construction indicates that the vessel was hand-made. It appears to be an essentially pre-Conquest form.

No. 320   Jar with everted rim of fairly hard, grog-tempered ware. Light grey core and dark grey surfaces. Traces of an incised horizontal groove set between narrow ridges on the lower neck. Later first to early-second century A.D.

South Enclosure Ditch (LWB–S24–7).

No. 321   Small jar with out-turned, slightly beaded rim of fairly soft, soapy grog-tempered ware. Grey core and orange-brown surfaces. Later first to early-second century A.D.

East Enclosure Ditch (LWB–T20–3, T21–4, T21–6, T21–7, U22–4, U22–5, V22–4, V23–4 and 78–21).

No. 322   Everted rim of sandy ware. Grey-buff core and orange-buff surfaces. Keston Kiln Ware, dateable to *c.* A.D. 60–85.

No. 323   Small jar with everted rim of sandy ware. Grey core and orange-brown surfaces. Keston Kiln Ware, dateable to *c.* A.D. 60–85.

No. 324   Large jar with internally thickened bead rim of shell-tempered ware. Grey-buff core and orange-buff surfaces. Later first to early-second century A.D.

No. 325   Jar with flattened bead rim of sandy ware. Grey core and orange-buff surfaces. Keston Kiln Ware, dateable to *c.* A.D. 60–85.

No. 326   Large jar with internally thickened bead rim of shell-tempered ware. Grey-brown core and orange-brown surfaces. Later first to early-second century A.D.

No. 327   Jar with bead rim of sandy ware. Grey and buff sandwiched core and grey-black surfaces. Keston Kiln Ware, dateable to *c.* A.D. 60–85.

No. 328   Large storage jar with everted rim of hard, sandy, grog-tempered ware. Pink-brown core with orange-brown surfaces and grooved neck. Later first to early-second century A.D.

No. 329   Small jar with internally thickened bead rim of sandy ware. Grey and light brown sandwiched core and dark grey surfaces. Keston Kiln Ware, dateable to *c.* A.D. 60–85.

No. 330   Large storage jar with everted rim of sandy, grog-tempered ware. Orange core and surfaces. Later first to early-second century A.D.

No. 331   Small jar with internally thickened bead rim of sandy ware. Grey-brown core and surfaces. Keston Kiln Ware, dateable to *c.* A.D. 60–85.

No. 332   Large jar with slightly out-turned, thickened bead rim of sandy, grog-tempered ware. Grey core and orange-buff surfaces. Later first to early-second century A.D.

No. 333   Small jar with flattened bead rim of sandy ware. Light grey core and grey-black surfaces with grooved and cordoned shoulder. Keston Kiln Ware, dateable to *c.* A.D. 60–85.

No. 334   Small jar with bead rim of sandy, grog-tempered ware. Grey-buff core and orange-buff surfaces with incised chevron pattern on shoulder. Late-first to early-second century A.D.

No. 335   Jar with internally thickened bead rim of shell-tempered ware. Grey-brown core and brown-black surfaces. Later first to early-second century A.D.

No. 336   Base of probable globular beaker of hard, sandy ware. Light orange-brown core and orange surfaces coated with a dark red slip. Horizontal, incised groove above the foot. Perhaps from a vessel similar to Camulodunum Form 91. Keston Kiln Ware, dateable to *c.* A.D. 60–85.

No. 337   Lid or platter with recessed rim of sandy ware. Grey-brown core and surfaces. Keston Kiln Ware, dateable to *c.* A.D. 60–85.

No. 338   Small jar with internally thickened bead rim of hard, thin-walled shell-tempered ware. Dark grey-brown core and surfaces. Dateable to the later first to early-second century A.D.

No. 339   Jar with slightly everted rim of sandy ware. Grey-brown core and patchy grey-brown surfaces.

No. 340   Squared, everted rim of sandy ware. Grey-brown core and surfaces.

No. 341   Lid of sandy ware with orange core and yellow-orange surfaces. Keston Kiln Ware, dateable to *c.* A.D. 60–85.

No. 342   Platter with slightly incurved rim and footring on base of sandy ware. Orange-brown core and grey-brown surfaces. Keston Kiln Ware, dateable to *c.* A.D. 60–85.

No. 343   Jar or bowl with upright, slightly recessed rim of grog-tempered ware with fine, white grit inclusions. Brown-black core and orange-brown surfaces. Later first to early-second century A.D.

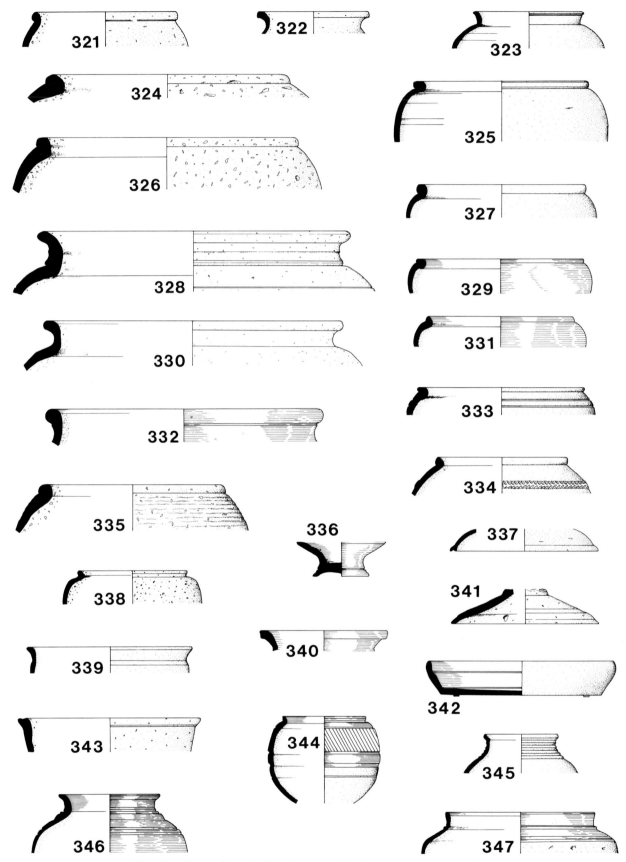

Fig. 66. *Pottery from South Enclosure Ditch and East Enclosure Ditch* ($\frac{1}{4}$).

No. 344   Globular beaker with bead rim of sandy ware. Brown-black core and buff-grey surfaces. Grooved shoulder and girth and incised, diagonal line decoration on lower shoulder. Keston Kiln Ware, dateable to *c.* A.D. 60–85.

No. 345   Small jar with everted rim of sandy ware. Grey-brown core and surfaces with shallow cordons on neck. Keston Kiln Ware, dateable to *c.* A.D. 60–85.

No. 346   Jar with everted rim. Grey-buff core and orange-brown surfaces. Two faint cordons at the base of the neck with a further cordon on the shoulder set between two shallow grooves. Keston Kiln Ware, dateable to *c.* A.D. 60–85.

No. 347   Jar or bowl with slightly everted rim of sandy ware. Brown core and grey-black surfaces with cordon on neck. Keston Kiln Ware, dateable to *c.* A.D. 60–85.

No. 348   Butt beaker with bulbous body of sandy ware. Dark grey core and buff-brown surfaces. A decorated zone has been formed by applying a rouletting wheel to the surface (see p. 155). Keston Kiln Ware, dateable to *c.* A.D. 60–85.

No. 349   Butt beaker rim of sandy ware with grey-brown core and surfaces. Keston Kiln Ware, dateable to *c.* A.D. 60–85.

No. 350   Jar with slightly everted rim of sandy ware. Light grey core and patchy grey surfaces with a wide cordon around the neck. Keston Kiln Ware, dateable to *c.* A.D. 60–85.

No. 351   Butt beaker rim of sandy ware with buff core and buff-brown surfaces. Keston Kiln Ware, dateable to *c.* A.D. 60–85.

No. 352   A sherd, probably from the shoulder of a vessel in flint-tempered fabric. It is decorated with deep finger-tip impression. Both surfaces are wiped with flints, visible and protruding. The internal surface and core are black (N2). The external surface is brown (2.5YR5/6–7.5YR5/6) and worn. (Fabric A). Pre-Conquest.

No. 353   Small vessel with slightly everted rim of sandy ware. Brown core and patchy brown surfaces. Keston Kiln Ware, dateable to *c.* A.D. 60–85.

No. 354   Shouldered jar with bead rim of sandy ware with brown-black core and surfaces. Traces of burnished exterior surface and cordon on shoulder. Keston Kiln Ware, dateable to *c.* A.D. 60–85.

No. 355   An internally expanded rim in flint-tempered fabric, angle uncertain. The internal surface is dark grey (N3) and wiped smooth with few flints visible or protruding. The external surface is dark grey to black (N3–N2) and wiped with flints protruding. The core is dark grey (N3). (Form 26, fabric A). Pre-Conquest.

Filling of Quarry Pit Complex (LWB–L29–5, L29–6, M29–5, M29–6, M31–9, N29–5, N29–8, N29–12, N29–13, N30–7, N30–8 and N31–7).

No. 356   An everted rim in sandy flint-tempered fabric. It has been fired light yellow-brown (7.5YR7/6) throughout. Both surfaces have been wiped smooth with few flints visible or protruding. (Form 29, fabric B). Pre-Conquest.

No. 357   Butt beaker rim of hard, sandy ware with grey-brown core and orange-buff surfaces. Keston Kiln Ware, dateable to *c.* A.D. 60–85.

No. 358   Butt beaker rim of sandy ware with pink-buff core and surfaces. Keston Kiln Ware, dateable to *c.* A.D. 60–85.

No. 359   Rim of small butt beaker of sandy ware with orange core and orange-brown surfaces. Keston Kiln Ware, dateable to *c.* A.D. 60–85.

No. 360   Butt beaker rim of hard, sandy ware. Pink-buff core and orange-pink surfaces. Keston Kiln Ware, dateable to *c.* A.D. 60–85.

No. 361   Butt beaker rim of hard, sandy ware with buff core and surfaces. Keston Kiln Ware, dateable to *c.* A.D. 60–85.

No. 362   Narrow-mouthed butt beaker with bulbous body of hard sandy ware. Light grey core and surfaces. A zone of roulette decoration on the body has been produced by means of one of the 'pottery wheels' found on the site. Keston Kiln Ware, dateable to *c.* A.D. 60–85.

No. 363   Butt beaker rim of sandy ware with grey core and buff-brown surfaces. Traces of a cordon on the shoulder. Keston Kiln Ware, dateable to *c.* A.D. 60–85.

No. 364   Butt beaker body-sherd of sandy ware. Orange-buff core and grey surfaces with rouletted 'wheel' decoration. Keston Kiln Ware, dateable to *c.* A.D. 60–85.

No. 365   Platter with slightly incurved rim of sandy ware. Orange-brown core and brown surfaces. Keston Kiln Ware, dateable to *c.* A.D. 60–85.

No. 366   Platter with incurved rim of sandy ware. Grey-brown core and grey-black surfaces. Keston Kiln Ware, dateable to *c.* A.D. 60–85.

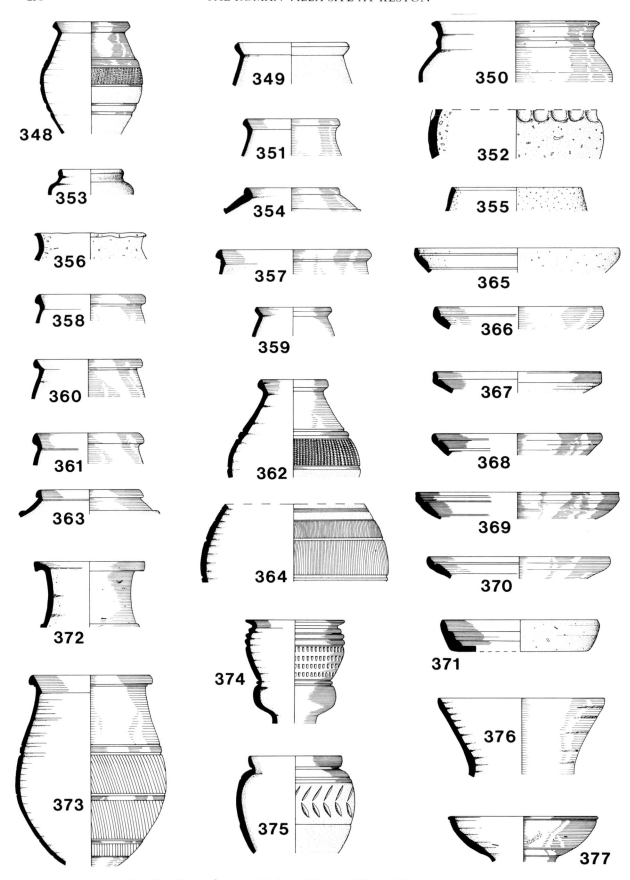

Fig. 67.   *Pottery from East Enclosure Ditch and filling of Quarry Pit Complex* ($\frac{1}{4}$).

No. 367   Platter with upright rim of hard, sandy ware. Orange-brown core and orange-brown, burnished surfaces. Keston Kiln Ware, dateable to *c.* A.D.60–85.

No. 368   Platter with slightly incurved rim of sandy ware. Grey-brown core and grey black surfaces. Keston Kiln Ware, dateable to *c.* A.D.60–85.

No. 369   Platter with upright rim of sandy ware. Grey-black core and orange surfaces with burnished exterior. Keston Kiln Ware, dateable to *c.* A.D.60–85.

No. 370   Platter with upright rim of sandy ware. Grey-brown core and grey-black, burnished surfaces. Keston Kiln Ware, dateable to *c.* A.D.60–85.

No. 371   Platter with upright rim of sandy ware. Grey-brown core and orange-brown surfaces. Keston Kiln Ware, dateable to *c.* A.D.60–85.

No. 372   Probable flagon with everted, squared rim of sandy ware. Orange core and orange-brown surfaces with traces of a cordon at the base of the neck. Similar to Camulodunum Form 140 (?). Keston Kiln Ware, dateable to *c.* A.D.60–85.

No. 373   Butt beaker of sandy ware. Buff core and surfaces decorated with zones of rouletting (Camulodunum Form 113). Gallo-Belgic import of no earlier than A.D.40 and most probably post-Conquest (see p. 197).

No. 374   Girth beaker of hard, sandy ware. Brown core and dark red surface decorated with cordons and stabbing and zones of burnishing. This type can be broadly paralleled at Camulodunum by Type 84/85, there dated A.D.10–61 (Ref. 247). Keston Kiln Ware, dateable to *c.* A.D.60–85.

No. 375   Beaker with everted rim of sandy ware with grey-buff core and buff surfaces. Decorated with two rows of angled slashes and an orange slip on the neck. Copying Camulodunum Form 114, there dated A.D.10–65 (Ref. 248). Keston Kiln Ware, dateable to *c.* A.D.60–85.

No. 376   Pedestal beaker with out-turned rim of hard, gritty ware. Grey-brown core and red-orange, burnished surfaces. Similar to Camulodunum Form 74/79 (Ref. 249). Keston Kiln Ware, dateable to *c.* A.D.60–85. See also No. 312.

No. 377   Open bowl or lid with small bead rim of sandy ware. Grey-brown core and brown-black surfaces with burnished exterior. Keston Kiln Ware, dateable to *c.* A.D.60–85.

No. 378   Large jar with bead rim of shell-tempered ware with orange-brown core and surfaces. Later first to early-second century A.D.

No. 379   Storage jar with heavy, internally thickened bead rim of shell-tempered ware. Grey-brown core and surfaces. Later first to early-second century A.D.

No. 380   Jar with bead rim of sandy ware. Blue-grey core and buff-brown surfaces, Keston Kiln Ware, dateable to *c.* A.D.60–85.

No. 381   Jar with bead rim of shell-tempered ware with some grog inclusions. Grey-brown core and surfaces. Later first to early-second century A.D.

No. 382   Jar with bead rim of shell-tempered ware. Grey-black core and surfaces. Later first to early-second century A.D.

No. 383   Small, flat-bottomed 'cup' with out-turned rim of hard, sandy ware. Dark grey core and orange-brown surfaces with somewhat pitted exterior. Keston Kiln Ware, dateable to *c.* A.D.60–85.

No. 384   Carinated bowl with everted rim of sandy ware. Grey-black core and surfaces with exterior slightly burnished with incised lattice decoration on rim. Keston Kiln Ware, dateable to *c.* A.D.60–85.

No. 385   Jar with everted rim of sandy ware. Grey-brown core and buff-brown surfaces with traces of a narrow cordon at the base of the neck. Keston Kiln Ware, dateable to *c.* A.D.60–85.

No. 386   Jar with everted rim of hard, sandy ware with sparse, fine shell-tempering. Orange brown core and buff-brown surfaces. Probably Keston Kiln Ware, dateable to *c.* A.D.60–85.

No. 387   Jar with slightly everted rim of hard, shell-tempered ware. Grey core and brown surfaces with slightly burnished exterior.

No. 388   Crudely-made jar with everted rim of sandy ware. Orange-brown core and surfaces with irregular grooves on neck. Keston Kiln Ware, dateable to *c.* A.D.60–85.

No. 389   Jar with inturned, thickened rim of shell-tempered ware. Dark grey core and grey-brown surfaces. Probably pre-Conquest.

No. 390   Hand-made jar or bowl with upright rim and rounded shoulder of coarse, shell-tempered ware. Black core with orange-brown interior surface and dark brown exterior. Pre-Conquest.

No. 391   Bowl with upright, slightly beaded rim of coarse, shell-tempered ware with black core and surfaces. Probably pre-Conquest.

No. 392   A globular vessel with a short everted rim in sandy shell-tempered fabric. Most of the shell fragments have dissolved, leaving voids in the surfaces of the sherd. The internal surface is light to dark grey (N5–N3) and worn. The external surface is grey to dark grey (N4–N3) and appears to have been burnished above the shoulder. Below this the surface is smooth and has been decorated with a horizontal groove 1.5 mm. thick

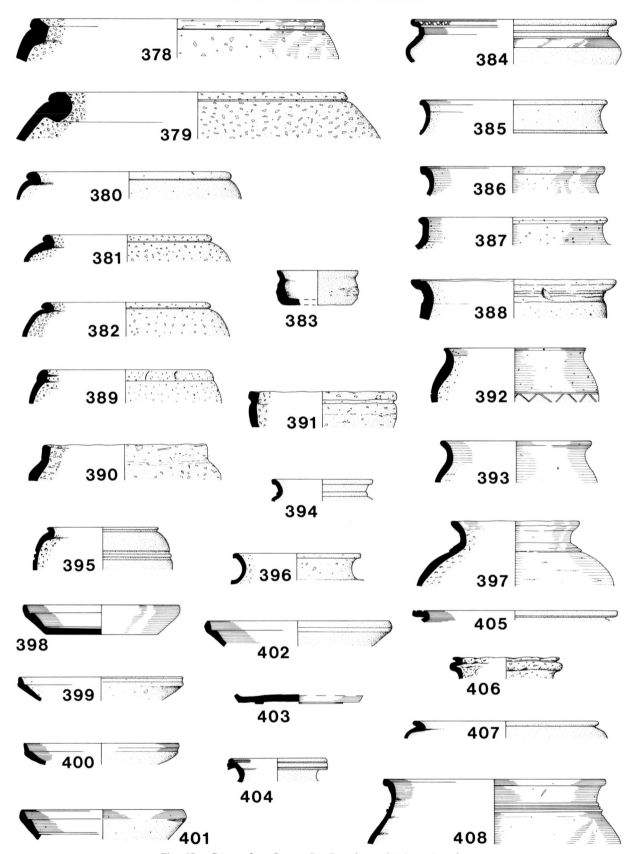

Fig. 68.   *Pottery from Quarry Pit Complex and Kiln Debris* ($\frac{1}{4}$).

below which are two diagonal grooves, possibly part of a design of hanging triangles. The core is grey to dark grey (N4–N3). (Form 33, fabric D). Pre-Conquest.

No. 393 An everted rim in fine glauconitic sandy fabric. The internal surface is black (N2) and has been burnished in a band around the rim to a depth of 2.5 cm. Below this the surface is dark grey (N3) and smooth. The external surface is black (N2) and burnished. The core is dark grey (N3). (Form 32, fabric G). Pre-Conquest.

Kiln Debris (LWB–M31–2, N31–18 and N31–19).

No. 394 Small jar with everted rim of hard, well-fired sandy ware. Dark grey core and surfaces with a small cordon on the neck. Probably an over-fired Keston Kiln product and dateable to *c.* A.D.60–85.

No. 395 Probable globular jar with bead rim of shell-tempered ware with grey-brown core and surfaces. There is a narrow cordon around the girth with shallow grooves on either side. Later first to early-second century A.D.

No. 396 Jar with everted rim of hard, slightly sandy ware with sprase shell-tempering. Dark grey core and light orange-brown surfaces. Probably Keston Kiln Ware and dateable to *c.* A.D.60–85.

No. 397 Narrow-mouthed jar with everted rim of soft, soapy, grog-tempered ware. Grey core and orange-brown interior surface with patchy grey and brown exterior with incised groove below the neck. Not obviously a Keston Kiln product, but probably dateable to the first century A.D.

No. 398 Platter with upright rim of sandy ware with grey-brown core and surfaces. Keston Kiln Ware, dateable to *c.* A.D.60–85.

No. 399 Platter with inturned rim of sandy ware. Grey-brown core and grey-black surfaces. Keston Kiln Ware, dateable to *c.* A.D.60–85.

No. 400 Platter with upright rim of sandy ware. Red-brown core and red, burnished surfaces, in imitation of *Terra Rubra*. Keston Kiln Ware, dateable to *c.* A.D.60–85.

No. 401 Platter with upright rim of sandy ware. Grey core and buff surfaces. Keston Kiln Ware, dateable to *c.* A.D.60–85.

No. 402 Platter with incurved rim of hard, sandy ware. Grey core and buff surfaces. Keston Kiln Ware, dateable to *c.* A.D.60–85.

No. 403 Two sherds of a platter base and footring of sandy ware. Brown core and orange-red surfaces, in imitation of *Terra Rubra*. One sherd bears a maker's stamp (No. 901). Keston Kiln Ware, dateable to *c.* A.D.60–85.

No. 404 Flagon rim of hard, sandy ware with light grey core and darker grey surfaces. A thoroughly Romanised ware, possibly intrusive here.

No. 405 Bowl with reeded rim of sandy ware with grey core and orange-buff surfaces. Keston Kiln Ware, dateable to *c.* A.D.60–85.

No. 406 Kiln waster consisting of the rim of a small, bead rim jar. Shell-tempered ware with mottled orange and dark brown fabric. The shoulder of the vessel has sagged during the firing process. It provides clear evidence for pottery making at Keston. The vessel type is very common on the site, dating from the later first to early-second century A.D.

No. 407 Jar or bowl with flattened bead rim of sandy ware with orange core and surfaces. Keston Kiln Ware, dateable to *c.* A.D.60–85.

No. 408 Large jar with everted rim of sandy ware. Orange core and surfaces with cordon on the neck. Keston Kiln Ware, dateable to *c.* A.D.60–85.

Soil Over Quarry Pit Complex (LWB–L29–4, M28–4, M29–5, M30–4, N28–6 and 7, N29–4 and N30–3).

No. 409 Small jar with everted rim of sandy ware. Grey core and grey-brown surfaces with an incised 'cross' on the body. Dateable to the late-first to early-second century A.D.

No. 410 Globular jar with small bead rim of grog-tempered ware. Brown core and orange-brown surfaces with applied bosses on the shoulder. Later first to early-second century A.D.

No. 411 Globular jar with small bead rim of hard, sandy ware. Light grey core and buff-brown surfaces with slight traces of a dark red slip on the exterior. Two faint cordons on the shoulder. Keston Kiln Ware, dateable to *c.* A.D.60–85.

No. 412 Rusticated jar with out-turned rim of coarse, sandy ware with grey-brown core and surfaces. Dateable to A.D. 50–120.

No. 413 Jar with bead rim of shell-tempered ware. Black core and dark grey surfaces. Dateable to the later first to early-second century A.D.

No. 414 Butt beaker rim of hard, sandy ware with grey-black core and surfaces. Keston Kiln Ware, dateable to *c.* A.D.60–85.

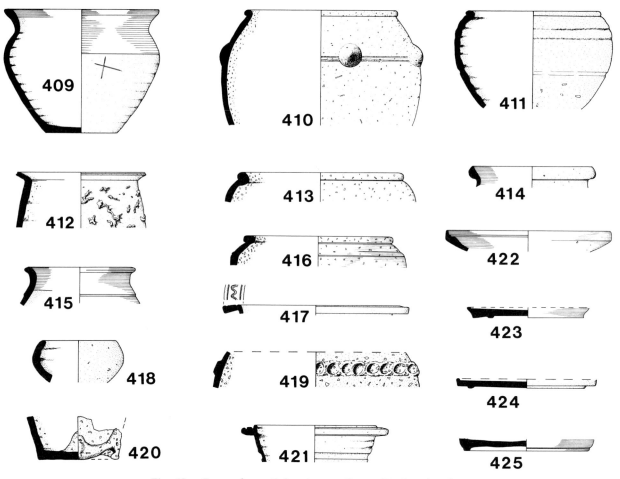

Fig. 69.   *Pottery from soil deposits over Quarry Pit Complex (¼).*

No. 415   Small jar with everted rim of sandy ware. Brown core and grey-brown surfaces with traces of burnishing on both sides. Keston Kiln Ware, dateable to *c.* A.D.60–85.

No. 416   Jar with flattened bead rim of shell-tempered ware. Brown core and black exterior surface with a faint cordon on the shoulder. Dateable to the later first to early-second century A.D.

No. 417   Bowl with reeded rim of sandy ware. Probably similar to No. 878. Orange-grey core and pink-grey surfaces. Incised zig-zag around top of rim and traces of a red slip on rim top. Keston Kiln Ware, dateable to *c.* A.D.60–85.

No. 418   Small 'cup' with weakly carinated shoulder and simple, internally thickened rim of sandy ware. Dark grey core and orange-brown exterior surface. Possibly a lamp-holder. Broadly similar to No. 383. Keston Kiln Ware, dateable to *c.* A.D.60–85.

No. 419   A sandy flint-tempered sherd, possibly from the neck of a vessel, with an applied cordon decorated with finger-tip impressions. The internal surface is grey-brown (N4–5YR6/3). The external surface is dark grey (N3) and the core grey (N4). (Fabric B). Pre-Conquest.

No. 420   Jar with heavily distorted base of shell-tempered ware. Light orange-brown core and surfaces with moderate amounts of added shell. This piece is clearly a waster, produced on the Keston site, and it seems that the vessel totally collapsed during the firing process. See also No. 406, a waster rim, probably from a similar vessel-type.

No. 421   Bowl with flanged, reeded rim of hard, sandy ware. Grey-brown core and patchy grey-brown surfaces. Generally dateable in West Kent to the second century A.D.

No. 422   Platter with upright rim of sandy ware. Grey-brown core and orange-brown surfaces. Keston Kiln Ware, dateable to *c.* A.D.60–85.

No. 423   Platter base of sandy ware with grey core, dark grey interior surface and buff-brown exterior. Keston Kiln Ware, dateable to *c.* A.D.60–85.

No. 424   Platter base of sandy ware with dark grey core and orange-red surfaces. Keston Kiln Ware, dateable to *c.* A.D.60–85.

No. 425   Platter base of slightly sandy ware with part of a central stamp (No. 902). Grey-brown core and buff-brown, well-burnished surfaces. Keston Kiln Ware, dateable to *c.* A.D.60–85.

Centre Enclosure, East and South Ditches (LWB–I27–2, J23–6, J23–8, K22–3, 77–10, 77–89, 77–91, 77–92 and 77–120).

No. 426   Large storage jar with thickened, everted rim of grog-tempered ware. Grey core and orange-buff surfaces. This is typical of the so-called Patch-Grove Wares, dateable in West Kent to the later first to second century A.D.

No. 427   Jar with out-turned, slightly under-cut rim of grog-tempered ware. Light grey and patchy orange-grey surfaces, burnished over and inside the rim. Dateable to the later first to early-second century A.D.

No. 428   Jar with bead rim and small, raised cordon on the lower neck, set between shallow grooves. The sherd exhibits the unusual dual fabric construction noted on a number of pieces from the site (No. 311). It seems clear that the beaded rim and the outer part of the neck of the pot, which are of sandy Keston Kiln Ware, had been added to an otherwise shell-tempered vessel. The core of the sherd has been fired to a grey-brown colour. The interior surface is light brown and the exterior dark grey-brown. The vessel is clearly a product of the Keston Kiln and may, therefore, be dated to the period *c.* A.D.60–85.

No. 429   Pedestal base, from a vessel of uncertain form, of sandy ware. Grey core with some dark red iron-stone/grog inclusions and dark brown surfaces. The fabric is typical of the Keston Kiln products and may be dated to *c.* A.D.60–85.

No. 430   Jar with everted rim of grog-tempered ware. Light grey core and dark grey surfaces with 'pitch' painted beneath the rim and a broad cordon below.

No. 431   Jar with bead rim and angled shoulder of shell-tempered ware. Dark grey core and surfaces. Dateable to the later first to early-second century A.D.

No. 432   Jar with small bead rim and pronounced shoulder of shell-tempered ware. Dark grey core with light brown interior surface and dark grey-brown exterior. Later first to early-second century A.D.

No. 433   Jar with small bead rim of shell-tempered ware. Brown-black core with buff interior surface and brown-black exterior with two horizontal grooves on the shoulder. Later first to early-second century A.D.

No. 434   Bowl with small bead rim of sandy ware. Orange core and orange-red surfaces with traces of a dark red slip on the exterior. There is a narrow cordon between horizontal grooves on the neck and three horizontal grooves decorate the body of the vessel. The fabric is typical of the Keston Kiln and may be dated to *c.* A.D.60–85.

No. 435   Lid of sandy ware with grey-brown core and patchy grey surfaces. Keston Kiln Ware, dateable to *c.* A.D.60–85.

No. 436   Lid of shell-tempered ware with grey-brown core and orange-brown surfaces.

No. 437   Lid of sandy ware with grey core and patchy grey surfaces.

No. 438   Jar with slightly out-turned, thickened rim of grog-tempered ware. Grey core and dark grey surfaces.

No. 439   Jar with slightly out-curved rim of sandy ware. Dark grey-brown core and grey, lightly burnished surfaces with traces of a cordon at the base of the neck.

No. 440   Jar with bead rim and upright neck of grog-tempered ware. Light grey core and brown-black surfaces, burnished beneath the rim. The vessel has a shoulder cordon.

No. 441   Jar with upright neck of hard, over-fired, sand-tempered ware. Black core and patchy red-black surfaces with well-burnished exterior and a cordon above the shoulder. Keston Kiln Ware, dateable to *c.* A.D.60–85.

No. 442   Platter with inturned rim of sandy ware. Dark grey core, dark brown-black interior surface and light orange-brown exterior with a dark red slip. Keston Kiln Ware, dateable to *c.* A.D.60–85.

No. 443   Platter with incurved rim of sandy ware. Red-brown core and surfaces with double grooves on the inner rim. Keston Kiln Ware, dateble to *c.* A.D.60–85.

No. 444   An inturned rim of sandy flint-tempered fabric. The surfaces are light brown (5YR7/6) and smooth with flints visible. The core is black (N2). (Form 1, fabric B). Pre-Conquest.

No. 445   Bowl with bead rim of sandy ware. Grey-brown core and patchy grey-brown surfaces. Keston Kiln Ware, dateable to *c.* A.D.60–85.

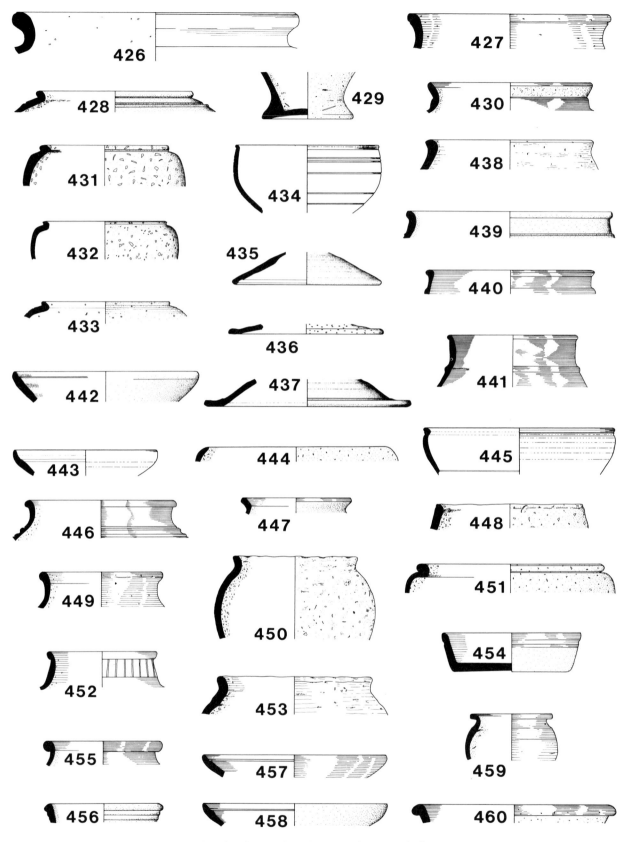

Fig. 70.   *Pottery from Centre Enclosure Ditch* ($\frac{1}{4}$).

Centre Enclosure, West Ditch (Gullies 'C' and 'D') (C23–2, C24– 4, C25–5, D19–2, D21–5, D21–6 and D23–3).

No. 446   Jar with everted rim of hard grog-tempered ware. Grey-brown core and surfaces with two shoulder cordons between grooves.

No. 447   Small jar with everted rim of sandy ware with brown core and brown-black surfaces.

No. 448   Flat-topped, slightly inturned rim of shell-tempered ware with brown-black core and surfaces. The rim form is typical of the pre-Conquest period.

No. 449   Jar with slightly everted rim of hard, grog-tempered ware. Grey-black core and grey-buff surfaces with exterior lightly burnished.

No. 450   Globular jar with slightly out-turned rim and rounded shoulder of hard, gritty, grog-tempered ware with occasional shell inclusions. Dark grey core and light grey-brown surfaces with lightly burnished exterior. Probably first century A.D.

No. 451   Jar with bead rim of shell-tempered ware. Grey-brown core and orange-brown surfaces. Later first to early-second century A.D.

No. 452   A necked jar in a fabric tempered with grog and fine shell fragments. The internal surface is dark grey (N3) and burnished. The external surface is burnished horizontally down to about 2.5 cm. below the rim, and this band is decorated with at least four vertical burnished lines which apear as dark grey (N3), contrasting with the grey (N4) background. Below this, the surface is dark grey (N3) and highly burnished. The core is also dark grey (N3). (Form 36, fabric J). Pre-Conquest.

No. 453   An everted rim in a shell-tempered fabric. Both surfaces are black (N2) and have been burnished with shell fragments visible. The core is dark brown to grey (10R5/3–N4). (Form 32, fabric G). Pre-Conquest.

No. 454   Bowl with upright rim of sandy ware. Light grey core and dark grey surfaces. Traces of burnishing survive on the inside of the vessel and there is a black burnished band below the rim. Probably third to fourth century A.D. and intrusive here.

No. 455   Small jar with rolled rim of sandy ware. Grey core and brown-black surfaces. Dateable to the second century A.D.

No. 456   Rim of probable ring-necked flagon of sandy ware. Grey-brown core and buff surfaces.

No. 457   Platter with upright rim of sandy ware. Grey-brown core and grey-black surfaces with dark red, slip-coated, burnished surfaces in imitation of *Terra Rubra*. Keston Kiln Ware, dateable to *c.* A.D.60–85.

No. 458   Platter with upright rim of sandy ware with grey-black surfaces. Keston Kiln Ware, dateable to *c.* A.D.60–85.

No. 459   Small beaker with everted rim of hard, grog-tempered ware. Grey core and orange-brown surfaces with lightly burnished exterior. This appears to be a Romanised form and fabric.

No. 460   Dish with bead rim of sandy ware with orange-brown core and grey-brown surfaces. Second century A.D.

Mixed filling of Centre and West Enclosure Ditches (LWB–D21–2, D21–3 and D22–4).

No. 461   About half of a large storage jar with heavy, flat-topped bead rim of shell-tempered ware. Light orange-brown core and light to dark brown surfaces. Later first to early-second century.

No. 462   Base of a probable pedestal beaker of sand-tempered ware. Dark grey and orange-brown sandwiched core with traces of a dark red slip on the surfaces. The fabric is typical of the Keston Kilns and is dateable to *c.* A.D.60–85.

No. 463   Butt beaker of hard, sandy ware. Light grey core and dark grey surfaces with burnished rim and exterior. The vessel has a shoulder cordon. Possibly Keston Kiln Ware and dateable to *c.* A.D.60–85.

No. 464   Out-turned, flat-topped rim of sparsely shell-tempered ware with grey-brown core and buff surfaces. The rim form is typical of the pre-Conquest period.

No. 465   Storage jar with heavy bead rim of shell-tempered ware with orange-brown core and surfaces. Later first to early-second century A.D.

No. 466   Shoulder of a storage jar of shell-tempered ware. Grey-brown core and buff-brown surfaces with a band of incised line decoration on the shoulder. The rim is missing.

No. 467   Large storage jar with heavy, flat-topped bead rim of shell-tempered ware. Grey-brown core and orange-brown surfaces. Probably similar to No. 461 and dateable to the later first to early-second century A.D.

Soil Cut by Early-Roman Pit 17 (LWB–K20–2).

No. 468   Jar with simple, upright rim of coarse, shell-tempered ware. Black core and patchy black-brown surfaces. Probably pre-Conquest.

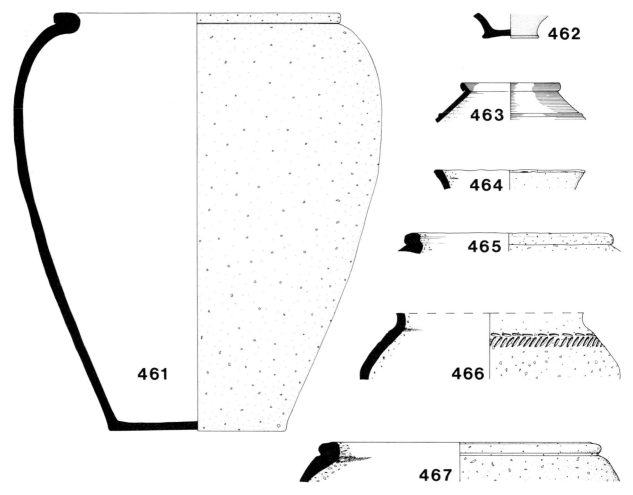

Fig. 71.   *Pottery from Gullies C and D and East Ditch of West Enclosure ($\frac{1}{4}$).*

Early-Roman Pit 17, Main filling (LWB–K20–3).

No. 469   Narrow-mouthed jar with slightly outcurved rim of sandy ware. Grey black core and surfaces with well-burnished exterior and a narrow shoulder cordon. Keston Kiln Ware, dateable to *c.* A.D.60–85.

No. 470   Narrow-mouthed beaker with small rim of sandy ware. Grey-brown core and buff-brown surfaces with a pronounced cordon on the shoulder. Possibly Keston Kiln Ware and, therefore, dateable to *c.* A.D.60–85.

No. 471   Lid of fine sandy ware. Light grey core and grey surfaces with burnished exterior. Keston Kiln Ware, dateable to *c.* A.D.60–85.

No. 472   Jar or bowl with bead rim of fine sandy ware. Grey core and surfaces with shoulder cordon and burnished lattice decoration below. Keston Kiln Ware, dateable to *c.* A.D.60–85.

No. 473   Platter with slightly inturned rim of sandy ware. Grey core and dark grey surfaces with burnished interior and rim. Keston Kiln Ware, dateable to *c.* A.D.60–85.

No. 474   Upright, flat-topped rim of sandy ware with light grey core and grey surfaces.

No. 475   Jar with out-turned bead rim of fine sandy ware. Light grey core and dark grey surfaces, burnished inside and beneath the rim.

No. 476   Large storage jar with heavy, flat-topped bead rim of shell-tempered ware. Grey-brown core and surfaces. Later first to early-second century A.D.

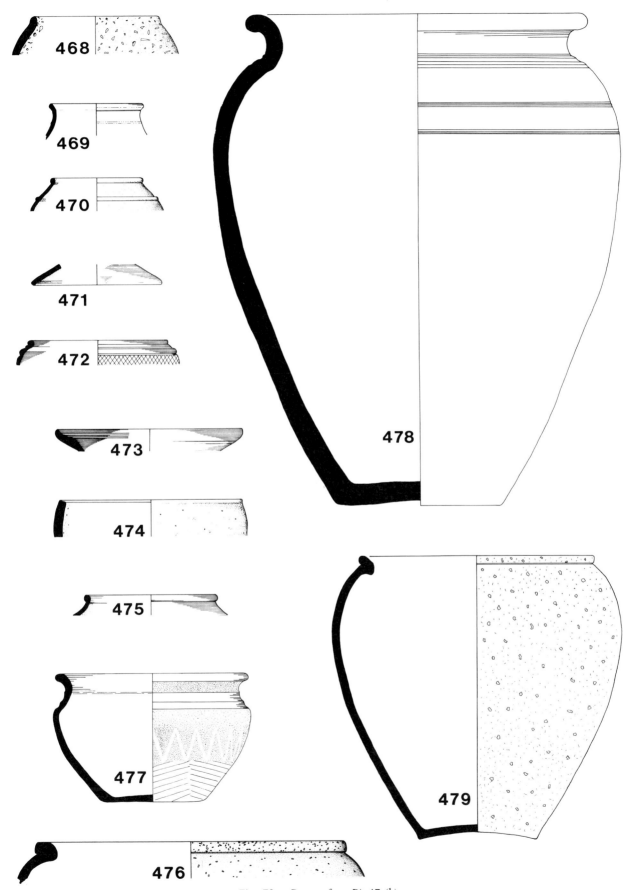

Fig. 72. *Pottery from Pit 17* ($\frac{1}{4}$).

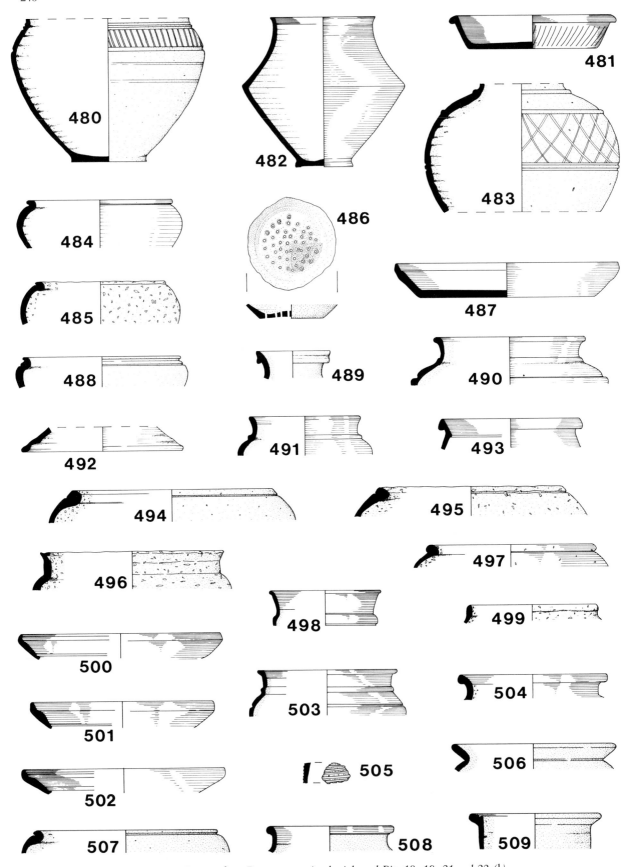

Fig. 73. *Pottery from Roman cremation burials and Pits 18, 19, 21 and 22* ($\frac{1}{4}$).

Early-Roman Pit 17, Lower filling (LWB–K20–4).

No. 477   Substantially complete bowl with thickened, everted rim and zig-zag decoration on the body.

No. 478   Substantially complete storage jar of unusually large size with everted rim of grog-tempered ware. The jar has cordons on the neck and shoulder and orange-brown surfaces. Dateable to the later first to second century A.D.

No. 479   Substantially complete jar with internaly thickened bead rim of shell-tempered ware with buff-brown surfaces. Dateable to the later first to early-second century A.D.

Roman Cremation Burial 1 (LWB–B22–3).

No. 480   Jar of sandy ware with brown core and grey surfaces. The shoulder is decorated with near-vertical, burnished lines. The rim is missing. Later first century A.D.

No. 481   Shallow dish with bead rim of sandy ware. Brown core and well-burnished, brown-black surfaces. Exterior decorated with burnished, angle lines. Probably dateable to the mid-second century A.D.

Roman Cremation Burial 3 (LWB–Z–7).

No. 482   Complete carinated jar with slightly outcurved rim of smooth ware. Grey core and grey-brown surfaces. Probably a product of the North Kent Marshes and dateable to the second half of the first or the early-second century A.D.

Early-Roman Pit 18 (LWB–J21–3 and 4).

No. 483   Narrow-mouthed jar of fine sandy ware with orange-brown core. There is a horizontal cordon at the base of the neck and on the shoulder. Set between the shoulder cordon and two horizontal grooves around the body of the pot is a zone of burnished criss-cross decoration, fairly irregularly applied. The rim is missing. Keston Kiln Ware, dateable to c. A.D.60–85.

No. 484   Bowl with flattened bead rim of sandy ware. Light grey core and dark grey surfaces with slightly burnished exterior. Keston Kiln Ware, dateable to c. A.D.60–85.

No. 485   Jar with small, flattened bead rim of shell-tempered ware. Grey-brown core and dark grey-brown surfaces. There is a shallow, horizontal groove below the shoulder. Later first to early-second century A.D.

No. 486   Base of a strainer or collander perforated with three, roughly concentric rings of small holes, made before firing. Hard, light buff-brown sandy ware from the Keston Kilns and dateable to c. A.D.60–85.

No. 487   Platter with upright rim of sandy ware. Grey-black core and orange-buff surfaces with dark red slip coating in imitation of *Terra Rubra*. Keston Kiln Ware, dateable to c. A.D.60–85.

No. 488   Jar with slightly beaded rim of sandy ware. Dark grey core and surfaces with a cordon between grooves below the rim. Keston Kiln Ware, dateable to c. A.D.60–85.

No. 489   Flagon rim of fine sandy ware with orange core and orange-buff surfaces. The rim form appears to be copying those of early imported flagons (Camulodunum Form 140 etc). Keston Kiln Ware, dateable to c. A.D.60–85.

No. 490   Probable globular jar with everted rim of fine sandy ware. Brown-grey core and dark grey surfaces. There is a slight cordon on the neck and a wide, horizontal groove on the shoulder. Keston Kiln Ware, dateable to c. A.D.60–85.

No. 491   Jar with slightly outcurved rim of sandy ware. Light grey core and dark grey-black surfaces with slightly burnished exterior. There is a bold cordon on the neck. Keston Kiln Ware, dateable to c. A.D.60–85.

Early-Roman Pit 19 (LWB–D23–2).

No. 492   Lid of fine sandy ware with dark grey-brown core and dark grey-black burnished surfaces. A broad groove on the inside allowed a close fit with the main vessel. Possibly Keston Kiln Ware and, therefore, dateable to c. A.D.60–85.

No. 493   Genuine Gallo-Belgic butt beaker rim of hard, sandy ware. Grey core and cream-buff surfaces. Dateable to the Claudio-Neronian period. (See p. 197).

No. 494   Jar with bead rim of shell-tempered ware with some grog inclusions. Grey core and brown-black surfaces. Dateable to the later first to early-second century A.D.

No. 495   Jar with bead rim of grog-tempered ware with some shell inclusions. Dark grey core and light orange-brown surfaces. Later first to early-second century A.D.

No. 496   Jar with flattened, slightly out-turned rim of coarse, shell-tempered ware, dark grey core and interior surface with brown exterior. This is essentially a pre-Conquest form and is dated earlier than No. 495. It is likely to be residual.

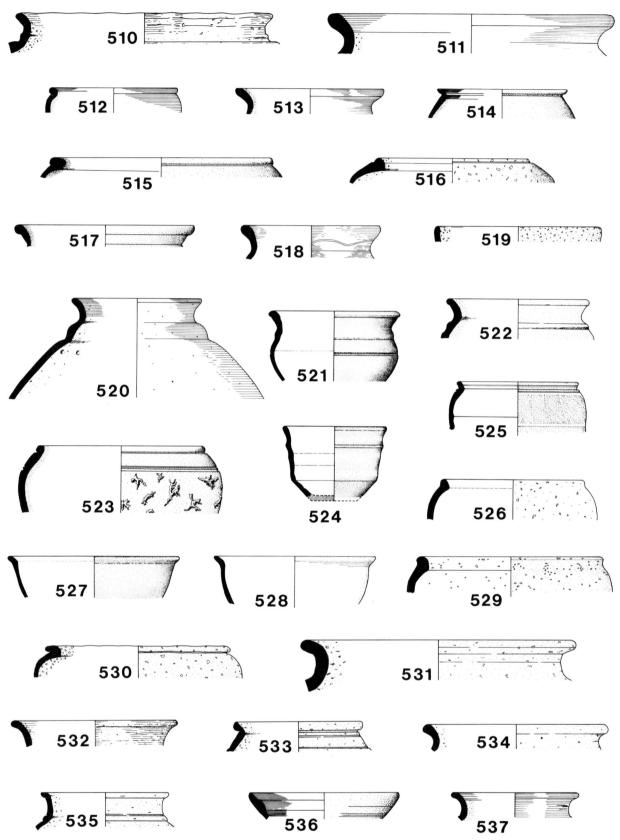

Fig. 74.   *Pottery from South Timber Building, Centre Timber Building, Centre Flint Structure, Lower East Metalling and Two-Post Structure 'A' ($\frac{1}{4}$).*

Early-Roman Pit 21 (LWB–M36–3 and M36–10).

No. 497 Jar with thickened bead rim of shell-tempered ware. Brown core and brown-black surfaces. Later first to early-second century A.D.

No. 498 Small jar with slightly outcurved rim of sandy ware. Dark grey core and dark grey, lightly burnished surfaces. There is a wide cordon on the shoulder. Keston Kiln Ware, dateable to *c.* A.D.60–85.

No. 499 A plain externally thickened, upright rim of an inturned neck of flint-tempered fabric. The sherd is small and the angle and diameter uncertain. Both surfaces are dark grey to black (N3–N2) and smooth with few flints visible. The core is dark grey (N3). (Form 15, fabric A). Pre-Conquest.

No. 500 Platter with inturned rim of hard, sandy ware. Dark grey core and patchy light grey surfaces with burnished interior. Keston Kiln Ware, dateable to *c.* A.D.60–85.

No. 501 Platter with upright rim of hard, sandy ware. Dark grey core and orange-brown surfaces with traces of a dark red colour-coat. Keston Kiln Ware, dateable to *c.* A.D.60–85.

No. 502 Platter with upright rim of hard, slightly sandy ware. Dark grey core and dark grey-black, burnished surfaces. Keston Kiln Ware, dateable to *c.* A.D.60–85.

No. 503 Jar with slightly out-turned neck and bead rim of hard, slightly sandy ware. Dark grey core and dark grey-brown surfaces with burnished exterior. There is a raised cordon at the base of the neck and an incised groove on the shoulder. Keston Kiln Ware, dateable to *c.* A.D.60–85.

No. 504 Jar with out-turned, thickened rim of hard, grog-tempered ware. Orange-brown core and buff-brown surfaces.

Early-Roman Pit 22 (LWB–S22–8 and S22–9).

No. 505 A wall sherd of flint-tempered fabric. It has been fired black (N2) throughout. The internal surface is smooth with flints visible, the external surface is decorated with at least five grooves, from a deep combed design. (Fabric A). Pre-Conquest.

No. 506 Jar with sharply out-turned rim of hard, sandy ware. Light grey core and slightly darker grey surfaces with traces of an orange-brown coating on the exterior surface. Dateable to the mid to late-second century A.D.

No. 507 Jar with small bead rim of fairly hard, sandy ware. Light grey core and dark grey-brown surfaces. Later first to early-second century A.D.

No. 508 Jar with slightly outcurved, bead rim of hard, sandy ware. Dark grey core and lighter grey-brown surfaces. Later first to early-second century A.D.

No. 509 Bowl with flanged rim of a hard, sandy ware. Light grey core and darker grey surfaces. Dateable to the later first to early-second century A.D.

South Timber Building, Daub Spread (LWB–M34–15).

No. 510 Storage jar with out-turned rim of grog-tempered ware. Mottled, grey-brown with orange-brown surfaces. Broad, slight cordon on the neck. 'Patch Grove' Ware, dateable to the later first to second century A.D.

South Timber Building, Post-pit 5 (LWB–N34–3 and N34–5).

No. 511 Large storage jar with outcurved rim. Fairly soft, slightly soapy, grog-tempered ware. Light orange-brown core, orange internal surface and dark grey-brown exterior. A well known 'Patch Grove'-type vessel, dateable to the later first or second century A.D.

No. 512 Small jar with bead rim of sandy ware. Dark grey core and dark grey-black surfaces. Exterior slightly burnished. Keston Kiln Ware, dateable to *c.* A.D.60–85.

No. 513 Jar with everted rim of hard, grog-tempered ware. Light grey core and orange surfaces. Patch Grove Ware, dateable to the later first to second century A.D.

No. 514 Jar with slightly recessed rim of fine sand-tempered ware. Light grey core and grey surfaces. Dateable to the first half of the second century A.D.

Centre Timber Building, Fill of Post-pits (LWB–O24–6, P24–3, Q22–9, R22–3 and T22–10).

No. 515 Jar with flattened, bead rim of sandy ware. Light grey core and orange-buff surfaces. Dateable to the later first to early-second century A.D.

No. 516 Jar with slightly beaded rim of sparsely shell-tempered ware. Grey-brown core with orange interior and brown exterior. Dateable to the later first to early-second century A.D.

No. 517 Jar with slightly outcurved, thickened rim of grey-buff sandy ware with grey surfaces.

No. 518   Jar with everted rim of grog-tempered ware. Grey core and orange-buff surfaces. Patch Grove Ware dateable to the later first century to second century A.D.

No. 519   Small plain rim in flint-tempered fabric. The rim is irregular and the angle uncertain; but it probably belongs to an open bowl. It has been fired dark grey (N3) throughout. Both surfaces are smooth with flint inclusions visible. (Form 38, fabric A). Pre-Conquest.

Flint Rubble associated with Centre Flint Structure (LWB–K27–3, K27–5, K27–6 and J27–5).

No. 520   Large, narrow-mouthed jar with everted rim of grog-tempered ware. Grey core and brown surfaces with a wide cordon on the neck. Slight traces of burnishing on the exterior. Quite possibly a 'Belgic' pedestal urn and most probably dateable to the first century A.D.

No. 521   Bowl with outcurved rim of sandy ware. Dark grey core and light grey-brown surfaces. There is a cordon on the neck, with a slight groove below and a deeper groove around the shoulder. Dateable to the later first century A.D.

No. 522   Jar with everted rim of fine sandy ware. Light brown core and interior, with dark grey-brown exterior. There is a slight horizontal cordon on the neck. Keston Kiln Ware dateable to c. A.D.60–85. (From the soil under the flint rubble).

No. 523   Bowl with upright, slightly beaded rim of sandy ware. Grey core and light grey surfaces. There is a double horizontal groove on the shoulder. Below this there is a 'rusticated' decoration, similar to that on No. 412. Dateable to c. A.D.50–120.

No. 524   Cup with upright rim of grey-brown sandy fabric with patchy grey surfaces. There is a horizontal cordon below the rim.

No. 525   Small jar or bowl with bead rim and double groove below. Sandy ware with a light grey core, light grey interior surface and dark grey exterior with a band of burnished lattice decoration. Keston Kiln Ware, dateable to c. A.D.60–85.

No. 526   Jar with bead rim of shell-tempered ware with grey-brown core and surfaces. Dateable to the later first to early-second century A.D.

No. 527   Bowl with outcurved rim of sandy ware with orange-brown core and surfaces. Possibly Keston Kiln Ware which is dateable to c. A.D.60–85.

No. 528   Bowl with outcurved rim of sandy ware with orange-brown core and patchy brown surfaces. Possibly Keston Kiln Ware and similar to No. 527.

No. 529   Storage jar with an internally thickened bead rim of shell-tempered ware. Grey-brown core with patchy grey surfaces. Dateable to the later first to early-second century A.D.

Soil under Lower East Metalling (LWB–AA24–15).

No. 530   Jar with a slightly flattened bead rim of coarse, shell-tempered ware. Light grey core and light orange-brown surfaces. Dateable to the later first to early-second century A.D.

No. 531   Large storage jar with everted rim of grog-tempered ware. Mottled grey core with orange-brown surfaces. Patch Grove Ware, dateable to the later first to second century A.D.

Lower East Metalling (LWB–AA23–10, AA24–3 and AA24–13).

No. 532   Jar with everted rim of grog-tempered ware. Light brown core with burnished, grey-brown surfaces.

No. 533   Narrow-mouthed jar or beaker with a sharply out-turned, thickened rim of sandy, grog-tempered ware. Light grey core with orange-brown surfaces and traces of a raised cordon at the base of the neck.

No. 534   Jar with everted, thickened rim of grog-tempered ware. Light grey core and orange surfaces. A typical Patch Grove form dateable to the later first to second century A.D.

No. 535   Jar with outcurved, slightly thickened rim of grog-tempered ware. Hard, thin grey fabric with dark grey-brown surfaces. There is a faint horizontal groove and cordon at the base of the neck.

No. 536   Platter with an upright rim of sandy ware. Brown-black core and grey-black surfaces. Interior slightly burnished. Keston Kiln Ware dateable to c. A.D.60–85.

Two-Post Structure 'A' (LWB–77–139).

No. 537   Jar with outcurved rim of sandy, grog-tempered ware. Light grey-brown core with dark grey-brown surfaces. There is a narrow cordon on the neck.

Roman Water Storage Pond (LWB–78–56).

No. 538   Small jar with everted rim of grog-tempered ware. Light grey core with dark grey-brown surfaces. There is a slight horizontal cordon on the neck. Dateable to the mid-first to early-second century A.D.

No. 539   Small jar with outcurved, thickened rim of sandy ware. Orange-brown core and surfaces. Dateable to the late-first to early-second century A.D.

No. 540   Dish with bead rim of sandy ware. Dark grey core and surfaces. Dateable to the mid to late-second century A.D.

No. 541   Decorated wall sherd in hard orange fabric, with a dark grey-brown colour-coat. A raised swirl or spiral on the exterior seems to represent part of a floral design. Probably Nene Valley Ware of second to early-third century date.

No. 542   Jar with sharply everted rim of sandy ware. Hard, grey core and internal surface with orange-brown exterior. There is an incised cross cut on the inside of the rim after firing. Dateable to the mid to late-second century A.D.

Soil over Roman Water Storage Pond (LWB–78–47).

No. 543   Jar with sharply out-turned, thickened and undercut rim of hard sandy ware. Dark grey core and light grey-brown surfaces. Dateable to the late-second to mid-third century A.D.

No. 544   Jar with everted rim of sandy ware. Orange-brown core and surfaces.

No. 545   Jar with outcurved, squared and undercut rim of hard sandy ware. Grey core and surfaces.

No. 546   Dish with flanged rim of hard, sandy, grog-tempered ware. Light grey-brown core and internal surface with grey exterior. Dateable to the fourth century A.D.

No. 547   Jar with outcurved, recessed rim of hard, sandy ware. Light grey core and somewhat abraded surfaces. Dateable to the third to fourth century A.D.

No. 548   Small jar with outcurved, hooked rim of hard, coarse sandy ware. Cream core and surfaces. 'Cream Sandy Ware', dateable to the fourth century A.D.

North-West Ditch of Villa Enclosure, Lower filling of East Arm (LWB–76–44).

No. 549   Dish with straight sides and upright rim of hard, sandy ware. Grey-brown core and grey-black burnished surfaces with an external groove below the rim. Dateable to the mid-second to mid-third century A.D.

North-West Ditch of Villa Enclosure, Middle filling of East Arm (LWB–76–35).

No. 550   Jar with everted rim of sandy ware. Grey-black core with patchy grey surfaces. Dateable to the mid-second to mid-third century A.D.

No. 551   Jar with almost upright rim of hard, grog-tempered ware. Light grey core with patchy orange-buff surfaces.

North-West Ditch of Villa Enclosure, Upper filling of East Arm (LWB–76–4).

No. 552   Dish with straight sides and heavy bead rim of sandy ware. Dark grey core and surfaces, with burnished surfaces. Dateable to the later second century A.D.

No. 553   Jar with upright neck and outcurved, thickened rim of sandy ware. Grey-brown core with burnished brown-black surfaces and faint grooves at the base of the neck. Dateable to the late-first to mid-second century A.D.

No. 554   Flagon with outcurved rim and traces of a handle. Fine pink-red ware, with orange-red surfaces in a cream slip.

No. 555   Jar with everted rim of sandy ware. Grey-black core with light grey-brown surfaces. Inside of rim and exterior burnished. Dateable to the second half of the third century A.D.

No. 556   Lid of orange-brown sandy ware with orange-buff surfaces.

No. 557   Dish with straight sides and upright rim of coarse sandy ware. Grey-black core and brown-black surfaces. Exterior decorated with burnished interlocking arcs. Dateable to the second century A.D.

No. 558   Jar with everted rim of sandy ware. Grey-brown core with patchy grey surfaces.

No. 559   Bottle with outcurved, thickened rim of sandy ware. Dark grey core and light grey surfaces.

No. 560   Dish or bowl with thickened bead rim of sandy ware. Brown-black core with orange-brown surfaces and burnished exterior. Dateable to the later second century A.D.

North-West Ditch of Villa Enclosure, Lower filling of North Arm (LWB–F4–4).

No. 561   Bowl with flanged rim of sandy ware. Grey-brown core and dark grey-black burnished surfaces. Dateable to the mid-third century A.D. to the fourth century A.D.

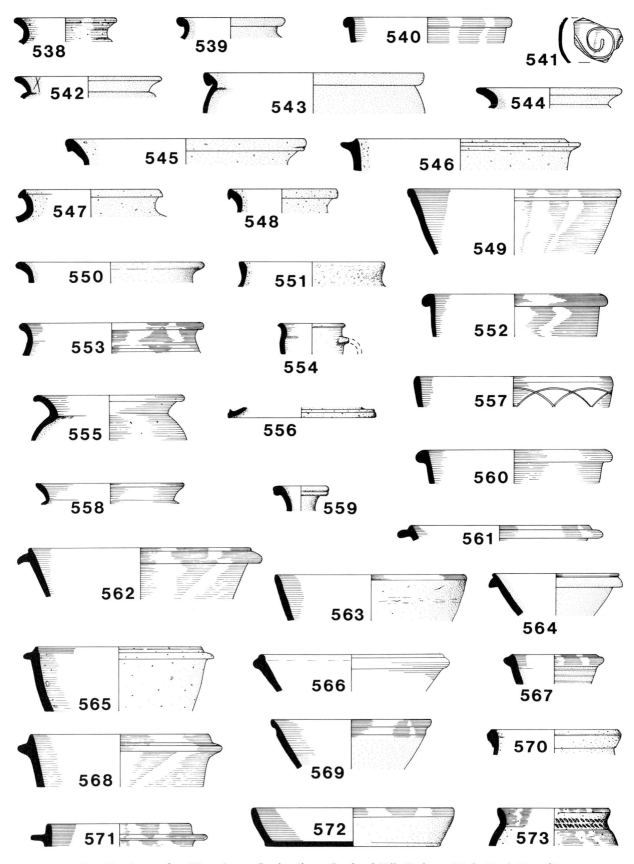

Fig. 75.   *Pottery from Water Storage Pond, soil over Pond and Villa Enclosure Ditch, North-West* (¼).

North-West Ditch of Villa Enclosure, Upper filling of North Arm (LWB–E4–2, H6–3, J7–2, 76–3 and 76–178).

No. 562   Bowl with flanged rim of sandy ware. Dark grey core with patchy grey-brown surfaces. Dateable to the mid-third to fourth century A.D.

No. 563   Dish with straight sides and upright rim of sandy ware. Light grey core with patchy light grey external surface and a black slip over the rim and interior. Alice Holt Ware, Class 6A, dateable to *c.* A.D.180–270.

No. 564   Small bowl with rounded flanged rim of sandy ware. Grey-buff core with patchy grey surfaces and traces of black slip over the flange. Dateable to the mid-third to fourth century A.D.

No. 565   Bowl with flanged rim of coarse, gritty, grog-tempered ware. Light grey-brown core and dark brown surfaces with traces of burnishing on the interior. Dateable to the fourth century A.D.

No. 566   Dish with flanged rim of hard, gritty, grog-tempered ware. Dark grey-brown core with grey-black surfaces and burnished exterior. Dateable to the fourth century A.D.

No. 567   Small dish with flanged rim of sandy ware. Light grey core and surfaces with traces of a burnished slip over and inside the rim. Alice Holt Ware, Class 5B, dateable to the third to fourth century A.D.

No. 568   Dish with flanged rim of sandy, grog-tempered ware. Grey core and patchy orange-brown surfaces, burnished over the flange. Dateable to the fourth century A.D.

No. 569   Straight-sided dish with upright rim and broad groove below of sandy ware. Grey core and surfaces with a white slip on the interior. Alice Holt Ware, broadly dateable to the third and fourth centuries A.D.

No. 570   Probable jar with upright, thickened rim of sandy grog-tempered ware. Brown-black core and surfaces.

No. 571   Bowl with a well-developed flanged rim of hard, grog-tempered ware. Light grey core and brown-black surfaces with traces of burnishing. Dateable to the fourth century A.D.

No. 572   Dish with straight sides and upright rim of fine, sandy ware. Grey core and surfaces with burnished interior. Alice Holt Ware, Class 6A.4, dateable to the late-third to mid-fourth century A.D.

No. 573   Small jar with everted rim of gritty, grog-tempered ware. Grey-brown core and brown-black surfaces with two rows of stabbed decoration below the rim. Dateable to the fourth century A.D.

No. 574   Large storage jar with heavy, undercut rim of sandy ware. Grey-buff core and orange-grey surfaces with slip-coated exterior. Alice Holt Ware, Class 1C, dateable to the third and fourth centuries A.D.

No. 575   Large storage jar with heavy, undercut rim of sandy ware. Grey core and grey-buff surfaces. Alice Holt Ware, Class 1C and similar to No. 574.

No. 576   Jar with everted rim of gritty, grog-tempered ware. Brown-black core and interior with orange-brown exterior. Traces of burnishing on the inside of the vessel. Dateable to the fourth century A.D.

No. 577   Small jar with everted rim of sandy ware. Black core and grey-black surfaces, burnished inside the rim. Keston Kiln Ware, dateable to *c.* A.D.60–85.

No. 578   Jar with outcurved rim of hard, grog-tempered ware. Grey-black core and surfaces. Dateable to the fourth century A.D.

No. 579   Jar with sharply everted rim in hard, sandy grog-tempered ware. Light grey core with patchy grey surfaces. Dateable to the fourth century A.D.

No. 580   Small jar with everted rim of sandy, grog-tempered ware. Grey-brown core with patchy brown-black surfaces. Dateable to the fourth century A.D.

No. 581   Jar with out-turned rim of grog-tempered ware. Dark grey core with brown-black surfaces. Traces of burnishing inside the rim. Dateable to the fourth century A.D.

No. 582   Jar with outcurved, thickened rim of sandy ware. Light grey core with grey-black surfaces.

No. 583   Small jar with out-turned rim of sandy ware with small red grog inclusions. Grey-brown core and brown-black surfaces.

No. 584   Jar with outcurved rim of sandy ware. Light grey core with patchy grey surfaces and a white slip over and inside the rim. Alice Holt Ware, dateable to the third to fourth century A.D.

No. 585   Jar with outcurved thickened rim of sandy ware. Orange-brown core with light grey-brown surfaces, burnished beneath the rim. There is a narrow cordon on the shoulder. Dateable to the first half of the second century A.D.

No. 586   Small bowl with out-turned, thickened rim and bulbous wall of sandy ware. Orange core with light grey-brown surfaces and burnished exterior. Dateable to the late-first to early-second century A.D.

No. 587   Jar with outcurved rim of sandy ware. Grey-black core, with light grey surfaces and traces of burnished slip over and inside the rim. Alice Holt Ware, dateable to the third to fourth centuries A.D.

No. 588   Jar with everted rim of sandy ware with red grog inclusions. Grey-brown core with grey-black surfaces. Exterior burnished. Dateable to the later third to fourth century A.D.

No. 589   Jar with squared, undercut rim of sandy ware. Light grey core and surfaces with traces of a white slip-coating. Alice Holt Ware, Class 1A.12, dateable to the third century A.D.

No. 590   Narrow-mouthed jar with lobed rim of sandy ware. Grey core and surfaces with traces of dark grey slip. Alice Holt Ware, Class 1A, datable to the third to fourth century A.D.

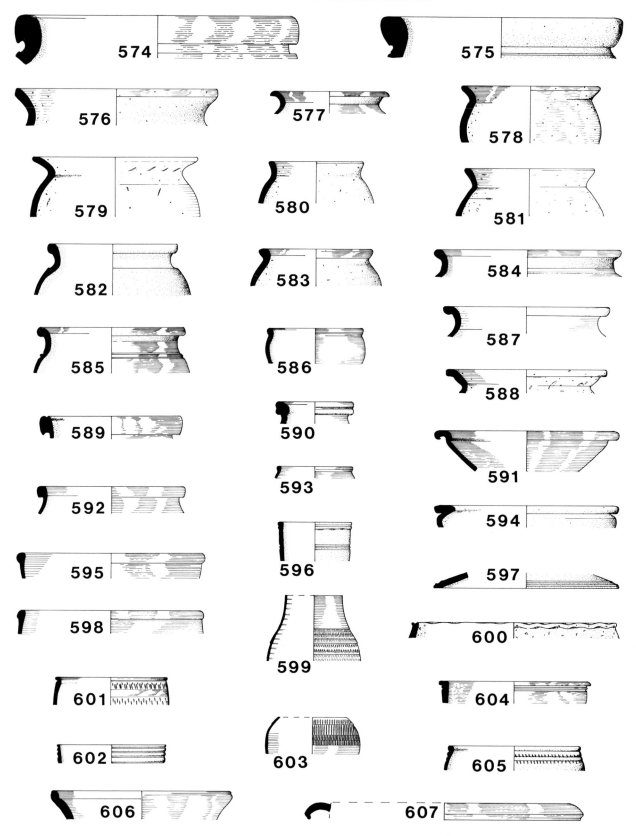

Fig. 76.   *Pottery from Villa Enclosure Ditch, North-West ($\frac{1}{4}$).*

No. 591   Shallow bowl with flanged rim of hard, fine, sandy ware. Blue-grey core and orange surfaces with orange-brown colour-coat. New Forest Ware, Type 61.2, dateable to *c.* A.D.340–370.

No. 592   Jar with upright neck and squared rim of sandy ware. Grey-brown core and grey surfaces with a white slip over the exterior and inside the rim. Alice Holt Ware, Class 1A.6, dateable to the late-second to third century A.D.

No. 593   Beaker with small bead rim of fine sandy fabric. Pink-buff core and surfaces with orange-brown colour-coat. Probably dateable to the third century A.D.

No. 594   Bowl with flanged rim of sandy ware. Light grey core with patchy grey surfaces. This vessel appears to be an Alice Holt Ware strainer pot, Class 5C.1, dateable to the period *c.* A.D.150–250.

No. 595   Bowl with bead rim of sandy ware. Orange-buff core and surfaces with traces of an orange colour-coat. Oxfordshire Ware, Type C.45, dateable to *c.* A.D.270–400.

No. 596   Beaker with an upright, thickened rim of sandy ware. Orange core and surfaces with incised grooves beneath the rim.

No. 597   Lid of sandy ware, with light grey core and patchy grey-brown surfaces.

No. 598   Bowl with bead rim of sandy ware. Pink-orange fabric with orange-brown colour-coat. Oxfordshire Ware, Type 82, dateable to the late-third to fourth century A.D.

No. 599   Body sherd of a rouletted beaker in a thin sandy ware. Light grey-brown fabric with brown-black colour-coat. Dateable to the mid-third to fourth century A.D.

No. 600   A small fragment from an inturned rim in a flint and shell-tempered fabric. The top is decorated with finger-tip impression and this has caused an irregular external thickening to the rim. The sherd has been fired dark grey (N4) throughout. Both surfaces have been wiped smooth with few shell fragments visible. (Fabric E). Pre-Conquest and clearly residual here.

No. 601   Beaker with small bead rim of fine, sandy ware. Orange core and orange-brown surfaces with a zone of rouletted decoration below the rim and on the body.

No. 602   Thin-walled beaker with upright rim of fine, sandy ware. Light grey core and buff surfaces. Exterior decorated with grooves and cordons.

No. 603   Wall sherd from a beaker of fine, sandy ware. Orange-buff core with pale orange-buff surfaces showing signs of a brown colour-coat. The exterior bears rouletted decoration. Oxfordshire Ware, Type C.23 dateable to *c.* A.D.270–400.

No. 604   Small jar or beaker with upright neck and out-turned rim of sandy ware. Orange core and surfaces and traces of a dark red slip. Two horizontal grooves below rim on exterior. Keston Kiln Ware, dateable to *c.* A.D.60–85.

No. 605   Small jar of fine ware beaker with bead rim of slightly sandy ware. Drab orange core and orange-buff surfaces. There are two horizontal cordons below the rim, each with a band of rouletted decorated below.

No. 606   Platter with incurved rim. Fine white fabric with worn grey surfaces. Imported *Terra Nigra*; Camulodunum Form 14. Dateable to *c.* A.D.50–70 and clearly residual in the present context (see Specialist Report, p. 197).

No. 607   Bowl with flanged rim of sandy ware. Grey core with orange surfaces and traces of an orange-red colour-coat. Oxfordshire Ware, probably Type C.47 and dateable to the later third to fourth century A.D.

North-East Ditch of Villa Enclosure, Lower filling (LWB–76–64 and 65).

No. 608   Narrow-mouthed jar with outcurved, squared rim of hard, sandy ware. Orange-pink core and cream-buff surfaces. There is a single raised cordon at the base of the neck with a band of roulette decoration above and below. Similar bands of rouletting occur on the rim and shoulder.

No. 609   Flagon or flask with thickened rim of sandy ware. Orange fabric with traces of a cream slip. Dateable to the late-first to early-second century A.D.

North-East Ditch of Villa Enclosure, Middle filling (LWB–76–50).

No. 610   Base of beaker of fine, smooth ware. Red fabric with dark brown colour-coat, possibly discoloured by burning. Dateable to the mid-third to fourth century A.D.

North-East Ditch of Villa Enclosure, Upper and General fillings (LWB–76–38, 76–61, 76–63, 78–2, 78–34, 78–36, 78–37 and 78–48).

No. 611   Dish with straight sides and upright rim of sandy ware. Orange-brown and grey sandwiched core with patchy grey surfaces. A horizontal groove has been cut below the rim on the exterior. Dateable to the mid-second to mid-third century A.D.

No. 612   Jar or beaker with upright neck and outcurved, thickened rim in a smooth grey fabric with dark

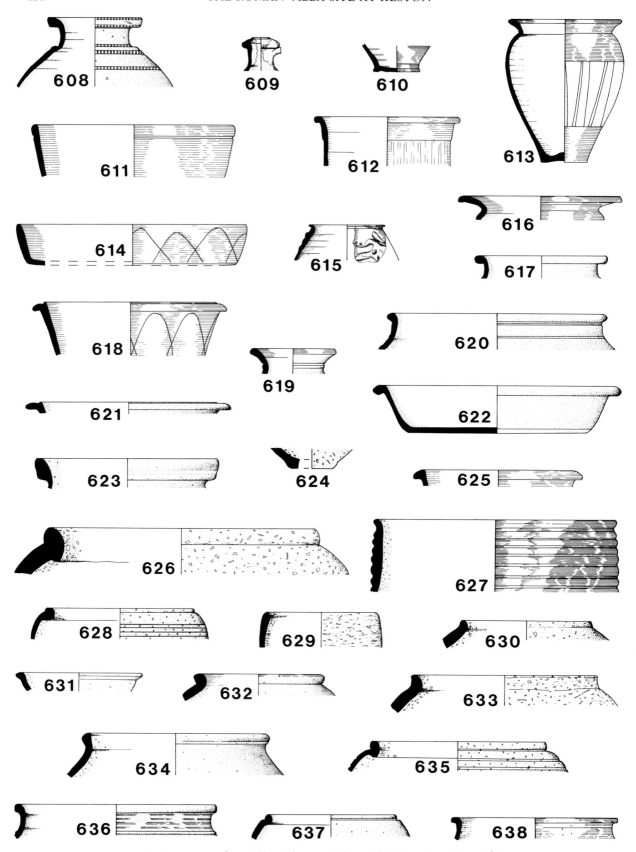

Fig. 77. *Pottery from Villa Enclosure Ditch, North-East and South-East ($\frac{1}{4}$).*

grey-brown abraded surfaces. There is a horizontal groove on the neck with very faint traces of incised vertical decoration below this. Possibly North Kent Marsh Ware, of late-first or second century A.D. date (see also No. 884).

No. 613 Substantially complete jar with a flared rim of sandy ware. Sandwiched red-brown and grey core with patchy light grey surfaces. The body is decorated with pairs of incised vertical lines. Dateable to the mid-second to early third century A.D.

No. 614 Dish with straight sides of sandy ware. Grey-brown core and surfaces. Exterior decorated with burnished overlapping arcs. Dateable to the second century A.D.

No. 615 Probably 'Hunt Cup' with cornice-rim of smooth white ware. Grey colour-coated surfaces with barbotine decoration of uncertain form on the exterior. Nene Valley Ware dateable to the later second to early-third century A.D.

No. 616 Jar with flared rim of sandy ware. Sandwiched orange and brown core with patchy brown surfaces and burnished interior. Dateable to the third century A.D.

No. 617 Jar with flattened rolled rim of sandy ware. Sandwiched brown and light grey core with patchy brown surfaces. Dateable to the late-first to early-second century A.D.

No. 618 Dish with flanged rim of sandy ware. Brown-black core and surfaces with burnished interior and burnished arc decoration on the exterior. Dateable to the third century A.D.

No. 619 Narrow-mouthed jar or flask with everted rim of sandy ware. Light grey core and surfaces with a narrow cordon on the neck.

No. 620 Large jar with slightly outcurved, rolled rim of sandy ware. Buff-brown core and grey-brown surfaces with an incised double horizontal groove beneath the rim. Probably dateable to the third century A.D.

No. 621 Dish with flanged rim of sandy ware. Grey-brown core with patchy grey-buff surfaces. Dateable to the third century A.D.

No. 622 Dish with bead rim of hard sandy fabric. Sandwiched light and dark grey core with dark grey surfaces. Dateable to the late-second century A.D.

No. 623 Jar with squared rim of coarse, sandy ware. Yellow-cream core with cream surfaces. 'Cream Sandy Ware', dateable to the fourth century A.D.

No. 624 A flat base in sandy flint and organic-tempered fabric. The surfaces are smooth and sandy with few flints visible. The sherd is dark grey (N4) with a grey-brown (5YR5/3) external margin. (Fabric B). Pre-Conquest and clearly residual here.

No. 625 Dish with bead rim of hard, sandy ware with some large quartz inclusions. Grey-brown core and dark grey surfaces. Dateable to the mid to late-second century A.D.

South-East Ditch of Villa Enclosure, Lower filling (LWB–X24–12, Z23–8, DD21–6 and DD21–8).

No. 626 Large storage jar with heavy, internally thickened bead rim. Coarse shell-tempered ware with light orange-buff core and orange-buff surfaces. Later first to early-second century A.D.

No. 627 Large, straight-sided jar with small, out-turned rim in hard, grog-tempered fabric. Light grey core and dark grey burnished surfaces. Below the rim the wall of the vessel exhibits a series of well-formed horizontal cordons, giving the vessel a 'corrugated' appearance.

The overall form of this vessel is characteristic of 'Belgic' material in south-east England, although the type is not particularly common. The type itself may be comparable to Thompson's Group B4–1, dateable to the period either side of the Roman Conquest. 'Belgic' grog-tempered wares in general do not occur especially frequently in this part of West Kent. See No. 520 for another probable 'Belgic' form from the Keston site.

No. 628 Small jar with internally thickened bead rim of hard, fine, shell-tempered ware. Blue-grey core with pink-orange surfaces. Dateable to the later first to early-second century A.D.

No. 629 Small, hand-made cup or bowl with upright, slightly thickened rim of coarse, shell-tempered ware. Brown-black core and surfaces. Probably pre-Conquest.

No. 630 Narrow-mouthed jar with small, upright rim of hard, shell-tempered ware. Dark grey core and orange-brown surfaces. Dateable to the first century A.D.

No. 631 Small shallow bowl with bead rim of sandy ware. Orange core and surfaces, heavily abraded.

South-East Ditch of Villa Enclosure, Middle filling (LWB–BB22–7).

No. 632 Narrow-mouthed jar with bead rim of coarse sandy ware. Red-brown core and surfaces. Keston Kiln Ware, dateable to c. A.D.60–85.

No. 633 Jar with slightly everted bead rim of hard shell-tempered ware. Dark grey core and patchy orange-brown surfaces.

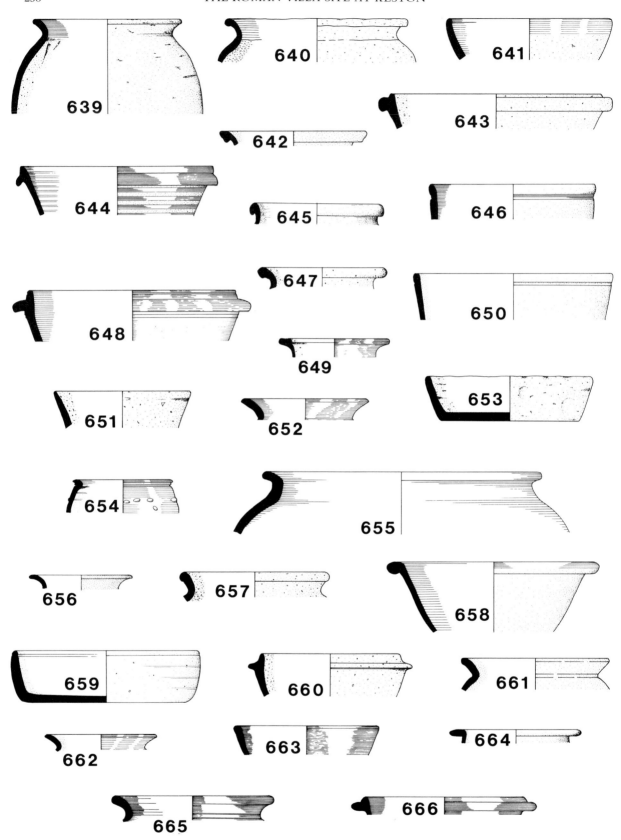

Fig. 78.   *Pottery from West Masonry Building and North Timber Building* ($\frac{1}{4}$).

South-East Ditch of Villa Enclosure, Upper filling (LWB–Z23–5, BB22–6 and CC21–8).

No. 634   Jar with out-turned, thickened rim of sandy ware. Grey core and orange surfaces. Dateable to the late-first to early-second century A.D.

No. 635   Jar with internally thickened bead rim of sparsely shell-tempered ware. Grey-buff core and surfaces, with two horizontal grooves on the shoulder. Dateable to the later first to early-second century A.D.

No. 636   Jar with everted rim of sandy ware. Grey-buff core and grey surfaces showing signs of burnishing.

No. 637   Small jar with bead rim of sandy ware. Blue-grey core with grey-black surface. Dateable to the later first to early-second century A.D.

No. 638   Jar with out-turned rim of hard, sandy ware. Sandwiched light grey and brown core with dark grey-brown surfaces. Dateable to the early-second century A.D.

West Masonry Building, Hearth Pit (F.225) (LWB–B18–6).

No. 639   Jar with everted rim of hard, grog-tempered ware. Grey core and grey-brown surfaces. Dateable to the fourth century A.D.

No. 640   Jar with everted rim of hard, coarse, grog-tempered ware. Brown core and grey surfaces. Dateable to the fourth century A.D.

No. 641   Straight-sided bowl with simple upright rim of hard, sandy ware. Light grey core and cream-brown surfaces, with a band of burnishing extending below the rim on the exterior.

West Masonry Building, Fill of Cellar (LWB–C20–2).

No. 642   Jar with outcurved, squared and undercut rim of fine, sandy ware. Brown core with orange-brown surfaces. Probably dateable to the late-second to early-third century A.D.

No. 643   Dish with heavy flanged rim of hard, sandy ware. Light grey-brown core, cream-brown interior surface and dark grey exterior. Probably dateable to the late-third century A.D.

Soil over West Masonry Building (LWB–A25–2 and B27–2).

No. 644   Dish with flanged rim of sandy ware. Grey-buff core and surfaces. Dateable to the later third to fourth century A.D.

No. 645   Jar with undercut, bead rim of sandy ware. Light grey core and blue-grey surfaces. Probably dateable to the third century A.D.

No. 646   Dish or bowl with upright rim of sandy ware. Yellow-buff core and surfaces, decorated with double incised lines below the rim. Dateable to the third century A.D.

No. 647   Small jar with rolled rim of coarse, gritty ware. Brown-black core and surfaces. Probably dateable to the third century A.D.

No. 648   Dish with flanged rim of sandy ware. Light grey core with blue-grey surfaces and traces of slip over the rim. Alice Holt Ware, Class 5B, dateable to the later third to fourth centuries A.D.

No. 649   Probable small jar with flanged rim of hard, slightly sandy ware. Orange-brown core and interior surface with dark grey exterior.

No. 650   Bowl with straight sides and upright rim of hard, sandy ware. Grey core and grey-brown surfaces. There is a slight horizontal groove on the exterior below the rim. Dateable to the third to fourth century A.D.

No. 651   An out-turned rim in sandy, flint-tempered fabric. The surfaces are smooth, with few flints visible and the sherd has been fired dark grey (N3) throughout. (Form 26, fabric B). Pre-Conquest and clearly residual here.

No. 652   Jar with flared rim of sandy ware. Grey-buff core with patchy grey-brown surfaces and white slip on the inner rim. Alice Holt Ware dateable to the later third and fourth centuries A.D.

North Timber Building, Beam Slot F.949 (LWB–76–221).

No. 653   Dish with straight sides and simple upright rim of hard, grog-tempered ware. Grey-brown core and surfaces. Dateable to the fourth century A.D.

No. 654   Upper part of a decorated beaker of hard, white ware with dark grey slip on both surfaces. Traces of barbotine decoration suggest that this is probably a 'Hunt Cup'. Nene Valley Ware dateable to the later second to early-third century A.D.

North Timber Building, Filling of Main Post Pits (LWB–76–205 and 77–235).

No. 655   Large storage jar with everted rim of hard, gritty ware. Orange-brown core with dark grey-black surfaces. Exterior lightly burnished. Dateable to the later first to early-second century A.D. (Post-hole 17).

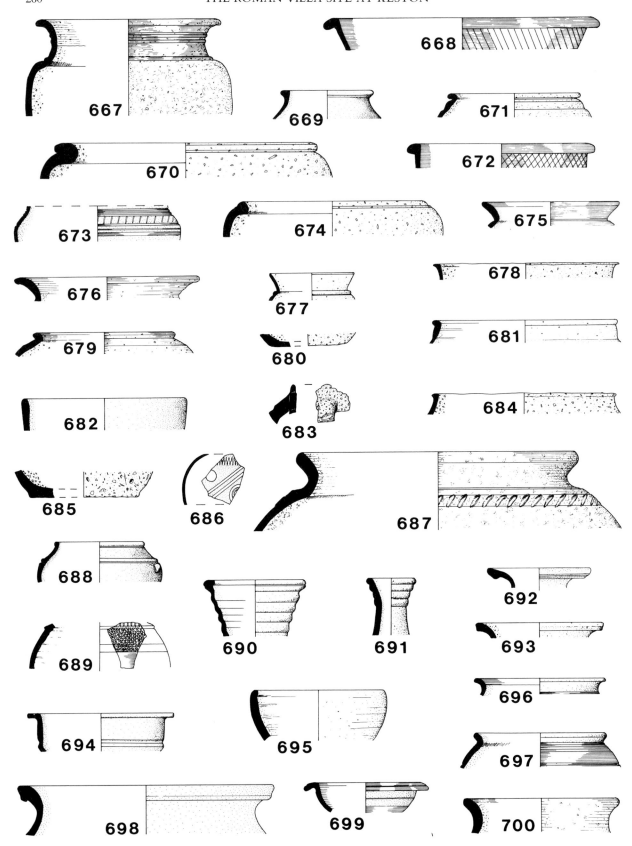

Fig. 79.   *Pottery from Roman Fences and South Tank* (¼).

No. 656   Small jar or beaker with outcurved rim of hard, sandy ware. Light grey core and slightly darker grey surfaces. Dateable to the second century A.D. (Post-hole 20).

North Timber Building, Filling of Main Post-pipes (LWB–76–169, 77–230 and 77–257).

No. 657   Jar with out-turned rim of coarse, gritty, grog-tempered ware. Dark grey-brown core and dark grey surface. Dateable to the fourth century A.D. (Post-hole 12).

No. 658   Bowl with heavy bead rim of sandy ware. Grey core and surfaces with burnished interior. Dateable to the early-third century A.D. (Post-hole 19).

No. 659   Dish with slightly convex sides and upright rim of hard, fine, sandy ware. Cream fabric with grey-brown slip-coated surfaces. New Forest Ware dateable to the late-third to fourth century A.D. (Post-hole 12).

No. 660   Bowl with flanged rim of coarse, gritty, grog-tempered ware. Dark grey core with light orange-brown surfaces. Dateable to the fourth century A.D. (Post-hole 12).

No. 661   Jar with out-turned rim of hard, sandy ware. Light grey core and slightly darker grey surfaces. Dateable to the mid-second to third century A.D. (Post-hole 12).

No. 662   Small thin-walled jar with everted rim of sandy ware. Hard, grey core with orange-brown surfaces, coated with a dark grey slip. (Post-hole 18).

Soil Over North Timber Building (LWB–76–37).

No. 663   Dish with straight sides of sandy ware. Grey and brown sandwiched core and grey-black surfaces. Dateable to the third to fourth century A.D.

No. 664   Dish or bowl with flanged rim of sandy ware. Grey-buff core and patchy buff surfaces. Dateable to the second century A.D.

No. 665   Jar with everted rim of sandy ware. Light grey core and surfaces. Dateable to the late-second to early-third century A.D.

No. 666   Bowl with flanged rim of sandy ware. Brown-black core and surfaces. Dateable to the later third to fourth century A.D.

Centre Fence, Filling of Post-pipes (LWB–76–83 and 76–86).

No. 667   Jar with everted rim of soft, grog-tempered ware. Grey core and dark brown surfaces with burnished shoulder and neck. The exterior is decorated with a double cordon on the neck and a single cordon on the shoulder. Dateable to the first century A.D. (F.840).

No. 668   Dish with a well-formed bead rim of hard, sandy ware. Dark grey core and dark grey surfaces showing signs of light burnishing. Faint traces of burnished line decoration on the exterior and top of rim. Dateable to the mid to late-second century A.D.

South Fence, Filling of Post-hole F.306 (LWB–N20–4).

No. 669   Beaker with small, thickened, out-turned rim of hard, sandy ware. Cream core and surfaces.

East Fence, Filling of Post-pits (LWB–P19–4, P21–8, P21–11, P22–6 and P23–9).

No. 670   Storage jar with internally thickened bead rim of shell-tempered ware. Grey core with orange surfaces. Dateable to the later first to early-second century A.D. (F.408).

No. 671   Small jar with flattened bead rim and rippled shoulder of grog-tempered ware. Grey-brown core with orange-brown surfaces. (F.411).

No. 672   Dish with bead rim of sandy ware. Brown-black core and surfaces, with burnished lattice decoration under the rim. Dateable to the later second century A.D. (F.411).

No. 673   Wall sherd from a probable carinated bowl of hard, sandy ware. Blue-grey core and grey-black surfaces. Burnished vertical lines occur on the shoulder between zones of horizontal burnishing. Dateable to the late-first to mid-second century A.D. (F.411).

No. 674   Jar with internally thickened bead rim of hard, grog-tempered ware with some shell inclusions. Dark grey core and orange-brown surfaces. Probably dateable to the later first to early-second century A.D. (F.412).

No. 675   Jar with outcurved rim of hard, sandy ware. Dark grey core with grey surfaces and a white slip on the exterior. Alice Holt Ware, dateable to the later third to fourth century A.D. (F.414).

No. 676   Jar with outcurved rim of fairly soft, grog-tempered ware. Mottled grey-brown core with light orange-brown surfaces. Dateable to the later first to early-second century A.D. (F.414).

No. 677   Poppy-head beaker with out-turned rim and well-formed cordon on the neck of smooth ware. Dark grey core with grey surfaces. A product of the North Kent Marsh Kilns and dateable to the second century A.D. (F.416).

East Fence, Filling of Post-pipes (LWB–P19–5, P23–7 and 78–73).

No. 678   An out-turned rim with externally projecting flat top in flint-tempered fabric. The sherd is black (N2) throughout with a brown (5YR6/6) patch on the exterior. Both surfaces have been wiped, with flints protruding. (Form 30, fabric A). Pre-Conquest. (F.409).

No. 679   Narrow-mouthed jar with flattened bead rim of grog-tempered ware. Grey-brown core and surfaces. The surfaces are burnished. Dateable to the first to early-second century A.D. (F.416).

No. 680   A fragment of a flat base in flint-tempered fabric. The wall surfaces are dark grey (N4) and smooth with few flints visible. The core is dark brown (5YR4/3). Beneath the base numerous flint grits are visible. (Fabric A). Pre-Conquest. (F.1557).

West Fence, General filling of Post-holes (LWB–O20–5 and 6 and P22–3).

No. 681   Jar with slightly inturned bead rim of sandy ware. Sandwiched orange-brown and grey core with patchy brown surfaces. (F.433).

No. 682   Straight-sided dish or bowl of coarse, sandy ware. Grey-black core with buff surfaces. (F.433).

No. 683   A handle in flint-tempered fabric. The surfaces are brown to dark grey (5YR6/6–N3) and wiped with flint inclusions visible and protruding. The core is black (N2). Fracture marks at the point where the handle joins the wall indicate that the handle was added as a coil of clay pressed into a hole in the wall. A broad diagonal impression on the top of the handle may represent deliberate decoration. (Form 41, fabric A). Pre-Conquest. (F.405).

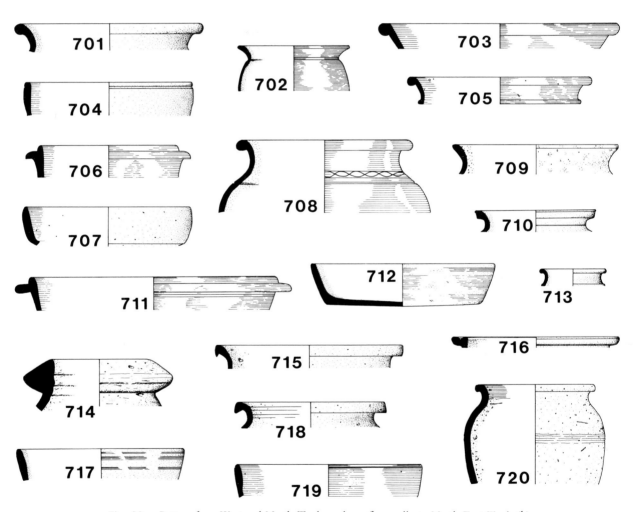

Fig. 80.   *Pottery from West and North Tanks and overflow gully to North-East Tank ($\frac{1}{4}$).*

No. 684   An inturned rim with externally expanded flat top in flint-tempered fabric. The sherd is small and the diameter uncertain. Both surfaces are worn and flints protrude. The surfaces are light orange (5YR7/6) and the core is light grey (N8). (Form 12, fabric A). Pre-Conquest. (F.405).

No. 685   A flat base in flint-tempered fabric. The sherd has been fired grey (N5) throughout. Both surfaces are worn with flints protruding. (Fabric A). Pre-Conquest. (F.405).

North Fence, Filling of Post-hole F.912. (LWB–76—164).

No. 686   Wall sherd from a decorated beaker in a hard, fine sandy fabric. Sandwiched grey and dark red core with dark grey slip on both surfaces. The exterior surface is decorated with dots, lines and circles in cream slip with a horizontal rouletted band above. Dateable to the late-second to third century A.D.

Filling of South Tank (LWB–J34–13, J35–4 and I35–4).

No. 687   Large storage jar with everted rim of hard, grog-tempered ware. Mottled grey core and orange-buff surfaces with a band of angled slashes on the shoulder. This is Patch Grove Ware, very common in West Kent and may be dated to the later first to the end of the second century A.D.

No. 688   Beaker with small bead rim of sandy ware. Buff core and surfaces. The vessel has a raised cordon on the shoulder with an irregular applied knob below, probably accidental. Keston Kiln Ware, dateable to *c.* A.D.60–85.

No. 689   Decorated body sherd of a beaker in sandy ware. Grey-brown core with orange-buff surfaces. Rouletted decoration on the exterior.

No. 690   Large ring-necked flagon of sandy ware. Light grey core with grey-buff surfaces. Southwark Type 1B.4 (Ref. 250), dateable to the first half of the second century A.D.

No. 691   Small ring-necked flagon of sandy ware. Blue-grey core and surfaces. Southwark Type 1B.6 (Ref. 251), dateable to the first half of the second century A.D.

No. 692   Flagon or flask with out-turned slighly hooked rim of hard, sandy ware. Dark grey core and interior surface with mottled light grey and brown exterior.

No. 693   Small jar with everted rim of sandy ware. Light grey core and surfaces.

No. 694   Bowl with flanged rim of hard, sandy ware. Orange core and orange-buff surfaces. There is a broad groove and a horizontal cordon at the base of the neck and a deeply incised groove on top of the rim. Dateable to the late-first to early-second century A.D.

No. 695   Bowl with curving wall and upright rim of sandy ware. Grey core and surfaces. Dateable to the fourth century A.D., but intrusive in this context.

No. 696   Small jar with everted rim of sandy ware. Orange-buff core with yellow-buff surfaces. Dateable to the late-first to early-second century A.D.

No. 697   Small jar with short everted rim of hard, sandy ware. Orange-brown core with grey-brown surfaces. Horizontal burnished lines decorate the neck and there is a groove on the shoulder. Dateable to the late-first to early-second century A.D.

No. 698   Large jar with outcurved, squared and slightly undercut rim of hard, coarse, sandy ware. Light grey core and cream-yellow surfaces. This sherd appears to belong to the 'Cream Sandy Wares', dateable to the fourth century A.D. It must be intrusive in its present context.

No. 699   Small bowl with slightly down-turned flanged rim of hard, sandy ware. Buff core and surfaces. The sherd is somewhat distorted and the vessel must have been a 'second' if not a 'waster'. Keston Kiln Ware, dateable to *c.* A.D.60–85.

No. 700   Jar with everted rim of hard, grog-tempered ware. Mottled grey core and buff-orange surfaces. A ware related to the 'Patch Grove' series, dated to the later first to second century A.D.

Filling of West Tank 1 (LWB–F19–2, F19–4, F19–5 and F19–7).

No. 701   Jar with outcurved, thickened rim of sandy ware. Light grey core and grey-brown surfaces. Probably third century A.D.

No. 702   Small, thin-walled beaker with flared rim of sandy ware. Grey-buff core with patchy grey-brown surfaces. Dateable to the mid-second century A.D.

No. 703   Dish with bead rim of sandy ware. Buff core with patchy brown-black surfaces. Dateable to the mid to late-second century A.D.

No. 704   Dish or bowl with upright rim of sandy ware. Grey-buff core with buff-orange surfaces and incised horizontal groove below the rim. Dateable to the second century A.D.

No. 705   Jar with outcurved bead rim of hard, sandy ware. Sandwiched light grey and orange core with light grey-brown surfaces. Traces of a raised cordon survive at the base of the neck.

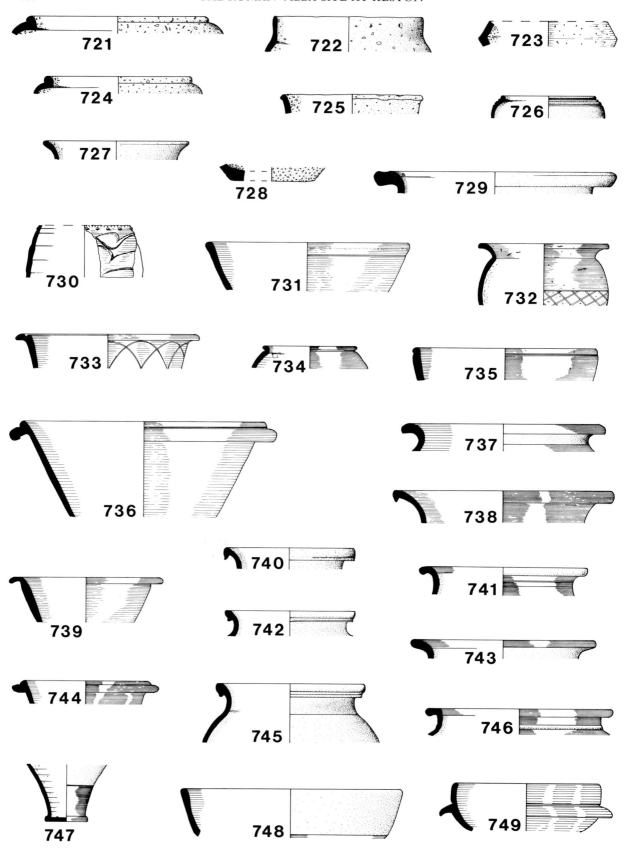

Fig. 81.   *Pottery from soil deposits between Lower and Upper East Metalling and Ditch 21a* ($\frac{1}{4}$).

No. 706   Dish with flanged rim in hard, coarse sandy fabric. Dark grey core and grey surfaces. Rim and internal surface burnished. Dateable to the late-third or fourth century A.D.

Filling of West Tank 2 (LWB–F19–9).

No. 707   Dish with straight sides and upright rim of sandy ware. Orange-brown core with grey-brown surfaces. Dateable to the third to fourth century A.D.

No. 708   Jar with slightly outcurved bead rim of hard, sandy ware. Brown core and grey surfaces; lightly burnished on the exterior and with a burnished double wavy line decorating the base of the neck. Late-second to third century A.D.

No. 709   Jar with everted rim of grog-tempered ware. Mottled grey core with buff-orange surfaces. Patch Grove Ware, dateable to the later first to second century A.D.

Filling of West Tank 3 (LWB–F19–3).

No. 710   Small jar with everted, squared rim of sandy ware. Light grey core with blue-grey surfaces. Dateable to the mid-second to third century A.D.

No. 711   Bowl with flanged rim of sandy ware. Grey-brown core with grey-black surfaces. Dateable to the later third to fourth century A.D.

No. 712   Dish with straight sides and upright rim of sandy ware. Brown-black and grey-brown surfaces with burnished arc decoration on the underside of the base. Dateable to the late-second to mid-third century A.D.

Filling of the North Tank (LWB–76–136, 76–144 and 77–219).

No. 713   Small jar or beaker with everted rim of sandy ware. Orange-brown core with grey-brown surfaces.

No. 714   Amphora rim of sandy ware with grey core and buff-orange surfaces. This type of rim is typical of the South Spanish amphorae (Dressel Form 20 etc.).

No. 715   Jar with outcurved, hooked rim of sandy ware. Light grey core and orange-brown surfaces. Dateable to the late-second to early-third century A.D.

No. 716   Probable bowl with deeply recessed rim of sandy ware. Grey-buff core with blue-grey surfaces. Dateable to the late-third to fourth century A.D.

No. 717   Dish with upright rim of sandy ware. Grey-brown core and surfaces. Dateable to the third century A.D.

No. 718   Jar with outcurved hooked rim of sandy ware. Buff-brown core with patchy grey-brown surfaces. Dateable to the late-second to mid-third century A.D.

No. 719   Dish with upright rim of sandy ware. Grey-buff core with patchy grey surfaces. Dateable to the third century A.D.

Filling of Overflow Channel, North-East Tank (LWB–77–261).

No. 720   Jar with everted rim of hard, grog-tempered ware. Grey core with grey-brown surfaces. Dateable to the fourth century A.D.

Soil Deposits between the Upper and Lower East Metalling (LWB–X23–8, X24–11, Z22–6, AA23–6, AA23–7 and BB22–5).

No. 721   Jar with bead rim of shell-tempered ware. Brown core and brown-black surfaces. Dateable to the later first to early-second century A.D.

No. 722   Crudely-made jar or bowl with upright rim of coarse, gritty ware with some flint inclusions. Orange-grey core and patchy orange and grey-brown surfaces. (Fabric B). Pre-Conquest.

No. 723   A carinated shoulder in sandy flint-tempered fabric. The surfaces are red-brown (2.5YR5/6) and are now worn but appear to have been smooth with few flints visible. The core is dark grey (N4). (Fabric B). Pre-Conquest.

No. 724   Small jar with bead rim of shell-tempered ware. Grey-brown core and buff-brown surfaces. Dateable to the later first to early-second century A.D.

No. 725   A small fragment of an everted rim in flint-tempered fabric. The surfaces are dark grey (N3) and the core dark brown (5YR4/2). The internal surface is worn. The external surface is wiped smooth with few flints visible. (Form 27, fabric A). Pre-Conquest.

No. 726   Small bowl with bead rim of sandy ware. Grey-buff core and surfaces with incised grooves below the rim. Dateable to the later first to early-second century A.D.

No. 727   Jar with everted rim of sandy ware. Grey core and red-brown surfaces.

No. 728   A flat base in flint-tempered fabric. Both surfaces are worn and flints protrude. The internal surface is dark red (10YR5/8). The external surface is dark grey (N3) and the core black (N2). (Fabric A). Pre-Conquest.

Late-Roman Ditch 21a, middle filling (LWB–77–225).

No. 729   Bowl with a large flanged rim of sandy ware. Light grey core and patchy grey surfaces. Alice Holt Ware dateable to the later third to fourth century A.D.

No. 730   Wall sherd of a beaker of fine, sandy ware. Cream-white fabric with blue-black colour-coat. The exterior is decorated with rouletting and barbotine foliage and dots. Nene Valley Ware, dateable to the second to third century A.D.

No. 731   Straight-sided dish with upright rim of sandy ware. Sandwiched light grey and light brown core with burnished grey-brown surfaces. Dateable to c. A.D.140–240.

No. 732   Jar with everted rim of coarse, sandy ware. Grey-black core and surfaces. The neck and shoulder are burnished with burnished lattice decoration below. Dateable to c. A.D.150–240.

No. 733   Bowl with flanged rim of coarse, sandy ware. Grey-black core and surfaces. Exterior burnished and decorated with incised arcs. Dateable to the third century A.D.

Late-Roman Ditch 21a, Upper filling (LWB–76–46, 76–57, 77–218 and 77–220).

No. 734   Fine-ware beaker with out-turned, thickened rim of hard white ware. Dark grey colour-coat. Nene Valley Ware dateable to the second or third century A.D.

No. 735   Upright dish with grooved bead rim of sandy ware. Grey-brown core and grey-black surfaces with burnished interior. Dateable to the later second century A.D.

No. 736   Large bowl with flanged rim, about one third complete. Hard sandy ware with light brown core and grey surfaces. Top of flange slightly burnished. Dateable to the late-third to fourth century A.D.

No. 737   Jar with everted rim of sandy ware. Orange-brown core with patchy brown-black surfaces.

No. 738   Jar or bowl with outcurved, hooked rim of fine, sandy ware. Yellow-orange core with buff-yellow surfaces. Traces of an orange-red colour-coat survive. Probably third century or later.

No. 739   Small bowl with flanged rim of gritty ware. Grey-brown core with brown-black surfaces showing signs of burnishing.

No. 740   Jar with outcurved, hooked rim of sandy ware. Grey core and burnt grey-black surfaces. Dateable to the later second to mid-third century A.D.

No. 741   Jar with everted rim of sandy ware. Light grey core and patchy grey surfaces. Probably Alice Holt Ware and dateable to the third to fourth century A.D.

No. 742   Jar with outcurved lobed rim of sandy ware. Orange-brown core with patchy brown-black surfaces. Dateable to the late-second to mid-third century A.D.

No. 743   Jar with flared rim of sandy ware. Light grey core and surfaces, burnished inside the rim. Alice Holt Ware, dateable to the later third to fourth century A.D.

No. 744   Small bowl with flanged rim of sandy ware. Light grey core and medium grey surfaces. There is a deep groove in the upper surface of the flange. Dateable to the later third to fourth century A.D.

No. 745   Jar with outcurved, hooked rim of sandy ware. Brown-black core and surfaces with an incised horizontal groove on the shoulder. Dateable to the late-second to mid-third century A.D.

No. 746   Jar with flanged rim of sandy ware. Grey-brown core with grey-black surfaces.

No. 747   Base of beaker of thin, fine sandy ware. Orange core with dark orange-brown slip-coating on both surfaces and a zone of dark grey slip-coating on the upper part of the exterior. Dateable to the third century A.D.

No. 748   Dish with straight sides and simple upright rim of hard, sandy ware. Grey core with dark grey surfaces. Dateable to the mid-second to early-third century A.D.

No. 749   Bowl with flanged rim in hard, fine sandy ware. Orange-red core and surfaces. There is no sign of a surface slip and this piece is not obviously an Oxfordshire kiln product, despite its close similarity in form to the common Type C51 bowl. Dateable to the later second to fourth century A.D.

Late-Roman Recut, Ditch 21b, Lower filling (LWB–77–224).

No. 750   Jar with heavy, flattened bead rim of sandy ware. Orange core and patchy grey-brown surfaces showing signs of burnishing.

No. 751   Decorated wall sherd from a 'Hunt Cup' of fine white ware. Dark grey slip-coating. The exterior shows the rear portion of an animal above a band of rouletting. Nene Valley Ware, dateable to the later second to early-third century A.D.

No. 752   Small beaker with bead rim of thin, fine sandy ware. Pink-orange fabric with glossy green-brown colour-coat. Dateable to the third century A.D.

Late-Roman Recut, Ditch 21b, Middle filling (LWB–77–231 and 77–249).

No. 753   Flask with flared rim of sandy ware. Buff-grey core and surfaces with traces of a black slip. Possibly Alice Holt Ware, dateable to the third to fourth century A.D.

No. 754   Jar with out-turned rim of coarse, sandy ware with occasional inclusions of flint grit. Dark grey core with light grey interior surface and orange-red exterior. There are traces of incised decoration on the lower rim in the form of angled slashes.

Late Roman Recut, Ditch 21b, Upper filling (LWB–77–205, 77–215, 77–221, 77–222, 77–223 and 77–251).

No. 755   Bowl with flanged rim of sandy ware. Grey-black core and surfaces with burnished arcs on the exterior. Dateable to the third century A.D.

No. 756   Dish or bowl with small bead rim of fine, sandy ware. Orange fabric with traces of an orange-red slip, rather worn. Probably Oxfordshire Ware of Types 44–46, dateable to the late-third to fourth century A.D.

No. 757   Beaker with cornice rim of hard, fine, slightly sandy ware. White core with dark grey slip over both surfaces. The exterior shows traces of barbotine decoration of uncertain form. Nene Valley Ware and possibly part of a 'Hunt Cup', of later second to early-third century date.

No. 758   Bowl with flanged rim of coarse sandy ware. Grey core with dark grey, lightly burnished interior and orange-brown exterior. Dateable to the later third to fourth century A.D.

No. 759   Bowl with flanged rim of smooth cream-white ware. Orange-brown slip-coated surfaces, somewhat worn. Dateable to the later third to fourth century A.D.

No. 760   Base of small globular beaker of sandy ware. Pink-orange core with brown-black surfaces coated with a dark brown slip. Dateable to the third century A.D.

No. 761   Bowl with flanged rim of sandy ware. Dark grey core and surfaces. Traces of burnishing on the upper part of the flange. Dateable to the later third to fourth century A.D.

No. 762   Base of an imitation Gallo-Belgic platter with a raised footring of hard, sandy ware. Dark grey-black core and underside and red-brown upper surface. The upper surface bears a rouletted band of decoration consisting of eight or nine rows of dots set between two concentric grooves. Keston Kiln Ware, dateable to c. A.D. 60–85.

No. 763   Beaker with 'collared' rim of thin, fine sandy ware with orange core and orange-brown colour-coat. Dateable to the third century A.D.

No. 764   Dish with flanged rim of sandy ware with light grey core and surfaces. Probably Alice Holt Ware, dateable to the later third to fourth century A.D.

No. 765   Dish or bowl with heavy bead rim of sandy ware with grey-black core and surfaces. Dateable to the later second century A.D.

No. 766   Base and wall of beaker in fine, thin sandy ware. Pale blue-grey core and brown-black colour-coat. Dateable to the third century A.D.

No. 767   Bowl with flanged rim of coarse, sandy ware. Dark grey-brown core with grey-black surfaces showing signs of burnishing and traces of burnished arcs on the exterior. Later second to third century A.D.

No. 768   Jar with everted, squared rim of sandy ware with grey-brown core and brown-black surfaces. Dateable to the late-second to third century A.D.

No. 769   Bowl or dish with slightly out-turned rim of sandy ware. Orange-buff core and grey-black surfaces with an incised line under the rim. Dateable to the mid-second to third century A.D.

No. 770   Large bowl with bead rim of sandy ware. Grey-brown core and patchy brown-black surfaces with traces of burnishing. Dateable to the second half of the second century A.D.

Late-Roman Ditch 7 (LWB–78–24, 78–25, 78–39 and 78–45).

No. 771   Dish or bowl with flanged rim of grog-tempered ware. Grey-brown core and surfaces. Dateable to the fourth century A.D.

No. 772   Small jar or beaker with outcurved, slightly beaded rim of coarse, sandy ware. Grey core and surfaces with traces of an external cream-white slip extending over the rim. Possibly Alice Holt Ware of late-third to fourth century date.

No. 773   Large jar with flared rim of coarse, gritty, grog-tempered ware. Light grey core and dark grey-black surfaces. Dateable to the fourth century A.D.

No. 774   Dish with straight sides and simple, upright rim of hard, sandy ware. Dark grey core and dark grey-black surfaces with an external horizontal groove below the rim. Dateable to the mid-second to mid-third century A.D.

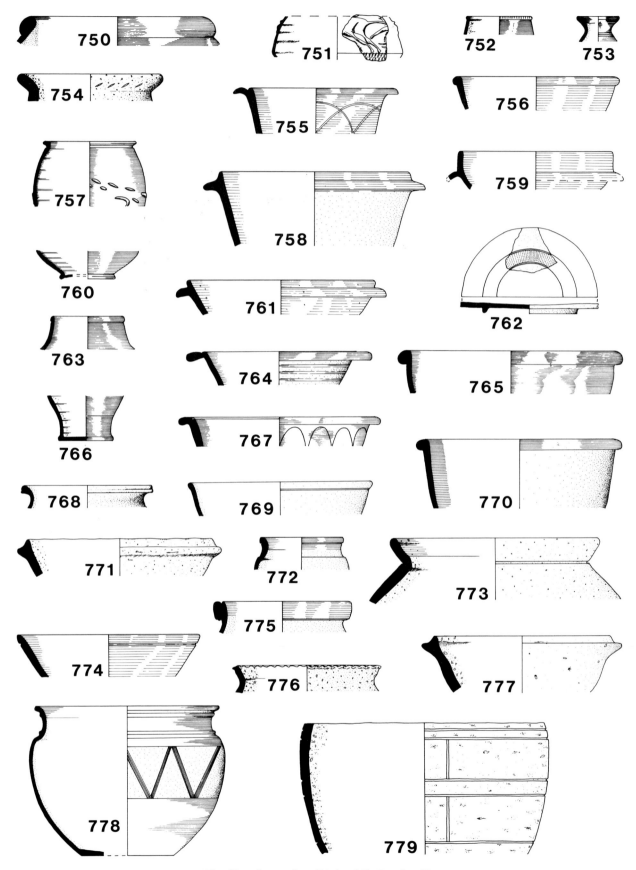

Fig. 82. *Pottery from Ditches 21b, 7 and 1 (¼).*

No. 775   Jar with squared, slightly undercut rim of sandy ware. Grey core and surfaces with traces of a worn grey slip on the upper part of the rim. Alice Holt Ware, Class 1C.5, dated A.D. 300–350.

No. 776   An everted rim in flint-tempered fabric. The sherd is small and the angle and diameter are uncertain. The top of the rim is decorated with diagonal finger-tip impressions. Both surfaces are worn with flints protruding. The internal surface is grey-brown (7.5YR6/4). The external surface is light grey (N5) and the core dark grey (N3). (Form 31, fabric A). Pre-Conquest.

Late-Roman Ditch 1 (LWB–77–9 and 77–12).

No. 777   Crudely-made bowl with flanged rim of grog-tempered fabric with occasional white flint grit inclusions. Light grey core and surfaces. Dateable to the fourth century A.D.

No. 778   Globular jar with outcurved rim of fine, sandy ware. Sandwiched light grey and brown core with dark brown interior surface and dark grey exterior. Exterior decorated with a raised cordon below the rim and at the base of the neck, and there is a band of burnished angled lines around the body. Keston Kiln Ware, dateable to c. A.D.60–85 and clearly residual here.

No. 779   Jar with simple, upright, flat-topped rim of hard, grog-tempered ware. Grey core and dull orange surfaces; seemingly a Patch Grove type ware. The exterior of the vessel is decorated with incised, horizontal and vertical grooves, dividing the wall into a series of plain rectangular panels. This is an unusual vessel for which no local parallels are known. Probably first or second century A.D.

Soil over South Masonry Building (LWB–F33–2, F34–6, G33–2, G34–5, H33–2, H33–4, H34–5, I35–2, I35–3, J34–2, J34–6, J35–2, J35–3, J36–6, K33–3 and L34–2).

No. 780   Large, plain storage jar, probably hand-made, of hard, coarse, grog-tempered ware. The rim has been formed by adding a roughly applied strip of clay to the top of the vessel. Orange-brown core and interior surface with buff-brown exterior. Dateable to the fourth century A.D.

No. 781   Jar with everted rim of hard, grog-tempered ware. Light grey-brown core and patchy dark grey surfaces. On the exterior surface, the neck and shoulder of the vessel are burnished and there is a zone of irregular burnished lattice decoration below this. Dateable to the fourth century A.D.

No. 782   Large jar with thickened, everted rim of sandy ware. Grey-brown core and grey-black surfaces. Probably third century A.D.

No. 783   Bowl with flanged rim of sandy ware. Grey-brown core and grey-black surfaces, decorated with burnished horizontal lines. Later third to fourth century A.D.

No. 784   Large jar with outcurved, squared rim of hard, coarse, sandy ware. Light cream-grey core and cream-yellow surfaces. 'Cream Sandy Ware', dateable to the fourth century A.D.

No. 785   Bowl with flanged rim of sandy ware with buff core and burnished, grey-black surfaces. Later third to fourth century A.D.

No. 786   Wall sherd from a large jar of hard, coarse, sandy ware. Light grey core and yellow-buff surfaces. Exterior decorated with closely-spaced horizontal rilling. 'Cream Sandy Ware', probably similar to No. 784, dateable to the fourth century A.D.

No. 787   Bowl with flanged rim of sandy ware with dark pink-buff core and a burnt, dark grey-black exterior surface. The flanged rim has been partially formed by a deep groove cut around the top of the vessel. Probably third to fourth century A.D.

No. 788   Large jar with everted rim, slightly distorted during firing. Sandy ware with grey-brown core and patchy grey surfaces and burnishing over the rim. Dateable to the third to fourth century A.D.

No. 789   Flagon with rippled neck of sandy ware with orange-buff core and grey surfaces. Dateable to the late-third to fourth century A.D.

No. 790   Bowl with flanged rim of sandy ware. Grey-buff core and brown, colour-coated surfaces. Nene Valley Ware dateable to the late fourth century A.D.

No. 791   Jar with heavy, everted rim of sandy ware. Grey-brown core and grey surfaces.

No. 792   Jar with squared, everted rim of coarse, sandy ware with grey-brown core and surfaces. Dateable to the late-third to fourth century A.D.

No. 793   Dish with bead rim of sandy ware. Grey-brown core and grey-brown burnished surfaces. Mid to late-second century A.D.

No. 794   Jar with everted rim of coarse, grog-tempered ware. Light grey core and interior surface and brown exterior. Dateable to the fourth century A.D.

No. 795   Jar with flared rim of grog-tempered ware. Brown-black core and patchy brown, burnished surfaces showing signs of burning.

No. 796   Small jar or bowl with everted rim of sandy ware. Grey-brown core and patchy grey surfaces with a shallow cordon between grooves on the shoulder. Dated to the early-second century A.D.

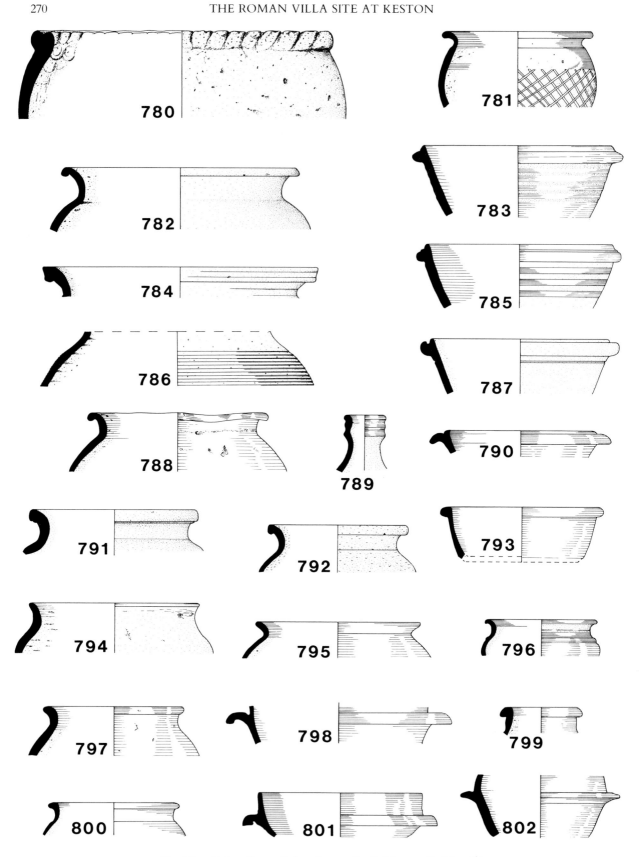

Fig. 83.   Pottery from soil deposits over South Masonry Building ($\frac{1}{4}$).

No. 797 Jar with everted rim of sandy ware. Grey core and surfaces with slightly burnished exterior.

No. 798 Bowl with hooked flanged rim of hard, fine, sandy ware. Orange core with dark orange-red slip-coating on both surfaces. Oxfordshire Ware, Type C51, dated *c.* A.D.240–400.

No. 799 Small jar with bead rim of hard brown fabric with some red grog inclusions. Dark grey-black surfaces. Dateable to the third to fourth century A.D.

No. 800 Jar with flattened, everted rim of sandy ware. Grey core and grey-black surfaces with signs of burnishing on the exterior.

No. 801 Bowl with flanged rim of hard, fine, sandy ware. Grey core and red, slip-coated surfaces, discoloured by burning. Oxfordshire Ware, Type C.51. Dateable to the late-third to fourth century A.D.

No. 802 Bowl with flanged rim of sandy ware with grey-brown core and orange-brown surfaces.

No. 803 Large storage jar or dolium with squared, slightly undercut rim of sandy ware. Light grey-brown core and surfaces. Probably Alice Holt Ware. Third or fourth century A.D.

No. 804 Bowl with upright rim of hard, cream fabric with light grey-brown exterior surface and dark grey interior. Both surfaces have been slip-coated. Probably New Forest Ware of late-third to fourth century A.D.

No. 805 Bowl with internally thickened, flat-topped bead rim of hard, sandy ware. Light grey and orange-brown sandwiched core with dark grey surfaces. Exterior and top of rim burnished. Later first to early-second century A.D.

No. 806 Large storage jar with squared, undercut rim. Light grey core and darker grey surfaces. Alice Holt Ware, dateable to the late-third to fourth century A.D.

No. 807 Dish with straight sides and slightly incurved rim of gritty ware. Orange-brown core and burnished black surfaces. Dateable to the third century A.D.

No. 808 Lid of sandy ware with grey core and grey-black surfaces. Keston Kiln Ware, dateable to *c.* A.D.60–85.

Upper East Metalling (LWB–T24–3, Y23–5, Y24–2 and AA23–12).

No. 809 Dish with flanged rim of sandy ware. Brown core and interior surface with dark grey-black exterior. Dateable to the later third to fourth century A.D.

No. 810 Bowl with straight sides and simple, upright rim of hard, gritty, grog-tempered ware. Grey core with dark brown interior surface and black exterior. Dateable to the fourth century A.D.

No. 811 An out-turned rim in fine flint-tempered fabric. It is dark grey (N4) throughout. The surfaces are smooth with flints visible. (Form 27, fabric A). Pre-Conquest.

No. 812 Dish with flanged rim of sandy ware with light grey core and dark grey surfaces. Late-third to fourth century A.D.

Soil over Upper East Metalling (LWB–U24–4, U24–7, Z23–3 and EE20–3).

No. 813 An everted rim from a jar in fine glauconitic sandy fabric. The internal surface is almost totally worn away, but the surviving portion shows that it was dark grey (N4) and burnished. The external surface is dark grey to black (N3–N2) and highly burnished. The core is dark grey (N3). (Form 32, fabric G). Pre-Conquest.

No. 814 Jar with squared, everted rim of coarse, sandy ware. Light grey core and yellow-buff surfaces. 'Cream Sandy Ware', dateable to the fourth century A.D.

No. 815 Dish with flanged rim in a hard, sandy fabric. Light grey core and dark grey surfaces, slightly burnished internally. Late-third to fourth century A.D.

No. 816 Small jar with everted rim of sandy ware. Orange and buff sandwiched core and grey surfaces. Dark grey burnished bands on upper rim internally and on neck and lower rim externally. Possibly Alice Holt Ware, dateable to the late-third to fourth century A.D.

No. 817 Jar with upright, slightly beaded rim of grog and fine shell-tempered ware. Grey-brown core and abraded red-brown surfaces. Dateable to the first to second century A.D.

No. 818 Jar with outcurved rim of hard, grog-tempered ware. Dark grey core and dark grey-black surfaces with traces of soot on the exterior. Dateable to the fourth century A.D.

No. 819 A plain rim with flat top in flint-tempered fabric. The sherd is small and the angle and diameter uncertain. Both surfaces are burnished with flints visible and the sherd has been fired dark grey (N3) throughout. (Form 3, fabric A). Pre-Conquest.

No. 820 Jar with outcurved, bead rim of sandy ware. Orange-brown core and grey-brown surfaces with traces of a grey slip on both surfaces and burnishing on the exterior. Probably dateable to the third century A.D.

No. 821 A rim, from an open bowl or lid, of flint-tempered fabric. The internal surface has been wiped and the flint tempering is visible. The external surface has been wiped with flints protruding. The sherd has been fired dark grey to black (N3–N2) throughout. (Form 39, fabric A). Pre-Conquest.

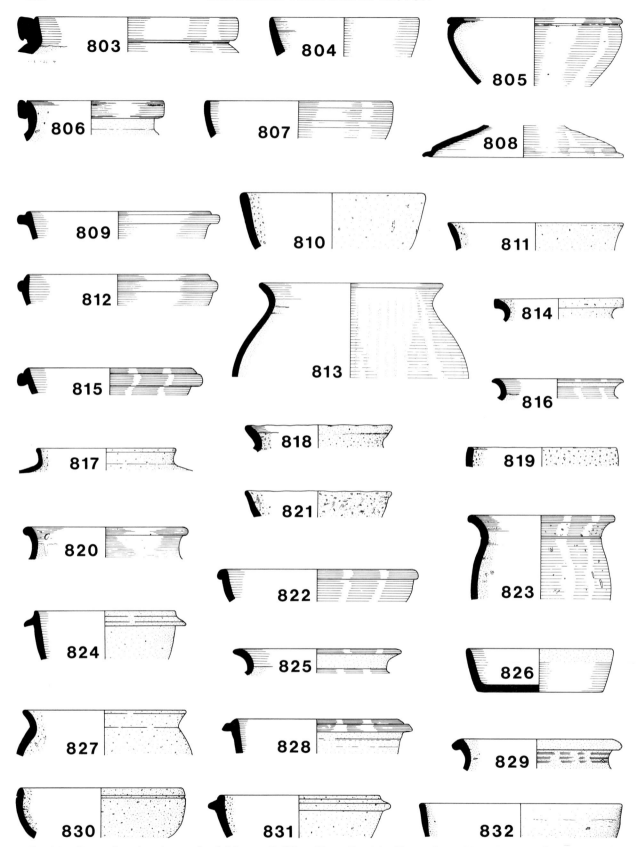

Fig. 84. *Pottery from deposits over South Masonry Building, Upper East Metalling, soil over Upper East Metalling, External Corn Drying Oven, Late Hut over the North Timber Building and Ditch 14.*

External Corn Drying Oven (LWB–78–9, 78–27 and 78–44).

No. 822   Dish or bowl with small bead rim of fine, sandy ware. Orange core and surfaces with dark red slip, somewhat worn. Oxfordshire Ware, Types 44–46, copying samian form Dr.31. Late-third to fourth century A.D. Similar to No. 756. (Fill of heating chamber, F.1508).

No. 823   Jar with outcurved rim and weak shoulder of fairly hard, grog-tempered ware. Dark grey core with mottled light and dark grey-brown surfaces. There are traces of light burnishing on the interior of the rim. Dateable to the fourth century A.D. (Fill of heating chamber, F.1508).

No. 824   Bowl with flanged rim of hard, grog-tempered ware. Light grey core with light to dark grey interior surface and mottled orange-grey exterior. Dateable to the fourth century A.D. (Fill of stoke-pit, F.1510).

No. 825   Jar with everted rim of hard, sandy ware. Grey core and surfaces with a white slip applied to the interior of the rim and at the base of the rim externally. Alice Holt Ware, probably third century A.D. (Fill of stoke-pit, F.1510).

No. 826   Dish with straight sides and plain, upright rim of hard, sandy ware. Light grey-brown core and dark grey surfaces with traces of burnishing on the interior. Dateable to the third to fourth century A.D. (Fill of stoke-pit, F.1510).

Fill of Late Hut Terrace within North Timber Building (LWB–77–246 and 77–265).

No. 827   Jar with outcurved rim of fairly hard, grog-tempered ware. Dark grey core and dark grey-brown interior surface and light orange-brown exterior. Dateable to the fourth century A.D.

No. 828   Bowl with flanged rim of sandy ware. Light grey core and surfaces with burnishing on inside and top of rim. Traces of white slip on the flange. Alice Holt Ware, Class 5B, dated late-third to fourth century A.D.

No. 829   Jar with heavy bead rim of hard, sandy fabric. Light cream-grey core and medium to light grey surfaces.

No. 830   Convex-sided bowl with simple, upright rim of hard, coarse, sandy ware. Cream-yellow fabric with a shallow, horizontal groove on the exterior surface below the rim. Probably 'Cream Sandy Ware' of fourth century date.

No. 831   Bowl with flanged rim of fairly hard, coarse, sandy grog-tempered ware. Light grey core with light grey to medium grey surfaces. Dateable to the fourth century A.D.

Ditch 14, West Arm (LWB–77–212).

No. 832   Straight-sided dish with simple, upright rim of sandy ware. Brown core and patchy grey-brown surfaces. Dateable to the later third to fourth century A.D.

Miscellaneous Features.

No. 833   A shouldered jar with an open flaring rim in shell and organic-tempered fabric. The internal surface is grey (N4–N3) and wiped with flint and shell fragments protruding. The external surface is light grey-brown (N7–7.5YR6/4) and wiped with few flint and shell fragments visible. The shoulder is decorated with a row of finger-tip impressions. The core is dark grey (N3). (Form 26, fabric C). Pre-Conquest. (West Masonry Building, Pit D; LWB–B24–4).

No. 834   Large jar with heavy rolled rim of sandy ware. Light grey core and grey-buff surfaces with a zone of irregular, lattice decoration on the shoulder. (West Masonry Building, Pit C; LWB–B25–2).

No. 835   Jar with out-turned, flat-topped rim of shell-tempered ware. Dark grey core and light grey-brown surfaces. Dateable to the pre-Conquest period. (West Masonry Building, Pit C; LWB–B24–4).

No. 836   Upright rim of shell-tempered ware with brown core and patchy brown surfaces. Pre-Conquest. (West Masonry Building, Pit C; LWB–B24–2).

No. 837   Small globular jar with out-turned, thickened rim of fine, sandy ware. Orange-red core and surfaces. The exterior is decorated with a raised cordon at the base of the neck and on the shoulder and a broad zone of lattice decoration on the body. Smaller version of No. 778. Keston Kiln Ware, dateable to c. A.D. 60–85. (West Masonry Building, Pit cutting Centre Enclosure Ditch; LWB–C23–6).

No. 838   A small everted rim jar with a flat base in sandy shell-tempered fabric. The shoulder is decorated with a stamped and grooved design: a horizontal band of interlocking arcs bounded above by two horizontal grooves and dotted lines and below by one horizontal groove and dotted line. Between each pair of interlocking arcs is a pair of stamped concentric circles. The internal surface is worn, the external surface is smooth, even polished. Most of the sherds are light brown (5YR6/4). Some which are light grey (N6) may have been refired. (Form 35, fabric D). Pre-Conquest. (Hollow cutting West Enclosure Ditch, near north-east corner; LWB–76–198).

No. 839   An everted rim in fine glauconitic fabric. The sherd is worn and has been burnt. The internal surface is grey (10R4/1) and smooth. The external surface is red-brown (2.5YR5/6) with patches of grey (N4), and

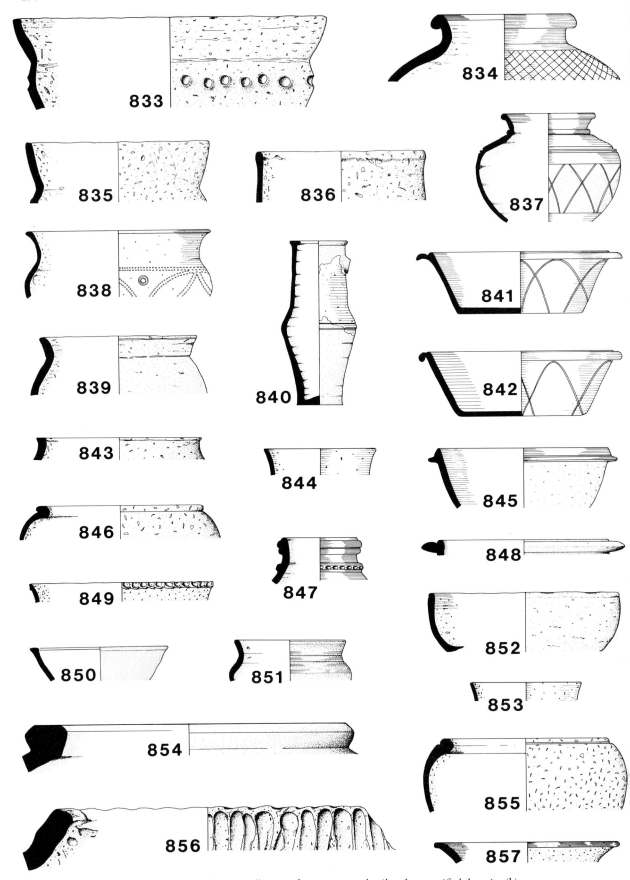

Fig. 85.   *Pottery from miscellaneous features, general soil and unstratified deposits* (¼).

was orignally smooth. The core is dark grey (N3) and there is a rusty brown (2.5YR6/8) margin beneath both surfaces. (Form 32, fabric G). Pre-Conquest. (West Enclosure, Pit F.205; LWB–C23–4).

No. 840   Complete profile of a medieval jug of hard, sandy ware. Yellow-buff core and surfaces with splashes of a dense emerald green lead-glaze. This seems to be Cheam Ware and is likely to be of 14th century date. (West Masonry Building, Pit D; LWB–A24–2 and A24–3).

No. 841   Substantially complete bowl with flanged rim of coarse, sandy ware. Grey-black core and black surfaces with burnished interior. Burnished arcs on the exterior surface and burnished loops on the underside of the base. On the inside of the base, a series of radially arranged score marks have been cut into the surface of the vessel after firing. Dateable to the third century A.D. (Pit/post-hole cutting North Tank; LWB–76–176).

No. 842   Bowl with flanged rim of sandy ware. Grey-black core and black surfaces with burnished arc decoration on the exterior. Dateable to the third century A.D. (Pit/post-hole cutting North Tank; LWB–76–176).

No. 843   Jar or bowl with flattened, upright rim of shell and grog-tempered ware with dark grey core and orange surfaces. Pre-Conquest. (Fill of Minor Ditch 19 adjacent South Masonry Building; LWB–N36–2).

No. 844   A gently everted rim in sandy, flint-tempered fabric. The sherd is small and the angle uncertain. Both surfaces are now worn but were evidently black (N2) and burnished with few flints visible. The core is black (N2) and there is a dark grey (N3) external margin. (Form 27, fabric B). Pre-Conquest. (Pit F.1021; LWB–77–59).

No. 845   Bowl with flanged rim of hard, grog-tempered ware. Dark grey-brown core with dark grey, slightly burnished interior surface and grey-brown exterior. Dateable to the fourth century A.D. (North Timber Building, Late Hut Terrace, fill of Pit F.1200; LWB–77–256).

No. 846   Jar with flattened bead rim of hard, shell-tempered ware with some grog inclusions. Dark grey core and light brown surfaces. Dateable to the later first to early-second century A.D. (Post-hole F.1089; LWB–77–120).

No. 847   Narrow-mouthed jar or flask with lobed rim of hard, sandy ware. Light grey-brown core and grey surfaces with traces of a dark grey slip on the exterior. There is a raised cordon on the neck bearing finger-tip decoration. Alice Holt Ware, dateable to the late-third to fourth century A.D. (South Masonry Building, adjacent pebble surface; LWB–N33–3).

No. 848   Bowl with flanged rim of sandy ware with light grey core and surfaces. Alice Holt Class 5B.1 of earlier third century date. (Post-hole F.1079; LWB–77–80).

No. 849   A small everted rim in flint-tempered fabric. The exterior of the rim is decorated with shallow finger-tip impressions. Both surfaces are orange (2.5YR6/6), and worn with flint inclusions protruding. The core is light grey (N5). (Form 31, fabric A). Pre-Conquest. (Post-hole F.1532; LWB–78–50).

No. 850   Bowl or lid with thickened, flat-topped rim of fairly hard, sandy ware. Grey core and surfaces with lightly burnished exterior. Probably Keston Kiln Ware, dateable to *c.* A.D.60–85. (Fill of Pit F.413; LWB–P21–10).

No. 851   Globular jar or bowl with everted rim of sandy ware. Grey-buff core and patchy grey surfaces showing signs of burnishing on the exterior. (Post-hole F.40; LWB–J34–9).

No. 852   Bowl with convex sides and upright rim of hard, coarse, sandy ware. Dark grey core and black surfaces. Exterior shows signs of sooting. Dateable to the fourth century A.D. (Post-hole F.1550; LWB–78–67).

No. 853   A fine gently everted rim in flint-tempered fabric. The sherd is small and the diameter uncertain; but the thin wall (3 mm. thick) suggests that it belonged to a small bowl or cup. The surfaces are smooth, almost polished, with few flints visible. The sherd has been fired dark grey to black (N3–N2) throughout. (Form 29, fabric A). Pre-Conquest. (Four-post Structure 2, Post-hole F.605; LWB–X20–3).

Plough Soil, Hillwash and General Soil Deposits

No. 854   Large storage jar with heavy, flat-topped bead rim of sandy, grog-tempered ware. Pink-brown core and pink-orange surfaces. Dateable to the later first to early-second century A.D. (LWB–78–69).

No. 855   Jar with bead rim of shell and grog-tempered ware. Brown-black core and surfaces with traces of burnishing. Dateable to the later first to early-second century A.D. (LWB–P22–7).

No. 856   Large hand-made, storage vessel with inturned rim of hard, grog-tempered ware. Light grey-brown core with orange-brown interior and patchy brown-black exterior. The exterior of the vessel is decorated with vertical finger-impressions. This vessel is broadly similar to No. 780. Dateable to the fourth century A.D. (LWB–I31–3).

No. 857   Jar with everted rim of sandy ware. Grey-brown core and brown-black surfaces with burnishing inside the rim. (LWB–DD21–3).

No. 858   A thick sherd with a smooth plain edge in flint-tempered fabric. It could be from the rim of a storage jar, or from the edge of slab of fired clay. The sherd is worn and, if it is from a rim, its diameter is unknown. It

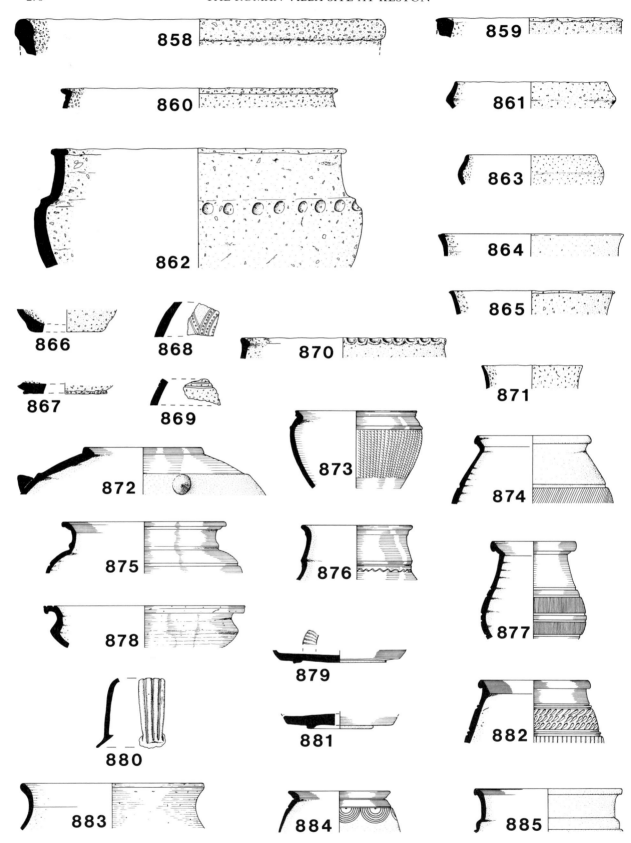

Fig. 86.　*Pottery from unstratified and general soil deposits* ($\frac{1}{4}$).

has been fired orange-brown (5YR7/6) throughout. The surfaces are wiped and flints protrude. One surface in particular has abundant flints protruding. (Form 25, fabric A). Pre-Conquest. (LWB–T23–5).

No. 859   A very worn fragment of a plain rim in flint-tempered fabric. The sherd has been fired light orange (5YR7/8) throughout and flint inclusions protrude. (Form 16, fabric A). Pre-Conquest. (LWB–U22–3).

No. 860   A rim with flat top and external projection in flint-tempered fabric. Both surfaces are brown (7.5YR6/6) and wiped with flints protruding. The core is black (N2). (Form 10, fabric A). Pre-Conquest. (LWB–T23–3).

No. 861   The rim and carinated shoulder from a bipartite vessel in flint and shell-tempered fabric. The sherd is small and the diameter uncertain. The internal surface is brown (5YR6/4), smooth and horizontally burnished inside the shoulder, with few flints visible. The external surface is smooth and partially worn, with flints visible. It is grey (5YR5/1) around the shoulder and brown (5YR5/3) around the rim. The core is grey (N5). (Form 11, fabric E). Pre-Conquest. (LWB–T21–2).

No. 862   A shouldered jar with upright neck and a flat-topped rim with external projection in shell-tempered fabric. Both surfaces have been wiped with shell temper visible. The internal surface is light brown (5YR7/5). The core is dark grey (N3) and the external surface grey-brown (5YR6/2). The shoulder is decorated with a row of finger-tip impressions. (Form 18, fabric C). Pre-Conquest. (LWB–L24–5).

No. 863   A plain inturned rim of hard flint-tempered fabric. The sherd is small and the diameter unknown. The internal surface is black (N2) and smooth with flint temper visible. The external surface is light brown (5YR7/6) and has been wiped with flint grits protruding. The colour of the core varies from light brown to black (5YR7/6–N2). (Form 11, fabric A). Pre-Conquest. (LWB–U20–2).

No. 864   A rim with flat top and external expansion in fine sandy flint-tempered fabric. The sherd is small and the angle uncertain; it could be everted or inturned. It has been fired black (N2) throughout. Both surfaces are smooth with few flints visible. (Fabric B). Pre-Conquest. (LWB–S20–3).

No. 865   An everted rim with flat top and external expansion in flint-tempered fabric. Both surfaces have been wiped and the flint temper protrudes. The internal surface and core are black (N2) and the external surface was evidently brown (5YR7/4) but is now worn with black (N2) showing through. (Form 29, fabric A). Pre-Conquest. (LWB–J19–2).

No. 866   A flat base in flint-tempered fabric. Both surfaces are orange-brown (2.5YR5/6) and worn with flints protruding. The core is grey (N3). Beneath the base numerous flint fragments protrude. (Fabric A). Pre-Conquest. (LWB–U22–3).

No. 867   A fragment of a flat base in flint-tempered fabric. The internal surface is dark grey (N3) and has been wiped leaving the flint tempering visible. Beneath the base the surface is black (N2) with abundant flints protruding. The core is dark grey-brown (5YR5/2). (Fabric A). Pre-Conquest. (LWB–U20–2).

No. 868   A wall sherd in fine glauconitic sandy fabric. The external surface is grey (N4), smooth and decorated with a grooved and dotted curvilinear design. The internal surface is grey (N5) and burnished. The core is light grey (N6). (Fabric G). Similar to No. 222. Pre-Conquest. (LWB–V22–2).

No. 869   A wall sherd in fine flint-tempered fabric. Both surfaces are worn and grey-brown (N3–5YR6/4) and the core is dark grey (N3). The exterior is decorated with two parallel grooves, 1.5 mm. wide and 3 mm. apart. These may be horizontal, as illustrated in the figure, or curvilinear if the sherd was originally set at another angle. (Fabric A). Pre-Conquest. (LWB–T23–3).

No. 870   A rim with finger-tip decoration in flint-tempered fabric. The sherd is small and the angle and diameter uncertain. The internal surface is dark grey (N3) and wiped smooth with flints visible. The external surface is dark grey to black (N3–N2) and smooth with few flints visible. The core is grey (N4) and there is a rusty brown (2.5YR5/6) external margin. (Fabric A). Pre-Conquest. (LWB–S24–4).

No. 871   A gently everted rim from a small bowl or cup of fine flint-tempered fabric. Both surfaces are worn with flints visible. The internal surface is black (N2) with a patch of the brown (5YR6/6) margin showing through near the rim. The exterior is now mainly brown (5YR6/6), the original dark grey (N3) surface having been largely worn away. The core is grey (N4). (Form 29, fabric A). Pre-Conquest. (LWB–O22–2).

No. 872   Large, narrow-mouthed globular jar with slightly squared bead rim of hard, sandy ware. Brown core and orange-red surfaces. There is a faint cordon on the shoulder with a large applied conical boss below. The vessel is burnished between the cordon and the rim. Similar to No. 410. Probably Keston Kiln Ware, dateable to c. A.D.60–85. (LWB–L32–4).

No. 873   Small globular beaker with out-turned rim of hard, sandy ware. Light grey-brown core and orange-brown surfaces coated with an orange-brown slip on the interior surface. There is a horizontal cordon on the shoulder and vertical 'wheel' decoration below. The 'wheel' decoration is more usually found on butt beakers and has been applied by means of one of the small clay discs recovered from the excavations (see page 155). Similar to Camulodunum Form 91. Keston Kiln Ware, dateable to c. A.D.60–85. (LWB–K21–2).

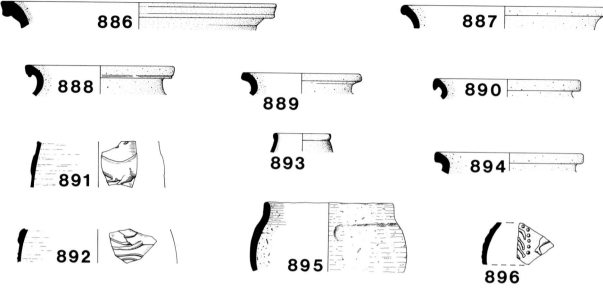

Fig. 87.   *Pottery from unstratified and general soil deposits (¼).*

No. 874   Butt beaker of sandy ware with orange-buff core and orange-brown surfaces. There is a horizontal groove above the shoulder with a zone of fine, angled combing below. Keston Kiln Ware, dateable to *c.* A.D.60–85. (LWB–N29–6).

No. 875   Probable globular jar with everted rim of slightly sandy ware with buff-brown core and orange-brown surfaces. There is a raised horizontal cordon at the base of the neck and a shallow groove on the shoulder. Similar to No. 490. Keston Kiln Ware, dateable to *c.* A.D.60–85. (LWB–N31–10).

No. 876   Long-necked jar with outcurved rim of hard, sandy ware. Dark grey core and orange-buff surfaces. There is an angular cordon at the base of the neck. The neck is burnished and a dark red slip has been applied to the cordon and wall below. Through the slip, a horizontal groove has been scored under the cordon and a somewhat irregular wavy line below this. Keston Kiln Ware, dateable to *c.* A.D.60–85. (LWB–M32–4).

No. 877   Narrow-necked butt beaker of fine, hard sandy ware. The bulbous body is decorated with horizontal cordons set between grooves with bands of fine, vertical combing between. Keston Kiln Ware, dateable to *c.* A.D.60–85. (LWB–N31–10).

No. 878   Carinated bowl with flanged, reeded rim of hard, fine, sandy ware. Dark orange-red core and surfaces with slight traces of burnishing on the exterior. Broadly similar to No. 384. Keston Kiln Ware, dateable to *c.* A.D.60–85. (LWB–N31–10).

No. 879   Base of imitation Gallo-Belgic platter of hard sandy ware. Dark grey core and dark brown surfaces. There is a shallow footring on the underside, whilst on the upper surface a band of rouletting, produced by one of the pottery wheels found on the site, surrounds a central stamp (No. 899). Keston Kiln Ware, dateable to *c.* A.D.60–85. (LWB–L26–8).

No. 880   Handle of hard, slightly sandy ware. Light cream-grey core with cream surfaces. Three slightly irregular vertical lines have been scored along the length of the handle on the outside. Probably Keston Kiln Ware, dateable to *c.* A.D.60–85. (LWB–N31–10).

No. 881   Base of imitation Gallo-Belgic platter with footring. Coarse, sandy ware with grey core and pink-buff surfaces. Keston Kiln Ware, dateable to *c.* A.D.60–85. (LWB–K32–2).

No. 882   Butt beaker of hard, sandy ware. Grey core and orange-brown surfaces, burnt black on the exterior. Two horizontal cordons on the neck are separated by three lines of closely-spaced, angled slashes. Keston Kiln Ware, dateable to *c.* A.D.60–85. (LWB–N31–10).

No. 883   Jar with everted rim of soft, soapy, grog-tempered ware. Mottled grey core and brown, slightly burnished surfaces. Late first to early-second century A.D. (LWB–P22–7).

No. 884   Small jar or beaker with out-turned rim of smooth grey ware. Light grey surfaces with exterior decorated with a row of compass-drawn arcs. This type of decoration is typical of 'London Ware', although the present sherd is probably a regional imitation, quite possibly from the North Kent Marshes. (See also No. 612). Late-first to early-second century A.D. (LWB–024–1).

No. 885   Jar with tall neck and small, out-turned, thickened rim of hard, fine, sandy ware. Dark grey core and light grey-brown surfaces with traces of soot on the interior. There is a bold horizontal cordon at the base of the neck. (LWB–N31–10).

No. 886   Large jar with everted, squared rim of hard, coarse, sandy ware. Light grey core and cream-grey surfaces. 'Cream Sandy Ware', dateable to the fourth century A.D. Similar to No. 784. (LWB–J33–1).

No. 887   Jar with undercut, everted rim of very granular sandy ware with grey core and grey-buff surfaces. 'Cream Sandy Ware', dateable to the fourth century A.D. (LWB–1).

No. 888   Jar with everted, undercut rim of hard, coarse, sandy ware. Light grey core with cream-buff surfaces. 'Cream Sandy Ware', dateable to the fourth century A.D. (LWB–I34–1).

No. 889   Jar with everted rim of coarse, sandy ware with buff core and cream-buff surfaces. 'Cream Sandy Ware', dateable to the fourth century A.D. (LWB–1).

No. 890   Jar with undercut rim of coarse, sandy ware with orange-buff core and cream surfaces. Similar to No. 888. 'Cream Sandy Ware', dateable to the fourth century A.D. (LWB–1).

No. 891   Body sherd from a 'Hunt Cup' of Nene Valley Ware. Hard, white fabric with dark grey slip on both surfaces. The decoration depicts the front part of a running animal. Similar to No. 751. Hunt Cups are dateable to the later second to early-third centuries A.D. (LWB–76–8).

No. 892   Body sherd from a 'Hunt Cup' of Nene Valley Ware. Hard, orange fabric with applied cream decoration, coated with a dark grey slip on both surfaces. The decoration shows the lower portion of a running animal with scroll-work lines below. The decoration is broadly similar to No. 891. Dateable to the later-second to early-third century A.D. (LWB–M33–7).

No. 893   Small beaker with upright, thickened rim of sandy ware with orange core and surfaces. (LWB–E4–1).

No. 894   Jar with squared, everted rim of coarse, sandy ware. Light grey core and cream-buff surfaces. 'Cream Sandy Ware', dateable to the fourth century A.D. This vessel appears to be a slightly larger version of the form represented by No. 889. (LWB–1).

No. 895   Globular jar or bowl of fairly crude construction with simple, upright rim of hard, sandy ware. Dark grey core and exterior surface with dark brown interior. The exterior is slightly burnished.
    The dating of this vessel is not clear. It may well relate to the burnished jars found in late-Iron Age contexts on the site (No. 209, 212, 215 etc.) but it is also similar to some of the Saxon material recovered from the sunken hut (West Kent Nos. 464–467). On balance, the general absence of Saxon pottery from other contexts on the site suggests that this is a late-Iron Age vessel. (LWB–Z21–3).

No. 896   Wall sherd from a beaker of fine, sandy ware. Orange core and surfaces with traces of a pink-orange colour-coat, decorated with an indeterminate applied barbotine design. (LWB–E4–1).

Potter's Stamps on Keston Kiln Ware Platters by Valerie Rigby.

No. 897   Bordered Mark. Central, within two fine incised circles on the upper surface of a platter, no evidence of a footring. Typical fabric, rather under-fired; partially oxidised brown surfaces; highly burnished upper surface, very abraded lower.
    The stamp impression is incomplete. The die-face is unusually small. It appears to consist of repeated V-motifs within a border and is one of the most common and widely found die-styles in southern Britain. Examples are mainly concentrated on sites north of the Thames, but do occur to the south of Canterbury, also Southwark and Chichester and Fishbourne, Sussex. (Fill of Quarry Pit Complex; LWB–N29–5).

No. 898   Unbordered Mark. Off-centre, within a single burnished circle on the upper surface of a small footring platter. Burnt, discoloured and abraded fine quartz sand-tempered fabric, no finish survives.
    The stamp impression is very abraded, but it appears to be an unbordered Mark, with alternating I and X motifs. The die-style is fairly common in south-eastern Britain, occurring at Ashton, Northants; Bierton, Bucks; London and Winchester, Hants. (General Soil Deposit, south-east of Lower East Metalling; LWB–BB24–7).

No. 899   Unbordered Mark. Central, within a bordered wreath of 'cord' impressions (typical of those produced with the roulette 'wheels' found on the site) on the upper surface of a small platter with functional footring (See No. 879). Fine quartz sand-tempered ware, with additional fine black grog or glauconitic inclusions; grey core with partially oxidised, self-coloured, brown surfaces; traces of a burnished finish.
    The stamp impression is incomplete. It appears to consist simply of repeated V-motifs made up of unusually broad strokes. This is the most common and widely found die-style in southern Britain being represented more or less wherever stamps have been found, in Bedfordshire, Buckinghamshire, Essex, Gloucestershire, Hampshire, Middlesex, Northamptonshire, Oxfordshire, Wiltshire and is also recorded from Murston, Kent. (Unstratified Quarry Pit Complex; LWB–L26–8).

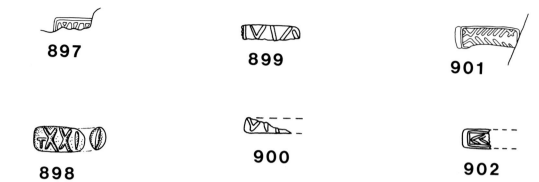

897   **899**   **901**

898   **900**   **902**

Fig. 88.   *Stamps on Keston Kiln ware platters ($\frac{1}{1}$).*

No. 900   Unbordered Mark, from the same die as No. 899. Central, within two fine incised circles on the upper surface of a platter with a footring. Similar fabric fired to dark grey in reducing conditions; burnished upper surface, unfinished lower. (Soil over Quarry Pit Complex; LWB–L29–4).

No. 901   Bordered Mark. Central, within two fine incised circles on the upper surface of a small platter with a functional footring. (See No. 403). Typical fabric but with traces of a red slip on the upper and lower surfaces; incomplete oxidation occurred during firing and there is a grey core, with light orange under-surfaces. The finished fabric in its original state must have looked remarkably like an imported product in Terra Rubra 1(B), with glossy, coral red surfaces (Ref. 252).

An almost complete although abraded impression, which like No. 902 reads vertically and produces a fern-leaf motif. This stamp is from a different much larger die than No. 902, however. Similar, but unbordered Marks have been recorded at Mount Bures, Essex; Winterton, Lincs; Needham, Norfolk and Duston, Northants. (Kiln Dump; LWB–N31–9).

No. 902   Bordered Mark. Central, within two fine incised circles on the upper surface of a platter with a functional footring. Typical fabric, partially oxidised buff surfaces; highly burnished upper, unfinished lower.

Like No. 897, the die-face is narrow. The stamp impression is very fragmentary and difficult to interpret. It appears to consist of double strokes which when read vertically produce a fern-leaf motif, similar to that produced by some of the roulette 'wheels' from the site (although experiments show that this was almost certainly not the method used). Such a motif is unique, although it does resemble the larger stamp, No. 901. (Soil over Quarry Pit Complex; LWB–M29–5).

Stamped amphora handle, wall sherds with graffiti and chaff-tempered vessels.

No. 903   Stamped handle from an amphora, probably of globular South Spanish type. Coarse, sandy fabric with buff core and orange-buff surfaces. From a similar form of amphora to No. 714. (Soil over Upper East Metalling; LWB–AA24–12).

No. 904   Wall sherd of sandy ware with grey-brown core and black-brown surfaces. Two letters have been scratched on the exterior of the sherd after firing. The first is substantially complete and consists of an 'R'. To the right of this an angled stroke must represent part of the next letter, possibly an 'A'. (Upper filling of North-West Ditch of Villa Enclosure, North Arm; LWB–76–178).

No. 905   Wall sherd of early-Roman grog-tempered ware with grey core, grey-brown surfaces and a burnished lattice decoration on the exterior. A graffito has been scratched on the exterior after firing. This consists of two crossed lines with a 'D' or 'P'-shaped mark at the intersection, just possibly a crude Chi-Rho mark. (East Fence, fill of Post-pipe F.418; LWB–P24–8).

No. 906   Small vessel with slightly out-turned rim of chaff-tempered ware with buff core and orange-buff surfaces. (Fill of Quarry Pit Complex; LWB–N29–8).

No. 907   Small vessel with slightly out-turned, thickened rim of chaff-tempered ware. Buff core and orange-buff surfaces. (Unstratified, Quarry Pit area; LWB–N31–10).

Vessels of similar form and fabric to Nos. 906–907 have been discovered in Canterbury and several other sites, mostly in East Kent. The precise function and overall form of these vessels remains uncertain but they are consistently in 'Belgic' and early-Roman deposits. No. 906 comes from the filling of the first century Quarry Pit Complex and No. 907 was found unstratified in the same area, with much other first century pottery. The early-Roman dating of the material thus, once more, seems confirmed. (See p. 205).

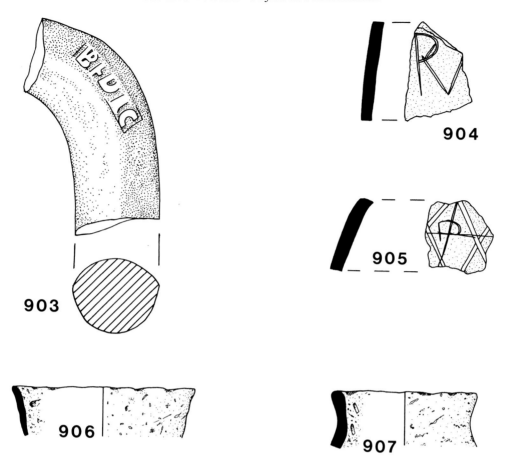

Fig. 89.   *Stamped amphora handle; wall sherds with graffiti and chaff-tempered vessels ($\frac{1}{2}$).*

H) THE MORTARIA (Figs. 90 and 91, Nos. 908–932).

Some 153 mortaria sherds were recovered from Lower Warbank Field. Of these, 25 have been drawn (Nos. 908–932) including two stamps (Nos. 917 and 932). The entire collection was submitted to Mrs K. Hartley for study but her main report has not been completed in time for inclusion here. A note on one of the stamped sherds (No. 917) has been received, however. This is printed below but details of the remaining pieces will be held over until the second Report on the site is published. The context of the illustrated sherds is given in the following list:

No. 908   Filling of Quarry Pit Complex (LWB–N29–8).
No. 909   Post-Pit 5, South Timber Building (LWB–N34–3).
No. 910   Flint Rubble, Centre Flint Structure (LWB–J27–5).
No. 911   Lower filling, North-West Ditch of Villa Enclosure (LWB–E4–4).
No. 912   Upper filling, North-West Ditch of Villa Enclosure (LWB–76–3).
No. 913   Upper filling, North-West Ditch of Villa Enclosure (LWB–H6–3).
No. 914   Filling of cellar, West Masonry Building (LWB–B20–6).
No. 915   Robber-trench, West Masonry Building (LWB–B21–3).
No. 916   Unstratified, West Masonry Building (LWB–Z–1).
No. 917   Soil over Lower East Metalling (LWB–BB21–3). Mrs K. Hartley has provided the following note on this stamped piece:

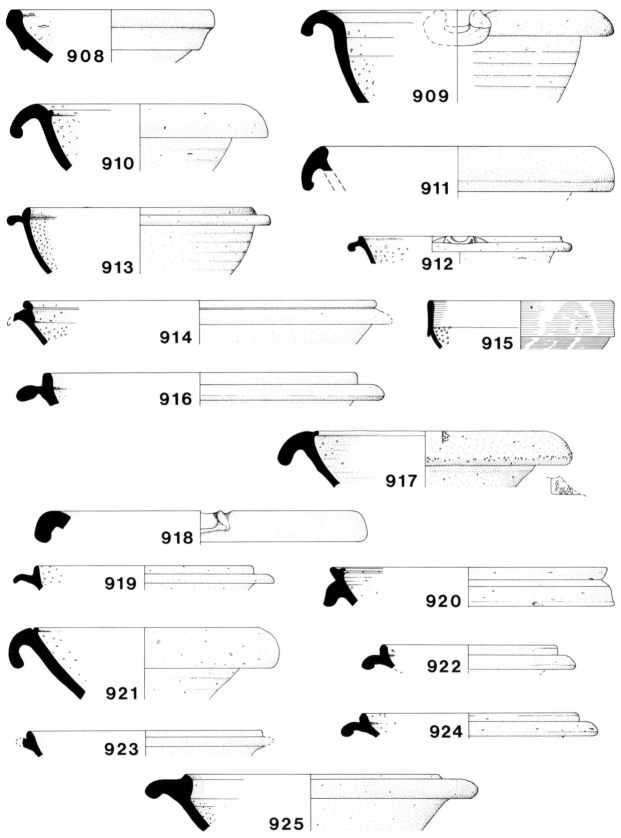

Fig. 90.   *Roman Mortaria* ($\frac{1}{4}$).

Three joining sherds making over one third of the upper part of a mortarium in softish, buff-cream fabric with pink core and quartz, flint and some orange-brown and calcareous inclusions. The trituration is largely flint and quartz and the upper side of the flange is gritted. The poorly impressed potter's stamp is from one of at least ten dies used by Q. Valerius Veranius. A stamp from the same die is published from Fishbourne (Ref. 253). Deep and clear impressions of this stamp give DOG (or C) AERIA FAC in very tiny letters between the two main lines, possibly for 'made in Dogaeria', a name not otherwise recorded. Veranius worked at one time in the Bavai area but the bulk of his production was elsewhere, probably in north-east Gaul, and most of his mortaria are in Britain. He was the most important of a number of potters who worked in the same tradition (Ref. 254; Group 2). His main production was in the period A.D. 65–100 and all of his mortaria in Britain belong to this period.

No. 918   Soil between Upper and Lower East Metalling (LWB–Z24–6).
No. 919   Upper filling Ditch 21b (LWB–77–205).
No. 920   Filling of Ditch 7 (LWB–78–3).
No. 921   Unstratified, South Masonry Building (LWB–J35–10).
No. 922   Late Hut Terrace, North Timber Building (LWB–77–210).
No. 923   Late Hut Terrace, North Timber Building (LWB–77–210).
No. 924   Late Hut Terrace, North Timber Building (LWB–77–211).
No. 925   West Tanks 2/3 (LWB–77–165).
No. 926   West Tanks 2/3 (LWB–77–165).
No. 927   Overflow channel (F.1198), North-East Tank (LWB–77–260).
No. 928   Fill of External Corn Drying Oven (LWB–78–9).
No. 929   Filling of Ditch 4 (LWB–K28–4).
No. 930   General soil deposit (LWB–K28–2).
No. 931   Unstratified, 1968 (LWB–K30–6).
No. 932   Unstratified, 1976 (stamped) (LWB–76–1).

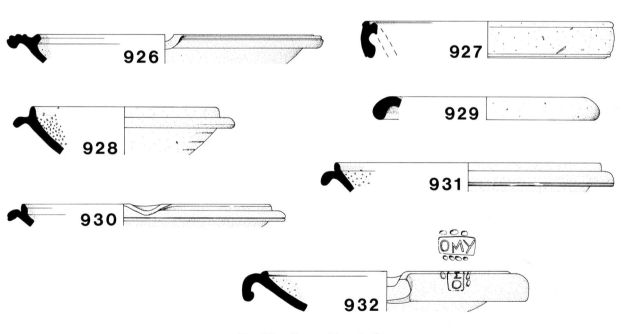

Fig. 91. *Roman Mortaria* ($\frac{1}{4}$).

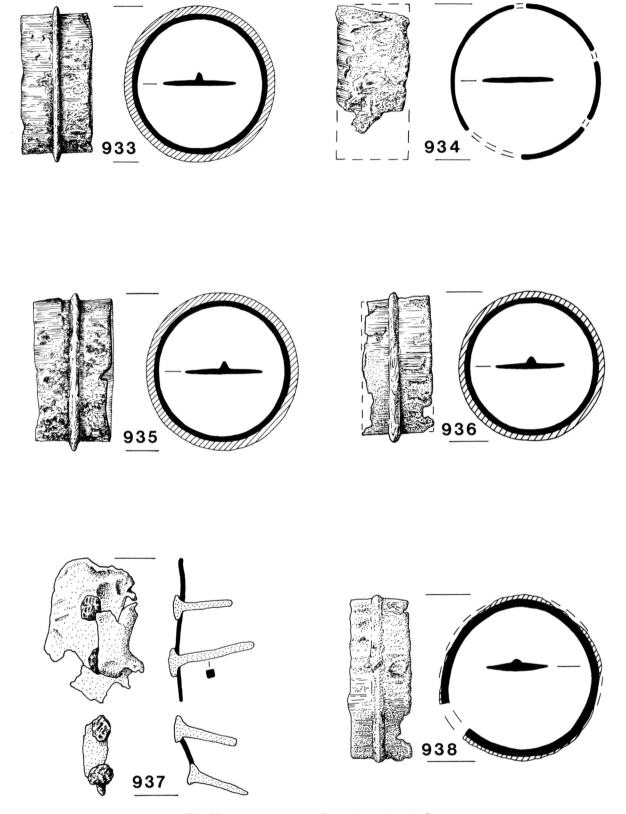

Fig. 92. *Iron water-pipe collars and a lead patch ($\frac{1}{2}$).*

I) THE IRON WATER-PIPE COLLARS (Fig. 92, Nos. 933–938).

It seems clear that the settlement at Keston was always supplied with fresh water from the natural springs which occur just above the site. During the main villa periods (VI and VII) this water was carried to various parts of the complex by a network of wooden pipes, joined with iron collars. The decay of the wooden pipes themselves, followed by centuries of ploughing has effectively destroyed details of the overall system. However, a number of the iron pipe-collars were revealed *in situ* and two separate pipe-lines are represented by these. Five of the twelve water-pipe collars recovered have been illustrated here (Nos. 933–938). All of these except No. 938 come from the eastern pipe-line. In form, all of the collars are similar, having an internal diameter ranging between 65 mm. and 77 mm. With the exception of No. 934 all have external, central stop ridges. Mineralized wood is preserved on most pieces.

Manning (Ref. 255) notes two common sizes of iron water-pipe collar in Roman Britain and the present examples belong to the smaller of these. Other villa sites producing *in situ* pipe collars, include Fishbourne (Ref. 256), Bignor (Ref. 257), Chilgrove I (Ref. 258), Eccles (Ref. 259), Gadebridge Park (Ref. 260) and Dicket Mead (Ref. 261), thus indicating that all of these sites were provided with a piped water supply. Such pipe-lines are generally found supplying bath-houses, yet this does not appear to have been the case at Keston, on the evidence of the surviving pipe-lines.

No. 933   Complete iron water-pipe collar, with an internal diameter of about 68 mm. Traces of an external stop-ridge remain and mineralized wood occurs on the surface. From the eastern water-pipe trench, tentatively dated to Period VI (LWB–L22–2).

No. 934   Fragments of an iron water-pipe collar with an estimated original diameter of about 77 mm. There appears to be no external stop-ridge on this example but mineralized wood is again present. From the eastern water-pipe trench, tentatively dated to Period VI (LWB–I28–26).

No. 935   Complete iron water-pipe collar, with an internal diameter of about 67 mm. The external stop-ridge is again present and traces of mineralized wood occur. From the eastern water-pipe trench, tentatively dated to Period VI (LWB–J26).

No. 936   Complete iron water-pipe collar, with an internal diameter of about 66 mm. The external stop-ridge remains and traces of mineralized wood occur. From the eastern water-pipe trench, tentatively dated to Period VI (LWB–J25–2).

No. 937   Sheet of lead of irregular shape, pierced by four iron nails. The piece appears to have been used as a patch, originally nailed over a split in a wooden pipe of the western water pipe-line. A similar lead patch was discovered on the line of a wooden pipe-line at Dicket Mead, near Welwyn (Ref. 262) (P.C.7).

No. 938   Almost complete iron water-pipe collar, with an internal diameter of about 75 mm. Traces of an external stop-ridge survive and fragments of mineralized wood adhere to the surface. From the western water-pipe trench, tentatively dated to Period VI (P.C.5).

J) THE ANIMAL BONE (not illustrated)
by Alison Locker

1) Introduction.
The animal bones recovered from the excavations in Lower Warbank Field during 1968–1978 varied in their stratigraphical reliability on this shallow chalkland site. For this reason the assemblage has been divided into two main stratigraphic groups (Groups 'A' and 'B'). The Group 'A' material, accounting for approximately three-quarters of the total bone recovered, came from the less well stratified contexts, where it was clear from the evidence on site that there had been at least some later disturbance of the deposits. The Group 'B' material came from the better stratified contexts on the site, although even here subsequent examination has revealed some apparently intrusive material.

The bones within Group 'B' have been subjected to a more detailed study than the material in Group 'A' and only the Group 'B' material is described in detail here. Nevertheless, the Group

'A' bone shows many similarities with the Group 'B' material and it seems clear that the bulk of it is generally derived from the late-Iron Age or Romano-British settlements.

I would like to thank Kim Bryan and Barbara West (British Museum, Natural History) for making available reference material.

2) THE GROUP 'A' BONE.

Although the bone from Group 'A' was not recorded in as much detail as that of Group 'B' it appeared that there were many similarities between the two groups, both in the species recovered, butchery techniques and the occurrence of red deer and the use of antler. A complete female red deer skull was found in the soil over the South Masonry Building and a single fallow deer (dama dama) antler tine was identified from soil over the North Timber Building. Human infant remains and a few adult skull fragments were found isolated in small numbers with the animal bones. There was no indication of complete burials, and it is not unusual to find infant bones mixed in with the domestic food debris.

An interesting find from the topsoil at one point was the mandible of a juvenile macaque (macaca sp.) in which the third permanent molar was about to erupt. It was not possible to determine whether this was the species common to India/Burma/North Vietnam or the Barbary Ape of North Africa. It seems fairly certain that this is a recent animal that came from the adjacent Keston Foreign Bird Farm, which closed in the 1970s.

THE GROUP 'B' BONE.

The Group 'B' bone numbered some 2,467 fragments and these mainly seem to represent domestic food debris. The bulk of the material came from the fillings of the ditches associated with the villa complex of Periods VI and VII. Also possibly assignable to the earlier villa period is the bone from the post-holes of the fence-lines of Period VI, but much of this material is more probably derived from earlier Periods, being residual in its excavated context. Material more certainly relating to the pre-villa settlement includes quantities of bone from the late-Iron Age (Period III) and early-Roman (Period IV) Pits, the West Enclosure Ditch of Period IIIb, the East Enclosure Ditch of Period IV and the post-holes of the Centre Timber Building of Period V.

The following species were identified: ox (bos domestic), ovicaprid (ovis domestic/capra domestic), goat (capra domestic), pig (sus domestic), horse (equus domestic), red deer (cervus elaphas), roe deer (capreolus capreolus), ox-sized, ovicaprid-sized, dog (canis domestic), rabbit (oryctolacus cuniculus), brown hare (lepus capensis), pine marten (martes martes), domestic fowl (gallus domestic) and turkey (meleagris gallopavo). In addition four fragments of human bone, 91 oyster (ostrea edulis) fragments, 57 snails and one belemnite fossil were recoverd. Tables 42–44 indicate the most commonly identified species in each major feature.

Some degree of intrusion is evident in these contexts, indicated by the presence of rabbit in some deposits. A turkey tarsometatarus from the upper fill of the North-West Ditch of the Villa Enclosure indicates the intrusion of post-medieval material since this species (kindly identified by Roger Jones, Ancient Monuments Laboratory) was not introduced to this country from North America until the 17th century. It seems quite likely that it is a recent intrusion derived from the adjacent Keston Bird Farm.

a) The Iron Age Pits (Period II and Period IIIa).

The Iron Age bone (Periods II and III) is dominated by ovicaprid remains from Pit 9 (Period IIIa). Much of the bone in Pit 9 comprises immature ovacaprid remains, some of which were of neonatal size and others, judging from dates for epiphyseal fusions (Ref. 263) of under 10 months. At least four of these immature individuals were present and all parts of the skeleton were represented. These may be the remains of lamb carcases cooked whole, or in sides or quarters. A small number of ox fragments was also identified, two pig mandible fragments and a dog mandible and tibia showing a healed fracture. One radius and three ovicaprid tibia shafts were burnt, as were 20 other fragments. Five fragments of human skull were also found in this feature.

Two partially complete skeletons of ovicaprid were recovered from the upper filling of Pit 9. The mandible from the youngest animal showed little wear on the deciduous fourth premolar and the first permanent molar was just beginning to erupt. The second individual, the more complete of the two, showed slightly more wear on the deciduous fourth premolar and the permanent first molar had slight wear. The estimated values for these mandibles are >13e and >15e respectively (Ref. 264). Amalgamating the data from both tooth eruption and epiphyseal fusion (Ref. 265) both individuals appear to be under a year old, with the younger of the two nearer six months. The older animal is largely complete, while the younger is represented by a single mandible, scapula, humerus, radius and pelvis.

No butchery marks were present except for knife cuts on the left scapula, just above the neck, across the mid area of an astragalus, and on one mid rib fragment. The former two knife cuts were found on the more mature animal. Rodent knawing was observed on the ilium neck of the right pelvis. A porous horn core base indicated that at least one of the two animals was horned. It has been suggested that these animals may be the remains of a religious offering.

The bone from the remaining Iron Age pits represents a small group of domestic food debris totalling 30 fragments with equal numbers of ox and ovicaprid remains and two fragments of pig.

Pits 2 and 11 only contained a small quantity of bone. In Pit 11 (Period IIIa) a single ox tooth, a pair of pig scapulae and eleven fragments of ovicaprid, largely limb bones and two immature mandibles were recovered. Four burnt fragments were also found. The Pit 2 (Period II) material was also fragmentary, with three ox fragments, an ovicaprid metapodial and eight burnt fragments.

Pit No.	Ox	Ovic.	Pig	Horse	Dog	Unid.	Bird	Hum.	Mouse	Totals
Pit 2	3	1	–	–	–	8	–	–	–	12
Pit 9	16	128	2	–	2	63	–	5	–	216
Pit 11	1	11	2	–	–	4	–	–	–	18
Pit 17	4	80	8	1	16	–	5	–	1	115
TOTAL	24	220	12	1	18	75	5	5	1	361

Table 42. Animal species in Iron Age and early-Roman pits.

Key to species abbreviations:
Ovic. = Ovicaprid   Unid. = Unidentifiable   Hum. = Human

b) The early-Roman Pits (Period IV).
The animal bone recovered from pits assigned to Period IV was generally small and fragmentary. Nevertheless, the contents of two of these pits (Pit Nos. 17 and 23) are worthy of some further note.

Pit 17
This was notable for the large number of ovicaprid remains it contained. Goat was identified from four skulls and an immature skull fragment as well as some other immature ovacaprid remains. The partial skeleton of a single dog was from an individual of shoulder height 23.8 cm. Five limb bones from an immature gallinaceous bird were identified. A house mouse skull was found in this pit; this species is thought to have been introduced in the Roman period.

The dog skull from the lower filling showed the rather dome-like skull and reduced dentition resulting from a foreshortened maxilla as seen in the lap dog found in the Shaft near the Tombs in

1962 (Ref. 266). All the molars were in wear, but only two premolars had erupted on the left and only the fourth premolar on the right. Using Harcourt's cephalic and snout indices these show a higher ratio of skull width relative to its height, and a shorter snout length relative to the head than other Romano-British dogs measured by Harcourt (Ref. 267). Comparisons with modern skeletons of small dogs indicates that selective breeding retains foetal features such as domed skulls and a lack of sagittal crests in adulthood.

Pit 23 (F.946).
This contained most of an ovicaprid skeleton for which the estimated shoulder height was 54 cm. (Ref. 268). No butchery was apparent except for knife cuts across the anterior surface of an astragalus, across the lateral surface of a calcaneum, and on five rib fragments. All limb fragments were fused and apart from one mandible fragment, no skull remains were present.

The importance of the ovicaprid groups in the late-Iron Age and early-Roman periods, particularly in Pits 9 and 17, is clear. In terms of domestic refuse, the goat and juvenile ovicaprid remains could represent carcasses utilised and disposed of in a single event, rather than the remains of a number of meals spread over time. Ross cites examples of European sites of La Tène date where pits containing partial animal skeletons are associated with ritual sanctuary enclosure (Ref. 269). Ritual association could be a possible explanation of the presence of immature ovicaprids.

c) The Centre Timber Building (Period Va).
Only 19 bones were recovered from the post-holes, including ovicaprid mandible and limb fragments, a few ox and ox-sized remains and a single pig metapodial.

d) Features assigned to the Main Villa Complex (Periods VI and VII).
Details of the main bones present are given in Table 43. Of special note was a complete humerus from the South-East Villa Enclosure Ditch most closely resembling polecat, in particular pine marten. It compares well with the specimen in the Newton Collection, B.M.N.H., and was larger than the comparative material of the domestic ferret. The total length of this bone was 69.2 mm.

Two femur fragments of human infant were found in the North-West Villa Enclosure Ditch, and a fragment of adult human skull in the South-East Villa Enclosure Ditch.

Context	Ox	Ovic.	Goat	Pig	Horse	Red Deer	Roe Deer	Ox-S	Ov-S	Dog	Rabb.	Hare	Totals
West Enc. (P.IIIb)	141	88	1	44	5	–	1	126	67	4	28	1	506
East Enc. (P.IVa)	29	11	–	5	–	1	1	27	4	–	–	–	78
TOTALS	170	99	1	49	5	1	2	153	71	4	28	1	584

Table 43. Comparative table showing the numbers of bones of most common species identified in the ditches of the West and East Enclosures

Key to species abbreviations:
Ovic. = Ovicaprid   Ox-S = ox-sized   Ov.S = Ovicaprid-sized   Rabb. = Rabbit

e) Miscellaneous.

In an undated miscellaneous pit (F.947) situated immediately to the west of the North Timber Building were found the remains of a single ox skull. The left occipital/frontal area and fragmented horn cores were from a very large individual. The estimated basal circumference of the left horn core was 310 mm. which is within the lower range given for *Bos primegenius* (aurochs) males by Grigson (Ref. 270). It seems likely that this skull is at least of Bronze Age origin, though whether it is in a primary position or is redeposited by later activity is not clear. The only other bone from this feature is the proximal and midshaft area of a right tibia of ox (not of auroch size) which may suggest redeposition is the more likely interpretation.

Hare, which could have been expected to be more numerous, was only represented by a single scapula fragment from the West Enclosure Ditch.

Intrusions into the Roman deposits were suggested by the presence of rabbit in 12 contexts, including most of a skeleton in the West Enclosure Ditch. Also intrusive was the turkey bone previously mentioned.

Context	Ox	Ovic	Goat	Pig	Horse	Red Deer	Roe Deer	Ox-S	Ov-S	Dog	Rabb.	Hare	Total
North-West Villa Enc. Ditch	77	10	–	28	8	6	–	113	46	–	–	–	288
North-East Villa Enc. Ditch	42	10	–	6	1	–	1	129	6	–	–	–	195
South-East Villa Enc. Ditch	134	9	–	5	1	3	–	61	27	129	6	–	375
Centre Fence	5	2	–	–	–	–	–	–	–	–	–	–	7
East and West Fences	18	15	–	1	1	–	–	9	7	1	6	–	58
North Fence	–	1	–	–	–	–	–	1	–	–	–	–	2
Ditches 21A and 21B	71	20	–	46	2	7	–	82	29	1	–	–	258
Totals	347	67	–	86	13	16	1	395	115	131	12	–	1183

Table 44. Distribution of most common animal bone in Group 'B'. Features assigned to Periods VI and VIII

4) BUTCHERY

Ox remains predominate, particularly in the ditch deposits (especially the West Enclosure Ditch of Period IIIb and the North-West and South-East Villa Enclosure Ditches). The largest quantities of bone came from the Villa Enclosure Ditches and the bulk of this material must be derived from the villa complex of Periods VI and VII. The heavy fragmentation of the ox bone is largely the result of butchery which in some cases is clearly evidenced by chop marks. Scapulae had been chopped across the blade and more commonly across the neck and across the base of the spine. Humeri were chopped across the midshaft and across the distal end. Little butchery was observed on the radius; one was chopped proximally, and another split down the shaft. Similarly two ulnae were chopped across the proximal ends and one across the midshaft. One metacarpal was split proximally. On the hind limb the pelvis was chopped across the acetabulum and the femur across the midshaft. Tibiae were also chopped across the midshaft and one was split distally. One astragalus was chopped across the mid area, a metatarsal was chopped across the midshaft and one was split. Vertebrae showed evidence of chopping, sometimes axially. Evidence of skinning was seen in knife cuts on a frontal skull fragment, the medial side of an ulna above the articulation, the proximal end of a metacarpal, and across the mid area of an astragalus. Knife cuts on limb bones may also be the result of the cutting of tendons. The quantity of bone is rather too low to suggest any butchery patterns, but some aspects of ox butchery occur repeatedly and are also echoed among the contaminated Roman material of Group 'A'. These include the chopping of scapulae across the neck and at the base of the spine as well as knife cuts seen repeatedly across the astralagus.

Ovicaprid remains were fewer and also less fragmented than ox, which is a reflection of carcass size. Goat was only identified from horn core fragments (probably male) from the West Enclosure Ditch, and the Boessneck index (Ref. 271) used on metapodials indicated that these bones belonged to sheep. A humerus was chopped obliquely across the shaft, and two radii were split. A femur was chopped proximally and a tibia across the midshaft. Some vertebrae were chopped and split axially.

Pig was largely represented by loose teeth and mandible fragments. Although limb fragments were fragmented little direct evidence of butchery was seen. An ulna was chopped across the midshaft, and a tibia across the proximal end.

Red deer were butchered on the limb bones. A scapula had a knife cut at the base of the spine, a humerus was chopped across the trochlea at the distal end and had a knife cut across the shaft. A metacarpal had been chopped across the distal condyles, and had been cut by a knife across the shaft. On the hind limb, a femur had been chopped proximally, and on a tibia, across the shaft. Antler fragments showed signs of working. One in particular was a piece of tine that had been chopped, had a hole punched into it, and also showed evidence of slight polish. This piece had then been discarded unfinished and had been gnawed by rodents. Roe deer limb fragments did not show any butchery marks. One tine fragment had been chopped. All the above mentioned deer remains come from ditch deposits.

Neither horse nor any of the other remaining species identified showed any evidence of butchery or knife cuts.

5) AGEING

The ageing of mandibles was carried out using the system devised by Grant (Ref. 272) in which the eruption and state of wear is attributed with a numerical value which is totalled for each mandible.

Ox mandibles were frequently too fragmentary for a value to be calculated; however, incorporating four estimates, 15 mandibles were aged of which eleven had a value of over 40 which Grant suggests is around 3.5–4 years (Ref. 273). This indicates that most cattle were adult and used primarily for traction, milk and breeding with meat as a secondary function. This maturity is also reflected in epiphyseal fusion.

Although ovicaprid remains were less numerous they were less fragmented and 18 mandibles were aged. Of these eleven were older than the 31–32 stage which Grant suggest is 3–3.5 years and was a peak kill-off stage in some of the Portchester Castle material (Ref. 274); three were at this stage, and two immature mandibles were also present. This suggests, although again it is a very small sample, that wool and breeding were of primary importance rather than meat.

Pig mandibles were also fragmentary, only nine could be aged, none of which showed any great degree of wear on the third permanent molar and included one very young individual in which the first permanent molar was visible, but not erupted. Measurement of four fully erupted third molars from the West Enclosure Ditch of Period IIIb suggested that these were all from domestic animals.

All horse remains were from fully mature animals represented by both limbs and mandible fragments.

6) SIZE

Measurements were taken according to Jones (Ref. 275), which enabled the calculation of four withers heights for cattle:

Radius	– 106.6 cm.	(Ref. 276)
Metacarpal	– 115.0 cm.	(Ref. 277)
Metacarpal	– 101.5 cm.	
Metatarsal	– 112.2 cm.	

These heights compare well with the size range found at Gorhambury Villa (Ref. 278) and the lower end of the range for Magiovinium; both sites are located in Hertfordshire (Ref. 279).

Three ovicaprid withers heights could be calculated:

Metacarpal	– 66.3 cm.	
Metacarpal	– 53.7 cm.	(Ref. 280)
Metatarsal	– 53.9 cm.	

These were shown by Boessneck's index (Ref. 281) to be from sheep and indicate some diversity in size which may be a sex difference. The two lower sizes are slightly smaller than those from Gorhambury (Locker unpub.), Magiovinium (Ref. 282) and Gadebridge (Harcourt 1975, Ref. 283), but the larger specimen is within the upper range for Magiovinium (Ref. 284).

Two complete horse metacarpals from two of the enclosure ditches suggested wither heights of:

160.2 cm.	Kiesewalter	(Ref. 285)
132.0 cm.	Kiesewalter	

These are approximately equivalent to animals of 15.2 hh and 13 hh, the former qualifies as a horse, the latter is a pony.

None of the red deer bones was complete enough for total lengths to be measured. However the following measurements have been included:

Radius proximal width	= 51.5 mm.
Humerus distal trochlea breadth	= 51.5 mm.
Humerus max. distal breadth	= 57.5 mm. (same bone)
Metacarpal proximal breadth	= 38.5 mm.
distal breadth	= 41.3 mm.
Metatarsal distal breadth	= 38.3 mm.

The total length of a roe deer metacarpal was 164.0 mm.

A dog tibia from the West Enclosure Ditch of Period IIIb was from an animal of shoulder height 57.5 cm. (Ref. 286). A complete skeleton from Pit 17 of late-1st century date (Period IV) represented an adult animal of approximately 25 cm. The pathological dog skeleton from the South-East Villa Enclosure Ditch of Period VI had unfused epiphyses and therefore was not measured.

The domestic fowl bones were also measured; the following total lengths were taken:-

Coracoid	= 57.0 mm.
Humerus	= 77.5 mm.
Ulna	= 78.0, 77.3, 77.5 mm.
Carpometacarpus	= 42.5 mm.
Femur	= 86.9, 86.8 mm.

The skeleton of a single individual was found in a layer of the South-East Villa Enclosure Ditch. The bird was spurred and represents a cock bird or possibly a capon (Ref. 287).

7) PATHOLOGY

Only one example of pathology was recorded from most of an immature dog skeleton from the South-East Villa Enclosure Ditch. Using both the dentition and epiphyseal fusion dates given by Silver (Ref. 288) this animal was around ten months old. The left pelvis showed sever exostoses around the infused acetabulum. The left femur was unaffected but the right showed a swelling and distortion of the shaft suggestive of a traumatic injury, such as a fracture which later became infected. West (pers. comm.) has suggested the distortion of the left pelvis may be a result of the extra weight being carried on this limb while the right leg would have been held clear of the ground. The dates given for the fusion of appendicular skeletons by Silver suggest there has been some delay in the fusion of the left pelvis (the right pelvis is absent) this may also be the result of extra stress on this limb. There seems to be no reason to link this skeleton, or the other ones from this group, with any ritual deposit as has been suggested for the skeletons found in Pit 17 (see p. 287). There is no evidence for the cause of death in this immature animal, which may have been deliberately culled as the movements in its hind limbs would always have been severely restricted.

K) A SAMPLE OF CARBONISED PLANT REMAINS (not illustrated) by Gordon Hillman

A single sample of floated plant remains, from the late-Roman ditch (Ditch 21) (LWB–76–222) over the North Timber Building, comprised the following:–

Triticum spelta (spelt wheat)	– spikelet forks	1 (typical)
	– glume bases	2 (typical)
	– grains in good condition	2 (both germinated)
	– grains in poor condition	*c.* 6 (? germinated)
Avena sp. (wild or cultivated oat)	– grains	1 (embryo end only)
Lolium temulentum (darnel)	– grains	1 (upper half only)

Nothing else was present.

The oat cannot be identified to species in the absence of the lemma-base. On the basis of size, the grain would fit any one of the species *Avena sativa*, *A. fatua* and *A. ludoviciana* if one allows for the differences in size between upper and lower grains in the individual spikelets of each species. Certainly, the grain is too large for the other British species of *Avena* or the other genera of the tribe Avenae with which it might otherwise be confused.

Darnel was once a common weed of cereals and still afflicts crops in southern Europe. This was doubtless its status at Keston. Its unpopularity with farmers was on account of its grains commonly becoming infected with mycelium of the poisonous fungus *Endocladium temulentum*. The infected grains grow to almost the same size as the grains of many wheats and ryes and cannot, therefore, be removed by the traditional sieving operations. The association of an infected grain with the Keston wheat is therefore not unexpected.

The germinated state of the charred spelt grains can be explained in many ways, though perhaps the most obvious interpretations are as follows. Firstly, a wet summer and/or a belated harvest could have led to lodgeing, a malady to which spelt is particularly prone, and some of the grain would then have sprouted in the ears. The germinated grains from Keston could have been charred accidentally during the kilning of whole ears which commonly preceded the primary threshing. Secondly, the grain may have been sprouted deliberately to produce malt. Subsequent kilning of the malted grains often resulted in a few grains getting charred. Thirdly, the Keston grains may simply have sprouted in storage, particularly if they were among the dregs left on the floor of a damp barn or granary. Sweepings from a granary floor are quite likely to end up on a fire and any grains will then be charred. Similarly, any stored grain that showed signs of sprouting would have been kilned immediately to avoid total spoilage, and occasional grains are again likely to have been charred.

It is impossible to opt for any one explanation for the germination and carbonisation of the grain. As for the use intended for the spelt grown at Keston, no excavation in Britain has yet produced evidence for the form in which spelt was eaten (or drunk). In more recent times, spelt products have included malt (for beer or spirits), soft groats, griddle-cakes, a heavy bread, roasted (popped) grain and, most famous of all, the *grunkernmahl* of Wurttemberg. Spelt cultivation in Britain appears to have largely died out during the Dark Ages and commercial production has now been abandoned, even in its last refuge – in Southern Germany. Any of these could have been produced at Roman Keston.

CHAPTER VI

DISCUSSION

PERIOD I.

A general scatter of some 500 struck flints, only about 6% of which were worked or utilized to any extent, was found across much of the site. Similar light scatters occur in several fields in the adjacent Keston and West Wickham areas and simply suggest non-intensive usage during a short time in the late Neolithic or Early Bronze Age (nominally about 2000 B.C.)

PERIOD II (600–200 B.C. – Fig. 5).

It is clear that the first fixed form of settlement occurred on this site in the Middle Iron Age, *c.* 600–200 B.C. The evidence came from two areas, one just south-east of the centre of the excavated area and the other about 200 feet to the north, roughly on the site of the North Roman cemetery. The former contained two shallow storage-pits, at least one post-hole, a substantial quantity of domestic pottery and a La Tène I brooch (*c.* 450–200 B.C.). The evidence from the latter was confined to a scatter of residual pottery.

Damage to the site in the Roman period and also later ploughing may have removed further evidence and the two discrete areas may in fact represent a single, much larger site. Clearly, the general area did not contain deep pits or ditches of Middle Iron Age date, for the lower parts of these would certainly have survived. On the available evidence, therefore, it is only possible to suggest a scattered site of modest proportions and limited features and finds. The total absence of any related ditches strongly suggests that the site was not enclosed and a simple open farmstead seems to be implied. Evidence for such Middle Iron Age farmsteads occurs rarely in Kent, perhaps at Highsted (Ref. 289) and Minnis Bay (Ref. 290), but seems much better known in Wessex.

PERIOD III (50 B.C.–A.D. 50 – Fig. 5).

It seems likely from the available evidence that the Period II settlement at Warbank, Keston ended about 200 B.C. and that the site was effectively abandoned for the next 150 years. Coincidentally, or not, this is roughly the time when the great hillfort at nearby Holwood was constructed and at its greatest significance. At Warbank the available evidence suggests that the site was re-occupied from about 50 B.C. and that it remained in use for at least the next 500 years. The Period III settlement is considered, on the available evidence, to have spanned from about 50 B.C. to about A.D. 50.

The total evidence for the Period III settlement at Keston includes at least 13 storage-pits, ten four-post structures, one six-post structure, a possible sub-rectangular hut, two ditched enclosures, various post-holes and several hearths below the tombs. Nearly 800 stratified potsherds were recovered from Lower Warbank Field (excluding the pottery from the distrubed ditches of the West Enclosure). The sherds represent at least 190 different vessels, while five Potin coins and several important small-finds were also recovered. Most of these features and finds can be classified, mainly on stratigraphic and circumstantial grounds, into two broad phases (Period IIIa and Period IIIb).

All the pits and posted structures are regarded as Period IIIa and the great majority of these were located in a compact area in the south-east corner of the excavated site, covering the pits of Period II. What must be highly significant, is that the pits and posted structures, so far revealed, flank the north and west sides of a large block of unexcavated ground. It seems certain from this that the Period III features extend into this area and indeed may be centred upon it. At the very least the features span an area about 220 feet east–west and at least 100 feet north–south. On the present evidence, therefore, it is likely that the main Period IIIa settlement lay exclusively on the middle slopes of Lower Warbank Field.

It seems that the Period IIIa settlement was at least partially superseded by the South Enclosure and the West Enclosure, here regarded as Period IIIb. Of these, the West Enclosure was probably the most substantial and it seems to have survived in some form, into the early part of Period IV. The South Enclosure, of which only the northern corner was found, cut through Pit 6 and this clearly indicates that at least part of this area had a changed use. Overall, the creation of these new enclosures seems to represent a fairly major reorganisation of the site and indeed ditched enclosures were also a major feature of the succeeding Period IV in the post-Conquest period.

The absence of ditches associated with the Period IIIa settlement strongly suggests that, like Period II, it was unenclosed and probably formed part of an open farmstead. The presence of both pits and four-post structures, the former for underground storage and the latter probably for above ground storage, suggests that grain was produced on the site. A rotary quern from Pit 9 also suggests that grain was processed on the site and it seems likely that a network of small fields then existed in the immediate area of the settlement. The presence of loom-weights and at least one spindle-whorl suggests that sheep were kept for their wool and two ovicaprid skeletons from Pit 9 probably confirm this.

The creation of enclosures during Peiod IIIb, is reminiscent of the situation at nearby Farningham Hill (Ref. 291), where a farmstead site of broadly similar date has been totally excavated. There, a ditched enclosure, covering about half an acre, enclosed a single post-built round-house and a series of 24 storage-pits. The West Enclosure at Keston seems comparable to that at Farningham Hill, but only one possible hut (West Timber Structure) was found within it close to a wide eastern entrance. Little can be said about the extent of the South Enclosure and it may be that both enclosures were intended as cattle compounds. What seems clear is that no certain domestic huts were located for Periods IIIa or IIIb and that if these have not been destroyed by subsequent land-use, they must have existed beyond the limits of the present excavation. The possible hut inside the West Enclosure consisted of ten post-holes which formed only two sides of a sub-rectangular structure which was at least 16 feet by 9 feet, as surviving, moreover its date is not totally certain.

It is not impossible that some of the features assigned to Period IIIa actually belong to Period IIIb, but none of these was found to occur within the enclosed areas. The occupation represented by the Period III features seems to have continued unbroken into Period IV, when new enclosures were created across the site. Pit digging also continued (Pits 17–22 of Period IV). The chronological distinction between Periods III and IV, therefore, is not clearcut, which implies continuity between the two periods, despite the Roman invasion. The precise relationship of Period III to the Iron Age hillfort at Holwood (1,000 yards to the north-east of the site) is not known, but will be further considered in the second Report on Keston.

PERIOD IV (A.D. 50–160 – Fig. 9).

It seems clear that the Period III enclosures, pits and four-post structures were, mainly on the dating evidence, substantially superseded by a series of new features. These included two enclosures, extensive quarry pits, kiln-debris, several pits and a small cemetery. These have been divided into two phases, the earlier (Phase a) dating from about A.D. 50–100 and the later (Phase b) to about A.D.100–160.

These features were found scattered over most of the site and probably extend beyond the limits of the excavation, certainly at the south-east corner. Not much can be said about the partially destroyed East Enclosure except that it was probably sub-rectangular and at least 100 by 25 feet. No structures were found inside the enclosure ditches, but it is probable that any which had existed were removed by later ploughing. On other sites, such small enclosures may have contained small huts and related features, which collectively would have constituted small

Romano-British farmsteads. The site at Eastwood, Fawkham, was clearly of this type and several others are known across West Kent (Ref. 292). At Keston the pottery, discarded as domestic rubbish into the ditches, clearly indicates nearby occupation, though this could equally have come from outside the enclosure. If the enclosure did not contain structures then it is likely that it served as a cattle compound.

The Quarry Pit Complex lay in an open area towards the southern end of the site, about 85 feet south-west of the contemporary East Enclosure. It measured about 75 by 30 feet and consisted of a series of irregular hollows dug into the underlying natural chalk. These are interpreted as minor quarries. It is just possible that the chalk was extracted for building purposes, but no corresponding chalk structures of the appropriate date are known at Keston. It is more likely, however, that the chalk removed was dug for agricultural purposes, probably to lime adjacent clay soils. Pliny, writing about A.D. 70 (Ref. 293) remarks that the Belgae dug deep shafts for chalk to spread on the land. Clearly, the quarry-pits cannot be regarded as shafts, but rather a shallow form of open-cast mining. After quarrying had ceased the pits and hollows were filled with mixed soils containing domestic and industrial debris.

A consideration of all the samian ware, small-finds and coarse pottery recovered from the filling of the Quarry Pit Complex, shows that none is certainly later than A.D. 100. The great bulk of the material can be dated to the second half of the 1st century A.D., though there are a few residual objects of earlier date. There can be little doubt that the filling took place during the latter part of the 1st century A.D., particularly as Flavian samian ware is represented.

Exactly when the successive minor pits and hollows were dug is less clear. They are here identified as minor chalk quarries and these could have been dug over either a short period, or over many years. All, or most, probably post-date the late-Iron Age pit (Pit 16) and from the available evidence it seems that the quarries were probably dug sometime during the period A.D. 50–80 and filled no later than about A.D. 100. The soils above the quarries also contained 1st century pottery, as well as later material including four coins of 3rd or 4th century date. The pits were certainly filled and levelled at an early date for they were sealed by a dump of kiln-debris and also by the foundations of the Centre Flint Structure (Period Vb), dated to the mid to later 2nd century A.D. (see below).

The Quarry Pits also contained slight evidence of some industrial processes. This included black-smithing debris in the form of hearth-bottom slags and in addition fragments of crucibles containing copper-alloy residues. These suggest small-scale iron and bronze working on the site, perhaps predictable on a farmstead site.

Much more unusual for such a site, was substantial evidence for the manufacture of domestic pottery, from what may now be regarded as the Keston Kiln. Although there is evidence for the production of a range of kitchen wares here it seems that a significant part of the process was concerned with the manufacture of a range of fine-wares imitating imported pottery, the market for which must have been rather more limited than for the kitchen wares. The date-range seems to have been A.D. 60–85.

The later part of Period IV (Phase b) included the construction of the Centre Enclosure, to the north and west of the Quarry Pits and East Enclosure, respectively. This occupied a largely open area, but its west side overlapped the partially silted ditches of the West Enclosure (Period III). It was broadly sub-rectangular, about 65 feet wide and 95 to 125 feet in length with an open north side.

The enclosed area contained a series of pits and post-holes and a small metalled area, mostly later than Period IV. These included 21 pits, of which three specialised pits with clay lining were water storage-tanks associated with the main villa of Periods VI and VII. Pit 19 seems to have been filled during the period A.D. 80–90 and is likely to just predate the Centre Enclosure. Of the miscellaneous pits inside, only three (F.1096, 1102 and 1111) produced more than five sherds of dateable pottery and one of these also produced a coin (Coin No. 38, from F.1096). From their contents these three pits are of 3rd or 4th century date and clearly post-date the enclosure. The remaining 17 pits produced either only a few indeterminate potsherds or, more frequently, nothing at all. These cannot, therefore, be assigned to any specific period. The same is the case for many of the 56 post-holes revealed within the enclosure. Apart from a setting of post-holes relating to Four-Post Structure 8 (Period III) and a row of post-holes representing a major fence-line of the Period VI villa complex (South Fence), few of the post-holes produced any significant dating evidence. Two did produce sufficient pottery to indicate that they were of late-3rd to 4th century date (F.1114 and F.1125) and these must again post-date the present enclosure. Of the remainder little more may be said except to note that they formed no significant alignments or concentrations. From this it would seem that most of these pits and post-holes formed part of the wide scatter of miscellaneous minor features that covered much of the site and the very limited dating evidence suggests that they belong to a broad date-range.

In terms of dating evidence the substantial stratified material from the ditches of the Centre Enclosure, suggests that these were filled by about A.D. 160 and the general absence of later material, apart from a few intrusive objects, must be significant. The great bulk of the ceramic material dates from A.D. 50–160 and, allowing for some of this being residual material, it seems likely that this enclosure was created at the end of the 1st century A.D., or very early in the 2nd century A.D.

The site was further extended during Period IV–Phase b by the creation of a small cremation cemetery some 30 feet west of the Centre Enclosure. Three burials were located and these actually occupied part of the internal area of the, by then, abandoned West Enclosure (Period III). This cemetery, of late-1st century and early-2nd century date, is further evidence in itself of the Period IV settlement and it probably lay a discrete distance from the main area of occupation.

Outside the two enclosures and beyond the quarry pits and small cemetery were at least seven scattered pits (Pits 17–23), that also related to Period IV. It seems probable that some of these were intended for the storage of grain, thus continuing the pre-Conquest tradition (Period III). Two pits, however, are of particular interest for they seem to have had a specialised, probably ritual, function. Pit 17 was a small shaft which contained a skeleton of a dog, two goat skulls and three partially complete pots. The pottery and the domestic rubbish in the upper filling of the shaft all dates to the last forty years of the 1st century A.D. and the pit was probably filled at the very end of that century. Pit 23 was small and contained the curled up skeleton of a sheep/goat.

The combined evidence for Period IV suggests a settlement consisting of scattered elements covering most of the known site. It seems very likely that this was a large native farmstead, engaged in a range of agricultural and small-scale industrial activities, the latter including the manufacture of pottery.

Period IV seems to have come to a fairly abrupt end in the middle years of the 2nd century A.D., when the entire site was replanned and a series of major timber buildings erected (Period V – see below). The contrast between the Period IV and V layouts was thus particularly marked, but the dating evidence does not suggest that the two periods were separated by an abandonment phase.

PERIOD V (A.D. 160–200 – Fig. 14).

The scattered elements of Period IV over most of the site, seem to have been superseded at about A.D. 160 by a major reorganisation. The central new element included three large wooden buildings, regarded as Phase a, with several lesser, but related features or structures, regarded as Phase b. The new layout, so sharply contrasting with the scattered earlier elements suggests either new owners or the substantial adoption of Romanised forms of planning and the creation of a proto-villa estate.

What is clear is that although the three buildings are widely spaced they appear to be set around a central open area, which may reasonably be considered as forming a yard or garden and although only about three-quarters of this area was excavated, the circumstantial evidence is convincing. Several points of significance on the relative positions of the buildings around such a notional yard, or garden, emerge. Whilst any of these could be coincidental, when taken together they make a good case for the three main buildings having been laid out to a pre-conceived, overall plan.

In the first place the area chosen for the buildings and their notional yard was in the southern part of the site, framed between the present-day 395 foot, and the 412 foot contours. This now produces a fall of about 17 feet, giving an even gradient of about 1 in 14. The Roman buildings do not, however, follow the modern contours, probably much altered by ploughing since Roman times, but rather at an angle to them. It seems probable from the positions of the three buildings, that they marked the north, west and south sides, respectively, of a broadly rectangular area. The structures on the north and south sides (the Centre Timber Building and the South Timber Building) are both broadly set across the slope of the hillside and are only 9° off being parallel to each other. The building on the west side (the West Timber Building) was, however, placed on the highest point of the selected area, but was aligned down the slope and formed rough right-angles with the projected lines of the other two buildings. It was anyway the largest building of the group, it also had some painted walls and it also dominated the area. This was clearly the principal building, being domestic in character and indeed it faced south-east in a manner much prefered by many major Roman domestic rural buildings.

In addition to the juxta-positioning of the buildings, it seems significant that the line of the west wall of the Centre Timber Building, if projected southwards, falls exactly on the east wall of the South Timber Building. Similarly, the projected line of the south wall of the West Timber Building, if projected eastwards, bisects the space between the Centre and South Timber Buildings. Furthermore, the north wall of the West Building is roughly in line with the south wall of the Centre Building. Finally, the Lower East Metalling enters this notional yard area exactly at the centre of the east side, mid-way between the Centre and the South Timber Buildings. All this suggests a degree of planning.

In reality, however, any precisely rectangular layout was not achieved. The 9° difference between the main axes of the Centre and South Buildings distorts the shape slightly, but more significant is the positioning of the West Building, which apparently lies some 14° off a symmetrical axis. These variations in laying-out may well have been caused by the slope of the ground, with the original surveyors taking insufficient account of this when measuring out the area. The distance between the West and Centre Buildings is 140 feet and between the West and South Buildings 130 feet. The South and Centre Buildings are 104 feet apart.

It is reasonable to suppose that the sides of the notional yard area, between the three principal buildings, were marked in some way. The most obvious method would be by means of either a ditch, a fence or a hedge. No ditches, however, were found and although fence-lines have been identified on the site, these are quite certainly part of the succeeding Period VI villa complex and do not relate to Period V. Nevertheless, that some broadly comparable arrangement also occured in Period V seems very likely. This would anyway be a most sensible arrangement, keeping the farm animals from straying and preventing wild animals from reaching the internal area. Despite this, however, there is no clear archaeological evidence for any fence-lines on the site in Period V. If these had been as substantial as those of Period VI it seems highly probable that they would have survived and it appears, therefore, that any fences around the Period V area must have had posts sufficiently small not to have penetrated the natural chalk to any depth. Alternatively, hedges may have been employed and these would leave no archaeological traces.

The exact course of any such Period V hedge or fence-lines cannot be certain. Perhaps the most likely arrangement, however, would have been to run straight alignments from the corners of the main buidings. Whether these buildings stood entirely within such an enclosure, or whether a smaller enclosed area was set between their inner walls cannot be decided. It does seem quite possible, however, that the line between the east wall of the South Building and the west wall of the Centre Building represents the actual course of the eastern boundary of the yard, in which case most of the Centre Building would have lain outside the enclosed area. A boundary line in this area seems to have been broadly maintained in Period VI when the East and West Fences were erected. The South Fence of Period VI was only a fairly short distance from the suggested northern boundary of the Period V yard and this too may approximately preserve the earlier line.

Indeed, the entire fenced compound of Period VI, defined by the East, Centre and South Fences lies immedieately to the north of the notional area covered by the Period V yard, almost as if the larger overall area enclosed during Period VI was created by adding a fenced compound to the north side of an existing Period V yard.

The three timber buildings (Table 45) were all constructed with large upright, circular posts, earthfast and deeply buried in the ground. These posts formed rectangular, oblong frames of either four, five or six bays. The buildings varied in length from 36'6" to 59'8" and in width from 19'9" to 21'4", the measurements being taken from the centres of each of the relevant posts. This suggests that the length of the tie-beams across the widths of the buildings was mostly in the 20–21 feet range, whilst the bay spacing was between about 9 and 10 feet and this suggests the minimum size of the wall-plate beams. Certainly the bays would have been infilled, except for functional openings and there is some evidence to suggest that both the West Timber Building and the South Timber Building were at least partially infilled with daub. No direct evidence of the form of the roof-frames was found, but these could have been pitched or flat, the former more likely and that covered with tile or thatch. Nor are the heights of the buidings known. It seems clear that some 40 major trees would have been required to provide just the basic uprights for the buildings and clearly many more to provide the rest of these large structures.

The overall length and width dimensions of the buildings seem to have a fairly close relationship to known Roman dimensions, though none is precise. The three buildings may have been laid out with lengths of 38, 50 or 60 Roman feet, respectively and the widths 20–22 Roman feet. The bay spacing, however, clearly varied between the buildings by as much as one Roman foot.

Structure	Length	Width	Area sq. ft.	Number of Posts	Number of Bays
West Timber Building	59'8"	21'4"	1,272	16	6
Centre Timber Building	49'0"	21'3"	1,041	14	5
South Timber Building	36'6"	19'9"	720	10	4
North Timber Building (excluding aisles)	70'0"	23'0"	1,652	24	9

Table 45. Comparative data of the three Period V timber buidings and the North Timber Building of Period VI.

The terms of function the larger West Timber Building had at least partially painted walls and surely must have been the main domestic house, exactly as was the Period VI house which replaced it. Its elevated position overlooked the whole site. The other two, smaller, structures were probably ancillary farm buildings used perhaps for storage, animals or for working tasks. Both flanked the eastern end of the notional yard, lower down and in full view of the main house.

Broadly similar timber-framed buildings to those identified here as Period Va, have been found on other Romano-British sites. At Latimer, Bucks, a large rectangular timber building, at least 30'6" by 24'6" was found beneath the main masonry villa. It has been dated, tentatively, to about A.D. 80–120 (Ref. 294). At Chew Park, Somerset a timber-house, some 38 feet by 15 feet internally was found and this has been broadly dated to the first-second century A.D. and may even be just pre-Conquest (Ref. 295). Its large post-holes were spaced at intervals of about 8 feet. At Gorhambury, Herts, a large rectangular aisled barn has been located and this seems to be of pre-Conquest origin (Ref. 296).

In terms of the other structures, here all Period Vb, the two incomplete walls of the Centre Flint Structure fall within the limits of the notional yard and unequally between all three major buildings. The buiding technique used, flint footings under a presumed timber-frame, was new at Keston, but what survived was only about 14 by 4 feet and a larger building could be represented.

The metalled trackway (Lower East Metalling), seemingly aligned on the centre of the notional yard, can on pottery and circumstantial grounds be assigned as Period Vb. It seems to represent a trackway heading north-east away from the site.

The clay-lined Water Storage Pond at the north-east corner of the site has also been dated on pottery evidence as Period Vb. It may have served as a cattle-pond for animals grazing away from the main area of the building. Finally, the small area of metalling (F.873) at the north-west and the two Two-Post Structures (A and B) have on general sequential evidence and on somewhat limited pottery evidence, been dated to Period Vb. All seem to be minor elements of the site, though it should be noted that both Two-Post Structures fall within the notional yard and may have served as drying-racks.

Little absolute dating evidence was found for the three wooden buildings themselves, but the relative dating seems convincing. Clearly the large West Timber Building overlay the small cremation cemetery (Period IV), the South Timber Building overlay at least two pits (also Period IV) and the Centre Timber Building seems to have superseded the South Enclosure (Period III). However, it cannot be proved that the three buildings were exactly contemporary, but the circumstantial evidence strongly suggests that they formed part of a single, coherent plan. The combined pottery evidence, the horizontal stratigraphy and the overall circumstantial evidence suggests that Period V ended about A.D. 200 to be substantially replaced by the Period VI layout.

PERIOD VI (A.D. 200–300 – Fig. 17).

The proto-villa layout (Period V above) was largely superseded by a second and much larger reorganisation of the whole site at about A.D. 200. This saw the full development of the villa on a grand scale with many new and sophisticated elements. These included a large new masonry house (West Masonry Building); a large new agricultural building (North Timber Building) north-east of it; deep boundary ditches on the north and south sides; several major fences, piped-water and underground storage-tanks and also the creation of a major domestic cemetery, including monumental tombs, on rising ground to the north. These major changes seem to reflect greater wealth, a higher social status, or perhaps new owners.

This major new layout also seems to have resulted in the demolition of the Centre Timber Building and the Centre Flint Structure, both of which would otherwise have been left inconveniently at the centre of the grand new scheme.

It seems clear that the Period V West Timber Building, identified as the main house on the site, was destroyed by fire about A.D. 200. This necessitated rebuilding, in masonry in the same position, and it is likely that most of the other major changes and additions were triggered off by this event. Even so, it is possible that some of the changes may not have taken place at exactly the same time, but all can be attributed to Period VI. At least the Period V South Timber Building seems to have been retained during Period VI.

What is certainly clear is that the new layout included two delimiting enclosure ditches on the north side, forming the site boundary there. One was L-shaped in plan (Villa Enclosure Ditch, North-West) and partly defined the north-west corner of the site. Another (Villa Enclosure Ditch, North-East) marked the broad eastward continuation and the two were separated by a gap some 28 feet in width. The total distance covered by the two ditches (as so far known) is about 240 feet. The gap between the ditches must represent a broad entrance causeway and this seems to mark the major uphill axis of the site. Indeed, a line bisecting this entrance runs parallel to the front of the West Masonry Building and also leads to the cemetery area, thus linking these two major elements.

Just why the North-West Ditch returned southwards to flank this axis is less clear, but it could have helped control the movement of farm animals. Significantly, the North-East Ditch had been constructed to fit closely around the North Timber Building, where it would also have served to collect surface water on the uphill side.

The corresponding boundary ditch on the south side (Villa Enclosure Ditch, South-East) lay about 120 feet from that on the north side and roughly parallel to it. Its eastward extension, beyond the limit of excavation, may turn to join the extension of the north ditch, probably at right-angles and perhaps with a central entrance. The westward continuation of the South-East Ditch is uncertain, for it did not reappear in the main area of excavation and it must either have ended or turned southwards. Villa sites elsewhere are known to have been enclosed by boundary ditches and examples occur at Ditchley (Ref. 297); Sandwich (Ref. 298) and Frocester Court (Ref. 299). In general these delimit the main area of the villa buildings with the related field systems lying beyond.

Within the overall enclosure ditches lay the two principal new buildings of Period VI on the north and west sides. These two structures were set at an angle of about 115° to each other and occupied two sides of a broadly rectangular area, with the pre-existing Period V South Timber Building lying on the third side. This arrangement seems to represent an enlarged version of the Period V layout. The building on the west side was clearly the main house and it must be significant that the buildings on the north and south sides were each about 90–100 feet from it. The North Timber Building contained a series of large corn-drying ovens and seems to have been agricultural in function, perhaps a massive barn or granary. Both the West Masonry Building and the North Timber Building will be discussed in detail in the second Report on the Keston excavations, together with the excavation report on the cemetery.

Of additional significance, in terms of the overall layout is a series of fences, the lines of which were clearly marked by sockets for wooden posts. The Centre Fence, L-shaped in plan, joined the west and north buildings and created a clear boundary for the northern side of what seems to have been a large courtyard some 150 feet on its north–south axis.

The new plan thus created by the three buildings and the Centre Fence is fan-shaped, splaying outwards away from the main house on the west side and an enlargement of the notional Period V yard. This arrangement is known at a small number of villa sites in Britain, but it has been suggested as a continental introduction and is certainly more common in northern Gaul. In Kent, the fan-shaped pattern also occurs at Darenth, a villa site about ten miles north-east of Keston. (Ref 300). This large courtyard was itself sub-divided by a South Fence which, in conjunction with the East/West Fence, created a four-sided corral or paddock, about 120 feet by 45 feet.

What is less clear is the exact function of the East and West Fences, though it is likely that the East Fence was original and replaced by the West Fence. The line of the former clearly originated on the west post of the main entrance of the North Timber Building, suggesting that access to it was only required from the east (outer) side. The southern end of this fence-line, if projected, would have missed the east end of the South Timber Building.

No wells for drawing water were discovered anywhere on the site and indeed the steep slope and height of the hill above the local water-table, would have required these to have been very deep. However, in Period VI at least, water was brought onto the site by two separate water-pipe systems, both originating higher up the hill. These probably brought in constant supplies of fresh water from springs on the hill above, one of which still flows today.

In addition, a series of four large rectangular clay-lined pits was found on the Roman site and these seem to represent deep water-storage tanks. Significantly, one of the pipe-lines (the West Water-pipe) seems to have discharged directly into one of the tanks (West Tank), whilst two other tanks (the South and North-East Tanks) incorporated overflow channels. A continuous flow of water may be implied. These tanks appear to cover both Periods VI and VII. The south Tank appears to have been added at the west end of the earlier South Timber Building, which had survived from Period V. It probably served that building and its adjacent area. The set of West Tanks had been built close to the north wing of the West Masonry Building and close to the Centre Fence (both Period VI) and is unlikely to be earlier. These tanks probably served that building, perhaps including its bath-house and also the adjacent area. The North Tank and the North-East Tank were cut through the ruins of the North Timber Building (Period VI) and are therefore later (Period VII).

Ploughing was found to have severely damaged the two water pipe-lines which were only represented by short lengths of shallow gullies containing occasional iron collars. The latter had once formed connectors between wooden pipes, since decayed. It seems likely that additional pipe-lines may have been destroyed. The East Water-pipe may have served the South Tank and it may be that this pipe-line had originally joined the West Water-pipe further uphill to run to a common source. At other sites, Roman pipe-lines often followed irregular courses so some variation in the alignments at Keston is likely. The most sensible line for the pipes to take would have been across the wide causeway between the enclosure ditches on the north side and indeed both head in that general direction.

Sometime before the end of Period VI, the northern boundary ditches must have been substantially silted. A new fence (North Fence) was placed across the causeway between the ditches and two of its posts had been cut into the upper silt of the ditches. A gate may have been incorporated into this fence to allow continued access. Period VI seems to have ended at about A.D. 300 when some degree of contraction of the site seems to be indicated (see below).

PERIOD VII (A.D. 300–400 – Fig. 30).

Whilst Period VI represents the Roman villa complex in its most expansive form during the period A.D. 200–300, it seems clear that the fourth century saw a partial contraction, here regarded as Period VII. This new phase seems to have started at about A.D. 300 when the great North Timber Building, with its large internal corn-drying ovens, was burnt down. It must be significant that this largely agricultural building was not reconstructed and this could reflect a change in the type of agriculture, or even a major reduction in land being farmed. At about much the same time the great aisled building on the Darenth villa estate was drastically reduced in area during its Period V (Ref. 300) and this could be a reflection of a wider decline.

At Keston, the main West Masonry Building probably continued in use during the fourth century, though little datable evidence (of any period) was found within it. It is, however, clear that the main cemetery (Period VI) on the villa site was abandoned in the fourth century when large quantities of domestic rubbish were being piled near the stone mausolea. Presumably, an alternative cemetery was created nearby.

The most obvious advance of the fourth century was the replacement of the South Timber Building (Period V) by a larger structure in masonry, the South Masonry Building. This occupied the same site, more than quadrupled the area and also sealed the South Tank (Period VI) beneath its floors and walls. The new building, probably some 69 feet by 43 feet, covered a total area of about 3,000 sq. ft. It consisted of a pair of matching rooms, about 19 ft. sq., separated by a passage just 5 feet wide and flanked on all sides by passage, or verandah. It seems to have been a domestic building, but rather more modest than the main house to its north-west. It clearly resembles the East Block of the complex of buildings on the nearby Roman villa site at Darenth, a site partially excavated by the West Kent group in 1969. The Darenth building, of almost identical plan, slightly larger and was also adjacent to the main house on the site, was clearly domestic in character. Its precise function is less clear, but it has sometimes been termed a 'guest-house' or even taken as evidence of possible dual-ownership of the villa estate. Coincidentally, or not, the Darenth villa also developed with a fan-shaped layout.

Another structural element designated to Period VII is the Upper East Metalling, which appears to be a late replacement of the east-west road first built during Period V. An extra area of corresponding metalling, shown as the Centre Metalling, probably joined this road at a near right-angle and may have led to the front of the West Masonry Building.

Of minor structures relating to Period VII, several occur in a group in the vicinity of the destroyed North Timber Building. The most significant is a probable hut that seems to have occupied a wide hollow cut through the south-east corner of the original building. It contained a large hearth and traces of iron-working. Nearby were two large clay-lined tanks, the North-East Tank and the North Tank, again both cutting deeply through the ruins of the North Timber Building. These must have held large quantities of water, available for industrial, agricultural or domestic purposes. Just south of the hut was a small double-chambered corn-drying oven and flanking it on the north and east sides two large ditches, Ditch 7 and Ditch 21a. Both may have served to take storm-water, but Ditch 7 could also have taken water from the original overflow from the North-East Tank. Ditch 21b was later recut through the silt of Ditch 21a and also through the filling of the North-East Tank so at least two phases of use are indicated.

There is little firm evidence for the exact demise of the Roman villa estate at Keston. Little of very late Roman date has been found and the latest coin recorded is of the House of Valentinian, minted no later than A.D. 378. Hence, a terminal date either at the end of the fourth century or early in the fifth century seems likely.

The occurence of a fine Saxon hut, dated A.D. 450–550, close to the physical centre of the Roman site is a discovery of great importance. It clearly shows settlement on the site, at the very least on a small scale, in the 5th or 6th centuries (Period VIII). This seems to be the last settlement on the site and the area has certainly been open farmland for many centuries. Post-Saxon activity (Period IX) is represented by three large robber-pits and three shallow ditches, probably old field boundaries. The focus of settlement in late-Saxon, Norman and later times was the parish church about 500 yards to the south-east of Warbank Field. If settlement at Keston generally was continuous, then movement from the Warbank site to the church area must have taken place in the 7th–9th centuries. If not continuous, then a fresh settlement must have been created during these centuries fortuitously 500 yards from the original long-established site.

BIBLIOGRAPHICAL REFERENCES

Ref. No.	Subject	Author	Publication
1	Archaeological sites in the Keston Area	Crozier, P. and Philp, B.J.	*The Archaeology of the Bromley Area* (1985), p. 14.
2	London to Lewes Roman Road	Margary, I.D.	*Roman Roads in Britain* (1973), p. 59.
3	London to Lewes Roman Road	Margary, I.D.	*Roman Ways in the Weald* (1956), p. 124.
4	Romano-British sites	–	See Ref. 1, p. 8–11.
5	Bath-house, Baston Manor	Philp, B.J.	*Excavations in West Kent, 1960–1970* (1973), p. 80.
6	Orpington villa	Philp, B.J.	*Kent Arch. Review*, No. 94 (1988), p. 74–78.
7	Titsey villa, Surrey	Leveson-Gower, G.	*Surrey Arch. Collection 4* (1869), p. 214–237.
8	Beddington villa, Surrey	Adkins, L. and R.	Beddington Roman Villa, *Current Archaeology* (1983), No. 88, p. 155–157.
9	Early excavations at Keston	Kempe, A.J.	*Archaeologia*, XXII (1828), p. 336.
10	Early excavations at Keston	Corner, G.	*Archaeologia*, XXXVI (1855), p. 120.
11	Early excavations at Keston	Wheeler, R.E.M. *et al.*	*Victoria County History (Kent)*, Vol. 3, p. 119.
12	Early excavations at Keston	Piercy Fox, N.	*Arch. Cant.*, LXIX (1955), p. 96.
13	Early excavations at Keston	Dunkin, J.	*Outlines of the History and Antiquities of Bromley in Kent* (1815), p. 45–58.
14	Early discoveries at Warbank	–	See Ref. 9.
15	Early discoveries at Warbank	–	See Ref. 9, p. 337.
16	Early discoveries at Warbank	–	See Ref. 13.
17	Early excavations at Keston	–	See Ref. 9.
18	Early excavations at Keston	–	See Ref. 9.
19	Early excavations at Keston	–	See Ref. 10.
20	Cremation at Warbank	–	See Ref. 12.
21	Early excavations at Keston	–	*Athenaeum*, Oct. 28th (1893).
22	Early excavation at Keston	Ward Perkins, J.B.	*Arch. Cant.*, L (1938), p. 164.
23	Excavations in Eight Acre Field	–	See Ref. 12.
24	Early excavations at Keston	–	See Ref. 12, p. 184–191.
25	Keston Tombs excavations	Mynott, E.	*Kent Arch. Review*, No. 9 (1967), p. 8.
26	Keston Tombs excavations	Philp, B.J.	*Kent Arch. Review*, No. 11 (1968), p. 10.
27	Keston Tombs excavations	Philp, B.J.	*Current Archaeology*, No. 14 (1969), p. 73.
28	Lower Warbank excavations	Mynott, E.	*Kent Arch. Review*, No. 14 (1968), p. 8.
29	Lower Warbank excavations	Mynott, E.	*Kent Arch. Review*, No. 15 (1969), p. 6.
30	Lower Warbank excavations	–	*Kent Arch. Review*, No. 18 (1969/70), p. 13.
31	Lower Warbank excavations	Philp, B.J.	*Kent Arch. Review*, No. 21 (1970), p. 21.
32	Lower Warbank excavations	Mynott, E.	*Kent Arch. Review*, No. 49 (1977), p. 215.
33	Stone coffin, Keston	Mynott, E.	*Kent Arch. Review*, No. 54 (1978), p. 88.
34	Ritual shaft, Keston	Philp, B.J.	*Kent Arch. Review*, No. 82 (1985), p. 35.
35	New building at Keston	Philp, B.J. and Garrod, D.	*Kent Arch. Review*, No. 89 (1987), p. 194.
36	West Kent Group	–	See Ref. 5, p. 1.
37	Pottery type-series	–	See Ref. 5.
38	Flint assemblages	–	See Ref. 5, p. 14–51.
39	Neolithic sites	–	See Ref. 5, p. 5.
40	Ritual quern burial	Merrifield, R.	*The Archaeology of Ritual and Magic* (1987), p. 33.
41	Iron Age farmsteads	Philp, B.J.	*Excavations in the Darent Valley, Kent* (1984), p. 33.
42	Early excavations, Lower Warbank	–	See Ref. 12, p. 96.

43 Iron Age sites   –   See Ref. 41.

44 Iron Age enclosures   Philp, B.J.   *Excavations at Faversham,* 1965 (1968), p. 65.

45 Iron Age enclosures   Hurd, H.   *Arch. Cant,* XXX (1914), p. 309.

46 West Timber Structure   –   See Ref. 31.

47 Superstructure of pottery kiln   Anthony, I.E.   Excavations in Verulam Hills Field, St. Albans, 1963–64, *Hertfordshire Archaeology* 1 (1968), p. 9–50.

48 Ditched villas   Ralegh Radford, C.A.   The Roman Villa at Ditchley, Oxon, *Oxonesia, i,* (1936), p. 24–69.

49 Ditched villas   Parfitt, K.   *Kent Arch. Review* No. 60 (1980), p. 238.

50 Ditched villas   Price, E.G.   *Current Archaeology,* No. 88 (1983), p. 140.

51 Gallic features of villas   Black, E.W.   The Roman Villas of South East England, *B.A.R.* 171 (1987), p. 139.

52 West Masonry Building   –   See Ref. 10, p. 120.

53 West Masonry Building   –   See Ref. 9.

54 West Masonry Building   –   See Ref. 42.

55 West Masonry Building   –   See Ref. 10.

56 West Masonry Building   –   See Ref. 51.

57 Wooden floors   Neal, D.S.   The Excavation of the Roman Villa in Gadebridge Park, Hemel Hempstead, 1963–68 (1974), *Society of Antiquaries Rept. XXXI,* p. 49.

58 Corn drying ovens   Morris, P.   Agricultural Buildings in Roman Britain, (1979), *B.A.R.* 70, p. 5.

59 Corn drying ovens   –   See Ref. 5, p. 128.

60 Fence-lines   –   *Current Archaeology,* No. 87 (1983), p. 116.

61 Fence-lines   –   See Ref. 50, p. 144.

62 Fence-lines   Down, A.   The Roman Villas at Chilgrove and Upmarden (1979), *Chichester Excavations* Vol. 4, Fig. 33.

63 Fence-lines   –   See Ref. 62, p. 43, Fig. 8.

64 Fence-lines   Philp, B.J.   Forthcoming.

65 Water pipe-lines   –   See Ref. 62, p. 66.

66 Water pipe-lines   Frere, S.S.   *Britannia,* XIII (1982), p. 142.

67 Water pipe-lines   Detsicas, A.P.   *Arch. Cant.,* LXXXII (1967), p. 165.

68 Water pipe-lines   Tester, P.J.   *Arch. Cant.,* LXXVI (1961), p. 91.

69 South Masonry Building   –   See Ref. 10.

70 Wooden floors   –   See Ref. 57.

71 South Masonry Building   –   See Ref. 10.

72 South Masonry Building   Payne, G.   *Arch. Cant.,* XXII (1897), p. 49–84.

73 Bowl furnace   –   See Ref. 58, p. 182.

74 Anglo-Saxon hut   –   See Ref. 5, p. 156.

75 Anglo-Saxon hut   Jones, M.U.   *Antiquaries Journal,* LIV, part II (1974), p. 183.

76 Anglo-Saxon hut   Addyman, P. and Leigh, D.   *Med. Arch.* XVII (1973), p. 1.

77 Saxon place-name, Keston   Copely, J.G.   *Archaeology and Place-names in the 5th and 6th Centuries, B.A.R.* 147 (1986), p. 55.

78 Grubenhäuser in Britain   Leeds, E.T.   *Early Anglo-Saxon Art and Archaeology* (1936), p. 21.

79 Saxon huts, Mucking   Jones, M.U.   *Antiquaries Journal,* XLVIII (1968), p. 210.

80 Saxon huts, Sutton Courtney   Leeds, E.T.   *Archaeologia,* XCII (1947), p. 79.

81 Saxon huts, West Stowe   West, S.E.   *Med. Arch.,* XII (1968), p. 161.

82 Saxon huts, Canterbury   Frere, S.S.   *The Civitas Capitals of Roman Britain* (1966), p. 91.

83 Saxon weaving loom   Leeds, E.T.   *Archaeologia,* LXXVI (1926), p. 75.

84	Saxon huts, Bishopstone	Armstrong, J.R.	*Weald and Downland Open Air Museum* (1971), p. 26.
85	Saxon lead-weight	–	See Ref. 79, p. 210.
86	Saxon lead-weight	Wheeler, R.E.M.	*London Museum Catalogue, No. 6* (1935), p. 136.
87	Coins	–	See Ref. 5, p. 158.
88	Potin coins	–	*Kent Arch. Review No. 22* (1970), p. 58.
89	Potin coins	Allen, D.F.	*The Iron Age and its Hillforts* (1971), p. 146, Fig. 32.
90	Dating of Potin coins	Haselgrove, C.	*Iron Age Coinage in South-East England (1987), B.A.R. 174.*
91	Potin coins	–	See Ref. 44, p. 84.
92	Potin coins	–	See Ref. 41.
93	Potin coins	Detsicas, A.P.	*Arch. Cant.*, LXXXI (1966), p. 188.
94	Potin coins	–	See Ref. 89, p. 146.
95	Potin coins	–	See Ref. 89.
96	Triangular arrowhead	Evans, J.	*The Ancient Stone Implements of Great Britain* (1872), p. 349, Fig. 331–333.
97	Triangular arrowhead	Stead, I.M.	Excavations at Winterton and other Roman Sites in North Lincs., *D.o.E. Arch. Rept. 9* (1976), p. 250, Fig. 135, 1, p. 250.
98	Triangular arrowhead	Green, S.	*Lithics*, No. 5 (1984), p. 31.
99	Arrowheads	–	See Ref. 98. p. 19 and 33.
100	Small-finds	–	See Ref. 5.
101	Clay loom-weights	Elsdon, S.	*Iron Age Pottery Group Newsletter* No. 3, p. 3.
102	Clay loom-weights	Bell, M.	*Sussex Arch. Coll.*, Vol. 114, p. 290, Fig. 44.
103	Clay loom-weights	Potter, T.W.	*Britannia*, XII (1981), p. 130, Fig. 23,1.
104	Clay loom-weights	–	See Ref. 41, p. 35, Fig. 14,8.
105	Clay loom-weights	–	See Ref. 5, p. 73, Fig. 19, 156.
106	Pottery kilns	Woods, P.J.	*Britannia* V (1974), p. 274.
107	Early kiln furniture	Swan, V.	*The Pottery Kilns of Roman Britain* (1984), p. 60.
108	Kiln furniture	–	See Ref. 107.
109	Baked clay slabs	Wheeler, R.E.M. and T.V.	Verulamium: A Belgic and two Roman Cities (1936) Soc. of Antiquaries Rept. XI, p. 178.
110	Kiln furniture	–	See Ref. 109.
111	Pottery tray	Rawes, B.	*Britannia*, XII (1981), p. 72, Fig. 10,7.
112	Pottery production, Eccles	Detsicas, A.P.	In Roman Pottery Studies in Britain and Beyond (1977), *B.A.R.* 30.
113	Pottery roulette from Eccles	Detsicas, A.P.	*Antiquaries Journal 54* (1974), p. 305–306.
114	Slag	McDonnell, G.	*Current Archaeology No. 86* (1986), p. 83.
115	Antler tine	–	See Ref. 5.
116	Antler pick	Bushe-Fox, J.P.	Second Report on the Excavations on the Site of the Roman Town at Wroxeter, Shropshire, 1913, (1914), *Society of Antiquaries Rept. II*, p. 20, Fig. 2, Pl IX.
117	Antler pick	Wheeler, R.E.M.	Maiden Castle, Dorset (1943), *Society of Antiquaries Repts. XII*, p. 308.
118	Antler rakes	–	See Ref. 5, p. 143, Fig. 46.
119	Antler rakes	Philp, B.J.	*Kent Arch. Review No. 32* (1973), p. 46.
120	Bone toggles	Cunliffe, B.	Danebury: An Iron Age Hillfort in Hants (1984), Vol. 2, *C.B.A. Rept, No. 52*, p. 378–380.
121	Bone pins	Crummy, N.	*Britannia*, X (1979), p. 157.
122	Bone pins	–	See Ref. 121.

123	Bill-hooks	Rook, T.	*Hertfordshire Archaeology*, Vol. 9, p. 150, Fig. 60, 34.
124	Bill-hooks	Rees, S.	*Ancient Agricultural Implements* (1981), p. 67.
125	Bill-hooks	Wheeler, R.E.M.	*London in Roman Times* (1946), Pl. XXXIV.
126	Pruning-hook	Webster, G.	*Bristol and Gloucester Arch. Soc. Transactions*, XCIX (1981), p. 52, Fig. 11, 18.
127	Pruning-hook	Frere, S.S.	*Britannia*, XIII (1982), p. 180, Fig. 28,22.
128	Pruning-hook	–	See Ref. 62, p. 155, Fig. 48,32.
129	Pruning-hook	Brodribb, A.C., Hands, A.R. and Walker, D.R.	*Excavations at Shakenoak Farm, near Wilcote, Oxfordshire*, Vol. I (1971), p. 102, Fig. 34, 23.
130	Spearhead	Brailsford, J.V.	*Hod Hill*, Vol. I (1962), p. 5, Pl.V.
131	Iron stylus	Manning, W.	*Catalogue of Romano-British Ironwork in the Museum of Antiquities, Newcastle Upon Tyne* (1976), p. 34, Fig. 21.
132	Ox goad	Wheeler, R.E.M. and T.V.	Report on the Excavations of the Prehistoric, Roman and Post Roman Site at Lydney Park, Glos, (1932), *Society of Antiquaries Rept. IX*, p. 74, Fig. 8,6.
133	Ox goad	Pitt Rivers, A.L.F.	*Excavations in Cranborne Chase i* (1887), Pl.XXIX,10.
134	Ox goad	–	See Ref. 109, p. 212.
135	Ox goad	Frere, S.S.	*Verulamium Excavations*, III (1984), p. 87, Fig. 38.
136	Ox goad	–	See Ref. 117, p. 288.
137	T-clamp	–	See Ref. 131, p. 40, Fig. 25, 157.
138	Brooches	Hattatt, R.	*Iron Age and Roman Brooches* (1985), p. 56, Fig. 24.
139	Brooches	Collingwood, R.G. and Richmond, R.A.	*The Archaeology of Roman Britain* (1969), p. 295, Fig. 102.
140	Colchester Brooches	Hawkes, C.F.C. and Hull, M.R.	Camulodunum: First Report on the Excavations at Colchester 1930–39 (1947), *Society of Antiquaries Rept. XIV*, p. 312.
141	Colchester Brooches	–	See Ref. 138, p. 26.
142	Iron bow-brooch	–	See Ref. 140.
143	La Tène I brooch	Cunliffe, B.W.	*Iron Age Communities in Britain* (1974), p. 144.
144	La Tène I brooch	–	See Ref. 138, p. 10–12.
145	Thistle brooch	–	See Ref. 139, p. 293.
146	Thistle brooch	–	See Ref. 140, p. 316.
147	Langton Down brooch	–	See Ref. 140, p. 317.
148	Langton Down brooch	–	See Ref. 139, p. 292.
149	La Tène III brooch	Hull, M.R. and Hawkes, C.F.C	Corpus of Ancient Brooches in Britain (1987), *B.A.R.* 168, p. 193–196.
150	Plate brooch	Meates, G.W.	*The Lullingstone Roman Villa*, Vol. II, p. 65, Fig. 24, 61.
151	Plate brooch	–	See Ref. 138, p. 141, Fig. 60,518.
152	Dolphin brooch	–	See Ref. 138, p. 72.
153	Dolphin brooch	–	See Ref. 138.
154	Colchester brooches	–	See Ref. 138, p. 26, Fig.12.
155	Penannular brooch	–	See Ref. 139, p. 300, Fig. 106.
156	Colchester brooch	–	See Ref. 141, p. 310.
157	Colchester brooches	–	See Ref. 138.
158	Twisted wire bracelet	–	See Ref. 150, p. 65, Fig.25,72.

159	Bronze bracelet	Stead, I.M. and Rigby, V.	*Baldock: The Excavation of a Roman and pre-Roman Settlement* (1986), p. 126, Fig. 52.
160	Jet bracelet	Crummy, N.	The Roman Small Finds from the Excavations in Colchester, 1971–79, *Colchester Arch. Rept. 2*, p. 35, Fig. 37, 1498, 1496.
161	Jet bracelet	Whiting, W, Hawley, W. and May, T.	*Report on the Excavations of the Roman Cemetery at Ospringe, Kent* (1931), Pl.LVII.
162	Jet bracelet	Penn, W.A.	*Arch.Cant.* LXXIX (1964), p. 187, Fig. 5,16.
163	Bronze bell	–	See Ref. 160, p. 127.
164	Bronze finger-ring	–	See Ref. 41.
165	Bronze fitting	–	See Ref. 160, p. 80.
166	Bronze fastening	–	See Ref. 159, p. 134.
167	Shale palette	–	See Ref. 160, p. 57, Fig. 61, 1867.
168	Lamp chimney	Parsons, J.	*Kent Arch. Review No. 27* (1971), p. 202.
169	Quernstone distribution	–	See Ref. 51, p. 117–119.
170	Millstones at Darenth	–	See Ref. 5, p. 143.
171	Water mill (?) at Darenth	–	See Ref. 41, p. 89.
172	Saddle-quern	–	See Ref. 41, p. 36, Fig. 14,11.
173	Samian	Marsh, G.	London's Samian Supply and its Relationship to the Development of the Gallic Samian Industry (1981), *B.A.R. International Ser.* 123, p. 173–238.
174	Samian	Oswald, F. and Pryce, T.D.	*An Introduction to the Study of Terra Sigillata* (1920).
175	Samian	Ricken, H.	Die bilderschüsseln der Kastelle saalburg und Zugmantel (1934), *Saalburg, 8*, p. 130–182.
176	Samian	Atkinson, D.	A Hoard of Samian Ware from Pompeii (1914), *Journal of Roman Studies*, 4, p. 27–64.
177	Samian	–	See Ref. 176.
178	Samian	Hermet, F.	*La Graufesenque* (1934), p. 40, Pl. 27.
179	Samian	Knorr, R.	*Südgallische Terra-Sigillata-Gefässe von Rottweil* (1912).
180	Samian	Forrer, R.	Die römischen Terrasigillata-Töpfereien von Heiligenberg-Dinsheim und Ittenweiler im Elsass (1911) *Mittelungen der Gesellschaft für Erhaltung der Geschichtlichen Denkmäler im Elsass,* 2 ser, 23, p. 525–768.
181	Samian	Dannell, G.B.	In Excavations at Fishbourne 1961– 1969, Vol II, The Finds (1971), *Repts, Res. Com. Soc. Antiq.* XXVII, p. 260–316.
182	Samian	Stansfield, J.A. and Simpson, G.	*Central Gaulish Potters* (1958).
183	Samian	Rogers, G.B.	Poteries sigilées de la Gaule Centrale, 1; les motifs non-figurés, *Gallia Supp,* 28.
184	Pottery typology	–	See Ref. 5, p. 60.
185	Coarse pottery	–	See Ref. 41.
186	Coarse pottery	Pollard, R.J.	In Ref. 150.
187	Coarse pottery	Pollard, R.J.	*The Roman Pottery of Kent* (1988).
188	Coarse pottery	–	See Ref. 150.
189	Coarse pottery	Thompson, I.	Grog-tempered Belgic pottery of South-east England (1982), *B.A.R. 108*, p. 753.
190	Coarse pottery	–	See Ref. 41.
191	Coarse pottery	–	See Ref. 189.
192	Coarse pottery	Piercy Fox, N.	*Arch. Cant., LXXXIV* (1969), p. 185.

193	Coarse pottery	–	See Ref. 5.
194	Coarse pottery	Lyne, M.A.B. and Jeffries, R.S.	The Alice Holt-Farnham Roman Pottery Industry (1979), *C.B.A. Res. Rept.* 30.
195	Coarse pottery	–	See Ref. 195.
196	Coarse pottery	Philp, B.J.	*Kent Arch. Review*, No. 61 (1980), p. 12.
197	Coarse pottery	–	See Ref. 186.
198	Coarse pottery	–	See Ref. 41, p. 100.
199	Coarse pottery	Cunliffe, B.W.	Excavations at Portchester Castle, Vol. I (1975), *Soc. of Antiquaries Rept.* XXXII.
200	Coarse pottery	Stead, I.M. and Rigby, V.	Baldock Excavations 1968–72, *Brit. Mon.* 7, p. 232.
201	Coarse pottery	Birchell, A.	*P. P. S.*, Vol. 31 (1965), p. 241–367, Fig. 12, No. 97.
202	Coarse pottery	Young, C.J.	Oxfordshire Roman Pottery (1977), *B.A.R.* 43.
203	Coarse pottery	Fulford, M.G.	New Forest Roman Pottery (1975), *B.A.R.* 17.
204	Coarse pottery	Going, C.	Pers. comm.
205	Coarse pottery	Palmer, S.	*Excavation of the Roman and Saxon Site at Orpington* (1984).
206	Coarse pottery	Parfitt, K.	forthcoming.
207	Coarse pottery	Green, M.J.	*Kent Arch. Review*, No. 66 (1981), p. 128.
208	Coarse pottery	–	See Ref. 112.
209	Coarse pottery	–	See Ref. 113.
210	Coarse pottery	Richardson, B. and Tyers, P.	*Britannia* XV (1984), p. 133–142.
211	Coarse pottery	Down, A.	*Chichester Excavations*, 3 (1978), Fig. 103.
212	Coarse pottery	Woods, P. and Hastings, S.	*Rushden: the Early Fine Wares* (1984), pp. 40–46, 122–132, 165–166.
213	Coarse pottery	–	See Ref. 112.
214	Chaff-tempered ware	MacPherson Grant, N.	*Kent Arch. Review*, No. 61 (1980), p. 2.
215	Chaff-tempered ware	Barford, P.	*Kent Arch. Review*, No. 69 (1982), p. 204.
216	Iron Age pottery	Barrett, J.C.	In Excavations at a Neolithic Causewayed Enclosure, Orsett, Essex (1975), *P. P. S.* 44, Fig. 41, 48.
217	Iron Age pottery	–	See Ref. 143, A.8,1.
218	Iron Age pottery	–	See Ref. 216, p. 268–288.
219	Iron Age pottery	Harding, D.W.	*The Iron Age in the Upper Thames Basin* (1972), Pl.58.
220	Iron Age pottery	–	See Ref. 143, A.9 and A.10.
221	Iron Age pottery	–	See Ref. 219, p. 79.
222	Iron Age pottery	Marien, M.E.	*La nécropole à tombelles de Saint-Vincent* (1964), p. 157–8.
223	Iron Age pottery	Longley, D.	Excavations at Runnymede Bridge (1980), *Surrey Arch. Soc. Research Volume*, No. 6, Pl. 143, type 4b.
224	Iron Age pottery	O'Connell, M.	Petters Sports Field, Egham (1986), *Surrey Arch. Soc. Research Volume*, No. 10, p. 72.
225	Iron Age pottery	–	See Ref. 216, Fig. 40,35.
226	Iron Age pottery	–	See Ref. 216, Fig. 41,74.
227	Iron Age pottery	–	See Ref. 143, A.9,1.
228	Iron Age pottery	Jones, M.U. and Bond, D.	In The British Later Bronze Age (1980), *B.A.R.* 83(ii), p. 471–482.
229	Iron Age pottery	De Sweaf, W. and Bourgeois, J.	Un habitat du La Tène la à Lede (Aalst, Flandre orientale) (1986), *Scolae Archaeologicae*, No. 3, Fig. 17.

230	Iron Age pottery	Elsdon, S.	Later Bronze Age Pottery from Farnham, a reappraisal (1982), *Surrey Arch. Collections*, LXXIII, Fig. 4,11.
231	Iron Age pottery	–	See Ref. 228, p. 477.
232	Iron Age pottery	–	See Ref. 143, p. 52.
233	Iron Age pottery	–	See Ref. 41, p. 48, decoration (b).
234	Iron Age pottery	–	See Ref. 41, Nos. 142 and 138.
235	Iron Age pottery	–	See Ref. 41, p. 45, form 2.
236	Iron Age pottery	Thompson, I.	*Grog-tempered 'Belgic' Pottery of South-eastern England* (1982), p. 190–209.
237	Iron Age pottery	–	See Ref. 236, p. 10.
238	Iron Age pottery	–	See Ref. 41, p. 49, decoration (e).
239	Iron Age pottery	Elsdon, S.	Stamped Iron Age Pottery (1975), *B.A.R.* 10.
240	Iron Age pottery	–	See Ref. 236, p. 223–4.
241	Iron Age pottery	–	See Ref. 5, Fig. 24.
242	Iron Age pottery	–	See Ref. 236, p. 198–209.
243	Iron Age pottery	–	See Ref. 5, p. 60–63, Nos. 81–83, 88.
244	Iron Age pottery	–	See Ref. 236, p. 256–267.
245	Coarse pottery	Couldrey, P. C.	In Ref. 41.
246	Coarse pottery	–	See Ref. 140, p. 231.
247	Coarse pottery	–	See Ref. 140, p. 233.
248	Coarse pottery	–	See Ref. 140, p. 239.
249	Coarse pottery	–	See Ref. 140, p. 231.
250	Coarse pottery	Marsh, G. and Tyers, P.	In *Southwark Excavations 1972–74, II* (1978), p. 549.
251	Coarse pottery	–	See Ref. 250, p. 550.
252	Coarse pottery	–	See Ref. 159, p. 223.
253	Mortaria	Cunliffe, B.W.	Excavations at Fishbourne, 1961–69 (1971), *Society of Antiquaries Rept,* XXVII, p. 204–207, Fig. 82,8.
254	Mortaria	–	See Ref. 112, p. 5–17.
255	Water-pipe collars	–	See Ref. 131, p. 40, Fig. 24,151.
256	Water-pipe collars	–	See Ref. 253, p. 128, Fig. 55,4,5.
257	Water-pipe collars	–	See Ref. 127, p. 181, Fig.28,27.
258	Water-pipe collars	–	See Ref. 62, p. 158, Fig. 51,60.
259	Water-pipe collars	–	See Ref. 67.
260	Water-pipe collars	–	See Ref. 57, p. 27.
261	Water-pipe collars	–	See Ref. 123, p. 152, Fig. 61,4.
262	Water-pipe collars	–	See Ref. 123, p. 152, Fig. 61,4.
263	Animal bone	Silver, I.A.	The Ageing of Domestic Animals (1969), *Science in Archaeology*.
264	Animal bone	Grant, A.	Appendix A: The Use of Tooth Wear as a Guide to the Age of Domestic Animals, in Excavations at Portchester Castle, Vol. 1, *Repts. Res. Comm. Soc. Antiq.* XXXII, p. 437–450.
265	Animal bone	–	See Ref. 263.
266	Animal bone	Piercy Fox, N.	*Arch. Cant.* LXXXII, p. 184.
267	Animal bone	Harcourt, R.	The Dog in Prehistoric and Early Historic Britain (1975), *Journal of Archaeological Science*, Vol. 1, p. 151–175.
268	Animal bone	Teichart, M.	Osteometriche Untersuchungen zur Berechnung der Widerristhohe bei Schafen (1975), *Archaeological Studies, Amsterdam*, p. 51–69.

269 Animal bone   Ross, A.   *Pagan Celtic Britain* (1967).

270 Animal bone   Grigson, C.   The Uses and Limitations of Differences in Absolute Size in the Distinction between the bones of Aurochs (*Bos primegenius*) and domestic cattle (*Bos taurus*), (1969), *The Domestication and Exploitation of Plants and Animals*, p. 277–279.

271 Animal bone   Boessneck, J.   Osteological Differences between Sheep (*Ovis aries Linne*) and Goat (*Capra hircus Linne*) (1969), *Science in Archaeology*, p. 331–358.

272 Animal bone   –   See Ref. 264.

273 Animal bone   Grant, A.   The Animal Bones (1975), in Ref. 264, p. 378–408.

274 Animal bone   –   See Ref. 273.

275 Animal bone   Jones, R.T., *et al*   Ancient Monuments Laboratory, D.o.E. Computer Based Osteometry, Data Capture User Manual (1), *Ancient Monuments Laboratory Report No.* 3342.

276 Animal bone   Matolsci, J.   Historische erforschung der Korpergorss der Rindes aus Grund von ungarischen Knockematerial (1970), *Tierzuchtg, u. Zuchtungsbiol*, Vol. 87, p. 89–137.

277 Animal bone   Fock, J.   *Metrische Untersungen an Metapodien Einiger Europaischer Rinderassen Gedruckt mit Genemigung der Tierarzlichen Fakultat der Universitat Munchen* (1966).

278 Animal bone   Locker, A.   Forthcoming.

279 Animal bone   Locker, A.   In *Excavations at Magiovinium*, forthcoming.

280 Animal bone   –   See Ref. 268.

281 Animal bone   –   See Ref. 271.

282 Animal bone   –   See Ref. 279.

283 Animal bone   –   See Ref. 267.

284 Animal bone   –   See Ref. 279.

285 Animal bone   Kieswalter   In Kritische Amerkungen zur Widerrishohenberechnung aus Langemassen vo-und fruhgeschichtlicher Tierknochen, *Saugetierkundliche Mitteilungen*, 22, p. 325–348.

286 Animal bone   –   See Ref. 267.

287 Animal bone   West, B.   Chicken Legs Revisited (1985), *Journal of the Association for Environmental Archaeology*.

288 Animal bone   –   See Ref. 263.

289 Iron Age farmsteads   Tatton-Brown, T.   *Arch. Cant.* XCII (1976), p. 236–238.

290 Iron Age farmsteads   Worsfold, F.H.   *P. P. S.* Vol. 9 (1943), p. 28–47.

291 Iron Age site, Farningham Hill   –   See Ref. 41, p. 29.

292 Romano-British Farmsteads   Philp, B.J.   *Arch. Cant.* LXXVIII (1963), p. 55.

293 Shafts   Pliny   *Lib.*, XVII (8).

294 Timber-framed buildings   Branigan, K.   Latimer: Belgic, Roman, Dark Age and Early Modern Farm, p. 57.

295 Timber-framed buidings   Rahtz, P. A. and Greenfield, E.   Excavations at Chew Valley Lake, Somerset (1977), p. 35 *D.O.E. Report No. 8*

296 Timber-framed buildings   –   See Ref. 60.

297 Ditched villas   –   See Ref. 48.

298 Ditched villas   –   See Ref. 49.

299 Ditched villas   –   See Ref. 50.

300 Period VI villa arrangement   –   See Ref. 5, p. 119.

INDEX

311

PLATES

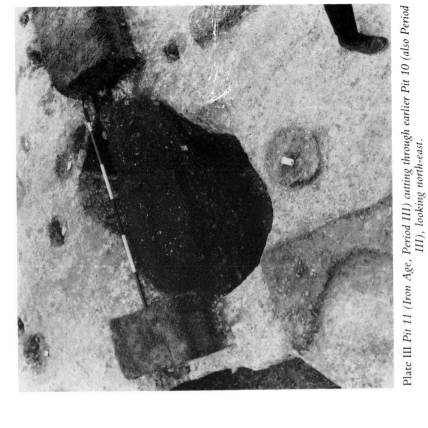

Plate III *Pit 11 (Iron Age, Period III) cutting through earlier Pit 10 (also Period III), looking north-east.*

Plate II *Pit 6 (Iron Age, Period III), half sectioned looking south-west. Shallow Ditch of South Enclosure (P. IIIb) cuts through upper pitfill on far side.*

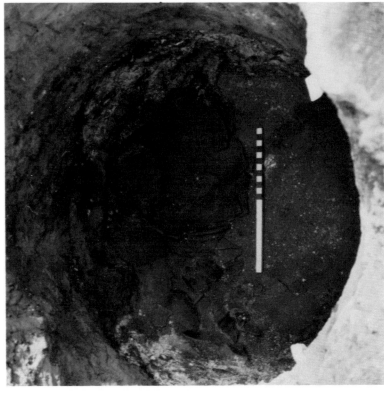

Plate V Pit 17 (Roman Ritual Shaft 'A', Period IV); showing broken pottery
vessels lying on the bottom.

Plate IV Pit 16 (Iron Age, Period III) cut by the later complex of quarry pits
(Period IVa) looking south-west.

Plate VI *Pit 23, the Roman sheep/goat ritual(?) burial (Period IV).*

Plate VII *Excavations at Keston in 1854 from the south, with the South Masonry Building in the foreground, the West Masonry Building (to the left) and the circular mausoleum on the hill above.*

Plate VIII *The West Masonry Building (Period VI); showing detail of the N.E. Room, looking north-west.*

Plate IX *The West Masonry Building (Period VI); showing detail of Room 'D' of the bath-suite, looking south-west.*

Plate X *The West Masonry Building (Period VI); showing masonry of the south-east wing of the bath-suite (east end), looking north-east.*

Plate XI *The North Timber Building (Period VI); showing the north-west corner of the structure, with beam-slots marked by rods and the damaged north Corn-Drying Oven near the centre.*

Plate XIII *The North Timber Building (Period VI); showing detail of the south Corn-Drying Oven, with central channel (marked by rods), side channels and lateral vents.*

Plate XII *The North Timber Building (Period VI); showing the Corn-Drying Ovens, looking west.*

Plate XV The Villa Enclosure Ditch (North-West), Period VI, showing the east arm, looking south, from its junction (foreground) with the north arm and a flint-packed post-hole of the North fence (Period VI) in one of the baulks.

Plate XIV The North Timber Building (Period VI); showing detail of the south Corn-Drying Oven, with vents in the side chambers.

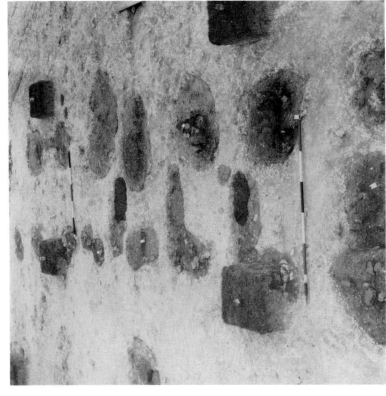

Plate XVII *The East and West Fences (Period VI), showing some of the post-holes and related parallel 'slots'.*

Plate XVI *The Centre Fence (Period VI), showing some of the post-pits and post-pipes, looking west, cutting a linear pre-Roman animal burrow.*

Plate XIX The South Masonry Building (Period VII) after excavation in 1968, looking east.

Plate XVIII The South Masonry Building (Period VII) under excavation in 1968, looking south-east.

Plate XXI The South Masonry Building (Period VII); showing detail of the north-west internal corner of the corridor walls, with inserted partition wall.

Plate XX The South Masonry Building (Period VII) looking south-east, showing the inserted passage across the north corridor and the earlier South Tank (Period VI) beyond.

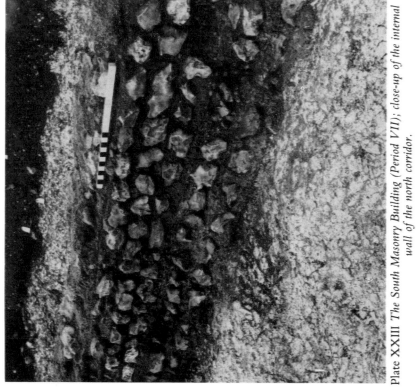

Plate XXIII *The South Masonry Building (Period VII); close-up of the internal wall of the north corridor.*

Plate XXII *The South Masonry Building (Period VII); showing detail of the north corridor, looking north-west.*

Plate XXV *The External Corn-Drying Oven (Period VII), partly excavated, looking east.*

Plate XXIV *Ditch 7 (Period VII), looking south.*